Cities and Suburbs:

Selected Readings in Local Politics and Public Policy

Edited by

Bryan T. Downes
Michigan State University

Wadsworth Publishing Company, Inc. Belmont, California

Preface

This book of readings addresses itself to important questions infrequently raised or systematically discussed in the classroom but increasingly asked in society as the problems of our central cities and suburbs continue to mount:

1. Why have such problems arisen?
2. How have local governments responded to these problems?
3. Why have they responded in a particular manner?
4. What factors either impede or facilitate a positive and innovative policy response by local decision makers to the policy problems they currently confront in different issue areas?
5. Have local governments been able to effectively cope with or successfully solve the critical problems they face?

In the classroom, attention is too often on the problems and too rarely on their origins and the reasons for failure to solve or cope with them. But for this volume, I have assumed that what political scientists should seek to explain are *policy outcomes*. This includes not only *public policy*, or the authoritative actions (decisions) of local governments; but also *policy outputs*, or the service levels affected by public policy; and *policy impacts*, or the effect policy has on people's lives, the alleviation of particular problems, and/or citizen demands for policy change. Once these three policy outcomes have been analyzed and explained, we will be in a much better position to evaluate the performance of local governments, as well as answer the questions listed above.

In addition, unlike most others, this collection of readings focuses attention on both central-city and suburban politics. These selections provide an excellent cross section of current research on local municipalities and their politics, and though not exhaustive, many important theoretical, conceptual, methodological, and empirical concerns are suggested. Despite considerable variation in research strategies and methods, most of the selections are basically comparative empirical studies. (A number of case studies have also been included because they describe and/or attempt to explain ongoing processes and behavior in greater detail.)

In the introductory essay, the basic theoretical scheme and model used to organize presentation of the selections is set forth, as is an inventory of key concepts and variables in current use by researchers. I discuss the policy-making approach to the study of local municipalities, plus the four concepts that provide the focal point for the major subdivisions within the volume.

By using concepts in the policy-making model heuristically to organize presentation of the various sections, I have attempted to solve one of the critical problems that plague most collections of articles, and students attempting to make use of them—their lack of organization and continuity. For example, in Part One, selections focus on some of the distinctive similarities and differences in the contextual—ecological, demographic, economic, etc.—characteristics of central cities and their suburbs. These are factors which may influence the types of problems confronting local municipalities, cleavages that give rise to and nourish community conflict, and the nature of demands made upon local decision makers.

Part Two focuses on the formal legal rules and procedures under which local governments operate, and differences in the arrangement, organization, and type of governmental and nongovernmental structures one finds in central cities and suburbs. These are factors which may have a significant effect on the form which political conflict takes, as well as on the nature of citizen participation and influence in the policy-making process at the local level.

In Part Three, various aspects or components of the policy-making process are examined: political attitudes and participation in the policy-making process; group activities and the formation of coalitions; who governs, or the nature of political leadership in central cities and suburbs; and how these as well as other phenomena influence the decision-making process in city councils and school boards.

In Part Four, researchers investigate how the factors discussed in Parts One, Two, and Three influence the type of policy problems that arise in central cities and suburbs and/or the public policies actually pursued by local governments. And in the Conclusion, some of the shortcomings of current research on local government and politics are discussed. In addition, future directions are suggested which theorizing, concept formation, and empirical inquiry might or perhaps should take.

As a further assistance to you, each part is prefaced by a brief introduction in which I again discuss the major cluster of variables taken up, and briefly introduce the readings. Also, additional related readings are suggested.

Finally, each selection is prefaced by its own brief, sometimes critical, introduction, pointing out relationships discussed and major conclusions reached by the author(s); important questions raised in the selection; and the implications, when applicable, of the research findings for the realization of democratic politics at the local level; and placing the selection in the context of the larger concerns of the section and volume. Additional relevant materials are also presented.

I am indebted to the numerous authors and publishers who allowed me to reprint their original materials. Without their cooperation this collection of readings would not have been possible. I also appreciate the assistance given by two graduate students, Stephen W. Burks and Lewis Friedman, in the initial selection and evaluation of articles. To the numerous undergraduates and graduate students who have since read and commented on the selections finally included, I acknowledge my gratitude. I would also like to acknowledge my appreciation for the extremely constructive criticism given the original manuscript by Peter A. Lupsha (Yale University), Robert H. Salisbury (Washington University), J. David Greenstone (University of Chicago), and Harry M. Scoble (UCLA). The comments of Edward S. Greenberg (Stanford University) on the final manuscript were also helpful and encouraging. I especially thank the numerous students who in long hours of discussion have been enthusiastic "foils" for many ideas I have tried to incorporate into this volume. Thanks must also go to various work-study students who were particularly helpful in developing the manuscript, and to the secretaries in the political science department at Michigan State University for their assistance in the final stages of the manuscript's preparation. Finally, without the encouragement of Robert Gormley of Wadsworth Publishing Company, the editorial comments of Kevin Gleason, and the patience and assistance of my most constructive critic, my wife Sheri, this volume would never have been completed in its present form.

Contents

Introduction The policy-making approach to the study of local municipalities

We will begin this introductory essay with a brief, critical look at some of the traditional concerns of students of local government, followed by a review of some of the divergent trends in recent empirical research on local politics and public policy, in which attention will be focused on the various phenomena that contemporary political scientists have used to explain similarities and differences in local-level public-policy decisions. A very general model of politics will be set forth. The subsequent discussion and elaboration of this policy-making model will enable us not only to summarize various determinants of public-policy decisions at the local level, but also to incorporate them into a common conceptual framework, one that provides a preliminary inventory of key concepts and variables currently being used in research on local politics. Although reading the selections in this volume will give you a more exact understanding of the relationships among key components of the local-level policy-making model, you should be acutely aware of the serious gaps in our understanding of central-city and suburban politics.

Traditional concerns: the study of local government

Students and practitioners of local government tend to become victims of their traditions, to be dominated by their habit patterns. They become blinded by their own "truths" and their own environs. Perhaps persons engaged in local government research need to engage regularly in professional introspection and "extrospection." Research analysts might profitably spend some of their time testing the validity of currently accepted conclusions and implicit assumptions.[1]

[1] Allan R. Richards, "Local Government Research: A Partial Evaluation," *Public Administration Review*, vol. 14, no. 4 (Autumn 1954), p. 274.

This statement should alert you to how theory and research in an area of inquiry can be influenced by traditional concerns, assumptions, and findings. For example, the total literature on municipal government is vast, but until recent years, significant scholarly, and particularly empirical, studies have been rare. Using historical and legal data, traditional students of the subfield of political science, municipal government, devoted primary attention to the formal authority and institutions of local government and political reforms.[2] The basic strategy followed in many early studies was to describe existing governmental arrangements and evaluate them according to whether or not they gave rise to economical and efficient government. If they did not, changes in form of government, in how local officials were to be elected, and so on, were prescribed.

This "tinkering" with the formal rules and procedures under which local governments operated was disappointing theoretically.[3] Largely the result of a narrow approach and a concern with immediate solutions, it was also due to the use of a number of unverified, highly questionable assumptions about the changes in government performance that would be forthcoming if a particular form of government, such as the council manager plan, were adopted by a local municipality. Although legal rules and procedures (laws) do structure the formal organization of government, they in no way assure "good government." (For example, might not the imposition of a particular legal form, no matter how logical or reasonable, have negative as well as positive political effects? And might not criteria other than those of economy and efficiency be used to evaluate changes in governmental form?)

Students of municipal government were most concerned with how governments *ought* to function. They devoted very little attention to describing or attempting to explain their actual operation. Perhaps if they had, their prescriptions for change would not have been so narrow and simplistic. In any case, research in this "lost world of municipal government," as it has been so aptly characterized by Lawrence Herson, fell short of the minimum contemporary requirements for systematic empirical inquiry in the social sciences.[4] Such research has been criticized for its normative and prescriptive nature, its insularity from the mainstream of social and political inquiry, its use of outdated and untenable assumptions, and its failure to provide adequate standards of proof. Studded with facts gathered with little regard for the construction of general explanatory theories, it is at the same time beset with prescriptions for change that have been advanced without having been verified empirically as efficacious.[5]

[2] This approach is discussed further in: Wallace S. Sayre and Nelson Polsby, "American Political Science and the Study of Urbanization," in Philip M. Hauser and Leo F. Schnore (eds.), *The Study of Urbanization* (New York: John Wiley, 1965), pp. 115-156.

[3] Robert T. Daland, "Bibliographical Article: Political Science and the Study of Urbanism," *The American Political Science Review*, vol. 51, no. 2 (June 1957), p. 492. This is an excellent, though somewhat dated, review article.

[4] Lawrence J. Herson, "The Lost World of Municipal Government," *The American Political Science Review*, vol. 51, no. 2 (June 1957), pp. 330-345.

[5] *Ibid.*, p. 330.

While almost no systematic empirical research on the policy-making process or political change was hitherto undertaken by students of municipal government, this is particularly true of those studies influenced by the reformist movement of the late nineteenth and early twentieth centuries. Today, this tradition still serves to direct attention away from examination of the policy-making process—the interactions taking place among individuals and groups in a community that result in public-policy decisions—and analysis of political change.[6] As a result, few conceptual frameworks, or models, have been developed that focus attention not only on the formal rules and procedures of local governments and on governmental institutions, but also on the policy-making process and policy outcomes. In addition, political change at the local level remains a largely neglected area of inquiry.

Recent concerns: the study of local politics and public policy

Although public policy, or the authoritative actions (decisions) of local city councils, have long been of concern to students of municipal government, only recently have political scientists begun to empirically examine those phenomena which influence the initiation, adoption, and implementation of such policies. Neglected has been investigation of the impact of nonlegal and noninstitutional factors on the political attitudes and behavior of municipal residents and their political leaders and on the actions of local governments.

Even as late as 1957, there had been no adequate study of the urban policy-making process.[7] The few case studies that had been undertaken did little more than list common types of interest groups, leaving unexamined the extent of their impact and the impact of other factors on public policy. Studies of municipal policy decisions were mainly public administration cases dealing with a particular problem, and were carried out in a few large cities, like New York, Chicago, and Philadelphia.[8] This meant that the policy-making process and resulting policy decisions of most central cities and their suburbs were simply not studied.[9]

[6] Bryan T. Downes and Timothy M. Hennessey, "Theory and Concept Formation in the Comparative Study of Urban Politics: Problems of Process and Change," paper delivered at the 1969 Annual Meeting of the American Political Science Association, New York (September 1969). Hennessey discusses this problem further in his selection in the conclusion to this volume.

[7] Daland, "Bibliographical Article," *op. cit.*, p. 508.

[8] For example see: Harold Stein (ed.), *Public Administration and Policy Development: A Case Book* (New York: Harcourt, Brace & World, 1952).

[9] Some early studies include: Robert S. Lynd and Helen Merrell Lynd, *Middletown: A Study of Modern American Culture* (New York: Harcourt, Brace & World, 1929); Arthur J. Vidich and Joseph Bensman, *Small Town in Mass Society: Class, Power, and Religion in a Rural Community* (Princeton: Princton University Press, 1958); Robert C. Wood, *Suburbia, Its People and Their Politics* (Boston: Houghton Mifflin, 1958); William M. Dobriner (ed.), *The Suburban Community* (New York: G.P. Putnam's, 1958); and A.H. Birch, *Small-Town Politics: A Study of Political Life in Glossop* (London: Oxford University Press, 1959).

Today, however, and as Herbert Jacob and Michael Lipsky point out in a 1968 review article,[10] local politics as a subfield within political science is no longer "Dullsville." "Rather than being the laggard of the discipline that some political scientists perceived it to be, the study of . . . local politics has reentered the mainstream of political research."[11] Since 1957, numerous empirical case studies of municipal policy-making have appeared,[12] which have been classified by Peter Rossi as employing one or more of three basic research strategies.[13] The first focuses on the characteristics of decision makers and attempts to relate social and personal differences among elected or appointed political leaders to their policy choices.[14] The second moves away from the actual decision makers and examines the various groups or "partisans" (influentials) involved in a particular decision, seeking to find in their actions vis-à-vis the decision makers the ultimate determinants of policy decisions.[15] Finally, a third strategy stays close to actual decisions. It

[10]Herbert Jacob and Michael Lipsky, "Outputs, Structure, and Power: An Assessment of Changes in the Study of State and Local Politics," *The Journal of Politics*, vol. 30, no. 2 (May 1968), pp. 510-538.

[11]*Ibid.*, p. 510.

[12]For a survey of the literature on community policy-making since 1950, see: Charles Press, *Main Street Politics: Policy Making at the Local Level* (East Lansing, Mich.: Institute for Community Development, 1962); and Government Affairs Foundation, Inc., *Metropolitan Communities: a Bibliography with Special Emphasis upon Government and Politics* (Chicago: Public Administration Service, 1956). Supplements to this initial volume appeared in 1960, 1967, and 1969. Some representative studies would include: Martin Meyerson and Edward C. Banfield, *Politics, Planning and the Public Interest: The Case of Public Housing in Chicago* (New York: The Free Press, 1955); Wallace S. Sayre and Herbert Kaufman, *Governing New York City: Politics in the Metropolis* (New York: Russell Sage Foundation, 1960); Roscoe C. Martin and Frank J. Munger *et al.*, *Decisions in Syracuse: A Metropolitan Action Study* (New York: Doubleday, 1961); Edward C. Banfield, *Political Influence* (New York: The Free Press, 1961); Peter H. Rossi and Robert A. Dentler, *The Politics of Urban Renewal: The Chicago Findings* (New York: The Free Press, 1961); and Warner E. Mills, Jr., and Harry R. Davis, *Small City Government: Seven Cases in Decision-Making* (New York: Random House, 1962). For relevant reviews see: Charles R. Adrian, "Metropology: Folklore and Field Research," *Public Administration Review*, vol. 21, no. 3 (Summer 1961), pp. 148-156; Gladys M. Kammerer, "The Politics of the Metropolis: Still a Frontier," *Public Administration Review*, vol. 23, no. 4 (December 1963), pp. 240-246; and Robert Gutman and David Popenoe (eds.), "Urban Studies," *The American Behavioral Scientist*, vol. 6, no. 6 (February 1963).

[13]Peter H. Rossi, "Community Decision-Making," in Roland Young (ed.), *Approaches to the Study of Politics* (Evanston, Ill.: Northwestern University Press, 1958), pp. 363-382. Also see: Peter H. Rossi, "Theory, Research, and Practice in Community Organizations," in Charles R. Adrian (ed.), *Social Science and Community Action* (East Lansing, Mich.: Institute for Community Development, 1960), pp. 9-24.

[14]By *decision* or *policy makers* we mean those elected or appointed officials who have the authority, that is, the legal right to make decisions that are binding on community residents. Some representative studies employing this approach would include: Harold D. Lasswell and Daniel Lerner (eds.), *World Revolutionary Elites* (Cambridge: M.I.T. Press, 1967); Donald R. Matthews, *The Social Background of Political Decision-Makers* (New York: Random House, 1954); and James David Barber, *The Lawmakers: Recruitment and Adaptation to Legislative Life* (New Haven: Yale University Press, 1965).

[15]For example see: Edward C. Banfield and James Q. Wilson, *City Politics* (Cambridge: Harvard University Press, 1963); Robert H. Salisbury, "The Dynamics of

employs decisions as a reference point and seeks to understand the policy choices of decision makers as the outcome of relatively complex group processes.[16]

Although these case studies are seldom guided by any explicitly stated conceptual framework or model, they seek to explain. As a result, the proponents of each of these "approaches" to the study of public policy have presented convincing arguments for the importance of their findings for some decisions and for some decision makers. They have also been quick to disclaim the generalizations of researchers employing other strategies. However, political scientists should probably spend less time arguing about whether there is a structure of power or whether the social background of decision makers influences their behavior.[17] Instead, they should be more concerned with the conditions under which each explanation best fits the policy decisions being examined.[18] For example, Robert Dahl's concern over "who governs" is interesting and important, but an even more important question for students of politics is: Who governs, where, when, and with what effects in central cities and suburbs?[19]

Other recent studies have drawn our attention to several additional phenomena that may have an important impact on the policy-making process at the local level, and hence on public policy. For instance, a group of researchers has begun to examine how contextual differences among local communities are related to differences in their tax and expenditure policies.[20] Size of city, density of population, rate of population growth, median family income, and per capita assessed valuation have been found to influence the level of expenditures in most cities. Henry Schmandt and Ross Stephens present additional support for the hypothesis that a community's

---

Reform: Charter Politics in St. Louis," *The Midwest Journal of Political Science*, vol. 5, no. 3 (August 1961), pp. 260-275; Floyd Hunter, *Community Power Structure: A Case Study of Decision Makers* (Chapel Hill: University of North Carolina Press, 1953); Robert H. Dahl, *Who Governs?: Democracy and Power in an American City* (New Haven: Yale University Press, 1961); and Robert Presthus, *Men At The Top: A Study of Community Power* (New York: Oxford University Press, 1964).

[16] Very few researchers have adopted this particular approach. One notable exception is: James David Barber, *Power in Committees: An Experiment in the Governmental Process* (Chicago: Rand McNally, 1966).

[17] This position is most forcefully presented by: James Q. Wilson, "Problems in the Study of Urban Politics," in Edward H. Buehrig (ed.), *Essays in Political Science* (Bloomington: Indiana University Press, 1966), p. 131. See also the discussion and literature cited in: Nelson W. Polsby, *Community Power and Political Theory* (New Haven: Yale University Press, 1963); and Willis D. Hawley and Frederick M. Wirt (eds.), *The Search for Community Power* (Englewood Cliffs, N.J.: Prentice-Hall, 1968).

[18] Rossi, "Community Decision-Making," *op. cit.*, p. 379.

[19] Wilson, "Problems in the Study of Urban Politics," *op. cit.*, p. 133. See also the introductory essay in: Terry N. Clark (ed.), *Community Structure and Decision-Making: Comparative Analyses* (San Francisco: Chandler Press, 1968).

[20] For instance see: Harvey E. Brazer, *City Expenditures in the United States* (New York: National Bureau of Economic Research, 1959); Glenn W. Fisher, "Revenue and Expenditure Patterns in Five Large Cities," *Quarterly Review of Economics and*

wealth or resources, measured in terms of per capita income, assessed valuation, and median value of owner-occupied dwellings, are far more important determinants of total and per capita expenditures than total population or density.[21]

One of the most sophisticated and comprehensive attempts to analyze how community contextual differences influence differences in tax and expenditure policies has been the study by Oliver Williams and his associates at the University of Pennsylvania.[22] After classifying suburbs in the Philadelphia Metropolitan Area according to population density and locational criteria, they examine statistically the relationship between contextual variables and the fiscal responses of local municipalities. The factors they found most closely associated with variation in expenditures were the proportion of young adults in the population, land-use composition, population density, and social rank. Although they found no suburban prototype—economic function, wealth, and social characteristics were mixed in a diverse fashion—they did find these contextual differences to be consistently related to differences in municipal policy decisions.

However, these and similar studies suffer very serious conceptual and theoretical shortcomings.[23] When not altogether absent, the concepts used in this research are frequently badly conceived and ill-defined. There has also been a general failure to specify the exact nature of the theoretical linkages that exist between contextual phenomena and fiscal policy. (That is: How and why do these contextual factors bring about particular fiscal policies?) In addition, such studies leave much of the variation in public policy unexplained.

Nevertheless, as do similar studies of the American states, they encourage a mode of inquiry that has long been advocated but seldom practiced.[24] They demonstrate the potential for systematic comparison of interesting and meaningful hypotheses, using central cities and suburbs as units of analysis. They

---

Business, vol. 3, no. 3 (Autumn 1963), pp. 61-72; Glenn W. Fisher, "Determinants of State and Local Government Expenditures: A Preliminary Analysis," *National Tax Journal*, vol. 14, no. 4 (December 1961), pp. 349-355; Louis H. Masotti and Don R. Bowen, "Communities and Budgets: The Sociology of Municipal Expenditures," *Urban Affairs Quarterly*, vol. 1, no. 2 (December 1965), pp. 39-58; Thomas R. Dye, "Governmental Structure, Urban Environment, and Educational Policy," *The Midwest Journal of Political Science*, vol. 11, no. 3 (August 1967), pp. 353-380; and Alan K. Campbell and Seymour Sacks, *Metropolitan America: Fiscal Patterns and Governmental Systems* (New York: The Free Press, 1967).

[21] Henry J. Schmandt and G. Ross Stephens, "Local Government Expenditure Patterns in the United States," *Land Economics*, vol. 34, no. 4 (November 1963), pp. 397-406; and Henry J. Schmandt and G. Ross Stephens, "Revenue Patterns of Local Governments," *National Tax Journal*, vol. 15, no. 4 (December 1962), pp. 432-436.

[22] Oliver P. Williams, Harold Herman, Charles S. Liebman, and Thomas R. Dye, *Suburban Differences and Metropolitan Policies: A Philadelphia Story* (Philadelphia: University of Pennsylvania Press, 1965).

[23] Some of these are discussed in: Richard I. Hofferbert, "Elite Influence on Policy Formation: A Model for Comparative Inquiry," paper delivered at the 1968 Annual Meeting of the American Political Science Association, Washington, D.C. (September 1968), p. 5.

[24] *Ibid.*, pp. 1-3.

also raise some doubts about the relevance of many "structural" variables, such as the rules and procedures under which local governments operate (including forms of government), that political scientists have long valued for their ability to explain public policy. Finally, such studies direct increased attention to the importance of contextual variables, a set of phenomena that political scientists have long neglected.

One of the first attempts to comparatively examine the interrelationship between contextual and political characteristics of local municipalities was undertaken by Oliver Williams and Charles Adrian in the late 1950s.[25] They examined how various community contextual characteristics and several aspects of the policy-making process were related to the policy preferences of four medium-sized cities in Michigan. In an attempt to differentiate the policy roles of local government, they developed a fourfold typology: (1) promoting economic growth, (2) providing and securing greater life amenities, (3) maintaining existing services only, and (4) arbitrating among conflicting interests. They found that policy roles adopted in each of the four municipalities were primarily a function of the socioeconomic characteristics of their populations and the extent to which recruitment for political offices was structured by political groups. Communities with higher socioeconomic-status populations had a more structured recruitment process and councils that were more likely to promote economic growth and greater amenities.

One of the primary problems with this study was its failure to clearly delineate the variables examined and to specify their interrelationships. It was unclear how the explanatory factor used by the authors, the structuring of political recruitment, was related to such basic community contextual characteristics as the social and economic structure of the four cities. Is the first variable independent, or does it intervene and mediate the effect of the latter factors on public policy? Recent research has also been plagued by this problem of poor delineation, even though it has moved beyond studying a few communities.[26] One of the primary reasons for this is that such research has not been guided by any explicitly stated conceptual framework or model which clearly specifies the nature of the relationships among the key concepts and the variables being studied. In addition, the typology used by Williams and Adrian fails to meet the two basic requirements for such constructs. In order for a typology to be logical and meaningful, as well as useful for empirical research, the criteria used in distinguishing diverse types of policy must give rise to categories that are at once *mutually exclusive* and *jointly exhaustive.*[27]

[25] Oliver P. Williams and Charles R. Adrian, *Four Cities: A Study in Comparative Policy Making* (Philadelphia: University of Pennyslvania Press, 1963).

[26] For instance see: Robert L. Crain, *The Politics of School Desegregation* (Chicago: Aldine, 1968); and Robert L. Crain, Elihu Katz, and Donald B. Rosenthal, *The Politics of Community Conflict: The Fluoridation Decision* (Indianapolis: Bobbs-Merrill Co., 1969); and Francine F. Rabinovitz, *City Politics and Planning* (New York: Atherton, 1969).

[27] See the discussion of this problem in: Arthur L. Kalleberg, "The Logic of Comparison: A Methodological Note on the Comparative Study of Political Systems," *World Politics*, vol. 19, no. 1 (October 1966), pp. 69-82.

A model for studying policy-making at the local level: relevant concepts and concerns

One of our critical needs in the subfield of local government and politics is for comparative empirical studies that employ a common conceptualization of politics—a broader conceptualization than the one used traditionally by students of municipal government. Such studies will require the construction of appropriate conceptual frameworks and models that incorporate this broader perspective, to guide systematic inquiry. Once this has been done and sufficient comparative research carried out, we will begin to have a better understanding of why local-governmental decision makers do or do not initiate, adopt, and implement particular public policies. We may also know a great deal more about the various phenomena that either impede or facilitate policy change.

Let us first, however, briefly examine the essential characteristics of a model. A model simply sets forth a number of concepts in which one is interested and specifies the relationships among them.[28] It is a representation of reality, and in our case it directs our attention to those factors thought to have an important influence on policy outcomes. Despite the generality and abstractness of the model, the development of such a conceptual tool and the elaboration of the major concepts incorporated in it are among the first steps on the long road to the construction of empirical political theory (or theories)—theory that explains why local communities initiate, adopt, and implement particular public policies. In addition, the model provides a very general set of working hypotheses that require further specification and systematic testing.

It is my intention in this portion of the essay to set forth and discuss a general and, I hope, more adequate conceptualization of politics at the local level. This strategy is predicated on the assumption that adequate models of politics at one point in time (static models) must precede or at least be developed in conjunction with models of political change (dynamic models).[29]

In developing such a comprehensive framework to guide future research, we can draw upon the work previously reviewed. For example, we can view the three types of factors—decision-maker characteristics, group or "partisan" activities, and organizational contexts—identified by Peter Rossi, as potential

---

[28] Whether or not the factors included in our model form a "system," even in an analytic sense, is an empirical question, and cannot be assumed prior to systematic research to determine the actual interrelationship and degree of interaction among the various categories of variables. On this point I differ—that is, disagree—with both David Easton and Talcott Parsons and with other systems "theorists." For example see Easton's attempt to differentiate real and analytic systems in: David Easton, *A Framework for Political Analysis* (Englewood Cliffs, N.J.: Prentice-Hall, 1965). See also: Talcott Parsons and Edward A. Shils (eds.), *Toward a General Theory of Action* (New York: Harper & Row, Publishers, 1951); and Talcott Parsons, *The Social System* (New York: The Free Press, 1951).

[29] Wilbert E. Moore, "A Reconsideration of Theories of Social Change," *American Sociological Review*, vol. 25, no. 6 (December 1960), p. 817.

explanatory variables. Furthermore, the analysis and understanding of any particular decision is not likely to be as useful theoretically as examining determinants of types of policy decisions.[30] Research on the various phenomena that may influence municipal policy should also be comparative. Thus, decision makers operating within different institutional and community settings should be compared as they make decisions on various types of public-policy questions.[31] Such a revised approach requires a merging of earlier perspectives into a broader one. It also requires a sampling of local municipalities, decision makers, and public-policy issues. To continue undertaking diverse studies at the local level will be theoretically meaningless unless they are concerned with explaining a common dependent variable, such as public policy and/or other policy outcomes.[32]

For example, in developing such a framework, we can assume that public policy is one of the primary dependent variables that political science seeks to explain.[33] The objective becomes to incorporate within a comparative framework some of the phenomena that may account for differences (or similarities) in the policy decisions of individual municipal governments. The investigator focuses on the types of policy adjustments that municipalities make in response to differences in their demographic, ecological, social, economic, and political characteristics.

Moving from left to right in the model presented in Figure 1, we can assume that community contextual characteristics may influence the development of different rules, procedures, and political structures.[34] In addition, these same contextual factors may directly affect various aspects or components of the policy-making process and the public policies actually undertaken by local

[30] Rossi, "Community Decision-Making," *op. cit.*, p. 380. See the literature cited in footnotes 73, 74, and 75 for a more detailed discussion of specific "types" of public policies.

[31] For a discussion of research which adopts this particular perspective, see the various articles in: Clark (ed.), *Community Structure and Decision-Making, op. cit.* See also: Bryan T. Downes, "Suburban Differentiation and Municipal Policy Choices: A Comparative Analysis of Suburban Political Systems" (unpublished doctoral dissertation: Washington University, St. Louis, 1966).

[32] Oliver P. Williams, "A Typology for Comparative Local Government," *The Midwest Journal of Political Science*, vol. 5, no. 2 (May 1961), p. 150. See also: Albert J. Reiss, "The Sociological Study of Communities," *Rural Sociology*, vol. 24, no. 2 (June 1959), pp. 118-130.

[33] For a discussion of this position see: James A. Robinson, "The Major Problems of Political Science," in L.K. Caldwell (ed.), *Politics and Public Affairs* (Bloomington: Institute of Training for Public Service, 1962), pp. 161-188; and Wilson, "Problems in the Study of Urban Politics," *op. cit.*

[34] A similar model is discussed in: Richard E. Dawson and James A. Robinson, "Inter-Party Competition, Economic Variables, and Welfare Policies in the American States," *The Journal of Politics*, vol. 25, no. 2 (May 1963), pp. 265-289; and James A. Robinson, "The Major Problems in Political Science," *op. cit.* See also: Thomas R. Dye, *Politics, Economics, and the Public: Policy Outcomes in the American States* (Chicago: Rand McNally, 1966). One of the very real shortcomings of the analysis undertaken by these researchers has been their inability to adequately conceptualize (and measure) various dimensions of the policy-making process. For a thorough critique of these and related studies see: Timothy M. Hennessey, "Considerations of Theory and Concept Formation in Comparative Political Analysis," paper delivered at the 1969 Annual Meeting of the Midwest Political Science Association, Ann Arbor (April 1969).

governments. However, the influence of community contextual character-istics upon policy outcomes may be mediated by a municipality's rules, procedures, and political structures and/or its policy-making process. Public policy, as well other policy outcomes in the model, may be the result of the interaction among: community contextual characteristics; rules, proce-dures, and political structures; and the policy-making process. Or, as the outer solid lines indicate, community contextual characteristics may influence policy outcomes directly without being mediated by structural or process factors.

Each section in this volume focuses on one of the four major concepts in this model. The various selections discuss some of the relevant components of each concept and explore their political implications, particularly their impact on public policy. Because of the generality of the model and the discussion that follows it will remain for these selections to specify in greater detail the exact nature of the relationships among the four concepts in the model. A reading of these materials should also point out some of the major gaps in policy-making research and, hence, in our understanding of how and why these factors influence policy outcomes in central cities and their suburbs.

Several concepts have been used in the model in Figure 1 and in the above discussion that now require further clarification. Each of these concepts, which are simply abstract ideas generated after examination of local communities and existing research on local government and politics, represents a general category (or cluster) of variables:

1. Basic municipal contextual characteristics (demographic, economic, and the like);
2. Municipal rules, procedures, and political structural characteristics (the formal rules and procedures under which local governments operate, as well as the type and number of governmental and non-governmental political structures—institutions and groups—operating in local municipalities);
3. Characteristics of a municipality's policy-making process (citizen political attitudes and behavior, political participation, the nature of political leadership, the structure of power and influence, and the nature of the decision-making process through which scarce resources are authoritatively allocated);
4. Municipal policy outcomes (public policy, policy outputs, and policy impacts).

The municipal context

Politics always takes place within some environmental or geographic context (setting or milieu).[35] The game of local politics is played within the geographic confines of specific governmental units, such as cities, suburban townships, counties, special districts, and so on. Although *social* scientists

---

[35] Easton, *A Framework for Political Analysis, op. cit.,* pp. 59-77. Although I am not interested in differentiating local political systems from the environment in which they function as Easton is, this does provide a preliminary discussion of various components of the environmental context within which politics takes place.

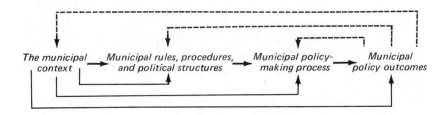

Figure 1.   A model for studying policy outcomes in local municipalities

have argued for some time about the important influence contextual characteristics may have upon political structures, processes, and policy outcomes, *political* scientists have only recently begun to consider contextual variables.

Even though we are now beginning to study the impact various ecological, demographic, socioeconomic, and cultural conditions within a community have on its political life, it is still unclear just how contextual factors influence local politics. This is largely the result of a failure to specify the exact nature of the theoretical linkage between these factors. Although researchers continually point to these phenomena as being important for political scientists to study, they seldom specify theoretically and then document empirically why they are politically important. This may be either because their impact is minimal or because we have only begun to consider the exact nature of the relationship between contextual conditions and local politics.

Like the other three concepts we shall discuss, the notion of a municipal context can be further analyzed into a number of important components. First, we can distinguish an *ecological component*: the physical environment or the geographic characteristics of local communities. In their selection in Part One, Edward Banfield and James Q. Wilson indicate how such factors as physical resources, topography, climate, and access to appropriate means of transportation had an important impact on the initial location and early growth of local communities. But today such physical characteristics as a deteriorating physical plant—poor housing, industrial, commercial, educational, and recreational facilities—have important implications for the policy problems facing many central-city governments, as well as for the demands being made upon them for particular policy changes. In suburban areas, access to transportation facilities plus the availability of municipal services and land may have an important influence on commercial- and industrial-location decisions. Such decisions may in turn have a rather direct impact on the resource base of a particular suburban community.

A second or *demographic component* of a community's context has to do with the general characteristics of a municipality's population: size, median age, growth rate, density, distribution, and other vital statistics such as rates of unemployment, birth, death, and crime. In their selection, Banfield and Wilson document how many of these factors have changed over time, as the United States became first an urban and subsequently a metropolitan nation. They also indicate how communities with large populations densely concentrated into a given geographic area may be faced by very different policy problems than a municipality with a smaller population dispersed over a similar geographic area.

Perhaps of equal importance for local politics is the way in which populations are distributed. Particularly relevant are class, racial, and ethnic patterns in a community. In relatively heterogeneous communities, such spatial patterning may have important implications for community cleavages and the nature of political conflict, while more homogeneous communities may not have to deal with such cleavages and resulting antagonisms. James S. Coleman, in his article in Part Three, documents how population diversity and resulting cleavages can have an important impact on the nature of community conflict, conflict that local political leaders may be called upon to resolve. Of further interest may be the percentage of young adults in a municipality's population, for research has found that this particular age group tends to eschew governmental services.[36]

A third, the *socioeconomic component*, refers primarily to the median socioeconomic rank or status of a community's population. We consider this factor separately because so much research has called attention to the important effects it may have on local politics.[37] In his article in Part One, Walter Williams, documenting how differences between "haves" and "have-nots" have been accentuated in Cleveland, Ohio, since 1960, is particularly concerned with the policy implications of this change in Cleveland's municipal context.

The relationship of an individual's socioeconomic status—that is, his educational level, occupation, and income—to his political attitudes and behavior has been amply documented by political researchers.[38] In Part Two, Frederick Wirt investigates the relationship of the socioeconomic status of suburban residents to their voting behavior, while in Part Three, Harlan Hahn examines the racial attitudes of different social-class groupings in Detroit, Michigan. In their selection in Part Three, Oliver Williams and his associates document how this factor also appears to structure the preferences of suburban residents for certain public policies. The median socioeconomic status or rank of a municipality's population has also been found to influence

[36] Williams, Herman, Liebman, and Dye, *Suburban Differences and Metropolitan Policies, op, cit.;* and Bryan T. Downes, "Suburban Differentiation and Municipal Policy Choices: A Comparative Analysis of Suburban Political Systems," in Clark (ed.), *Community Structure and Decision-Making, op. cit.,* pp. 243-267.

[37] See the studies cited in footnotes 25 and 26.

[38] Lester W. Milbrath, *Political Participation: How and Why Do People Get Involved in Politics?* (Chicago: Rand McNally, 1965); Angus Campbell, Philip E. Converse, Warren E. Miller, and Donald E. Stokes, *The American Voter* (New York: John Wiley, 1960); and Basil B. Zimmer and Amos H. Hawley, *Metropolitan Area Schools: Resistance to District Reorganization* (Beverly Hills: Sage Publications, 1968).

the extent and nature of political participation, the pool of available leaders, and the nature of the group infrastructure in a local community.

The *economic component* of a community's context refers to the nature of its economic base, whether it is manufacturing, diversified manufacturing, retail, or whatever. The diversification of a municipality's economic base may influence the extent to which economic notables are a viable source of political leadership.[39] Furthermore, the nature of the ownership of the key modes of production—whether they are local and/or national—may have important implications for the manner and extent to which businessmen participate in a community's policy-making process. In Part One, Leo F. Schnore also indicates that employing, intermediate, and residential suburbs each contain residents of quite different socioeconomic status from those of the other types.

A final component that social scientists have investigated may be labeled the *cultural component.*[40] This refers to the comprehensive set of attitudes, values, and beliefs citizens hold. Of particular interest to political scientists are the orientations community residents have toward government (their locally elected political leaders), toward the regime (the aggregate of basic governmental structures and the norms of this polity), or toward the community in which the government and regime operate.[41] These orientations, many of which are quite enduring, frequently involve the value citizens place on certain types of governmental action, on the legitimacy of various group demands, on the utility of political participation, and on appropriate forms political activity should take. They are largely a product of socialization experiences that individuals have gone through in the family, their schools, on the job, and so on.[42] In her article in Part Three, Jewel Prestage is particularly concerned with how the nature of the socialization process experienced by black Americans has influenced their political attitudes and behavior. This is an important concern because the continued existence of a political system depends on the extent to which citizens internalize norms and attitudes supportive of the system.

[39] Claire W. Gilbert, "Community Power and Decision-Making: A Quantitative Examination of Previous Research," in Clark (ed.), *Community Structure and Decision-Making, op. cit.,* pp. 139-156. See also: William V. D'Antonio, William H. Form, Charles P. Loomis, and Eugene C. Erickson, "Institutional and Occupational Representation," and Donald A. Clelland and William H. Form, "Economic Dominants and Community Power: A Comparative Analysis," in Hawley and Wirt (eds.), *The Search for Community Power, op. cit.,* pp. 319-329 and 78-87.

[40] This component, *political culture,* is discussed in: Gabriel A. Almond and G. Bingham Powell, Jr., *Comparative Politics: A Developmental Approach* (Boston: Little, Brown and Co., 1966), pp. 42-72. See also: Gabriel A. Almond and Sidney Verba, *The Civic Culture: Political Attitudes and Democracy in Five Nations* (Princeton: Princeton University Press, 1963).

[41] For a more detailed discussion of these orientations see: Richard E. Dawson, "Political Socialization," in James A. Robinson (ed.), *Political Science Annual, 1966* (Indianapolis: Bobbs-Merrill Co., 1966). In this review article Dawson also cites most of the relevant literature.

[42] Kenneth P. Langton, *Political Socialization* (New York: Oxford University Press, 1969).

The cultural component of a community's context, then, can link the individual directly to the polity. This is particularly true when the general attitudes, values, and beliefs citizens hold about their leaders, governmental structures, and community influence their political behavior and the extent to which they participate in the policy-making process. Research at other levels of the American polity has shown that such orientations may have an important influence. However, very little research on the specific influence of this dimension of a municipality's context has been undertaken at the local level.

As you can see from this discussion, the articles included in Part One simply introduce some of the critical differences and similarities in the contextual characteristics of central cities and their suburbs. Although the political implications of these contextual phenomena are briefly discussed, in-depth examination of the exact nature of their impact on local politics has been left to later selections in Parts Two, Three, and Four.

Municipal rules, procedures, and political structures

As we indicated in the first portion of this essay, our conceptualization of this second cluster of variables is inadequate, even though political scientists have expended a great deal of time studying both the formal rules and procedures and the political structures found in local communities.[43] However, let us differentiate—at least in an initial fashion—several components that we have placed under this rubric, components that political scientists have indicated may have important effects on political processes and outcomes.

Our first component is that of the *formal rules and procedures*, most often embodied in city charters and state statutes, under which local government units operate. In Part Two, Roscoe Martin discusses the rather direct impact that state intergovernmental relationships may have on the formal rules and procedures adopted by local municipalities. He also examines how such relations may place certain restraints or parameters on just what local units of government can do. Other researchers, such as Robert Alford and Harry Scoble, have discussed some of the factors that impede a city's ability to change its form of government. They examine whether certain contextual characteristics like social heterogeneity, class composition, growth, and mobility are related to the form of government a local municipality adopts, and then conjecture about how these factors either impede or facilitate

[43] There are some very serious shortcomings in the treatment of this particular cluster of variables by political researchers. There has been a basic failure to specify and then empirically verify what it is about the adoption of particular rules and procedures or the existence of certain political structures in a local municipality which results in particular policy outcomes. How and why do these factors influence the policy-making process and resulting policy decisions? A somewhat more enlightened perspective on this problem can be found in: Peter H. Rossi, "Power and Community Structure," in Clark (ed.), *Community Structure and Decision-Making, op. cit.,* pp. 129-138.

changes in governmental form. In his article in the concluding section, James W. Clarke addresses himself to this same question.

What impact do these formal rules and procedures have on the policy-making process and policy outcomes? Some researchers have argued that, varying considerably from community to community, they may structure the distribution of authority, responsibility, access, and power or influence in a local municipality.[44] For example, Jean Stinchcombe, in her selection in Part Three, is concerned with the effect that the adoption of reformed structures has on local political leadership. Robert Lineberry and Edmund Fowler, in their selection in Part Four, on the other hand, examine the impact reformed and unreformed governmental structures have had on the fiscal policies of American cities. The selection by J. David Greenstone and Paul E. Peterson plus the one by Terry Clark are also concerned with the influence this factor may have on the distribution and/or allocation of scarce resources.

Other researchers have focused their attention on how the degree of professionalism among city employees and the extent to which they are insulated from political control by civil service, the type of electoral system (partisan or nonpartisan), and the manner in which local political leaders are elected (wards and/or at-large), may influence the policy-making process and hence the public policies actually pursued by local governments. However, as Charles Adrian has observed:

> Structural arrangements do have an effect on government, but they neither guarantee good government nor prevent it. The forms are important because they affect the pattern of influence of various groups upon policy making. The specific structure in any given case helps to establish behavior patterns and attitudes toward power that definitely affect the process whereby decisions are made.[45]

Our second component encompasses the *political structures*, both governmental and nongovernmental, operating in local municipalities. Of particular interest are the type of local party system and its degree of organization, the degree of interparty competition, and the extent to which political recruitment is structured by political parties or similar groups. Fred Greenstein, in his article in Part Two, describes some of the factors that have brought about changes in political parties at the local level. Frederick Wirt, on the other hand, examines the growth of interparty competition both within and between suburban communities.

In addition, we are interested in the number and type of interest groups active in a local municipality, that is, the extent to which a community has a well-developed "infrastructure." A community's infrastructure and the nature of its local party system may both have important consequences for the

---

[44] Because local municipalities are "creatures of the state," many of the rules and procedures under which local governments operate originally were enacted by state legislatures. A thorough discussion of the possible effects these factors can have on political structures, processes, and outcomes can be found in: Roscoe C. Martin, *The Cities and the Federal System* (New York: Atherton Press, 1965).

[45] Charles R. Adrian, *Governing Urban America*, 2nd ed. (New York: McGraw-Hill Book Co., 1961), p. 197.

articulation, aggregation, and communication of political demands, and more generally upon the way in which the game of politics is played at the local level. Wallace Sayre and Herbert Kaufman, in their selection in Part Two, discuss the complex infrastructure that exists in New York City. However, as this article points out, each component of New York's infrastructure varies considerably in the manner and extent to which it is involved in the policy-making process. Although each component does perform important political functions, our lack of understanding of the role they play in the local polity is probably matched only by our lack of meaningful empirical research on the impact that such structures and the formal, legal, constitutional rules and procedures have on the policy-making process and policy outcomes.

It should be made clear that neither contextual factors nor the formal rules and procedures of local government operation explain why central cities and suburbs initiate, adopt, and implement certain public policies—though these factors may place certain limits or parameters on governmental action (by limiting available resources; conditioning needs, preferences, and political behavior; influencing access to political decision makers; and so on).[46] But on the other hand, the political "infrastructure" in a community can have a rather direct impact on the policy-making process and policy outcomes. However, at present we know very little about how a municipality's political structures impinge on these aspects of politics at the local level.

The policy-making process

The policy-making process refers to that set of interactions among individuals and groups in a community that results in governmental decisions. It is in many ways the core of politics at the local level—a dynamic process involving conflict as well as cooperation; involving also communication and power and influence relationships. The policy-making process "is a sequence of activities which results in the selection of one course of action, [sometimes] from a set of socially defined alternative courses of action which are intended to bring about a particular future state of affairs."[47] It is a

---

[46] The concepts *municipal needs, resources,* and *preferences* are discussed in: Williams, Herman, Liebman, and Dye, *Suburban Differences and Metropolitan Policies, op. cit.,* p. 78. For example, "municipal needs" refer to those conditions within a municipality which by themselves generate needs for certain public policies. They are essentially objective conditions, such as total population, density, and population increase, which set upper and lower limits on policy decisions.

[47] Richard C. Snyder and Glenn D. Paige, "The United States Decision to Resist Aggression in Korea: The Application of an Analytic Scheme," *Administrative Science Quarterly,* vol. 3, no. 4 (December 1958), p. 347. Our concept, policy making, is very similar to the Snyder-Paige concept of decision making. The decision-making process, as defined by Snyder and Paige, includes the actions and interactions that produce or give rise to the authorities' ultimate choice of a particular policy over its rivals. For a review of related literature see: Richard C. Snyder and James A. Robinson, *National and International Decision-Making* (New York: Institute for International Order, 1963).

process wherein ideals, individuals, events, and political considerations are analyzed to meet a problem situation.

The policy-making process can be viewed as a series of interrelated stages spanning a period of time. At each state, elected political leaders or decision makers must make a number of decisions. For analytic purposes and in order to understand this complex of decisions within decisions, we can break down the policy-making process into the following distinct stages:[48]

1. Identification of the problem: its formulation and articulation of initial demand(s);
2. Authoritative consideration of initial demand(s);
3. Developing possible alternative policy solutions;
4. Evaluation of each solution—policy deliberation—and the consequent organization of political support;
5. Authoritative consideration and decision to adopt (or not adopt) a particular public policy;
6. Making known or public the policy decision; and
7. Implementation of the public policy, coupled with subsequent learning and revision.

The policy-making process can also be broken down into a number of components: factors that may influence decisions made during each of the above listed stages.[49] First, when one begins to study the policy-making process in a local municipality, he may direct attention to the impact which *citizen attitudes and opinions* have on governmental decisions. As Harlan Hahn indicates in his article in Part Three, such attitudes and opinions are particularly relevant when citizens are called upon to approve referenda or vote for political candidates. We know that the attitudes about candidates and policy issues held by citizens, and their level of interest in local politics, directly influence whether or not, or how, they will vote or otherwise participate politically.[50] In addition, Oliver Williams and his associates, in their selection in Part Three, found a congruence between the policy preferences of suburban residents in the Philadelphia Metropolitan Area communities and their political leaders. A similar congruence was also found between resident-leader policy preferences and the public policies actually pursued by these suburban governments.

However, for a number of reasons, most citizens do not actively participate beyond the simple act of voting at the local level. Only a small percentage attempt to directly influence public-policy decisions by participating in other political activities. The extent and nature of *citizen political participation,*

---

[48] This is a composite scheme which has been extracted from: Robert E. Agger, Daniel Goldrich, and Bert E. Swanson, *The Rulers and the Ruled: Political Power and Impotence in American Communities* (New York: John Wiley, 1964); and Orville G. Brim and David C. Glass *et al., Personality and Decision Processes: Studies in the Social Psychology of Thinking* (Stanford: Stanford University Press, 1962).

[49] This breakdown, although somewhat arbitrary, appears to focus on significant aspects of the policy-making process which have been discussed and studied by political researchers. However, we also point out those aspects of this process which political scientists have failed to study in their research.

[50] See the literature cited in footnote 38.

then, is the second component of the policy-making process we are interested in examining.[51] This is primarily because such participation may have important effects on both the level of community controversy and on how scarce resources are authoritatively allocated—who gets what, where, when, and how.[52] For example, in her article in Part Three, Jewel Prestage examines some of the factors that influence black political participation at the local level, particularly how the attitudes and opinions held by black Americans affect whether and in what way they participate in local politics. On the other hand, in his article in the same section, James Q. Wilson discusses the impact increased citizen participation has had on urban-renewal decisions.

Political scientists, however, have devoted their greatest attention to "conventional" forms of political participation—voting behavior, party and interest-group activity, running for political office, and so on. As a result, they have generally neglected to study "less conventional" forms, such as sit-ins, boycotts, demonstrations, civil disobedience, violence, and so on.[53] Accordingly, they have generally failed to examine their impact on the policy-making process and resulting policy outcomes. Yet blacks and other minority groups, who have traditionally been excluded from meaningful participation in the policy-making process, are increasingly resorting to these forms of participation in order to articulate, aggregate, and communicate their demands for political change.[54] Rather than simply viewing such participation in negative terms, political scientists should devote greater attention to their obvious political objectives.[55]

Some citizens do participate in the conventional policy-making process in ways other than voting. For example, many belong to groups that may become involved in the policy-making process in some way. Such groups, but particularly their leaders, may actively articulate, aggregate, and communicate demands—as well as information—to political decision makers, and attempt to mobilize sufficient support to influence public-policy decisions. Although we know a great deal about the number and types of groups found in different

[51] For a discussion of some of the more positive implications of increased citizen participation in the area of education see: Marilyn Gittell, "Community Control of Education," *Proceedings of the Academy of Political Science*, vol. 29, no. 1 (July 1968), pp. 60-71. See also: Alvin Boskoff and Harmon Zeigler, *Voting Patterns in a Local Election* (New York: Lippincott, 1964); and Crain, Katz, and Rosenthal, *The Politics of Community Conflict, op. cit.*

[52] For a discussion of this perspective see: Harold Lasswell, *Politics: Who Gets What, When, How* (Cleveland: Meridian Books, 1958).

[53] Jerome Skolnick, *The Politics of Protest* (New York: Ballantine Books, 1969). This is a notable exception to this generalization. See also: Michael Lipsky, "Protest as a Political Resource," *The American Political Science Review*, vol. 62, no. 4 (December 1968), pp. 1144-1158.

[54] See the discussion in: Bryan T. Downes, "Black Protest and Urban Racial Violence: Confrontation Politics," in James A. Riedel (ed.), *New Perspectives on State Politics* (Waltham, Mass.: Blaisdell, 1971).

[55] Harlan Hahn, "The Political Objectives of Ghetto Violence," paper delivered at the 1969 Annual Meeting of the American Political Science Association, New York (September 1969).

kinds of local municipalities, we know very little about how they go about influencing policy decisions.[56]

Group activities and the formation of coalitions, then, becomes the third component of the policy-making process in which we are interested.[57] In his article in Part Three, Robert Salisbury discusses how the formal structure of government has influenced coalition formation in St. Louis, Missouri. In another selection in Part Three, Michael Lipsky examines how effective relatively powerless groups in our society have been in mobilizing the support of third parties and hence sufficient political resources to influence public policy. Although he concludes that protest has not been a very viable political resource, Lipsky does argue that in the long run it may be one of the most effective means for developing powerful political groups among the poor.

When examining the policy-making process at the local level, one should be aware that at each stage in that process different individuals and groups, in either an organized or ad hoc fashion, become active; coalitions form, and influence is exerted.[58] However, in most communities a great deal of influence is only potential. On most issues only a few individuals and groups actively make use of their political resources to directly influence policy outcomes. In fact, the sequence of activities that has been outlined, in which citizens more or less spontaneously organize to protest some felt injustice and carry that protest through publicity and organized demands to authorities formally vested with the power to redress their grievances, may simply be inaccurate or inapplicable. The process is usually more complicated, and the flow of action is often in the reverse direction, with demands being initiated, sustained, and communicated to decision makers by other political leaders.[59] One is likely to find a great deal of variation, then, from city to city and from issue to issue in the extent to which citizens, groups, and political leaders actively participate in the policy-making process and attempt to influence the behavior of decision makers.

In addition, most citizens have only indirect influence on policy decisions—either through elections or because some decision makers keep the real or imagined preferences of constituents constantly in mind when deciding what policies to adopt or reject.[60] However, through such legal procedures as the initiative, referendum, and recall, citizens can have rather

[56] See the volumes listed in footnote 12.

[57] On the problem of coalition formation see: Mancur Olson, Jr., *The Logic of Collective Action* (Cambridge: Harvard University Press, 1965).

[58] See the excellent discussion of influence in: Ronald L. Nuttall, Erwin K. Scheuch, and Chad Gordon, "On the Structure of Influence," in Clark (ed.), *Community Structure and Decision-Making, op. cit.*, pp. 349-380. In this selection these authors develop a typology of influence. They distinguish between individuals and groups with *manifest, potential, and reputed influence* according to whether the actors concerned have actual access to relevant resources and whether or not others involved in the policy-making process credit them with this possession.

[59] For example see: James Q. Wilson, *Negro Politics: The Search for Leadership* (New York: The Free Press, 1960).

[60] Dahl, *Who Governs?, op. cit.*, pp. 163-165, 270-275. Kenneth Prewitt, in a paper soon to be published, argues quite persuasively that at the local level, elections are *not* a very adequate means of holding public officials accountable. According to Prewitt, this is

direct influence on some public-policy decisions. When such means are used to influence public policy, the attitudes and opinions that citizens hold about policy issues and their elected political officials have important implications. The fourth and least-studied component of the policy-making process has to do with *political communications.* Who says what, through which channel, to whom, with what effects?[61] Single and group citizen demands, if they are to have any impact at all, must not only be articulated and supported but also communicated to relevant political leaders. Similarly, as discussion of a particular policy issue progresses, information must be gathered and disseminated to citizens and political leaders. Obviously, control of the communications media may have important consequences for just who gets heard in a local community. However, research has shown that face-to-face interpersonal communication is probably the most important source of information and opinion for most local residents, as well as a more effective means of influencing behavior.[62] In analyzing the way in which the communication function is carried out in a local community, particularly the "flow" of opinion, information, and influence, one must be aware of (1) the source, (2) channels used, (3) the content of the communication, (4) intended audience, and (5) the consequences, whether intended or unintended, generated by the communication.

Social scientists have spent a great deal of time studying the fifth component of the policy-making process, that is, the *structure of power and influence* and the general *nature of political leadership* in local communities.[63] In their article in Part Three, Peter Bachrach and Morton S. Baratz attempt to place in critical perspective the differences between sociologists and political scientists as to the locus of community power. In so doing, they point out how power has "two faces," neither of which sociologists see and only one of which political scientists take into account in their research.

We do know a great deal about the nature of power and influence, the varying forms it takes, and the factors that affect the centralization/decentralization of influence. However, social scientists have only begun to

---

primarily because many city councilmen are *initially appointed* to office and an even larger number *voluntarily retire* from office. Therefore, they have few ties with the electorate. Of course, as office holders develop political ambition and/or an interest in staying in political office, elections can be a very effective means of holding elected political leaders accountable.

[61] Harold D. Lasswell, "The Structure and Function of Communication in Society," in Lyman Bryson (ed.), *The Communication of Ideas* (New York: Harper & Row, Publishers, 1948), p. 37. See also the discussion in: Karl W. Deutsch, *The Nerves of Government: Models of Political Communication and Control* (New York: The Free Press, 1963); and Richard R. Fagen, *Politics and Communication* (Boston: Little, Brown and Co., 1966).

[62] One of the first studies to document this fact was: Bernard R. Berelson, Paul F. Lazarsfeld, and William N. McPhee, *Voting: A Study of Opinion Formation in a Presidential Campaign* (Chicago: University of Chicago Press, 1954). See also: Elihu Katz and Paul F. Lazarsfeld, *Personal Influence: The Part Played by People in the Flow of Mass Communications* (New York: The Free Press, 1955).

[63] See the literature cited in: Hawley and Wirt (eds.), *The Search for Community Power, op. cit.* In this essay, by *authority* we mean the legal right to act or to require

investigate the impact that particular power structures (leadership configurations) have upon public policy. We know something about who governs, where, and when, but very little about what difference it makes who governs.[64] For example, Marilyn Gittell in her selection in Part Three, documents some of the consequences of a narrow consensual elite of professional experts for educational policy in New York City. By way of contrast, Jean Stinchcombe points out some of the implications for urban-renewal policy which the fragmentation of power and influence plus an apathetic and divided leadership has had in Toledo, Ohio. Terry Clark continues this line of inquiry in Part Four, reporting on a comparative study conducted in fifty-one American cities in which he examined the relationship between the centralization/decentralization of influence and public policy in a number of issue areas.

We have already indicated how researchers have found that few individuals and groups exert direct influence over public policy. This is primarily because resources, such as time, wealth, access, prestige, reputation, expertise, numbers, and so on, tend to be distributed unequally in most communities.[65] Some individuals and groups possess much of such resources, while others, such as the poor and other minorities, possess almost none. Because they lack requisite resources and/or interest, most individuals and groups do not participate in the policy-making process at any stage. Only a few appear willing and able to bargain effectively in the political arena. In addition, participation may be further inhibited because the costs involved, for either the individual or group, may far outweigh the benefits received as a result of particular policy decisions.

There is some variation from issue to issue and from municipality to municipality in the extent of participation and the degree to which individuals and groups participate in different issue areas. Nevertheless, the general consensus among students of community power is that, even though there may be more competition among political leaders in some communities because of issue specialization, there is very little direct mass citizen and group involvement in the policy-making process at the local level. In addition, and as Bachrach and Baratz point out in their article in Part Three, meaningful citizen participation in and hence influence over public policy may also be hindered by either overt or covert attempts by those with power to keep certain issues from being discussed and/or certain individuals and groups out

---

others to act. *Influence*, on the other hand, refers to the ability to act or to cause others to act in accordance with one's intention. Authority may or may not give rise to influence, that is, the legal right to require action may or may not be sufficient to evoke it. Political influence, then, refers to the ability of individuals and groups to bring about changes in attitudes and behavior of those actors involved in the policy-making process and hence in the public policies actually pursued by local governments. In this discussion the concepts *power* and *influence* will be used interchangeably.

[64] For further discussion of this point see: Clark (ed.), *Community Structure and Decision-Making, op. cit.*, pp. 3-126, 139-156.

[65] See the discussion in: Hunter, *Community Power Structure, op. cit.*; Dahl, *Who Governs?, op. cit.*; and Presthus, *Men at the Top, op. cit.*

of the decisional arena.[66] This is the so-called "second face of power," which they discuss.

The sixth and final component of the policy-making process, the *decision process*, can be considered the focal point of this process at the local level. In city councils and on school boards, inputs of demands and supports that originate among citizens, groups, and leaders are acted upon by elected political officials, in such a way that it is possible for the polity to persist and for the council or school board to produce outcomes that meet the demands of at least some citizens while retaining the support of most. Through the decision process in city councils and school boards, elected political leaders translate demands and supports into authoritative decisions.[67]

There have been few attempts to analyze empirically the various factors that influence the behavior of those involved in city council and school board decision-making or to assess the functionality of their behavior for the resolution of political conflict. For example, do city councils respond to demands made upon them by individuals and groups? If they do respond, how and why do they react in a particular manner? These are two questions that have generally been neglected by students of local politics. It is simply naive and also misleading to assume that city councils and school boards always respond to demands made upon them.

Political scientists have begun to systematically examine the decision process in other settings and at different levels of government. But at the local level, and despite a longstanding interest in political leadership, students of politics have only begun to investigate factors that influence the perceptions, attitudes, and actions of those individuals who sit on city councils and school boards.[68] For example, in a selection in Part Three, I investigate the nature of issue conflict and consensus in a number of suburban city councils in St. Louis County, Missouri. I was particularly interested in whether rapid increase in a suburb's population gives rise to exclusive values, divergent interests, and strains that may be reflected in higher levels of issue conflict and/or factionalism, and hence less consensus in its city council. Although the data lent some tentative support to this hypothesis, I found it necessary to qualify the original hypothesis in several important respects. In another article in Part Three, Robert Crain and David Street examine some of the factors that influence the attitudes and behavior of school board members, and hence their decisions, in the area of school desegregation. They found that both the attitudes held by board members and the extent to which they agreed on an appropriate course of action had an important impact on the resolution of conflict in this particular issue area.

[66] See also: Peter Bachrach, "Nondecision Making and the Urban Racial Crisis," paper delivered at the 1969 Annual Meeting of the American Political Science Association, New York (September 1969).

[67] See the discussion of this "conversion" process in: David Easton, *A Systems Analysis of Political Life* (New York: John Wiley, 1965).

[68] For an exception see: Bryan T. Downes, "Municipal Social Rank and the Characteristics of Local Political Leaders," *Midwest Journal of Political Science*, vol. 12, no. 4 (November 1968), pp. 514-537.

Municipal policy outcomes

Public policy, policy outputs, and policy impacts are the three policy outcomes in which we are interested. Political scientists have studied public policy for some time. Initially, they were primarily concerned with the content of alternative policies. Since the late 1950s, however, attention has shifted to the analysis of the policy-making process and, to some extent, examination of the impact which various aspects of this process have on public policy.

Ira Sharkansky has suggested that we should also begin to inquire into the relationship among *public policy*, or the actions of government; *policy outputs*, or the service levels affected by these actions; and *policy impacts*, or the effect the service has on a given problem or population.[69] His initial research suggests that in many cases the actions of government may not have much effect on policy outputs or service levels. They may not even have the intended impact on a given population, such as alleviating demands for certain types of policy change. For example, one could argue quite persuasively that programs such as urban renewal and public housing have done very little to alleviate the basic problems of the poor, let alone upgrade housing conditions, change attitudes and behavior, or reduce demands. In his selection in Part Three, James Q. Wilson shows quite clearly how urban-renewal programs have simply intensified community conflict and increased the demands of the poor for additional policy changes. Nevertheless, very few studies have systematically examined the relationship among these three policy outcomes. As a consequence, we know very little about the impact (if any) which particular public-policy decisions have on urban problems and the people living in central cities and suburbs. Without such knowledge we are in a very poor position to evaluate the success or failure of government programs and hence, governmental performance. I would argue that these are research concerns which should receive greater attention in the future. In particular, we should consider the following question: What difference does policy make on people's lives?

As a result, our primary focus in this volume is upon public policy. Many selections, particularly those in Part Four, discuss public policy at the local level. They either examine why central cities and suburbs currently face certain policy problems, or attempt to explain the public policies actually pursued by these local units of government. For example, Alan Campbell and Philip Meranto examine the important effect contextual changes may have on educational policy. They are concerned particularly with the impact population changes have on the growing disparity between the needs and resources of many central-city school districts. Robert Lineberry and Edmund Fowler examine the impact reformed and unreformed governmental structures have

---

[69]This distinction is made in: Ira Sharkansky, "Environment, Policy Output, and Impact: Problems of Theory and Method in the Analysis of Public Policy," Paper delivered at the 1968 Annual Meeting of the American Political Science Association, Washington, D.C. (September 1968). See also the materials in: Austin Ranney (ed.), *Political Science and Public Policy* (Chicago: Markham, 1968).

on municipal fiscal policies, while J. David Greenstone and Paul Peterson investigate their influence on the distribution of goods and services or political power—the two somewhat contradictory goals of the war on poverty.

Other selections in Part Four examine the important effects citizen attitudes and behavior or political leadership may have on public policy in selected issue areas. In sum, when these important determinants of public policy are combined with those discussed in previous sections, it becomes quite clear that the problem of explaining why particular central cities and/or suburbs pursue divergent (or similar) policies is extremely complex.

In addition, after a reading of these selections, it will be apparent that although we do know something about the determinants of specific policies, we know very little about their impact on broader types of public policy. Consequently, much of the research in this area is not very cumulative. In order to overcome this particular problem, greater attention will have to be devoted to more adequate conceptualization of public policy, including the development of more useful typologies.[70]

Public policy, then, represents a community's commitment to specific goals and objectives.[71] In a formal sense, such policy is ultimately made by elected and appointed political leaders, that is, decision makers, in a local community.[72] Municipal policies are usually set forth formally in resolutions, ordinances, and local laws, but sometimes they are simply the result of informal agreement or understanding. They may affect the whole community, as is usually the case in tax matters, or only a single family, as would be true when a citizen requests that the street be repaired in front of his home. Although most policy decisions are simply routine and are not conflict-provoking, some are adaptive or even innovative and may involve a great deal of controversy.[73] Furthermore, municipal policy may emphasize the maintenance of existing services only, provide and secure greater life amenities, promote economic growth, maintain existing social character, and/or simply arbitrate among conflicting interests.[74] Policies may also redistribute

[70] This point is made in: Lewis A. Froman, Jr., "An Analysis of Public Policies in Cities," *The Journal of Politics,* vol. 9, no. 1 (February 1967), pp. 94-108.

[71] Dawson and Robinson, "Inter-Party Competition," *op. cit.,* p. 267.

[72] Rossi, "Community Decision-Making," *op. cit.,* p. 363. In this case, the particular type of issue defines the relevant decision or policy maker(s) according to rules laid down by law and/or custom.

[73] For a discussion of this typology see: Gladys Kammerer, "Role Diversity of City Managers," *Administrative Science Quarterly,* vol. 8, no. 4 (March 1964), pp. 421-442. Other related typologies include: Ernest A.T. Barch and Stuart D. Johnson, "Community Power and a Typology of Social Issues," *Social Forces,* vol. 38, no. 4 (October 1969), pp. 29-32; Aaron B. Wildavsky, "The Analysis of Issue Contexts in the Study of Decision-Making," *The Journal of Politics,* vol. 24, no. 4 (November 1962), pp. 717-732; and Peter Bachrach and Morton S. Baratz, "Decisions and Non-Decisions: An Analytic Framework," *The American Political Science Review,* vol. 57, no. 3 (September 1963), pp. 632-642.

[74] This typology is developed in greater detail in: Oliver P. Williams, "A Typology for Comparative Local Government," *op. cit.,* pp. 150-164; and Oliver P. Williams and Charles R. Adrian, *Four Cities, op. cit.*

scarce resources, regulate behavior, or bring about changes in the formal local-government rules and procedures and governmental structures.[75] Public policies are the primary outcome of the policy-making process, and represent the authoritative allocation of scarce resources and values in a community.[76]

Conclusion

Figure 2 represents an attempt to pull together and specify the various components and variables we have just discussed. At the most general level, our working hypothesis stipulates that there are consistent relationships between contextual and political differences which characterize local municipalities and their policy outcomes. After reading the selections that follow and my comments on them, you should be more aware of the exact nature of these relationships. However, you will also be acutely aware of the serious gaps in our understanding of the relationships among the factors presented in Figure 2.

One of the purposes in setting forth and discussing the policy-making model is that our conceptualization forces students and researchers to at least be cognizant of the variety of contextual, structural, and process factors that may influence public-policy outcomes at the local level. Most previous research has focused on only one or perhaps two important determinants of the public-policy decisions of local governments. It is to be hoped that our model will allow students of local politics to go beyond the concerns of past research, thereby increasing our understanding of the phenomena that give rise to policy problems and influence municipal-policy outcomes. The model, as set forth initially in Figure 1 and elaborated in Figure 2, clearly delineates some of the concepts and variables one might incorporate into such an analysis. It also specifies, although in only a very general manner, their relationships to the primary dependent variable we are attempting to explain.

We hope that students of local politics will begin to systematically examine the linkages among the concepts and variables in the model. This is something they have generally failed to do in the past. For example, greater attention should be devoted to investigating the impact that contextual factors, the formal rules and procedures under which local units of government operate, and political structures have upon the attitudes and behavior of local political leaders. Of particular interest would be their influence on

[75] For a discussion of these particular types of policies see: Robert H. Salisbury, "The Analysis of Public Policy: A Search for Theories," in Ranney (ed.), *Political Science and Public Policy, op. cit.*, pp. 151-175.

[76] This is similar to the conception set forth in: Easton, *A Framework for Political Analysis, op. cit.*; and Gladys M. Kammerer, Charles D. Farris, John M. DeGrove, and Alfred B. Clubok, *The Urban Political Community: Profiles in Town Politics* (Boston: Houghton Mifflin Co., 1963). For a discussion of this process which draws more heavily upon economic theory see: Joyce M. Mitchell and William C. Mitchell, *Political Analysis & Public Policy: An Introduction to Political Science* (Chicago: Rand McNally, 1969); and R.L. Curry, Jr., and L.L. Wade, *A Theory of Political Exchange: Economic Reasoning in Political Analysis* (Englewood Cliffs, N.J.: Prentice-Hall, 1968).

Figure 2.   *Breakdown of model concepts plus selected variable listing*

The municipal context	*Municipal rules, procedures, and political structures*	*Municipal policy-making process*	*Municipal policy outcomes*
Ecological component: *Physical resources, topography, size of territory, climate, etc.* Demographic component: *Population size, age, growth, density, distribution (class, ethnic, and racial patterns), etc.* Social component: *Social rank of population, community wealth, etc.* Economic component: *Economic base, etc.* Cultural component: *Attitudes, values, and beliefs citizens hold about the community, the regime, and government at the local level, etc.*	Formal (and informal) rules and procedures affecting: *Form of government, type of electoral system (partisan or non-partisan), manner in which local political leaders are elected (at-large and/or by wards), etc.* Governmental and nongovernmental political structures: *Number and type of interest groups, extent of organized group activity (nature of infrastructure); type and organization of the local party system plus the extent to which political recruitment is structured, degree of inter-party competition, etc.*	Citizen political attitudes and opinions. The extent and nature of political participation. Group activities and the formation of coalitions. The nature of the political communications system: *Who says what, through which channel, to whom, with what effects?* Structure of power/ influence (Who governs?): *Centralization/ decentralization of power/ influence, etc.* Characteristics of political leaders *(Distinguish between those of influentials and policy makers and aggregate): background, role perceptions, policy attitudes, etc.* Council or school board decision-process characteristics.	Public policy: *Fiscal policies (tax, revenue, expenditure policies); breakdown of general and specific policies pursued in various functional areas; differentiate types of policies (adaptive-control, areal-segmental, distributive-redistributive-regulative, etc.) according to explicit criteria (other than functional); differentiate policy emphasis of community (encouraging economic growth, providing greater life amenities, maintaining existing services only, maintaining existing social character, arbitrating conflicting interest), etc.* Policy outputs. Policy impacts.

leader participation in the decision-making process, and the effects of such participation on the policy decisions made by local city councils and school boards.

Because public-policy and other policy outcomes are the primary dependent variables that political scientists should seek to explain, it is important to increase our understanding by investigating within a comparative framework some of the variables that account for differences or similarities in the public policies pursued by municipal governments. For those interested in social engineering and/or making government more responsive to citizen and group demands, such an understanding should provide important clues as to where, when, and how to intervene most effectively in the policy-making process in your local communities. However, we should also be devoting greater attention to analysis of the impact which public policies have on the lives of people residing in central cities and suburbs and on the alleviation of urban problems.

Part one   The context of local politics: central cities and suburbs

Politics always takes place within some environmental or geographic context. Social scientists have argued for some time about the important impact contextual factors may have on local political structures, the policy-making process, and public-policy outcomes. For example, researchers in state politics and political development have documented how such contextual factors as urbanization, economic development, extension of the communication media, and a population's level of educational attainment may influence political participation, the development of a group infra-structure, political leadership, and public-policy decisions of a state or nation. However, it has not been at all clear just how contextual factors influence local politics. This may be because their impact is minimal, or because political scientists have only begun to consider exactly how ecological, demographic, economic, and cultural conditions are related to local political life.

The readings in this section are intended to introduce some of the critical differences and similarities in the contextual characteristics of central cities and their suburbs. Although the political implications of these contextual factors will be briefly discussed, in-depth examination of the exact nature of their impact on local political life will be left to later selections.

First, Banfield and Wilson are most explicitly concerned with the political implications of contextual differences brought about by historical changes in the metropolis. Of particular interest is how population changes give rise to cleavages, cleavages which Banfield and Wilson assume generate community conflict. Such conflict is politically important because local political leaders must often attempt to resolve or at least manage it.

Williams, on the other hand, is concerned with empirically documenting the accentuation of a single cleavage in Cleveland, Ohio. Since 1960 the gap between "haves" and "have-nots" has increased quite drastically. The extreme differences that have developed in the educational level, income, and occupational status of these two groupings of central-city residents have a number of policy implications that Williams also explores.

Finally, Schnore examines status differences among employing, intermediate, and residential suburbs. He concludes that suburban communities are becoming increasingly heterogeneous, at least in terms of the contextual characteristics he examined.

The City as a Setting for Politics

Edward C. Banfield
James Q. Wilson

The common contextual differences between central cities and their suburbs, particularly in older and larger metropolitan areas, are indeed striking. However, as this selection from City Politics *indicates, such differences took many years to develop. Edward C. Banfield and James Q. Wilson examine some of the historical changes in the contextual characteristics of cities in the United States. They trace the development of a "typical" American city from its initial location and early growth to the dispersal of people, industry, and commerce outward from a central core area. They document the urbanization process as it took place in the United States, and the subsequent growth of metropolitan America.*

Such contextual changes have had and continue to have important political implications, not only in terms of their profound impact on the policy problems facing many cities and suburbs, but also on conflict and consensus in the metropolis. Homogeneous communities tend to frequently exhibit consensus over matters of public concern. However, as Banfield and Wilson indicate, most central cities and many suburbs are quite heterogeneous. They are made up of populations that vary in socioeconomic status, racial and ethnic composition, and political affiliation. These contextual differences form the community's basic divisions or cleavages, providing the possible basis for the emergence of community conflict, which local governments must attempt to manage or resolve.

Will the principal divisions or cleavages in the metropolis be accentuated by further contextual changes? What impact will the continued exodus of whites to the suburbs have on city-suburban, racial, and partisan conflicts? What is likely to be the future role of the central city in American society if the trends described by Banfield and Wilson continue in their present direction? Should government do anything to reverse the trends described or should it simply be content to manage and resolve conflicts that arise between individuals and groups over matters of public concern? These are all questions that should be considered as you read and discuss this selection.

Introduction

Politics arises out of conflicts, and it consists of the activities—for example, reasonable discussion, impassioned oratory, balloting, and street fighting—by which conflict is carried on. In the foreground of a study of city politics, then, belong the issues in dispute, the cleavages which give rise to them and nourish them, the forces tending toward consensus, and the laws, institutions, habits, and traditions which regulate conflict. But these cannot be understood without some account of the factors conditioning them. The city is an arrangement of people in space. Certain developmental tendencies are inherent in it, and it is subject to external pressures as well. The nature of the arrangement (and of the pressures and tendencies) fixes in a general way the form and content of the conflict that goes on within the city.

To speak of "the American city" generically may strike the reader as implausible, even though it is only general features that we propose to discuss. To most Americans the differences among cities, especially the larger ones, are probably more conspicuous than the similarities. Boston, so it seems, could hardly be more different from Houston, or Atlanta, or even Cincinnati. Chicago is a world apart from Philadelphia and another world apart from Los Angeles. Everyone knows that New York is *sui generis*—a world city.

The differences are, indeed, striking. Nevertheless there are enough important underlying similarities to make discussion of a typical situation and a typical set of problems worthwhile. It must be kept in mind, however, that what is true of the "typical" city may not be true of a particular one and certainly will not be the *whole* truth about any city.

The typical city exists within a metropolitan area. The Census in 1960 defined 212 such areas in the United States for statistical purposes, ranging in size from the New York area with almost 600 local governments and 10,694,633 people to the Meriden, Connecticut, area with few local governments and 51,850 people. For our present purposes, a metropolitan area consists of a central city, several suburban cities (residential or industrial or both, and of various sizes) and, in the interstices between the cities, villages and unincorporated places. The metropolitan area is often coextensive with a county, but it may include parts of two or three (in a few cases even more) counties. What makes it a unity, to the extent that it is one, is a common

Reprinted by permission of the publishers from Edward C. Banfield and James Q. Wilson, *City Politics* (Cambridge, Massachusetts: Harvard University Press, Copyright, 1963), pp. 7-17, by the President and Fellows of Harvard College and The Massachusetts Institute of Technology.

orientation—cultural and political, perhaps, but mainly economic—toward the central city. The central city is called "central" because it is the object of this common orientation. Where there is a discontinuity in the pattern of settlement, it is this that usually fixes the boundaries of the metropolitan area: beyond a certain point urban settlement ceases and there is a gap of many miles to the next urban settlement. In some cases, however, there is no discontinuity: settlements extend without interruption, some being oriented toward one large city and some toward another. Rather arbitrarily in such cases (for the orientation of the cities is usually ambiguous and the line of demarcation between them is not clear), it is said that one part of the contiguous bloc of settlement constitutes one metropolitan area and another part constitutes a second.

No metropolitan area has a general-purpose government serving the whole of it. There are in many places governments which perform one or two functions (e.g., sewage disposal) for the whole of a metropolitan area, and there are two or three general-purpose governments (e.g., Dade County, Florida) that serve a considerable part of the metropolitan area. But one cannot at present speak of "metropolitan government" as a thing that exists in the United States. Government in the metropolitan area (not "of" it, for there is no government *of* it as such) consists of municipal corporations of various kinds. The most common are city governments, school districts and similar bodies organized to perform special functions, and counties.

Developmental history[1]

As a rule, the central city is the oldest part of the metropolitan area. It is apt to be on a river or a well-protected harbor. Every sizable city requires a large flow of water to carry away its waste products (this is true even if the waste is nothing more than the effluent of a modern sewage disposal plant), and this would be a sufficient reason for cities to be located close to rivers, lakes, and oceans. But there is an additional reason why the larger cities are near water: most of them were founded before there were railroads, and transportation was then mainly by water.

The oldest part of the central city, the point from which its expansion began, is closest to the river or harbor. This is where the core of the city is likely to be now. The central business district—"downtown"—the place where office buildings, banks, theaters, and restaurants are thickest and at which all transportation lines converge—is, if not the exact site of the first settlement, at least adjacent to it.

When the central cities were laid out, people traveled on foot. Accordingly, everyone—factory hands, clerks, and merchants—lived close to the center of things. Although there was limitless space to be had outside the city, the city was built at a very high density. Streets were narrow, lots were small, and

[1] For this account we owe a general debt to Raymond Vernon, *The Myth and Reality of Our Urban Problems* (Cambridge, Mass.: Joint Center for Urban Studies, 1962).

houses were crowded together. The rich lived on the hills, a few minutes by carriage from their places of business. The poor were crowded together in the mudflats along the river front, close to their work, or in whatever open spaces they could find around warehouses and breweries. The middle class, perforce, lived on the edges of the city, a safe distance from the noise, confusion, and immorality of the waterfront.

Late in the nineteenth century, changes in transportation changed the form of the city. People began to travel on electric trolleys or trains rather than by foot. This meant that their residences could be farther away from their places of work. The growth of the railroads tended also to cause the city to spread out. Taking advantage of rail transportation, many industries left the waterfronts and located beyond what were then the city boundaries. Meanwhile central business districts were growing. The skyscraper was invented (following the invention of structural steel and of the electric elevator), and as great insurance, banking, and industrial empires came into being, the centers of cities filled with offices and office workers. In its essential elements, however, the structure of the city remained as it had been. The rich and the poor continued to occupy the core (the rich in the desirable and the poor in the undesirable locations) and the middle class settled the outskirts.

The city's rapid growth required raising large sums in taxes. The burden was by no means intolerable, however, because it could spread over the real estate of the thriving central business district and the property of solid citizens in the outlying residential neighborhoods. Furthermore, municipal boundaries were flexible. The city annexed outlying neighborhoods as fast as they were populated; the residents of these neighborhoods were anxious to be annexed because they depended on the central city for services.

Beginning in the 1920's, another change in the technology of transportation accelerated the dispersion of the city. Widespread use of the automobile enabled the middle class to move outside the city. During the preceding decades this class, growing in numbers and income, had built new homes within the city. These were mostly three- and four-story row houses and single dwellings on very small lots, located along the lines of the electric railways. The density of population in these middle-class neighborhoods was high. The freedom of movement that the automobile gave encouraged the middle class to begin almost at once to leave the "crowded city" for the suburban countryside, where one could have "a place of one's own." Around the city "dormitory suburbs" sprang up, the populations of which commuted to the central business district of the city. This "flight to the suburbs" still continues.

To some extent the movement out of the central city expressed (and expresses) the desire of offspring of immigrant parents to cut themselves off both from the slum or semi-slum, and from status attributes that it more or less symbolized. To some extent, too, it expressed the desire for more living space and for the satisfactions of rural life. There was also an economic factor at work. It was more costly to create the kind of houses and neighborhoods that were wanted in the central city, where lots were too small and houses had to be rebuilt, than to start afresh in a new suburb. Central-city neighborhoods that were only twenty or thirty years old were, by the standards of the more prosperous 1940's and 1950's, obsolete. Nothing, therefore, could prevent the mass migration of the middle class from the central city and its abandonment of most of the housing built in the first decades of the century.

From the New Deal on, the flight to the suburbs was encouraged, although inadvertently, by the federal government. The Federal Housing Administration (created in 1934) and, since World War II, the Veterans Administration, have insured (and hence subsidized) loans for the purchase of houses. Because both agencies were concerned about the soundness of the loans they guaranteed, they virtually limited them to the financing of *new* homes, which meant, for all practical purposes, homes in the new suburbs. By 1959 the FHA had "helped to make it possible for three out of every five American families to own their own homes."[2]

The movement to the suburbs began long before expressways were built to make automobile travel convenient. No matter how congested the roads, there were plenty of people ready to commute. The heavy subsidization of expressway construction by the state and federal governments was intended in part to bring new life to the downtown business districts of the central cities. The cities tore themselves open to make way for new superhighways in order to attract shoppers back to their big department stores. The improvement in transportation, however, had the unintended effect of encouraging even more people to live outside the city while working in it, or—in more and more cases—to live *and* work outside it.[3]

The central-city housing left by the middle class has been taken over by the poor. The densest slums in the center of the city have lost population and the better neighborhoods in the outlying sections have gained it. This has been going on for many years, but the rate has been dramatic in the last decade or so. In Philadelphia, for example, a district between the two rivers, the oldest, poorest, and most overcrowded part of the city, lost almost 20 percent of its population between 1950 and 1960 and now contains 72 percent fewer people than it did a hundred years ago. Figure 1 shows the Philadelphia trend in the 1950's. A similar trend could be shown for many large American cities.

The rapid spreading out has made the slum increasingly visible in recent years and has given many middle-class people the impression that there is a new and growing "slum problem." Actually, the cities have fewer slum dwellers now than ever before. The difference is that the slums are now less dense and less centralized. From the standpoint of the poor, this is a very good thing. A family that used to live in a decaying tenement with fifty or a hundred other families thinks itself (and is) much better off in a place that is

[2] U.S. Federal Housing Administration, "The FHA Story in Summary, 1934-1959" (FHA 375).

[3] For a summary of the effects of the highway program, see U.S. Department of Commerce, "Studies of the Economic and Social Effects of Highway Improvement," *Final Report of the Highway Cost Allocation Study,* part 6, House doc. 72, 87th Congress, 1st session, 1961.

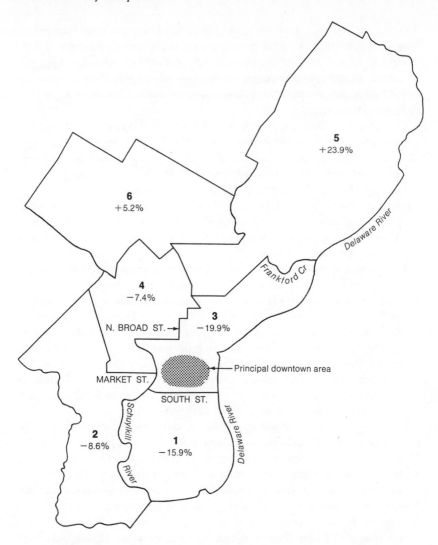

Figure 1. Population changes in Philadelphia by Congressional district, 1950-1960.
Source: U.S. Bureau of the Census, **Congressional District**
Data Book *(87th Congress),* **1961.**

merely dilapidated and that is lived in by only two or three other families.
But to those middle-class people who are not yet ready to move out of the
transitional neighborhoods or who look back nostalgically from the suburbs
at the "nice" neighborhoods where they grew up, the "invasion" of the slum
dwellers seems a catastrophe.

That the slum dwellers are mostly Negroes (and, in a few cities, Puerto
Ricans) makes the spread of the slum all the more conspicuous, and, for some
people, all the more horrifying. The existence of large stocks of both jobs and
poor housing (poor by middle-class standards, that is) has enabled a great
many Negroes to come to the central cities from the small towns of the

South. As Table 1 illustrates, migration and a high rate of natural increase have dramatically increased the number and proportion of Negroes in many cities.

Table 1. Percentage of nonwhites in large cities, 1950 and 1960* plus 1965 (estimates)†

City	1950	1960	1965	City	1950	1960	1965
Boston	5.3	9.8	13	Milwaukee	3.6	8.9	11
Chicago	14.1	23.6	28	New York City	9.8	14.7	18
Cincinnati	15.6	21.8	24	Philadelphia	18.3	26.7	31
Cleveland	16.3	28.9	34	Pittsburgh	12.3	16.8	20
Dallas	13.2	19.3	21	Richmond	31.7	42.0	—
Detroit	16.4	29.2	34	San Francisco	10.5	18.4	—
Houston	21.1	23.2	23	St. Louis	10.0	28.8	36
Kansas City	12.3	17.7	22	Washington	35.4	54.8	66
Los Angeles	10.7	16.8	17				

*In most places, the number of nonwhites who are not Negro is insignificant. Source: 1960 Census of the Population, vol. PC (1)-1B.
†Report of the National Advisory Commission on Civil Disorders.

Until recently, Negroes found it almost impossible to get housing outside of segregated slums. It was poor whites, not Negroes, who left the slums for the neighborhoods that the middle-class suburbanites vacated. Negroes got additional housing if they got it at all, by "taking over," sometimes at the risk of life and limb, one block after another on the perimeter of their slums. Late in the 1950's, however, the supply of housing caught up with the backlog of demand that had been generated by the war and by the large number of new families formed in the postwar period. Furthermore, the United States Supreme Court ruled in 1948 that "restrictive covenants" in property deeds could no longer be enforced to prevent the sale of homes to Negroes. White sellers then had both an incentive and an opportunity to sell to Negroes. Negroes have since been increasingly able to spread out into declining areas everywhere in the central cities and older suburbs.[4]

About half the jobs in an urban area exist to supply wants that arise because of the presence of the urban dwellers. As people move to suburbs, many jobs therefore go with them. Industry also tends to move outward when the central city ceases to be the only source of a labor supply. The central business district then becomes more and more a place for such businesses as require frequent face-to-face communication with a large and varied clientele. A businessman, for example, may find it indispensable to be where he can talk face to face with bankers, public officials, and other businessmen. But the record-keeping departments of his firm may very well be decentralized to the suburbs where land is cheaper and where many typists, business machine operators, and accountants live.

[4] See Davis MacEntire, *Residence and Race* (Berkeley and Los Angeles: University of California Press, 1961).

All these changes have created acute problems for the central cities. Their tax bases have shrunk from the loss of industry, business, and middle-class homeowners. But demands for city services have not decreased. Indeed, the replacement of the middle class by the lower has necessitated increased expenditures for fire, police, welfare, education, and other services. . . .

Living in the suburbs does not, however, prevent the owners and managers of the largest enterprises of the central city from participating actively in its affairs. To members of this elite, the central city—or rather its central business district—is not only the locus of their wealth but also the center of their cultural lives and the symbol of values that they cherish. Although they continue as business and civic leaders, the members of this elite are as a rule disqualified by their residence in the suburbs for elective and appointive office in the city. For this reason, it is no longer easy to find wealthy and cultivated people to serve on boards of education, housing and redevelopment authorities, park boards, and the like.

The middle-class people whose stake in the central city was never so large—who do not own department stores or newspapers and are not trustees of its hospitals and museums—tend to lose all interest in it when they move to the suburbs. For many of them it symbolizes a social status they have transcended. It is a place where "undesirables" live, and it is run by "corrupt politicians." The suburbanite commonly feels no responsibility to contribute to the financial support of the central city.

What has happened to the central cities has happened to many of the older suburbs and small cities as well. These have also begun to decay at the center as residents of old neighborhoods have moved out in search of more spacious, convenient, aesthetically satisfying, and prestigious places to live. Lower-class and lower-middle-class people, including, of course, Negroes, wait watchfully for housing to be "down-graded." Poor whites (but not Negroes) tend to "leapfrog" the newer suburbs to take root near the centers of the older suburbs, and to convert these neighborhoods that are obsolete by the standards of the middle class into slums and semi-slums.

It is often assumed that the flight of the middle class to the suburbs, urban sprawl, poor housing, unsatisfactory race relations and other characteristically urban problems exist chiefly in the large cities, especially such great metropolitan centers as New York, Chicago, and Los Angeles. Actually, as James G. Coke has shown with respect to Illinois, all of the same problems are to be found,[5] often in more marked degree, in many small cities. The difference is that in the large cities there is lively concern and protest about conditions that go almost unnoticed in the small ones. This, Coke very convincingly argues, is to be explained largely by political factors—especially the existence in the large cities of a larger number of highly organized and articulate special-interest constituencies, a larger number of policy-oriented professionals, and voluntary associations devoted to some form of community problem-solving.

[5] James G. Coke, "The Lesser Metropolitan Areas of Illinois," *Illinois Government*, no. 15, November 1962, published by the Institute of Government and Public Affairs, University of Illinois, Urbana, Ill.

Newburgh, New York, the city that broke into the national news in 1961 by defying the generally accepted standards for city welfare programs, is an example of a small place in the toils of these changes. Originally a whaling port on the Hudson River, it was long a predominantly middle-class trading center for the surrounding farm country. In recent years, prosperity and automobiles encouraged many of the better-off people to move out of town. This made it possible for less prosperous people to move into the places they had vacated. Eventually Negro migratory fruit pickers settled in four ancient waterfront slums. Suddenly Newburgh found itself with a serious financial problem. The assessed value of its central business district, an important part of the tax base, declined $945,000 in three years. Meanwhile, welfare expenditures rose rapidly; in 1961 the city was spending about $1,000,000, one third of its budget, for welfare (federal and state grants reimbursed it for 55 percent of this). Two thirds of the persons now on relief are Negroes. Some Newburghers blame the city's troubles on the Negroes, and it was against the Negro, of course, that the stringent welfare code was directed in 1961. That the poor must live somewhere and that they may be better off in Newburgh than they were in other places is not something which Newburgh, occupied as it is with its own troubles, is likely to consider.[6]

In 1960, most suburbs were still almost entirely white. Whereas in 1930 three percent of the suburban population of the twelve largest metropolitan areas was nonwhite, five percent was nonwhite in 1960. In seven of these twelve areas, there was in these thirty years only a slight increase in the proportion of nonwhite to white in the suburbs. In five areas—Philadelphia, Pittsburgh, Washington, Cleveland, and Baltimore—the proportion of non-whites in the suburbs declined.[7]

The differences between the central-city and suburban populations are of profound importance politically.[8] The central-city populations, which are often heavily Catholic, Negro, and lower-class, tend to be Democratic and to tolerate or even favor the old-style machine politics of bosses. The newer residential suburbs (there are, of course, industrial suburbs as well) tend to be Republican, to favor high levels of public service, and to be devoted to "good government."[9] The suburbanite is as anxious to turn his back on the tradition of the "boss" as on the old slum tenement. But not all suburbs have the same political composition, and all are subject to rapid change. As the middle class empties into the new suburbs and the lower class into the deteriorating portions of the older ones, the Republicanism of some suburbs is being diluted. In some cases this is at least partially offset by the tendency of those

[6]*Time*, June 29, 1961, p. 17, and *New York Times*, Sept. 17, 1961, p. 64.

[7]*New York Times*, May 7, 1961.

[8]Central cities, industrial suburbs, and old suburbs belong in one category in opposition to all the rest of the metropolitan area, i.e., newer suburbs and unincorporated areas. See Leo F. Schnore and Robert R. Alford, "Forms of Government and Socioeconomic Characteristics of Suburbs," *Administrative Science Quarterly*, June 1963, pp. 1-17.

[9]We have put "good government" in quotation marks here and elsewhere to indicate that we refer to the doctrines of the reform movement, not to what we ourselves regard as good government.

who leave the central city to be upwardly mobile individuals who adapt to the suburban environments by becoming Republican or "independent." Some suburbs will become Democratic, but others will become even more solidly Republican. The central cities, however, are likely to remain at least as Democratic as before. The relatively few people who move into them will be mostly lower-class whites, Negroes, and Puerto Ricans.

Even if these population differences did not exist, there still would be important political differences between the central cities and the suburbs. That some people live on one side of a boundary and some live on the other is enough in itself to make an important difference. Those who live in one place (say the suburbs) do not want to be taxed to support facilities and services in another place (say the central city).

The politics of almost every facet of urban government—of metropolitan organization, of housing, of race relations, of transportation, of finance—bears a close relation to the much larger question, which is often outside the view of the interests most actively concerned, of the future of the central city, and, indeed, of the structure and character of urban life. Not far below the surface in all of these matters lie the questions: Is the central city to become the possession of the lower class and of the minority groups or is it to be restored to the middle class? If it is to be restored to the middle class, where is the lower class to live? If it is not restored to the middle class, what will happen to the centers of economic and cultural life in the cores of the central cities? If these centers lose their vitality, how will the pre-eminent role that the central city has played in the creation and dissemination of culture be filled in the future?

The Crisis Ghetto

Walter Williams

Is our nation moving toward two societies—one black, one white, separate and unequal—as the National Commission on Civil Disorders concluded in its 1968 report? Walter Williams' analysis of 1965 data from a special census further documents, at least in Cleveland, Ohio, the emergence of "two Americas." This census reveals Cleveland's contrasting prosperity and decay. For instance, the area Williams labels the "Crisis Ghetto" has moved even further away from the rest of the city on all major economic indices since 1960. Although some have-nots have escaped the vicious cycle of poverty found in Cleveland's hard core ghetto, most remain.

Other research has shown that the accentuation of this important contextual characteristic—the basic cleavage between haves and have-nots—is not restricted to Cleveland. What are the political implications of such findings? First, one very real possibility is that a sharpening of economic differences between the races can only add to the potentially explosive nature of the ghetto and increase the overall level of antagonism and conflict between central-city and suburban residents. Second, such findings raise a number of important policy questions for local political leaders to consider. For example, can anything be done to alleviate the deteriorating economic position of the poor in our nation's ghettos? Williams discusses a number of possible policy alternatives, but places primary emphasis on the need for basic changes in ghetto institutions as well as institutions outside the "Crisis Ghetto." Will other changes also be required?

Introduction

The riot in the Hough section of Cleveland, Ohio, occurred in July 1966. Not much more than a year earlier, in April 1965, the Bureau of the Census had conducted a special census for Cleveland that showed unexpected social and economic changes in the five years since 1960. (See Figure 1.) What was most significant was a sharp economic polarization among the city's Negroes. A substantial number had moved up to a more affluent life; but the group in the worst part of the ghetto was at a level of poverty that was actually *below* the one recorded in 1960. Who rose and who stayed behind, and why?

What is most startling about the changes revealed by Cleveland's special census is their magnitude. These five years saw rapidly rising real income and falling unemployment for the city as a whole—but not for the very poor. The gap between haves and have-nots widened strikingly; and the most rapid widening was among Negroes—between those outside the slums who were rising, beginning finally to cash in on the American dream, and those still in the hard-core ghetto, on limited rations of income and hope.

In the special census nine neighborhoods at the bottom economically were grouped together and called the "Neighborhood." (See Figure 2.) The rest of the city, in which the prospering middle and upper classes are concentrated, was called the "Remainder of Cleveland." In Cleveland, however—as in the Inferno—there are different levels on the path downward, and one area of the Neighborhood is especially bad. This is the "Crisis Ghetto." It is predominantly Negro. Hough is part of it—on the edge.

The group that rose most swiftly in the period 1960-1965 were the Negroes who did not live in the Neighborhood. In 1960 they numbered 22,000. By

Reprinted from *Trans*-action, Vol. 4, No. 9 (September 1967), pp. 33-42, by permission of the publisher and author. Copyright © 1967 by *Trans*-action magazine, St. Louis, Missouri.

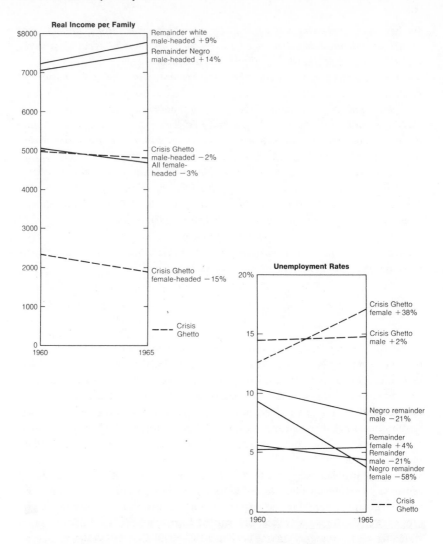

Figure 1. Cleveland: five-year changes in real income and unemployment.

1965 their number had almost doubled. In all Cleveland they had achieved the greatest economic gains, showing that the door of opportunity, for some at least, was opening wider. (And also providing a convenient, but unwarranted, rationalization against help for the less fortunate—for if some Negroes could rise so quickly through their own efforts, why not all?)

At the opposite end of Cleveland's economic spectrum we find a grim picture. The number of Negro children in poor female-headed households increased sharply. By 1965 nearly two-thirds of these poor Negro youths in female families were in the Crisis Ghetto. Further, the Crisis Ghetto's average resident was in worse economic straits than in 1960. Unemployment was higher, income lower, and a larger percentage of the population was poor.

In relative terms the Crisis Ghetto was further away from the rest of the city than in 1960 in terms of major economic indices. For instance, the income gap between the Crisis Ghetto and the next economic stratum (the other five sections of the Neighborhood) had spread visibly. The range of median real incomes for the four sections of the Crisis Ghetto and the five sections in the rest of the neighborhood was as shown in the table below.

Range of median incomes	1960	1965
Crisis ghetto	$3,170-4,900	$3,000-4,160
Rest of neighborhood	$5,450-6,230	$5,460-6,500

Hence the top of the Crisis Ghetto income range is now $1,300 short of the next economic tier, in contrast to $550 in 1960. And that next tier itself had suffered in income terms over the five-year period relative to the Remainder of Cleveland.

Thus, at least in Cleveland, the census validated our fears of the emerging "two Americas." If this portrays what is happening in other cities, it is most disturbing.

The Crisis Ghetto's potential for generating earned income has declined a great deal since 1960. Those economic units with lowest earning potential—female-headed families and aged people—have increased in absolute numbers, while those with the greatest earning potential (younger male-headed families) have diminished sharply. The Crisis Ghetto has become a concentration point not merely for the poor, but for the hard-core poor—those with least hope or opportunity of being anything else.

The widening gap

The increasing distance between Cleveland's majority and its disadvantaged segment is frequently hidden in the overall economic indices of the city. Averaging the increasingly prosperous and the stable poor seems to give a "rise" to everybody. But the almost unchanged poverty rate between 1960 and 1965 masks within different groups large movements that have further split the population. Between 1960 and 1965, the poverty rate:

—declined markedly among male-headed families while it increased among female-headed families;
—fell for white people, but remained almost unchanged for Negroes;
—yet showed a much greater decline (almost 40 percent below the 1960 level) for non-Neighborhood Negroes than for any other group (the whites outside the Neighborhood experienced a 12 percent decrease);
—and rose sharply in the Crisis Ghetto while it fell in the Remainder of Cleveland.

Another important change was in the *kinds* of poor families and poor people in the Crisis Ghetto. Between 1960 and 1965, the number of poor people fell by roughly 14,000. But members of Negro female-headed families increased by almost 12,000 persons (all but the merest handful of whom were found in the Neighborhood) while persons in families headed by Negro males and white males and females decreased by 26,000. As a consequence of these population changes in the five-year period, members of Negro female-headed families increased from one-fifth to one-third of Cleveland's poor. And in 1965, 60 percent of these poor, Negro, female-headed family members lived in the Crisis Ghetto.

Changes in the structure of industry have hurt the Crisis Ghetto. As Louis Buckley notes in discussing the plight of the low-skilled city laborer:

> The changes in the demand for labor in our central cities have been in the direction of expansions of industries requiring well educated white collar workers and a relative decline in the industries employing blue collar unskilled and semi-skilled workers.

Many of these modern industries have fled to the suburbs. Unfortunately, public transportation has not followed, so ghetto residents have difficulty getting out to suburban jobs.

Further, an increasing percentage of the Crisis Ghetto's residents are in families whose heads have the least likelihood of increasing materially their earned income. In general, the two groups with the most limited economic

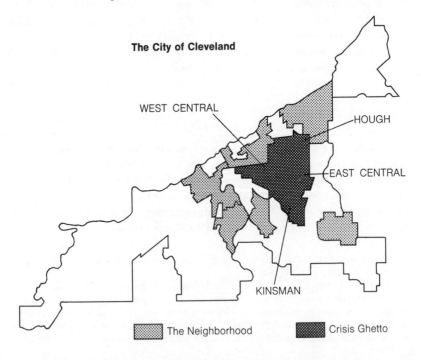

The City of Cleveland

WEST CENTRAL

HOUGH

EAST CENTRAL

KINSMAN

The Neighborhood   Crisis Ghetto

Figure 2.   The haves and the have-nots: The years between 1960 and 1965 saw rapidly rising real income and falling unemployment for the city of Cleveland as a whole—but not for the very poor. The gap between the haves and the have-nots widened strikingly.

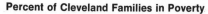

Percent of Cleveland Families in Poverty

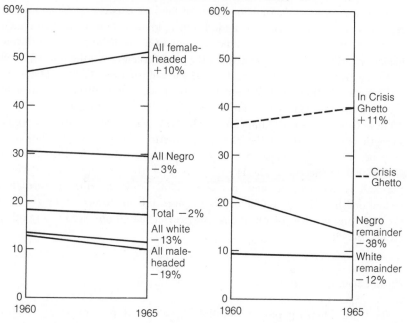

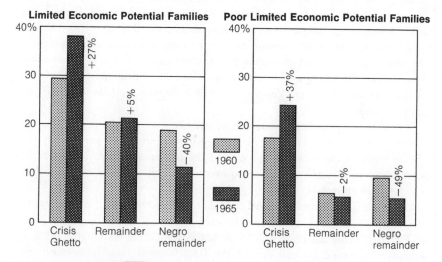

potential are family units (our definition of unit includes single persons living alone) headed by women and by the aged. These groups rose significantly over the five-year period as a percentage of the Crisis Ghetto population. (See Figure 2.) Not only do these two groups seem *least* likely to earn much more than at present—but they seem the *most* likely group to suffer an actual as well as a relative decline in earned income. In short, they have the lowest chance to improve their financial position, and the highest probability of declining. Once a unit in this limited potential group becomes poor, by definition, it is likely to remain so. This persistent poverty is the eroding evil.

Real income in the Crisis Ghetto declined by 2 percent for male-headed families and 15 percent for female-headed families between 1960 and 1965. At the end of the five-year period unemployment rates for both men (14.6 percent) and women (17.2 percent—up over one-third since 1960) were higher, standing at nearly three times the city's average; and the poverty level had risen from 36 to 40 percent. In 1965 the average Crisis Ghetto inhabitant was worse off than he had been in 1960, both absolutely and relative to others in the city. (The pattern of deterioration is shown in Figure 2.)

These facts have major implications. On the one hand, those with economic strength or potential *can* flee the Crisis Ghetto. (True, if Negro, they may only be allowed to escape to a better Negro area.) But it is also clear that entrapment in the Crisis Ghetto springs directly from poverty. The price over the wall is primarily money, not skin color. However, once poverty has locked one into the Crisis Ghetto, the chances of being forced to remain—and the bad consequences of remaining—are greater than if one lived in any other area of the city.

Population decline

The Crisis Ghetto population declined by about 20 percent during the five years (from 170,000 to 134,000 persons), and this exodus might seem to imply an explanation for the decline and the change. After all, if the more able, above-average people leave, averages should move down.

But exodus, by itself, cannot explain enough. Certainly the population decrease cannot be used to explain the absolute *increases* since 1960 of a few hundreds in the number of female-headed families, and of some 3,000 poor persons in such families. Yet that is what happened; and we have no pat explanation for it.

Nor does the population decrease necessarily counterbalance the possible adverse effects coming from the declining economic situation, particularly the rise in weak economic units as a part of the total population. These people seem likely to face the Crisis Ghetto over an extended period of time. What are the consequences?

The deleterious effects of a hard-core ghetto spread beyond the economy to the total environment—to schools, to street associations, to the preservation of life itself. This last point was driven home when three Washington medical schools threatened to pull out of the D.C. General Hospital because the meager budget provided almost medieval services. Even to be sick in the Crisis Ghetto is far more dangerous than in the suburbs. So, from birth to death the ghetto marks each person, and cuts his chances either to escape or survive. The Crisis Ghetto lacks the precise boundaries and imposed restrictions of the European ghettos of the past; but it is, nevertheless, an existing reality that limits and blights the lives of its inhabitants as effectively as did the old ghettos and pales.

Is this pattern confined to Cleveland? Only in Cleveland was a special census made for the city as a whole. But figures available for 1960-65 for

South Los Angeles (which includes Watts and in an economic sense is like the Cleveland Neighborhood) also show a decrease in real income per family, a small increase in the percent of poor people, and a decrease in the male and increase in female unemployment rates (the Crisis Ghetto differs only in that it shows a very small male unemployment increase). Further, Negro female family members became a far more significant proportion of South Los Angeles poor (we do not have city-wide data) increasing from 37 percent to 48 percent. While the number of poor people in Negro female-headed households rose by 9,500 (roughly 25 percent) the number of poor among white male, white female, and Negro male-headed families all decreased.

At the national level poor Negro female-headed family members have increased both absolutely and as a proportion of the total poor population. For 1960 and 1966, the number of poor persons (in millions) for these categories are shown in the table that follows.

	1960		1966	
	Number in Millions	*% of total poor*	*Number in Millions*	*% of total poor*
Negro female-headed family members	3.2	8%	3.8	12%
All other poor persons	35.7	92	28.9	88
Total poor persons	38.9	100	32.7	100

The non-Neighborhood Negro has advanced greatly in the five years between the two censuses—more, as noted, than any other Cleveland group. Of course, this great improvement can be partly explained by residential segregation. The white on the rise goes to the suburbs—and out of the Cleveland census area—while his Negro counterpart must stay in the city. Still, there is no doubt that the Negroes escaping the Neighborhood are advancing as a group more rapidly than any within the city limits, and closing in on the Remainder of Cleveland whites. Even more striking than their increasing prosperity were their increasing numbers—from 22,000 to 41,000. They now account for 15 percent of the Negro population.

The Cleveland data indicate that economic discrimination has declined in Cleveland since 1960. Is this only in the upper and middle level jobs or has discrimination lessened across the board? I believe it may have lessened somewhat across the board; but this may not help the Crisis Ghetto Negroes unless direct action is taken to overcome their difficulties. Any decrease in overt economic discrimination, of course, is encouraging. However, it is absurd to think that this change *alone*—even if the reduction in discrimination had been far greater than I expect it was in Cleveland—will set right all the damage of the past. The liabilities of the Crisis Ghetto Negroes caused by past discrimination—poor education, lack of skills, poor health, police records— would still hold them back in the job market. In fact, the reduction in discrimination *alone* may exacerbate the split between the various strata of Cleveland Negroes.

Earlier discrimination possibly served as a lid for the advancement of *all* Negroes, squeezing them closer together in income and opportunity despite differences in skills and potentials. But once the lid was lifted, especially during boom years, the more skilled, educated, and able rose much more rapidly than the others. So the gap widened. Unless something is done the more able Negroes should continue to widen their lead until they too become part of the symbols of success that have so far evaded the Crisis Ghetto Negroes and make failure ever more visible and disturbing.

At the opposite pole, though population in the Crisis Ghetto declined by one-fifth, Negro female-headed families increased by 8 percent, children in these families by 25 percent (16,900 to 21,000), and children in *poor* Negro female-headed families by 30 percent (13,100 to 17,000). Of the 21,000 children of female-headed families in the Crisis Ghetto, 17,000 are living below the poverty level. And it is this increasing group of female-headed families that suffered the largest real income decline of the five-year period, falling from $2,300 to $1,950 per family per year. That is, at the later survey date (1965), the average Crisis Ghetto female-headed family had an income *per week* of just over $37.50.

The implications of these statistics are appalling. There were 3,900 *more* poverty-stricken children in the ghetto in 1965 than 1960—in a population 36,000 less—and there is no reason to believe that this trend is not continuing or accelerating. These children can do least to improve their condition—yet they must have tremendous influence on the future of the Neighborhood, and of all Cleveland.

Poor Negro children in female-headed families are the great tragedy of the Crisis Ghetto. They constitute 13 percent of all persons there, 30 percent of all the children. They make up over half of the members of the poor limited-potential families.

There has been tremendous movement in and out of the Crisis Ghetto—at least four out of every ten departed or died in the five years. But the option of movement is not a random phenomenon affecting all equally. It seems available at will to some and almost completely closed to others—and most tightly closed to adults with limited economic potential, and their children.

Although the percentage of people with limited economic potential in the Crisis Ghetto is about twice as large as the population in the Remainder of Cleveland, the percentage of poor among them—standing at nearly 25 percent—is about *five* times as large. (See Figure 2.)

Recent prosperity has removed many from the rolls of the needy, but those remaining may be far more discontented than when most of their neighbors were also poor. "Relative deprivation" is a very real force. For example, the classic study of this phenomenon made during World War II showed that there was more jealousy and dissatisfaction in an Air Force fighter squadron noted for rapid promotions ("boy colonels") than in a military police unit with few promotions. This feeling of being ignored, discriminated against, and isolated, while all around others rise, may create a far more explosive situation than when many are in the same boat, as during the Depression.

The Cleveland Census reveals the city's contrasting prosperity and decay. Sharp differences emerge within the Negro population. The rapid income increase for non-Neighborhood Negroes probably indicates less economic discrimination. Also, while residential segregation remained strong, the white flight to the suburbs opened up some of the desirable Cleveland residential areas. For example, Lee Miles, an area with many expensive dwellings, changed from 28 to 72 percent Negro in five years (21,000 Negroes by 1965). Many strong economic units fled the ghetto.

As many fled to better circumstances, others became more ensnarled. And by 1965 the most disadvantaged group had grown to a very significant portion of the total Crisis Ghetto population. Particularly depressing is the increase of poor Negro young people in the economically weak female-headed homes—young people whose bondage becomes more oppressive as the rest of the city grows more prosperous.

Income and incentive

What can be done? What can be our long term goals?

The ghetto male, frequently with limited skills, enters the job market with grave liabilities. Often the job does not pay him enough to support his family and has little prospect of leading to a living wage. The longer the man works, the longer he fails as a provider. His marriage will frequently deteriorate. As Elliot Liebow has suggested in *Tally's Corner*, the unprovided-for family becomes a continuous symbol of a man's inability to fulfill the demands of his society—to be a man. So he opts out, and the sparse existence of the female-headed family has begun.

Job and training programs for men in the Crisis Ghetto are thus a first order need. Employment that yields a living wage over time seems to be the best bet for *preventing* family break-up, and *re-establishing* stable families.

Many broken homes, however, are not going to be reestablished. Consequently, the female-headed family, as the Cleveland data show so starkly, will face a particularly exposed financial position. The mother may well seek a relationship with a man that has some prospect of offering family stability and also additional income. Unfortunately, the "eligible" males are often the failures from prior marriages. The woman enters a tenuous relationship with the very unrealistic hope that it will work into a real family situation. The result is often another child.

Programs thus must be aimed at providing greater economic stability to the female-headed family. Job programs should be readily accessible for women as well as men. This means that major efforts for establishing day care centers are needed. Yet, work is not the answer for all these women. Also needed are better programs of income maintenance which will provide the family a reasonable income.

It is clear that our long run goals should be to prevent the breakup of families. But, many families are beyond the prevention of this sort. Further, the Negro mother has shown remarkable strength as a family head. Her great weakness has been in producing sufficient income, and the resultant poverty has had an adverse effect on the family. If these deficiencies can be overcome by work or transfer income, many of these mothers may be able to properly motivate their children. If freed from poverty, the inner strength of the matriarchal Negro family may begin to assert a positive effect upon the Crisis Ghetto.

We see the alternative in current trends. The poor in the Crisis Ghetto are falling further behind. Not only distance is building up between the two poles, but tension as well—as with electrodes approaching a sparking point.

If what is happening in Cleveland is also happening in other cities, we must multiply this tension, and the danger signals, by a large factor. If by inaction we consign the misery of the parents in the Crisis Ghettos to their children, the sickness of the central cities must fester and grow worse. Hough may be a pale prelude to other, greater Houghs—a short dramatic prologue, announcing that the tragedy has begun.

Further reading suggested by the author

Tally's Corner by Elliot Liebow (Boston: Little, Brown, & Co., 1967). An anthropological field study of Negro street-corner men which seems relevant to the study of family formation by females.

Negroes in the Cities by Karl E. Taeuber and Alma F. Taeuber (Chicago: Aldine Publishing Co., 1965). A wealth of statistical data on Negro migration patterns and racial segregation in large urban areas is presented.

The Moynihan Report and the Politics of Controversy by Lee Rainwater and William L. Yancey (Cambridge, Mass.: M.I.T. Press, 1967). A discussion of the Moynihan controversy, including the debate over poverty versus cultural inheritance.

Planning for a Nation of Cities edited by Sam Bass Warner, Jr. (Cambridge, Mass.: M.I.T. Press, 1966). See particularly chapters on the expressive style and the problems of transition from country to city.

The Social and Economic Characteristics
of American Suburbs

Leo F. Schnore

Through his research, Leo F. Schnore has contributed a great deal to our understanding of the critical contextual characteristics of central cities and their suburbs. For example, although it has frequently been assumed that suburbs contain populations ranking higher in socioeconomic status than the central cities they surround, Schnore has found this is only true of white populations in larger and older metropolitan areas. Age and, to a lesser extent, size of the central city appear to be the best predictors of the existence of city-suburban status differences.

In a later study, of status differentials among the nonwhite *population, Schnore found another important factor in addition to age and size of the central city. This was the regional location of the Urbanized Area. Only when region was controlled did status differences appear among nonwhites, and then only in the North and West. In the South, nonwhites failed to show the usual city-suburban status differences because, as opposed to the North and West, poor and less advantaged nonwhite residents have traditionally lived on the periphery of the city. Although many nonwhites have migrated to central cities in the South, many still live on the edges of large and small, old and new, Southern cities.*

In the study reported in this article, Schnore examines suburbs to discover whether contextual differences systematically correspond to the classification of suburbs by their primary economic function. Drawing upon 1960 Census data, he finds significant variation in the contextual characteristics of employing, intermediate, and residential suburbs. Perhaps the most clear-cut set of differences were those having to do with socioeconomic status. Measures of income, education, and occupational standing all showed the same results in suburbs in the New York Metropolitan Area and in the twenty-five largest urbanized areas in the United States.

It appears from this and other research that in the last thirty years suburbs lying outside the corporate limits of most large central cities have become increasingly diversified. Successive waves of middle-class and more recently lower middle-class, migrants, and the decentralization of manufacturing and commercial activities into the suburban zone, have brought about increased contextual differentiation and functional specialization among such communities. Suburbia is no longer a "looking glass" for the character, behavior, and culture of middle-class America.

What are the political implications of these findings? It is assumed here and pointed out in later articles that the status differences identified by Schnore have important implications not only for disputes, antagonisms, and conflicts that arise between residents of central cities and their suburbs, but also for those that arise between residents of different suburbs. Such differences may also influence, albeit indirectly, the policy-making process and public policies actually pursued by local municipalities.

Introduction

In the traditional popular image, "the suburb" is nothing more than the dwelling place of commuters who work in the near-by central city. While it is certainly correct to characterize many outlying subcenters as little more than "bedroom cities," a realistic portrayal must reflect the fact that "dormitory towns are only one species of suburb."[1] Some suburbs are literally manufacturing centers, devoted to light or heavy industry, while others are given over to the provision of such specialized services as education or recreation; as such, they represent significant centers of employment, drawing workers from other subcenters and even from the central city itself. Indeed, the range of economic specialization that can be discerned among suburbs is virtually as wide as that observable among other cities.

Despite the great variety of suburban functions, however, it has proved useful to distinguish two main types of suburb—employing and residential. This distinction made an early appearance in the literature of urban sociology, notably in the work of Taylor and that of Douglass.[2] Subsequent research has demonstrated the utility of this simple dichotomy. Harris has shown that "the commonest types of suburb are housing or domitory suburbs and manufacturing or industrial suburbs,"[3] and it has been further shown that these two basic types differ with respect to a number of important social, economic, and demographic characteristics, including their rates of population growth.[4] It is the purpose of this study to discover whether or not systematic differences existed between suburbs according to functional type as of 1960, and (if so) to delineate suburban profiles by reference to characteristics enumerated in the 1960 Censuses of Population and Housing. In

Reprinted from *The Sociological Quarterly,* vol. 4, no. 2 (Spring 1963), pp. 122-134 by permission of the publisher and author. This study was supported by the research phase of the University of Wisconsin Urban Program, under the terms of a grant from the Ford Foundation.

[1] Coleman Woodbury, "Suburbanization and Suburbia," *American Journal of Public Health,* 45:2 (Jan., 1955).

[2] Graham R. Taylor, *Satellite Cities* (New York and London: D. Appleton, 1915); Harlan Paul Douglass, *The Suburban Trend* (New York and London: Century, 1925), and his "Suburbs," in *The Encyclopaedia of the Social Sciences* (New York: Macmillan, 1934), 14:433—35.

[3] Chauncry D. Harris, "Suburbs," *American Journal of Sociology,* 49:6 (May, 1943).

[4] Leo F. Schnore, "The Functions of Metropolitan Suburbs," *American Journal of Sociology,* 61:453—58 (Mar., 1956), and his "The Growth of Metropolitan Suburbs," *American Sociological Review,* 22:165—73 (Apr., 1957).

short, it is our intention to retest one of the more neglected hypotheses advanced by Louis Wirth in his well-known essay, "Urbanism as a Way of Life":

> An industrial city will differ significantly in social respects from a commercial, mining, fishing, resort, university, and capital city. A one-industry city will present different sets of social characteristics from a multi-industry city, as will an industrially balanced from an unbalanced city, a suburb from a satellite, a residential suburb from an industrial suburb. . . .[5]

One of the new questions in the 1960 Census concerned the workplace of each employed person. Initially, we had hoped to make use of this item in order to make a precise identification of individual suburbs according to type. Unfortunately, the tabulation and publication of information on workplace makes use of such gross categories that it proved impossible to use these materials in the way that was originally contemplated. Workplaces are simply classified as lying inside or outside the worker's county of residence, and the only individual incorporated places that are recognized are those of 50,000 or more inhabitants—essentially the central cities of the Standard Metropolitan Statistical Areas and Urbanized Areas. In a few of these areas, however, workplace data can be used to characterize suburbs in a very rough fashion. In those few cases in which the central city is a separate county (e.g., San Francisco) or a quasi county (e.g., St. Louis) it is possible to estimate the number of suburban commuters who work there. A person living in a New York suburb and working in the city itself, for example, will have to cross a county line, since the five boroughs making up the city are themselves separate counties. As a consequence, the proportion of a particular New York suburb's working population that is registered as "working in a county other than the county of residence" includes all those who commute to the central city together with those who travel to other employing centers in different counties. Thus the proportion working outside the county of residence serves as a rough index of the suburb's functional status, i.e., as an employing or a residential subcenter. A suburb with a high proportion of its employed population working outside the county is very probably a residential suburb. At the same time, a suburb with a very low proportion working in another county is quite likely to be an employing subcenter providing jobs for its own residents, if not for others as well. In any event, close inspection of the data for New York's suburbs indicated that this proportion would serve as a useful basis of classification. Let us examine the results.

The suburbs of New York

In Table 1, 74 incorporated places of 10,000 or more inhabitants lying within the New York–Northeastern New Jersey Urbanized Area have been

---

[5] Louis Wirth, "Urbanism as a Way of Life," *American Journal of Sociology*, vol. 44 (July, 1938); reprinted in Paul K. Hatt and Albert J. Reiss, Jr. (eds.), *Cities and Society* (Glencoe, Ill.: The Free Press, 1957), p. 49.

*Table 1. Social and Economic Characteristics of Suburbs
in the New York Urbanized Area, 1960*

	Type of suburb		
	Employing	*Intermediate*	*Residential*
A. Age and ethnic composition			
1. *Percentage foreign-born*	12.9	12.7	11.9
2. *Percentage nonwhite*	10.6	7.8	1.5
3. *Percentage aged 65 or more*	10.2	9.6	9.4
B. Fertility and dependency			
4. *Nonworker-worker ratio*	1.27	1.33	1.41
5. *Fertility ratio*	391	401	376
6. *Percentage with children under 6*	26.0	27.6	25.9
C. Socioeconomic status			
7. *Percentage completed high school*	40.9	42.9	50.6
8. *Percentage in white-collar occupations*	44.9	47.2	58.0
9. *Median family income*	$7,051	$7,337	$8,994
D. Population growth			
10. *Median rate of increase*	5.7	17.5	32.1
11. *Percentage of places losing population*	24.0	25.0	8.0
12. *Percentage migrant 1955–60*	11.8	14.0	20.1
E. Housing characteristics			
13. *Percentage built between 1950 and 1960*	16.8	20.8	24.4
14. *Percentage owner occupied units*	50.3	55.0	67.7
15. *Percentage one-family units*	48.5	50.1	63.9
No. of suburbs	25	24	25

classified as belonging to one of three types of suburb. Places with less than 25 per cent of their employed populations working outside the county of residence are labeled "employing" suburbs. At the other extreme, places with 37.5 per cent or more workers commuting across a county line are characterized as "residential" suburbs; on average, a place in this category sends almost 50 per cent of its employed labor force into another county. Finally, a third "intermediate" or "mixed" category is recognized, wherein intercounty commuters make up 25 to 37 per cent of its resident working population. Recognition of this third category permits a more rigorous test of the hypothesis to the effect that there exist systematic differences between employing and residential suburbs; if such differences exist, the values registered for the intermediate type should fall somewhere between those found for the two polar types.[6] In fact, Table 1 shows that a number of systematic differences according to type do characterize the suburbs of New York. . . .

[6] The "intermediate" type recognized in this paper should not be confused with the "balanced" type of suburb identified by Douglass, wherein jobs and workers are approximately equal in number.

The employment-residence ratio

Unfortunately, the procedures used in classifying New York's suburbs cannot be employed in other areas. In most cases, the central city is located in the same county as the suburbs surrounding it. As a consequence, these suburbs cannot be readily characterized as "employing" and "residential" in accordance with the census data on workplace. Even the detailed tabulations of workplace—wherein commuter trips to central cities of 50,000 and over will be separately identified—will not permit an exact classification of suburbs according to type, since work trips to places other than central cities will not be separately reported.

For these reasons, we have turned to another source of information as a means of classifying suburbs according to functional type. We have used the "employment-residence ratio" computed by Jones and Collver for all incorporated places of 10,000 or more inhabitants in 1950; as they indicate, "the employment-residence ratio was obtained by comparing the number of workers employed in the city in 1954 in manufacturing and trade with the number of employed residents reporting these same occupations."[7] Cities are differentiated, then, on the basis of the net daily movement of workers into and out of them. A place with a high ratio tends to have many more jobs than employed workers, and can be fairly characterized as an employing subcenter. On the other hand, a place with a low employment-residence ratio has more workers than jobs available locally, and can be aptly categorized as a residential subcenter.

In all, the 25 largest Urbanized Areas contain exactly 300 suburbs for which employment-residence ratios have been calculated. The list in Table 2, ordered by population size, shows the number of suburbs found in each of the 25 Urbanized Areas of more than 750,000 inhabitants in 1960.

Once again there is the problem of establishing "cutting points." For present purposes, suburbs with employment-residence ratios of 101 or more were classified as "employing" subcenters. Those with ratios falling between 51 and 100 are termed "intermediate," and those ratios of 50 or less are treated as "residential" suburbs.[8] As it happens, this procedure yields three groups of approximately equal size.

Table 3 shows the economic base of each suburb according to functional type. It will be seen that the employing suburbs are heavily specialized in manufacturing; in fact, if one adds together the first three categories—manufacturing, industrial, and diversified suburbs in which manufacturing predominates—one finds four out of every five employing suburbs represented. At the other extreme, residential suburbs are heavily specialized in the

---

[7]Victor Jones and Andrew Collver, "Economic Classification of Cities and Metropolitan Areas," in Orin F. Nolting and David S. Arnold (eds.), *The Municipal Yearbook, 1959* (Chicago: The International City Managers' Association, 1959), p. 72.

[8]Jones and Collver suggest that cities with ratios below 50 should be treated as "dormitory suburbs," and they point out that "all but three of these cities are located within SMA's and only four are manufacturing or industrial cities."—*Ibid.*, p. 71.

Table 2.   *Number of suburbs in each of 25 Urbanized Areas*
of more than 750 inhabitants, 1960

Urbanized Area	Population 1960	Number of suburbs in study
New York—Northeastern New Jersey	14,114,927	74
Los Angeles—Long Beach, Calif.	6,488,791	34
Chicago—Northwestern Indiana	5,959,213	30
Philadelphia, Pa.—N.J.	3,635,228	14
Detroit, Mich.	3,537,709	22
San Francisco—Oakland, Calif.	2,430,663	18
Boston, Mass.	2,413,236	16
Washington, D. C.—Md.—Va.	1,808,423	4
Pittsburgh, Pa.	1,804,400	22
Cleveland, Ohio	1,784,991	12
St. Louis, Mo.—Ill.	1,667,693	12
Baltimore, Md.	1,418,948	0
Minneapolis—St. Paul, Minn.	1,377,143	4
Milwaukee, Wis.	1,149,997	7
Houston, Texas	1,139,678	3
Buffalo, N.Y.	1,054,370	5
Cincinnati, Ohio—Ky.	993,568	4
Dallas, Texas	932,349	4
Kansas City, Mo.—Kans.	921,121	1
Seattle, Wash.	864,109	1
Miami, Fla.	852,705	4
New Orleans, La.	845,237	1
San Diego, Calif.	836,175	3
Denver, Colo.	803,624	2
Atlanta, Ga.	768,125	3

provision of retail trade and services. Over half these places are retail trade centers, and if one combines the last three categories—retail trade centers, diversified centers in which retail trade predominates, and service centers—one finds four out of every five of the residential suburbs so classified. As expected, the intermediate suburbs represent a greater mixture of places from the standpoint of their economic bases. These materials suggest that in working with subcenters classified according to their employment-residence ratios we are dealing with more or less distinctive types of suburb which play dissimilar roles in the metropolitan economy.

Table 3.   *Economic base of suburb by type*

Economic base	Type of suburb		
	Employing	Intermediate	Residential
Percentage Mm (manufacturing)	70.6	33.3	2.0
Percentage M (industrial)	3.9	7.1	2.0
Percentage Mr (diversified, with manufacturing predominant)	7.8	16.2	13.1
Percentage S (service)	2.9	2.0	5.1
Percentage Rm (diversified, with retail trade predominant)	5.9	23.2	23.2
Percentage Rr (retail trade)	8.9	18.2	54.6
Total	100.0	100.0	100.0
Number of suburbs	102	99	99

Social and economic characteristics
of 300 suburbs

Table 4 provides summary profiles of 300 employing, intermediate, and residential suburbs, using the employment-residence ratios as the basis of the typological distinction. The characteristics shown include all those previously analyzed for the suburbs of New York.

Age and ethnic composition[9] As in the case of New York, suburbs generally appear to vary systematically with respect to certain compositional

Table 4. *Social and economic characteristics of suburbs*
in the 25 largest Urbanized Areas, 1960

	Type of suburb		
	Employing	Intermediate	Residential
A. Age and ethnic composition			
1. Percentage foreign-born	10.5	8.5	7.7
2. Percentage nonwhite	7.0	6.2	2.4
3. Percentage aged 65 or more	9.7	9.0	9.1
B. Fertility and dependency			
4. Nonworker-worker ratio	1.41	1.44	1.44
5. Fertility ratio	421	437	422
6. Percentage with children under 6	27.8	29.2	28.2
C. Socioeconomic status			
7. Percentage completed high school	43.2	48.2	55.8
8. Percentage in white-collar occupations	44.6	49.8	58.5
9. Median family income	$6,869	$7,510	$8,210
D. Population growth, 1950–60			
10. Median rate of increase	6.0	18.1	26.9
11. Percentage of places losing population	30.4	24.2	16.2
12. Percentage migrant 1955–60	13.8	16.7	17.4
E. Housing characteristics			
13. Percentage built between 1950 and 1960	24.1	29.4	31.6
14. Percentage owner-occupied units	57.7	63.1	71.4
15. Percentage one-family units	62.3	68.2	75.9
No. of suburbs	102	99	99

[9]The proportions nonwhite and aged 65 and over were taken from U.S. Bureau of the Census, *U.S. Census of Population: 1960, General Population Characteristics* (Washington, D.C.: U.S. Government Printing Office, 1961), Table 13 for each state. Unless otherwise indicated, the remaining characteristics were taken from U.S. Bureau of the Census, *U.S. Census of Population: 1960, General Social and Economic Characteristics* (Washington, D.C.: U.S. Government Printing Office, 1961), Tables 32 and 33 for each state. These two publications are Chapters "B" and "C" respectively, and will be so identified in subsequent references. Unless otherwise indicated, the values shown are unweighted means for the type of suburb in question.

features. Employing suburbs contain not only higher proportions of foreign-born inhabitants, but they also contain larger percentages of nonwhites. The nonwhite representation in residential suburbs is again notably lower than in the other types. With respect to age composition, employing suburbs tend to have larger proportions of older inhabitants, but the other two types do not differ much in this respect.

Fertility and dependency[10]   Similarly, residential and intermediate types of suburb are not clearly distinguished with respect to dependency, for their nonworker-worker ratios are identical. This ratio, seen in Panel B, is only slightly lower for employing suburbs. These findings represent a departure from the patterns exhibited by New York's suburbs, where a rather clear gradient was in evidence. Like New York's suburbs, however, the larger sample reveals the highest fertility ratios in the intermediate type of suburb; employing and residential suburbs have child-woman ratios that are lower and virtually identical. Similarly, the proportions of married couples with children under six years of age are lower in the two polar types of suburb, with a higher proportion found in the suburbs of the intermediate type. Again, these findings reproduce the patterns observed when only the 74 New York suburbs were under scrutiny.

Socioeconomic status   The New York sample also proved to be typical with respect to differentials in socioeconomic status between suburbs of varying type.[11]   Panel C in Table 4 shows that the highest proportion completing high school is found in the residential suburbs. Similarly, the largest relative number of employed persons in white-collar occupations is found in this same type of suburb. Finally, income differentials are again very pronounced. A gap in excess of $1,300 dollars separates the median incomes of employing and residential suburbs, with the latter type clearly favored.

Population growth[12]   We have already referred to evidence to the effect that the growth of residential suburbs outstripped that of employing suburbs during the 1930's and 1940's. During the 1950's, according to Panel D, this differential clearly persisted. While employing subcenters grew an average of only 6 per cent over the 1950-1960 decade, residential suburbs grew by

---

[10]The source of the fertility ratio was Chapter "B", Table 13. This measure is also commonly known as "the child-woman ratio."

[11]Leo F. Schnore, "Satellites and Suburbs," *Social Forces*, 36:121—27 (Dec., 1957).

[12]For growth rates between 1930 and 1940, see Harris, *op. cit.* Suburban growth between 1940 and 1950 is examined in Schnore, "The Growth of Metropolitan Suburbs," *op. cit.*, and in his "Components of Population Change in Large Metropolitan Suburbs," *American Sociological Review*, 23:570—73 (Oct., 1958). The growth rates for 1950—1960 were computed on the basis of data taken from U.S. Bureau of the Census, *U.S. Census of Population: 1960*, vol. 1, *Characteristics of the Population*, Part A, "Number of Inhabitants" (Washington, D.C.: U.S. Government Printing Office, 1961), Table 8 for each state. The rates of growth were adjusted for annexations of territory and population between 1950 and 1960 by reference to Table 9. For the importance of this adjustment, see Leo F. Schnore, "Municipal Annexations and the Growth of Metropolitan Suburbs, 1950—1960," *American Journal of Sociology*, 67:406—17 (Jan., 1962).

almost 27 per cent. Again, suburbs of intermediate type registered intermediate gains. We also see that three out of every ten employing suburbs
actually lost population during the decade, while only half as many
residential suburbs registered losses during the same interval. Again, as in the
case of the New York sample, residential suburbs were generally more likely
to contain migrants, i.e., people who lived in different counties in 1955 and
1960.

Housing characteristics[13]   The final array of characteristics examined here
refers to housing in employing, intermediate, and residential suburbs. Panel E
reveals higher proportions of new housing (built between 1950 and 1960) in
residential suburbs; this finding, of course, is in accordance with the
expectation formed on the basis of examining differentials in population
growth. Another set of differences that was anticipated—largely on the basis
of New York suburban experience—has to do with housing tenure. Panel E
shows that dwelling units in residential suburbs are more likely to be
occupied by owners than by renters. Finally, the three types of suburb differ
systematically with respect to type of residential structure. While lower
proportions of dwelling units are of the one-family style in employing and
intermediate suburbs, fully three out of every four units are designed for
single-family occupancy in residential suburbs. As in most of the preceding
comparisons, then, the housing data for all 300 suburbs reflect the patterns
observed in the more limited sample drawn from the environs of New York.

Summary and conclusions

The massive shifts in population denoted by the concept of "suburbanization" have been thoroughly documented in demographic research.[14] Moreover, detailed case studies have reminded us of the diversity of suburbs in
America.[15] As Riesman has observed, however, "we cannot link nation-wide
data on changes in metropolitan areas with Whyte's descriptions of how Park
Forest feels toward its pro tem inhabitants. This is the characteristic situation
in sociology today—that research in the macrocosmic and in the microcosmic
scarcely connect, scarcely inform each other."[16] This study represents an
effort at portraying what is typical in contemporary suburbia while simultaneously giving attention to variations within the broad category "suburb."

[13] All of the housing data were taken from U.S. Bureau of the Census, *U.S. Census of
Housing: 1960*, volume 1, *States and Small Areas* (Washington, D.C.: U.S. Government
Printing Office, 1962), Table 1 for each state.

[14] See, for example, Amos H. Hawley, *The Changing Shape of Metropolitan America:
Deconcentration Since 1920* (Glencoe, Ill.: The Free Press, 1956).

[15] See, for example, William H. Whyte, Jr., "The Transients," in his *The Organization
Man* (New York: Simon and Schuster, 1956), Part VII; John R. Seeley, R. Alexander
Sim, and E. W. Loosley, *Crestwood Heights: The Culture of Suburban Life* (New York:
Basic Books, 1956); and Bennett M. Berger, *Working-Class Suburb* (Berkeley and Los
Angeles: University of California Press, 1960).

[16] David Riesman, "The Suburban Dislocation," *Annals of the American Academy of
Political and Social Science*, 314:125 (Nov., 1957).

We have followed the sociological tradition by identifying two major types of suburb—employing and residential. For purposes of analysis, however, we have recognized a third—and intermediate type. Some fifteen social and economic characteristics were then examined, first in a sample of 74 suburbs surrounding New York City and subsequently in a group of 300 suburbs found within the 25 largest Urbanized Areas.

The values observed for thirteen of these fifteen characteristics tended to increase or decrease systematically as one moved from one type of suburb to the next. In other words, the characteristics of the intermediate class of suburbs tended to fall somewhere between those of employing and residential suburbs. The exceptions to this pattern both involved characteristics reflecting suburban fertility—the child-woman ratio and the proportion of married couples with children under six years of age. Both of these measures turned out to be higher (in both samples) for intermediate suburbs than in employing or residential subcenters.

Perhaps the most clear-cut set of differences were those having to do with socioeconomic status. Measures of income, education, and occupational standing all showed the same results in both samples, i.e., the highest values were registered in the residential suburbs, somewhat lower values in the intermediate class, and the lowest values in the employing category. Other measures with a "status" connotation—proportions foreign-born and nonwhite, and proportions in owner-occupied and single-family dwelling units—showed similar patterns.

Finally, this study has demonstrated the continuation of a long-term trend with respect to population growth. Growth differentials favoring residential suburbs continued to characterize the fifties, just as they did the thirties and the forties. While it is undeniable that suburbs vary in many respects, it is equally clear that these variations are quite systematic and predictable.

Additional suggested readings:
The context of local politics

John C. Bollens and Henry J. Schmandt, *The Metropolis: Its People, Politics and Economic Life* (New York: Harper & Row, Publishers, 1965).

Kenneth B. Clark, *Dark Ghetto: Dilemmas of Social Power* (New York: Harper & Row, Publishers, 1965).

James S. Coleman, *Community Conflict* (New York: The Free Press, 1957).

William M. Dobriner, *Class in Suburbia* (Englewood Cliffs, N. J.: Prentice-Hall, 1963).

Bryan T. Downes, "Social and Political Characteristics of Riot Cities: A Comparative Study," *Social Science Quarterly*, vol. 49, no. 3 (December 1968), pp. 504-520.

Editorial Research Reports on the Urban Environment (Washington, D.C.: Congressional Quarterly, Inc., 1969).

Charles N. Glabb and A. Theodore Brown, *A History of Urban America* (New York: Macmillan Co., 1967).

Nathan Glazer and Daniel Patrick Moynihan, *Beyond the Melting Pot: The Negroes, Puerto Ricans, Jews, Italians, and Irish of New York City* (Cambridge: M.I.T. Press, 1963).

Jean Gottmann, *Megalopolis: The Urbanized Northeastern Seaboard of the United States* (Cambridge: M.I.T. Press, 1961).

Scott Greer, *The Emerging City: Myth and Reality* (New York: The Free Press, 1962).

Jeffrey K. Hadden and Edgar F. Borgatta, *American Cities: Their Social Characteristics* (Chicago: Rand McNally, 1965).

Michael Harrington, *The Other America: Poverty in the United States* (Baltimore: Penguin, 1963).

Philip M. Hauser and Leo F. Schnore, *The Study of Urbanization* (New York: John Wiley, 1965).

Christen T. Jonassen and Sherwood H. Peres, *Interrelationships of Dimensions of Community Systems: A Factor Analysis of Eighty-two Variables* (Columbus: Ohio State University Press, 1960).

Blake McKelvey, *The Urbanization of America, 1860-1915* (New Brunswick: Rutgers University Press, 1963).

———, *The Emergence of Metropolitan America, 1915-1966* (New Brunswick: Rutgers University Press, 1968).

Thomas F. Pettigrew, *A Profile of Negro America* (Princeton: D. Van Nostrand Co., 1964).

J. John Phalen and Leo F. Schnore, "Color Composition and City-Suburban Status Differences: A Replication," *Land Economics*, vol. 41, no. 1 (February 1965), pp. 87-91.

Report of the National Advisory Commission on Civil Disorders (New York: Bantam Books, 1968).

The Report From the National Commission on the Causes and Prevention of Violence (New York: Award Books, 1969).

Leo F. Schnore, *The Urban Scene: Human Ecology and Demography* (New York: The Free Press, 1965).

Sam Bass Warner, Jr., *The Private City: Philadelphia in Three Periods of Its Growth* (Philadelphia: University of Pennsylvania Press, 1968).

Part two Rules, procedures, and political structures in central cities and suburbs

What is the nature of the formal rules and procedures under which local units of government operate and the political structures one finds in local communities? How have these rules, procedures, and political structures changed over time? What are the factors that have brought about such changes? These are the primary questions to which the selections in this section are addressed. We will leave to later sections investigation of the impact that these as well as other factors may have on the policy-making process and policy outcomes.

All central cities and suburbs operate under certain formal rules, most often set forth in city charters, state statutes, and local laws. Such rules stipulate the formal, legal procedures under which local governmental units must operate. For example, they indicate the form a city's government must take and how local public officials are to be elected; they vest authority in certain elected or appointed officials and institutions; they assign functional responsibilities; and so on. Many researchers assume that local units of government actually operate in accordance with these and other formal legal prescriptions. Although this is an extremely questionable assumption, it still undergirds a great deal of "empirical" research.

As Martin indicates in the first article in Part Two, the actions of state legislatures can have a rather direct impact on the formal rules and procedures adopted by local municipalities. States frequently require local units of government to adopt, and hence operate under, certain rules and procedures. This is primarily because local governments have long been considered "creatures of the state." In most states, however, as local municipalities increase in population they are given some choice as to which rules and procedures to adopt. When such options exist, adoption of specific rules and procedures by a municipality becomes a matter of public policy. In addition, it is frequently a policy change that requires citizen approval at the polls. James Clarke, in his selection in the conclusion to this volume, examines some of the contextual and political factors related to decisions to consider and adopt a new form of government by forty-three third-class cities in Pennsylvania.

In this first selection, then, Martin examines the historical development of the relationship between cities and states. He finds that over the years something like a federal system has evolved between municipalities and their state governments. Martin also discusses how other intergovernmental relationships, particularly those with the federal government, influence the actual operation and activities of local governments. He concludes that today local governments have become significant "handmaidens" of both state and national governments.

Are there other contextual characteristics besides intergovernmental relationships that influence the formal rules and procedures under which local governments operate? One group of researchers has found that such municipal contextual characteristics as population size, growth rate, heterogeneity, and socioeconomic status are rather consistently related to form of government, method of electing city councilmen, and type of ballot used (partisan or nonpartisan). For example, with regard to the correlates of governmental form, Alford and Scoble conclude that white, Anglo-Saxon, Protestant, growing, and high-mobility cities are likely to be manager cities; ethnically and religiously diverse but low-mobility industrial cities are likely to be mayor council cities; and the commission form is associated with declining population, low mobility, a low white-collar composition, a low educational level, and low ethnic and religious diversity.[1] Although Alford and Scoble do not argue that any of these contextual characteristics "cause," in any direct sense, the adoption of a particular form of government, they do conclude their analysis with the following statement:

> We may conceive of both population growth and mobility as intervening variables, serving to loosen the social and political ties of persons to their community and rendering ineffective those characteristics of the population which would otherwise bring forth political demands. Class composition and social heterogeneity or homogeneity are stable long term characteristics of a city's population.[2]

They argue that high-mobility, heterogeneous cities should experience considerable pressure for change in their form of government, as should growing but heavily blue-collar cities.

Although a series of plausible reasons for the relationships found between contextual characteristics and governmental form are offered by Alford and Scoble, who also conjecture about how these factors may result in pressure for change, such reasons are probably best viewed as hypotheses in need of further testing. What types of information would have to be collected in

---

[1] Robert R. Alford and Harry M. Scoble, "Political and Social Characteristics of American Cities," in *The Municipal Yearbook, 1965* (Chicago: The International City Managers' Association, 1965), pp. 82-98.

[2] *Ibid.*, pp. 96-97.

order to test such hypotheses? Why should the contextual characteristics mentioned above be related to the rules and procedures guiding the operations of local governments? A reading of the article by Lineberry and Fowler in Part Four and that by Clarke in the Conclusion should give you some insight into this question.

In addition to the lack of adequate explanations for the particular relationships they have found between municipal contextual characteristics and formal rules and procedures, the above-mentioned studies also make several questionable assumptions—for example, that the more heterogeneous a community's population, the more highly politicized its government is likely to be, particularly if the sources of social and political diversity have channels for political expression. In this sense, a form is "politicized" when it encourages and allows interest group representation and "professionalized" when it facilitates efficient implementation of goals. Thus, the council manager plan (plus nonpartisan at-large elections) is assumed to be more professional than either the commission or mayor council plans. It is also assumed to be less politicized, since adoption of the manager plan implies that dominant social groups agree on the major goals of city government. Unfortunately, no evidence is ever presented about actual differences in performance of city services, or that certain groups actually have less potential influence over city decisions under the council manager form than under other governmental plans.

There is also a set of structures in local communities, seldom referred to in constitutional documents or laws, that perform vital political functions. These structures may influence the recruitment of individuals for public office, as well as the articulation, aggregation, and communication of political demands. The remaining three articles in this section discuss these governmental and nongovernmental structures, that is, the institutions and groups one finds in varying numbers and forms in local municipalities. However, we are only beginning to learn about the various factors that influence the development of a particular group infrastructure in central cities and their suburbs.

The selection by Sayre and Kaufman examines the complex group infrastructure of New York City, but tells us very little about the factors which led to its development. Greenstein, on the other hand, discusses in detail the various factors which have brought about significant changes in the nature and role of political parties at the local level. Although the structures described in these selections do perform important political functions, each varies considerably in the extent to which it is involved in the policy-making process. Wirt concludes this discussion by examining some of the factors which have brought about greater partisan differentiation among suburban communities in the last ten years.

The Place of Cities in the American Federal System

Roscoe C. Martin

What effect do the actions of governments at other levels, state and national, in the American federal system have upon the nature and outcomes of politics in local, city and suburban, municipalities? In this selection from The Cities and the Federal System, *Roscoe C. Martin examines this question—an important one, because the activities of federal and state governments are having an increasingly direct impact on the politics and public-policy decisions of local municipalities. Intergovernmental relationships, therefore, are one of the more important components of the environmental context that may influence local political life.*

Legally, cities and suburbs have long been considered "creatures of the state." State legislatures have frequently circumscribed the authority of municipal units of government by enacting laws that specify their general duties and responsibilities, the form of government they must adopt, their taxing authority, and the extent of bonded indebtedness. Such laws have a direct influence on the formal rules and procedures that guide the operations of city and suburban governments. They also place limits on the authority of local officials. However, some cities, particularly larger ones, have achieved a measure of legal independence through home rule, their sheer voting strength in the state, and recent reapportionment of state legislatures. Martin argues that over the years something like a federal system has evolved between the states and their local governments.

Although cities and suburbs are constitutionally not members of the federal partnership, in operational terms the situation is quite different. The distribution of authority among the federal government, the constituent states, and local units of government has never been subject to final disposition. In practice, the American federal system has remained open-ended, flexible, and adaptive. For example, since the 1930s the evolution of cooperative federalism has brought about significant increases in the extent to which public responsibilities are shared by two or more levels of government. The vigorous practice of cooperative federalism has made cities and suburbs significant "handmaidens" of both state and national governments.

Even though a great deal of flexibility appears inherent in the American federal system, there are definite limits to cooperative action. For example, many cities and some suburbs have turned to higher levels of government for assistance, because the problems they confront cannot be solved with local resources alone. The states having largely ignored such requests for aid, the federal government has therefore been forced to assume responsibility in certain problem areas, such as civil rights, poverty, and apportionment. Despite such actions, however, the federal and state governments have generally been unwilling to undertake extensive cooperative action with local municipalities to solve the problems currently confronting many cities and suburbs in America. Query: will the federal and state governments become more responsive to the demands of municipal units of government in the future?

Introduction

The cities and the states

The spirit of local independence ran high in America at the time of the Revolution, as indeed it does to this day. The hard-won fruits of rebellion were considered to be local gains, and any enterprise not associated with the immediate community was regarded with suspicion. Government in particular was held close to the bosom of the people. They had won the right to control their own affairs, which to the greatest degree possible were to be vested in the seeable, touchable government of the small community.

If we consider the sacredness attached to individual freedom and by easy transfer to close-at-home government, it is not surprising that local government early came to enjoy a certain sanctity in the popular esteem. Nor is it a matter for wonder that a legal doctrine was conjured up to buttress little government. The transition from confidence and satisfaction in local institutions to veneration of them was natural; the next step was somewhat more difficult, but it, too, was taken in time. It led to the enunciation and broad acceptance of the doctrine of the inherent right of local self-government.

This doctrine, evolved early as a local counterweight to the centralizing tendencies set in motion by the new state governments, enjoyed wide support during the first decades of the Republic. In coldly practical terms, its acceptance in law would have resulted in local government anarchy for the new nation. It was rejected in favor of the doctrine of state supremacy vis-à-vis its local governments. It is worthy of note that this rejection signaled a reversal of the teachings of colonial history; for by it the anterior governments, the local communities, were made secondary and the derivative governments, the states, became primary.

The local governments, and particularly the growing cities, were loath to accept this metamorphosis, and they continued sporadically to assert their prior rights and privileges with respect to local affairs. Three-quarters of a century passed before the ghost of inherent local rights was authoritatively laid to rest. This was accomplished by the Supreme Court of Iowa, which in 1868 incorporated the following passage in a historic decision:

> Municipal corporations owe their origin to, and derive their powers and rights wholly from, the legislature. It breathes into them the breath of life, without which they cannot exist. As it creates, so may it destroy. If it may destroy, it may abridge and control. Unless there is some constitutional limitation on the right, the legislature might, by a single act, if we can suppose it capable of so great a folly and so great a wrong, sweep from existence all the municipal corporations in the State and the *corporation* could not prevent it. We know of no limitation on this right so far as the corporations themselves are concerned. They are, so to phrase it, the mere *tenants at will* of the legislature.[1]

The decision of the Iowa court was subsequently upheld by the Supreme Court of the United States. It continues, however, to be known as Dillon's Rule, after the Iowa justice who originally decided the case and wrote the preceding passage.

Dillon's Rule has been tested many times by cities seeking loopholes or limitations in it, but it continues as the ruling principle governing the legal status of the cities. Barring a state constitutional grant or guarantee (a contingency covered by the rule as originally stated), the city has no rights apart from or above those granted by state law. Legally it is a creature of and is utterly dependent on the state. Harking back to the alternatives available to the framers of the Constitution in 1787, the state is therefore unitary rather than federal in structure in the eyes of the law.

But practice often departs from law, either by blinking legal dogma or by modifying it in application. Nowhere is this aphorism better illustrated than in the position of the city vis-à-vis the state. The law has it that the city is the creature of the state, but practice accords the city a considerable measure of independence. One factor which mitigates the harshness of the legal rule resides in the persistence of tradition; for the ghost laid to rest by Judge Dillon almost a century ago appears recurrently to set forth its case and plead its cause. The right of local self-government is among the hardiest of American traditions.

Above the sense of outrage at any infringement of local autonomy is the fact that the state itself has moved to grant its cities certain basic rights. The principal (but not the sole) vehicle by which such a grant is conveyed is "home rule," a device by which the state concedes to its cities (or counties) more or less autonomy over local affairs. The device varies in nature and scope; its extreme form is found in the grant of power to the city to draft and adopt its own charter. Home-rule rights may be spelled out in either constitutional provision or statutory law, and may be either broad or limited. The constitution of Missouri since 1875 has contained a provision giving the

[1] *City of Clinton v. Cedar Rapids and Missouri River Railroad Company,* 24 Iowa 455 (1868); quotation at p. 475.

cities wide latitude with respect to the adoption and amendment of their charters. Other states granting their cities a broad measure of home rule are California, Michigan, and Texas. To date, about half of the states have placed in their constitutions provisions giving their cities home-rule powers over charter formation and change. Cities in many states therefore enjoy a measure of autonomy through home rule.

Nor is the political strength inherent in the city to be overlooked. Again sheer numbers are on the side of the cities, and will be increasingly so; for if almost 70 per cent of the nation's people reside in the cities, then two-thirds or more of the voters, actual or potential, likewise reside there. Political control of the state by the cities is widely suspected; in 1964 the Republican candidate for governor of Illinois charged that the Democratic incumbent owed his election to and was indeed the tool of the Chicago Democratic machine. Any candidate for statewide office in New York must make his peace early with New York City; it has been more than forty years since New York has had a governor who was not a resident of or at least not closely identified with its largest city. In any election where sheer number of votes is controlling, the influence of the cities is great and undoubtedly will increase in the future.

A development in immediate prospect concerns the impending reapportionment of state legislatures. Reapportionment, if and when achieved, in itself will produce no millennium, although in time it will make the legislatures more representative and in turn will produce a legislative body more attuned both to urban needs and to current issues. In further consequence it will mitigate the time drag in dealing with urban problems. The cities are destined to play an increasingly important role in the affairs of the states, in considerable part because of legislative reapportionment.

Organizations of cities and city officials likewise provide the cities with instruments for the wielding of political influence. The league of cities and the association of mayors will almost always command a respectful hearing at the state house. Even the legislature, which because of the apportionment system has not had cause to fear the strength of the cities in the past, listens to the spokesmen of these organizations with more than ordinary respect. The cities of course do not speak with one voice, for differences do exist—between New York City and the upstate New York urban centers, as an example. Nevertheless they have little difficulty uniting to resist state assaults on urban prerogatives. Local differences are set aside in the face of a common enemy.

The cities are not nearly so supine as Judge Dillon's statement would lead us to believe. Something quite like a federal system has grown up within the states; for while the law calls for state supremacy, practice has produced a considerable measure of municipal autonomy. As a matter of law, the states could of course modify this system in any way they might see fit, but in point of fact they would find it difficult to abridge any important right enjoyed by the cities. Now and again a state takes punitive action against a city (usually one governed by the political party not in control of the state house), but such occurrences are so rare and the storm they provoke so violent as simply to underline the significant change which practice has brought about in the Dillon Rule: *de jure* the state is supreme, *de facto* the cities enjoy considerable autonomy. The intrastate federal system rests largely upon custom fortified by statutory law, but it is none the less stable for that. Custom provides a strong foundation for most institutional practices, while a body of legislative law which is not subject to repeal and which can be amended only with the concurrence of its subjects affords almost as firm a base as the constitution itself.

The cities and the nation

There is a general disposition for observers to dismiss the subject of the place of the cities in the federal system with the brisk conclusion that cities are not members of the federal partnership. In a technical sense this is true, for the Constitution of the United States nowhere accords recognition to local governments. In operational terms, however, the situation is quite different, for the cities have played a significant part in the functioning of the federal system for many years. This has prompted one student of the subject to observe, "Local governments—rural, urban, and suburban—are part and parcel of the American federal system"[2] The author argues that the practice of cooperative federalism has long since brought the cities—indeed, all local governments—within the orbit of the federal system notwithstanding explicit recognition was withheld by the framers of the Constitution. Thus they have been accorded *de facto* recognition as members of the federal partnership, though denied constitutional status.

The quasi-federal system that exists within the states is concrete and persuasive evidence that the position of the cities is considerably stronger than the law lets on. There are also certain recent and current developments—the mass of the urban population, the number and size of the cities, and the velocity of urban government—that point to significant strengthening in the position of the cities. It will be remembered that in 1960 there were 332 cities with 50,000 or more people, and that these cities contained 35 per cent of the nation's total population. In that same year the five largest cities (a million or more each) had a total population of some 17.5 million, approximately 10 per cent of the country's total. Chicago had 35 per cent of all the people in Illinois, New York City more than 46 per cent of the total population of New York State. In the states containing the five largest cities, the proportion of the population residing in metropolitan areas ran from 73 per cent (Michigan) to almost 87 per cent (California).

By other measures also the larger cities in particular make their influence felt in their several states. In 1961 Chicago contained 30 per cent of Illinois' total assessed value of property subject to local general property taxation; the comparable figure for New York City was 61 per cent. As in the case of

[2] Daniel J. Elazar, "Local Government in Intergovernmental Perspective," in *Illinois Local Government*, a publication of the Institute of Government of the University of Illinois, *University of Illinois Bulletin*, vol. 58 (May 1961), p. 24.

population, the larger metropolitan areas dominated the assessed property values of their states. For the states containing the five largest cities, the proportion of assessed values lying within the metropolitan areas ran from somewhat less than 74 per cent (Illinois) to 91 per cent (New York). In public employment, New York City had well over twice as many employees as New York State, Chicago had almost two-thirds as many as Illinois, and Detroit had close to half as many as Michigan.

The importance of the cities is likewise reflected in the role they play in the national economy. In terms of expenditures, indebtedness, and services performed—in terms, that is, of the criteria used to measure economic activity—that role is increasingly influential. Whether they thrive or languish is a matter of first importance to the nation. No longer can the national government permit the economies of the cities to run at idling speed, for the national economy tends increasingly to reflect the aggregate of the urban economies.[3]

In yet another direction the cities play a role of national importance. In the distant past urban governments served almost exclusively urban needs, fulfilling the traditional role of local units in the American system of government. Then came the states, then the nation, to utilize existing governments with their established organizations and procedures. Today much of the activity of the city reflects the demands of state and national programs, for the vigorous practice of cooperative federalism has made of the cities in significant part handmaidens to higher governments. In many important action areas the cities have become instruments of national policy through service as administrators of national programs.

The more urgent metro-problem areas . . . require resources of an order and kind not commanded by state and local governments. With respect to such problems it is fruitless to debate what is urban, what is state, and what is national, for they represent a confluence of concern by all governments. This fact has been recognized at the national level, where many programs—in the fields of public housing, urban renewal, and water quality management, to name but three—have been launched with an eye to the alleviation of these urban-national problems. President Johnson, taking note of the convergence of national and urban concerns, not only has promised further vigorous action by the government in Washington but also has taken positive steps to implement that promise.

Other concerns than that of the cities are of course relevant to this discussion. One is that of the states, whose interest in urban problems and capacity for dealing with them will vary. Another is that of the national government, which in some respects is closer to the cities than the states themselves. In contemplating the stake of the nation in the cities, and more particularly the future course of federal-city relations, three factors suggest themselves as worthy of special consideration. First is the increasing political strength of the city. National holders of elective office are not likely readily

---

[3] A.A. Berle, Jr., has argued this point persuasively in an article entitled "Reflections on Financing Governmental Functions of the Metropolis," *Proceedings of the Academy of Political Science*, vol. XXVII, no. 1 (May 1960), pp. 66-79.

to forget—nor to be allowed to forget—the needs of the cities. Second are significant current modifications in the practice of federalism in the face of long-standing and in some areas serious shortcomings in governmental performance. In *An American Dilemma,* Gunnar Myrdal was generous in his appraisal of the American Dream, but there is growing public dissatisfaction with the gap that separates what we profess from what we do, what could be from what is. Third is the rapid and continued increase in the nation's wealth, which reflects itself in mounting resources available for the support of public programs. These factors point toward the nationalization of problems previously held to be urban and toward increased reliance on the cities as active participants in their administration. This is not the place to argue the case for direct access by the cities to the national government, but it is not premature to suggest that there are currents in being which bid fair to work important changes in the traditional relations among the three levels of government in the American system.

Quest for operational effectiveness

The search for workable arrangements—that is, for adaptations which would translate legal forms into structures and procedures adequate to meet operational needs—has followed two major lines. The first has produced a maze of governmental units which in 1962 numbered 91,236; by census definition all of these except the nation and the fifty states are local governments. They are, of course, central to an analysis of the subject of governmental adaptation to program requirements, but they are not of immediate relevance to the study at hand. Of greater concern is the second line of search, which relates to the amplification of the federal system.

In broad outline, the nature of the American system was generally understood by 1875. The Civil War had determined the union to be a federal one, while the Dillon Rule had declared the cities subject in all fundamental particulars to their respective states. The basic partners in the American system therefore were the nation and the states. Even if we omit mention of what the Constitution neglected to say, it seems reasonably clear in what it did say regarding the respective powers of the two. The list of powers conferred upon the national government appeared adequate to foreseeable needs, while the residual powers seemed to make the states a bottomless repository of authority over all things else. Although it was never contemplated by those who conceived the federal system that the nation and the states would pursue completely separate and distinct courses, a judicial doctrine resting essentially upon that concept had gained almost universal currency. It resided in the notion of dual federalism, summarized by Chief Justice Roger B. Taney in 1858 in these words:

And the powers of the General Government, and of the State, although both exist and are exercised within the same territorial limits, are yet separate and distinct sovereignties, acting separately and independently of each other, within their respective spheres.[4]

This concept of federalism, which, though at its height perhaps a century ago, has been embraced throughout most of our national history, appeared the more logical by reason of the seemingly clear-cut division of powers in the Constitution.[5]

As legal doctrine dual federalism enjoyed general acceptance over the course of many years; but as a description of the federal system in operation it came to be recognized as artificial. The notion of two parallel streams of government, one labeled state, the other national, with little or no crossover from one to the other, simply was not in accord with the way the federal system operated. Some reserved powers were discovered to gain in significance if shared by the states with the central government, whereas the latter found itself the beneficiary of state collaboration in many areas in which it enjoyed delegated powers. There was, moreover, the broad sea of concurrent powers—powers that might be exercised by either state or nation, or both. With respect to concurrent powers in particular, the states and the central government frequently found themselves in a position of interdependence, with each profiting by turn from the collaboration of the other.

The concept of dual federalism appears scarcely adequate to describe the network of interrelations that grew up between the two major federal partners. "Cooperative federalism" would seem a more apt term. This phrase has gained wide currency during the last quarter-century, in reference particularly to the "new federalism" of the New Deal.[6] It signifies the common sharing of public responsibilities by two or more "levels" of government. The sharing may be national-with-state (or the reverse), national-with-state-with-local, state-with-local (though technically this is an intrastate rather than a federal matter), or federal-with-local. The Tennessee Valley Authority, which through a network of "agreements of cooperation" has brought literally scores of governments together in collaborative action in the Tennessee Valley, is a prime exemplar of cooperative federalism. Cooperative federalism describes a confused, even a chaotic, arrangement, and it has to recommend it initially only the fact that it also describes operating relations among the governments—relations that have existed since the early days of the Republic.

---

[4] *Ableman v. Booth,* 21 Howard 506 (1858); quotation at p. 516.

[5] The literature of federalism is vast, learned, diverse, and in some part illogical and contradictory. The Workshop in American Federalism of the University of Chicago, under the leadership of the late Professor Morton Grodzins, has produced a number of studies which suggest a fairly drastic revision of our thinking about the nature of federalism. In particular, these studies question sharply the applicability of the doctrine of dual federalism throughout much of our history. On Professor Grodzins' nomination and my invitation, Professor Daniel J. Elazar, a former member of the Workshop, prepared a memorandum for my use in this study. I found this memorandum useful, though it goes without saying that Professor Elazar is not to be taxed with responsibility for what I have said here.

[6] See especially Jane Perry Clark, *The Rise of a New Federalism* (New York: Columbia University Press, 1938).

As a concept it lacks the neatness of the notion of dual federalism, but it has the advantage of a foundation in reality.

Cooperative federalism has been shown by Elazar to have prevailed from the early 1800s in such areas as "the extension of internal improvements, the maintenance of a sound nationwide fiscal system, the establishment of appropriate educational facilities, and, to a more limited extent, the provision of necessary public welfare aids." He mentions the joint stock company and the cooperative survey as two of the major means by which cooperation among governments was achieved in the early days, and illuminates numerous cases of inter-level cooperation achieved by these (and other) means.[7]

As practiced throughout the nineteenth century, cooperative federalism possessed certain characteristic features. First, it rested upon a common concern among governments in public programs of wide significance. A program which through generality of interest might be considered national but at the same time was possessed of immediate state or local importance or had a direct and demonstrable local impact was the natural starting point for an agreement among governments to share responsibility. Second, intergovernmental cooperation served, in the nineteenth century as now, as a device for matching resources with needs. In important program areas the only resources available were those of the general government, whereas the needs frequently were quite particular. Third, the instrument most commonly employed for encouraging and implementing cooperative arrangements was the grant-in-aid. Throughout the last century the grant was usually in land; with the substantial depletion of the public domain shortly after the beginning of this century, money grants came into vogue. The central government possessed all the public land and recently has enjoyed a substantial superiority in the matter of money revenue. It has, therefore, been in a position to act as chief instigator and supporter of cooperative federalism. Fourth, the practice of cooperation has combined national standards with state and local responsibility for administration. This has had the effect of placing a floor under performance without destroying local responsibility for what have been, in impact at least, local problems. Fifth, the setting of standards has entailed a measure of national supervision in the matters both of fiscal management and of achievement of program goals, and this has raised recurrently the question of centralization. These features suggest the nature of cooperative federalism as it has been practiced almost from the beginning of our history.

The participants in these cooperative activities have been identified, by implication at least: they were, first, the national government and the states. It is highly significant, at the same time, that the cities played a not-unimportant role in these cooperative arrangements. The city of Norfolk participated, together with the states of Virginia and North Carolina (and

[7]Daniel J. Elazar, "Federal-State Collaboration in the Nineteenth Century United States," an unpublished paper prepared for delivery at the 1962 annual meeting of the American Political Science Association, Washington, D.C. The quotation appears at page 5. For a more extended discussion, see his *The American Partnership* (Chicago: University of Chicago Press, 1962).

private investors as well), in a joint stock company to implement an Army Engineers plan for the Dismal Swamp Canal as early as 1816; and Hartford benefited from cooperative support for an asylum for the deaf and dumb founded the next year.[8] If the cities were not often singled out as major partners in the practice of cooperative federalism, it was because they were not of much size or separate consequence during most of the nineteenth century and their problems were those common to general local government rather than those of the highly differentiated urban society of today. Because their problems had not yet become specialized, as a rule they were handled in the normal course of dealing with general public issues. Even so, the cities were practicing partners in many cooperative programs from the early 1800s, and in some they were signatories, so to speak, of the agreement on which cooperation rested.

Cooperative federalism has gained wide acceptance of recent years as a term newly popularized to describe the ever increasing practice of cooperation among national, state, and local governments. In point of fact, however, cooperation has characterized the practice of federalism from the early years of the Republic. The Constitution provided for a dual system, but from the beginning dual federalism was more legal myth than operational reality. Clearly the constitutional system required to be energized by a workable set of understandings and arrangements to fill the voids and smooth the harsh edges of legal federalism. The dualism of Justice Taney was transformed into an operationally effective system by cooperative federalism, a device typically American in its pragmatism.

Two observations may be made in conclusion. First, cooperation among different levels of government has been so widely practiced and so well known over the decades as to have gained matter-of-course acceptance. Not much point was made of cooperative federalism in the nineteenth century precisely because it was a universal phenomenon. Second, the question of what government assumes responsibility for action in case of need is of small concern to the citizen. Federal centralization, states' rights, local self-government—these and kindred shibboleths have little significance so long as health programs are run well, streets are fixed, and school is kept. The Federal Council on Intergovernmental Relations demonstrated more than twenty years ago that the citizen's concern is for service defined in terms of answers to felt needs, rather than for legal or ideological justifications. Cooperative federalism is a term which, it may be supposed, lies beyond the vocabulary of the average citizen, but it nevertheless describes the kind of government he is used to. Alexander Pope's much-abused couplet in praise of pragmatism has more relevance here than in most places where it is employed.

An evolving federalism

The federal system wherever found is experimental and inexact, whether as concept or as practice. As corollaries it is also flexible, highly adaptive, and

[8] Daniel J. Elazar, "Federal-State Collaboration . . . ," *op. cit.,* pp. 5, 11.

ever changing. This is true for example of the federal systems of Canada and Australia, where the relationship between the central government and the states is a matter of constant concern and continuous probing. The federal system was designed to effect a marriage of centrality and diversity; because these concepts (and public understanding of them) vary from country to country and from time to time, there can be nothing static about federalism.

It comes as no surprise that American federalism fits into the common pattern. It is an evolving arrangement for the division of powers and the distribution of responsibilities among governments of different levels. Far from being rigidly bound by philosophical or ideological conceptions, the federal system is a pragmatic scheme that not only permits but also requires adjustments to meet the varying needs of changing times. American federalism, in practice if not in theory, reflects sensitively shifts in presidential leadership, which is chiefly responsible for accelerating or braking adaptation in the system. It is also sensitive to changes in the composition of the Supreme Court, which must be relied upon both for legal interpretations and for legitimating action when it is challenged. The federal system thus reacts positively to change in all its forms—social, economic, political. It is a major instrumentality for adjusting the relations among nation, states, and localities so as to make and keep government in its totality abreast of the needs of the people.

If the federal system is inexact in concept and flexible in practice, it is at the same time possessed of unplumbed depths and untested limits in respect of possibilities for adjustment. When widely felt wants have emerged to command a national consensus on action, ways have been found to meet them. War and depression have produced the most spectacular readjustments in federal-state-local relations, but the modifications introduced all along to make federalism a working reality have been important too. Many modifications of high significance have been introduced under the mantle of cooperative federalism, which in various guises has been engaged in the business of making the federal system operational for at least a century and a half. That federalism will prove equal to future challenges presently unforeseen may be confidently expected; the case of Puerto Rico, recently brought into association with the union as a commonwealth—a status without precedent in either law or practice—is suggestive on this point. It is difficult to believe that American federalism will not prove equal to future demands to be made upon it.

It is significant that, notwithstanding marked modifications in both the law and the practice of federalism, the distinguishing features of the federal system persist in America. Relations among the members of the American partnership are not what they were, or what they were expected to become, in 1800, yet it cannot be truly said that any partner has suffered a loss of fundamental rights or that any has gained in stature at the expense of another. Quite specifically the states, whose leaders now and then complain about latter-day trends, cannot be demonstrated to have forfeited any right to action or to responsibility in any field in which they have had the power and the will to act. If they have on occasion forfeited the right to *in*action, that is because they have misread the signs of the times or misjudged the conscience of the American people. But that is another story, one more appropriate for telling elsewhere. What is important here is that it be understood that America's federal system has found ways to adapt to new conditions without loss by its partners of any essential rights or prerogatives. The evolution of federalism has been more in practice than in theory; it has reflected pragmatic responses to urgent stimuli rather than abandonment of or modification in fundamental philosophical concepts.

In a commencement address delivered at the University of Michigan on May 22, 1964, President Johnson spoke of the overwhelming problems of the cities in the context of the federal system. These problems, he concluded, "require us to create new concepts of cooperation—a creative federalism—between the National Capital and the leaders of local communities."[9] The ingredients for the creative federalism envisioned by the President are ready at hand. They include principally freedom from commitment to a static doctrine, a fluid concept of federalism, and a willingness to experiment. It does not seem likely that the form of the federal system will be modified in any important way because that does not appear necessary, but the practice of federalism could change significantly in our time.

In contemplating the possible directions and the likely extent of change, we will find it useful to weigh the relative capacities of the partners in federalism against the foreseeable tasks that lie ahead. Let us particularize the question: What are the interests of the national government, the state, and the city in the problems of a metropolitan society? What resources—leadership, vigorous and effective organization, skilled and experienced manpower, demonstrated success in governing, money—is each prepared to plough into the war to make America's cities livable? How deep, how firm, and how effective is any commitment that may be undertaken likely to prove? These are the kinds of questions that are relevant to the President's call for a creative federalism. They are most pertinent and most timely when asked of the states.

[9] As reported in *The Washington Post*, May 23, 1964, A6:3.

Contestants for the Prizes of a City's Politics

Wallace S. Sayre
Herbert Kaufman

Before we begin our discussion of the policy-making process in central cities and their suburbs, it is useful to have some idea of the number, type, and organization of groups in such communities, because these structures are among the primary participants (contestants or actors) in the game of local politics. By becoming involved in such groups, individuals can translate their values, commitments, interests, and attitudes into political action—which may influence the outcomes of local politics.

In this selection from Governing New York City, *Wallace S. Sayre and Herbert Kaufman discuss the various structures involved in New York City's politics. The selection was chosen for several reasons. First, it described a wide variety of groups which may participate in the policy-making process at the local level. The group infrastructure in a city like New York is very complex and the governmental and nongovernmental contestants exceedingly diverse.*

You should consider, however, how the group infrastructure may vary in other municipalities. Obviously, when one moves from a large heterogeneous city like New York to smaller, more homogeneous municipalities, one discovers that the number and type of contestants can change considerably. For instance, in smaller communities, neighborhood associations and ad hoc groups of citizens may be the primary nongovernmental participants in the policy-making process. In addition, political parties may be relatively unimportant actors in such communities. Scott Greer and Peter Orleans have found that the number and type of voluntary nongovernmental groups—the "parapolitical structure" of a community—vary considerably because of differences in life style between municipalities. Differences in the degree of urbanization of a community, the social rank of its population, and its ethnic composition were found to have important implications for the kinds of structures one is likely to find involved in the policy-making process.

A second reason for selecting this article is that Sayre and Kaufman discuss the functions various groups perform in the larger polity, as well as some of their internal characteristics. Left unanswered, however, is a very interesting question: How are the attitudes of individual group members translated into political action? They also do not systematically discuss the factors which affect a particular group's ability to influence public-policy decisions. Sayre and Kaufman do indicate, however, that group conflict is regulated to some extent by a basic consensus among key participants on how the game of politics should be played.

Finally, Sayre and Kaufman point out that not all contestants are continually involved in the policy-making process. To discriminate among the kinds of involvement of various groups, they use two criteria, (1) the scope of a group's political interest, and (2) the frequency of a group's political intervention. Continual political intervention on a broad range of issues is very costly. Therefore, each group, particularly its leadership, must weigh the costs of political action against the possible benefits it can receive.

As one might expect from the nature of the stakes, there is, within the context of agreement that unites the people of the city, a steady and vigorous competition for the rewards of political action.

The contestants fall into five groups: the party leaders, the public officials, the bureaucracies, the nongovernmental groups (including the press and the other mass media of communication), and the officials and bureaucracies of the state and federal governments involved in city affairs.

None of these categories is monolithic. Each has several components, and each component functions with considerable autonomy, although some categories have a nominal unity of mission and leadership. Nevertheless, because the elements here grouped into categories share many common attributes, they may be treated as classes for the purpose of organizing the discussion.

Party leaders

Efforts are made in some cities to operate the electoral system on a nonpartisan basis. New York City, by contrast, has always been committed to the political party as a central institution in its governing processes. Party leaders, in consequence, are major participants in the city's politics.

A political party as an institution consists of two main elements: its members and its officers or functionaries. Party members may be dedicated partisans, or usually loyal members, or persons only lightly attached to their party. The main business of the parties is conducted by its officers, who make up the party organization. The party leaders are the contestants with whom we are here concerned.

The functions of party leaders

The services that city party leaders perform are fourfold. First, by their controls over nominations, thus presenting in the general election only one candidate for each office, they reduce to manageable proportions the number of choices each voter is called upon to make. If the party organizations did not winnow out aspirants to office, and if their nominees did not ordinarily stand a better chance than independent candidates of emerging victorious, there might well be dozens of names for each post. Not only might such a situation overwhelm the electorate, but it would also increase the probability of a city government splintered into fragments without majority support.

Second, the leaders of the party organizations serve the city electoral system by keeping it competitive. In New York City they produce candidates even when the chances of winning seem slight. There is always an element of risk for anybody in or seeking office. In New York City even the strongest bastions have occasionally fallen, even the safest constituencies have sometimes been captured by the opposition. This uncertainty keeps candidates and officials more responsive to popular demands than they would be otherwise. The party organizations sometimes function as recruiters as well as

Reprinted from *Governing New York City: Politics in the Metropolis* (New York: Russell Sage Foundation, 1960), pp. 67-89, by permission of the publisher and authors.

filters and in so doing help create an atmosphere in which elections fulfill their many purposes.

Third, the party leaders serve candidates by providing the machinery needed to win votes. Even candidates for positions with the smallest constituencies—seats in the state Assembly, the lower house of the state legislature—must make their appeals to at least fifteen thousand voters in the smallest districts and from two to four times as many in more populous districts, while candidates whose constituencies comprise the entire city (for example, Mayor, President of the City Council, Comptroller; for statewide offices, including Governor and United States Senator; and for President and Vice President of the United States) must think in terms of electorates of two to three and a half million city voters. Sometimes, in a safe district, a nominee may not have to campaign at all; his party's label may be all he needs to win even though he himself, as a person, is virtually unknown. At other times, and invariably for the more prominent elective offices, candidates who fail to make their names and affiliations, if not their programs, familiar to the people run serious risks of being defeated even in areas regarded as almost certain.

Since every electoral contest in the city involves such large numbers of voters, acquainting electorates with candidates requires the services of an organization skilled and experienced in this kind of campaigning. Even a candidate with a great deal of money, a candidate with supporters who can afford to buy publicity and hire many people to help him, may be at a disadvantage in a stuggle with a party unit that has been functioning as a team over a long period, knows its area intimately and has established lines of access and contact with the voters, and can, if necessary, enlist the support of prominent and influential ticket leaders of their own party to assist in their local cause. Organization itself, no less than money and manpower, is a valuable resource in the conduct of electoral campaigns. It is this resource, and often the others as well, that the party leaders put at the disposal of their candidates.

Fourth, in thus serving their candidates, the party organizations also serve the city's voters. In carrying the appeals of nominees to the public, party workers make it possible for voters to gain some familiarity with the personalities and issues in elections with little or no effort by the voters. They also familiarize the public with their respective party emblems and the programs with which the parties are associated. Thus, if an individual voter has for some reason not been reached by the parties' propaganda efforts, or has paid no attention to the candidates in the course of the campaigning, he can still form some reasonably reliable expectations about the behavior of the several candidates should they be elected to office. Without party organizations in a city the size of New York, voters would be deprived of many clues to the future actions of the candidates on which electoral choices presumably rest. To be confronted with the obligations to make selections among total unknowns is tantamount to having no option at all. The party leaders help to rescue the voters from this possible futility.

In New York City the services performed by the party organizations for candidates and electorate are by no means confined to contests for local office. On the contrary, it is the same organizations, the same party workers, who do the basic campaign jobs whether city, county, state, or federal positions are at stake. Their ranks may be swelled by temporary volunteers when major offices are to be filled, and their operations may be paralleled by various kinds of citizens' associations and similar groups of more or less amateur politicians, but the backbone of every campaign conducted in the city for every office from state assemblyman to President of the United States is the regular organizations of the established parties. It is on these regular, frontline troops of party warfare that every candidate who hopes to win votes in the city is compelled to depend, regardless of the office he seeks.

Although elections are the chief business of the party leaders, elective office is not the only prize of politics with which they are connected. Because of their influence over voters—that is, their vote-getting capabilities—party officials can make claims upon the elected officials whose victories they were instrumental in engineering, and such claims will almost always be heard and often satisfied. The claims extend to the selection of personnel to fill appointive positions and to the wide range of governmental decisions through which the other rewards of the political system are distributed. In part, these demands are asserted on behalf of party supporters, particularly for those leaders of groups whose help has been significant in votes, financial contributions, or useful public endorsement. Claims are also made by the party leaders for themselves, and they are often the recipients in the distribution of rewards. . . .

Public officials

Public officials do not, once they have achieved office, cease their quest for the prizes of political action. On the contrary, they often intensify their efforts. They seek to consolidate or broaden their constituencies. They aspire to increase their own autonomy and bargaining power in the political system. They seek favorable alliances with other participants. They utilize their positions as springboards to higher positions, in the fashion common to members of all large organizations. They exert influence on governmental decisions dealing with public moneys—sometimes to further the agencies in which they serve, sometimes to promote programs to which they are psychologically and materially committed, sometimes to advance their own rates of compensation or other personal interests. They figure significantly in the formulation of decisions about governmental services, for these affect their prestige, their promotional opportunities, their work, their bargaining power. They seek many of the ideological and intangible rewards connected with governmental action, such as the satisfactions of public service and status in the community. All the stakes of politics, in short, are goals of those officials who are "in" the government as much as they are the objectives of those who manage the political parties or serve as members of the bureaucracies or who as "outsiders" are served or regulated by government.

The distinctive role of public officials

Public officials, however, are in a special position in the political process. They promulgate the official decisions of government and supervise the performance of the acts that translate the words of the formal decisions into deeds and objects. They are thus distributors of the rewards of politics as well as beneficiaries of the system and, therefore, are the targets of all who are interested in shaping public policy. They occupy the center of the governmental arena.

Statements of general policy binding on the people of the community take the form of duly authenticated constitutional amendments, statutes, executive orders, administrative regulations and directives, and other documents emanating formally from officialdom. And in them are imbedded decisions concerning the sharing of the prizes of politics-decisions about governmental services and regulations, about taxation and spending and borrowing, about organs of government and their powers and procedures, about individual citizen rights and privileges, about public employee appointments, promotions, punishments, and dismissals.

A group of many parts

Although public officials as a group occupy a unique position in the governmental process, they are not a homogeneous group. They do not constitute a monolithic organization. On the contrary, they are divided into many segments having different loyalties, different perspectives, different aspirations, different—sometimes competing—objectives, different sources of influence, different jurisdictions. Seldom, if ever, do they function as a single unit.

Division by branches of government Executives, legislators, and judges all are public officials, but their separation into comparatively independent organs makes for differences among them. They are subject to divergent pressures. Different expectations as to their roles on the part of the public and of their specific constituencies exert influence. The separate branches are sometimes rivals for control of public policy, and they are generally touchy about infringements on their powers. As individuals, they are unequally visible, chief executives being constantly in the limelight, most legislators, judges, and lesser executives operating in relative anonymity compared to the chief executives. Their functions and traditions vary. Executives have tended to assume the mantle of initiative in government, legislators the role of suspicious and restraining guardians, judges the posture of impartial referees. Necessarily, they often work cooperatively with each other and sometimes even slip into each other's roles. But the establishment of three branches of government separates the members of each from the members of the others in important respects treated in detail later on. The distinctions manifest themselves in the relations of the Mayor with the Board of Estimate of the city, and with the City Council; the relations of the Governor with the chambers of the state legislature; the contacts between the President and Congress. All these divisions have significant consequences for the roles of the officials and for the government and politics of New York City.

Mode of accession and tenure   Government officials are further classified according to whether they are elected or appointed, and whether their tenure in office is uncertain or stable. The manner in which they come to office and their job security produce disparate values and perceptions. Their own expectations and the expectations of others concerning their roles differ, and these differences produce competition as well as cooperation.

The number of elective officers is not large—less than four hundred; counting all elective officials voted for in the city, from state assemblyman to President of the United States. These officials have widely varied constituencies, and their terms of office range from two years for assemblymen and United States Representatives to fourteen years for some judges.

The number of appointed officials is much larger. Their total is in the thousands. They range from high-ranking executives and judges to minor functionaries of temporary significance. Some appointive officers serve at the pleasure of those who appoint them, some have fixed terms. Federal judges are appointed for life. Insofar as tenure may be a factor in the capacity of officials to ignore pressures from all sources, the federal judges are in the strongest position; they stay on while elected officials, and many appointed ones, come and go.

Functional Differences   Public officials are further differentiated by the kinds of services they perform, and the kinds of people for whom they perform them. Life for officials in the line agencies is different from that in the overhead or staff agencies. The officials who lead these different lives do not always display complete harmony with each other.

What is more, the agencies, whether line or overhead, have become highly specialized. In the city government alone, more than fifty bureaus serve the public in a variety of ways, and some ten overhead agencies guide and supervise their operations. Public officials who head these agencies must often deal with clusters of fairly autonomous bureaus, each organized around a specialty. The officials heading these organizations must usually develop strong attachments to their agencies and to the programs they conduct. They become jealous of their jurisdictions, aggressive in their leadership against the competing claims of other officials heading other agencies.

Public officials as a heterogeneous class   In sum, while it is useful to speak of "government" as an institution from which decisions emerge, each decision is promulgated and supervised by particular sets of officials. These officials are not a solid, undifferentiated, tightly integrated body; they are an aggregation of many parts, of many kinds. In the contest for the stakes of politics, it is the specific sets and combinations of officials, rather than the general class, that must be observed. But public officials are nevertheless major participants in the city's politics.

The organized bureaucracies

The employees who work in the city, whether for the federal, state, county, or city governments, are employed, for the most part, under some type of merit system—that is, a personnel system providing for entrance by examination, advancement by seniority and performance, wages and salaries under a job classification plan, and tenure during satisfactory service. In the six decades since the establishment of the Greater City and under the protections offered by the merit systems, the many separate bureaucracies in the city have slowly but steadily enhanced their claims to autonomy and have acquired status as major participants in the city's political life.

Their combined numbers are great—about 382,000 at the three levels of government in the city. Like the public officials, the bureaucrats have a special position in the political process. As individual employees and as the staffs of governmental bureaus they initiate small and great proposals for the formal signatures of officials, and in carrying out these and other policies and decisions they ordinarily possess great discretionary power. Like the officials, too, they are in the government and their agreement is usually essential to the goals of other major participants that require governmental action. As Luther Gulick has observed,

> Much of the actual discretion used in administration is used at the very bottom of the hierarchy, where public servants touch the public. The assessor who walks into the home and sees the furniture and the condition of the house, the policeman who listens to the motorist's story, the health inspector who visits the dairy, the income tax auditor who sees the return and interviews the taxpayer—all these people are compelled to exercise discretion, and more important discretion from the point of view of the citizen, than many other functionaries much farther up in the organization.[1]

In these ways the bureaucracies play key parts in setting the quality, the direction, and the intensity of governmental service and regulation, functioning not simply as claimants seeking satisfaction of their own demands, but also as dispensers of rewards or penalties.

But it is as organized, self-conscious, and cohesive groups that the bureaucracies have achieved status as participants in the city's political system. These associations are quite numerous. The membership of some of them is large. The power of others is measured by unusual cohesives or by strategic location in the city's governmental or political process. Thus, the associations of teachers, policemen, firemen, transit workers, and sanitation workers represent numbers which have great political significance, while the social workers, lawyers, engineers, accountants, and other relatively small groups depend for influence upon their professional unity and their strategic roles in the administration of public agencies. All seek allies inside or outside the government itself. Their skills as contestants in the city's politics have steadily increased. In many situations their power is a crucial factor in determining how the prizes are distributed.

[1] Gulick, Luther, "Politics, Administration, and 'the New Deal,' "*Annals of the American Academy of Political and Social Science*, vol. 169, September, 1933, p. 62.

The bureaucracies are not monolithic

The bureaucracies share an important characteristic with the categories of party leaders and the public officials. Like them, the bureaucracies are not a monolithic category. Instead, like the public officials, they are separated by governmental levels, by functional differences, by a variety of closed personnel systems. Although they are found primarily in the executive branch of each of the three levels of government, the individual departments and bureaus tend to become strongholds of particular professions and trades.

As a result, there is not one large, unified bureaucracy in the city, but a number of separate bureaucracies. From time to time, some of them join with one another in a cooperative endeavor to achieve some common goal. Far more frequently, however, they function without much reference to one another, or in competition or conflict with one another.

The ranks of the bureaucracies are intersected by the many kinds of associations and societies into which they group themselves, or with which some among them affiliate. The workers in some departments and agencies—in the Sanitation Department and the New York City Transit Authority, for example—are strongly unionized and are affiliated with the labor movement. Professional personnel—doctors, lawyers, engineers, nurses, social workers, and others—are, on the other hand, generally members of the separate associations that speak for their specialties. Cutting across departmental lines are other types of organizations, the public service unions—the Civil Service Forum, the American Federation of State, County, and Municipal Employees. Still another type is represented by the Patrolmen's Benevolent Association. Associations of police officers from sergeant to captain function in the Police Department in much the same fashion as labor unions. Similar associations are found in the Fire Department. Indeed, it was even customary, during the depression decade, for eligibles—those who had passed civil service examinations and were registered on civil service eligible lists—to form numerous separate associations to promote their interests. In many of the larger agencies there are also religious fraternities—Catholic Holy Name Societies, Protestant St. George Societies, and Jewish Shomrim Societies—made up of employees of the same faith. These, too, often have political goals.

The bureaucracies are thus crisscrossed by all manner of groupings. There are groups whose functions derive from the existence and nature of the public bureaucracies—associations of public personnel administrators, civil service specialists and lawyers, labor relations lawyers specializing in governmental employee relations, civil service newspapers, civil service examination "cram" schools. Though not themselves part of the machinery of government in many cases, such groups promote the self-consciousness of bureaucrats as a segment of government and society, and stimulate the self-identification of parts of the bureaucracies as separate and distinct entities.

In the city's political contest, the several organized bureaucracies have come of age as leading and influential participants. They are divided and often competitive among themselves, but each major grouping has the capacity and inclination to assert its own separate and autonomous bargaining power, to offer inducements to allies, and to claim the privileges of its role as a member of the third category of major participants in the political life of the city.

Nongovernmental groups

Each of the thousands of governmental decisions reached yearly by party leaders, public officials, and the bureaucracies affects a possible interest of some New Yorkers. This is true not only of decisions impinging directly on the public—laws and ordinances, executive orders, judicial decisions, rules, regulations, adjudications and orders of administrative agencies—but also of many kinds of action often described as "internal" or "managerial"—budget directives, personnel directives, organization and reorganization plans. It is a rare piece of duly authenticated official paper that does not lead somebody to the conclusion that he, as a result of it, has either lost or gained ground in the struggle for political prizes. Concern with who get public office or employment and what they do when they have it is thus not confined exclusively to officials and employees themselves, or to party leaders. Private citizens, by definition not in the government, are deeply interested in what governments do. Though not often themselves seekers of public office, they may organize to intervene energetically in the decisions of who will occupy these positions. Though these organizations are not political parties, they are not far removed in tactics or accomplishments. Though not so large as the city electorate, and incapable by themselves of turning out government officials as an electorate can and does, they probably wield greater influence on the day-by-day activities of public officials and the bureaucracies than does the electorate as such. Though most of these groups do not think of themselves as political, they are often deeply involved and actively participant in the political process. No discussion of government and politics is complete without an analysis of these nongovernmental groups as contestants for the rewards of political action.

Spokesmen for legitimate interests

More than a century ago de Tocqueville commented on the tendency of Americans to form associations for every purpose; he was struck by the plenitude and variety of voluntary groups in American society and politics. Were he to return today and survey New York City, he would discover not only that the tendency still flourishes, but that it has, if anything, intensified over the years. No careful census of these nongovernmental groups in the city has ever been made, but the number seems to run at least to tens of thousands. This estimate comprises only those groups sufficiently well organized to have letterheads, telephones, and/or to appear in some published directory. Just these visible and respectable groups add up to an impressive total.

They are not all alike, of course. Some of them have a long history and have had a reputation of power and influence for decades; others are clearly transient and limited in power. They vary in membership from a few score to many thousands. To finance their activities, some nongovernmental groups depend on contributions by a limited number of sponsors, others on donations from the general public, and still others upon dues levied on their members. Their operating budgets range from a few hundred to several hundred thousand dollars a year. The work of smaller, less well-financed groups is generally performed by part-time, volunteer, and amateur workers. Some of the larger, or the more affluent, associations employ permanent, full-time, highly paid professional staffs and provide them with research and secretarial and clerical assistance. The differences among these organizations seem endless; no two groups are identical.

Many groups at one time or another attempt to exert influence on the selection of public officials and bureaucrats, on particular governmental programs, on individual governmental decisions and actions, or on any combination of these. Only a handful, however, are concerned primarily with government. The overwhelming majority are mobilized around other central interests, and active participation in the city's political process is merely one subsidiary phase of much broader sets of activities. Many organizations in the city are established as occupational groups to protect and promote the common interest of those engaged in particular kinds of work. These are the business and professional associations and the labor unions, of which there are thousands. Many others are organized on status lines, building their memberships on the basis of what people are rather than what they do. The most prominent and numerous of these are associations of persons of the same religion, national origin, or race, and the veterans' organizations. Others are territorial in character, some being identified with particular streets (the Fifth Avenue Association, the Twenty-third Street Association), others with particular neighborhoods. Some concentrate on individual governmental or social functions—for instance, health (usually a single disease), welfare (including a host of private charities), or education.

In addition, *ad hoc* groups spring up in relation to specific issues, such as fluoridation of water supplies, hazards to children, and the so-called baby-carriage brigades of mothers who throw road blocks across busy intersections of the city to compel the installation of traffic signals or the assignment of traffic patrolmen. Such groups may also force the modification of local conveniences, typified by the outraged birdwatchers who successfully prevented the destruction of a grove in Central Park favored by migrating birds, as well as by the indignant parents who stopped the transformation of a Central Park lawn from a play area used by their children into a parking lot.

At most, only a handful of associations can be identified as groups whose chief orientation is toward government and whose activities are confined almost exclusively to studying and influencing the conduct of government. The others intervene in the city's political process only when their special interests are at stake, devoting most of their energies to the relations of their members with each other and with other nongovernmental institutions.

This classification of the many kinds of interests of the legitimate nongovernmental groups in the city suggests the reason why every official decision and action, no matter how trifling it may seem, arouses a response from some element of the population. It suggests also the myriad patterns of coalition and conflict that can be expected to develop over time. Most nongovernmental groups can be classed as logically in one category as another. Borough-wide business associations and professional societies, for example, stress their territorial nature at some times and their occupational nature at others. Religious, welfare, and labor agencies behave now as status groups and now as functional groups. Many groups that make common cause with respect to one policy may end up on opposite sides of the fence when another is involved. In fact, it is often difficult to predict which stand a given group will take because one of its interests may lead it in one direction, another in a contrary direction. The context of the city's politics and its governmental decision-making is therefore always complicated and volatile.

Another useful way of looking at the city's nongovernmental groups is to examine the scope of their interests and the degree of persistence with which they pursue those interests. The groups can thus be plotted on a chart formed by the intersection of two scales (see Figure 1): a horizontal scale of scope of political interest ranging from narrow to broad, and a vertical scale of degree of persistence ranging from high to low.

In the first quadrant fall those groups with a wide range of interests and a record of continual intervention in the formulation of political and governmental decisions. This quadrant is sparsely populated, for it is confined

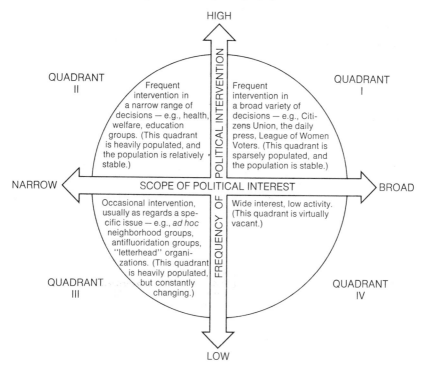

Figure 1. Classification of nongovernmental groups by scope of political interest and frequency of political intervention in governmental decision-making

primarily to the city's civic groups and the communication media. The second quadrant comprises the groups displaying high persistence in relatively narrow segments of the whole spectrum of political action. While it contains groups of every kind, the most prominent class is those groups defined above as having functional interests. The second quadrant is more heavily populated than the first, but far less so than the third. The third quadrant includes all those groups that participate only intermittently in the political or governmental process, and only in relation to decisions that impinge directly and heavily on their special interests. The great bulk of the nongovernmental groups in the city are found here. The fourth quadrant is almost empty, for there are few groups that have a broad range of political interests yet intervene only intermittently in governmental decisions.

Any single group in the first quadrant is likely to have a greater impact on a larger number of governmental decisions than any single group in the other quadrants. Similarly, any single group in the second quadrant is likely to affect a larger number of decisions than any single group in the third quadrant. It may well have greater influence on a particular decision within its special area of competence than any group in any quadrant, but it will normally play a role in fewer decisions than any group in the first quadrant. A group in the third quadrant may occasionally be exceedingly influential in an individual instance, but the number of such instances is likely to be low. Groups in the fourth quadrant rarely exercise much influence at all.

Some political issues bring out large numbers of groups, most bring out a few who are directly interested, a few bring out only the civic groups, and the civic groups may well turn up to take sides on any issue. The most significant fact for the city's politics, perhaps, is that there are few enduring alliances uniting any substantial number of these groups. They are incurably pluralistic, competitive, specialized in their interests, jealous of their separate identities.

The underworld

Twenty-five years ago Denis W. Brogan,[2] an English observer of the American political scene, noted the importance of what he called "the three B's"—betting, booze, and brothels—in state and local politics in this country. The repeal of prohibition has greatly reduced the importance of bootlegging, although some still continues by evaders of liquor tax and customs laws. Illegal gambling, organized prostitution, and narcotics sales remain significant factors in the politics of the city, and organizers of these trades must be reckoned among the nongovernmental contestants for the rewards of political action.

The gross business of these three "trades" in New York City is often alleged to run to hundreds of millions of dollars annually. Since the activities from which these revenues, whatever their actual magnitude, are derived are proscribed by law, the chief political concern of the organizations engaged in

[2] *Government by the People.* Harper and Bros., New York, 1933, pp. 240-245.

them is to ease the stringency of law enforcement. While they naturally conduct their operations clandestinely, they cannot afford to be too secretive, for they might thus escape their customers as well as agents of the law. Consequently, they must induce some appropriate governmental officials and bureaucrats to be tolerant of them while they are plying their trades and lenient with them when they are apprehended.

Two other types of underworld enterprise seemingly brought to a high stage of development in the past quarter century are business racketeering and labor racketeering. The "business" groups often assume the guise of trade associations of the kind that regulate conditions in an industry and defend the interest of the industry both economically and politically. Under this protective coloration, some alleged business associations have taken to providing "services" for their members, which often means nothing more than that they will refrain from committing violence upon their victims if the victims join the association and contribute regularly to it. In the same fashion the "labor" gangs often disguised as unions threaten work stoppages and violence in order to exact tribute from employers. In trucking and on the waterfront these methods have been employed to prevent action by employers and insurance companies against organized and large-scale pil-ferage. Both kinds of racketeers have been known to use their gains to influence some party leaders, public officials, and bureaucrats, particularly to safeguard themselves against suppression by law enforcement. Strenuous efforts are made by business associations, labor unions, and law enforcement agencies to eliminate these illegitimate organizations. But stamping out criminal elements masquerading as legitimate groups has proved not to be an easy task; they continue to exist and to wield an influence in some sections of the political arena.

These underworld groups concentrate a very high proportion of their energies and resources on mitigating the severity of law enforcement. There are some political tactics and strategies these groups cannot use because they are anxious to stay out of the public eye, but, in trying to get friendly people into office and affecting the behavior of those already in office, their practices are not fundamentally different from those of other nongovern-mental groups. Many respectable individuals and nongovernmental groups resort to techniques in their endeavors to sway the behavior of public servants (such as inspectors, tax assessors, and law-enforcement officers) that are hardly distinguishable in kind from those of underworld groups. Legitimate groups and underworld groups can be distinguished from each other, but nongovernmental groups of all types share many characteristics in connection with their strivings for the rewards of political action.

The special role of the press

Like the other institutions of the city, the mass communication media are often profoundly affected by governmental actions and decisions. In this respect, they are classed with other nongovernmental groups.

In other respects, however, they are special and a class apart. In the first place, they are not merely contestants in the great game of the city's politics, they are also the principal channel through which all other contestants reach the general public; hence, they have a great impact—usually deliberately, sometimes inadvertently—on some governmental and party decisions. In the second place, the popular image of government and politics depends heavily on the information supplied by the communication media. The whole tenor, the atmosphere, of political contest is colored by their presentations and portrayals. While it perhaps cannot be said that the mass media are more powerful than other nongovernmental participants in the political and governmental process, it is clear that they occupy a unique position. . . .

The communication media, and particularly the newspapers, are like the political parties in the sense that they are instruments on which the democratic governmental system depends but are not part of the official machinery of that system. At the same time, being business enterprises, they resemble in status and behavior other nongovernmental groups. In this dual capacity they are not only able to claim some of the rewards of political action for themselves, but they also figure prominently in the process by which the rewards of other contestants are distributed.

Officials and bureaucrats of the state and federal governments

As we have seen earlier, the public officials and the organized bureaucracies of the city are each an important class of participants in the city's politics. So, too, are many of the public officials and the bureaucracies of the state and federal governments. These officials and bureaucracies are, of course, primarily participants in their own separate political and governmental systems, but the intervention of many of them in the city's political system is sufficiently frequent and important to give them the status of major participants in the city system.

Almost every federal and state governmental agency has an office in the city. Several state agencies have their main offices here. State and federal courts are located in the city. More than 130,000 members of state and federal bureaucracies work in the city. Since the public officials who direct these activities and the bureaucracies who perform them make a multitude of decisions concerning governmental services to be provided, the governmental regulations to be imposed, the spending and collecting of public money, the distribution of public office and employment, they become perforce major participants in the city's political system, dealing continuously or frequently as the case may be with city officials, bureaucracies, party leaders, the leaders of the city's nongovernmental groups and the press, as well as directly with the citizens to whom they provide services or whose behavior they regulate.

The city's political system also has representatives in the state and federal systems. There are the city's delegation in the United States House of Representatives, the claims the city has upon the two United States Senators from New York, and the federal executives and judges whose appointments depend upon their connections with the city's political system. There are, further, the city's delegations to the two houses of the state legislature, the claims of the city upon the statewide elected executives (the Governor and others) and upon the state's elected judges whose electoral constituencies include the city, and the appointed state executives and judges whose selection and tenure is connected with its political system.

The officials and bureaucracies of the state and federal governments become major participants in the city's government and politics in several important ways. They distribute some of the prizes of office and employment for which the other contestants compete—for example, federal judgeships, postmasterships, state executive posts. They provide governmental services to the people of the city, in competition with or in addition to services provided by the city government—for example, postal service, highway construction. They initiate, administer, and exercise discretion under numerous statutes and rules governing many opportunities and liabilities of the city's residents. They grant or refuse to grant large sums of money for the support of city government activities (for example, federal aid in urban renewal, state aid for general governmental support, education, and many other city government programs). They supervise city officials and bureaucrats in many ways: through state legislative statutes, the regulations and rules of state executive and administrative agencies, the power to investigate, to criticize, and even to remove city officials. These are the ever-present, powerful levers with which federal or state officials and bureaucracies exercise their influence as participants in the city's political and governmental contest.

The officials and the bureaucracies of the state and federal governments, as contestants in local politics, share many of the characteristics of the other participants. They are not a monolithic group. Party lines often divide them. Function separates them. Differences in mode of selection and conditions of tenure introduce additional divisions among them. The degree of their dependence upon, or relative autonomy from, the city's political system produces different behavior. Their separate career aspirations are another source of differing attitudes and actions among both officials and bureaucrats. In short, like the other major categories of contestants, they are also pluralistic in composition, competitive with each other, playing their roles in the city's politics as many separate sets of officials and bureaucrats, each relating its strategy to the particular environment in which it finds itself. But, as a distinguishable category of participants, the state and federal officials and bureaucrats constitute a set of important contestants in the city's political life.

The electorate

In the last analysis, the whole pattern of the distribution of the stakes of city politics is shaped by the electorate of the city.[3] Every electoral contest

---

[3] As will be seen later, voters can be regarded as a number of electoral constituencies rather than as one. Elective government offices, party posts, and nominations made in

for government or party office, or for a nomination, is decided ultimately by the relevant constituency of voters. They thus determine who will fill the key positions in the political system, and they thereby determine which office seekers and officeholders will be rewarded. Moreover, their electoral choices profoundly affect the selection of appointive personnel and the lines of access and communication and pressure carefully developed over the years between elections by all the contestants—nongovernmental as well as party and official—for the stakes of political power. The preferences and behaviors of the electorate change often enough to keep the entire system highly fluid. By their actions, the voting constituencies can work more drastic transformations in the disposition of the stakes of politics than any other participants in the political process.

Party leaders, officials, candidates, and others envisage and solicit the support of a great variety of constituencies within the electorate: borough-conscious constituencies, ethnic constituencies, racial constituencies, religous constituencies; home-owning constituencies, rent-paying constituencies, tax-conscious constituencies; partisan constituencies and "independent" consti-tuencies; and so on through a seemingly endless series. These are usually, to the extent they exist at all, amorphous sets of forces. They influence the stakes of politics largely as indirect factors in the calculations and strategies of other contestants.

Only in the most general sense, then, can these specialized electorates be said to share in those stakes. Their claims are so diffuse, their heterogeneity so pronounced, their tolerance for the neglect of campaign promises so generous, and the connection between their nebulous mandates and the day-to-day decisions and activities of governmental officials and party officers so tenuous, that it is difficult to identify anything that might meaningfully be called a reward. The city's voters speak in a thunderous voice, but largely in generalities. Yet whatever any contestant gets, or is denied, can be traced in the end to what the electoral constituencies do.

The loose-knit organizations of party leaders, the multitude of officeholders and office seekers, the numerous organized and specialized bureaucracies, the plethora of nongovernmental groups, the media of mass communication (especially the press), and the many-faceted city electorate constitute the dramatis personae of the vast and intricate spectacle that is the govern-ment and politics of New York City. Each category is itself immensely complicated, and the interactions among them are exceedingly complex. The stakes they pursue are high, as befits the first city of the nation and of the world, a city created by the competitive as well as the cooper-ative efforts of eight million people.

---

primary elections all have different constituencies. Different numbers of voters appear in different years, when different offices are at stake, and, in any given election or primary, the number of ballots cast for different offices in any given election district also will vary.

The broad context of agreement

Portraying the city's politics as a contest among individuals and groups focuses attention on its most exciting and dynamic elements—the rivalry, competition, conflict, bargaining, and maneuvering; the alliances and coalitions; the victories and defeat—out of which public policy emerges. Even in totalitarian societies, where the opportunities for ordinary citizens to assert their demands and to organize to press for them without the sanction of the ruling cliques are tightly circumscribed, there are some evidences that this bargaining process occurs. In a democratic polity such as New York City enjoys, prevailing political values not only tolerate such a contest, they encourage it. Most New Yorkers doubtless regard it not as a privilege, but as a *right*, and many consider it a *duty*, to participate. Widespread contest over office and over governmental decisions is thus not a pathology of democratic government, but a sign of its vigor. The study of opposing forces in New York City politics is in this sense an inquiry into the operation of a democracy.

But the analogy of the contest must not be carried too far. The city is not an example of a Hobbesian "war of all against all." The contest takes place in an environment of agreement, within a matrix of accepted rules and a context of cooperation. The observer who lifts his eyes to the broader scene can hardly fail to be struck also by the degree of concord, mutual accommodation, and good will characteristic of the city. Bargaining and mutual concession, not stubborn rigidity, are also hallmarks of its politics.

The Changing Pattern of
Urban Party Politics

Fred I. Greenstein

Political parties are one of the more important nongovernmental structures that have long been involved in the policy-making process in central cities and their suburbs. What role does the political party play in contemporary local politics? What functions do parties perform? What changes have taken place in their organization and the extent to which they are involved in local politics? Why have these changes taken place? Fred I. Greenstein addresses himself to these and related questions in this selection.

In discussing some of the significant changes which have taken place in the organization and activities of political parties, Greenstein points out that disciplined urban party organizations, capable of controlling politics and government in their communities, have been one of the more important indigenous political developments in the United States. According to him, this particular political form could not have arisen had it not been for certain broad cultural patterns, such as the absence of strong traditional authorities. Although these cultural patterns were necessary, they are not sufficient to explain the development of urban party machines. The immediate determinants were the organizational requirements of urban growth, the inability of existing city governments to meet these requirements, the presence of a market—among businessmen and voters—for the service of the old-style politician, and the existence of universal suffrage.

Old-style political parties have declined only partly as a consequence of direct attacks on them by municipal reformers. A variety of social and political changes have sapped the resources of the political machine and in many communities have reduced voter interest in the resources still available to such organizations. Greenstein argues that further insights into the functions of old-style parties may be had by looking at their present-day alternatives—the politics of nonpartisanship and new-style reform politics within the Democratic party.

What are the political implications of the changes which Greenstein documents in this article? Specifically, what has been the impact of these changes on political recruitment and the articulation, aggregation, and communication of citizen demands at the local level? What influence has the demise of partisan and the emergence of nonpartisan politics in many municipalities had upon political parties? Do political parties still remain active? If parties are not active, do existing groups perform their traditional functions or do new structures emerge?

Introduction

Highly organized urban political parties are generally conceded to be one of America's distinctive contributions to mankind's repertory of political forms. Just as the two major national parties in the United States are almost universally described in terms of their *disorganization*—their lack of an authoritative command structure—the municipal parties have, until recently, been characterized by most observers in terms of their hierarchical strength. E. E. Schattschneider once summarized this state of affairs in the memorable image of a truncated pyramid: a party system which is weak and ghostlike at the top and solid at the bottom.[1]

This essay deals with the disciplined, largely autonomous local political parties which sprang up in many American cities in the nineteenth century.

Reprinted from *The Annals of the American Academy of Political and Social Science*, vol. 353 (May 1964), pp. 1-13, by permission of the publisher and author.

[1] E. E. Schattschneider, *Party Government* (New York, 1942), pp. 162-169.

Much of the literature on these political configurations is heavily pejorative, concerned more with excoriation than explanation. Even the basic nomenclature, "boss" and "machine," is laden with negative connotations, although recently there has been a turn toward nostalgic romanticization of the "vanishing breed" of city bosses.[2]

Here, for reasons which I shall indicate, the attempt shall be to delineate rather than to pass moral judgment: What was the nature of old-style urban party organization? Why did this political pattern develop and how did it operate? What contributed to its short-run persistence in the face of reform campaigns? Under what circumstances have such organizations disappeared and under what circumstances have they continued into the present day—or even undergone renaissances? What are the present-day descendents of old-style urban party organizations?

Analytic delineation invariably involves oversimplification. This is doubly necessary in the present case, because our knowledge of the distribution of types of local party organization is scant. We have no census of local political parties, either for today or for the putative heyday of bosses and machines. And there is reason to believe that observers have exaggerated the ubiquity of tightly organized urban political parties in past generations, as well as underestimated somewhat their contemporary prevalence.

Old-style party organization: definitional characteristics

Ranney and Kendall have persuasively argued that the imprecision and negative connotations of terms like "boss" destroy their usefulness. What, beyond semantic confusion, they ask, can come from classifying politicians into "bosses" versus "leaders"? Such a distinction leads to fruitless preoccupation with the purity of politicians' motives rather than the actuality of their behavior; it overestimates the degree to which figures of the past such as Richard Croker, William Tweed, and Frank Hague were free of public constraints; and it obscures the fact that *all* effective political leaders, whether or not they are popularly labeled as bosses, use quite similar techniques and resources.[3]

Granting these points, it still seems that a recognizable and noteworthy historical phenomenon is hinted at by the venerable terms "boss" and "machine." If the overtones of these terms make us reluctant to use them, we might simply speak of an "old style" of party organization with the following characteristics:

---

[2] Among the better known accounts are Frank R. Kent, *The Great Game of Politics* (Garden City, N. Y., 1923, rev. ed., 1930); Sonya Forthall, *Cogwheels of Democracy* (New York, 1946); Harold F. Gosnell, *Machine Politics* (Chicago, 1937); and the many case studies of individual bosses. For a recent romanticization, see Edwin O'Connor's novel, *The Last Hurrah* (Boston, 1956).

[3] Austin Ranney and Willmoore Kendall, *Democracy and the American Party System* (New York, 1956), pp. 249-252.

1. There is a disciplined party hierarchy led by a single executive or a unified board of directors.
2. The party exercises effective control over nomination to public office, and, through this, it controls the public officials of the municipality.
3. The party leadership—which quite often is of lower-class social origins—usually does not hold public office and sometimes does not even hold formal party office. At any rate, official position is not the primary source of the leadership's strength.
4. Rather, a cadre of loyal party officials and workers, as well as a core of voters, is maintained by a mixture of material rewards and *nonideological* psychic rewards—such as personal and ethnic recognition, camaraderie, and the like.[4]

The rise of old-style party organizations

This pattern of politics, Schattschneider comments, "is as American as the jazz band . . . China, Mexico, South America, and southern Italy at various times have produced figures who played roles remotely like that of the American boss, but England, France, Germany, and the lesser democracies of Europe have exhibited no tendency to develop this form of political organization in modern times."[5] What then accounted for the development of old-style party organization in the United States?

The Crokers, Tweeds, and Hagues and their organizations probably could not have arisen if certain broad preconditions had not existed in American society and culture. These include the tradition of freewheeling individualism and pragmatic opportunism, which developed in a prosperous, sprawling new society unrestrained by feudalism, aristocracy, monarchy, an established church, and other traditional authorities. This is the state of affairs which has been commented on by countless observers, even before de Tocqueville, and which has been used to explain such disparate phenomena as the failure of socialism to take hold in the United States, the recurrence of popularly based

---

[4] This last definitional criterion explicitly departs from the characterization of a "machine" in James Q. Wilson's interesting discussion of "The Economy of Patronage," *The Journal of Political Economy,* Vol. 59 (August 1961), p. 370n., "as that kind of political party which sustains its members through the distribution of material incentives (patronage) rather than nonmaterial incentives (appeals to principle, the fun of the game, sociability, etc.)." There is ample evidence that for many old-style party workers incentives such as "the fun of the game," "sociability," and even "service" are of central importance. See, for example, Edward J. Flynn, *You're the Boss* (New York, 1947), p. 22; James A. Farley, *Behind the Ballots* (New York, 1938), p. 237; and the passage cited in note 8 below. The distinction between "material" and "nonmaterial" incentives would probably have to be discarded in a more refined discussion of the motivations underlying political participation. So-called material rewards, at base, are nonmaterial in the sense that they are valued for the status they confer and for other culturally defined reasons.

[5] *Op. cit.,* p. 106.

assaults on civil liberties, and even the peculiarly corrosive form which was taken by American slavery.[6]

It also is possible to identify five more direct determinants of the form that urban party organization took in the nineteenth century, three of them consequences of the Industrial Revolution and two of them results of political institutions and traditions which preceded industrialization.

Massive urban expansion

Over a relatively brief span of years, beginning in the mid-nineteenth century, industrial and commercial growth led to a spectacular rise in the number and proportion of Americans concentrated in cities. A thumbnail sketch of urban expansion may be had by simply noting the population of urban and rural areas for each of the twenty-year periods from 1840 to 1920:

	Urban population	Rural population
	(in millions)	
1840	1.8	15.2
1860	6.2	25.2
1880	14.1	36.0
1900	30.1	45.8
1920	54.2	51.6

These statistics follow the old Census Bureau classification of areas exceeding 2,500 in population as urban. Growth of larger metropolitan units was even more striking. In 1840 slightly over 300,000 Americans lived in cities—or, rather, a single city, New York—with more than a quarter of a million residents; by 1920 there were twenty-four cities of this size, containing approximately 21 million Americans.

The sheer mechanics of supporting urban populations of this magnitude are, of course, radically different from the requirements of rural life. There must be extensive transportation arrangements; urban dwellers are as dependent upon a constant inflow of food and other commodities as an infant is on the ministrations of adults. A host of new administrative functions must be performed as the population becomes urbanized: street construction and maintenance, bridges, lighting, interurban transportation, sanitary arrangements, fire-fighting, police protection, and so forth. Overwhelming demands suddenly are placed on governments which, hitherto, were able to operate with a minimum of effort and activity.

[6] See, for example, Edward A. Shils, *The Torment of Secrecy* (Glencoe, Ill., 1956) and Stanley M. Elkins, *Slavery* (Chicago, 1959, reprinted with an introduction by Nathan Glazer, New York, 1963).

Disorganized forms of urban government

The forms of government which had evolved in nineteenth-century America were scarcely suitable for meeting the demands of mushrooming cities. Governmental structures reflected a mixture of Jacksonian direct democracy and Madisonian checks and balances. Cities had a multitide of elected officials (sometimes they were elected annually), weak executives, large and unwieldy councils and boards. The formal organization of the cities placed officials in a position permitting and, in fact, encouraging them to checkmate each other's efforts to make and execute policies. Since each official was elected by appealing to his own peculiar constituency and had little incentive to co-operate with his associates, the difficulties caused by the formal limitations of government were exacerbated. In a period when the requirements for governmental action were increasing geometrically, this was a prescription for chaos.

Needs of businessmen

A third aspect of mid-nineteenth-century American society which contributed to the formation of old-style party organizations was the needs of businessmen. There was an increasing number of merchants, industrialists, and other businessmen, licit and illicit, who needed—and were willing to pay for—the appropriate responses from city governments. Some businessmen wanted to operate unrestrained by municipal authority. Others desired street-railway franchises, paving contracts, construction work, and other transactions connected with the very growth of the cities themselves.

Needs of dependent populations

The needs of the bulk of the nineteenth-century urban population were not for profits but for the simple wherewithal to survive and maintain a modicum of dignity. It is difficult in the relatively affluent society of our day to appreciate the vicissitudes of urban life several generations ago: the low wages, long hours, tedious and hazardous working conditions, and lack of security which were the lot of most citizens. Even for native-born Americans, life often was nasty and brutish. But many urbanites were first- and second-generation immigrants who, in addition to their other difficulties, had to face an alien culture and language. Between the Civil War and the First World War, the United States managed somehow to absorb 25 million foreigners.

Unrestricted suffrage

Urban dwellers were not totally without resources for their own advancement. The American tradition of unrestricted male franchise was, in the long run, to work to their advantage. Although it doubtless is true that few city dwellers of the day were aware of the importance of their right to vote, politicians *were* aware of this. Because even the lowliest of citizens was, or could become, a voter, a class of politicians developed building upon the four conditions referred to above: the requirements of organizing urban life, the inability of existing governments to meet these requirements, and the presence of businessmen willing to pay for governmental services and of dependent voting populations in need of security from the uncertainties of their existence.

The old-style urban party leader was as much a product of his time and social setting as was the rising capitalist of the Gilded Age. Building on the conditions and needs of the day, the politician had mainly to supply his own ingenuity and co-ordinating ability in order to tie together the machinery of urban government. If a cohesive party organization could control nominations and elect its own agents to office, the formal fragmentation of government no longer would stand in the way of municipal activity. The votes of large blocs of dependent citizens were sufficient to control nominations and win elections. And the financial support of those who sought to transact business with the city, as well as the revenues and resources of the city government, made it possible to win votes. The enterprising politician who could succeed in governing a city on this basis was a broker *par excellence*; generous brokers' commissions were the rule of the day.

The importance of out-and-out vote-buying on election day as a source of voter support can easily be overestimated. Party organizations curried the favor of voters on a year-long basis. In a day when "better" citizens espoused philosophical variants of Social Darwinism, urban politicians thought in terms of an old-fashioned conception of the welfare state. In the familiar words of Tammany sachem George Washington Plunkitt:

> What holds your grip on your district is to go right down among the poor families and help them in the different ways they need help. I've got a regular system for this. If there's a fire in Ninth, Tenth or Eleventh Avenue, for example, any hour of the day or night, I'm usually there with some of my election district captains as soon as the fire engines. If a family is burned out I don't ask whether they are Republicans or Democrats, and I don't refer them to the Charity Organization Society, which would investigate their case in a month or two and decide they were worthy of help about the time they are dead from starvation. I just get quarters for them, buy clothes for them if their clothes were burned up, and fix them up til they get things runnin' again. It's philanthropy, but it's politics, too—mighty good politics. Who can tell how many votes one of these fires bring me? The poor are the most grateful people in the world, and, let me tell you, they have more friends in their neighborhoods than the rich have in theirs.[7]

[7]William L. Riordon, *Plunkitt of Tammany Hall* (originally published in 1905; republished New York, 1948 and New York, 1961; quotations are from the 1963 edition), pp. 27-28.

With numerous patronage appointees (holders not only of city jobs but also of jobs with concerns doing business with the city), party organizations could readily administer this sort of an informal relief program. And, unlike many latter-day charitable and governmental relief programs, the party's activities did not stop with the provision of mere physical assistance.

> I know every man, woman and child in the Fifteenth District, except them that's been born this summer—and I know some of them, too. I know what they like and what they don't like, what they are strong at and what they are weak in, and I reach them by approachin' at the right side.
>
> For instance, here's how I gather in the young men. I hear of a young feller that's proud of his voice, thinks that he can sing fine. I ask him to come around to Washington Hall and join our Glee Club. He comes and sings, and he's a follower of Plunkitt for life. Another young feller gains a reputation as a baseball player in a vacant lot. I bring him into our baseball club. That fixes him. You'll find him workin' for my ticket at the polls next election day. Then there's the feller that likes rowin' on the river, the young feller that makes a name as a waltzer on his block, the young feller that's handy with his dukes—I rope them all in by givin' them opportunities to show themselves off. I don't trouble them with political arguments. I just study human nature and act accordin'.[8]

This passage reflects some of the ways in which party activities might be geared to the *individual* interests of voters. *Group* interests were at least as important. As each new nationality arrived in the city, politicians rather rapidly accommodated to it and brought it into the mainstream of political participation. Parties were concerned with the votes of immigrants virtually from the time of their arrival. Dockside naturalization and voter enrollment was not unknown.

But if the purpose of the politicians was to use the immigrants, it soon became clear that the tables could be turned. In Providence, Rhode Island, for example, a careful study of the assimilation of immigrant groups into local politics shows that, within thirty years after the arrival of the first representative of a group in the city, it began to be represented in the councils of one or both parties. Eventually, both of the local parties came to be dominated by representatives of the newer stocks. Thus, in 1864 no Irish names appear on the lists of Democratic committeemen in Providence; by 1876 about a third of the names were Irish; by the turn of the century, three-quarters were Irish. In time, the Republican party became the domain of politicians of Italian ancestry.[9] Perhaps the most dramatic example to date of urban party politics as an avenue of upward social mobility was in the antecedents of President Kennedy, whose great-grandfather was an impoverished refugee of the Irish potato famine, his grandfather a saloon keeper and a classical old-time urban political leader, his father a multimillionnaire businessman, presidential advisor, and ambassador to the Court of St. James's.

[8]*Ibid.*, pp. 25-26.
[9]Elmer E. Cornwell, Jr., "Party Absorption of Ethnic Groups: The Case of Providence, Rhode Island," *Social Forces*, Vol. 38 (March 1960), pp. 205-210.

When the range of consequences of old-time party organizations is seen, it becomes apparent why moral judgments of "the boss and the machine" are likely to be inadequate. These organizations often were responsible for incredible corruption, but they also—sometimes through the very same activities—helped incorporate new groups into American society and aided them up the social ladder. The parties frequently mismanaged urban growth on a grand scale, but they *did* manage urban growth at a time when other instrumentalities for governing the cities were inadequate. They plied voters, who might otherwise have organized more aggressively to advance their interests, with Thanksgiving Day turkeys and buckets of coal. But, by siphoning off discontent and softening the law, they probably contributed to the generally pacific tenor of American politics. It seems fruitless to attempt to capture this complexity in a single moral judgment. One can scarcely weigh the incorporation of immigrant groups against the proliferation of corruption and strike an over-all balance.

[handwritten margin note: Haymarket? Pullman? Lawrence? Etc?]

Why reformers were "mornin' glories"

Stimulated by high taxes and reports of corruption and mismanagement on a grand scale, antiboss reform movements, led by the more prosperous elements of the cities, became increasingly common late in the nineteenth century. Compared with the regular party politicians of their day, reformers were mere fly-by-night dilettantes—"mornin' glories."[10] They lacked the discipline and the staying power to mount a yearlong program of activities. Perhaps more important, the values of the reformers were remote from—in fact, inconsistent with—the values of the citizens whose support would be needed to keep reform administrations in office. Reformers ordinarily saw low taxes and business-like management of the cities as the exclusive aim of government. To the sweatshop worker, grinding out a marginal existence, these aims were at best meaningless, at worst direct attacks on the one agency of society which seemed to have his interests at heart.

The decline of old-style party organization

Although in the short run old-style party organizations were marvelously immune to the attacks of reformers, in recent decades the demise of this political form has been widely acclaimed. Because of the absence of reliable trend data, we cannot document "the decline of the machine" with precision. The decline does seem to have taken place, although only partly as a direct consequence of attempts to reform urban politics. Events have conspired to sap the traditional resources used to build voter support and to make voters less interested in these resources which the parties still command.

[10] Riordon, *op. cit.*, pp. 17-20.

*Decline in the resources of old-style
urban politicians*

Most obviously, job patronage is no longer available in as great a quantity as it once was. At the federal level and in a good many of the states (as well as numerous cities), the bulk of jobs are filled by civil service procedures. Under these circumstances, the most a party politician may be able to do is seek some minor form of preferment for an otherwise qualified job applicant. Furthermore, the technical requirements of many appointive positions are sufficiently complex to make it inexpedient to fill them with unqualified personnel.[11] And private concerns doing business with the cities are not as likely to be sources of patronage in a day when the franchises have been given out and the concessions granted.

Beyond this, many modern governmental techniques—accounting and auditing requirements, procedures for letting bids, purchasing procedures, even the existence of a federal income tax—restrict the opportunities for dishonest and "honest" graft. Some of these procedures were not instituted with the explicit purpose of hampering the parties. Legislation designed deliberately to weaken parties *has*, however, been enacted—for example, nomination by direct primary and non-partisan local elections, in which party labels are not indicated on the ballot. Where other conditions are consistent with tight party organization, techniques of this sort seem not to have been especially effective; old-style parties are perfectly capable of controlling nominations in primaries, or of persisting in formally nonpartisan jurisdictions. But, together with the other party weakening factors, explicit anti-party legislation seems to have taken its toll.

*Decline of voter interest in rewards
available to the parties*

Even today it is estimated that the mayor of Chicago has at his disposal 6,000 to 10,000 city patronage jobs. And there are many ways of circumventing good-government, antiparty legislation. An additional element in the decline of old-style organization is the increasing disinterest of many citizens in the rewards at the disposal of party politicians. Once upon a time, for example, the decennial federal census was a boon to those local politicians whose party happened to be in control of the White House at census time. The temporary job of door-to-door federal census enumerator was quite a satisfactory reward for the party faithful. In 1960 in many localities, party politicians found census patronage more bother than boon; the wages for this task compared poorly with private wages, and few voters were willing to put in the time and leg work. Other traditional patronage jobs—custodial work in city buildings, employment with departments of sanitation, street repair jobs—were becoming equally undesirable, due to rising levels of income, education, and job security.

[11] Frank J. Sorauf, "State Patronage in a Rural County," *American Political Science Review*, Vol. 50 (December 1956), pp. 1046-1056.

An important watershed seems to have been the New Deal, which provided the impetus, at state and local levels as well as the federal level, for increased governmental preoccupation with citizen welfare. The welfare programs of party organizations were undercut by direct and indirect effects of social security, minimum wage legislation, relief programs, and collective bargaining. And, as often has been noted, the parties themselves, by contributing to the social rise of underprivileged groups, helped to develop the values and aspirations which were to make these citizens skeptical of the more blatant manifestations of machine politics.

Varieties of contemporary urban politics

Nationally in 1956, the Survey Research Center found that only 10 per cent of a cross section of citizens reported being contacted personally by political party workers during that year's presidential campaign. Even if we consider only nonsouthern cities of over 100,000 population, the percentage is still a good bit less than 20.[12] This is a far cry from the situation which would obtain if party organizations were well developed and assiduous. But national statistics conceal a good bit of local variation. A survey of Detroit voters found that only 6 per cent of the public remembered having been approached by political party workers; in fact, less than a fifth of those interviewed even knew that there *were* party precinct officials in their district.[13] Reports from a number of other cities—for example, Seattle and Minneapolis—show a similar vacuum in party activity.[14]

In New Haven, Connecticut, in contrast, 60 per cent of the voters interviewed in a 1959 survey reported having been contacted by party workers.[15] The continuing importance of parties in the politics of this municipality has been documented at length by Robert A. Dahl and his associates.[16] New Haven's Mayor Richard C. Lee was able to obtain support for a massive urban redevelopment program, in spite of the many obstacles in the way of favorable action on such programs elsewhere, in large part because of the capacity of an old-style party organization to weld together the government of a city with an extremely "weak" formal charter. Lee commanded a substantial majority on the board of aldermen and, during the crucial period for ratification of the program, was as confident of the votes of Democratic aldermen as a British Prime Minister is of his parliamentary majority. Lee was far from

[12] Angus Campbell, Philip E. Converse, Warren E. Miller, and Donald E. Stokes, *The American Voter* (New York, 1960), pp. 426-427. The statistic for nonsouthern cities was supplied to me by the authors.

[13] Daniel Katz and Samuel J. Eldersveld, "The Impact of Local Party Activity on the Electorate," *Public Opinion Quarterly*, Vol. 25 (Spring 1961), pp. 16-17.

[14] Hugh A. Bone, *Grass Roots Party Leadership* (Seattle, 1952); Robert L. Morlan, "City Politics: Free Style," *National Municipal Review*, Vol. 38 (November 1949), pp. 485-491.

[15] Robert A. Dahl, *Who Governs?* (New Haven, 1961), p. 278.

[16] *Ibid.*; Nelson W. Polsby, *Community Power and Political Theory* (New Haven, 1963); Raymond E. Wolfinger, *The Politics of Progress* (forthcoming).

being a mere creative creature of the party organization which was so helpful to him, but he also was effectively vetoed by the party when he attempted to bring about governmental reforms which would have made the mayor less dependent upon the organization to obtain positive action.[17]

Further evidence of the persistence of old-style party activities came from a number of other studies conducted in the late 1950's. For example, in 1957 party leaders from eight New Jersey counties reported performing a wide range of traditional party services, in response to an ingeniously worded questionnaire administered by Professor Richard T. Frost.[18] There was even some evidence in the 1950's of a rebirth of old-style urban party activities—for example, in the once Republican-dominated city of Philadelphia, where an effective Democratic old-style organization was put together. Often old-style organizations seem to exist in portions of contemporary cities, especially the low-income sections. These, like the reform groups to be described below, serve as factions in city-wide politics.[19]

Why old-style politics persists in some settings but not others is not fully clear. An impressionistic survey of the scattered evidence suggests, as might be expected, that the older pattern continues in those localities which most resemble the situations which originally spawned strong local parties in the nineteenth century. Eastern industrial cities, such as New Haven, Philadelphia, and many of the New Jersey cities, have sizable low-income groups in need of traditional party services. In many of these areas, the legal impediments to party activity also are minimal: Connecticut, for example, was the last state in the union to adopt direct primary legislation, and nonpartisan local election systems are, in general, less common in industrial cities than in cities without much manufacturing activity.[20] Cities in which weak, disorganized parties are reported—like Seattle, Minneapolis, and even Detroit (which, of course, *is* a manufacturing center of some importance)—are quite often cities in which nonpartisan institutions have been adopted.

Some new-style urban political patterns

In conclusion, we may note two of the styles of politics which have been reported in contemporary localities where old-style organizations have become weak or nonexistent: the politics of nonpartisanship and the new "reform" factions within some urban Democratic parties. Both patterns are

---

[17]Raymond E. Wolfinger, "The Influence of Precinct Work on Voting Behavior," *Public Opinion Quarterly*, Vol. 27 (Fall 1963), pp. 387-398.

[18]Frost deliberately worded his questionnaire descriptions of these services favorably in order to avoid implying that respondents were to be censured for indulging in "machine tactics." Richard T. Frost, "Stability and Change in Local Politics," *Public Opinion Quarterly*, Vol. 25 (Summer 1961), pp. 231-232.

[19]James Q. Wilson, "Politics and Reform in American Cities," *American Government Annual, 1962-63* (New York, 1962), pp. 37-52.

[20]Phillips Cutright, "Nonpartisan Electoral Systems in American Cities," *Comparative Studies in Society and History*, Vol. 5 (January 1963), pp. 219-221.

of considerable intrinsic interest to students of local government. And, as contrasting political forms, they provide us with further perspective on the strengths and weaknesses of old-style urban politics.

The politics of nonpartisanship

The nonpartisan ballot now is in force in 66 per cent of American cities over 25,000 in population. Numerous styles of politics seem to take place beneath the facade of nonpartisanship. In some communities, when party labels are eliminated from the ballot, the old parties continue to operate much as they have in the past; in other communities, new local parties spring up to contest the nonpartisan elections. Finally, nonpartisanship often takes the form intended by its founders: no organized groups contest elections; voters choose from a more or less self-selected array of candidates.

In the last of these cases, although nonpartisanship has its intended effect, it also seems to have had—a recent body of literature suggests[21]—a number of unintended side effects. One of these is voter confusion. Without the familiar device of party labels to aid in selecting candidates, voters may find it difficult to select from among the sometimes substantial list of names on the ballot. Under these circumstances, a bonus in votes often goes to candidates with a familiar sounding name—incumbents are likely to be re-elected, for example—or even candidates with a favorable position on the ballot. In addition, campaigning and other personal contacts with voters become less common, because candidates no longer have the financial resources and personnel of a party organization at their disposal and therefore are dependent upon personal financing or backing from interest groups in the community.

Nonpartisan electoral practices, where effective, also seem to increase the influence of the mass media on voters; in the absence of campaigning, party canvassing, and party labels, voters become highly dependent for information as well as advice on the press, radio, and television. Normally, mass communications have rather limited effects on people's behavior compared with face-to-face communication such as canvassing by party workers.[22] Under nonpartisan circumstances, however, he who controls the press is likely to have much more direct and substantial effect on the public.

Ironically, the "theory" of nonpartisanship argues that by eliminating parties a barrier between citizens and their officials will be removed. In fact, nonpartisanship often attenuates the citizen's connections with the political system.

The Reform Democrats

The doctrine of nonpartisanship is mostly a product of the Progressive era. While nonpartisan local political systems continue to be adopted and, in fact,

[21] For a brief review of the relevant literature, see Fred I. Greenstein, *The American Party System and the American People* (Englewood Cliffs, N. J., 1963), pp. 57-60.

[22] Joseph T. Klapper, *The Effects of Mass Communication* (New York, 1960).

have become more common in recent decades, most of the impetus for this development results from the desire of communities to adopt city-manager systems. Nonpartisanship simply is part of the package which normally goes along with the popular city-manager system.

A newer phenomenon on the urban political scene is the development, especially since the 1952 presidential campaign, of ideologically motivated grass-roots party organizations within the Democratic party.[23] The ideology in question is liberalism: most of the reform organizations are led and staffed by college-educated intellectuals, many of whom were activated politically by the candidacy of Adlai Stevenson. In a few localities there also have been grass-roots Republican organizations motivated by ideological considerations: in the Republican case, Goldwater conservatism.

New-style reformers differ in two major ways from old-style reformers: their ideological concerns extend beyond a preoccupation with governmental efficiency alone (they favor racial integration and improved housing and sometimes devote much of their energy to advocating "liberal" causes at the national level); secondly, their strategy is to work within and take control of the parties, rather than to reject the legitimacy of parties. They do resemble old-style reformers in their preoccupation with the evils of "bossism" and machine politics.

There also is an important resemblance between the new reform politician and the old-style organization man the reformer seeks to replace. In both cases, very much unlike the situation which seems to be stimulated by nonpartisanship, the politician emphasizes extensive face-to-face contact with voters. Where reformers have been successful, it often has been by beating the boss at his own game of canvassing the election district, registering and keeping track of voters, and getting them to the polls.[24]

But much of the day-to-day style of the traditional urban politician is clearly distasteful to the new reformers: they have generally eschewed the use of patronage and, with the exceptions of campaigns for housing code enforcement, they have avoided the extensive service operations to voters and interest groups which were central to old-style party organizations. For example, when election district captains and other officials of the Greenwich Village Independent Democrats, the reform group which deposed New York

---

[23] James Q. Wilson, *The Amateur Democrat* (Chicago, 1962).

[24] There is another interesting point of resemblance between old- and new-style urban party politics. In both, an important aspect of the motivation for participation seems to be the rewards of sociability. Tammany picnics and New York Committee for Democratic Voters (CDV) coffee hours probably differ more in decor than in the functions they serve. An amusing indication of this is provided by the committee structure of the Greenwich Village club of the CDV; in addition to the committees dealing with the club newsletter, with housing, and with community action, there is a social committee and a Flight Committee, the latter being concerned with arranging charter flights to Europe for club members. See Vernon M. Goetcheus, *The Village Independent Democrats: A Study in the Politics of the New Reformers* (unpublished senior distinction thesis, Honors College, Wesleyan University, 1963), pp. 65-66. On similar activities by the California Democratic Clubs, see Robert E. Lane, James D. Barber, and Fred I. Greenstein, *Introduction to Political Analysis* (Englewood Cliffs, N. J., 1962), pp. 55-57.

Democrat County Leader Carmine DeSapio in his own election district, were asked the same set of questions about their activities used in the New Jersey study, strikingly different responses were made. (See Table 1.)

The successes of this class of new-style urban party politician have vindicated a portion of the classical strategy of urban party politics, the extensive reliance upon canvassing and other personal relations, and also have shown that under some circumstances it is possible to organize such activities with virtually no reliance on patronage and other material rewards. The reformers have tapped a pool of political activists used by parties elsewhere in the world—for example, in Great Britain—but not a normal part of the American scene. One might say that the reformers have "discovered" the British Labor constituency parties.

It is where material resources available to the parties are limited, for example, California, and where voter interest in these resources is low, that the new reformers are successful. In practice, however, the latter condition has confined the effectiveness of the reform Democrats largely to the more prosperous sections of cities; neither their style nor their programs seem to be successful in lower-class districts.[25] The areas of reform Democratic strength are generally *not* the areas which contribute greatly to Democratic pluralities in the cities. And, in many cities, the reformers' clientele is progressively diminishing as higher-income citizens move outward to the suburbs. Therefore, though fascinating and illuminating, the new reform movement must at least for the moment be considered as little more than a single manifestation in a panorama of urban political practices.[26]

Conclusion

The degree to which *old-style* urban party organizations will continue to be a part of this panorama is uncertain. Changes in the social composition of the

Table 1. *Services performed by New Jersey politicians and New York Reform Democrats*

	Percentage performing it often	
The service	*New Jersey*	*New York*
Helping deserving people get public jobs	72	0
Showing people how to get their social security benefits, welfare, unemployment compensation, etc.	54	5
Helping citizens who are in difficulty with the law. Do you help get them straightened out?	62	6

[25] DeSapio, for example, was generally able to hold on to his lower-class Italian voting support in Greenwich Village; his opponents succeeded largely by activating the many middle- and upper-class voters who had moved into new high-rent housing in the district.

[26] Probably because of their emphasis on ideology, the new reform groups also seem to be quite prone to internal conflicts which impede their effectiveness. One is reminded of Robert Michels' remarks about the intransigence of intellectuals in European socialist parties. *Political Parties* (New York, 1962, originally published in 1915), Part 4, Chap. 6.

cities promise to be a major factor in the future of urban politics. If, as seems possible, many cities become lower-class, nonwhite enclaves, we can be confident that there will be a continuing market for the services of the service-oriented old-style politician. Whether or not this is the case, many lessons can be culled from the history of party politics during the years of growth of the American cities—lessons which are relevant, for example, to studying the politics of urbanization elsewhere in the world.[27] In the nineteenth century, after all, the United States was an "emerging," "modernizing" nation, facing the problems of stability and democracy which are now being faced by countless newer nations.

[27]On the significance of the American experience with old-style urban politics for the emerging nations, see Wallace S. Sayre and Nelson W. Polsby, "American Political Science and the Study of Urbanization," Committee on Urbanization, Social Science Research Council, mimeo, 1963, pp. 45-48.

The Political Sociology of American Suburbia: A Reinterpretation

Frederick M. Wirt

Just how Republican are the suburbs surrounding most of our nation's central cities? In this study, Frederick M. Wirt reexamines the traditional view of suburbs as strongholds of Republicanism. On the basis of his protracted analysis of aggregate voting data from presidential, congressional, and mayoral elections in 154 suburbs, Wirt concludes that the stereotype of the Republican suburb was built either by examining a few special types of suburbs or by equating the Eisenhower success of the 1950s with permanent Republican growth. His data suggest that interparty competition is much more lively than the existing literature suggests.

Wirt also examines the relationship between various community contextual factors and suburban electoral behavior. He finds that in the suburbs he studied, the more extreme their socioeconomic characteristics the more likely their inhabitants will have similar partisan attachments. Especially strong is the relationship between high socioeconomic status and Republicanism. Wirt's research, like later studies, suggests that although initially only upper- and upper-middle-class Republicans fled the central city, more recently large numbers of middle- and lower-class Democrats have also left, and these later migrants do not appear to have changed their partisan attachments upon moving to the suburbs. In the suburban zone, we now find not only upper social ranking communities whose inhabitants tend to be overwhelmingly Republican, but also lower social ranking suburbs whose inhabitants tend to be predominantly Democratic, and many middle-class "competitive" communities in which we find varying concentrations of Republicans, Democrats, and Independents. When we refer to suburbs, then, we must be careful to distinguish among those local communities in both socioeconomic (contextual) and partisan (political-structural) terms, Wirt concludes.

These findings have a number of important implications not only for variations we might find in the extent and nature of party activity within each type of suburb but also for inter- and intracommunity antagonism and conflict. How do political parties capitalize on the partisan attachments of suburban residents? What are the effects of increased partisan differentiation in suburbia for conflict and consensus in local politics?

Partisan cleavages are frequently a source of discord at the local level. In addition, the game of politics may be played quite differently in communities in which parties are active. For example, as Greenstein suggests in the previous article, even though many suburbs are formally nonpartisan, political parties are often involved either overtly or covertly in local politics. Recent research on latent partisanship in nonpartisan elections in a group of San Francisco Bay Area communities, conducted by Heinz Eulau and Kenneth Prewitt, has shown this tends to be particularly true in middle-class competitive and lower-middle-class Democratic suburbs. Partisan activity is more manifest in such communities and hence government more politicized. On the other hand, in upper-class Republican suburbs, one finds little in the way of campaigning for political office, little active interest in council elections, and councilmen initially appointed rather than elected to the council. In effect, in these suburbs partisan activity is absent.

Despite nonpartisan labels, then, we must realize that parties may still be the primary recruitment agencies as well as accepted agents of interest aggregation. We should also be aware that partisan activities are more likely to occur in some suburbs than in others. According to Eulau and Prewitt, nonpartisanship is likely to give way to partisan activity in suburban communities if: (1) there is sufficient tension arising out of the coexistence of partisan and nonpartisan systems in the same locale, (2) the political situation is sufficiently competitive to warrant attempts at partisan activity in formally nonpartisan elections, and (3) a given partisan group feels sufficiently disadvantaged by the nonpartisan electoral format, yet is organizationally strong and enthusiastic enough to function as a mobilizing elite.

Introduction

Among the many consequences of American urbanism, the mass migration to the suburbs has been the most striking. These fringe towns orbit around megopolis, at once tied to it by gravitic bonds of commerce, transportation, and entertainment—and yet independent in many local affairs. A whole new literature has arisen about them, including a school of fiction depicting transplanted but rootless inhabitants who strive to find meaning in a life of metropolitan work, suburban civics, and newly adopted values. Non-fiction literature at the popular level has been of the whither-are-we-drifting variety, finding in these places a source of concern.

Social research into suburbs has dealt with their demographic characteristics, but surprisingly little depicts suburban political life. Lubell depicted the great Eisenhower support in suburbia in the 1950's. But he was uncertain that this was a permanent addition to the Republican party; rather it might be merely an expression of support of Eisenhower which other locales, such as core cities, were also showing.[1]

Despite his cautions as to the future of suburban politics, much popular writing tended to see these places as predominantly Republican. This condition was explained by a simple theory. New immigrants and their children had realized vital aspirations through political attachment to the New Deal, and as one consequence of their prosperity moved to better surroundings, eventually to the suburbs. Here they tended to switch political loyalty to the Republican party. They did so for several reasons: partly to adapt to the immediate environment of these areas, but mostly because Republicanism was one characteristic of upper-class Americans. For the newcomer, voting Republican was an act of identification symbolizing his arrival. This thesis of suburban Republican growth is termed by Robert Wood as the "conversion" theory, although he did not necessarily accept its validity as an explanation of what had occurred.[2]

But this interpretation is somewhat heterodox. It assumes that party identification is a transient attitude, but the work of the Survey Research Center demonstrated very convincingly that party identification is a stable aspect of attitude structure, changing permanently only under the traumatic impact of war and depression. So a second explanation, which Wood calls "transplantation," is sometimes employed. This interpretation argues that the newcomers to suburbia were lifelong Republicans carrying their sense of affiliation with them as they migrated.[3]

Reprinted from *The Journal of Politics*, vol. 27, no. 3 (August 1965), pp. 647-666, by permission of the publisher and author.

[1] Samuel Lubell, *Revolt of the Moderates* (Harper & Bros., N.Y., 1956).

[2] Robert C. Wood, *Suburbia: Its People and Their Politics* (Houghton Mifflin, Boston, 1958), Ch. 5. See also Fred I. Greenstein and Raymond E. Wolfinger, "The Suburbs and Shifting Party Loyalties," *Public Opinion Quarterly*, (Winter 1958-59), 473-82; Jerome G. Manis and Leo C. Stine, "Suburban Residence and Political Behavor," *ibid.*, 483-89.

[3] Wood, *op. cit.*, Ch. 5.

Before we explain the facts, we had better make sure we have the facts straight. How Republican *are* these suburbs? That is, is the increased suburban vote for Eisenhower over Dewey in 1948 evidence of Suburban Republicanism or of suburban support for Eisenhower? If it is only the latter, then it is fatuous to attempt to explain the inherent Republicanism of the suburbs, something assumed out of hand by *both* transplantation and conversion explanations.

Indeed, there is scattered evidence that indicates that suburbs are not as homogenously Republican as assumed. Edson and Janosik in separate articles noticed surprising numbers of Democrats in St. Louis and Bucks County suburbs before 1960.[4] Millet and Pittman found in two suburbs of Rochester, N. Y., no evidence of the conversion thesis.[5] Even Lubell, in a curious footnote, had earlier noticed that, "Some suburban returns I have analyzed point to a long-run trend to make the suburbs somewhat more Democratic, although not on any scale that would threaten Republican ascendancy in these communities."[6]

What might have been written off as a series of local anomalies, became more difficult to explain away in 1960. Fully 49 per cent of the suburban vote went for Kennedy. In only one metropolitan area (Kansas City) did Nixon's share of the suburban vote exceed Eisenhower's, while in seven areas Kennedy's share actually exceeded Nixon's (Boston, Detroit, Pittsburgh, St. Louis, St. Paul, San Francisco, and Washington) and in two the vote was even (Cleveland and Milwaukee).[7]

Another question not answered because not faced in both conversion and transplantation theses is: "How much of suburbia is upper middle class?" The key conceptual framework within which this question is explored here has been made explicit by two sociologists. William Dobriner puts it: "Perhaps one of the central theoretic problems growing out of suburbanization is the need to clarify . . . *the relationship between the suburb as an ecological variable and the elements of suburban organization and culture as class variables.*" Bennet Berger has pointed out the error of those scholars who, in equating Suburbia with Republicanism, analyzed "the social and economic position and aspiration of white-collar people; their conclusions had to do with suburbs. To what extent these two variables are coextensive is precisely the question that has been ignored."[8]

Clearly, we need to re-examine notions about the pervasiveness of suburban Republicanism. This article shall probe beyond gross voting data to

[4] Charles Edson, "The Suburban Vote," Senior Thesis, Harvard Univ., 1955, quoted in Wood, *op. cit.*, 144-45. G.E. Janosik, "The New Suburbia," *Current History*, August, 1956.

[5] John Millet and David Pittman, "The New Suburban Voter: A Case Study in Electoral Behavior," *Southwestern Social Science Quarterly*, (June, 1958), 33-42.

[6] *Op. cit.*, 276-77.

[7] *The 1960 Elections*, Republican National Committee (mimeo), 1961, 18-20.

[8] William Dobriner (ed.), *The Suburban Community* (Putnam, N. Y., 1958), xxii (emphasis in original); Bennett Berger, *Working-Class Suburb: A Study of Auto Workers in Suburbia* (Univ. of Calif. Press, Berkeley, 1960), 32.

(1) explore whether there is variety in suburbia, both in electoral and socio-economic terms, and (2) to suggest some implications of suburban politics for the course of American politics, generally.

Sources

The sources for this paper are aggregate data on election returns and census materials for 154 suburbs. These suburbs are from among the 260 so designated by Victor Jones and his associates in their extensive economic description of American cities.[9] The present author chose suburbs in the 10,000-25,000 population range in 1950 and employed 1960 census data (described later). My collection of electoral data began before 1960 and thus the 1950 population base was employed. But all census data analyzed below are drawn from Jones' post-1960 study. This population range was chosen because it constitutes the largest number of suburbs reported by Jones.

From these 260 suburbs[10] electoral data were received for 154 suburbs after four waves of mail questionnaires. These data covered the years 1932 and 1948-1960 for the offices of President, Congressman, and Mayor. Not all 154 suburb electoral results are complete; some municipalities were not legally in existence in 1932, some do not elect the Mayor (all of California, for example), and some reported that no old records are kept. However, it was possible for any suburb to return complete data on 21 elections. The temporal span thereby provided could show a base in 1932 before the New

Table 1. *Comparison of the means of respondent and non-respondent suburbs by 1960 Census indices*

	Respondent suburbs	Non-respondent suburbs	Difference
Percent non-white	7.4	7.6	0.2
Percent under $3000 income	11.7	11.2	0.5
Median age	32.0	31.0	1.0
Percent white collar	49.0	50.2	1.2
Percent owner occupied	67.2	68.8	1.6
Population (thousands)	21.3	23.9	2.6
Percent one-unit structures	75.1	78.4	3.3
Employment - residence ratio	94.6	91.2	3.4
Manufacturing percent	42.1	36.6	5.5
Percent homes built since 1950	26.0	34.1	8.1
Percent over $10,000 income	45.5	25.8	19.7
Percent population change, 1950	35.9	57.2	21.3
Percent migrant	48.4	19.3	29.1

[9] Victor Jones, Richard L. Forstall and Andrew Collver, "Economic and Social Characteristics of Cities," *Municipal Year Book, 1963* (International City Managers' Association, Chicago, 1963), 85-157.

[10] All southern suburbs were omitted except 2. It seemed likely when this study was begun that traditional Southern Democracy might operate in these suburbs and hence depress the national weight of suburban Republicanism.

Deal impact, the post-war changes (if any) and the post-Eisenhower changes (also if any). Further, for any year, and across the years, one could determine the influence of the particular office upon party success. Finally, we may see the degree of party competition over the whole period.

Limitations on inferences drawn from mail polls are well-known. Thus, no level of confidence analysis is possible in this report; the conditions of random sampling cannot be met by a mail poll. However, Table 1 provides some basis for a belief that the returnees were not wildly different from the non-respondents.[11]

The last three measures do show a wide discrepancy. But by overweighting returns with high income and high migrant type suburbs, these data are those most relevant to the popular image of suburbia.

Suburban electoral patterns

Because the assumption of suburban Republicanism underlies both the "conversion" and "transplantation" hypotheses, the first question is purely empirical: How Republican are American suburbs? Table 2 initiates the analysis.

Several conclusions are suggested here. Except at one or two points, these data do not reveal the high Republican percentages which suburbs are popularly thought to produce. The 1932-1948 comparison shows little Republican gain in the Presidential vote in percentage terms; but it would loom larger naturally in absolute terms as suburban population had increased considerably over 1932. Although there is a rough picture here of a suburban Republican surge for Eisenhower, it will be recalled that outside suburbia there was also an Eisenhower surge. Further note that this Eisenhower

Table 2. *Mean suburban GOP vote percentage for selected offices and years*

	President		Congress		Mayor	
	%	N	%	N	%	N
1932	51.3	79	54.9	80	59.1	34
1948	52.4	143	52.4	138	57.9	55
1950	–	–	56.0	141	64.4	42
1952	56.4	152	55.6	146	58.9	59
1954	–	–	52.4	147	56.9	41
1956	60.0	152	54.1	151	54.0	57
1958	–	–	49.0	105	40.9	23
1960	47.3	110	48.9	109	46.0	24

[11] The usual criticism of the unreliability of mail polls lies in that the failure of the non-respondent to reply may reflect a factor systematically differentiating him from respondents. But here we were polling not individuals *per se* but representatives of political *units*. In four waves, mayors, city clerks, county election boards, and secretaries of state were solicited. There seems unlikely to be any variable associated with these official roles which would differentiate between responding and non-responding sources.

increase in suburbia is accompanied by a parallel Republican *erosion* in the Congressional and Mayor vote, so that by 1960 the vote was split between the parties for all offices studied. Certainly these findings question whether the conversion theory is applicable if the assumption of Republican ascendancy cannot be factually sustained. Transplantation is still compatible with these data, although one possible inference, explored later, is that those coming to suburbia by the late 1950's were as much Democratic as Republican.

But such conclusions are gross, because the mean measures are deceptive. In order to reveal even more clearly the variation in suburban voting, Table 3 shows for each office and year the frequency distribution of Republican percentages. Such a schema permits scrutiny of a given year across offices or the reverse. Here 45-55% constitutes a marginal range, a benchmark used by many practising politicians. The two ranges either side of this middle position indicate a degree of party competition which may have different character-istics from the completely one-party system.

Examining this table by office, we find several conclusions available on suburban *presidential* voting. The share of presidential Democratic suburbs prior to Eisenhower paralleled that of the Republican suburbs, then dropped sharply in the 'fifties as the Republican share increased; but in 1960 the percent of Democratic suburbs rose again to exceed its pre-Eisenhower total as the Republican share dropped to its lowest point. Note that the weight of marginal suburbs remained roughly constant throughout, hovering around one-fifth. Turning to the *congressional* contests, a more stable picture appears. The Democratic share dropped somewhat during the Eisenhower elections as that of the Republicans increased, but in 1960 both parties had returned to the 1948 balance, with the Republican predominating, although not by a majority. Again, the weight represented by marginal suburbs remained constant, around one-fifth. Finally, in the *mayoralty* contests, what

Table 3. *Frequency distribution of Republican suburban vote for selected offices and years by percentage*

		N	0—34%	35—44%	45—55%	56—65%	66—100%
President	1932	79	14	24	18	19	25 = 100%
	1948	143	20	17	19	19	25
	1952	152	11	18	20	18	33
	1956	152	7	12	20	22	39
	1960	110	20	24	22	25	10
Congress	1932	79	9	19	22	22	29 = 100%
	1948	138	22	15	20	15	28
	1952	146	16	14	18	21	32
	1956	151	19	11	17	23	30
	1960	109	21	14	20	26	19
Mayor	1932	34	3	12	38	26	21 = 100%
	1948	55	9	13	25	27	25
	1952	59	7	19	27	24	24
	1956	57	11	14	39	19	18
	1960	24	4	12	54	21	8

can be seen in the more limited data is a drop in both Republican and Democratic shares as that represented by marginal suburbs by the late 'fifties loomed largest of all three partisan possibilities; further, more marginal suburbs appear here than in the other two contests.

In contrast to the premise of both the "conversion" and "transplantation" hypotheses of suburban Republican growth, the data in Tables 2 and 3 raise serious questions about whether the Republican vote has grown. Eisenhower did make a visible impact upon the suburban vote as he did upon the urban and rural vote, but even in his best year, 1956, there remained a sizeable minority of non-Republican suburbs, either marginal or heavily pro-Stevenson. The ephemeral nature of this vote is seen in the drastic Republican decrease in the 1960 election where the heavily Kennedy suburb predomina-ted over the marginal or heavily Nixon suburb. Nor is suburban Republicanism overwhelming in congressional voting, for it actually shows a slight, gradual decrease since 1950. And even in the mayoralty contests, the former Republican predominance is also in decline, so that by the 'sixties the marginal contest may well predominate.

Table 2 shows that by the election of 1960, in electoral contests on all three levels there was no heavy national Republican suburban vote. By 1960, Republicans had a somewhat larger share of the suburbs in Congressional votes and Democrats more in the Presidential vote. However one chooses to explain it, the contours of the vote indicate that Republicans did not dominate the suburbs. It is likely therefore that the stereotype of the Republican suburb was built either by examining a few special suburbs (discussed later) or by equating the Eisenhower success of the 'fifties with a permanent Republican growth. Indeed, the data suggest that inter-party suburban competition is more lively and energetic than the literature contemplates.

Suburban inter-party competition

The measurement of party electoral competition can be as crude as examining the vote for one office for one year or as sophisticated and laborious as the scholar can construct.[12] I have utilized the Ranney-Kendall typology[13] in which the discriminating variables are the percent of contests won by the second party and the size of that second party's vote. For this, the second party in a suburb need win but 26 per cent of the contests to be classified a "Two Party" suburb; of the remaining suburbs, some were classified "Modified One Party" if the second party won (a) over 30 per cent of the vote in 70 per cent of the elections, *and* (b) over 40 per cent of the vote in 30 per cent of the elections. If suburbs fell below these minimum criteria of competition, they were designated "One Party." We thus arrive at five types of suburbs: One Party Democratic (OPD), Modified One Party

[12]William H. Standing and James A. Robinson, "Inter-Party Competition and Primary Contesting: The Case of Indiana," *American Political Science Review*, (December, 1958), 1066-77, provide a sophisticated measure and review other measures.

[13]*Democracy and the American Party System* (Harcourt, Brace, N. Y., 1956), 161ff.

Democratic (MOPD), Two Party (TP), Modified One Party Republican (MOPR) and One Party Republican (OPR).

The continuum thereby employed has certain limitations. Not all suburbs in the population range returned electoral results, those returning did not always provide complete results, the 1934-1946 elections are omitted, and no account of frequency of turnover is provided as some have suggested as an important measure.[14] To the first two, one may merely comment that analysis must begin sometime and that Table 1 suggests a similarity in socio-economic base between sample and non-respondents. To the limitation of omission of the New Deal years, one may point out that inclusion of these (which would have cut down on the incidence of Republicanism) would distort changes, if any, in the postwar era.[15] To the limitation on providing no turnover measure, note that so few years are included here that such a measure would have a very flimsy empirical basis.

The degree of party competition in the Ranney-Kendall typology and in rough terms of percent of these contests won by Republicans is revealed in Table 4.

Table 4 shows the prevalence of Republican suburbs—roughly one-half all suburbs here studied. Yet, there exists another half of this sample which does not fit the usual picture of suburban politics. Almost one-third are Democratic (one in six is OPD) and one-sixth TP. Put another way, in every six suburbs, three are Republican but two are Democratic and one is Two Party.

Table 4.   Frequency distribution of suburban party competition types and Republican wins

Party type	N	%	% GOP Wins
OPD	27	17.5	5.0
MOPD	22	14.3	10.9
TP	25	16.2	48.2
MOPR	37	24.0	88.1
OPR	43	28.0	97.7
	154	100.0	58.7

[14] Joseph A. Schlesinger, "A Two-Dimensional Scheme for Classifying the States According to Degree of Inter-Party Competition," *American Political Science Review,* (December, 1955), 1120-28.

[15] Key has shown that after the "critical election" of 1928, a partisan realignment took place which lasted at least up to 1952, so that by 1932 we deal with a crystallized partisan cleavage which forms a base for post-war comparison. Cf. V. O. Key, "A Theory of Critical Elections," *Journal of Politics,* (February, 1955), 3-18. Samuel Lubell, *The Future of American Politics* (Harper & Bros., N. Y., 1952), earlier developed this thesis. Key, *op. cit.,* 9, fn. 7, cites evidence in Angus Campbell *et al., The Voter Decides,* (Row, Peterson & Co., Evanston, 1954), 100-103, that some Republicans voted Democratic in 1932 and 1936, although later switching back; this lends weight to the present author's contention that post-1932 inclusion of New Deal voting would inflate the weight of Democracy in the suburbs. As constituted, the schema here employed gives a greater chance to demonstrate any postwar suburban Republican growth.

Other computations, not here included,[16] demonstrate that prior to 1960: Eisenhower received from each of the three party type areas (D, TP, R) an increasingly larger share of votes; most Republican gain for either congressional or presidential candidates came from the most Republican suburbs; the partisan suburbs tended strongly to support their own candidates most consistently (despite some Democratic suburbs being pulled toward Eisenhower) while the TP suburb shifted most—as befits a truly competitive area; and despite the foregoing evidence of change, if one compares 1948 with the big Eisenhower year of 1956, 70 per cent of these suburbs appear in the same voting range. In short, there are surprisingly large numbers of non-Republican suburbs; in these there was some drift to Eisenhower; this Republican shift did not carry down strongly to congressional and mayoralty contests, and there are some suburbs that never moved Republican whether measured by winning contests or increasing percentage. With the 1960 election, this popularly exaggerated Republican suburban growth was reversed at all three offices.

The ecology of suburbia

Having isolated political differences among these suburbs and in so doing questioned the premise of monolithic Republicanism, we are now prepared to explore reasons for such differences. It is my contention that differences in suburban electoral behavior arise from differences in the socio-economic bases of these suburbs.

An approach to understanding these patterns may be found in introducing an ecological concept rarely treated in political analysis but quite familiar to sociology—the non-dormitory suburb. Political analysis has routinely treated the suburbs as though they were all similar. They are thought to be residential and peopled by middle-middle to upper-middle class or higher status; they contain only retail businesses, generally the hive-like shopping centers; the bread-winners leave *en masse* for the city in the morning and return to the split-level and dry martini in the evening. Readers of Whyte's *Organization Man* or almost any novel about suburbia will recognize these traits—or symptoms.

But there is another kind of suburb—the industrial. As early as 1925, H. Paul Douglass, writing on *The Suburban Trend*, recognized these two types, referring to the "suburb of consumption," the now familiar and publicized type, and the "suburb of production," the latter also lying adjacent to central cities but providing jobs for its own residents as well as others.[17] While the latter sends out goods and brings in persons, the suburb of consumption reverses this flow. This dichotomy received scant mention in

---

[16] See the author's "Suburban Patterns in American Politics," a paper presented in the 1960 American Political Science Association Convention.

[17] H. Paul Douglass, *The Suburban Trend* (Century Co., New York, London, 1925), 84-85.

the 1930's but was elaborated upon by C. D. Harris in a significant article a decade later.[18] During the 'fifties, sociologist Leo F. Schnore submitted the dichotomy to extensive analysis.[19]

Time does not permit here full treatment of Schnore's analysis, but a recapitulation of his findings is necessary. He relates a long history of these industrial suburbs; notes their presence in every part of the country; finds their identifying economic activity to be manufacturing (light or heavy), education and recreation, extraction (oil and mining) or governmental services; shows the residential suburb's rate of growth exceeded that of the industrial suburb (during the 1940's by almost twice, 31.9 per cent to 17.0 per cent); indicates that the former's increase is a function of better "housing opportunities," whereas the growth of regions and central cities is a function of more employment or economic opportunities; and concludes that as people will live where there are greater housing opportunities, preferring to drive to work or to nearby industrial suburbs or central city, the residential suburb will continue to grow at a higher rate than that of the industrial suburb.

As an initial approximation, the industrial-residential suburban dichotomy tells us that suburbs are not homogeneous. Dobriner, in his recent *Class in Suburbia*, exploring the bases of this heterogeneity, argues that:[20]

> There is such a diversity of suburb forms it is misleading to label all suburbs 'homogeneous.' Suburbs differ greatly in the circumstances of their creation, in the price and use of their real estate, their degree of transiency, their size and institutional complexity, and the income, life style, occupation, and educational level of their residents. . . . Unfortunately, many of the quasi-empirical studies of suburbs which gave rise to the homogeneity myth focused on upper-middle class areas around large central cities. *In fact, many suburbs are not essentially middle-class and accordingly do not exhibit those middle-class patterns too often mistaken as suburban patterns.*

It is Dobriner's contention that the variety of suburbs is a function of class characteristics, influenced primarily by "technological-economic" factors. "In the final analysis," Dobriner concludes, "suburbanites and city dwellers are joined together by common class bonds, and relatively few place factors separate them. It is unfortunate that the emphasis given to the few uniquely suburban situational features have blinded so many to this basic fact."[21]

---

[18]C. D. Harris, "Suburbs," *American Journal of Sociology*, 1943, 6.

[19]"The Functions of Metropolitan Suburbs," *ibid.*, (March, 1956), 453-58; "The Growth of Metropolitan Suburbs," *American Sociological Review*, (April, 1957), 165-73; "Satellites and Suburbs," *Social Forces*, (December, 1957), 121-27; "Components of Population Change in Large Metropolitan Suburbs," *American Sociological Review*, (October, 1958), 570-73. Cf. also, Walter T. Martin, "Ecological Change in Satellite Rural Areas," *American Sociological Review*, (April, 1957), 173-83; Leslie Kish, "Differentiation in Metropolitan Areas," *ibid.*, 388-98. For some methodological problems in suburban study, cf. Otis D. Duncan, "Research on Metropolitan Population: Evaluation of Data," *Journal of the Amer. Statistical Assn.*, (December, 1956), 5.

[20]*Op. cit.*, (Prentice-Hall, Englewood Cliffs, N. J., 1963), 13. Emphasis added.

[21]*Ibid.*, 59.

In the present study, we are not treating a "few uniquely suburban situational features" but 154 suburbs about which we have considerable electoral and socio-economic information. The previous part of this study has demonstrated political variety, both in electoral behavior and party competition. We are now ready to explore the bases of this variety.

Economic correlates of suburban politics

Voting studies almost without number, whether utilizing aggregate or survey data, have noted the relationship between economic indices and partisan voting. While the "party identification" thesis indicates that psychological factors can depress any one-to-one ratio between such economic factors as income and voting behavior, there still remains an association between such factors as high income and Republican voting. This association is not urged here as any sign of class conflict disguised as inter-party strife, but it is an association, and it has affected the behavior of party leaders in the conduct of campaigns.

The thesis now to be explored is that suburban political differences, like those of the core city, are associated with socio-economic differences. Suburbs which have the characteristics of upper-middle class will be more Republican that those suburbs having lower-middle and working class characteristics; but suburbs which are most heterogeneous will show more inter-party competition. The socio-economic variables employed are drawn from the Jones materials in the *Municipal Year Book, 1963*; the brief definitions of these variables given below are expanded upon at that source.[22]

The first analysis[23] bearing on this proposition . . . indicates that . . . Democratic suburbs are indeed concentrated in low income, low rental, and high manufacturing type suburbs, while the Republican suburb has the opposite characteristics. As the economic structure changes, so does the political. Thus, as the Income Level increases, the proportion of Democratic suburbs decreases regularly; almost two-thirds of the lowest income suburbs are Democratic (heavily OPD), while almost three-fourths of the highest income suburbs are Republican (heavily OPR).

[22] *Op. cit.*, 111-113.

[23] *Income Level* (IL) employs four quartile' ranges computed from 1960 for all cities over 10,000 by Jones *et al* with IL-1 the lowest and IL-4 the highest median family income. The *Rent Level* (RL) index relates the median gross monthly rent of a suburb to that of its SMA; RL-1 is $5 below the SMA median rent, RL-2 is in the range of ±$5 of the median, RL-3 $5 above, and RL-4 is more than twice the SMA median. *Functional Classification* distinguishes the proportions of different kinds of employment. Thus a Manufacturing (Mm) suburb has over 50% of all employment in manufacturing and *less* than 30% in retail trade; Industrial (M) has over 50% in manufacturing but *more* than 30% in retail trade; Diversified Manufacturing (Mr) has more employment in manufacturing than in retail trade but less than 50% of the aggregate; Diversified Retailing (Rm) has more in retailing than in manufacturing but the latter is at least 20% of the aggregate; Retailing (Rr) has more employment in retailing than in any other form and manufacturing is less than 20% of the aggregate; and Other (O) covers places where other employment predominates.

If the thesis that economic and political homogeneity are associated seems borne out here, the thesis that socio-economic heterogeneity produces greater inter-party competition is less supportable. . . .

In summary, the data show a rough association between the political complexion of suburbs and their economic characteristics. The more extreme the characteristics, the more likely the suburbs will have a similar political complexion; especially strong is this relationship between high economic indices and Republicanism. However, suburbs demonstrating intermediate economic characteristics are not associated mostly with inter-party competition, for such characteristics are spread among the various types of party competition. . . .

Several difficulties inhere in the nature of these three indices. First, the Income Level is based on *all* cities over 10,000 and not on suburbs in the range of our 154 suburbs. Further, the Income and Rent Level indices do not, by their natures, give us any indication of heterogeneity within any given suburb; any one of these suburbs at a given level might cover a wide variation in income or rent or it might have the same income or rent for all within it. Only Functional Classification permits us to determine heterogeneity. But this index, like the others (including Party Type), offers no fine discrimination in its scaling. What they do offer, however, is a first approximation that suburban political variety is related to variety in the suburban economic base.

Suburban politics: image and reality

This analysis raises serious doubts about the popular picture of suburbia and suggests that even the dichotomy of the industrial versus the residential suburb is an inadequate description. Not all suburbs by any means fit the popular description. . . .

A second question about the "conversion" thesis is whether in studying one kind of suburb we have made judgments about all kinds of suburbs. But aggregate analysis suggests variety in suburbia. We have seen the political variety in terms of party competition. Linked to this is socio-economic variety, as Table 5 indicates.

When one isolates suburbs by their partisan characteristics, there emerge striking differences in their other characteristics, as in Table 5. These data

Table 5.   Means of socio-economic factors by party types

	% White Collar*	Median Age*	% Under $3000 Income*	% over $10,000 Income*	E/R[†]	% Mfg.[†]	% GOP Wins[†]
OPD	39	29.8	15.8	46.1	111	54	5
MOPD	39	29.8	11.6	45.6	112	61	11
TP	44	31.0	12.8	45.0	92	51	48
MOPR	50	32.5	12.2	45.0	108	39	88
OPR	62	34.4	8.2	45.8	65	23	98

*N is respectively 25, 22, 24, 37, 43.
[†]N is respectively 27, 22, 24, 37, 43.
[†]N is respectively 27, 22, 25, 37, 43.

suggest a suburbia of surprising variety, thereby questioning a basic assumption of the conversion thesis.

Interpretations

In the preceding, there seems substantial evidence that when we speak of "suburban" we must distinguish among different kinds of suburbia in socio-economic and partisan terms. Each kind represents a different life-style; as Berger notes of his working-class suburb, "Most of the features of life reportedly characteristic of Levittown, Park Forest, and other suburbs of their kind are notable by their absence."[24] He found auto workers retaining their life-style when moving to a tract suburb—carrying lunch pails, not belonging to organizations, attending church less than the middle class, and no Republican switching. Campbell and his associates in *The American Voter* go further with survey data (albeit limited) to show "the absence of a really unique change in political allegiance among ex-urbanites [which] further indicates that movement out of the metropolitan centers cannot stand as the factor responsible for changes in partisan loyalties that cut across non-movers as well."[25] Instead of a mass conversion to Republicanism, a more discriminating process seems more likely.

Given the strength of partisan identifications, it seems possible that former city Democrats and Republicans carried their affiliations with them as they fled the city. Some sought suburbs of like-minded and like-situated people, and thus there developed working-class as well as elegant suburbs, each homogeneous in its distinctive party and economic contours. Other movers, with different partisan and economic backgrounds, came together in the same place to form a "mixed salad" suburb. From such combinations we can postulate a continuum of suburbs, ranged in terms of those factors here termed "life-style." Each life-style with its distinctive socio-economic syndrome is accompanied by a special partisan cast. At one end is Berger's working class suburb of Democratic cast, at the other end is the suburb of elegance with its Republican cast, and in between lie different mixes of life-styles with less predictable partisanships.

Probably the basic error in confusing all suburbs with heavy Republicanism is the failure to realize that not only the upper-middle class fled the city. The post-war world brought huge gains in income to all but the "one-third of a nation," now down to "one-fifth." Blue-collar and lower middle-class citizens also achieved the economic potential for new homes, realtors appeared to cater to their potentials, and the pressure of urban Negroes upon white housing added yet another motive for departing. Upon arrival, they came with a life-style, some of which, such as partisan identification, erodes very slowly or is transformed only by such traumatic events as wars and

[24] Berger, *op. cit.*, 23.

[25] *Op. cit.*, 459. The authors of this work did not treat suburbia as a special population category and thus "cannot accommodate in our analysis the crucially important qualitative differences among types of suburban communities." At 454, fn. 13.

depressions. What was there in the mere fact of a new locale to transform these deeply held views, particularly when some suburbs were so new? Place alone does not shape attitudes; it is the cultural milieu of a place that influences. But many suburbs were raw, new communities with no milieu yet formed, others offered a homogeneous culture which attracted the newcomer in the first place because it reflected his own life–style, and yet others were a mixed salad, offering few cultural directives that could influence uniformly the new arrival.

In other words, the exploding metropolis has created a suburban fall-out whose patterns in some respects duplicate those of the city. The city had known its working class, "silk stocking," and mixed wards, its residential and industrial districts, and its heavily Democratic, heavily Republican and marginal areas. This varied pattern of life-styles and partisanships is not unlike what we have seen in the data of this paper. True, there is a more Republican than Democratic cast to suburbia as a whole—but not in the most recent years and not for all offices. But we also have working class, elegant and mixed salad suburbs whose constituents are revealed with differing socio-economic characteristics, whose ecology reveals other differences, and whose politics question severely the notion of suburbia as a "political Jordan" from whose waters Democrats emerge in the image of the compleat Republican.

As suburban developments extend their tendrils farther from metropolis—to contact at some future point the tendrils of other metropolises—we may expect this pattern of continual life-style reduplication to accompany them.[26] In terms of political socialization, however, those making the trek do not demonstrate any massive conversion, but instead show signs that in their covered station wagon they carry their already engrained party affiliation. As the benefits of the affluent society spread even farther, there is a good likelihood that more Democrats will be in those wagons.[27]

---

[26] Even the city Negro wards are appearing tentatively in suburbia, e.g., Ludlow in the Cleveland area.

[27] 1964 Postscript:

Nothing in the 1964 returns challenged the previous findings of a renaissance of Democracy in suburbia: indeed these returns accentuate this movement. The Republican national decline in the 1964 election was even more sharp in the American suburban sample on which the preceding article was based.

Between 1960 and 1964, the median Republican vote for Goldwater in these suburbs fell to 33.8% (N = 119 suburbs) while the Republican median for Congressional voting declined slightly to 47.0% (N = 119). Goldwater carried only 16 of these suburbs (14.7%), while Republican Congressional candidates were securing a majority in 53 (44.5%). The Congressional changes from 1960 were possibly sharper than these measures reveal. Almost one-third (32%) remained roughly the same (±3%). But over one-half (56%) showed Republican Congressional decreases greater than 3%; in at least one-quarter of these suburbs. Republican voting was 10% or more percentage points less. Only 12% of the suburbs produced a Republican Congressional increase of over 3% in 1964.

Data are not yet available to determine whether the Republican suburban rate of decline in Presidential voting varied from that in core city or outside-metropolitan areas. But the 16% suburban decline between 1960 and 1964 is certainly greater than the *national* decline for those years (11%). Work in progress comparing the weight of suburban, core city, and outside-metropolis votes in postwar Presidential elections has

Additional suggested readings: rules, procedures, and political structures

Charles R. Adrian and Charles Press, *Governing Urban America* (New York: McGraw-Hill Book Co., 1968).

Edward C. Banfield, *Big City Politics* (New York: Random House, 1965).

Francis M. Carney, "The Decentralized Politics of Los Angeles," *The Annals of the American Academy of Political and Social Science,* vol. 353 (May 1964), pp. 107-121.

Lyle W. Dorsett, *The Pendergast Machine* (New York: Oxford University Press, 1968).

Heinz Eulau, Betty H. Zisk, and Kenneth Prewitt, "Latent Partisanship in Nonpartisan Cities," in M. Kent Jennings and L. Harmon Zeigler (eds.), *The Electoral Process* (Englewood Cliffs, N.J.: Prentice-Hall, 1966), pp. 208-237.

Daniel N. Gordon, "Immigrants and Urban Governmental Form in American Cities, 1933-60," *American Journal of Sociology,* vol. 74, no. 2 (September 1968), pp. 158-171.

Harold F. Gosnell, *Machine Politics Chicago Model* (Chicago: University of Chicago Press, 1968).

Scott Greer and Peter Orleans, "The Mass Society and the Parapolitical Structure," *American Sociological Review,* vol. 27, no. 5 (October 1962), pp. 634-646.

Herbert Hirsch, "Suburban Voting and National Trends: A Research Note," *The Western Political Quarterly,* vol. 21, no. 3 (September 1968), pp. 508-514.

Gladys M. Kammerer, Charles D. Farris, John M. DeGrove, and Alfred B. Clubok, *The Urban Political Community: Profiles in Town Politics* (Boston: Houghton Mifflin Co., 1963).

John H. Kessel, "Government Structure and Political Environment: A Statistical Note about American Cities," *The American Political Science Review,* vol. 56, no. 3 (September 1962), pp. 615-620.

Arthur Mann, *La Guardia Comes to Power, 1933* (Philadelphia: J. B. Lippincott Co., 1965).

Seymour J. Manndelbaum, *Boss Tweed's New York* (New York: John Wiley, 1968).

Roscoe C. Martin, *The Cities and the Federal System* (New York: Atherton Press, 1965).

Zane L. Miller, *Boss Cox's Cincinnati: Urban Politics in the Progressive Era* (New York: Oxford University Press, 1968).

produced a preliminary finding that of the three areas the suburban vote distribution has most nearly paralleled the national distribution. If this finding is reinforced in the 1964 election, it would seem to undergird the thesis that suburbia in its unsuspected variety is a mirror of multifaceted American politics.

Leo F. Schnore and Robert R. Alford, "Forms of Government and the Socioeconomic Characteristics of Suburbs," *Administrative Science Quarterly,* vol. 8, no. 1 (June 1963), pp. 1-17.

Lincoln Steffens, *The Shame of the Cities* (New York: Hill & Wang, 1957).

Anwar Syed, *The Political Theory of American Local Government* (New York: Random House, 1966).

Oliver P. Williams and Charles R. Adrian, *Four Cities: A Study in Comparative Policy Making* (Philadelphia: University of Pennsylvania Press, 1963).

James Q. Wilson and Edward C. Banfield, "Public-Regardingness as a Value Premise in Voting Behavior," *The American Political Science Review,* vol. 58, no. 4 (December 1964), pp. 876-887.

Raymond E. Wolfinger and John Osgood Field, "Political Ethos and the Structure of City Government," *The American Political Science Review,* vol. 60, no. 2 (June 1966), pp. 306-326.

Robert C. Wood, *Suburbia, Its People and Their Politics* (Boston: Houghton Mifflin Co., 1958).

Part three   The policy-making process in central cities and suburbs

The policy-making process, the core of politics at the local level, involves individuals and groups in a sequence of activities resulting in governmental decisions. The process can also be viewed as a series of interrelated stages taking place over a period of time, which involve interaction, cooperation and conflict, power and influence, communication, and political leadership.

Although it is difficult to capture in one set of readings both the complexity and diversity of the policy-making process in central cities and suburbs, I have attempted to introduce some of the more important components that political scientists have studied. For example, in general, how does the policy-making process in central cities differ from that of the suburbs? Are there any similarities? What factors influence the political attitudes and behavior of citizen and leader? How do citizen attitudes and participation influence public policy? What influence do citizens, groups, coalitions, and political leaders have on governmental decisions?

As one moves from the central city to suburban communities, he is likely to find important differences in the general style of politics, the extent of citizen involvement and participation in the policy-making process, partisanship, group activities, coalition formation, the way in which power is distributed, and political leadership. In addition, while large central cities frequently mirror the conflicts and dilemmas of the larger society, many suburbs exhibit a great deal of consensus reinforced by social homogeneity, though some are quite heterogeneous, making consensus harder to achieve. The policy-making process is generally more complex in the central city, while in suburban communities, local government is much smaller in scale and concerns itself with what appear to be "small events." Many of the issues in such communities appear quite trivial, particularly to those living in our problem-ridden central cities and in contrast to those confronting the larger society. However, they do have a significant effect on suburban residents, and therefore can and frequently do give rise to controversy.

In the initial introductory article to this part, Coleman discusses some of the factors that may give rise to and influence the course of community conflict. This selection serves as an excellent introduction to the policy-making process, a process which involves conflict as well as cooperation among individuals and groups attempting to influence the public-policy decisions of local city councils and school boards.

In the next three articles in this part, the influence that political attitudes and participation exert on the policy-making process and policy outcomes is examined. These selections also investigate some of the factors affecting such attitudes and participation in local-level politics, and point up some of the important implications of increased citizen involvement, particularly of previously disenfranchised groups, for municipal policy making. For instance, examining the voting behavior of Detroit residents on a series of referenda on racial questions, Hahn documents the very real problem of getting whites to support policies designed to integrate blacks into local neighborhoods. Williams and his associates, on the other hand, investigate the relationship between citizen and leader attitudes and public policy in Philadelphia suburbs. Wilson in turn discusses the implications of increased citizen participation on the particular issue of urban-renewal programs. Prestage concludes with a discussion of some of the factors which condition black political participation in local politics.

The next two articles examine various factors which influence the nature of coalition formation at the local level. First, Salisbury draws our attention to the critical role formal governmental arrangements have played in shaping the political coalitions which have emerged in St. Louis, Missouri. Second, Lipsky examines the viability of protest as a political resource. In so doing, he raises a number of important questions about the tactics and strategies presently being used by powerless groups not only to develop support among third parties and hence more viable coalitions capable of competing effectively in the political arena, but also to directly influence public-policy decisions.

The next three articles take up the question of who governs in central cities and suburbs—the structure of power and influence as well as the general nature of political leadership at the local level. Bachrach and Baratz begin by attempting to place in critical perspective differences between sociologists and political scientists as to the locus of community power. In so doing, they point out how power has "two faces," neither of which sociologists see and only one of which political scientists take into account in their research. Gittell then goes on to examine the nature of power and influence in a particular issue, education, documenting the preponderant influence that professionals, because of their technical expertise, have over school policy in New York City. This city, at least as far as educational policy is concerned, appears to be dominated by a narrow, convergent, consensual elite. By way of contrast, Stinchcombe points out some of the implications for public policy in an issue like urban renewal that fragmentation of power and influence and apathetic and divided leadership can have.

The two final selections in this section examine the decision-making process in city councils and school boards. This is in many ways the focal point of the policy-making process in local municipalities. In these decisional units, inputs of demands and supports which originate among citizens, groups, and influentials are acted upon by elected and/or appointed political leaders. Some factors impinge on the attitudes and behavior of the individuals who sit on city councils and school boards; these also are examined. First, in my own article, the nature of issue conflict and consensus in a number of suburban city councils in St. Louis County, Missouri, is investigated, with particular concern for how rapid increases in population are related to council conflict and consensus. In the final article, Crain and Street examine some of the factors which influence the attitudes and behavior of school board members, and hence their decisions in the area of school desegregation.

The Setting and the Initiation of Controversy in Local Communities

James S. Coleman

In this selection we turn once again to the topic of community conflict. Influenced by a number of factors, the initiation and development of controversy in local municipalities is a more complex process than previous selections have indicated. What are some of these factors?

This review of research on community conflict examines in detail the relationship found by various researchers to exist between a community's setting or context and the initiation and development of political controversy. Coleman is concerned with the actual development of community conflict, particularly with how controversy in local municipalities is conditioned by the conflict provoking the event, the community in which it takes place, and the area of life affected by the event.

Coleman also reviews possible internal and external sources of controversy and points out how such factors as clashes between different economic interests, changes in attitudes and opinions over time, population changes, and existing cleavages, may give rise to community conflicts. As time passes, new demands arise, issues change, and differences which were unimportant in the past become salient sources of conflict.

This selection serves as an excellent introduction to the policy-making process, a process which involves conflict as well as cooperation among individuals and groups attempting to influence public-policy decisions. Unlike previous selections, which are discussions of the significant contextual changes in the metropolis, this is a systematic examination of how these changes as well as other factors affect the actual initiation and development of controversy in local municipalities. Query: Do any of Coleman's hypotheses explain this process as it operates in your local community?

Introduction

Community involvement and controversy

Everybody knows that there are no controversies where there is nothing to quarrel about. Yet it is often overlooked that community disagreements are also a measure of community life. If communities held only the physical things of existence for their members, there would be no disagreement.

Communities differ widely in the degree to which community life is important enough to argue about. Within large cities, for example, there is usually considerably less to involve the residents in civic affairs than there is in a small, self-sufficient town. In a large city, a man's work is outside his neighborhood; often his children go to school outside that neighborhood; and in the extreme case, the neighborhood itself is hardly distinguishable as a unit. Thus, in the large cities, involvement in controversy is usually least widespread,[1] often confined to a few activists.

This relationship between the degree of involvement of the members of the community and the frequency of controversy is not confined to communities and cities. Other organizations exhibit the same tendencies. For example, when trade unions play an important part in their members' lives, one finds active internal politics, with lively factional fights, internal disputes, and challenges from the ranks. "Business unions," on the other hand, which do no

[1] Controversies surrounding desegregation of schools provide a good example of this. The greatest controversies have been in small towns, such as Milford, Delaware, and Clinton, Tennessee, in which a large part of the populace has risen in arms. In contrast, Baltimore and Washington, both with a higher proportion of Negroes than Milford, accomplished desegregation with only a small amount of picketing and other opposition by parents. See James Rorty (1954). Also, in controversies precipitated by right-wing attacks on the schools, it has been in the largest cities (Houston and Pasadena) that the critics, who constituted a minority, have succeeded in ousting the controversial person before most of the public was aroused and fought back. See David Hurlburd (1950), and the report on Houston by the National Defense Commission of the National Educational Association.

more than carry out wage negotiations, and whose members are little involved, are quiet, stable bureaucracies with little internal discord.[2]

Even more extreme in their bureaucracy and mass apathy are such voluntary organizations as consumer co-operatives, automobile clubs, professional societies, business associations, and veterans' groups. Such organizations, of only segmental importance to their members, seldom have membership opposition to administrative policies or to a proposed slate of officers. Opposition, if it comes at all, is usually from within the ranks of leaders; there is no controversy on the membership level, merely a "circulation of elites."[3]

Because controversy goes hand-in-hand with membership participation, the recent increase in community disputes should be not only a cause for concern about democratic processes, but at the same time an indication of a continued and perhaps reawakening interest in the local community. It may be that the movement to the suburbs, the increase in leisure time, and the consequent refocusing of life around the home and the neighborhood, have brought people back into community life, both psychologically and physically.

Kinds of events and the crises they create

Not every kind of event which deeply affects people in a community will create a conflict. Communities are beset by many kinds of crises—floods, storms, factory shutdowns, school controversies, vigilantism, political disputes, religious contention, crime waves, etc.—which may result in many kinds of responses, including conflict.

Floods, for example, most often generate united action within a community. An extended drought, on the other hand, might well throw a community into despair; far from uniting, drought defeats, as the dust storms of the thirties defeated the most energetic families and communities of the southwest plains. Economic depression can have a similar effect. The shutdown of a steel plant in Marienthal, a small city in Austria, reduced a lively and active town to an apathetic one whose members were listless and hardly interested in the life of their community (Lazarsfeld-Jahoda and Zeisel, p. 36 ff.).

In contrast, such crises as the Supreme Court desegregation edict, for example, or the floating of a school bond, or the charge "Communist" leveled at a public official, may create real controversy and conflict.

As these examples suggest, the *type of event* helps determine whether a crisis will unite a community, defeat it, or cause controversy. A flood, as we have said, seldom divides a community; it affects all men much the same, pits

---

[2] A recent case study of a union with an active democratic system discusses this point in detail, presenting much evidence to show that democracy in a union can hardly exist unless the occupational associations surrounding it fulfill a wide range of functions for the members. (See Lipset, Trow, and Coleman, 1956.)

[3] For a comprehensive study of the development of bureaucracies within organizations which were once active democracies, see Michels (1949).

them all against a common enemy. A school desegregation pronouncement, however, has diverse effects: it affects Negroes differently from whites, parents differently from people without children, prosegregationists differently from those who condemn segregation. Yet the crises are alike in that both permit action. In contrast, there arise problems for which communities have no solutions, such as the Okies' plight in the midst of drought or the Marienthalers' insoluble unemployment problem.[4]

Not only the type of event shapes the nature of the crisis; the kind of community in which it happens is equally important. The charge "subversive" against a schoolteacher will divide some communities into opposing camps, other communities will unite to protect the teacher, while still others will unite against the teacher.[5] Communities have widely different "styles of life" with which they approach problems, and these are important determinants of the course of conflict. One author (Walker, 1950, p. 26) reports that a town faced with the removal of its major plant responded actively and in a unified way, in part because "the people are self-sufficient and self-reliant, supplying most of their own needs and standing on their own feet in the face of emergencies."

Yet the response cannot be wholly explained by a "self-sufficient and self-reliant" people. Two other towns, equipped with similar independence of spirit, responded with bitter internal strife when faced with a seemingly simpler problem: the arrival of industrialization (Pope, 1942: Cressey, 1949). There are other factors, some psychological, others a matter of social organization. (In the city which successfully met a threatened plant removal the well-organized and active Chamber of Commerce was ready to meet the challenge.) In any case, numerous studies make evident that it is neither the kind of problem facing a community nor the community's characteristics which alone determines the pattern of conflict, but rather a conjunction of the two.

Events and incidents which lead to disputes

Criteria

If the differences in events and in communities which lead toward unification, division, or defeat are closely examined, the following three

---

[4] It may be, however, that problems insoluble *within* the community can be solved by recourse to some external power. Primitives turned to magic; some Marienthalers turned to radical political movements.

[5] Among the school controversies studied, all three of these responses could be detected, although neither of the extremes was met precisely. Port Washington, Long Island, where the liberal and conservative groups have often shifted control, each time by a tiny majority, is the best example of a community evenly split over school issues. The recent Scarsdale conflict comes close to being unified support of the school administration, for almost all the community organizations and leaders supported the administration, and as a climax to the conflict, a school board election drew the largest vote of confidence an incumbent board had ever received. The Houston school controversy is most nearly the other extreme of those examined. All these incidents are discussed more fully in later pages.

criteria become evident in the development of controversy out of an event: (a) The event must touch upon an important aspect of the community members' lives[6] —education of their children, their means of livelihood, religion, taxes, or something similar. Obviously, *different* areas of life are important to different communities, to different people within a single community, and at different periods of time. (b) The event must affect the lives of different community members differently. A tax proposal, for example, affects property-owners one way and non-property-owners another. (c) Finally, the event must be one on which the community members feel that action can be taken—not one which leaves the community helpless.

Given these three criteria, then, it is possible to say something about the events which will lead a given community to conflict, to unified action, or to demoralization. But what are some examples of conflict-producing events? A few are listed below:

1. In Northampton, Massachusetts, a controversy over fluoridation of the water supply began after the mayor appointed a commission and, following its recommendation, initiated a plan for carrying out fluoridation. Here the event which set off the controversy was the publication of a complete plan for fluoridation without prior public discussion of the proposal (B. and J. Mausner, 1955).

2. In other cities (e.g., Cincinnati, Seattle, Williamstown [Massachusetts]) a similar pattern appears: controversy began *after* machinery had been set up to carry out fluoridation (Mausner, 1955, p. 39).

3. In Norwalk, Connecticut, a controversy arose over the announcement by a community organization (the VFW post) of a plan to report to the FBI the names of those persons in the community whose activities were "not related to a strong America" (Groh, 1954).

4. In Athens, Tennessee, a group of World War II veterans attempted, as a reform group, to wrest political control from the entrenched regime (White, 1947). In other southern towns similar uprisings occurred in the early postwar years (Key, 1950, pp. 201-204).

5. In a number of southern towns which underwent rapid change from rural to industrialized areas, intense industrial conflict occurred. Although the precipitating incidents differ in different cases, the event which really presaged conflict in all cases was the advent of industrialization (Cressey, 1949; Pope, 1942).

6. In Scarsdale, New York, conflict over books in the public schools began when a local citizen became disturbed over what he felt to be the domestic menace of communism, and besieged the school board with complaints against books in the school library (Shaplen, 1950).

7. The Pasadena, California, conflict, which resulted in the ouster of the superintendent of schools, began ostensibly as a fight over a budget and tax assessment for the new school year. It had its real beginnings, however, soon after the superintendent arrived, in a number of small dissatisfactions with his administrative procedure, above all his inaccessibility to powerful persons in the community (Hurlburd, 1950).

---

[6]The event, of course, need not be important to all persons in the community; some controversies are carried on by only a minority of the community.

8. Other school controversies are precipitated by varied kinds of incidents. Some began by accusations from local citizens that a superintendent, principal, librarian, teacher, board member, or even P.T.A. member was subversive or suspect, or that "progressive education" was being practiced. In some of these cases, the initial information came from sources outside the community, that is, from one of the right-wing organizations which keep files on persons who have been members of left-wing groups, or from the files of a state or national investigating committee. But in most cases, it appears that the initial charges arose locally and only later, if at all, did material from the outside play a part.[7]

9. Other school controversies began when a speaker with right-wing or left-wing affiliations was invited to the community. Characteristically, heckling occurred during the speech, and the speaker's past associations were revealed in the discussion periods after the speech.[8]

10. A study of community conflict published in 1929 cited several examples of conflict arising when church-building and other activities by one church group in the community offended members of other churches (The Inquiry, 1929, p. 25, 31, 70, 81).

11. A study of abandonment of the city manager plan in four cities indicates that in each of the four, opposition to the plan was organized by a man on the fringe of the local business community who had been rebuffed in dealing with the city council. But this can hardly be called the sole precipitating incident; in all four cities, dissatisfaction had developed over the years, principally among the working class (Stene and Floro, 1953, pp. 21-39).[9]

12. In one New York town, the Republican city fathers selected the location of new water wells without going through the forms of democracy. Incensed community members held firmly to their democratic rights and an extended controversy ensued (The Inquiry, 1929, p. 60, 73).

13. In Milford, Delaware, Bryant Bowles made inflammatory speeches against desegregation and led the parents, children, and other townspeople into mass picketing. In Clinton, Tennessee, John Kaspar and Asa Carter delivered speeches which provoked a wave of violence against the integration of twelve Negro children in the Clinton high school. All three were outsiders to the communities involved (*Life*, 1954; *Southern School News*, 1956).

Internal and external sources

These and the other conflicts studied allow some generalizations about the kinds of incidents and events which set off disputes. In the first place, there is

[7]Controversies in Houston, Denver, and Eugene, Oregon, among others are in this class. See the report of the National Defense Commission of the National Educational Association on the Houston controversy (1953); also on Houston, "The Ebey Story," *The Nation* (1953). For Denver, see Martin (1951); for Eugene, Oregon, see Tugman (1951).

[8]The Englewood, New Jersey, controversy began this way, as did at least one of the several eruptions which have marked a long period of dispute in Port Washington, Long Island. See August J. Wiesner, Jr., (1951) and Louis Engel (1951).

[9]This phenomenon—tensions building up through lack of daily means of redress rather than dissipating through contact and controversy—has often been presented as a cause of radicalism of labor in large plants, taking the place of the feeling of friendliness to the employer which exists in the small shops where channels to management are both informal and open.

a clear distinction between disputes which arise *internally* and those which are a consequence of some *external* incident. The most completely internal include: the fluoridation controversies[10] (1, 2); the political uprising in southern towns (4); the church conflicts (10); abandonment of the city-manager plans (11); and location of the water wells (12). Not only were these incidents set off by community members themselves; the issues involved were purely local. A second group of conflicts were local in origin but fed on national issues: the Norwalk vigilantism (3); the Scarsdale and Pasadena school conflicts, and other school conflicts which centered around local school figures (6, 7, and 8). The incendiary incidents here came from sources within the community, though they did involve nationwide issues. Finally, a group of controversies must be laid primarily to external sources: industrialization in southern communities (5); conflicts resulting from the Supreme Court desegregation ruling implemented by state policies (13); and a few of the school controversies in which persons and propaganda from the outside began the controversy (9, 13).

This, then, is one important difference in the origin of community conflicts. Some need no external issue or incident to set them off, but are generated by processes internal to the community itself. In other cases, the community is more or less at the mercy of the world outside: a national climate of opinion like the recent fear of Communist subversion, industrial expansion or depression, a national law which contravenes the community's mores such as the Supreme Court ruling. This is not to say that a community can do nothing to affect the course of such controversies once they have begun. To be sure, it is a major premise of this report that much *can* be done, whether the conflict arises internally or externally. But when the problem arises from external sources, it is, in a sense, dumped on the community's doorstep.

As one might expect, community conflicts are now more often related to national affairs than they once were. In the 1929 book on community conflict mentioned above, about four out of forty community conflicts described could be said to be externally produced. In contrast, a great many present-day community conflicts—some of those cited above are indicative—have their sources outside the community. Whether we like it or not, the community is less often the locus of important social decisions than it once was. Even though school and church policy are still local matters, and community taxes remain important, the economic fate of a community often rests in the hands of men who have never passed through town.[11] Similarly, there is a continual shrinkage of the jurisdictional areas of community-level laws by

---

[10]In a few cases, the opponents of fluoridation utilized material distributed nationally as anti-fluoridation propaganda (see Vic Reinemer, 1955), but undoubtedly this has occurred on both sides in all fluoridation disputes, the proponents citing medical and dental authorities concerning its effectiveness, and the opponents citing evidence of its harmful effects.

[11]The Depression in the thirties was the first awakening of many formerly self-sufficient communities to the fact that their economic fate was firmly tied to that of the nation as a whole. Lynd's *Middletown in Transition* (1937) portrays well the inability of the community to comprehend this, and the attendant frustrations and despair it produced.

state and federal governments which find it necessary to have a consistent policy. Thus, the prospect for the future is toward an increase in the proportion of externally caused community controversies—although there are, and always will be, certain areas of social decision-making which are the province of the community or neighborhood.

The content of the issue and the area of life it affects

A second difference among the incidents which set off community disputes is in the area of life they affect. Three general areas can be roughly distinguished.

One is *economic*. Many communities have been split down the middle by economic issues. Whether a matter of livelihood (e.g., the movement of a factory to town), or the payment of taxes, or still a different issue, economic issues are likely to produce strong response.

Power or *authority* in the community constitutes a second important area of life. In the four city-manager disputes which led to abandonment of the city-manager plan, the increasing dissatisfaction with the plan had its origin in certain groups (primarily the working class) which felt in effect disenfranchised. Similarly, in the rebellion of southern veteran groups, the possibility of taking political power away from the machine led the veterans to initiate conflict. The cases are many, but the motives appear to be the same.

Nevertheless, in the struggle for power, often only a few are affected: those who stand to gain office, and those who stand to lose it. The structure of political authority often remains the same, and only those who have something at stake feel their pulses quicken as events lead to a dispute. How the rest of the community becomes involved—and, to be sure, it often does—is another matter, and one which will be treated later.

The third "area of life" is less easily defined, but may be thought of quite generally as *cultural values* or *beliefs*. The current school controversies are most often disputes between conflicting values or philosophies of education; the desegregation disputes are conflicts between two deeply felt beliefs— ingrained attitudes toward Negroes and equally ingrained attitudes toward equality of opportunity. The fluoridation plans which have generated controversy in so many towns apparently touched on values of individualism and anti-scientism in provoking the resistance which has occurred.[12] Differing values and doctrines may also be touched off by religious incidents, though these often include elements of community power and group hostility as well.

Besides these three major "areas of life," there is a fourth important basis on which people respond, deriving from attitudes toward particular *persons* or *groups* in the community, rather than from attitudes toward an incident,

---

[12] This is well documented for Northampton, Massachusetts, in one of the few opinion surveys carried out on cases of community conflict. The less educated, older, more individualistic, more science-resistant citizens voted against (and defeated) the fluoridation plan. (Bernard and Judith Mausner, 1955).

event, or policy. Existing antagonism between individuals, between clans, between ethnic groups, or between other groups in the community can lead people to take sides quickly—to say, "I'm against it because *he's* for it."

Many conflicts which appear to be centered around other issues are in fact a result of the existing hostility between two groups in the community. In such disputes, the particular issue involved can hardly be considered a unit in itself—it is only part of a continuing conflict, periodically active, the rest of the time languishing. These antagonisms are vestiges of previous disputes which often leave the community divided, and thus "load the dice" against peaceful resolution of future problems. The antagonism seems to keep the community alerted, open at any time to new dispute. Robin Williams (1947), in an excellent monograph on intergroup conflicts, shows some of the ways in which such antagonism opens the way to disruptive conflicts.

There is no suggestion intended that any given community conflict feeds on a single basis of response. On the contrary, often a conflict widens to include many bases of response. Nor is it true that a single incident which sets off a community conflict—say, a school bond proposal—receives all its response from the same source. One side may be largely involved through its economic interests in keeping taxes low; its opponents may be motivated by a particular philosophy of education. Even on the same side, there may be different bases of response for different men: some may be motivated by economic interests, some by a philosophy of education, and still others by a chance for power in the community.

Thus far our implicit approach has been something like this: an incident, event, or problem requiring solution faces a community, and meets differing responses among the members as it touches upon areas of life which act as *bases of response* to the event. These bases of response, primarily economic interests, power, and values, provide the initial dynamics for the controversy. They drive a nucleus of adherents to carry forward the dispute, to expand and intensify it until perhaps the whole community is involved. At this point, it is useful to examine variations in communities, that is, the social conditions underlying the response to one or another kind of incident.

Conditions for controversy

Differences in economic structure

Communities differ widely in their economic systems. Some are self-contained in the sense that men both live and work there. These include towns with small and diversified industry, agricultural towns (which form an economic unit with the surrounding farmland), and one-industry towns. Others are towns in which most men (with the exception of the few merchants and others who provide the necessary community services) live but do not work. Suburban communities provide the best example. (Westchester County communities, for instance, have been called the "bedrooms of New York City.") Finally, there are towns which are largely economic service organs for nonresident groups, e.g., resort towns whose primary industries exist to serve vacationers.

Naturally, different kinds of economically related incidents arise in different kinds of towns and evoke different kinds of response. In economically self-contained towns it is economic disputes which are most common and most intense, for here economic disputes often concern men's livelihoods, not only their taxes or some other ancillary economic issue. Such disputes ordinarily begin within the plant—between workers and management—though they may be initiated by all sorts of incidents.

The diverse and often inconsequential nature of incidents which set off economic disputes suggests that the incident itself is hardly important, that there has already been a strong predisposition to controversy. As students of labor relations well know, the strength of the response is only partly based on economic interests. Often it is compounded by the antagonism generated through the day-to-day relationships of labor and management in the plant.[13] This labor-management antagonism is a special and frequent case of the interpersonal and intergroup hostility which can arise between any two groups in the community. In some agricultural towns, farmer-merchant disputes similar to the quarrels of labor and management have broken out over similarly minor precipitating incidents. The farmers' distrust of merchants, particularly of banks and bankers, parallels the workers' distrust of management. The farmers' response, based both on economic interests and personal hostility, may help a trivial incident blossom into full-fledged conflict.[14]

Thus, towns with a self-contained economy can generate a most intense response to economically related incidents, a response based in part on economic interests, and in part on the antagonism created between different parts of an economic system. Farmers and workers, neither of whom have much control over their economic destinies, are the groups in which this antagonism is most often generated. (Not all controversies originating in economically self-contained towns concern economic matters, of course. Cleavages over values—religion or "subversion"—can split such towns just as they split the suburbs.)

In towns which do not constitute an economic unit, towns where men live but do not work, this kind of division is not generated; controversies set off

---

[13] There has been a considerable amount of work done in this area by students of industrial relations. Beginning with the Hawthorne studies in the nineteen thirties (see F.J. Roethlisberger and W.J. Dickson, 1939), and continuing to the present (see, for example, Kornhauser, Dubin, and Ross, 1954). This work has developed some fruitful insights which will be useful at various points in this study of community conflict.

[14] The collection of examples of community conflict published in 1929 contains two excellent cases of this. In one case, farmers were incensed over a town decision to remove the watering trough in the center of town, although most of the farmers came to town in cars. The conflict resulted probably not over the content of the decision but because it was made without consulting the farmers. In another case, farmers rebelled when the local creamery and bank invited them to a dinner in co-operation with an agricultural expert who had been working with the farmers. The farmers' reasons went like this: "If the bank and creamery are setting us up to a dinner, they're going to get it back out of us somehow." Such statements show clearly the latent hostility of the farmers to the merchants. The Inquiry, 1929, pp. 21, 22, 28, 29.

by economically related incidents seem to be less frequent and less intense. A man who lives in Long Island and commutes to work in New York will not take as the object of his economic frustrations the local merchant, business-man, or his next-door neighbor who works in another industry. It will be his employers, or perhaps "Wall Street financiers," but hardly others within his own community. It is true, however, that *tax* issues can be an important source of controversy in any community. It seems to be particularly impor-tant, in fact, in suburban communities where a high proportion of residents own their own homes.

The lack of economic class cleavage in many suburban towns does not imply that these towns are free from dispute. On the contrary, a high propor-tion of the community conflicts receiving national publicity in recent years have arisen in suburbs of large cities. But the incidents which have provoked these controversies, and the bases of responses which have drawn men into them, have often been quite different from those which divide economic classes. These controversies have centered around differing values: educa-tional values, political beliefs, and patriotic concerns. There are several reasons why men who live side by side in suburban communities should hold such different values. One is the great mobility these people have; another is the fact that the communities have often been settled in two or more "waves," creating "old residents" and "newcomers" who are frequently of different age groups, different ethnic groups, and live in different sections of town. Finally, if men commute to work at diverse tasks in a large city, their values may wander apart, with nothing to pull them back within a "range of tolerance." Suburbanites may live for years next door to someone with radically different views; they mind their own business until some important community decision must be made, or until someone attempts to impose his views on a community institution like the school system.

The third general economic type mentioned—service towns, particularly resort towns—are composed of "natives," a permanent, old-time group, and "outsiders," who are sometimes summer residents, sometimes year-rounders, but who in any case have come to town to rest or play, not to make a living. The responses which are touched off in these towns when an incident arises seem partly a consequence of economic resentments (for the "outsiders" are the primary customers of the "natives"), and partly a consequence of the extreme social barriers which isolate the two groups. Reports of the Peekskill riots (Rorty and Rauschenbusch, 1950) show a good example of conflict in this kind of town. They indicate how isolation was in part responsible for the hostility of the town to the resort colony.

Finally, another variation in economic structure must be mentioned—the variation between towns dominated by business interests and those dominated by political authority (through control of patronage, road con-tracts, and other local governmental contracting). In the latter, found most often in the nonindustrialized south, the absence of industry and the domi-nance of politics makes concern with politics much greater, and increases the likelihood that politically related incidents will set off controversy.

Thus, towns with different economic structures differ widely in the kinds of economic controversy they generate. At the same time, it can hardly be said that one kind of controversy is specific to a particular kind of community.

Changes in time

Certain bases of responses are more important at one time than another. In the 1929 book on community conflict, nine out of forty conflicts were directly related to church matters. In the contemporary conflicts reviewed, none appears to be centered around the church (though there are, to be sure, such controversies still continuing—controversies, for example, over relocation of churches in residential areas populated largely by people of different faiths). Religion seems to be a less important value and a less frequent basis of community conflict than it once was. Few communities today, for example, are so split religiously that Baptists and Methodists feel compelled to organize separate banks in a town which can hardly support one bank! The 1929 study reports such a case (The Inquiry, p. 70).

On the other hand, certain institutions, and the values which surround them, are just as strong today as they were thirty years ago. School controversies seem just as frequent (they contributed eleven of forty community controversies in the 1929 study), if not more so.

Besides long-run value changes, which affect the frequency of certain kinds of controversies, there is perhaps an even more important time effect—short-term changes in the social climate. A national climate of fear and distrust can provide a basis of response for numerous kinds of conflicts. After World War II, fear of Communist subversion acted as a kind of exposed "nerve"; when touched by an incident involving the schools, public health, and a host of other matters, it unleashed intense response. Of the conditions which tend to generate community conflict, such temporary climates of feeling seem to be among the most important. They appear to equip people with a kind of sensitivity to things which would leave them ordinarily unmoved. Often their greatest effect is on people who have been inactive in the community; that is, they bring into the controversy those community members who customarily remain on the sidelines.

Population shifts and heterogeneous values

At some time or another, mass migration may deposit a whole new group of people into an existing community. Often, these newcomers differ from the natives in their "styles of life"; they may have different religions, different cultural backgrounds, different occupations. The resulting "community" consists of two very dissimilar parts, and unless extraordinary measures are taken to integrate them, they can remain distinct groups for as long as a hundred years. Probably the two most outstanding examples of this phenomenon are the New England villages of the nineteenth century whose native

Americans faced immigrants of quite different backgrounds, and, in our time, the small, quiet, suburban villages outside large cities which are suddenly mushrooming with migrants from the city. Dissimilar as these two groups of communities are in other respects, they are alike in this; and this similarity alone means that some of the same kinds of incidents divide the towns: school appropriations, churches, taxes. Whenever a difference in values and in interests is created by the influx of new residents, it becomes a potential basis of conflicting response and sets the stage for precipitating incidents. An excellent study by Elin Anderson (1938) shows the effects of waves of immigration on one New England town; a series of articles in the *New York Times* by Harrison Salisbury (1955) on Yonkers, New York, shows the similar effects of migration on a suburb.

*Existing cleavages: the residuum of
past controversy*

A final difference which leads some communities to respond to an incident with conflict and allows others to pass it by is the past history of controversy in the community, which may have created mutual antagonisms or fostered unity. We repeat this because of its extreme importance in predisposing a community to respond to *any* kind of precipitating event, be it one of economic interests, of values, or of political power.

*General patterns in the initiation
of controversy*

When a well-developed theory of community conflict is constructed, it will be possible to say much more about the initiation and early stages of controversy. In particular, it will be possible to show how several elements combine to set off a controversy, just as a boy, a match, and a firecracker combine to set off an explosion. Such a theory will show the specific role that each element plays and will make explicit the *different* kinds of elements which help initiate controversy.

One crude example may indicate how valuable this could be for reducing controversy. In a number of recent school controversies (not all, by any means, but the Pasadena and Houston controversies at least), three elements seem to have been crucial in the initiation of the dispute:

(1) the existence in the community of a few extreme activists, who gain moral support, and sometimes information, leaflets, etc., from national sources; (2) the existence of a national climate of fear and suspicion concerning internal subversion; (3) the lack of close and continued relations between school administration and community organizations representing conservative as well as liberal segments of the population.

Evidence (discussed more fully later) suggests that if any one of these elements had been absent, controversy would never have begun. Thus, such controversies, in theory at least, could have been prevented in three ways, that is, through eliminating any one of the three elements.[15] Though the example is crude, it illustrates the potential value of such an approach.

Revolts against an administration:
the pattern of initiation

There is one large class of conflicts which can be thought of as revolts against an administration. These disputes, which include some of the fluoridation controversies, the school disputes cited in the example above, the disputes over continuation of the city-manager plan, and many industrial disputes, are characterized by the following:

1. *The administration in power becomes the defendant in the controversy which ensues.*

In the fluoridation controversies, this has been the town officials; in school controversies, the school administration (either the school board or the superintendent); in the disputes which led to abandonment of the city-manager plans, it has been the city-manager and usually the council as well; and in industrial disputes, the plant management.

2. *A few active oppositionists, men who are continually in opposition, oppose the administration. These men are sometimes motivated by the hope of power, but often they are ideologically committed to a "cause."*

In the recent school controversies, these have often been men who are sincerely convinced the schools are subversive, men who are against all modern trends in education, or whose whole political philosophy is far to the right of present-day parties. Though their "causes" may differ, the men are fully dedicated.[16] In labor-management disputes, the "oppositionists" are the active and ideologically-committed union leaders who never relax in their opposition to management. Like the dedicated right-wingers in the school controversies, their opposition to the "regime" is often based on a commitment to a cause which goes far beyond the immediate content of any dispute (Pope, 1942). In the four city-manager plan abandonments (Stene and Floro, 1953), the opposition leaders were evidently frustrated men on the fringes of the power elite. Their opposition appears to have been based completely on personal hostility and a desire for power. In the fluoridation controversies, the leader seems sometimes to have been a man with a desire for power; nevertheless, the leaders often included men who had little to gain personally but whose political philosophy moved them to oppose fluoridation as an infringement of individual rights.

---

[15] Whether in actual fact any one of the three ways could be used to prevent conflict depends on what elements one controls in the situation. Since those wishing to prevent conflict in such situations are usually persons in the school administration or sympathetic to the administration, the only one of these three elements which is even partly under their control is the third—the school-community relationship. It may be, of course, that the cost, in terms of an emasculated school policy, of placating certain community interests is greater than the administration would care to pay.

[16] The Scarsdale, Pasadena, Englewood, and Houston controversies best illustrate this among the school controversies examined here.

3. *A large group exists—often the majority of the people—who are ordinarily inactive, acquiescent to the administration, but not actively supporting it.*

In many school controversies, this is that large segment of the community, neither very liberal nor very conservative, which takes little interest or active part in school affairs. In the fluoridation episodes, the situation has been quite similar; the majority of the population is often apathetic, participating very little in community affairs. In the city-manager disputes leading to abandonment of the plans, voting statistics show that the working-class sections of town, constituting the majority of the population, were ordinarily quite apathetic, content to let the city government be elected without voting. (It was the large increase in the *number* of these working-class votes, not in their *distribution*, which accounted for the final abandonment [Stene and Floro, 1953, Chap. 6].) In labor-management disputes which became community conflicts, the workers as a whole, in contrast to their leaders, were usually apathetic.[17]

4. *An active group exists, usually a minority of the population, who continually support administration policies, and who were responsible for putting the administration in office in the first place.*

In school controversies, this includes the P.T.A., the school board, and other laymen who take part in school-community activities. In the fluoridation and city-manager controversies, these are usually the business and professional groups in town, organized and generally active in support of administration policies. In labor-management disputes, this is anyone from foremen on up who supports management within the company, and the community organizations which usually provide support for management from the community as a whole.

5. *The large passive group, or a part of it, [(3) above] becomes active in one of two ways:* (a) a change in the general climate of opinion, reinforced by national mass media and by current events, mobilizes certain basic values and dispositions (e.g., patriotism and resulting fear of subversion) which the passive majority has held continuously, but which have been dormant. The current events and attendant publicity act, in effect, to create a completely new atmosphere of suspicion, where values which were well accepted only a short time ago are liable to attack. In this atmosphere, the administration needs to commit only one tiny misstep and the suspicion will be directed against it; it is operating under a set of values antagonistic to those who brought it into power. (b) The administration commits a series of blunders in matters which are of considerable importance to the members of this passive majority, e.g., circumvention of democratic procedures by a city administration in setting up fluoridation plans or arbitrary exercise of power by management in industry.

---

[17]Exceptions to this occur when management policies are continually overbearing and provocative, or when social conditions particularly favor workers' action, e.g., among miners and longshoremen.

Be it changes in a national climate of opinion or changes in the local climate of opinion brought on by specific acts of the administration, the effect is the same: the inactive majority is made ready for action.

6. *The ideologically-committed, active oppositionist is now able to use this new hostile atmosphere to gain his ends.* He can now lead the large, mobilized group against the administration and its supporting minority. Seldom are his objectives and values those of the majority, but he uses them for his own purposes while they are active and in opposition to his adversary.[18]

In school controversies, for example, the majority seldom agrees with the educational or political philosophy of the right-wing leader even when it follows him. In the fluoridation controversies, the leaders are often chiropractors and others on the fringes of the medical profession who have private grudges. In labor-management disputes, the active, ideological union leaders have left-wing political goals quite different from the immediate economic gains of their followers.

This process of initiation of controversy seems to be a very general one, accounting for many of the controversies examined in the literature. The general pattern is revolt against the group in power; the mechanisms through which the revolt occurs seem to be those above. Unfortunately, perhaps, these mechanisms suggest manipulation of the masses by "evil" opposition. But a sophisticated administration often manipulates just as effectively to prevent conflict. For example: In many southern border states, school boards, school superintendents, and city governments co-operated to bring about school integration without incidents and without community conflict. During the period of integration, residents of these communities were asked, in conjunction with a national survey of attitudes toward Negroes, whether they favored integration. Two-thirds of the white population in these areas which had quietly integrated said that they opposed integration (Hyman and Sheatsley, 1952, p. 39). Thus the school and community administration had skillfully initiated a policy—often with apparent widespread public support—which was at variance with the privately expressed attitudes of a majority of the people.

Cases which lack one of the elements

Some incipient controversies, which never really became true controversies or in which the administration was never seriously threatened, demonstrate

---

[18] There is a parallel to this in internal union politics. In the 1930's, a small, radical, left-wing party, the Amalgamation Party, existed in the New York City printers' union. Until the printers felt the Depression, in the late 1930's, this party was composed of only a few activists, Communists or Communist sympathizers. When the economic pinch came, this party was able to use the existing climate of opinion to ride to power—upon the backs of the unemployed, so to speak. After 1940, the party again lost its following, and combined with one of the two major parties in the union. (See Lipset, Trow, and Coleman, 1956, p. 301-306.)

More generally, this seems to be the history of many small ideological parties in civil politics: to languish until the right climate of opinion arrives. This climate of opinion brings with it issues by which the small group of activists can attract a large and often heterogeneous group whose values are quite different from those of the "hard core." There are indications of this among Senator McCarthy's following: dispositions among the mass following were far removed from the ideological beliefs of the inner core.

why *each* initiating element must be present. In Scarsdale, New York, for example, dispute began when one citizen, sincerely convinced that books in the school libraries by Communists and leftists were aiding the cause of communism, attempted, first by himself, and then with the aid of a few fellow-citizens (a minister, a psychologist, a college professor, and others), to set up a watchdog committee to advise the Board of Education about books in the school library (Shaplen, 1950). After some controversy, during which the major governing organization and other organizations in town stood firmly against this committee, the Board of Education and the school superintendent repudiated all its efforts. At the next school board election, the incumbent members of the board were overwhelmingly reelected by the community. Although the attacks continued, the opposition was never able to gain concessions from the school board, and the right-wing supporters never constituted more than a tiny minority of the community. At no time was there a divided community; the administration never lost community support.

In Scarsdale, two important elements were present: a national climate of opinion and a dedicated opposition leader. But a third, the passive majority aroused against the school, was not. Scarsdale, an upper- and upper-middle-class community, has probably a higher proportion of community members active in its organizations than other towns throughout the country.[19] A close relationship existed between the community and its schools, as measured both in individual interest and in community-school organizations. Thus the formula lacked one major ingredient, the passively acquiescent majority which could be mobilized against the administration. The actively-supporting group [(4) in the schema above] was not a minority but the great majority of townspeople.

Similarly, in Denver, Colorado, two of the ingredients which created full-scale controversy in Pasadena and Houston were missing. The climate of opinion existed, but there was no avid right-wing leader to take advantage of it, though there were less radical and less dedicated oppositionists. Also, relations between the school system and the community, though not as close as those in Scarsdale, were close enough that the school's active supporters [(4) in the schema above] constituted a large segment of the Denver population.

These cases of controversy which never blossomed into successful revolt indicate the importance of each element in the genesis of controversy.

Patterns of initiation in other types of controversy

Not all community controversies develop along these lines. Port Washington, Long Island, for example, has been the scene of continual controversy

[19] It is a town of 14,000; the Town Club, which is the major governing body in town (as it "taps" men in the community to serve on the village board and school board) has a membership of 900.

between two factions—one favoring a traditional educational policy, the other a progressive one.

Desegregation controversies do not fit this pattern either; here the central issue is the conflict of *new* policy with established community beliefs. Riots like those in Cicero and Peekskill do not constitute revolt against an administration. Many other controversies, e.g., the continued disputes between new and old residents in Yonkers and other fast-growing suburbs, or the ethnic-related controversies in New England towns, are also quite different. It is clear that the pattern of initiation we have discussed holds only for a certain class of controversy; other controversies follow other patterns. It is one task of a theory of community controversy to make these patterns explicit, to show (much more precisely than we have done) how they *combine* to initiate a conflict. Such a theory would be of considerable value for the practical problems of community decision-making.

Bibliography

Abrams, Charles. "The Time Bomb That Exploded in Cicero," *Commentary,* XII, (Nov., 1951), 407-14.

Anderson, Elin W. *We Americans.* Cambridge: Harvard University Press, 1938.

Banfield, Edward C. *Government Project.* Glencoe: The Free Press, 1951.

Berelson, Bernard, Lazarsfeld, Paul F. and McPhee, William. *Voting.* Chicago: University of Chicago Press, 1954.

Bettelheim, Bruno and Janowitz, Morris. *Dynamics of Prejudice.* New York: Harper, 1950.

Blumenthal, Albert. *Small Town Stuff.* Chicago: University of Chicago Press, 1932.

Cantril, Hadley. *The Psychology of Social Movements.* New York: Wiley, 1941.

Cantril, Hadley, Gaudet, Hazel, and Herzog, Herta. *The Invasion from Mars.* Princeton: Princeton University Press, 1940.

Carter, Hodding. "A Wave of Terror Threatens the South," *Look Magazine,* XX, March 22, 1955, 32-36.

Charters, W. W., Jr., and Newcomb, Theodore M. "Some Attitudinal Effects of Experimentally Increased Salience of a Membership Group," in G. E. Swanson, T. M. Newcomb, and E. L. Hartley (eds.), *Readings in Social Psychology.* New York: Holt, revised edition, 1952.

Coleman, James. "Political Cleavage within the International Typographical Union." Unpublished Ph.D. dissertation, Columbia University, 1955.

——. "Multidimensional Scale Analysis." Submitted to *American Journal of Sociology,* 1957.

Coser, Lewis. *The Functions of Social Conflict.* Glencoe: The Free Press, 1956.

Per Z

671

S 36f

School Library Journal   Nov. 76

"Playing Favorites"

151

for   Pos 324

L&S 138-147
    147-168

Downs 400-423

Cressey, P. F. "Social Disorganization and Reorganization in Harlan County, Kentucky," *American Sociological Review,* XIV, (June, 1949), 389 *et seq.*

DeVoto, Bernard. "Norwalk and Points West," *Harper's,* CCVII, (April, 1954), 10-12.

Engel, Louis. "Port Washington, N.Y.," *Saturday Review,* ("The Public School Crisis") XXXIV (September 8, 1951), 6-20.

Farber, Maurice L. "The Armageddon Complex: Dynamics of Opinion," *Public Opinion Quarterly,* XV (1951-52), 217-24.

Festinger, Leon, Schacter, Stanley, and Back, Kurt. *Social Pressures in Informal Groups.* New York: Harper, 1950.

Foskett, John M. "Social Structure and Social Participation," *American Sociological Review,* XX (August, 1955), 431-38.

Gouldner, Alvin W. *Patterns of Industrial Bureaucracy.* Glencoe: The Free Press, 1954.

Groh, George W. "Norwalk, NATO, and the VFW: What's All the Hollering?" *The Reporter,* X (March 16, 1954), 28-30.

Hatch, D. L. "Changes in the Structure and Function of a Rural New England Community since 1900." Ph.D. dissertation, Harvard University, 1948.

Hessler, William H. "It Didn't Work in Cincinnati," *The Reporter,* IX, (December 22, 1953), 13-17.

Hicks, Granville. "Roxborough, Post-Truman," *Commentary,* XV (March, 1953), 227-35.

Homans, George. *The Human Group.* New York: Harcourt, 1950.

Hovland, Carl J., Lumsdaine, Arthur A., and Sheffield, Fred D. *Experiments in Mass Communication.* Princeton: Princeton University Press, 1949.

Hovland, Carl J., Janis, Irving L., and Kelley, Harold M. *Communication and Persuasion.* New Haven: Yale University Press, 1953.

Hughes, Everett C. *French Canada in Transition.* London: K. Paul, Trench, Trubner, 1946.

Hunter, Floyd. *Community Power Structure.* Chapel Hill: University of North Carolina Press, 1953.

Hurlburd, David. *This Happened in Pasadena.* New York: Macmillan, 1950.

Hyman, Herbert H., and Sheatsley, Paul B. "Some Reasons Why Information Campaigns Fail," in *Readings in Social Psychology,* G. E. Swanson, T. M. Newcomb, and E. L. Hartley (eds.). New York: Holt, revised edition, 1952.

—. "Attitudes on Desegregation," *Scientific American,* CXCV, (December, 1956), 35-39.

Jones, Alfred W. *Life, Liberty, and Property.* Philadelphia: Lippincott, 1941.

Katz, Elihu and Lazarsfeld, Paul F. *Personal Influence.* Glencoe: The Free Press, 1955.

Key, V. O. Jr. *Southern Politics.* New York: Knopf, 1950.

Kelley, Harold. "Two Functions of Reference Groups," in *Readings in Social Psychology,* Swanson, Newcomb, and Hartley (eds.). New York: Holt, revised edition, 1952.

Klapper, Joseph T. *The Effects of Mass Media.* New York: Columbia University, Bureau of Applied Social Research, 1950.

Kornhauser, Arthur, Dubin, Robert and Ross, Arthur M. *Industrial Conflict.* New York: McGraw-Hill Book, 1954.

Kriesberg, Martin. "Cross-Pressures and Attitudes," *Public Opinion Quarterly,* XIII (Spring, 1949), 5-16.

Lazarsfeld, Paul F., and Merton, Robert K. "Mass Communication, Popular Taste, and Organized Social Action," in *Readings in Social Psychology,* G. E. Swanson, T. M. Newcomb, and E. L. Hartley (eds.). New York: Holt, revised edition, 1952.

Lazarsfeld, Paul F., and Kendall, Patricia L. *Radio in Health Education.* New York: Columbia University Press, 1945.

Lazarsfeld-Jahoda, Marie, and Zeisel, H. *Die Arbeitslosen von Marienthal.* Leipzig: Hirzel, 1932, p. 36 and *passim.*

Lewin, Kurt. "Forces Behind Food Habits and Methods of Change." *Bulletin of the National Research Council,* 1943.

"Outsider Stirs Up Small Town Trouble," *Life,* XXXVII (October 11, 1954), 45-46.

Lipset, Seymour M. "Opinion Formation in a Crisis Situation," *Public Opinion Quarterly,* XVII, 1953, 20-46.

——, Trow, Martin, and Coleman, James. *Union Democracy.* Glencoe: The Free Press, 1956.

——, Lazarsfeld, Paul F., Barton, Allan H., and Linz, Juan, "The Psychology of Voting: An Analysis of Political Behavior," in *Handbook of Social Psychology,* Gardner Lindzey (ed.) Cambridge: Addison-Wesley, 1954.

Lundberg, George and Steele, Mary. "Social Attraction Patterns in a Village," *Sociometry,* I (January-April, 1938), 375.

Lynd, Robert S., and Lynd, Helen M. *Middletown in Transition.* New York: Harcourt, 1937.

Martin, Lawrence. "Denver, Colorado," *Saturday Review,* ("The Public School Crisis"), XXXIV, September 8, 1951, 6-20.

Mausner, Bernard and Judith. "A Study of the Anti-Scientific Attitude," *Scientific American,* CXCII (February, 1955), 35-39.

McKee, James B. "Organized Labor and Community Decision-making: A Study in the Sociology of Power." Unpublished Ph.D. dissertation, University of Wisconsin, 1953.

McPhee, William, "Community Controversies Affecting Personal Liberties and Institutional Freedoms in Education." Unpublished memorandum, Columbia University, Bureau of Applied Social Research, July, 1954.

Mead, George M. *Mind, Self, and Society.* Chicago: University of Chicago Press, 1934.

Menzel, Herbert and Coleman, James. "The Flow of Scientific Information in the Medical Community." Unpublished memorandum, Columbia University, Bureau of Applied Social Research, New York, 1955.

Merton, Robert K. and Lazarsfeld, Paul F. "Friendship as a Social Process," in *Freedom and Control in Modern Society,* Monroe Berger, Theodore Abel, and Charles Page (eds.), New York: Van Nostrand, 1954.

Merton, Robert K., West, Patricia S., and Jahoda, Marie. *Patterns of Social Life: Explorations in the Sociology of Housing.* Forthcoming.

Merton, Robert K. and Kitt, Alice S. "Contributions to the Theory of Reference Group Behavior," in *Continuities in Social Research,* Robert K. Merton and Paul F. Lazarsfeld, (eds.) Glencoe: The Free Press, 1950.

Merton, Robert K. *Mass Persuasion: The Social Psychology of a War Bond Drive.* New York: Harper, 1946.

Michels, Robert. *Political Parties.* Translated by E. Paul and C. Paul. Glencoe: The Free Press, 1949.

Morse, Arthur D. "Who's Trying to Ruin Our Schools?" *McCall's* (1951) reprinted in *Freedom and Public Education,* Ernest O. Melby and Morton Puner (eds.). New York: Praeger, 1953.

Mott, Frank Luther. "Newspapers in Presidential Campaigns," *Public Opinion Quarterly,* VIII (1944).

"The Ebey Story," *The Nation* (September 26, 1953), 242 *et seq.*

National Education Association. Report on Houston by the National Defense Commission, 1953.

Newcomb, Theodore M. *Personality and Social Change.* New York: Dryden, 1943.

Parsons, Talcott. *The Social System.* Glencoe: The Free Press, 1951.

Pope, Liston. *Millhands and Preachers.* New Haven: Yale University Press, 1942.

Queener, E. L. "The Development of Internationalist Attitudes Directed Toward Peace," cited in *Theory and Problems of Social Psychology,* David Krech and Richard S. Crutchfield. New York: McGraw-Hill, 1948, p. 156.

Reinemer, Vic. "Is Fluoridation a Marxist Plot?" *The Reporter,* XII (June 16, 1955), 28-30.

Roethlisberger, F. J., and Dickson, W. J. *Management and the Worker.* Cambridge: Harvard University Press, 1939.

Rorty, James. "Desegregation along the Mason-Dixon Line," *Commentary,* XVIII (December, 1954), 493-503.

——. "Thirty Days that Shook Norwalk," *Commentary,* XVII, (April, 1954), 330-36.

Rorty, James, and Rauschenbusch, Winifred. "The Lessons of the Peekskill Riots," *Commentary,* X (October, 1950), 309-23.

Rose, Arnold. *Studies in Reduction of Prejudice,* Chicago: American Council on Race Relations, 1947.

Salisbury, Harrison E. Four articles on Yonkers, N. Y., *New York Times,* April 18-21, 1955.

Sayles, Leonard R., and Strauss, George. *The Local Union.* New York: Harper, 1953.

Selznick, Philip. *TVA and the Grass Roots.* Berkeley: University of California Press, 1949.

Shaplen, Robert. "Scarsdale's Battle of the Books," *Commentary,* X, (December, 1950), 530-40.

Sherif, Muzafer. "Group Influences Upon the Formation of Norms and Attitudes," in *Readings in Social Psychology*, G. E. Swanson, T. M. Newcomb, and E. L. Hartley (eds.). New York: Holt, revised edition, 1952.

Simmel, Georg. *Conflict and the Web of Intergroup Affiliations.* Glencoe: The Free Press, 1955.

Southern School News, III, (October, 1956), p. 15.

Stene, Edwin K. and Floro, George K. *Abandonment of the Manager Plan.* Lawrence, Kansas: University of Kansas, 1953.

Stone, Harold S., Price, Don K., and Stone, Kathryn H. *City Manager Government in the United States.* Chicago: Public Administration Service, 1940.

The Inquiry, *Community Conflict.* New York, 1929.

Trow, Martin A. "Right Wing Radicalism and Political Intolerance: A Study of Support for McCarthy in a New England Town." Unpublished Ph.D. dissertation, Columbia University, 1957.

Tugman, W. M. "Eugene, Oregon," *Saturday Review,* ("The Public School Crisis") XXXIV (September 8, 1951), 6-20.

Walker, Charles. *Steeltown.* New York: Harper, 1950.

Warner, W. Lloyd and Associates. *Democracy in Jonesville.* New York: Harper, 1949.

Warner, W. Lloyd. *American Life: Dream and Reality.* Chicago: University of Chicago Press, 1953.

Warriner, Charles K. "Leadership and Society: A Study in Sociological Theory." Unpublished Ph.D. thesis, University of Chicago, 1953.

White, Theodore H. "The Battle of Athens, Tennessee," *Harper's,* CXCIV, (January, 1947), 194.

White, William Foote. *Street Corner Society.* Chicago: University of Chicago Press, 1943.

Wiesner, August J., Jr. "Englewood, N.J.," *Saturday Review* ("The Public School Crisis"), XXXIV (September 8, 1951), 6-20.

Williams, Robin. *The Reduction of Intergroup Tensions.* Bulletin 47. Social Science Research Council. New York: 1947.

Zimmerman, Carle C. *The Changing Community.* New York: Harper, 1938.

Suburban Attitudes, Opinions, and Local Policies

Oliver P. Williams
Harold Herman
Charles S. Liebman
Thomas R. Dye

This selection introduces for our consideration the first component of the policy-making process: citizen attitudes and opinions. What is the nature of citizen attitudes about local governmental activity? What do citizens conceive as the proper role for local government? Do these attitudes and policy preferences vary from community to community? What is the relationship between citizen attitudes and public-policy decisions? These are some of the questions considered in this selection—important questions to be kept in mind as you read and discuss this and subsequent articles.

Local communities can be distinguished according to differences in the attitudes of their residents. The authors of this selection taken from a larger study entitled Suburban Differences and Metropolitan Policies *systematically examine actual differences in the attitudes, opinions, and policy preferences of residents, elected public officials, and business and professional leaders in selected municipalities from the Pennsylvania portion of the Philadelphia Standard Metropolitan Statistical Area (which includes an area of western New Jersey). Using data drawn from questionnaires, they analyze the relationship between a municipality's social rank and these factors. The assumption underlying their study is that the social rank of a community reflects and/or structures citizen attitudes and opinions, and that such preferences have some influence on the policies undertaken by local governments.*

This analysis points up the very real differences from community to community in the attitudes, opinions, and policy preferences of suburban residents and their political leaders. For example, citizens in different communities varied considerably in their opinions about just what their municipality's government ought to be doing. About the proper role of their local government, respondents in high social ranking communities had very different expectations from individuals in low social ranking municipalities.

But does municipal policy actually reflect the attitudes and opinions of residents? These researchers conclude that in general it does. One reason for this is that locally elected leaders tend to have backgrounds similar to those of the individuals in the municipalities they represent, and also tend to share similar attitudes and policy preferences. This congruence of citizen and leader characteristics and attitudes further accentuates differences among suburban communities, with important implications for intermunicipal cooperation and conflict.

Finally, when these researchers asked various business and professional leaders their opinions about metropolitan cooperation, they found that the major differences in opinion were provoked by the extent of cooperation involved. With respect to the specific issues, all respondents favor cooperation where the services provided do not lead to the erosion of the formal separation and/or authority of the two municipal governments.

Introduction

. . . This chapter reports on two attitude and opinion surveys. In effect, it measures differences in the values that predominate in subareas of the metropolitan area. It uses survey techniques but retains the basic social-area orientation of the study. Specifically, the chapter measures differences in attitudes and opinions of residents and elected officials from municipalities of varying social rank and then relates these differences in predisposition to the policy differences that have been previously described. Secondly, the chapter examines the representativeness of the elected officials who constitute a municipality's formal policy makers. Representativeness in this sense refers to whether or not officials are similar to and share the value systems of their constituents. The broader question of public responsiveness and responsibility is reserved for later discussion. Finally, this chapter reports the results of a survey of opinions about metropolitan cooperation both in the abstract and in regard to specific areas of intergovernmental cooperation. . . .

Suburban residents and public officials: attitude differences

Five attitude batteries were used. Suburban residents and public officials were tested for local-cosmopolitan attitudes, nonpartisanship, anomie, conservatism, and ethnocentrism. . . .

Residents of high-social-ranking communities were, on the average, significantly more oriented to national affairs, were more opposed to government activity in the economic and social spheres, and were less hostile to out-groups than residents of low-social-ranking communities. In addition, attitudes of respondents with low-social-ranking characteristics who lived in high-social-ranking communities were more different from attitudes of

Reprinted from *Suburban Differences and Metropolitan Policies: A Philadelphia Story* (Philadelphia: The University of Pennsylvania Press, 1965), pp. 211-238, by permission of the publisher.

low-social-ranking respondents from low-social-ranking communities than were the attitudes of respondents with high-social-ranking characteristics in high-social-ranking communities. In other words, low-social-ranking respondents in high-social-ranking communities over-conform to the dominant values of their communities. There were insufficient respondents of high-social-rank characteristics living in low-social-ranking communities to draw any conclusions.

Suburban residents and public officials: opinion differences

The outstanding fact that emerges from a study of opinions of suburban respondents is that residents of different areas have very different opinions about governmental activity.[1] First of all, residents of high-social-ranking communities have different expectations of local government. They expect their governments to do different kinds of things and they become aroused over different kinds of issues. Secondly, as one might expect from the foregoing, place of residence serves to differentiate respondents in their replies to questions about specific metropolitan issues.

Differing expectations

On the basis of respondents' replies to the questions of which goals they felt were "very important" for local government, 3 distinct images or roles for government emerged: providing amenities, securing a low tax rate, and maintaining the social characteristics of the community. Respondents who thought that the goal of maintaining improved public services and the goal of providing esthetic amenities were very important goals for local government were judged to have amenity expectations. As indicated in Table 1 respondents from high-social-ranking municipalities were more concerned with amenities than respondents from low-social-ranking communities.

Residents were also asked about issues which were likely to get their community "most aroused." From high-social-ranking communities 58 percent of the residents said poor public service was such an issue. Only

[1] A more complete description of the two samples and the responses is found in Thomas R. Dye, *Certain Political Correlates of Social and Economic Differentiation Among Suburban Communities* (University of Pennsylvania, Unpublished doctoral dissertation, 1961). The sixteen municipalities grouped by social rank were: upper—Swarthmore, Lansdowne, Springfield, Haverford, Radnor, Nether Providence, middle—Yeadon, Folcroft, East Lansdowne, Norwood, Sharon Hill, lower—Chichester, Upper Chichester, Marcus Hool, Eddystone, Tinicum. While the social-class bias in the resident sample was largely controlled by grouping respondents, another very important variable influencing returns to mailed questionnaires, that of interest in the topic under investigation, continues to bias the resident response. Consequently in interpreting the material presented here, one must keep in mind that the resident respondents are probably more interested in, and concerned with, politics in general than the subpopulations they represent.

*Table 1.   Percentage of residents and public officials who judged
it very important for government to provide amenities*

| | Social-rank grouping of municipality | | |
	Upper	*Middle*	*Lower*
Residents			
Maintain improved public services	44.8	41.2	35.7
Provide esthetic amenities	50.0	38.2	32.1
Public officials			
Maintain improved public services	56.5	46.6	50.0
Provide esthetic amenities	47.8	33.3	28.5

49 percent of the residents from middle-social-ranking communities and 43 percent of the residents from low-social-ranking communities thought so.

Emphasis on the second value or role for local government, that of securing a low tax rate, was ascertained by determining which respondents thought the goals of acquiring business and industry and keeping tax rates down were very important goals for government. Respondents from high-social-ranking communities were not as concerned with this goal as respondents from low-social-ranking communities.

*Table 2.   Percentage of residents and public officials who judged it
very important for government to secure low tax rates*

| | Social-rank grouping of municipality | | |
	Upper	*Middle*	*Lower*
Residents			
Acquire business and industry	8.6	23.5	50.0
Keep tax rate down	56.9	79.5	82.0
Public officials			
Acquire business and industry	13.0	26.6	64.3
Keep tax rate down	43.5	80.0	79.0

From high-social-ranking communities, 41 percent of the residents thought that increasing taxes was an issue which was likely to get the community "most aroused." Comparable percentages for middle- and low-social-ranking communities are 66 and 79 percent. The value of providing industrial growth and a resultant low tax rate as opposed to a sacrifice in amenities was nicely juxtaposed in another question which asked, "Would you favor more industrial growth and more jobs for your local community even if it meant an increase in noise and traffic and industrial type buildings? Among residents from high-social-ranking communities, 18 percent favored the proposal and 82 percent opposed it. From the middle-social-ranking group 46 percent favored it and 54 percent opposed it. Among lower-social-ranking communities 78 percent favored it and 22 percent opposed it.

The value or role of maintaining the community's social characteristics and composition was ascertained by asking respondents whether they thought the goal of keeping undesirables out and the goal of maintaining the "quality" of residents were very important for local government.

High- and low-social-ranking communities do not express clear-cut differences with respect to this goal. The direction of response is different for the two questions. Sixty-two percent of the residents of high-social-ranking communities thought that keeping undesirables out was very important. Seventy-five percent of low-social-ranking community residents thought so as well. Comparable percentages for public officials were 70 and 86 percent. However, whereas 69 percent of residents from high-social-ranking communities thought that maintaining the "quality" of residents was a very important goal for local government, only 43 percent of residents from low-social-ranking communities thought so. Among public officials the percentage differences were much closer, 61 and 57 percent.

Table 3. *Percentage of residents and public officials who judged it very important for government to maintain the social characteristics of the community*

	Social-rank grouping of municipality		
	Upper	*Middle*	*Lower*
Residents			
Keep undesirables out	62.0	79.5	75.0
Maintain "quality" of residents	69.0	47.0	43.0
Public officials			
Keep undesirables out	69.6	73.2	85.5
Maintain "quality" of residents	60.8	66.6	57.0

The differences in the direction of the response to the two questions, maintaining quality of residents and keeping undesirables out, raises a problem; but before suggesting a solution, the overall impact of the response should be clear. Respondents from both high- and low-social-ranking communities thought that keeping undesirables out was a very important goal. Further, more residents from all types of communities thought that undesirables moving in was more likely to get their community very aroused than any other issue including zoning, increasing taxes, poor public service, metropolitan government, and unequal tax burdens. One might expect that the goal of keeping undesirables out, and the goal of maintaining the quality of residents, are both directed at the image of government as a maintainer of the social structure and, therefore, that the direction of response to these two questions among high- and low-social-ranking communities would be the same. Assuming a consistency among respondents, the responses indicate however that the two questions were perceived as having different meanings. Residents of low-social-ranking communities may be relatively unconcerned about maintaining the "quality" of residents, but they are clearly concerned about an influx of certain persons viewed as "undesirables." Residents of high-social-ranking communities favor keeping undesirables out and maintaining the quality of residents, although they are less concerned about the threat of "undesirables" than lowered "quality" of residents.

In summary, respondents from high-social-ranking communities expect their municipality to provide better public services and public amenities as well as to maintain the social structure. Respondents from low-social-ranking communities expect their local government to keep taxes low, are less concerned with amenities, and expect government to keep certain types of potential residents out. The term "undesirable" is, of course, an ambiguous one. To the suburban residents of northern industrial cities, especially those in lower social rank areas, it probably means "Negro."

In addition to those discussed above, respondents also differed sharply by social rank with respect to several other goals and issues. Thus, 81 percent of the residents from high-social-ranking communities and 87 percent of the public officials from these areas thought that protecting property values was a very important goal for government, while only 54 percent of the residents and 50 percent of the public officials from low-social-ranking communities thought so. Only 31 percent of the residents from high-social-ranking areas thought that unequal tax burdens was an issue over which their communities would get "most aroused," but 54 percent of the residents from low-social-ranking communities thought so.

Attitudes, opinions, and municipal policy

Does municipal policy actually reflect the attitudes and opinions of residents? Do low social-ranking communities, in fact, de-emphasize amenities, opt for low taxes and practice discrimination? With proper operational definitions the question is answered in the affirmative. The municipal policy analysis generally showed a relationship between expenditures for amenities and social rank. Even in industrial centers, where rich tax bases could cushion the effect of tax burdens on householders, expenditures for amenities were not stressed.

When the extraordinary needs of Industrial and Commercial Centers were statistically controlled, low-social-ranking municipalities were found to spend less for municipal services than other Suburbs. The differences in expenditures for public schools were most pronounced. That expenditure policies were in turn related to opinions about tax rates was verified in the analyses of tax effort and burden. Discounting the effect on tax rates of the school-aid subsidy, low-social-ranking municipalities were still inclined to maintain low tax rates at the expense of foregoing amenities, or perhaps, as in school expenditures, what high-social-ranking municipalities might consider necessities.

Residents of low-social-ranking communities probably pay higher percentages of their income for less municipal service than do citizens living in places at the other end of the scale. Economic motivations may thus explain the former's predisposition toward maintaining low tax rates. For present purposes, however, it is sufficient to note that this preference as measured by their opinions has been effectively transformed into municipal policy.

Sufficient data have not been presented in earlier chapters to compare opinions with regard to maintaining the social structure of the community and municipal policies. To some extent, the zoning policies pursued by high-social-ranking municipalites are an attempt to prescribe the character of future residents along lines of income and social status. A more obvious manifestation of the attempt to "keep out undesirables" is the practice of racial exclusion. Municipal ordinances are of decidedly lesser importance than informal citizen, group and public-official actions in pursuing this policy.[2]

The opinion survey found citizens from low-social-ranking municipalities more concerned with "keeping out undesirables" than residents from high-social-ranking municipalities. If opinion and action are related, in this case one might hypothesize that racial exclusion is practiced with more intensity by lower-social-ranking communities. But the practice and the effectiveness of policies of exclusion are not synonymous. A finding that there are more Negroes in lower- than high-social-ranking Suburbs would not constitute a refutation of the hypothesis.

Earlier in the study we reported a .845 coefficient of correlation between social rank and the residential market value per household. Thus the largest stock of inexpensive housing is concentrated in the lower-social-ranking Suburbs. The demand for housing among Philadelphia area Negroes centers in the lower price range. The higher-social-ranking Suburbs are in a sense protected from racial change by this economic barrier of high priced homes. Based upon economic considerations alone, one would expect higher-social-ranking Suburbs to be virtually all white, while lower-social-ranking Suburbs should have larger percentages of Negroes. The fact that this expectation is not fulfilled indicates non-economic forces are operative.

The Suburban racial composition by social-rank quartile is shown, for 1950 and 1960, in Table 4. The lowest quartile did indeed have the largest Negro population, numerically as well as proportionately, both in 1950 and 1960. It also experienced the largest increase in Negroes during the decade. This would support the view that the housing market is guiding the pattern of Negro migration. However, a closer examination of the pattern offers some qualifying indications.

The third-quartile Suburbs have a substantial supply of cheap housing too, yet they show a decline in Negro population despite the fact that they had the highest rate of increase in whites over the ten year period. But the fact remains that the lowest-social-ranking quartile did have the largest Negro influx.

[2]The nationally publicized entry of the first Negro family into a development in Folcroft dramatizes the often more subtle means of community response. Bathed in the light of publicity, the community eventually formally accepted the newcomers. However, the initial response indicated the predisposition of many, including some municipal employees, to affirm a policy of exclusion. And subsequent neighborhood pressures on merchants and others indicate that the issue is far from final resolution.

Table 4.   Suburbs: racial distribution by social-rank quartile, 1950 and 1960

Social rank	1950		
Quartile	White	Negro	% Negro of total
High			
1st N = 23	240,951	11,549	4.6
2nd N = 22	166,995	2,665	1.6
3rd N = 22	93,681	2,721	2.9
4th N = 23	201,229	27,903	13.9
Low			
Total	702,256	44,838	6.4

Social rank	1960		
Quartile	White	Negro	% Negro of total
High			
1st N = 23	393,828	12,180	3.1
2nd N = 22	253,557	3,854	1.5
3rd N = 22	184,248	2,474	1.3
4th N = 23	268,924	39,818	14.9
Low			
Total	1,099,657	58,336	5.3

Social rank	% increase 1950–1960		% of total increase	
Quartile	White	Negro	White	Negro
High				
1st N = 23	63.4	5.6	38.5	4.7
2nd N = 22	51.8	44.6	21.8	8.8
3rd N = 22	97.9	−9.2	22.9	−1.8
4th N = 23	33.2	42.7	16.8	88.3
Low				
Total	56.6	30.1	100	100

Table 5 shows the distribution of Suburbs by social-rank quartiles and percentage Negroes in the municipal population in 1960. Most of the Negro influx has been channeled into a few municipalities, while the rest of the fourth-quartile Suburbs remained virtually all-white. Two fourth-quartile Suburbs have no Negroes at all, 5 have under .1 percent, and 3 more have between .1 percent and 1 percent. On the other end of the scale, 3 lower-social-ranking Suburbs have 29.3 percent, and 76.1 percent Negroes respectively. While the over-all Suburban-Negro increase between 1950 and 1960 is concentrated in the fourth quartile, the fact is that Negroes were moving into relatively few of these 23 lower-social-ranking Suburbs. Interestingly, the lower-social-ranking Suburbs that remain all, or virtually all-white, are the smaller municipalities. Perhaps here the maintenance of a community exclusion policy through informal means is most possible.

Table 5. *Suburbs: distribution of percentage population Negro by social-rank quartiles, 1960*

Social rank	Percentage population Negro				
	Under 1%	1—5%	5—10%	10—15%	Over 15%
High					
1st quartile	7	10	5	1	0
N = 23					
2nd quartile	15	3	1	2	1
N = 22					
3rd quartile	17	3	1	0	1
N = 22					
4th quartile	10	6	2	2	3
N = 23					
Low					
Total suburbs	44	32	9	5	5

While the higher-social-ranking Suburbs have small Negro populations, the distribution among them compares favorably with the lower-social-ranking areas. The Negro population comprises approximately 5 percent of the Suburbs. There are as many higher social-ranking Suburbs (first-and second-quartile) with over 5 percent Negroes as there are lower social-ranking ones (third-and fourth-quartile). There are no first-quartile municipalities which practice total exclusion. The bulk of the first-quartile Suburbs approach the norm for all Suburbs in their Negro populations. There are some obvious factors which may explain this fact. There is a certain symbiosis between high-status local populations and a resident service class. In addition, a scattering of high-status Negroes does not represent the advance guard of many more potential residents of the high-status areas. Income factors safeguard against such an influx. Such speculation only serves to give some basis in social organization for the pattern observed.

In brief, the statistical evidence lends support to the hypothesis that there is effective exclusion of Negroes which is more operative in the low- than high-social-ranking areas. Given the income structure among Negroes and the presence of a large supply of inexpensive housing in the lower-social-ranking Suburbs, one would expect a wide dispersal of Negroes throughout these communities if market forces alone were operative. Instead, Negroes in the lower-social-ranking Suburbs are largely confined within a few communities. In the higher-social-ranking Suburbs with a more expensive housing stock, one would expect to find fewer Negroes. In fact, the Negro population in the first quartile is larger, constitutes a larger proportion of the population, and is more widely dispersed among municipalities than in quartiles farther down the social rank scale.

Suburban residents and their leadership

. . . These findings indicate that the social character of political leadership in suburban communities varies rather consistently with the social composition of these communities.[3] Decision-makers in different social types of communities are recruited from separate status levels and consequently bring to their respective roles diverse previous experiences. Separate sets of internalized values suggest that decision-makers in different types of communities will perceive, experience, and behave toward social and political issues in separate fashions. The accessibility of these decision-makers to various interests and diverse sources of information can also be expected to vary in a consistent manner. As a consequence, one can expect that a product of the correlation between community social structure and leadership will be variation in the policy choices of local government. The representative character of local leadership will reinforce the propensity of separate social types of communities to respond to metropolitan issues in diverse fashions.

Business and professional leaders: opinions about metropolitan cooperation

In relating differences in municipal behavior to differences in social rank, we have repeatedly skirted one question. Do communities of a given social rank show a preference for particular policies because large proportions of their residents share a certain occupational and educational status which is accompanied by one set of preferences; or are preferences the socialized choices of those groups of individuals with similar occupational and educational status *who flock together in a given community?* If the former, then municipal policy is nothing more than the expression of collective differences in the social status of individuals. If the latter, then the community becomes a truly meaningful unit for metropolitan analysis; for it is the community and people defined in terms of their choice of environment, and not merely different demographic categories of individuals, that impart distinctions to styles of local political life.

We have seen that low-status individuals living in high-social-ranking municipalities tend to adopt the outlook of the predominant high-status groups in the community. It appears that the opinions of these individuals are shaped as much or more by their environment as by their personal status. Some additional evidence of environment's influence was obtained from another

[3] Jennings summarizes this view of leadership in the following manner: "Both leadership and isolation appear as phenomena which arise out of individual differences in inter-personal capacity for participation and as phenomena which are indigenous to the specific social milieu in which they are produced. Individuals who in this community appear as leaders may or may not be found as leaders in another community of which they later become a part. . . ." Helen H. Jennings, *Leadership and Isolation* (New York: 1943); for an excellent review of the literature on leadership see Cecil A. Gibb, "Leadership," in Gardner Lindzey (ed.), *A Handbook of Social Psychology*, Vol. II (Reading, Mass.: Addison-Wesley, 1954). See also: Donald R. Matthews, *The Social Background of Political Decision-Makers* (New York: Doubleday, 1954); and Wendell Bell and Maryann I. Force, "Urban Neighborhood Types and Participation in Formal Associations," *American Sociological Review*, Vol. 21 (February, 1956), pp. 25-34.

preliminary survey that was designed with a different question in mind.[4] The object of this survey was to test the opinions on metropolitan issues of business elites residing in Philadelphia and its suburbs. In effect, the survey controlled for differences in social status, for all the respondents had high-social-ranking characteristics.

The sample from which opinions were elicited is composed exclusively of business and professional leaders who work in Philadelphia's central business district. Twenty-three of the respondents live in Philadelphia, the remaining 118 live in the suburbs. All but four of the suburban respondents live in high-social-ranking communities.

Respondents were asked who they felt was right in a conflict between Montgomery County and Philadelphia where the county objected to joining with Philadelphia for an area-wide transportation system under Philadelphia's terms. This particular issue had made the front pages of the metropolitan press at the time the questionnaires were mailed. Sixty-one percent of Philadelphia residents thought Philadelphia was right whereas only 30 percent of the Suburbanites thought so. Suburban responses in turn correlated with whether or not respondents commuted by train. Those commuting by train tended to think Philadelphia was right. Those commuting by car favored the Montgomery County position which at that time really meant no areawide transit agreement. A different question getting at reactions to mass transit was also posed in the Delaware County sample. Citizens were asked if they favored their county or local government spending tax money to improve mass transit in the area. Whereas 45 percent of the respondents from high-social-ranking communities favored the proposal only 32 percent of respondents from low-social-ranking communities favored it. In this case as well, commutation was a decisive factor. Those who commuted tended to favor the proposal. Since more high-social-ranking individuals than low-social-ranking individuals are commuters (blue collar workers tending to be employed in the community in which they reside or in adjacent Suburban communities rather than in the central city), the response may reflect self-interest or involvement more than social rank.

Respondents were asked whether they would favor area-wide government, assuming it would save money and help keep taxes down. Sixty-one percent of the Philadelphians favored the proposal, whereas only 18 percent of the Suburbanites did.

There was less of a division by place of residence on two other questions. Asked for their opinions on a regional authority for air-pollution control, 78 percent of central city residents responded favorably as compared to 64 percent of the suburbanities. Eighty-three percent of the Philadelphians and 70 percent of the suburbanites thought that non-residents who work in

[4] A more complete description of this sample and the results is found in: Charles S. Liebman, *Some Opinions of Business and Professional Leaders About Governmental Cooperation in the Philadelphia Metropolitan Area* (University of Pennsylvania, Fels Institute of Local and State Government, ditto, 1961).

Philadelphia should pay for Philadelphia services through such devices as a wage tax.

The last specific issue raised was the desirability of a regional park authority to maintain large parks open only to residents of the local areas. Fifty-six percent of Philadelphians favored regional parks and only 33 percent of the suburbanites did so.

Finally two general questions were posed. Respondents were asked whether they thought the Suburbs ought to cooperate more for the purpose of protecting themselves against the possibility of Philadelphia taking them over. Whereas 71 percent of the Philadelphians said no or thought there was no need for it, only 40 percent of the Suburbanites replied in the negative.

The last question asked whether, with respect to the present state of intergovernmental cooperation in the Philadelphia metropolitan area, respondents thought that Philadelphia and the suburbs should be merged, should cooperate more, that present cooperation was good enough, or that more cooperation might solve some problems but would lead to loss of suburban independence and consequently was not worth it. Seventy percent of the Philadelphians favored merger or more cooperation, and 30 percent favored the status quo. Among Suburbanites, 52 percent favored merger or more cooperation and 31 percent favored the status quo. The results indicate a surprisingly strong level of agreement among respondents when the referent is a general attitude rather than a specific proposal. In other words, the general question of more cooperation elicits a uniformly favorable response, although, as might be expected, Philadelphians are more favorable to it. An almost identical proportion of residents in both Philadelphia and the Suburbs are opposed to more cooperation. However, as was evident from prior questions, it is the nature of the cooperative activity which provokes major differences of opinion. With respect to the specific issues, all respondents favor cooperation where the services provided do not necessarily bring residents of the metropolitan area in closer contact with one another.

One may suggest that the differences in city and suburban responses are not at all surprising, that status does not eliminate self-interest, that there are substantive policy differences between Philadelphia and its suburbs, and that city and suburban elites interpret these differences in terms of a conception of self-interest that centers around place of residence. One could suggest that metropolitan areas provide a replica, in miniature, of the international field in which theories of "national interest" apply. Of course, then, place of residence would serve to distinguish opinions about metropolitan issues.

On the other hand, one may argue that opinions are not really formulated through rational calculations of self-interest, not even in the case of high-status business and professional leaders. What may be involved are deeper attitudinal differences that are perhaps only coincidentally related to place of residence. Philadelphians may just be more cosmopolitan than Suburbanites and so, in turn, may be more disposed toward a regional outlook. To test this possibility, business and professional leaders were given a local-cosmopolitan battery. While the results were interesting and in the expected direction, the need for categorizing and sub-classifying responses reduced the sample to dangerously few numbers. Accordingly, these results must be interpreted cautiously.

More of the Philadelphians were judged cosmopolitan than local and, conversely, more of the Suburbanites were judged local than cosmopolitan. While Suburban cosmopolitans were more regionally oriented than Suburban locals, when Philadelphia and Suburban cosmopolitans were compared, the former were still more predisposed toward regional action.

The significance of this survey lies in the repeated emphasis upon place of residence as a factor contributing to differences of opinion. Opinion differences are related to differences in attitude. Whether localism and cosmopolitanism enter into locational decisions, or are rather a product of location, city and Suburban residents of similar status do differ in attitude. The degree to which opinion differences also stem from rational calculations of self-interest is problematic, but to whatever extent they do, place of residence is certainly a factor in this calculation.

Rational self-interest is the basis for many of the proposals for metropolitan cooperation, if not reorganization. In many places, this appeal is directed toward business and professional elites through leadership programs and seminars that sometimes appear to be more an attempt to create a metropolitan elite or power structure than a recognition of existing leadership patterns. The assumption behind these efforts is often that reason can be effectively employed with elite groups, and that they will, by virtue of their status, appreciate appeals to regional rather than local self-interest. Our data suggest that high-status is not equivalent to regional consciousness and that, whether or not there is, or should be, a regional interest that appeals to all metropolitan elites, their opinions about general as well as specific aspects of metropolitan issues are significantly affected by place of residence.

Place of residence as an independent variable

Why might we expect residents of particular communities in a metropolitan area to possess differing attitudes or opinions? We have already seen that social status, an important determinant of the norms and values internalized by individuals, is spatially distributed in a consistent fashion. Persons of an equivalent position on a status scale occupy clustered places of residence. Persons of similar rank also tend to possess similar attitudinal attributes. Consequently, we may expect that the attitudes and opinions associated with class or status will also be spatially distributed in a consistent fashion. When a decentralized government structure is superimposed upon this distribution of attitudes, we can expect that the individual political units will reflect the dominant attitudinal characteristics of the constituency which they encompass.

However, the analysis of opinion differences by place of residence demonstrates that even holding constant for factors such as social rank, income, and place of work, respondents are still sharply divided by place of residence in many opinions about the metropolitan area. This suggests that place of residence is a causal factor in producing differences in opinions about governmental activity, and/or the choice of residence is intimately related to differences in attitude and political conviction. Although our evidence is not conclusive with respect to these possibilities, it is significant that choice of residence is not made randomly. The business and professional leaders were asked in what other municipalities they had considered residing before making their present choice. Only 19 percent of the Philadelphia residents and 26 percent of the Suburban respondents reported that they considered moving to any part of the metropolitan area other than the part in which they presently lived. Their range of choice was limited at the outset, although, given the high social rank of the respondents, the limitations must be thought of as self-imposed. We might expect, therefore, that residence in particular suburbs carries certain uniform value connotations and choice is made on this basis.[5]

Apparently, individuals in attempting to relate themselves to a specific social environment are likely to engage attitudes similar to those of the inhabitants of that environment. Identification with a particular community is achieved by adopting the dominant values of the community as one's own. This has the effect of reinforcing attitudinal differences among communities. Of course, there can be many forces operating to achieve and maintain homogeneity of opinion in any community. Conformity is enforced by various and subtle social mechanisms involving the acceptance or withholding of approval by one's neighbors. Homogenous attitudes are furnished social support which helps to reassure one of the wisdom of his views. Deviant opinions incite discord and deprive one of the self-confidence needed to face and overcome the possibility that one's neighbors consider his opinions foolish. The more important one's neighborhood social life is to him, the more dependent he is upon the acceptance and approval of persons living in proximity to him and the more the dominant attitudes of the community impinge upon his own.

Thus, in order to complete the description of the community as a force in shaping attitudes and opinions, we must move from social-area analysis into the study of social organization. Our data suggest the relevance of the community but cannot describe the process through which outlook is influenced by unique areal circumstances.

---

[5] For a development of this idea in specific economic terms see Charles M. Tiebout, "A Pure Theory of Local Expenditures," *Journal of Political Economy,* Vol. 64 (October, 1956), pp. 416-424.

Northern Referenda on Fair Housing:
The Response of White Voters

Harlan Hahn

Most whites are upset about current racial turmoil, confrontation, and the violence surrounding the pursuit of freedom and equality by black Americans. Although whites generally favor integration, at least in the abstract, their attitudes and behavior become much less favorable when blacks attempt to integrate all-white schools and neighborhoods. Through the use of the referendum, initiative, and recall, citizens at the local level frequently have the final say about the policies their local government can pursue. However, except for referenda on fair housing, Northern voters are rarely confronted with the task of making decisions on civil rights questions.

In order to realize their political objectives, blacks must frequently attempt to gain the support of white voters. Research on Atlanta, Georgia, for example, has documented the emergence of a fairly stable voting coalition between blacks and upper-class whites. However, the results of recent referenda provide little encouragement for those who feel that additional progress in the area of civil rights can be secured by circumventing the legislative process through direct appeals to the people. A notable exception to this would be in communities where blacks have a stable and cohesive electoral majority.

The research reported in this article by Harlan Hahn examines voting on fair housing and other local issues. Hahn also analyzes how the socioeconomic attributes of whites and their attitudes relate to their voting behavior on open housing and other civil rights questions. Evidence from previous studies suggests that racial prejudice and discrimination may be associated with decreasing social status. Hahn indicates the relationship appears more complicated than this, at least in the city of Detroit. Although urban working-class whites were opposed to fair housing, the greatest opposition came from the middle class and the least from the upper. Working-class whites were also more in favor of federal activity on behalf of school desegregation. Why do the various social-class groupings react in this manner?

At what point does conflict generated by civil rights issues have a decisive impact on local politics in the North? To the extent that controversy over such issues polarizes black and white segments of the urban electorate, conflict over minority rights has an extremely divisive effect on local politics. In many cities such a polarization has already occurred or is presently emerging.

However, data from this study indicate that disputes over civil rights need not have this polarizing effect, particularly when individuals of varying socioeconomic status hold different attitudes about such questions. It does mean that blacks and other minorities have to change their electoral coalition partners to match changes in the public policy issues over which they are concerned.

As you read this article, reconsider once again the major conclusion of the National Advisory Commission on Civil Disorders, that our nation is moving toward two societies—one black, one white, separate and unequal. The Commission made it quite clear, perhaps for the first time, that white, moderate, responsible America is where the trouble lies. As Tom Wicker of the New York Times *observed in his introduction to the Bantam edition of the report, "[the Commission] produced not so much a report on the riots as a report on America—one nation divided." White racism—the refusal of whites to accept blacks as human beings, social and economic equals, no matter how they might feel about Negro civil rights—is the root problem. "What white Americans," the report states, "can never fully understand—but what the Negro can never forget—is that white society is deeply implicated in the ghetto. White institutions created it, white institutions maintain it, and white society condones it." Thus, until the fact of white racism is admitted by the white society, it cannot conceivably be expunged, nor are we likely to see the commitment to material action on the unprecedented scale envisaged by the Commission that would shape a future compatible with the historical ideals of American society. "The major need is to generate new will—the will to tax ourselves to the extent necessary to meet the vital needs of the nation."*

For significant changes to take place in the position of blacks in our society, whites must demonstrate faith in the concept of Negro equality by indicating that they are truly willing for blacks, as blacks, to enter into a society that is both black and white. They must, therefore, demand that white institutions in both the public and private sectors do everything possible to further black equality—though there has been no significant, material response to the Commission's prescriptions. For as Stokely Carmichael and Charles Hamilton have observed in Black Power,

> *there is no black man in this country who can live "simply as a man." His blackness is an ever-present fact of this racist society, whether he recognizes it or not. It is unlikely that this or the next generation will witness the time when race will no longer be relevant in the conduct of public affairs and in public policy decision making. To realize this and to attempt to deal with it . . . puts one in the forefront of a significant struggle. If there is no intense struggle today, there will be no meaningful results tomorrow.*

Introduction

Although the exercise of political rights may provide an effective avenue to first-class citizenship, Negro Americans seldom have acquired sufficient electoral strength to achieve their objectives without additional support. As a

Reprinted from *The Western Political Quarterly*, vol. 21, no. 3 (September 1968), pp. 483-495, by permission of the University of Utah, copyright owners.

minority group in most Northern localities, Negro voters frequently have attempted to enlist the aid of whites in the pursuit of full equality and freedom. The efforts occasionally have been successful, but there have been growing recent indications that the responses of the white electorate to Negro political aspirations may reveal opposition and resistance rather than cooperation and support.

Political ties between Negroes and whites frequently have occupied a prominent role in the struggle for civil rights. In some Northern cities including Detroit, for example, Negro organizations and white reform groups or labor unions have joined to promote common political aims.[1] Yet, relatively little attention has been devoted to the positions on racial issues of various groups in the electorate. Perhaps fewer studies have been conducted on attitudes or voting behavior regarding questions of discrimination or prejudice in Northern than in Southern cities.[2]

The gains that have been secured in the urban areas of the North often have seemed to result from an aroused public conscience rather than from the vigorous exertion of white voters. Frequently, moreover, advocates of civil rights have encountered substantial resistance when proposals have been offered for equal educational opportunities, integrated housing, and impartial police practices. On such issues, the merged voting strength of Negroes and white liberals necessary to attain desired electoral goals often has been either lacking or ineffective.

In recent years, at least eleven Northern cities and states have held referenda on civil rights issues.[3] In eight of these cities or states, proposals in the interest of Negro citizens have been defeated by the voters. The results of recent ballots on specific issues of discrimination, therefore, have provided little encouragement for securing additional progress on civil rights by circumventing the legislative process through direct appeals to the people. Even more importantly, the strength of civil rights opponents in referenda has raised serious questions concerning the future course of local politics in the North.

Despite the importance of white reactions to the political goals of the Negro, little empirical data have been accumulated concerning the responses of white groups in Northern communities to issues concerning Negro rights. Some evidence has suggested that prejudice may be associated with decreasing socioeconomic status.[4] The association between social class and white

---

[1] James Q. Wilson, *Negro Politics* (Glencoe: The Free Press, 1960), pp. 28-31.

[2] See, for example, M. Kent Jennings and L. Harmon Zeigler, "A Moderates' Victory in a Southern Congressional District," *Public Opinion Quarterly,* 28 (Winter 1964), 595-603; Norman I. Lustig, "The Relationships Between Demographic Characteristics and Pro-Integration Vote of White Precincts in a Metropolitan Southern County," *Social Forces,* 40 (March 1962), 205-8; James W. Vander Zanden, "Voting on Segregationist Referenda," *Public Opinion Quarterly,* 25 (Spring 1961), 92-105.

[3] Sol Rabkin, "Civil Rights Initiatives and Referendum," unpublished paper presented at the California Conference on Fair Housing Laws, 1965.

[4] Hazel Gaudet Erskine, "The Polls: Race Relations," *Public Opinion Quarterly,* 26 (Spring 1962), 137-48; Herbert H. Hyman and Paul B. Sheatsley, "Attitudes Toward Desegregation," *Scientific American,* 211 (July 1964), 16-23; Paul B. Sheatsley, "White Attitudes Toward the Negro," *Daedalus,* 95 (Winter 1966), 217-38.

attitudes regarding Negroes, however, never has been totally clear or consistent.

An extensive investigation of national opinion data found that, when the effects of education were controlled, the relation between social status and prejudice often was reversed. Low status respondents generally were more likely to accept Negroes as neighbors, for example, than upper status whites at the same educational level.[5] Another survey in Detroit revealed no major differences between occupational groups in the distribution of tolerant attitudes, but it did disclose that white collar adults displayed fewer "strongly intolerant" feelings than blue-collar respondents.[6] Perhaps more important than the discrepancies in prior findings, however, has been the general absence of available information which would indicate how attitudes regarding civil rights might be translated into political activity or voting behavior on local issues.

Fortunately, some research has been conducted concerning voting on fair housing issues in California, which has been the scene of several referenda on this subject. One study of a 1963 referendum in Berkeley revealed that support for fair housing tended to be concentrated among males, renters, Democrats, persons with a postgraduate education, professional or semi-professional workers, and younger voters. On the other hand, 71 per cent of the home owners, 87 per cent of the Republicans, 81 per cent of the respondents with a high school education or less, and 85 per cent of the retirees or housewives opposed the fair housing ordinance.[7] While the results clearly were skewed by the peculiar educational characteristics of Berkeley which produced a higher proportion of advanced degrees than might be found elsewhere, the data suggested that opposition to fair housing proposals might be found among homeowners, Republicans, and the aged.

Another analysis of opinions regarding Proposition 14 in California found that voting on the referendum was strongly influenced by education, party affiliation, and regional differences within the state.[8] Although the seemingly inconsistent support for Proposition 14 provided by respondents with low educational attainments and Republicans tended to confirm the findings of the Berkeley study, the impact of regional factors on the distribution of attitudes in California underscored the importance of comparative analyses of white reactions to local fair housing controversies in the North.

While civil rights issues have arisen in numerous forms at various times and in different localities, the questions that have been submitted to the electorate in Northern referenda on fair housing have been remarkably

[5] Charles H. Stember, *Education and Attitude Change* (New York: Institute of Human Relations Press, 1961), pp. 81-87, 102-3, 133-37, 152.

[6] Bruno Bettelheim and Morris Janowitz, *Social Change and Prejudice* (Glencoe: The Free Press, 1964), p. 22.

[7] Thomas W. Casstevens, *Politics, Housing and Race Relations: The Defeat of Berkeley's Fair Housing Ordinance* (Berkeley: University of California, Institute of Governmental Studies, 1965), pp. 90-94.

[8] Raymond E. Wolfinger and Fred I. Greenstein, "The Repeal of Fair Housing in California: An Analysis of Referendum Voting," *American Political Science Review* (forthcoming).

similar. Proposition 14 to repeal the Rumford Act, which outlawed racial discrimination by real estate agents and the owners of apartment houses and homes built with public aid, appeared on the ballot in California as follows:

SALES AND RENTALS OF RESIDENTIAL REAL PROPERTY
Initiative constitutional amendment. Prohibits State, subdivision, or agency thereof from denying, limiting, or abridging right of any person to decline to sell, lease, or rent residential real property to any person as he chooses. Prohibition not applicable to property owned by State or its subdivisions; property acquired by eminent domain; or transient accommodations by hotels, motels, and similar public places.

A similar proposal submitted to the electorate in 1964 was the so-called Home Owners' Ordinance that appeared on the ballot in Detroit, Michigan, in the following form:

ORDINANCE DEFINING RIGHTS OF DETROIT RESIDENTS AND PROPERTY OWNERS.
The purpose and substance of the proposed Ordinance is as follows: to define certain rights of Detroit residents and owners of residential property to privacy, and to the free use, enjoyment and disposition of residential property; including the right of selection or rejection of any persons as tenants or purchasers; the free choice of real estate brokers and to require such brokers to follow the instructions of the owner; and to fix penalties for violations of the provisions of the Ordinance.

In both proposals, the principal emphasis was placed on the emotionally favorable concepts of the "rights" of the property owner and his "free choice" in the sale or rental of real estate. No mention was made either in the proposals or in the campaigns promoting them of race or of the civil rights legislation that prompted their submission to the electorate. Clearly, at least a minimal level of sophistication was required of voters in order to perceive the import of the proposals and their true meaning in contemporary politics.

While Proposition 14 was presented to the heterogeneous and dispersed California electorate, the Home Owners' Ordinance was placed before the large but somewhat more homogeneous voting population of Detroit. As a result, the referendum on the Home Owners' Ordinance in Detroit provided a unique opportunity for comparative analysis and for the examination of attitudes regarding the fair housing issue within a metropolitan community where important regional differences are excluded and where "the interplay of social stratification and . . . prejudice can be seen more precisely."[9] The purpose of this study will be to assess the impact of racial issues on patterns in local politics, to explore the association between socioeconomic status and attitudes on fair housing referenda, and to examine the effects of different civil rights questions at various social class levels.

[9]Bettelheim and Janowitz, *op. cit.,* p. 21

Voting on fair housing and local issues

In 1964, voters in the city of Detroit were presented with an unusual number of questions containing important civil rights implications. On the ballot at the primary election on September 1 were several issues and contests that had major consequences for race relations and local politics. The primary nomination that probably attracted the most attention was the victory of Congressman John Dingell, who was identified with a favorable record on Negro rights, over Congressman James Lesinski, the only Northern Democrat who had voted against the Civil Rights Act of 1964.[10] Perhaps equally significant, however, were the referendum results and the selection of a pair of candidates for the Detroit Common Council at the same election.

While civil rights advocates in Detroit were encouraged by the nomination of Congressman Dingell, they suffered a substantial setback in the passage of the Home Owners' Ordinance. Although the ordinance subsequently has been declared unconstitutional, the electoral success of the measure, which was promoted by an organization called the Greater Detroit Home Owners' Council, represented a major triumph for the forces in Detroit opposed to the movement of Negroes into predominantly white neighborhoods of the city. Another referendum which was decided in the same election resulted in the rejection of a proposed bond issue for the Wayne County public schools. Simultaneously, Detroit voters nominated Jackie Vaughn III, a Negro, and Thomas L. Poindexter, leader of the home owners' organization and principal author of the ordinance, as candidates for the city council. Racial considerations, therefore, probably played a significant role in at least two of the three major controversies at the primary election.

The general election on November 3, 1964, also yielded a number of seemingly inconsistent results which were of major significance to the cause of Negro rights. While Detroit voters expressed an overwhelming preference for Lyndon Johnson rather than Barry Goldwater, another member of Congress who had opposed the Civil Rights Act, they also elected Poindexter to the city council over Vaughn. At the same time, voters decided the closely fought competition between Republican George Romney and Democrat Neil Staebler for governor of Michigan; and they rebuffed a proposal to introduce the so-called Massachusetts ballot that would arrange candidates by the offices they were seeking rather than by party columns.

To assess the political configurations and voting patterns that existed in Detroit, the election returns from the 1,099 precincts in the city were examined and Pearsonian coefficients of correlation were computed between the percentages of the vote by precinct on the major contests of the 1964 elections. The results of this analysis revealed that support for the Home Owners' Ordinance was highly related to Republicanism, the choice of Poindexter for the city council, and opposition to the school bond proposal.

[10]Harreld S. Adams, "The Dingell-Lesinski 1964 Primary Race," *Western Political Quarterly*, 19 (December 1966), 688-96.

Predictably, perhaps, the highest associations with the vote for the Home Owners' Ordinance were found in the vote for Poindexter in both the primary (+.95) and the general election (+.96). In addition, electoral support for the ordinance was related to both the Goldwater vote (+.73) and the Romney vote (+.72). Perhaps most striking, however, was the high association between the vote for the Home Owners' Ordinance and the vote in opposition to the school bond proposal (+.87).

Significantly, elections that revolved about implicitly racial issues yielded higher associations with balloting on the school bond proposal than partisan campaigns or other referenda. While opposition to the school bonds was related to the Goldwater (+.54) and Romney (+.53) votes as well as to the vote for the Massachusetts ballot (+.48), the Poindexter vote in the primary (+.84) and general (+.85) elections revealed the strongest relationships with the vote against the school bond issue. The larger the vote by precinct opposing the school bonds, the greater was the vote for Poindexter and the Home Owners' Ordinance.

Apparently the vote in opposition to fair housing, as reflected by preferences for the Home Owners' Ordinance, attracted the opponents of other local issues. Although the campaign to defeat the ordinance was endorsed by many prominent religious, labor, and civic spokesmen in Detroit, the combined efforts of numerous leaders were insufficient either to stem the tide of the home owners' movement or to secure the adoption of the school bond proposal. Unlike other Northern cities, such as New York, Boston, and Chicago, Detroit had enjoyed a relative lack of notoriety as a center of civil rights agitation over educational policies by 1964. Yet the data suggest that there was a close association between the vote against the school bonds and the vote in support of the Home Owners' Ordinance. In part, the difficulty of persuading voters to reject a measure that might promote housing discrimination may have been related to the broader problem of securing voter acquiescence in programs to extend and improve public services.

Since the analysis of voting returns, even from relatively small and homogeneous precincts, might not have reflected precisely the behavior of individuals,[11] a separate investigation was undertaken in Detroit to identify the characteristics and sources of support for the Home Owners' Ordinance. A survey of 342 adults in Detroit was conducted in the spring of 1965 to examine attitudes on local political issues. Respondents were chosen by a replicate systematic sample of registered voters in 22 randomly selected precincts in all areas of the city. Although the sampling procedures were designed to insure an adequate cross-section of Detroit electors, the population was confined to registered voters because several questions concerned prior voting behavior.

The results of the survey tended to confirm the finding that attitudes in Detroit on the Home Owners' Ordinance and the school bond issue were highly interrelated. Most of the voters who stated that they had opposed the

[11]W. S. Robinson, "Ecological Correlations and the Behavior of Individuals," *American Sociological Review,* 15 (June 1950), pp. 351-57.

school bond proposal also disclosed that they had supported the Home Owners' Ordinance. Only 14.1 per cent reported voting against both referendum proposals. Among the respondents who offered an opinion on the two propositions, 73.4 per cent of the voters who opposed the Home Owners' Ordinance also expressed approval of the school bond plans. On the other hand, 61.1 per cent of the opponents of the school bonds were favorable to the ordinance.

In large measure, however, the close association between positions on the two issues seemed to reflect differences between Negro and white voters. Among Negroes, whose representation in the sample accurately reflected the racial composition of the city, 86.2 per cent reported that they had favored the school bonds and more than two-thirds stated that they had opposed the somewhat misleading Home Owners' Ordinance. Conversely, white voters supported the ordinance by 68.2 percent and rejected the school bond proposal by a somewhat smaller margin. While the movement for the Home Owners' Ordinance seemed to produce electoral divisions that were present on other issues as well, voting on the referendum questions was highly related to the racial characteristics of the electors.

Since voting behavior on the referenda seemed to reflect a basic cleavage between Negroes and whites, primary attention was directed at the dominant white voters who provided the principal opposition to fair housing as well as to other local issues. Among whites, the survey data also seemed to correspond with the results of the voting analyses. In a trial heat for mayor, as an example, 59.8 percent of the respondents who endorsed the incumbent Jerome P. Cavanagh favored the Home Owners' Ordinance, but 86.7 per cent of the small band of voters who preferred Councilman Poindexter reported that they supported the ordinance. Apparently the popular following that was generated by the home owners' movement stimulated relatively consistent support for the ordinance that bore its name.

Even more striking, perhaps, was the fact that approval of the Home Owners' Ordinance seemed to be related to dissatisfaction with the Detroit city government. While 63.6 per cent of the respondents who evaluated government in Detroit as very good or good favored the ordinance, 76.1 per cent of those who thought the city government was fair or poor endorsed the measure. The strongest opposition to fair housing, therefore, was evident among the white voters, including adherents of the home owners' movement, who resisted the adoption of other municipal proposals such as the school bond plans and who revealed dissatisfaction with the political activities of the city.

Socioeconomic status and positions on fair housing

While attitudes shaped by local factors clearly were related to positions on the Home Owners' Ordinance, opinions regarding fair housing may have reflected basic characteristics. In particular, the socioeconomic attributes of white voters may have had a profound impact on their preferences concerning fair housing and other civil rights questions. Since the referenda on the Home Owners' Ordinance and Proposition 14 were essentially similar, a rare opportunity for a comparative analysis to test such speculation was provided by survey data from both Detroit and California.[12]

Table 1 reveals the percentage of white voters in Detroit and California who supported and opposed the Home Owners' Ordinance and Proposition 14, respectively, by various demographic characteristics. In general, white electors in Detroit gave slightly more support to the Home Owners' Ordinance than their counterparts in California provided for Proposition 14. Yet, the data reveal striking similarities. Within all of the categories, the proportion of voters who supported or opposed the Home Owners' Ordinance and Proposition 14 stand in roughly the same relationship at each level in the results from both Detroit and California.

Table 1.   Characteristics of white voters and positions on the Home Owners' Ordinance in Detroit and Proposition 14 in California, 1964

	Home Owners' Ordinance support (Detroit)		Proposition 14 support (California)	
	Per Cent	*No.*	*Per Cent*	*No.*
Age				
21–29 years	66.7	21	63.6	154
30–39 years	62.1	29	59.9	192
40–49 years	73.7	38	58.3	199
50–59 years	63.2	38	57.5	134
60 or more years	70.2	47	61.9	126
Home ownership				
Owns	67.9	134	57.5	574
Rents	76.7	30	67.1	231
Party identification				
Democrat	63.6	121	56.7	333
Republican	82.1	39	64.9	450
Education				
0–8 grades	62.8	43	67.1	84
Some high school	66.7	39	64.8	105
High school graduates	76.9	39	61.9	265
Work beyond high school	71.7	46	60.5	286
College degree	50.0	12	48.4	64
Income				
Lower and lower middle	68.0	46	60.7	135
Middle	78.7	47	63.1	520
Upper middle	75.6	45	52.1	119
Upper	48.0	25	40.6	32

[12] The California data were based on a probability-quota sample survey of registered voters conducted by the Field Research Corporation in October 1964. The author wishes to express his gratitude to Thomas F. Pettigrew and J. Michael Ross of Harvard University for furnishing the California data and for granting permission to incorporate them in this study.

The data from the surveys in both areas tended to confirm some findings and to confute the generality of other conclusions from the few prior studies that have been conducted on fair housing referenda. Unlike the results from Berkeley, for example, neither the evidence from Detroit nor California seemed to sustain the contention that opposition to fair housing was associated with increasing age. No discernable or consistent pattern was apparent in the relationship between age and positions on either the Home Owners' Ordinance or Proposition 14.

In addition, the surveys in Detroit and California did not tend to substantiate the claim, also derived from information collected in Berkeley, that renters would be more likely to favor fair housing than home owners. Surprisingly, perhaps, both sets of data in Table 1 indicated that renters expressed somewhat stronger approval of the Home Owners' Ordinance and Proposition 14 than home owners. Intuitive support for the latter finding, however, can be provided by recalling that both propositions applied to the sale or rental of property and by examining the possible status anxiety of tenants. For an individual who has not yet achieved the station of home ownership and who may live in closer proximity to Negroes, the fear of Negro dominance in the neighborhood may be more severe than for home owners who are ensconced in the relative security of their domains. The maintenance of existing patterns of housing discrimination, therefore, may be more critical for a renter who has not yet satisfied the dream of owning his home than for a person who has attained his ambitions of property ownership.

One finding that was consistently discovered in all of the research that has been conducted on fair housing referenda thus far concerned the close association between party identification and voting behavior. In general, Republicans were more opposed to fair housing measures than Democrats. Whereas the political appeal to Republicans of arguments concerning "property rights" as well as party positions on fair housing legislation may have accounted for part of the relationship, the results did not tend to clarify the seemingly inconsistent patterns produced by partisan affiliations and socioeconomic status in regard to positions on fair housing.

The data from Detroit and California, however, did not sustain the implication of the Berkeley study that increasing support for fair housing was related to progressively more extensive educational backgrounds. In fact, the distribution of white attitudes in terms of education and income seemed to be curvilinear. Respondents whose educational careers ended with high school, or shortly thereafter, were more favorable to the Home Owners' Ordinance and Proposition 14 than persons who had never entered high school as well as those who had earned a college degree. Similarly, middle-income voters, as defined by arbitrary categories of family earnings, in both Detroit and California expressed more support for anti-fair housing measures than lower and lower middle-income or upper-income voters. The strongest opposition to the Home Owners' Ordinance and Proposition 14 was found among college graduates and upper-income whites, but resistance to both proposals also was greater among whites with lower incomes and educational attainments than among those in the middle ranges on both variables. The results of the surveys, therefore, did not tend to confirm the direct relationship between social class and tolerant attitudes that had been suggested by national surveys on racial issues unrelated to fair housing referenda. Perhaps the specific contexts of the referenda may have produced a different association between social class variables and attitudes regarding Negro rights than general survey questions.

In order to explicate the relation between social class and voting on fair housing, a special index of socioeconomic status was constructed from a three-dimensional matrix containing the traditional measures of social class, the income, education, and occupation of heads of households. The combined scores that culminated in the index also were employed to test the findings of national surveys concerning socioeconomic status and white attitudes on issues such as neighborhood and school integration. Table 2 reveals positions on the Home Owners' Ordinance and responses to standard Survey Research Center questions on neighborhood integration and federal support of school desegregation among whites in Detroit by socioeconomic status. The results generally did not corroborate the belief that the greatest intolerance to Negro rights might be found among white urban working class voters. While the opposition to fair housing expressed by middle class respondents still produced a slightly curvilinear distribution of positions on the Home Owners' Ordinance, the patterns of responses on the remaining two questions were extremely interesting, if somewhat contradictory.

Table 2. Socioeconomic status and positions on the Home Owners' Ordinance, neighborhood and school integration among white voters in Detroit, 1964

Socioeconomic status	Home Owners' Ordinance support		Government activity in school desegregation support		Neighborhood integration support	
	Per Cent	No.	Per Cent	No.	Per Cent	No.
Lower and lower middle	73.3	45	46.0	50	39.3	56
Middle	77.2	44	43.2	44	57.1	42
Upper middle	71.1	46	41.2	51	72.7	55
Upper	50.0	26	33.3	27	83.3	30

Lower and lower middle class whites voiced greater approval of federal activity in behalf of school desegregation than middle or upper class whites. At succeedingly higher socioeconomic levels, opposition to integration in the schools, which was generally greater in the Detroit survey than in other national studies,[13] tended to increase. The pattern was reversed, on the other hand, in regard to the question of residential integration. Lower and lower middle class whites were inclined to support the statement that "White people have a right to keep Negroes out of their neighborhoods if they want to," while middle and upper class whites increasingly endorsed the view that "Negroes have a right to live wherever they can afford to, just like white people."

[13] Sheatsley, *op. cit.*, pp. 219-21.

To some extent, the different patterns produced by the two questions may have been related to the emphasis that middle and upper class whites place on education and their relatively secure positions in the residential neighborhoods of the city. In addition, however, the contradictory tendencies yielded by the questions may have been affected by the knowledge and sophistication of the respondents. While neighborhood integration might have been a real and immediate concern of lower and lower middle class voters, school desegregation may have seemed to be a relatively remote and unimportant issue. For upper and middle class voters, on the other hand, the acknowledgement of opposition to residential integration may have been considered a less socially acceptable response than resistance to federal efforts to accomplish school desegregation.

To probe the extent to which varying levels of sophistication and information may have influenced voting on fair housing referenda, the positions on the Home Owners' Ordinance of respondents who took different positions concerning related civil rights issues were examined separately. Table 3 reports the voting choices of whites in Detroit on the Home Owners' Ordinance by socioeconomic status, controlling on attitudes regarding neighborhood and school integration. Although considerable caution must be exercised in the interpretation of these as well as other data in this study because of the relatively small number of cases in some of the cells, the patterns were exceedingly clear and consistent.

Table 3. Socioeconomic status and positions on the Home Owners' Ordinance by attitudes regarding neighborhood and school integration among white voters in Detroit, 1964

	School desegregation				
Federal government should support	*Per Cent*	*No.*	*Federal government should stay out of it*	*Per Cent*	*No.*
Lower and lower middle	72.1	11	*Lower and lower middle*	82.6	23
Middle	70.6	17	*Middle*	81.8	22
Upper middle	56.3	16	*Upper middle*	76.0	25
Upper	26.7	15	*Upper*	88.9	9

	Neighborhood integration				
Negroes have a right to live where they wish	*Per Cent*	*No.*	*Whites have a right to keep Negroes out*	*Per Cent*	*No.*
Lower and lower middle	57.1	14	*Lower and lower middle*	82.8	29
Middle	57.1	21	*Middle*	93.8	16
Upper middle	71.9	32	*Upper middle*	72.7	11
Upper	42.9	21	*Upper*	80.0	5

In general, voters who felt that the federal government should stay out of school desegregation and respondents who believed that whites have a right to keep Negroes out of their neighborhoods were more apt to support the Home Owners' Ordinance than whites who took favorable positions on civil rights. The strong association between support for the ordinance and intolerant positions on other questions concerning Negro rights at all socioeconomic levels suggested that the opponents of civil rights regarded the Home Owners' Ordinance in essentially racial terms. The results were basically similar to the conclusions reached by another study of attitudes concerning the Rumford Act and Proposition 14 in California: "The general finding that emerges is that people who are opposed to all forms of racial contact and to other civil rights legislation are very likely to be hostile to the Rumford Act, while the most 'extreme' minority on the the other side, those people who take the liberal position even when it is quite unpopular, are by no means as likely to be wholehearted supporters of the act."[14] In examining patterns of support for the anti-fair housing ordinance by socioeconomic status, however, some important differences became apparent in the positions taken by those who favored related civil rights issues.

Respondents who believed that the federal government should encourage school desegregation, and, to a lesser extent, those who felt that Negroes have a right to live where they wish, assumed different positions on the Home Owners' Ordinance by socioeconomic status. Among persons who favored federal enforcement of school desegregation, approval of the Home Owners' Ordinance tended to increase at progressively lower levels of socioeconomic status. The same pattern was not as clear among voters who favored residential integration, but upper class whites were more opposed to the Home Owners' Ordinance than lower or middle class respondents. Particularly interesting was the sharp reversal in positions on the ordinance exhibited by upper middle class whites who took a liberal or tolerant position on the broad question of neighborhood integration. Perhaps this finding also was related to the anxiety that the upper middle class may feel concerning the potential threat of integrated housing. Upper class whites probably were relatively protected from the possibility of Negro immigration into their neighborhoods, but upper middle class voters may have reacted to the greater vulnerability of their social and residential locations in the city. Although a large proportion of upper middle class whites agreed with the general proposition that Negroes should be allowed to live where they wish, they also expressed strong approval of the Home Owners' Ordinance.

While a majority of lower and middle class whites tended to support the Home Owners' Ordinance, regardless of their opinions concerning related civil rights issues, the voting behavior of upper class whites in particular was differentiated by their attitudes on neighborhood and school integration. Perhaps the differences may have been inspired by the relative sophistication of respondents at various socioeconomic levels. At least a minimal amount of knowledge was required of voters in order to understand that the issue of the Home Owners' Ordinance dealt with race relations as well as the "rights" of home owners and their "free choice" in the purchase or sale of real estate. The data indicated that increasing proportions of voters at ascending levels of socioeconomic status possessed such information. Apparently, for lower and lower middle class voters, the principal issues in the referendum were those which appeared on the ballot; but, as socioeconomic status increased, voters,

---

[14]Wolfinger and Greenstein, *op. cit.*

with the possible exception of the upper middle class whites who claimed that they favored neighborhood integration, seemed to reflect a growing appreciation of the broader implications of the proposition for race relations and civil rights.

Such an interpretation was at least partially supported by the findings of the study of attitudes regarding Proposition 14 and the Rumford Act in California. Data from the California Poll revealed that, while an overwhelming majority of the proponents of state fair housing legislation believed that the Rumford Act dealt with civil rights or equality in housing, 44 per cent of its detractors felt that it meant compulsion or a loss of freedom of choice. The authors concluded that "fair housing propaganda emphasizing the theme of racial discrimination is quite ineffective with many people, since their perspectives on the issue do not include acceptance of the fact of discrimination."[15] In addition, the Detroit survey indicated that the perceptiveness or sophistication of white voters regarding the fair housing question may have been closely related to socioeconomic status.

Summary and conclusions

Arguments against Negro rights seldom have been expressed solely as blatant prejudice. At various times, the doctrines of states' rights or freedom of choice in private associations have been promulgated either as ideological propositions or as guises for genuine bigotry. Except for the referenda on fair housing, however, Northern voters rarely have confronted the specific task of making decisions on the freedom to choose neighbors and associates or other related civil rights questions. While the results of the votes furnished little occasion for hope among civil rights advocates, the referenda have provided an unusual opportunity to assess white reactions to important controversies that affect Negro rights.

The conflict generated by civil rights related questions may have a decisive impact on local politics in the North. In Detroit, voting on the so-called Home Owners' Ordinance was closely associated with preferences on other local issues, such as school bonds, as well as both partisan and nonpartisan elections. Expressions of support for the ordinance also seemed to be related to dissatisfaction with the city government. In large measure, however, such findings seemed to reflect differences between Negro and white voters. While Negroes tended to support the school bond proposal, fair housing, and Negro or Democratic candidates, whites frequently took diametrically opposing positions. To the extent that conflict over anti-fair housing measures tends to polarize Negro and white segments of the urban electorate, controversies regarding Negro rights could have an extremely divisive, and perhaps a destructive, effect on local politics. The data indicated, however, that for a large proportion of white voters who took a favorable stand on other civil

[15] *Ibid.*

rights questions, the issues in the referenda on fair housing were not confined to Negro rights.

Support for the Home Owners' Ordinance and Proposition 14 was not limited to the urban working class which frequently has been cited as the principal source of white "backlash" against civil rights progress. In fact, major opposition to fair housing tended to concentrate in the middle ranges of the income and educational distributions. In addition, the data from Detroit and California failed to confirm the findings of a prior study in Berkeley that disapproval of fair housing was associated with increasing age or home ownership. One conclusion that did seem to emerge consistently from all of the studies of Northern referenda, however, concerned the strong association between opposition to fair housing and Republicanism. While the results may have been affected by partisan stands on legislation concerning housing discrimination, they also may have reflected the sentiments of lower and middle class Republicans who felt the primary issues in the referenda were property rights rather than rights for Negroes.

Different civil rights issues seemed to produce varying responses from white voters by socioeconomic status. While approval of federal enforcement of school desegregation diminished at ascending levels of socioeconomic status, support for neighborhood integration increased as social status was enhanced. The patterns may have been partially inspired by the proximity of racial problems, but they also may have been affected by the growing knowledge and sophistication of respondents at higher socioeconomic levels.

Conclusions drawn from surveys conducted in both Detroit and California indicated that the opponents of other civil rights issues also were strongly inclined to resist fair housing. Approval of the Home Owners' Ordinance in Detroit among whites who endorsed school and neighborhood integration, however, tended to vary according to socioeconomic status. With the striking exception of upper middle class whites who alleged that they favored residential integration, upper class voters who took a favorable stand on related civil rights questions were more likely to oppose the ordinance than their lower and middle class counterparts. Although the relatively small number of observations available at this stage of the analysis prevented extensive claims for the generality of the findings, the results were consistent with similar studies and with an interpretation of attitudes concerning civil rights questions that accounts for different perceptions and formulations of the issues.

Apparently a large proportion of the whites who voted on questions such as the Home Owners' Ordinance and Proposition 14 reacted primarily to the relatively superficial issue of free choice in the purchase or sale of property. At higher socioeconomic levels, however, voters who expressed tolerant attitudes on other issues seemed to be sufficiently sophisticated to recognize or reflect the broad inferences of such propositions for housing discrimination. The statement and the context of issues affecting Negro rights, therefore, may have a crucial impact on the outcomes of civil rights controversies. While the referenda on fair housing might have offered opportunities for the expression of prejudice, they also probably reflected the different social experiences that could have provided voters with an awareness or an appreciation of the fact of discrimination.

Planning and Politics: Citizen Participation in Urban Renewal

James Q. Wilson

Urban-renewal programs in the United States have made slow progress in recent years. The coalition of liberals, planners, mayors, businessmen, and real estate interests which originally pushed through many urban-renewal programs has begun to fall apart. In addition, citizen resistance to land clearance and renewal programs has been increasing. Citizen groups are also demanding that they be allowed to participate in shaping urban-renewal policy.

Wilson argues that if one's goal is urban renewal on any really large scale, then increased citizen interest in and antagonism toward land clearance and renewal have important implications. The more organized a lower-class neighborhood, the poorer the prospects for urban renewal. According to Wilson, this is primarily because most neighborhood groups are quite hostile toward most of the objectives of urban-renewal programs. While the whole notion of "planning with people"—that is, citizen participation in neighborhood renewal—may be an improvement over old-style urban redevelopment, which ignored or took little account of neighborhood interests, the enthusiasm with which this doctrine is being advocated may blur many of its important consequences, particularly for comprehensive city planning, future city development, and political controversy.

On the other hand, I would argue that citizen involvement and controversy has been very functional, primarily because it has brought about a reevaluation by professional planners, bureaucrats, and politicians of this particular approach to redeveloping physically blighted sections of our cities. Political conflict is not necessarily dysfunctional as Wilson seems to assume. The poor, who live in the most decaying areas of our nation's central cities, have the most to lose when extensive land clearance and redevelopment take place. They have good reasons for objecting to such programs, since it is they who will lose their homes and businesses, and who must find inexpensive housing, which is already in short supply in most central cities.

Wilson's extreme pessimism about the implications of increased citizen participation may be unwarranted, then, particularly if one views citizen participation and control as a means of bringing about changes in community institutions and programs which have been unresponsive to the needs of the poor. For example, Marilyn Gittell has argued that increased community control over several local school districts in New York City has not only stimulated wider local participation in the community and greater parent interest and involvement in school meetings and organizations, but also brought about significant changes in educational policy. She feels that the New York experience offers important evidence that suggests how the lack of participation by lower-class groups may simply reflect the failure of our political system to provide means, incentives, and channels for citizen participation and hence influence over policy decisions.

Should demands for community control, whether they be in the area of education or urban renewal, be viewed, therefore, as attempts to develop a new participatory system that seeks to restructure worn-out mechanisms for meeting traditional democratic goals? Should increased citizen participation also be viewed as one of the most realistic nonviolent means of bringing about political change in policy areas dominated by bureaucratic centralization, specialization, and professionalism?

Institutions unresponsive to citizen demands for policy change have been one of the primary causes of recent racial violence and conflict. It is therefore important that meaningful channels of communication be developed so that a dialogue among interested parties can take place on matters of public concern.

Introduction

Few national programs affecting our cities have begun under such favorable auspices as urban renewal. Although public housing was from the very first a bitterly controversial policy, redevelopment and renewal by contrast were widely accepted by both Democratic and Republican administrations and had the backing of both liberals and conservatives, labor and business, planners and mayors. Yet today, almost fourteen years after urban redevelopment was inaugurated as Title I of the the Housing Act of 1949, the program is beset with controversy and, what is even more dismaying to its supporters, lagging far behind its construction goals.

Reprinted from *Urban Renewal: The Record and the Controversy* by James Q. Wilson (ed.), pp. 407-421, by permission of the M.I.T. Press, Cambridge, Massachusetts. Copyright © 1966 by The Massachusetts Institute of Technology and the President and Fellows of Harvard College. A slightly revised version of an article which first appeared in the *Journal of the American Institute of Planners*, Vol. 29, No. 4 (November 1963), pp. 242-249.

Although there are nearly 944 federally-approved slum clearance and urban renewal projects scheduled for over 520 different communities, only a little more than half have proceeded to the point where the cities are authorized to begin assembling and clearing land. And most important, of all the projects authorized, only 65 have been completed.[1] In New York, the city which has been the most active in renewal programs of all kinds, all the publicly supported projects undertaken over the last quarter century cover less than one per cent of the city's surface.[2] Further, most of the projects completed can be found in or near the central business districts of cities rather than in residential areas, and they have often involved clearing, not slums, but deteriorating commercial and industrial structures.

Some of the reasons for the relatively slight accomplishments of urban renewal are not hard to find. Federally-sponsored projects such as renewal require dealing successfully with almost endless amounts of red tape; it has taken a long time for city governments and private developers to acquire the knowledge and experience required for this. Furthermore, even though the federal government pays most of the cost of assembling and clearing the land on which a project is planned, it is not always easy to find a private developer to whom the land can be sold.

An additional reason for slow progress in urban renewal is racial. Blighted areas are often Negro areas. The political and social problems involved in relocating Negroes in other areas of the city are often sufficiently formidable to make opposition to the renewal program as a whole very powerful.

But the most important reason for controversy and slow progress is the mounting disagreement over the methods and even the objectives of urban renewal. The coalition among liberals, planners, mayors, businessmen, and real estate interests which originally made renewal politically so irresistible has begun to fall apart. Liberals, who still see the rehabilitation of the central city as a prime goal for government, have begun to have doubts, particularly about redevelopment that involves wholesale clearance by bulldozers. They are disturbed by charges from many Negro leaders—whom liberals are accustomed to regarding as their natural allies—that liberals have aided and abetted a program which under the guise of slum clearance is really a program of Negro clearance. They have been disturbed and even angered by the elimination of whole neighborhoods, like the Italian West End of Boston by the reduction in the supply of low-cost housing to make way for high-cost housing built with federal subsidies; and by what they take to be the inhuman, insensitive, and unrealistic designs of some city planners. Jane Jacob's book, *The Death and Life of Great American Cities*, is expressive of one powerful segment of opinion in this regard.[3] The liberals are everywhere

[1] Housing and Home Finance Agency, *Housing Statistics: Annual Data*, April, 1962, p. 76.

[2] See Raymond Vernon, *The Myth and Reality of Our Urban Problems* (Cambridge, Mass.: Joint Center for Urban Studies of MIT and Harvard, 1962), p. 40.

[3] See also, as an example of liberal objections to renewal, Staughton Lynd, "Urban Renewal—for Whom?" *Commentary*, January, 1961, pp. 34-45. The consequences of urban renewal for the underprivileged in American cities are discussed in Peter Marris, "The Social Implications of Urban Redevelopment," *Journal of the American Institute of Planners*, XXVIII (August, 1962), 180-186.

demanding that redevelopment (that is, wholesale clearance) be abandoned in favor of rehabilitation—conserving as many existing structures as possible.

Mayors and other city officials in some cities (although not yet in all) have seen in these debates a sign that a program which began as "good politics" has turned into something which at best is difficult politics. When it seemed possible that a vigorous and ambitious mayor could place himself at the head of an alliance of liberals, planners, businessmen, and newspapers on behalf of restoring the central city, urban renewal became a top priority civic objective. An initial burst of enthusiasm greeted renewal in almost every city where the idea was broached. But after the first few projects were undertaken, the hidden political costs began to become evident. Voters who did not like being called slum-dwellers and who liked even less being forced out of their old neighborhoods began to complain. As the enthusiasm of the civic boosters began to wane, many mayors began to wonder whether they were going to be left alone on the firing line to answer for projects which the boosters had pushed them into in the first place.

What in many ways is the most interesting aspect of the controversy surrounding urban renewal is not the breakup of this coalition, however, but the growing resistance of neighborhoods to clearance and renewal programs. The growth of neighborhood resistance to urban renewal has been gradual and cumulative. Many of the earliest redevelopment projects were completed with little organized opposition. Somehow, however, people have learned from the experience of others, and today, in cities which have been engaged in renewal for several years, the planners often find prospective renewal areas ready and waiting for them, organized to the teeth. In Chicago, for example, the Lake Meadows redevelopment project met with relatively little organized indigenous opposition (although considerable opposition from forces outside the area). The Hyde Park-Kenwood project, undertaken a few years later, was greeted with considerably more opposition. Today, plans for the Woodlawn and Near West Side areas have been met with impassioned opposition from many of the residents of the neighborhoods involved. Similarly, the West End project in Boston had relatively little difficulty in dealing with people in the area; the project planned for Charlestown, begun some time later, has been—at least for the time being—stopped dead in its tracks by organized neighborhood opposition. Today, according to Robert C. Weaver, Administrator of the Housing and Home Finance Agency, "in nearly every major city in the country and many small cities there are heated debates over urban renewal projects that are underway or under consideration."[4]

Mr. Weaver might well be concerned over these debates, for federal policy requires local citizen participation in the formulation of local renewal plans before federal money can be spent on them. As he himself stressed on another occasion, "We mean [by citizen participation] not just a passive acceptance of what is being done, but the active utilization of local leadership and organization which can profitably assist in the community's efforts."[5]

[4] Quoted in *St. Louis Post-Dispatch*, February 27, 1963.
[5] From an address to the 50th Anniversary of the Family Service Association of America, New York City, November 13, 1961.

Local citizen participation on a city-wide basis is usually not difficult to obtain. "Civic leaders" representing various groups and interests in the community can always be assembled for such purposes. But getting the participation, much less the acquiescence, of citizens in the renewal neighborhood is something else again. Although federal law does not require participation at this level, the increased vigor of neighborhood opposition has made such participation expedient if not essential—particularly with the new emphasis on rehabilitation and self-help.

The Hyde Park-Kenwood experience

The fullest account we have of such participation is that found in the book, *The Politics of Urban Renewal,* by Peter H. Rossi and Robert A. Dentler. This study dealt with one neighborhood—Hyde Park-Kenwood in Chicago—which in many ways is remarkable if not unique. The site of the University of Chicago, it is heavily populated with University professors and business and professional people, all possessing an inordinate amount of education, experience, and skills, and all having a strong commitment to the community. From 1949 on, these people were organized into the Hyde Park-Kenwood Community Conference, a neighborhood group with a professional staff, dedicated to conserving the area against blight. Actual planning for the area was not, of course, done by this organization—that was beyond its resources—but by the planning staff of the University of Chicago and by various city agencies.

The Community Conference took a deep and continuing interest in the $30,000,000 urban renewal plan for the area and meticulously examined and discussed every part of it. Local and federal authorities judged the Conference to be an excellent example of genuine grass-roots participation in a major renewal effort. After the plan was finally approved by the Chicago City Council, it commanded widespread (although not unanimous) citizen acceptance, even though about 20 per cent of the buildings in the community were to be torn down.

In evaluating the work of this local citizens group, Rossi and Dentler conclude that the Hyde Park-Kenwood Community Conference played two important roles. First, it stimulated public awareness of the necessity and practicability of change and gave people confidence that something could be done to save their neighborhood. Second, the Conference managed to create a climate of opinion in which the actual planning was done, and, although it is impossible to tell exactly what impact this climate had on the planners, it is likely that the general mood of the community as articulated by the neighborhood organization influenced at least the most general goals that were embodied in the final plan.

But it is also important to note what the Conference did not do. According to this study, the organization did not play a crucial part in influencing the specific details of the plan. Instead, it created broad popular acceptance for a plan which was not entirely in keeping with its own objectives. Rossi and

Dentler conclude that the "maximum role to be played by a citizen-participation movement in urban renewal is primarily a passive one."[6]

Considering what I have said about the rising opposition of local neighborhoods to urban renewal, the acquiescence of this grass-roots organization seems to require explanation. In the narrowest terms, this support was due to the fact that the Hyde Park-Kenwood Community Conference represented that part of a very heterogeneous community which would ultimately benefit from renewal. The upper-middle-class professors, housewives, and business and professional men (both white and Negro) who made up the bulk of the Conference were mostly people who were going to remain in the community and whose peace, security, cultural life, and property values would probably be enhanced by a successful renewal plan. The persons who were to be moved out of the community and whose apartments and homes were to be torn down were usually lower-income Negroes who, with very few exceptions, were not part of the Community Conference.

But this narrow explanation in terms of self-interest is only partly true, for if low-income Negroes were not directly represented on the Conference they were often represented vicariously—at least in the eyes of the Conference members. Time and again the Conference, or leading members of it, pressed the city to provide middle- and low-income public housing in the renewal area in part to accommodate persons who would be displaced by demolition. The Conference was firmly committed to the idea of a multiracial community; some of its members were committed in addition to the idea of a multiclass community.

I would argue that this broader consideration was equally as important as the narrower one in explaining the positive and constructive role of the Conference. . . .

Social differences in citizen participation

Most neighborhoods which planners consider in need of renewal are not, however, like Hyde Park-Kenwood in Chicago and are not heavily populated with citizens like the ones who organized the Hyde Park-Kenwood Community Conference. Most renewal areas are likely to be low-income, often Negro sections, many of whose inhabitants are the opposite in almost every respect from the cosmopolitan elite of Hyde Park-Kenwood. Such people are more likely to have a limited time-perspective, a greater difficulty in abstracting from concrete experience, an unfamiliarity with and lack of confidence in city-wide institutions, a preoccupation with the personal and the immediate, and few (if any) attachments to organizations of any kind, with the possible exception of churches.[7] Lacking experience in and the skills

[6] Peter H. Rossi and Robert A. Dentler, *The Politics of Urban Renewal—The Chicago Findings* (New York: Free Press of Glencoe, 1961), p. 287.

[7] Cf. Seymour Martin Lipset, *Political Man* (Garden City, N.Y.: Doubleday & Co., 1960), chap. iv, and Robert Agger, *et al.*, "Political Cynicism: Measurement and

for participation in organized endeavors, they are likely to have a low sense of personal efficacy in organizational situations. . . . They are intimately bound up in the day-to-day struggle to sustain themselves and their families.

Such people are usually the objects rather than the subjects of civic action: they are acted upon by others, but rarely do they themselves initiate action. As a result, they often develop a keen sense of the difference between "we" and "they"—"they" being outside, city-wide civic and political forces which seek to police them, vote them, and redevelop them. It is quite natural that the "they" are often regarded with suspicion.

Although such people are not likely spontaneously to form organizations to define and carry out long-range very general civic tasks, it is wrong to assume that they are not likely to organize—or to allow themselves to be organized—for any purpose. The important thing is not that they are unorganizable, but that they can be organized only under special circumstances and for special purposes. Except for organizations which are in some sense extensions of the family and the church, lower-income neighborhoods are more likely to produce collective action in response to threats (real or imagined) than to create opportunities . . . They are likely to collaborate when each person can see a danger to him or to his family in some proposed change; collective action is a way, not of defining and implementing some broad program for the benefit of all, but of giving force to individual objections by adding them together in a collective protest. . . .

Community organization strategies

Among community organizers, two radically different strategies have been evolved to produce citizen participation under such circumstances. One recognizes the special character of depressed lower-income neighborhoods and seeks to capitalize on it. The most prominent and controversial exponent of this approach is Saul D. Alinsky, executive director of the Industrial Areas Foundation of Chicago. He has created in a lower-income, heavily Negro area near the University of Chicago an organization ("The Woodlawn Organization") built in large part upon the residents' fears of urban renewal. According to a recent account, "Alinsky eschews the usual appeals to homeowners' interests in conserving property values or to a general neighborhood spirit or civic pride—appeals, in his view, that apply only to middle-class neighborhoods." Instead, he "appeals to the self-interest of the local residents and to their resentment and distrust of the outside world."[8] . . .

Meaning," *Journal of Politics*, XXIII (August, 1961), 477-506. See also the vivid account of the culture of a lower-income Italian section of Boston in Herbert J. Gans, *The Urban Villagers* (New York: Free Press of Glencoe, 1963).

[8] Charles E. Silberman, "The City and the Negro," *Fortune*, LXV (March, 1962), 88-91. See also Saul D. Alinsky, "Citizen Participation and Community Organization in Planning and Urban Renewal," address before the Chicago chapter of the National Association of Housing and Redevelopment Officials, January 29, 1962.

By stimulating and focussing such fears, an organization is created which can then compel other organizations—such as the sponsors of an urban renewal project—to bargain with it. Often the only terms on which such negotiations are acceptable to the neighborhood organization are terms unacceptable to the sponsors of renewal, for they require the drastic modification or even abandonment of the renewal plan. When an organization is built out of accumulated fears and grievances rather than out of community attachments, the cost is usually the tearing up of any plans that call for really fundamental changes in the landscape. On the other hand, such an organization may be very effective in winning special concessions from city hall to remedy specific neighborhood problems.

Many, probably most, planners and community organization specialists reject Alinsky's tactics. To them, his methods produce and even exacerbate conflict rather than prevent it, alienate the neighborhood from the city as a whole rather than bring it into the normal pattern of civic action, and place a premium on power rather than on a co-operative search for the common good.

The alternative strategy of most community organizers is to stimulate the creation of neighborhood organizations which will define "positive" goals for their areas in collaboration with the relevant city agencies and in accord with the time schedule which binds most renewal efforts. In Boston, for example, efforts have been made to stimulate the formation of neighborhood associations which will provide citizen participation in (and citizen consent to) the plans of the Boston Redevelopment Authority (BRA). So far this strategy has had some success, but only in those areas where rehabilitation rather than clearance is to be the principal renewal tactic. In one Negro area, Washington Park-Roxbury, a middle-class Negro organization was given a BRA contract to help organize the neighborhood to discuss renewal plans calling for rehabilitation, spot clearance, and the construction of some lower-middle-income housing. The plans were approved. In Charlestown, an old Irish neighborhood, the original proposals of the BRA were rejected by a citizens' organization created by Action for Boston Community Development (ABCD), a city-wide welfare agency financed in part by the Ford Foundation. The BRA decided to modify the plans and dispense with the services of ABCD; the final plan, developed after protracted discussions between BRA planners and Charlestown residents, emphasized rehabilitation and was approved . . .

Implications for renewal programs

If one's goal is urban renewal on any really large scale in our cities, the implications of these observations are disturbing. The higher the level of indigenous organization in a lower-class neighborhood, the poorer the prospects for renewal in that area.

To say that the prospects are poorer does not, of course, mean that renewal will never occur with the consent of strong indigenous organizations in lower-class areas. But the difficulty is substantially increased, and a protracted, subtle, and assiduous wooing of neighborhood sentiment must first take place.[9] Perhaps this explains why, at least until very recently, most local urban renewal directors made no effort to encourage citizen participation except on a city-wide basis—with little or no representation from the affected neighborhood.[10]

In short, while the devotion of some planners today to the concept of "planning with people"—that is, citizen participation in neighborhood rehabilitation—may be an improvement over old-style urban redevelopment which ignored or took little account of neighborhood interests, the enthusiasm with which the new doctrine is being advocated blurs many important problems. The most important of these is that "planning with people" assumes on the part of the people involved a willingness and a capacity to engage in a collaborative search for the common good. The willingness is obviously almost never present when the persons involved will be severely penalized by having their homes and neighborhoods destroyed through wholesale clearance. Nor will that willingness be present when "rehabilitation" means, as it sometimes does, that the residents must at their own expense bring their homes up to standards deemed satisfactory to the renewal agency or have their homes taken from them. But what is less obvious is that it may not be present, even when such clearance is not envisaged, because of important class differences in the capacity to organize for community-wide goals. This means that middle-class persons who are beneficiaries of rehabilitation will be planned with; lower-class persons who are disadvantaged by rehabilitation are likely to be planned *without*.

The fact that some people will be hurt by renewal does not, of course, mean that there should be no renewal. There are scarcely any public policies which do not impose costs on someone. What it does mean is that planners might more frankly take such costs into account, weighing them against the benefits renewal may confer on individuals and the community. There is little except obfuscation to be gained from attempting to maintain, as the slogan "planning with people" implies, that urban renewal and perfect democracy are and always should be compatible; that not only can the city be revitalized, it can be revitalized with the consent of all concerned.

If we decide to try to obtain the consent of those neighborhoods selected for renewal, we had better prepare ourselves for a drastic reevaluation of the potential impact of that program. Adjusting the goals of renewal to the

[9] See the account of Alfred G. Rosenberg, "Baltimore's Harlem Park Finds 'Self-Help' Citizen Participation is Successful," *Journal of Housing,* XVIII (May, 1961), 204-209. The initial reaction in the neighborhood to a renewal plan was bitter and got worse for three years. Patient community organization managed to overcome some of this resistance after much effort.

[10] See the survey reported in Gerda Lewis, "Citizen Participation in Urban Renewal Surveyed," *Journal of Housing,* XVI (March, 1959), 80-87. Questionnaires returned by about half the local renewal directors in the 91 cities which had approved "workable programs" as of July 31, 1956, showed that "the residents of project areas . . . seem to be relatively uninvolved in urban renewal"; representation from these areas on citizens' committees dealing with renewal was "almost totally absent."

demands of the lower classes means, among other things, substantially reducing the prospects for assembling sufficiently large tracts of cleared land to make feasible the construction of dwelling units attractive to the middle-class suburbanite whom the city is anxious to woo back into its taxing jurisdiction. This, in turn, means that the central city may have to abandon the goal of recolonizing itself with a tax-paying, culture-loving, free-spending middle class and be content instead with serving as a slightly dilapidated way-station in which lower-income and minority groups find shelter and a minimal level of public services while working toward the day when they, too, can move out to a better life. That, of course, is in great part the function that at least the older central cities of this country have always performed, and until we run out of lower classes (a day unfortunately far in the future), that may be the function they must continue to perform.

Political effects

Not only does the question of citizen participation in urban renewal have important implications for the goals of planning and even for one's conception of the function of the central city; it also goes to the heart of a fundamental problem in the urban political process. Resolving this issue is not simply a problem in planning priorities, but in addition a problem in electoral politics.

American mayors today are faced with the problem of governing cities in which to a great extent the traditional sources of political power have been dispersed or eliminated. The old-style political machine is gone except in a very few big cities. Party organization generally is weak. Mayors must still assemble the power to govern but they can rarely do so today by relying on loyal party lieutenants who occupy the lesser city offices and who sit on the council. Instead, the mayor must try to piece together that power out of the support he can receive from city-wide interests, such as newspapers, civic associations, business organizations, and labor unions. Support from such sources, valuable as it is, does not always carry with it the assurance that the support of the rank-and-file voter will also be forthcoming. Average citizens have a way of not sharing (or sometimes not even knowing about) the enthusiasms of the top civic leadership.

To insure against this possibility, many "new-style" mayors are trying to build up new neighborhood associations and enter into relationships with old ones in order to provide themselves with a way of reaching the average voter and of commanding his support . . .

To the extent that these neighborhood associations are courted by mayors, they attempt to extract in return concessions on matters of city policy (such as street sweeping, garbage collection, or playground maintenance) which affect their areas. They see themselves as instruments for adapting the programs of an impersonal city bureaucracy to the various and often conflicting needs of neighborhoods. In a sense, they perform (for entirely different reasons, of course) the same function which the political machine once performed.

The neighborhood civic association is widely regarded as not only a new mechanism for representing citizen wants to the city bureaucracy, but a means of ending the political "alienation" of those citizens. Much has been written of late to suggest that a large and perhaps growing number of people are "alienated" from the American political process, but particularly from the political process in their communities. In Boston,[11] Cambridge,[12] Detroit,[13] Nashville,[14] upstate New York,[15] and various other places where studies have been made, the voters—usually (though not always) those with little income or education—feel, we are told, estranged from and even threatened by the political life of their cities. To the extent that this alienation exists (and the studies are not very precise on this), the neighborhood civic association is seen as an important way of giving the citizen a meaningful and satisfactory relationship with his community—a way, in short, of ending his "alienation."[16]

It is not yet clear, however, whether such neighborhood groups will provide a means whereby citizens overcome their "alienation" or whether they will simply provide a forum in which citizens can give expression to it. These groups, after all, are usually concerned about neighborhood, not city-wide, problems, and the member's attachment is often at most only to his immediate family and neighbors, not to the community as a whole. Neighborhood associations seek many goals in their dealings with city hall. Generally speaking, however, they want higher levels of community services but they oppose extensive physical changes in their areas, as would be caused by highway construction or urban renewal programs.

For city-wide officials, such as mayors and planners, the crucial problem is how to make attention to these neighborhood demands compatible with city-wide programs, almost all of which will, to some extent, impose hardships on some neighborhoods. The old-style political leaders who were bosses of city machines were not faced to the same degree with this problem. Whenever they could, they avoided the conflict between neighborhood and city by not proposing any extensive programs designed to appeal to city-wide

[11] Murray B. Levin, *The Alienated Voter* (New York: Holt, Rinehart & Winston, 1960), pp. 58-75. See also Murray B. Levin and Murray Eden, "Political Strategy for the Alienated Voter," *Public Opinion Quarterly*, XXVI (Spring, 1962), 47-63.

[12] See William A. Gamson, "The Fluoridation Dialogue: Is It An Ideological Conflict?" *Public Opinion Quarterly*, XXV (Winter, 1961), 526-37, and Arnold Simmel, "A Signpost for Research on Fluoridation Conflicts: The Concept of Relative Deprivation," *Journal of Social Issues*, XVII (1961), 26-36.

[13] Arthur Kornhauser, *Attitudes of People Toward Detroit* (Detroit: Wayne University Press, 1952), p. 28.

[14] E.L. McDill and J.C. Ridley, "Status, Anomia, Political Alienation and Political Participation," *American Journal of Sociology*, LXVIII (September, 1962), 205-213.

[15] Wayne E. Thompson and John E. Horton, "Political Alienation as a Force in Political Action," *Social Forces*, XXXVIII (March, 1960), 190-95 and Horton and Thompson, "Powerlessness and Political Negativism: A Study of Defeated Local Referendums," *American Journal of Sociology*, LXVII (March, 1962), 485-93.

[16] Cf. William C. Loring, Jr., Frank L. Sweetser, and Charles F. Ernst, *Community Organization for Citizen Participation in Urban Renewal* (Boston: Massachusetts Department of Commerce, 1957), pp. 232-238.

interests. When such programs were politically unavoidable, they resolved the inevitable conflict by "buying off" their neighborhood opponents. The bosses used the jobs, favors, and patronage which they controlled to enforce their wills on neighborhood political leaders and to compensate the neighborhood voters for their distress . . .

Citizen participation in urban renewal, then, is not simply (or even most importantly) a way of winning popular consent for controversial programs. It is part and parcel of a more fundamental reorganization of American local politics. It is another illustration—if one more is needed—of how deeply embedded in politics the planning process is.

Black Political Participation —> *written* 12/68

Jewel L. Prestage

In this selection, Jewel L. Prestage examines some of the factors that condition black political participation, particularly how the socialization process that blacks experience influences their political attitudes and behavior. First, Prestage makes it quite clear that because blacks have had a history of negative contacts with the larger white society, particularly its political, social, and economic institutions, they have a greater sense of personal alienation and political futility than do similarly located whites. Blacks also tend to place little trust in either national or local political institutions. However, not all blacks are equally alienated and distrusting. More affluent and better educated blacks are generally active supporters of existing institutions. This leads Prestage to conclude that black attitudes and perceptions may change quite drastically when "reality" changes.

Second, because many blacks have been excluded from participation in the political system as well as from sharing in the benefits of "the good life," Prestage raises the following question: Does such exclusion remove their obligation to obey and instead give rise to an obligation to disobey and revolt.

Third, she reiterates the conclusion of the President's Commission on Civil Disorders, which pointed out how white racism, that is, the racial attitudes and behavior of white Americans toward black Americans, has been largely responsible for the resort to militant protest and collective violence by black wrong

Americans. *If the race problem in America is to be solved, it must be solved by whites, for they created the problem and currently perpetuate it.* Although the Commission tells us little about how this can be done, Prestage indicates it may require a restructuring of the socialization process for blacks and whites if our commitment to democratic values is to be translated into actual practices.

Fourth, Prestage argues the Commission was essentially wrong when it implied that blacks were not seeking to change the American political system but merely attempting to gain full participation in it. She asks: Could it be that black rioters are simultaneously attempting to change the system and to gain full participation? Furthermore, would not full participation by blacks in itself represent a fundamental change in the system?

Fifth, some blacks are currently seeking to gain effective political power and influence over authoritative policy decisions. Given the magnitude of the needs of black people, however, does politics represent a viable means for ministering to these needs? If politics is relevant then what types of strategies will best serve the needs of the black community, North and South? If irrelevant, what are the alternatives?

James Q. Wilson, in Negro Politics, argues that black politics cannot be understood apart from the city in which it occurs. For example, the existence of a black machine in Chicago is dependent on the existence of a white machine. On the other hand, in Los Angeles and Detroit, where almost none of the elements of machine control exist, the politics of each city is characterized by ad hoc groupings which come into being in election years to elect good-government, economy-minded leaders, whose appeal must be based largely on personality, issues, and newspaper influence. When blacks participate in this kind of a political system, they do so at a very real disadvantage. Although published in 1960, Wilson's basic conclusion, derived from examining black politics in Chicago, Los Angeles, and Detroit, that political organization and leadership within the black community are shaped in large measure by the political organization of the city, is still basically valid today. One could also argue that the political strategies adopted by blacks in a particular city will be conditioned by the nature of that city's policy-making process, particularly the openness of the decision-making process, the responsiveness of its political institutions to demands for change, and the distribution as well as locus of political power.

The most important modification Wilson noted to his basic conclusion has to do with the time lag in the entry of blacks into positions of political influence. Powerful constraints work against black influence in civic and political affairs—race prejudice, class differences, geographic concentration, and a weak economic position. As a result, Wilson suggests that black influence over public policy decisions, at least in the cities he studied, has not grown in proportion to the number of black voters. As a result, black political leaders have not been very effective in bringing about changes in public policy. In recent years, increased fragmentation in the black community and the resulting inability of black leaders to organize their own people to collectively achieve political goals, coupled with the growing resistance of *whites to black demands for change, have served to further inhibit attempts by blacks to gain power and influence. Although advocates of black political power are now attempting to increase the influence of the black community at both the national and local levels, many of the same obstacles which historically stood in the way of achieving such influence are still operative.*

Whatever the political strategies adopted by blacks, then, whether coalition politics, separate black political parties, demonstrations, sit-ins, violence, or what, they must be devised with the following considerations in mind, according to Prestage:

1. *Political strategy for blacks must take into account the difficulties inherent in being a numerical minority.*
2. *Any therapeutic strategy must acknowledge the reality that blacks in the ghetto already constitute a separate society.*
3. *Given the general apathy and insensitivity of whites toward problems of blacks, it seems reasonable to suggest that any meaningful gains for blacks will come as a result of demands supported by evidence of black willingness to cause great inconvenience to the community at large if these legitimate demands are ignored.*
4. *It may be that the Commission placed too much emphasis on the material aspects of the black man's problem (and the material aspects are indeed important) and did not devote enough attention to such psychological needs as dignity, self-respect, and identity, and to the relationship between these needs and any corrective actions, political or otherwise.*
5. *It would seem that black strategy and black strategists ought not be constrained to political alternatives if these alternatives prove to be mostly disfunctional for blacks.*
6. *The problems faced by blacks are of such magnitude that the correctives must be radical.*

Prestage has presented an extremely useful analysis of some of the factors which may affect black participation in the policy-making process. She implies, and I think rightly so, that the lack of responsiveness of white institutions to the legitimate demands of black Americans has forced them to resort to more militant forms of protest, that is, unconventional political participation. If political institutions continue to be unresponsive in the future, what political strategies are blacks likely to adopt? How effective do you think such strategies will be in bringing about policy change?

Reactions to the *Report of the National Advisory Commission on Civil Disorders*[1] have been widespread and varied, both in terms of their sources

Reprinted from the *Social Science Quarterly*, vol. 49, no. 3 (December 1968), pp. 453-464, by permission of the publisher and author.

[1] National Advisory Commission on Civil Disorders, *Report of the National Advisory Commission on Civil Disorders* (New York: Bantam Books, 1968) (hereafter referred to as the *Report*).

and their content. This discussion is essentially an effort to relate the *Report* to some of the theories and research findings in three areas of political science; namely, political socialization, democratic theory, and black political strategy. Any value accruing from this effort will probably be the results of the questions raised rather than directions or answers given.

Political socialization

One of the comparatively new and rapidly developing fields of inquiry for political scientists is political socialization.[2] Greenstein defines political socialization as ". . . all political learning formal and informal, deliberate and unplanned, at every stage of the life cycle, including not only explicitly political learning but also nominally nonpolitical learning which affects political behavior . . . ."[3]

Because political socialization has been interpreted as involving "all political learning at every stage of the life cycle" the dimensions of research possibilities are indeterminable.[4] It has been suggested that a full-blown characterization of political socialization would include classifications of: (1) who learns, (2) what is learned, (3) the agents of political socialization,

---

[2] Major studies include Herbert Hyman, *Political Socialization* (Glencoe, Ill.: The Free Press, 1959); Fred Greenstein, *Children and Politics* (New Haven: Yale University Press, 1965); Gabriel Almond and Sidney Verba, *The Civic Culture* (Boston: Little, Brown and Company, 1965); Lewis Froman, "Personality and Political Socialization," *Journal of Politics,* 23 (May, 1961), pp. 341-352; David Easton and Robert D. Hess, "Youth and the Political System" in Seymour M. Lipset and Leo Lowenthal, eds., *Culture and Social Character* (New York: The Free Press of Glencoe, 1961), pp. 226-251; David Easton and Robert D. Hess, "The Child's Political World," *Midwest Journal of Political Science,* 6 (Aug., 1962), pp. 229-246; Roberta Sigel, "Political Socialization: Some Reactions on Current Approaches and Conceptualizations," paper read at the 62nd annual meeting of the American Political Science Association, New York City, September, 1966; John J. Patrick, "Political Socialization of American Youth: A Review of Research with Implications for Secondary School Social Studies," High School Curriculum Center in Government, Indiana University, Bloomington, Indiana, March, 1967, mimeographed paper; Jack Dennis, "Major Problems of Political Socialization Research," *Midwest Journal of Political Science,* 12 (Feb., 1968), pp. 85-114.

[3] Fred Greenstein, "Political Socialization," in *International Encyclopedia of the Social Sciences* (New York: Crowell-Collier Macmillan Publishing Company, 1968); Roberta Sigel defines political socialization as "the gradual learning of the norms, attitudes, and behavior accepted and practiced by the ongoing political system." See Roberta Sigel, "Assumptions About the Learning of Political Values," *Annals of the American Academy of Political and Social Science, 361 (Sept., 1965), pp. 1-9;* of political socialization, Gabriel Almond writes, "What do we mean by the function of political socialization? We mean that all political systems tend to perpetuate their cultures and structures through time, and that they do this mainly by means of the socializing influences of the primary and secondary structures through which the young of the society pass in the process of maturation." See Gabriel Almond and James Coleman, eds., *The Politics of Developing Areas* (Princeton, N.J.: Princeton University Press, 1960), p. 27.

[4] The varied nature of such studies may be discerned from the foci of the following studies: Philip E. Converse and George Dupeux, "Politicization of the Electorate in France and the United States," *Public Opinion Quarterly,* 26 (Spring, 1962), pp. 1-23; Fred Greenstein, "Sex-Related Political Differences in Childhood," *Journal of Politics,* 23 (May, 1961), pp. 353-371; M. Kent Jennings and Richard Niemi, "Family Structure and the Transmission of Political Values," *American Political Science Review,* 62

(4) the circumstances of political socialization, and (5) the effects of political learning.[5]

An understanding of the political socialization function is essential to the understanding and analysis of any political system, and the stability and continued existence of a political system depend, in no small measure, on the extent to which the citizenry internalizes political norms and attitudes supportive of the system.[6] Political socialization, then, is induction into the political culture,[7] the means by which an individual "comes to terms" with his political system. The *Report* would seem to suggest that "coming to terms" is an especially traumatic experience for black people in America.

Examined in the context of current findings of political socialization research, the *Report* gives rise to several crucial concerns. The nature of these concerns is implicit in the observations which follow.

First, the political world of American blacks is so radically different from the political world of American whites that it might well constitute a "subculture" within a dominant or major culture. Even though there has been a great volume of writing and research on political socialization, very little has been directed to political socialization of American blacks.[8] The studies suggest that black people tend to relate rather differently to the political system and have a far greater sense of personal alienation and political futility than do similarly located whites.[9] Ghetto residents, like other citizens, tend to

---

(March, 1968), pp. 169-184; Heinz Eulau, William Buchanan, Leroy G. Ferguson, and John C. Wahlke, "The Political Socialization of American State Legislators" in John Wahlke and Heinz Eulau, eds., *Legislative Behavior: A Reader in Theory and Research* (Glencoe: The Free Press, 1959); Edgar Litt, "Civic Education, Community Norms and Political Indoctrination," *American Sociological Review,* 28 (Feb., 1963), pp. 69-75.

[5] Fred I. Greenstein, *Children and Politics* (New Haven: Yale University Press, 1965), p. 12.

[6] Almond and Coleman, *Politics of Developing Areas,* p. 31.

[7] Almond and Verba state, "When we speak of the political culture of a society, we refer to the political system as internalized in the cognitions, feelings and evaluations of its population." Almond and Verba, *The Civic Culture,* p. 13.

[8] See Dwaine Marvick, "The Political Socialization of the American Negro," *Annals of the American Academy of Political and Social Science,* 361 (Sept., 1965), pp. 112-127; and Bradbury Seasholes, "Political Socialization of Negroes: Image Development of Self and Polity" in William C. Kvaraceus, ed., *Negro Self-Concept: Implications for School and Citizenship* (New York: McGraw-Hill Book Company, 1965), pp. 52-90.

[9] See Dwaine Marvick, *ibid.* When Negro respondents were matched with whites (counterpart groups) having similar socioeconomic characteristics, Negroes expressed considerably less confidence that they would receive "equal treatment" from governmental officials or from the police.

In a study of Gary, Indiana, James T. Jones found that more Caucasian children than Negro children agreed that "A person owes his first duty to the community and the nation and next to himself." James T. Jones, *Political Socialization in a Midwestern Industrial Community* (Ph.D. diss., Department of Political Science, University of Illinois, 1965), p. 228.

Roberta Sigel found that Negro children were considerably more upset and worried than white children over the assassination of President Kennedy. These differences maintained themselves even when partisanship and socioeconomic status were taken into account. Roberta Sigel, "An Exploration into Some Aspects of Political Socialization: School Children's Reaction to the Death of a President" in Martha Wolfenstein and Gilbert Kilman, eds., *Children and the Death of a President* (Garden City: Doubleday and Company, 1965), pp. 34-69.

formulate their attitudes toward the political system largely on the basis of their contact with the system. For example, ghetto blacks believe that police brutality and harassment occur in their neighborhoods to a much greater extent than whites believe that violations occur in white areas. In Detroit, for example, 91 per cent of the rioters believed anger at police had something to do with causing the riots.[10] It is not surprising that the policeman, primarily a symbol of law and order in white neighborhoods, is for ghetto people a symbol of injustice, inhumanity and of a society from which they are alien as well as alienated. Studies of white policemen assigned to ghetto areas indicate that black fears and reservations about the police may not be entirely imaginary.[11] Bobby Richardson, writing about police brutality in New Orleans, states "... brutality, man, is a state of mind, not just a whipping with a billy, although plenty of the brothers get beat up on. They know that brutality is the way you are treated and the way a policemen will arrest one man and not another. And the way he will talk to you and treat you. Brutality is just an extension of prejudice, and it is easier to brutalize one man than it is another."[12]

Similarly, blacks tend to be less trusting of their political systems (local and national) than do their white counterparts.[13] Surveys done in Newark reveal that both "rioters" and "non-involved" blacks have a high distrust of local government with 44.2 per cent and 33.9 per cent, respectively, reporting they could "almost never" trust the Newark government to do what is right. In Detroit, 75 per cent of the rioters and 58.7 per cent of the non-involved felt that "anger with politicians" had a "great deal" or "something" to do with causing riots.[14]

Especially crucial for students of political socialization is the proportion of blacks, rioters and non-involved, who indicated that the country was not worth fighting for in a major world war. In Detroit the percentages were 39.4 for rioters and 15.5 for the non-involved, while the Newark survey revealed these sentiments on the part of 52.8 per cent of the rioters and 27.8 per cent of the non-involved.[15] These figures are striking, especially those related to the non-involved blacks, and would seem to indicate substantial disaffection among blacks. Similar results were ascertained in a recent study of black

[handwritten margin note: Take issue w/ interpretations]

[10] *The Report*, p. 178.

[11] See the *Report*, p. 306. From a study by Albert Reiss, director of the Center for Research on Social Organization, University of Michigan, "In predominantly Negro precincts, over three-fourths of the white policemen expressed prejudice or highly prejudiced attitudes toward Negroes. Only one per cent of the officers expressed attitudes which could be described as sympathetic towards Negroes. Indeed, close to one-half of all the police officers in predemoninantly Negro high crime rate areas showed extreme prejudice against Negroes. What do I mean by extreme racial prejudice? I mean that they describe Negroes in terms that are not people terms. They describe them in terms of the animal kingdom."

[12] Robert Richardson, "Every Black Man is My Brother," *New Orleans Magazine* 2 (June, 1968), pp. 30-31; and see also Eldridge Cleaver, "Black People and Police Routine," *Black Politics: A Journal of Liberation* 1 (April-May, 1968), pp. 33-36.

[13] Marvick, "Political Socialization of the American Negro," *loc. cit.*

[14] *The Report*, p. 178.

[15] *Ibid.*

youth in Atlanta where 49 per cent took a negative stance on the proposition, "Black Americans should be proud to be fighting in Viet Nam."[16]

Given the above data, it is interesting to note the Commission's contrasting finding that rioters were not seeking to change the American system, but merely to gain full participation in it. However, the deep disaffection from the system by blacks and the continued reluctance of the system to accept blacks as full participants might lead one to question the Commission's conclusion. Could it be that black rioters were attempting to change the system and to gain full participation simultaneously? Or, more directly, would not full participation by blacks in itself represent a fundamental change in the system? Such reservations regarding the goals of rioters receive some support from the recent report of Mayor Richard Daley's committee to study Chicago's riots of April, 1968. This committee reported a growing feeling among blacks that "the existing system must be toppled by violent means." This feeling was said to have its strongest expression among black teenagers, where there is "an alarming hatred for whites." Such feelings were found to be based on the attitude that "the entire-existing political-economic-educational structure is anti-black."[17]

Assuming the blacks of the ghetto have internalized the American dream of freedom, equality and justice, there is small wonder that "coming to terms" with the system has produced deep alienation, frustration and despair. Throughout the history of this country, blacks have, for the most part, been excluded from full benefits of this society. The fact that the rest of the country has experienced progressive affluence (flagrantly paraded before blacks through mass media) while blacks became poorer is a story much too familiar to belabor here. In the face of "the American dream" of equal opportunity and abundance, blacks have been forced to live "the American nightmare" of poverty, discrimination and deprivation. Despite some progress, American blacks continue to live in this "credibility gap" and part of the results are distrust, estrangement and violence.[18]

Data from the Detroit survey indicate that all blacks included in the survey were not equally alienated and distrusting. Least alienated were the "counter-rioters," a major portion of whom (86.9 per cent) regarded the country as worth fighting for.[19] Of this group, 88.9 per cent felt that getting what you want out of life is a matter of "ability" rather than "being in the right place" as compared to 76.9 per cent of the rioters and 76.1 per cent of the non-involved.[20] The typical counter-rioter was described as an active

[16] James E. Conyers and William Farmer, *Black Youth in a Southern Metropolis* (Atlanta: Southern Regional Council, 1968), p. 13.

[17] "Survey of Chicago Riots Reveals 'Black Racism,' " *Baton Rouge Morning Advocate,* August 8, 1968, p. 12-D.

[18] "Characteristically, violence has been employed by those groups in the political system which feel that they have least to lose from chaotic upheaval, and which face an enormous gap between possessions and expectations." See Gabriel Almond and Bingham Powell, *Comparative Politics: A Developmental Approach* (Boston: Little, Brown and Company, 1966), p. 82.

[19] The *Report*, p. 178.

[20] *Ibid.*, p. 176.

supporter of existing social institutions and considerably better educated and more affluent than either the rioter or the non-involved. This would lead one to speculate that black attitudes or perceptions may be changed when "reality" changes.

Finally, the *Report* attributes responsibility for the present civil disorders to "white racism" in America, "the racial attitude and behavior of white Americans toward black Americans." The fact that a political system theoretically committed to democratic values finds itself embroiled in a major crisis resulting from undemocratic practices raises some fundamental questions regarding the real operative values of the system. How do white Americans reconcile theory and reality? What are the special problems which this situation suggests relative to political socialization of white Americans? Is resocialization of American whites a prerequisite for the fundamental policy changes recommended by the Commission? A number of scholars and writers, some black and some white, have long maintained that the race problem in America is essentially a white problem, created and perpetuated by whites.[21] If the problem is to be solved it must be solved by whites. As Myrdal stated many years ago, "all our attempts to reach scientific explanations of why the Negroes are what they are and why they live as they do have regularly led to determinants on the white side of the race line."

Coming to grips with the fundamental cause of the riots, white racism, is more a task for American whites than for blacks. The process will no doubt necessitate an admission on the part of white Americans that the American dream remains a dream, that full democracy in America is yet to be realized. In short, it will entail alteration of the American political culture, a re-examination of basic values and possibly a rewriting of American history to revise the image of blacks in the minds of whites and blacks. More fundamentally, it will possibly require a restructuring of the socialization process for blacks and whites if our commitments to democratic values are to be translated into actual practices. The question for which the *Report* provides no answer is "how can this be done?" It is in the delineation of the broad outlines of such a process that political science and other social science research can possibly make its most significant contribution.

Democratic theory

"Democracy is . . . characterized by the fact that power over significant authoritative decisions in a society is distributed among the population. The ordinary man is expected to take an active part in governmental affairs, to be aware of how decisions are made and to make his views known."[22]

[21] See James Baldwin, *The Fire Next Time* (New York: The Dial Press, 1963); Gunnar Myrdal, *An American Dilemma* (New York: Harper and Row, 1944); and *Ebony Magazine* (special issue), "The White Problem in America," 20, August, 1965.

[22] Almond and Verba, *The Civic Culture*, p. 19.

Any attempt to view the *Report* in the context of democratic theory would seem to raise an array of tantalizing questions,[23] one of which is the relationship between *political obligation* and *consent*.

In a democracy the basis of political obligation is consent.[24] Such consent implies a high level of citizen participation in the political process or at least the unrestricted right of the interested citizen to participate. Consequently, democratic political systems have traditionally institutionalized certain structures and practices that allow for the orderly and periodic involvement of citizens in decision-making. A brief examination of the record tends to substantiate the Commission's contention that throughout the course of American history, black men have been essentially "subjects" rather than "participants" in the political process.[25]

Black men arrived in America in 1619 and began what was to become a 244-year legacy of chattel slavery. Slaves were, by definition, nonparticipants in the political process. The lot of free Negroes was not markedly different from that of slaves. The end of the Civil War, the Emancipation Proclamation, and ratification of the Fourteenth and Fifteenth Amendments heralded the period of Reconstruction and relatively widespread participation in politics by black people. A return to white control and patterns of excluding Negroes from southern politics followed the Compromise of 1877 and withdrawal of federal troops from the South. Southern states revised their constitutions to deny the franchise to Negroes and as the Negro entered the twentieth century, his political future looked dismal and bleak.[26] Since 1900, blacks have staged an uphill battle in quest of full participation in the body politic. Most significant among legal victories for blacks have been the outlawing of white primaries in 1944, the passage of Civil Rights acts in 1957, 1960, and 1964, the Anti-Poll Tax Amendment in 1963 and finally the Federal Voting Rights Act of 1965.[27]

[23] For critical commentary on this general subject see Lane Davis, "The Cost of Realism: Contemporary Restatements of Democracy," *Western Political Science Quarterly,* 17 (1964), pp. 37-46; Jack Walker, "A Critique of the Elitist Theory of Democracy," *American Political Science Review,* 60 (June, 1966), pp. 285-295; Robert Dahl, "Further Reflections on the Elitist Theory of Democracy," *American Political Science Review,* 60 (June, 1966), pp. 296-305. See also Joseph Tussman, *Obligation and the Body Politic* (New York: Oxford University Press, 1960).

[24] For an extensive treatment of the principle of consent in the American political experience see David W. Minar, *Ideas and Politics: The American Experience* (Homewood, Ill.: The Dorsey Press, 1964), Ch. 4.

[25] "Subjects" are those individuals who are oriented to the political system and the impact which its outputs, such as welfare benefits, laws, etc., may have upon their lives, but who are not oriented to participation in the input structures. "Participants" are those individuals who are oriented to the input structures and processes, and engage in, or view themselves as potentially engaging in, the articulation of demands and the making of decisions. See Almond and Powell, *Comparative Politics,* p. 53.

[26] For a detailed account of this period, see John Hope Franklin, *From Slavery to Freedom* (New York: Alfred A. Knopf, 1967).

[27] See *Revolution in Civil Rights,* 3rd ed. (Washington, D.C.: Congressional Quarterly Service, 1967).

Perhaps the most reliable source of information on current black registra-
tion and voting in the South is the Voter Education Project of the Southern
Regional Council. According to its director, Vernon Jordan, the 1965 Voting
Rights Act has had a marked impact on voter registration among southern
Negroes. He states that significant gains have come in Alabama, Louisiana,
Georgia, South Carolina, Virginia, and Mississippi. In Mississippi, Negro
registration jumped from 8 per cent to nearly 60 per cent in just two and a
half years.[28]

The most recent figures on voter registration supplied by the Voter Education Project are presented in Table 1.

Also noteworthy is the election of over 200 blacks to public office in the
South since the Voting Rights Act was passed.[29] There are presently
50 blacks holding local, parish, and state offices in Louisiana, all elected since
1965.[30]

These accelerated advances in black registration and election are indeed
impressive, but they do not eradicate the voting problem. With the exception
of Texas, black registration percentages are still below white percentages in all
the states included in the Voter Education Project survey, and in many areas
blacks still experience substantial difficulties in gaining the franchise. Also,
the number of blacks holding statewide positions in government and political
parties is in no way proportionate to the number of blacks in the population.

Wilson observes, "that the political participation of the Negro in the North
is significantly higher than in the South but even so is lower than that of most

Table 1. *Voter registration in the South, Winter–Spring, 1968*

	White registered	Per cent white VAP* registered	Negro registered	Per cent Negro VAP* registered
Alabama	1,119,000	82.7	271,000	56.3
Arkansas	616,000	72.4	121,000	62.8
Florida	2,194,000	83.8	293,000	62.3
Georgia	1,450,000	80.6	334,000	54.5
Louisiana	1,122,000	87.0	301,000	58.5
Mississippi	655,000	88.9	264,000	62.5
North Carolina	1,555,000	77.5	293,000	53.2
South Carolina	567,000	63.6	183,000	49.3
Tennessee	1,434,000	80.6	225,000	71.7
Texas	3,532,000	72.3	540,000	83.1
Virginia	1,200,000	63.9	247,000	56.6
Totals	15,454,000	76.9	3,072,000	61.2

Source: Voter Education Project News, 2 (June, 1968).
*VAP = Voter Age Population.

[28]Vernon E. Jordan, "New Forces of Urban Political Power," *The New South*, 23
(Spring, 1968), p. 47.

[29]United States Commission on Civil Rights, *Political Participation* (Washington, D.C.:
U.S. Government Printing Office, 1968), p. 15.

[30]These include 8 constables, 9 justices of the peace, 11 party executive committee
members, 5 school board members, 6 city and town councilmen, 10 police jurors and
only one statewide officer, a member of the state House of Representatives. Source: List
of Negro Elected Officials of Louisiana prepared for Workshop for Louisiana Negro
Elected Officials held at Southern University, Baton Rouge, Louisiana, July 13, 1968.

other Northern population groups."[31] It ought to be pointed out that low participation in the North cannot be attributed to the type of legal restrictions historically operative in the South. Social science surveys have indicated that persons with low socioeconomic status tend to vote less than persons of higher socioeconomic status.[32] In addition, Negroes in the urban North are more geographically mobile than whites and are less likely to be able to satisfy residence requirements for voting. Nonpartisan elections, candidates running at-large and weak party organization also contribute to low turnout among low income voters. And it could well be that "the extent to which an individual feels effective as part of the institutionalized process may well determine the degree to which he participates in those processes. In sum, the individual's perception of his personal effectiveness should be supportive to the values he places on participation."[33] Thus, while there are no legal deterrents to Negro voting in the North, the cultural deterrents (income, education, occupation) are attributable to the system. That is, the prevailing social, economic and educational arrangements operate in a manner which relegates Negroes to this status, and as long as Negroes face these artificial barriers it is reasonable to assume that their level of political participation will not change.[34]

The extent of constraints on black participation, North and South, would seem to suggest an absence of consent by blacks and thus possible relief from obligations traditionally incumbent upon citizens in a democracy. Of interest in this connection is a recent re-examination of the principles of obligation and consent and related problems rendered by Pitkin.[35]

Pitkin, in a highly provocative treatise, holds that obligation depends not on any actual act of consenting, past or present, but on the character of the government. If it is just government, doing what a government should, then you must obey it. If it is unjust, then you have no such obligation. Or, your obligation depends not on whether you have consented but on whether the

[31] James Q. Wilson, "The Negro in American Politics: The Present" in John P. Davis, ed., *The American Negro Reference Book* (Englewood Cliffs, N.J.: Prentice-Hall, Inc., 1966), p. 431.

[32] See Angus Campbell *et al.*, *The American Voter* (New York: John Wiley and Sons, Inc., 1964).

[33] James T. Jones, *Political Socialization in a Midwestern Industrial Community*, pp. 218-219.

[34] This point is developed in Philip Meranto, "Negro Majorities and Political Power: The Defeat of an All-Negro Ticket in East St. Louis" prepared for Herbert Hill, ed., *The Revolt of the Powerless: Negroes in the Cities* (New York: Random House, forthcoming); in earlier studies similar projections had been made regarding Negro registration and voting in the South. Donald R. Matthews and James W. Prothro, "Social and Economic Factors and Negro Voter Registration in the South,"*American Political Science Review,* 57 (March, 1963), pp. 24-44. On the national scene, there are one black U.S. Senator and five black Representatives (Adam Powell excluded). About 80 blacks were among over 2,600 delegates and alternates at the 1968 Republican Convention and some 301 were among 5,611 delegates and alternates at the Democratic Convention. "Has the GOP Written off Black Votes," in *Pittsburgh Courier,* nat'l ed., August 17, 1968, p. 1; and "Negro Delegates to Confab Shows Gain, Chairman Says" in Baton Rouge *Morning Advocate,* August 15, 1968, p. 18-A.

[35] Hanna Pitkin, "Obligation and Consent—I," and "Obligation and Consent—II," *American Political Science Review,* 59 and 60 (Dec., 1965 and March, 1966), pp. 990-999; pp. 39-52.

government is such that you ought to consent to it. Are its actions consistent with the type of government men in a hypothetical state of nature would have consented to establish and obey? Pitkin's study would suggest that any assessment of the riots and the rioters would of necessity involve grappling with these kinds of concerns.

The propensity among blacks to disobey certain basic canons of the political system has produced strains in the system which threaten to destroy its very foundation. Could this propensity derive fundamentally from the unwillingness of the system to incorporate blacks as full partners in the political process? Cook has projected that "on the empirical level, a tradition of exclusion from participation in the political system breeds disrespect for, and disloyalty to, that system."[36] "Men rarely question the legitimacy of an established order when all is going well; the problem of political obligation is urgent when the state is sick. . . ."[37]

Does exclusion from participation, coupled with exclusion from benefits of "the good life" of the system, not only remove the obligation to obey, but also give rise to the obligation to disobey or revolt? These queries are relevant, but they are also difficult in as much as they solicit precise guidance in specific and varied kinds of situations. Pitkin underscores the inadequacy of classical democratic theory as well as her own theory on consent by noting that both provide insufficient cues for determining what authority to resist and under what conditions. In the same way, both provide only imperfect guidelines for assessing and evaluating the consistency between civil disorder of the magnitude of riots and the obligation of citizens to obey the authority of society invested with the duty of enforcing the law.

Black political strategy

Scoble suggests that Negro leadership and politics represent a quest for effective political power. Negro politics can be best understood if viewed as pursuit of power and influence over authoritative policy decisions.[38] On the other hand, Wilson, in a recent article on the subject, writes, "Because of the structure of American politics as well as the nature of the Negro community, Negro politics will accomplish only limited objectives. This does not mean that Negroes will be content with those accomplishments or resigned to that political style. If Negroes do not make radical gains, radical sentiments may grow."[39] The crucial problem of the black man in the American political

---

[36] Samuel D. Cook, "The Negro and the American Political System: Obligation and Resistance," (unpublished paper presented at the Conference on Political Obligation and Resistance to Authority, Gatlingburg, Tennessee, April 18-20, 1968), p. 1.

[37] S.I. Benn and R.S. Peters, *Social Principles and the Democratic State* (London: George Allen and Urwin, 1959), pp. 299-300.

[38] Harry Scoble, *Negro Politics in Los Angeles: The Quest for Power* (Los Angeles: Institute of Government and Public Affairs, University of California, 1967), p. 2.

[39] See James Q. Wilson, "The Negro in Politics" in Kenneth B. Clark and Talcott Parsons, eds., *The Negro American* (Boston: Houghton Mifflin Company, 1966), p. 444. He notes that "American political institutions provide no way for the organized political pressure of a particular disadvantaged group to reshape in any fundamental sense social

arena seems to revolve around the magnitude of the needs of the black people (as set forth in the *Report* and elsewhere), in relationship to the limited potential of politics as a vehicle for ministering to those needs.[40] More succinctly put, it now seems incumbent upon black men to decide if politics, in the traditional sense, is now more of an irrelevancy rather than an imperative in the search for solutions to their problems. If politics is relevant, then what types of strategies will best serve the needs of the black community, North and South? If irrelevant, what are the alternatives?

Questions of strategy are significant and there are those who feel that this aspect of the black protest movement has not received sufficient attention from leaders in that movement. In fact, the alleged absence of a programmatic element in radical politics in America today, especially the black protest movement, provoked Lasch to state, "The very gravity of the crisis makes it all the more imperative that radicals try to formulate at least a provisional theory which will serve them as a guide to tactics in the immediate future as well as to long range questions of strategy."[41] Along the same general lines, Crozier points out that America is now committed to the omnipotence of reason and the black protest movements are out of step with that development. Very pointedly, he reflects that "it is no longer possible to make good through mere numbers, through the vote or through manual labor, but only through the ability to play the game of modern calculation. And in that area the Negro is still fundamentally disadvantaged. The more rational the society becomes, the more he loses his foothold."[42] Could it be that traditional politics characterize the black subculture while a more rational-calculating variety of politics has long been the pattern in the dominant political culture?[43]

The literature of the discipline and popular periodicals are replete with suggestions of appropriate strategies and/or programs for solving the race problem. Some of the more popularly suggested and researched strategies include black-liberal white coalitions, black-conservative white coalitions, fluctuating or *ad hoc* coalitions, separate black political parties, Black Power, ghetto power.[44] No examination of this proliferation of literature can be

and economic conditions. . . . That politics seems irrelevant to their daily pre-occupation is not necessarily an expression of neurotic withdrawal . . . but may well be the rational conclusion of a reasonably well-informed citizen." Also, see Carey McWilliams, "Protest, Power and the Future of Politics," *Nation*, 206 (Jan. 15, 1968), pp. 71-77.

[40] On the changing nature of the black protest, see Bayard Rustin, "From Protest to Politics: The Future of the Civil Rights Movement," *Commentary* (Feb., 1965), pp. 25-31.

[41] Christopher Lasch, "The Trouble with Black Power," *The New York Review of Books*, 10, February 29, 1968, p. 14.

[42] Michel Crozier, "America Revisited: The Lonely Frontier of Reason," *Nation*, 206 (May 27, 1968), p. 693. See also Harold Cruse, *The Crisis of the Negro Intellectual* (New York: William Morrow and Company, Inc., 1967).

[43] This writer's personal ambivalence on this question leads to the belief that some effort to apply developmental theory to the study of black politics in America would seem to provide interesting and meaningful research possibilities.

[44] On the white conservative-black coalition in Atlanta, see Edward C. Banfield, *Big City Politics* (New York: Random House, 1955), pp. 18-36. The coalition of blacks with liberal whites in Houston, Texas, is reported by Harry Holloway, "Negro Political Strategy: Coalition or Independent Power Politics," a paper in this issue of the *Quarterly*.

made in this limited commentary. Nor will any full-blown theory or strategy be offered. However, it does seem reasonable to submit that any strategy designed to redefine the status of black people in America must of necessity be devised with certain considerations.

First, political strategy for blacks must take into account the difficulties inherent in being a numerical minority. Minority strategy must be highly flexibly based, to a large degree, on the fluctuating attitudes and actions of the white majority in any given setting. It must also be directed toward overcoming traditional constraints on the exertion of effective power by Negroes endemic to the black community itself. Second, any therapeutic strategy must acknowledge the reality that blacks in the ghetto already constitute a "separate society,"[45] and must address itself seriously to black charges of control by "alien, outside" agents. Indigenous control of the ghetto and similar demands cannot be summarily dismissed as, for example, "old wine in new bottles."[46] Third, given the general apathy and insensitivity of whites toward problems of blacks, it seems reasonable to suggest that any meaningful gains for blacks will come as a result of *demands*, supported by evidence of black willingness to cause great inconvenience to the community at large if these legitimate demands are ignored. Fourth, it might be that the Commission placed too much emphasis on the material aspects of the black man's problem (and the material aspects are indeed important) and did not devote enough attention to such psychological needs as dignity, self-respect and identity and to the relationship between the latter and any corrective actions, political or otherwise. Taking these psychological dimensions into account will probably necessitate innovations in and restatements of traditional concepts and theories regarding democracy, civil disobedience, protest, and other forms of political activity. New tactics, new rhetoric and new sources of leadership will most probably emerge and must be accommodated by the system.[47] Fifth, and in a similar view, it would seem that black strategy and black strategists ought not be constrained to political alternatives if these alternatives prove to be mostly dysfunctional for blacks, and there is

See also Ronald Moskowitz, "Education and Politics in Boomtown," *Saturday Review*, February 17, 1968, pp. 52-54, 66-67. James W. Wilson suggests that blacks form coalitions on an issue-to-issue basis. See "The Negro in Politics" in Parsons and Clark, *The Negro American*, pp. 434-435. Also see Bayard Rustin, "Black Power and Coalition Politics," *Commentary*, 42, (Sept., 1966), pp. 35-40; Stokely Carmichael and Charles V. Hamilton, *Black Power: The Politics of Liberation in America* (New York: Random House, 1967); Floyd McKissick, "Programs for Black Power" in Floyd B. Barbour, ed., *The Black Power Revolt* (Boston: Porter Sargent Publisher, 1968), pp. 179-181; Hubert M. Blalock, Jr., *Toward a Theory of Minority Group Relations* (New York: John Wiley and Sons, Inc., 1967).

[45] Kenneth B. Clark, *Dark Ghetto* (New York: Harper & Row, 1965).

[46] See W.H. Ferry, "Blacktown and Whitetown: The Case for a New Federalism," *Saturday Review*, June 15, 1968, pp. 14-17.

[47] In the last decade, black sit-ins, mass marches and general obstruction of operations of various governmental and educational enterprises have become commonplace. These tactics have found widespread acceptance by nonblack groups such as students against university administrations and protesters against the draft. It would seem reasonable to suggest that similar creativity with regard to tactics will characterize the black struggle in the future.

a growing body of opinion which holds that they may well be. Finally, the magnitude of the problems faced by blacks is such that the correctives must be radical. If radical programs are not adopted, the Kerner Report may be more a prelude to, rather than a summation of, the worst race riots in the history of this nation, for there seems to be little reason to believe that black rioters will be satisfied with anything less than radical corrective action.

Interests, Parties, and Governmental Structures in St. Louis

Robert H. Salisbury

In this article, Robert H. Salisbury draws our attention to the critical role which formal governmental arrangements may play in shaping coalition formation and conflict in a local municipality. In St. Louis, around a somewhat bifurcated local governmental structure, two broad coalitions of interests have formed. The first centers around the county offices, the Board of Education, and the Board of Aldermen, but also includes locally oriented labor unions, blacks, neighborhood organizations, and lower-income people generally. Patronage is the lifeblood of this coalition which, according to Salisbury, has rather particularistic and restricted interests.

The second coalition is made up of downtown business interests plus middle- and upper-middle-class residents of the city. It tends to have broader policy concerns in areas such as civic progress, economic development, and urban renewal. This coalition of interests tends to cluster around the mayor's office. This executive-centered coalition represents a new convergence of power that has evolved in many cities in the United States and, according to Salisbury, actively seeks out solutions to problems regarded as critical to a city's growth; the coalition has therefore become the primary initiator of programs that involve major allocations of both public and private resources. However, to succeed, it must be actively led by the mayor. One of the factors which may distinguish one city's political system from another, then, is the energy, imagination, and cohesion of this newly convergent elite and its ability to mobilize resources to solve community wide problems.

In St. Louis, frequent clashes between these two coalitions give rise to a great deal of conflict. Such conflict, however, is generally covert and only becomes manifest when certain issues, such as charter reform, metropolitan reorganization, and taxation, arise in the city. In addition, conflict between the two coalitions has been institutionalized within the Democratic party and is not fought out between competing parties as it has been in some cities. Intercoalition conflict, therefore, is of an intra- rather than interparty nature.

Salisbury concludes by pointing out how there is no way to prove categorically that the formal structure of government in St. Louis is the crucial variable in determining what particular form coalition formation and conflict has taken in the city. Query: Do similar (or perhaps different) coalitions of interests cluster around the principal governmental office holders in other central cities and suburbs? If so, formal governmental arrangements, that is, the form of government in a city, may play an important role in determining the nature of local coalitions, thereby influencing the scope and intensity of political conflict at the local level.

Political scientists have been troubled in recent years by just what it is they mean when they talk about a political party. Whether the discussion concentrates on the American scene or includes comparative data from other countries, the ambiguity of party as an analytical tool remains. Particularly difficult and very largely untouched by specific empirical analysis are the relationships which connect core party organizations, the social and economic interest group configuration, and the formal governmental structure of a community. Whereas some political scientists have assumed the crucial importance of the formal structure in shaping the political life of the community, others have tended to regard structure as largely irrelevant and to argue instead that the only significant variables were embraced in interest group activity. This paper will offer a synopsis of the situation in one city, St. Louis, Missouri, in an effort to suggest the ways in which the three factors mentioned are interrelated.

The burden of the argument here is that a somewhat peculiar bifurcated structure of local government plays a crucial role in shaping the nature and scope of political conflict in the city. Two broad interest groupings in St. Louis, each composed of rather loosely allied groups and each pursuing different sets of goals in the political arena, are enabled to live under the same party label by the fact that each grouping can control one segment of the governmental structure and from that control secure the portion of its goals most vital to it. Neither group gains complete satisfaction thereby, but the consequence is that the two groups are not forced into the full range of sharp competition that a more centralized and monolithic structure might require.

Reprinted from *The Western Political Quarterly*, vol. 13, no. 2 (June 1960), pp. 498-507, by permission of the University of Utah, copyright owners.

The interests

The constellation of social and economic interests which make up the body politic of St. Louis is like in some ways and in some ways unlike that of other major American cities. In common with other metropolitan centers, the St. Louis area has experienced rapid growth in the post-World War II period, but unlike most other cities, this growth has taken place almost entirely outside the city limits, which were fixed by constitutional provision in 1876. The growth of the St. Louis area, further, has not kept pace with many other parts of the country, particularly because the hinterland of the city has not grown much. Consequently, St. Louis business leaders have been concerned to bring new industry to the city, and this effort has spurred the desire, shared by other metropolises, to solve traffic and transit problems, to renovate and rehabilitate slum areas, and to revive the downtown business district.

In common with many cities, St. Louis has experienced a great influx of Negroes and "mountain whites" in recent years with a resulting increased demand for various types of municipal services. As elsewhere, these "new immigrants" play the same role in relation to ward organizations of the party that nationality groups did in past decades. The tight and inflexible boundaries of the city have, at the same time, meant that St. Louis has lost upper income population to the suburbs. The combination of an increasingly lower income population and the desire to attract new industry and therefore to keep tax rates at reasonable levels has left the city in almost perpetual financial embarrassment in the postwar period, an embarrassment alleviated only by the imposition of an earnings tax of 1 per cent on all income.

If one looks at the major economic interests in the city, one can begin with familiar categories, labor and business, and discover some degree of conflict between these two groups. Yet no analysis can explain St. Louis politics satisfactorily by relying solely upon labor-management conflict. Labor, for example, is not monolithic. The largest unions are the Teamsters, the Building Trades, the Machinists, and the Auto Workers, while a number of smaller unions also play some role. These unions differ considerably in their local political significance. The Teamsters are the most active locally and the most controversial. They have a fairly fully articulated set of goals for St. Louis which includes general expansion of services for low income groups and which emphasizes heavily the betterment of race relations and equality for Negroes. The militance of the Teamsters, with its ideological flavor, is in contrast to the unphilosophical bread-and-butter concerns of the Building Trades which seek jobs and contracts and find that extensive political alliances are of great assistance in securing these goals. They are not really interested in most of the program of the Teamsters, and the Teamster leaders sometimes express contempt for the unconcern with policy exhibited by the "pork chop" unions. Nevertheless, each group finds that under present conditions their channels of action often bring them into working agreements with each other on political questions. The UAW and the Steelworkers differ from each of the two types of labor groups mentioned above, since they are largely unconcerned with local politics. Their union interests are not much affected by decisions in the local arena, and though their leaders sometimes go through political motions, neither these unions nor the management of the plants where they work are normally active on the St. Louis political scene.

The business community is likewise divided along a number of lines. Dominating the public view are the industrial, banking, and commercial leaders of locally controlled large businesses, the "downtown" business community. These are the men who need more industrial development in the city, these are the men who have significant stakes in the rehabilitation of the slums and the consequent revival of the core city, and these are the men who also form the social elite of the city. The interests of this configuration are articulated by the metropolitan daily press, and they are identified with "Progress" and "Good Government," while they are against the "Politicians." The bulk of the middle and upper-middle income residents of the city and the professional, religious, and educational leadership tend strongly to identify their interests with those of this business elite.

The small business community, on the other hand, does not. Composed of small downtown enterprises like parking lot operators and of neighborhood commercial establishments, this group is concerned with specific, individual treatment at the hands of governmental authority. Specific tax measures, provision of stop signs, regulation of on- and off-street parking, zoning, and the like are their primary goals, and they very often line up with organized labor groups in political alliance against the "downtown" interests.

The social composition of the city is noteworthy in two main respects, the impact of the Negro influx and the ethnic make-up of the city. More than one-fourth of the city's population today is Negro, and Negroes are achieving increasing political power. Six wards of the city's twenty-eight are represented by Negroes, and significant influence is exerted in at least three others. Desegregation of swimming pools, schools, and, to some extent, of places of public accommodation has followed the rise of Negroes to influence. Until the New Deal and again during most of the 1940's the Negro community was predominantly Republican, but since 1949 Negro wards have produced overwhelming margins for any candidate bearing the Democratic label.

Nationality groups have not played as important a role in St. Louis politics as in many cities. St. Louis experienced a large German immigration and a significant Irish immigration during the mid-nineteenth century. For decades these two groups formed the backbone of the Republican and Democratic parties respectively. But the "late immigrants" from Eastern and Southern Europe largely by-passed St. Louis in favor of the heavy industrial centers. Thus the European "ethnics" in the city have had nearly a century to become assimilated, and today, except for one Italian ward, it is difficult to find many traces of genuine nationality identification. The heavily Catholic religious heritage of St. Louis remains, but national origin seems to have little meaning in St. Louis politics.

St. Louis thus displays two broad configurations of interests. On one side are the locally oriented labor unions, Negroes, neighborhood businessmen, and lower income people generally. This grouping focuses its attention primarily on the specific bread-and-butter issues of jobs, stop signs, spot zoning, and the like, and exhibits a sharp antipathy toward any suggestion of increased tax rates. Downtown business interests and the middle and upper-middle income residents, on the other hand, are primarily interested in broader policy questions—economic growth, urban renewal—and their approach to problems of fiscal solvency is more sympathetic to the needs for more tax revenue.

The structure of government

The structure of St. Louis government is *sui generis* in many respects. The city is governed under a charter adopted by the voters in 1914. Some important aspects of the city's business, however, are not under home rule control. The police department, for example, is controlled by a Board of Police Commissioners appointed by the governor, and a Board of Election Commissioners is similarly appointed. Originally, the device was adopted to enable a pro-Southern state administration to have police control in a Unionist city. Later it allowed a Democratic state administration to have patronage to dispense in a normally Republican city. The contemporary significance of this arrangement is quite different as will be noted later. In the city a moderately strong mayor administers nearly ten thousand employees of whom he can appoint some seventeen without regard to civil service requirements. An elected comptroller acts jointly with the mayor and the president of the Board of Aldermen, elected at large, to form the Board of Estimate and Apportionment which prepares the city budget, a budget which the Board of Aldermen may cut but not increase. The budget includes in its provisions many of the most vital policy decisions affecting the city, and the mayor is certainly the key figure in its preparation. The Board of Aldermen is composed of the president and twenty-eight representatives elected one each from the twenty-eight wards. The mayor and the members of the Board of Aldermen each serve four-year terms. The aldermen, of course, must pass all ordinances for the city, but even though a majority of the Board often opposes the mayor on policy issues, the latter clearly dominates the policy-making process.

Almost entirely separate from this portion of the city government are the so-called "county offices." St. Louis, like Baltimore, is not a part of any county. Nevertheless, under state law, the functions ordinarily performed by county officials must be performed in St. Louis by officials like sheriff, collector of revenue, license collector, recorder of deeds, magistrates, and others who are elected by the voters and are completely outside the control of the city administration or the city charter. These officials make few policy decisions of any importance, but taken together they provide nearly one thousand non-civil service jobs, and, as one of the few remaining sources of patronage in the city, they are prizes of great importance to those who are interested in patronage.

The Board of Education should also be mentioned here. It, too, is outside the budgetary control of the city. The Board is elected separately and its tax rate is determined through separate referendum elections. It, too, controls a substantial pool of patronage jobs in its building and maintenance departments, and patronage rather than educational policy is the major issue in Board of Education elections.

Thus the structure of St. Louis government contains two largely separate sets of offices. One is centered in the mayor's office and is the natural focus of attention for those interested in broad problems of municipal policy. The other is based upon the county offices, Board of Education, and Board of Aldermen and consists essentially of a patronage pool and a means for securing individual favor with very little responsibility for policy.

The party situation

St. Louis has undergone two rather remarkable political metamorphoses during the past three decades. The first it shared with many other metropolitan centers, the change from consistent Republicanism to overwhelming Democracy as the New Deal coalition produced sizable pluralities on the local level. The shift to the Democrats embraced practically all elements of the community, but perhaps the most notable changes took place among the Negroes, and among many of the German areas of the city. Silk stocking and delivery wards alike went Democratic during the thirties. But although the state and national Democratic tickets continued to carry the city comfortably, during the next decade, from 1941 to 1949, the Republicans returned to power on the local scene. We need not examine the reasons for this switch except to note that it took in much of the city, especially the Negroes, and it was backed by much of downtown business and the metropolitan press. This Republican swing carried the party into the mayor's office (by a two-to-one majority in 1945), swept the Board of Aldermen nearly clean of Democrats, and helped elect Republicans to Congress, although the Democrats hung on to some local offices and Roosevelt won handily.

The period of Republican control ended in 1949, however, and since that time the Democratic sweep of all offices at all levels, save only a maximum of four aldermanic seats, has been complete. This time the Negro wards shifted overwhelmingly to the Democrats and have shown no sign of defecting despite that tendency in some other cities. The upper income areas—smaller now than formerly—have shown remarkable Democratic strength, largely undisturbed by the Eisenhower era. The lower income sections of the city, which include the Negro areas, are staunchly Democratic, to the extent that the Republicans are badly demoralized and have difficulty in finding either candidates or money to make a serious race for any political office in the community.

Yet this cyclical variation in the fortunes of the two parties does not conform to the configuration of interests in the community. As outlined above, the city is broadly divided along some sort of quasi-class basis into two groupings; labor, low income, small, neighborhood business, and at least recently Negroes, against large downtown business, the forces of "Progress," with the daily papers as spokesmen and the so-called "newspaper wards" as sources of voting strength. This general division of the community interests has not changed greatly during the past decade except perhaps as the proportion of Negroes has increased while the old German Republicans have lost their ethnic identity. But these changes surely do not account for (a) the massive shifts in the strength of each party over a relatively short period of time, or (b) the absence of fairly sharp and relatively even competition between the two parties for local office. For this latter fact is perhaps most prominent; namely, that when one party has been dominant, the other party is moribund. This is especially true of the Republicans since 1949. With a constellation of interests that normally might be expected to support Republican candidates, the latter lose by margins exceeding three-to-one.

Interest, party, and structure in St. Louis

We cannot here go into all the reasons for the variation in party fortunes and the recent lack of Republican success. But we do want to examine the forms of institutionalization of this division of interests in the community. If it has not taken the form of inter-party conflict, how has it been expressed? The answer is that two fairly distinct groupings have appeared *within* whichever party was dominant in a particular period, one representing the larger business groups, the newspaper ward areas, and the forces of "Progress" generally, while the other is characterized by the "Politicians" who are spokesmen for a medley of lower-income, labor, small business, and minority groups. Such a division was notable within the Republican ranks during the late 1940's. Such a division is quite obvious within the Democratic ranks today. *This division is not only one of conflict over economic and social interests in the community, it is also manifested in the formal structure of government.*

In both the Republican and the Democratic parties the intra-party division has followed essentially the same lines. On the one side, the downtown business groups and the other interests associated with them have found their representation in the office of mayor primarily, usually with co-operation from the comptroller and the president of the Board of Aldermen. All these officials are elected on a city-wide basis with substantial newspaper attention to their campaigns which tend to cost considerable sums of money for publicity. These three, forming the Board of Estimate and Apportionment, make the key fiscal decisions of the city, and, however hard they try, the Board of Aldermen can alter these decisions only at the margins. Moreover, the mayor, as mentioned before, is by all odds the most significant policy-making official in the city. It is policy, of course, with which the large business constellation is concerned—broad civic policy affecting the location of industry, general tax rates, availability of full city services, the social climate of the community necessary to attract technical personnel for their businesses, and the social climate of the community necessary to preserve the status of an old-line, social elite whose autonomy of local operation is being eroded by the nationalization of business and labor alike. It is this group which wants civic reform and civil service, which sponsors the many Citizens Committees to study local problems, and so on. The group is not reactionary or even particularly conservative in the usual meanings of those terms. Some of its leaders are liberal Democrats on the national scene, and many are outspoken defenders of equality for Negroes on all levels. Its co-operation with organized labor is never more than lukewarm, but again, on the national scene, the Teamsters and the Building Trades, the dominant labor groups locally, are not noted for their liberalism.

The other side is likewise focused on a set of public officials, the holders of the "county offices," supplemented by the dominant group on the Board of Aldermen. The county offices are filled in city-wide elections too, thus giving them the same formal constituency as the mayor and his associates. But these elections are not attended by wide publicity, they are held in conjunction with November general elections instead of the municipal elections in the spring, and the chief requisite of victory is a dependable vote delivered by an effective ward organization. The newspapers take little part in these elections and correspondingly have little influence on them. Instead they are dominated by the so-called "delivery wards" of the city, generally, the lower income and Negro wards. Again this was true when the Republicans controlled these offices as well as now when the Democrats are supreme.

The complex of interests which supports these political leaders also finds it important to have influence with the aldermen. In the wards inhabited by lower income residents aldermen are selected in the same way as the county officeholders; nomination dependent largely upon the support of the ward committeemen and election dependent upon an effective ward organization. Many county office-holders are also ward committeemen and the alliance between these elements of the core party organization is firm. By and large, this element of the party is not particularly concerned with broad social or economic policy as such. It is concerned rather with the immediate needs of effective ward organization, and these needs are not notably different today than they traditionally have been. Patronage remains the lifeblood of the organization and, of course, the county offices are sources of significant patronage in the city. Consequently, control of these offices is vital to the organization. For the same reason, control of the Board of Education is important. More than that, however, the county office element of the party is concerned with the needs of its electoral supporters as the latter interpret these needs. This means broadly *individual favor*. Jobs are crucial, but so also are specific contracts for building contractors, stop signs and parking regulations, assistance in getting into a public housing project, route location for a throughway, and so on. Assistance for individuals in need, the classic basis of urban political organization, remains the basis for this wing of the party, and such assistance is necessarily funneled through the particular set of offices which this wing seeks to control; jobs through the county offices and Board of Education, and individual attention from the Board of Aldermen achieved through a log-rolling system know locally as aldermanic .courtesy. These are the concerns of Negroes, low income groups, the politically active elements of the local labor movement, and of many kinds of small businesses. Thus there is not much question of which element in the party these groups will support in a situation of conflict between the two party groups.

One interesting thing about this division, both of interests in the city and of offices, is that conflict between the two groupings is minimized. The group focused on the mayor is not interested in patronage, although from time to time its conception of good government requires that it advocate the further extension of civil service. By the same token, the county office group and many of its electoral supporters are profoundly indifferent to most matters of public policy. Aldermanic courtesy does create conflict, since the granting of individual favors—e.g., a stop sign in front of a confectionery—often runs counter to broader policy concerns—e.g., a master traffic plan. Nevertheless, there are many areas of policy and of patronage where each element of the party is content to let the other element control. Each group needs the other. The county office people need the financial support for their precinct workers which the mayor-led group contributes to the party. The mayoral group needs the support of the delivery wards to get many of its policy goals put into effect. This mutual need is sufficient at least to permit the two groups to share the same party label, and perhaps to require it.

But there is always latent and sometimes manifest conflict between the two groups. Issues like the distribution of the tax load, recognition of labor organizations among municipal employees, and particularly charter reform, which might threaten the existence of the patronage offices, all activate not only the office-holders within the party but, more importantly, bring into operation most of the interest groups in the community which ally with one or the other faction. On such questions the mayoral group is sharply opposed by the majority of the aldermen as well as by the dominant elements in the city committee of the party, the ward committeemen—county office forces. The tendency toward conflict is reinforced by the fact that each group tends to view the other as an unholy conspiracy aimed at destroying its opponents. As it happens in St. Louis this conflict often takes the geographical form of what is nearly a north-south split with the south side and west end supporting the mayoral faction while the north side is the heart of the county office group strength.

A word should be said about the rather special effect that the structure of the police department, headed by a Board appointed by the governor, has on the political scene. Two consequences are apparent. In the first place, influence with the police department follows from influence with the governor, and consequently, successful gubernatorial candidates are much sought after figures in St. Louis politics. Secondly, although the police department is run on the merit system, there is a substantial amount of patronage available in the form of assignments and promotions. This patronage is, of course, of more interest to the county office group than to the mayoral group and the former seeks it more assiduously. In this quest the county office group joins forces with the representatives from St. Louis to the state legislature in an alliance that is facilitated by the dependence of the state legislators upon ward committeeman endorsement in order to win office. The close liaison between the state delegation and the county office forces means that the county offices themselves, established by state statute, are safe, and that the desires of the city administration for new state legislation will often get a cool reception from a state delegation allied with the opposing faction of the party. When the St. Louis delegation to the legislature is not united in behalf of the city's demands, they have little chance of passage, and policy requests from the St. Louis administration are blocked most often not by rural opposition, as so often is alleged, but by the county office faction of the St. Louis party.

Perhaps there is no way to prove categorically that the formal structure of government is the crucial variable in determining the particular form which the interest conflict in St. Louis politics has taken. Certainly the total political process in the city is complex. Yet it can scarcely be doubted that if the county offices did not exist and their meager functions were performed by regular administrative agencies of the city, the contending interest groupings in the city would have to find other channels for the satisfaction of their needs. Without the county offices there would be no patronage and hence ward organizations would be weakened. In that event, those interest groups, notably labor, which now work through the ward organizations, would be forced to play an even more direct role in the political process than they do now. Without the county offices there would be only one really important office through which to exert political power, for whatever purposes, and that would be the office of mayor. The aldermen, without effective ward organizations, would need to turn more directly to the interest groups of their wards, and again the conflict between the two broad interest configurations of the city would become more open. If the office of mayor became the chief and virtually the only prize for the contending groups, then it would seem that at least two consequences would follow, given the interest group line-up as it now exists in St. Louis. First, the two groupings which now form factions within the party would divide into two separate parties. This process might be slow. It might be effected through the use of "Blue Ribbon" slates running against "politician" slates, or it might in time result in the revival of the Republican party. In any case, the conflict would be more open than it is now. Secondly, it would be more continuous and involve a broader range of issues. Whereas now there is a substantial area of autonomous operation left to each faction, if the mayor's office were the only prize, then victory and the battle to achieve victory would cover all the issues in which the two sets of interests are even potentially in conflict. Either one side would win or it would lose, and there would be none of the present partial victories for both sides, which, however frustrating they are sometimes, at least give some satisfactions and some basis for compromise and mediation to each group.

If the present alignment of interests were altered in any significant way, a development which the militant and volatile character of the Teamsters and the increasing numbers and self-consciousness of Negroes make possible, the significance either of the present structure or of any alternative arrangements would be altered too. Under the present conditions, however, this analysis seems to be valid and, indeed, is confirmed by each major political event in the city. Any discussion of the effects of a really different structure, of course, must be speculative, since the proposal to change the structure so as to abolish the county offices will be met with sharp resistance by those groups which utilize the offices to advantage.

If the data reviewed here permit one to offer a tentative statement about the relationships between interests, party, and structure, it would appear that the interest group system is, as the Bentleyans argue it must be, basic. At the same time, however, the governmental structure affects in crucial ways the manner in which these interests will be articulated into political parties, and in so doing it plays an important role in determining the scope and intensity of political conflict in the community. It seems doubtful whether one could say that a particular structural form would in every case bring about a particular party system or give a particular shape to the conflict, since the structure and the interest configuration interact in each case. If the interest groups of St. Louis were more amorphous and diffuse and not joined in any bimodal pattern, even the most centralized structure of strong mayor control could not be expected to produce sharply competing parties. On the other hand, the present, somewhat diffuse structure would not appreciably moderate the conflict if St. Louis were divided into rigid class groupings of a quasi-feudal nature. Perhaps the study of the relationships of interests, parties, and structure in other cities will permit comparative analysis of a manageable range of data, and in turn lead us to more confident generalizations about the problem.

Protest as a Political Resource

Michael Lipsky

Michael Lipsky raises a number of important questions about the tactics and strategies currently being used by relatively powerless groups in our society to influence policy decisions. Is protest a viable political resource for such groups? How effective has protest by blacks and other minority groups been in bringing about policy change? What are the factors which may impede the effectiveness of protest? Should protest be viewed as a means of directly influencing public policy or as a tactic for building organizations which can then exert their own influence?

First, Lipsky points out that the primary problem facing the powerless in our society is their lack of political resources. The poor have very little to bargain with politically. Therefore, protest becomes a means of attempting to activate third parties to enter the political process on the side of the protestors. Obviously, if the orientations of third parties are sufficiently similar to those of the protesting group, the formation of a viable coalition capable of undertaking coordinated action is greatly facilitated.

Second, Lipsky makes it quite clear that protest designed to activate third parties whose values and goals differ from those of the protest group is a very unreliable political tactic for bringing about policy change, with problems involved in building a coalition quite different from those involving coalitions among similarly oriented groups. This is due to the tensions which arise because of the protest leader's need to appeal to four basic constituencies at the same time. He must: (1) nurture and sustain an organization, (2) adapt to the mass media, (3) try to develop and sustain the impact of the protest on third parties, and (4) try to directly influence the targets of the protest.

1968! { Third, Lipsky argues that in responding to protest, public officials tend to give symbolic reassurances to protest groups rather than real concessions, because those on whom they most depend are generally satisfied with appearances of action. Although protest groups learn how to dramatize an issue, they seldom are able to present data or proposals that public officials will consider objective or reasonable. Therefore, such groups frequently possess "negative" rather than "positive" influence, that is, they are more likely to succeed in vetoing than initiating a policy proposal.

Possibly   Finally, Lipsky points out that because of the ineffectiveness of protest, it should probably be viewed as a tactic for creating political organizations rather than a means of directly influencing public policy. Such organizations would eventually develop sufficient political resources so that either individually or collectively they could exert influence over public-policy decisions. Lipsky argues that the formations of coalitions among groups which share similar values and goals is particulary desirable if the poor want to participate meaningfully in policy-making at the local level.

However, protest can be viewed as an important means of bringing about changes in the political consciousness of protest participants, as well as achieving certain short-run objectives. The development of group consciousness can provide the basis for a more cohesive political organization, and may ultimately be the most important contribution of minority protest. Nevertheless, in the long run, success of the black power and other minority movements will depend on the acquisition of stable political resources by black and minority organizations. For without such resources, these organizations will be unable to compete effectively in the political arena.

The frequent resort to protest activity by relatively powerless groups in recent American politics suggests that protest represents an important aspect of minority group and low income group politics.[1] At the same time that Negro civil rights strategists have recognized the problem of using protest as a meaningful political instrument,[2] groups associated with the "war on poverty" have increasingly received publicity for protest activity. Saul Alinsky's Industrial Areas Foundation, for example, continues to receive invitations to help organize low income communities because of its ability to mobilize poor people around the tactic of protest.[3] The riots which dominated urban affairs in the summer of 1967 appear not to have diminished the dependence of some groups on protest as a mode of political activity.

This article provides a theoretical perspective on protest activity as a political resource. The discussion is concentrated on the limitations inherent in protest which occur because of the need of protest leaders to appeal to four constituencies at the same time. As the concept of protest is developed

Reprinted from *The American Political Science Review,* vol. 62, no. 4 (December 1968), pp. 1144-1158, by permission of the publisher and author. This article is an attempt to develop and explore the implications of a conceptual scheme for analyzing protest activity. It is based upon my studies of protest organizations in New York City, Washington, D.C., Chicago, San Francisco, and Mississippi, as well as extensive examination of written accounts of protest among low-income and Negro civil rights groups. I am grateful to Kenneth Dolbeare, Murray Edelman, and Rodney Stiefbold for their insightful comments on an earlier draft. This paper was developed while the author was a Staff Associate of the Institute for Research on Poverty at the University of Wisconsin. I appreciate the assistance obtained during various phases of my research from the Rabinowitz Foundation, the New York State Legislative Internship Program, and the Brookings Institution.

[1] "Relatively powerless groups" may be defined as those groups which, relatively speaking, are lacking in conventional political resources. For the purpose of community studies, Robert Dahl has compiled a useful comprehensive list. See Dahl, "The Analysis of Influence in Local Communities," *Social Science and Community Action,* Charles R. Adrian, ed. (East Lansing, Michigan, 1960), p. 32. The difficulty in studying such groups is that relative powerlessness only becomes apparent under certain conditions. Extremely powerless groups not only lack political resources, but are also characterized by a minimal sense of political efficacy, upon which in part successful political organization depends. For reviews of the literature linking orientations of political efficacy to socio-economic status, see Robert Lane, *Political Life* (New York, 1959), ch. 16; and Lester Milbrath, *Political Participation* (Chicago, 1965), ch. 5. Further, to the extent that group cohesion is recognized as a necessary requisite for organized political action, then extremely powerless groups, lacking cohesion, will not even appear for observation. Hence the necessity of selecting for intensive study a protest movement where there can be some confidence that observable processes and results can be analyzed. Thus, if one conceives a continuum on which political groups are placed according to their relative command of resources, the focus of this essay is on those groups which are near, but not at, the pole of powerlessness.

[2] See, e.g., Bayard Rustin, "From Protest to Politics: The Future of the Civil Rights Movement," *Commentary* (February, 1965), 25-31; and Stokely Carmichael, "Toward Black Liberation," *The Massachusetts Review* (Autumn, 1966).

[3] On Alinsky's philosophy of community organization, see his *Reveille for Radicals* (Chicago, 1945); and Charles Silberman, *Crisis in Black and White* (New York, 1964), ch. 10.

here, it will be argued that protest leaders must nurture and sustain an organization comprised of people with whom they may or may not share common values. They must articulate goals and choose strategies so as to maximize their public exposure through communications media. They must maximize the impact of third parties in the political conflict. Finally, they must try to maximize chances of success among those capable of granting goals. The tensions inherent in manipulating these four constituencies at the same time form the basis of this discussion of protest as a political process. It is intended to place aspects of the civil rights movement in a framework which suggests links between protest organizations and the general political processes in which such organizations operate.

I. "Protest" conceptualized

Protest activity as it has been adopted by elements of the civil rights movement and others has not been studied extensively by social scientists. Some of the most suggestive writings have been done as case studies of protest movements in single southern cities.[4] These works generally lack a framework or theoretical focus which would encourage generalization from the cases. More systematic efforts have been attempted in approaching the dynamics of biracial committees in the South,[5] and comprehensively assessing the efficacy of Negro political involvement in Durham, N.C., and Philadelphia, Pa.[6] In their excellent assessment of Negro politics in the South, Matthews and Prothro have presented a thorough profile of Southern Negro students and their participation in civil rights activities.[7] Protest is also discussed in passing in recent explorations of the social-psychological dimensions of Negro ghetto politics[8] and the still highly suggestive, although pre-1960's, work on Negro political leadership by James Q. Wilson.[9] These

---

[4] See, e.g., Jack L. Walker, "Protest and Negotiation: A Case Study of Negro Leadership in Atlanta, Georgia," *Midwest Journal of Political Science*, 7 (May, 1963), 99-124; Jack L. Walker, *Sit-Ins in Atlanta: A Study in the Negro Protest*, Eagleton Institute Case Studies, No. 34 (New York, 1964); John Ehle, *The Free Men* (New York, 1965) [Chapel Hill]; Daniel C. Thompson, *The Negro Leadership Class* (Englewood Cliffs, N.J., 1963) [New Orleans]; M. Elaine Burgess, *Negro Leadership in a Southern City* (Chapel Hill, N.C., 1962) [Durham].

[5] Lewis Killian and Charles Grigg, *Racial Crisis in America: Leadership in Conflict* (Englewood Cliffs, N.J., 1964).

[6] William Keech, "The Negro Vote as a Political Resource: The Case of Durham," (unpublished Ph.D. Dissertation, University of Wisconsin, 1966); John H. Strange, "The Negro in Philadelphia Politics 1963-65," (unpublished Ph.D. Dissertation, Princeton University, 1966).

[7] Donald Matthews and James Prothro, *Negroes and the New Southern Politics* (New York, 1966). Considerable insight on these data is provided in John Orbell, "Protest Participation among Southern Negro College Students," *The American Political Science Review*, 61 (June, 1967), 446-456.

[8] Kenneth Clark, *Dark Ghetto* (New York, 1965).

[9] *Negro Politics* (New York, 1960).

and other less systematic works on contemporary Negro politics,[10] for all of their intuitive insights and valuable documentation, offer no theoretical formulations which encourage conceptualization about the interaction between recent Negro political activity and the political process.

Heretofore the best attempt to place Negro protest activity in a framework which would generate additional insights has been that of James Q. Wilson.[11] Wilson has suggested that protest activity be conceived as a problem of bargaining in which the basic problem is that Negro groups lack political resources to exchange. Wilson called this "the problem of the powerless."[12]

is threat of "revolt" a resource?

While many of Wilson's insights remain valid, his approach is limited in applicability because it defines protest in terms of mass action or response and as utilizing exclusively negative inducements in the bargaining process. Negative inducements are defined as inducements which are not absolutely preferred but are preferred over alternative possibilities.[13] Yet it might be argued that protest designed to appeal to groups which oppose suffering and exploitation, for example, might be offering positive inducements in bargaining. A few Negro students sitting at a lunch counter might be engaged in what would be called protest, and by their actions might be trying to appeal to other groups in the system with positive inducements. Additionally, Wilson's concentration on Negro civic action, and his exclusive interest in exploring the protest process to explain Negro civic action, tend to obscure comparison with protest activity which does not necessarily arise within the Negro community.

Assuming a somewhat different focus, protest activity is defined as a mode of political action oriented toward objection to one or more policies or conditions, characterized by showmanship or display of an unconventional nature, and undertaken to obtain rewards from political or economic systems while working within the systems. The "problem of the powerless" in protest activity is to activate "third parties" to enter the implicit or explicit bargaining arena in ways favorable to the protesters. This is one of the few ways in which they can "create" bargaining resources. It is intuitively unconvincing to suggest that fifteen people sitting uninvited in the Mayor's office have the power to move City Hall. A better formulation would suggest that the people sitting in may be able to appeal to a wider public to which the city administration is sensitive. Thus in successful protest activity the *reference publics* of protest *targets* may be conceived as explicitly or

---

[10] A complete list would be voluminous. See, e.g., Nat Hentoff, *The New Equality* (New York, 1964); Arthur Waskow, *From Race Riot to Sit-in* (New York, 1966).

[11] "The Strategy of Protest: Problems of Negro Civic Action," *Journal of Conflict Resolution*, 3 (September, 1961), 291-303. The reader will recognize the author's debt to this highly suggestive article, not least Wilson's recognition of the utility of the bargaining framework for examining protest activity.

[12] *Ibid.*, p. 291.

[13] *Ibid.*, p. 291-292.

implicitly reacting to protest in such a way that target groups or individuals respond in ways favorable to the protesters.[14]

It should be emphasized that the focus here is on protest by relatively powerless groups. Illustrations can be summoned, for example, of activity designated as "protest" involving high status pressure groups or hundreds of thousands of people. While such instances may share some of the characteristics of protest activity, they may not represent examples of developing political resources by relatively powerless groups because the protesting groups may already command political resources by virtue of status, numbers or cohesion.

It is appropriate also to distinguish between the relatively restricted use of the concept of protest adopted here and closely related political strategies which are often designated as "protest" in popular usage. Where groups already possess sufficient resources with which to bargain, as in the case of some economic boycotts and labor strikes, they may be said to engage in "direct confrontation."[15] Similarly, protest which represents efforts to "activate reference publics" should be distinguished from "alliance formation," where third parties are induced to join the conflict, but where the value orientations of third parties are sufficiently similar to those of the protesting group that concerted or coordinated action is possible. Alliance formation is particularly desirable for relatively powerless groups if they seek to join the decision-making process as participants.

The distinction between activating reference publics and alliance formation is made on the assumption that where goal orientations among protest groups and the reference publics of target groups are similar, the political dynamics of petitioning target groups are different than when such goal orientations are relatively divergent. Clearly the more similar the goal orientations, the greater the likelihood of protest success, other things being equal. This discussion is intended to highlight, however, those instances where goal orientations of reference publics depart significantly, in direction or intensity, from the goals of protest groups.

Say that to protest some situation, A would like to enter a bargaining situation with B. But A has nothing B wants, and thus cannot bargain. A then attempts to create political resources by activating other groups to enter the conflict. A then organizes to take action against B with respect to certain goals. *Information concerning these goals must be conveyed through*

---

[14] See E.E. Schattschneider's discussion of expanding the scope of the conflict, *The Semisovereign People* (New York, 1960). Another way in which bargaining resources may be "created" is to increase the relative cohesion of groups, or to increase the perception of group solidarity as a precondition to greater cohesion. This appears to be the primary goal of political activity which is generally designated "community organization." Negro activists appear to recognize the utility of this strategy in their advocacy of "black power." In some instances protest activity may be designed in part to accomplish this goal in addition to activating reference publics.

[15] For an example of "direct confrontation," one might study the three-month Negro boycott of white merchants in Natchez, Miss., which resulted in capitulation to boycott demands by city government leaders. See *The New York Times*, December 4, 1965, p. 1.

communications media (C, D, and E) to F, G, and H, which are B's *reference publics.* In response to the reactions of F, G, and H, or in anticipation of their reactions, B responds, *in some way,* to the protesters' demands. This formulation requires the conceptualization of protest activity when undertaken to create bargaining resources as a political process which requires communication and is characterized by a multiplicity of constituencies for protest leadership.

A schematic representation of the process of protest as utilized by relatively powerless groups is presented in Figure 1. In contrast to a simplistic pressure group model which would posit a direct relationship between pressure group and pressured, the following discussion is guided by the assumption (derived from observation) that protest is a highly indirect process in which communications media and the reference publics of protest targets play critical roles. It is also a process characterized by reciprocal relations, in which protest leaders frame strategies according to their perception of the needs of (many) other actors.

In this view protest constituents limit the options of protest leaders at the same time that the protest leader influences their perception of the strategies and rhetoric which they will support. Protest activity is filtered through the communications media in influencing the perceptions of the reference publics of protest targets. To the extent that the influence of reference publics is supportive of protest goals, target groups will dispense symbolic or material rewards. Material rewards are communicated directly to protest constituents.

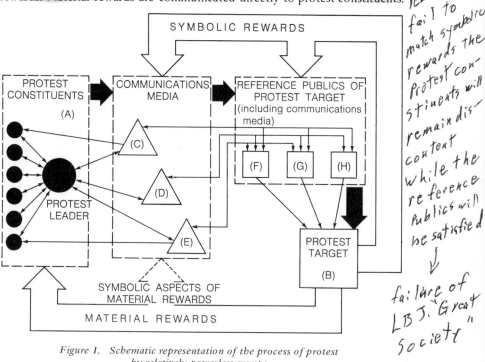

Figure 1. Schematic representation of the process of protest by relatively powerless groups

Symbolic rewards are communicated in part to protest constituents, but primarily are communicated to the reference publics of target groups, who provide the major stimuli for public policy pronouncements.

The study of protest as adopted by relatively powerless groups should provide insights into the structure and behavior of groups involved in civil rights politics and associated with the "war on poverty." It should direct attention toward the ways in which administrative agencies respond to "crises." Additionally, the study of protest as a political resource should influence some general conceptualizations of American political pluralism. Robert Dahl, for example, describes the "normal American political process" as

> one in which there is a high probability that an active and legitimate group in the population can make itself heard effectively at some crucial stage in the process of decision.[16]

Although he agrees that control over decisions is unevenly divided in the population, Dahl writes:

> When I say that a group is heard "effectively" I mean more than the simple fact that it makes a noise; I mean that one or more officials are not only ready to listen to the noise, but expect to suffer in some significant way if they do not placate the group, its leaders, or its most vociferous members. To satisfy the group may require one or more of a great variety of actions by the responsive leader: pressure for substantive policies, appointments, graft, respect, expression of the appropriate emotions, or the right combination of reciprocal noises.[17]

These statements, which in some ways resemble David Truman's discussion of the power of "potential groups,"[18] can be illuminated by the study of protest activity in three ways. First, what are the probabilities that relatively powerless groups can make themselves heard effectively? In what ways will such groups be heard or "steadily appeased"?[19] Concentration on the process of protest activity may reveal the extent to which, and the conditions under which, relatively powerless groups are likely to prove effective. Protest undertaken to obstruct policy decisions, for example, may enjoy greater success probabilities than protest undertaken in an effort to evoke constructive policy innovations.[20]

Second, does it make sense to suggest that all groups which make noises will receive responses from public officials? Perhaps the groups which make noises

---

[16] *A Preface to Democratic Theory* (Chicago, 1956), pp. 145-146.

[17] *Ibid.*

[18] *The Governmental Process* (New York, 1951), p. 104.

[19] See Dahl, *A Preface to Democratic Theory*, p. 146.

[20] Observations that all groups can influence public policy at some stage of the political process are frequently made about the role of "veto groups" in American politics. See *Ibid.*, pp. 104 ff. See also David Reisman, *The Lonely Crowd* (New Haven, 1950), pp. 211 ff., for an earlier discussion of veto-group politics. Yet protest should be evaluated when it is adopted to obtain assertive as well as defensive goals.

do not have to be satisfied at all, but it is other groups which receive assurances or recognition. Third, what are the probabilities that groups which make noises will receive tangible rewards, rather than symbolic assurances?[21] Dahl lumps these rewards together in the same paragraph, but dispensation of tangible rewards clearly has a different impact upon groups than the dispensation of symbolic rewards. Dahl is undoubtedly correct when he suggests that the relative fluidity of American politics is a critical characteristic of the American political system.[22] But he is less precise and less convincing when it comes to analyzing the extent to which the system is indeed responsive to the relatively powerless groups of the "average citizen."[23]

The following sections are an attempt to demonstrate the utility of the conceptualization of the protest process presented above. This will be done by exploring the problems encountered and the strains generated by protest leaders in interacting with four constituencies. It will be useful to concentrate attention on the maintenance and enhancement needs not only of the large formal organizations which dominate city politics,[24] but also of the ad hoc protest groups which engage them in civic controversy. It will also prove rewarding to examine the role requirements of individuals in leadership positions as they perceive the problems of constituency manipulation. In concluding remarks some implications of the study of protest for the pluralist description of American politics will be suggested.[25]

II. Protest leadership and organizational base

The organizational maintenance needs of relatively powerless, low income, ad hoc protest groups center around the tension generated by the need for leadership to offer symbolic and intangible inducements to protest participation when immediate, material rewards cannot be anticipated, and the need

[21] See Murray Edelman, *The Symbolic Uses of Politics* (Urbana, Ill., 1964), ch. 2.

[22] See Dahl, *Who Governs?* (New Haven, 1961), pp. 305 ff.

[23] In a recent formulation, Dahl reiterates the theme of wide dispersion of influence. "More than other systems, [democracies] ... try to disperse influence widely to their citizens by means of the suffrage, elections, freedom of speech, press, and assembly, the right of opponents to criticize the conduct of government, the right to organize political parties, and in other ways." *Pluralist Democracy in the United States* (Chicago, 1967), p. 373. Here, however, he concentrates more on the availability of options to all groups in the system, rather than on the relative probabilities that all groups in fact have access to the political process. See pp. 372 ff.

[24] See Edward Banfield, *Political Influence* (New York, 1961), p. 263. The analysis of organizational incentive structure which heavily influences Banfield's formulation is Chester Barnard, *The Functions of the Executive* (Cambridge, Mass., 1938).

[25] In the following attempt to develop the implications of this conceptualization of protest activity, I have drawn upon extensive field observations and bibliographical research. Undoubtedly, however, individual assertions, while representing my best judgment concerning the available evidence, in the future may require modification as the result of further empirical research.

to provide at least the promise of material rewards. Protest leaders must try to evoke responses from other actors in the political process, at the same time that they pay attention to participant organizational needs. Thus relatively deprived groups in the political system not only receive symbolic reassurance while material rewards from the system are withheld,[26] but protest leaders have a stake in perpetuating the notion that relatively powerless groups retain political efficacy despite what in many cases is obvious evidence to the contrary.

The tension embraced by protest leaders over the nature of inducements toward protest participation accounts in part for the style adopted and goals selected by protest leaders. Groups which seek psychological gratification from politics, but cannot or do not anticipate material political rewards, may be attracted to militant protest leaders. To these groups, angry rhetoric may prove a desirable quality in the short run. Where groups depend upon the political system for tangible benefits, or where participation in the system provides intangible benefits, moderate leadership is likely to prevail. Wilson has observed similar tendencies among Negro leaders of large, formal organizations.[27] It is no less true for leadership of protest groups. Groups whose members derive tangible satisfactions from political participation will not condone leaders who are stubborn in compromise or appear to question the foundations of the system. This coincides with Truman's observation:

> Violation of the "rules of the game" normally will weaken a group's cohesion, reduce its status in the community, and expose it to the claims of other groups.[28]

On the other hand, the cohesion of relatively powerless groups may be strengthened by militant, ideological leadership which questions the rules of the game and challenges their legitimacy.

Cohesion is particularly important when protest leaders bargain directly with target groups. In that situation, leaders' ability to control protest constituents and guarantee their behavior represents a bargaining strength.[29] For this reason Wilson stressed the bargaining difficulties of Negro leaders who cannot guarantee constituent behavior, and pointed out the significance of the strategy of projecting the image of group solidarity when the reality of cohesion is a fiction.[30] Cohesion is less significant at other times. Divided leadership may prove productive by bargaining in tandem,[31] or by

---

[26] As Edelman suggests, cited previously.

[27] *Negro Politics*, p. 290.

[28] *The Governmental Process*, p. 513.

[29] But cf. Thomas Schelling's discussion of "binding oneself," *The Strategy of Conflict* (Cambridge, Mass., 1960), pp. 22 ff.

[30] "The Strategy of Protest," p. 297.

[31] This is suggested by Wilson, "The Strategy of Protest," p. 298; St. Clair Drake and Horace Cayton, *Black Metropolis* (New York, 1962, rev. ed.), p. 731; Walker, "Protest and Negotiation," p. 122. Authors who argue that divided leadership is dysfunctional have been Clark, p. 156; and Tilman Cothran, "The Negro Protest Against Segregation in the South," *The Annals*, 357 (January, 1965), p. 72.

minimizing strain among groups in the protest process. Further, community divisions may prove less detrimental to protest aims when strong third parties have entered the dispute originally generated by protest organizations.

The intangible rewards of assuming certain postures toward the political system may not be sufficient to sustain an organizational base. It may be necessary to renew constantly the intangible rewards of participation. And to the extent that people participate in order to achieve tangible benefits, their interest in a protest organization may depend upon the organization's relative material success. Protest leaders may have to tailor their style to present participants with tangible successes, or with the appearance of success. Leaders may have to define the issues with concern for increasing their ability to sustain organizations. The potential for protest among protest group members may have to be manipulated by leadership if the group is to be sustained.[32]

The participants in protest organizations limit the flexibility of protest leadership. This obtains for two reasons. They restrict public actions by leaders who must continue to solicit active participant support, and they place restraints on the kinds of activities which can be considered appropriate for protest purposes. Poor participants cannot commonly be asked to engage in protest requiring air transportation. Participants may have anxieties related to their environment or historical situation which discourages engagement in some activities. They may be afraid of job losses, beatings by the police, or summary evictions. Negro protest in the Deep South has been inhibited by realistic expectations of retribution.[33] Protests over slum housing conditions are undermined by tenants who expect landlord retaliation for engaging in tenant organizing activity.[34] Political or ethical mores may conflict with a proposed course of action, diminishing participation.[35]

On the other hand, to the extent that fears are real, or that the larger community perceives protest participants as subject to these fears, protest

[32] This observation is confirmed by a student of the Southern civil rights movement: "Negroes demand of protest leaders constant progress. The combination of long-standing discontent and a new-found belief in the possibility of change produces a constant state of tension and aggressiveness in the Negro community. But this discontent is vague and diffuse, not specific; the masses do not define the issues around which action shall revolve. This the leader must do." Lewis Killian, "Leadership in the Desegregation Crisis: An Institutional Analysis," in Muzafer Sherif (ed.), *Intergroup Relations and Leadership* (New York, 1962), p. 159.

[33] Significantly, Southern Negro students who actively participated in the early phases of the sit-in movement "tended to be unusually optimistic about race relations and tolerant of whites [when compared with inactive Negro students]. They not only *were* better off, objectively speaking, than other Negroes but *felt* better off." Matthews and Prothro, *op. cit.*, p. 424.

[34] This is particularly the case in cities such as Washington, D.C., where landlord-tenant laws offer little protection against retaliatory eviction. See, e.g., Robert Schoshinski, "Remedies of the Indigent Tenant: Proposal for Change," *Georgetown Law Journal,* 54 (Winter, 1966), 541 ff.

[35] Wilson regarded this as a chief reason for lack of protest activity in 1961. He wrote: ". . . some of the goals now being sought by Negroes are least applicable to those groups of Negroes most suited to protest action. Protest action involving such tactics as mass meetings, picketing, boycotts, and strikes rarely finds enthusiastic participants among upper-income and higher status individuals": "The Strategy of Protest," p. 296.

may actually be strengthened. Communications media and potential allies will consider more soberly the complaints of people who are understood to be placing themselves in jeopardy. When young children and their parents made the arduous bus trip from Mississippi to Washington, D.C., to protest the jeopardizing of Head Start funds, the courage and expense represented by their effort created a respect and visibility for their position which might not have been achieved by local protest efforts.[36]

Protest activity may be undertaken by organizations with established relationship patterns, behavior norms, and role expectations. These organizations are likely to have greater access to other groups in the political system, and a demonstrated capacity to maintain themselves. Other protest groups, however, may be ad hoc arrangements without demonstrated internal or external relationship patterns. These groups will have different organizational problems, in response to which it is necessary to engage in different kinds of protest activity.

The scarcity of organizational resources also places limits upon the ability of relatively powerless groups to maintain the foundations upon which protest organizations develop. Relatively powerless groups, to engage in political activity of any kind, must command at least some resources. This is not tautological. Referring again to a continuum on which political groups are placed according to their relative command of resources, one may draw a line somewhere along the continuum representing a "Threshold of civic group political participation." Clearly some groups along the continuum will possess some political resources (enough, say, to emerge for inspection) but not enough to exercise influence in civic affairs. Relatively powerless groups, to be influential, must cross the "threshold" to engage in politics. Although the availability of group resources is a critical consideration at all stages of the protest process, it is particularly important in explaining why some groups seem to "surface" with sufficient strength to command attention. The following discussion of some critical organizational resources should illuminate this point.

Skilled professionals frequently must be available to protest organizations. Lawyers, for example, play extremely important roles in enabling protest groups to utilize the judicial process and avail themselves of adequate preparation of court cases. Organizational reputation may depend upon a combination of ability to threaten the conventional political system and of exercising statutory rights in court. Availability of lawyers depends upon ability to pay fees and/or the attractiveness to lawyers of participation in protest group activity. Volunteer professional assistance may not prove adequate. One night a week volunteered by an aspiring politician in a housing clinic cannot satisfy the needs of a chaotic political movement.[37] The need

---

[36] See *The New York Times,* February 12, 1966, p. 56.

[37] On housing clinic services provided by political clubs, see James Q. Wilson, *The Amateur Democrat: Club Politics in Three Cities* (Chicago, 1962), pp. 63-64, 176. On the need for lawyers among low income people, see e.g., *The Extension of Legal Services to the Poor,* Conference Proceedings (Washington, D.C., n.d.), esp. pp. 51-60; and "Neighborhood Law Offices: The New Wave in Legal Services for the Poor," *Harvard Law Review,* 80 (February, 1967), 805-850.

for skilled professionals is not restricted to lawyers. For example, a group seeking to protest an urban renewal policy might require the services of architects and city planners in order to present a viable alternative to a city proposal.

Financial resources not only purchase legal assistance, but enable relatively powerless groups to conduct minimum programs of political activities. To the extent that constituents are unable or unwilling to pay even small membership dues, then financing the cost of mimeographing flyers, purchasing supplies, maintaining telephone service, paying rent, and meeting a modest payroll become major organizational problems. And to the extent that group finances are supplied by outside individual contributions or government or foundation grants, the long-term options of the group are sharply constrained by the necessity of orienting group goals and tactics to anticipate the potential objections of financial supporters.

Some dependence upon even minimal financial resources can be waived if organizations evoke passionate support from constituents. Secretarial help and block organizers will come forward to work without compensation if they support the cause of neighborhood organizations or gain intangible benefits based upon association with the group. Protest organizations may also depend upon skilled non-professionals, such as college students, whose access to people and political and economic institutions often assist protest groups in cutting across income lines to seek support. Experience with ad hoc political groups, however, suggests that this assistance is sporadic and undependable. Transient assistance is particularly typical of skilled, educated, and employable volunteers whose abilities can be applied widely. The die-hards of ad hoc political groups are often those people who have no place else to go, nothing else to do.

Constituent support will be affected by the nature of the protest target and whether protest activity is directed toward defensive or assertive goals. Obstructing specific public policies may be easier than successfully recommending constructive policy changes. Orientations toward defensive goals may require less constituent energy, and less command over resources of money, expertise and status.[38]

III. Protest leadership and communications media

The communications media are extremely powerful in city politics. In granting or withholding publicity, in determining what information most people will have on most issues, and what alternatives they will consider in response to issues, the media truly, as Norton Long has put it, "set . . . the civic agenda."[39] To the extent that successful protest activity depends upon

[38] An illustration of low income group protest organization mobilized for veto purposes is provided by Dahl in "The Case of the Metal Houses." See *Who Governs?* pp. 192 ff.

[39] Norton Long, "The Local Community as an Ecology of Games," in Long, *The Polity*, Charles Press, ed. (Chicago, 1962), p. 153. See pp. 152-154. See also Roscoe C.

appealing to, and/or threatening, other groups in the community, the communications media set the limits of protest action. If protest tactics are not considered significant by the media, or if newspapers and television reporters or editors decide to overlook protest tactics, protest organizations will not succeed. Like 'the tree falling unheard in the forest, there is no protest unless protest is perceived and projected.

A number of writers have noticed that the success of protest activity seems directly related to the amount of publicity it receives outside the immediate arena in which protest takes place. This view has not been stated systematically, but hints can be found in many sources. In the literature on civil rights politics, the relevance of publicity represents one of the few hypotheses available concerning the dynamics of successful protest activity.[40]

When protest tactics do receive coverage in the communications media, the way in which they are presented will influence all other actors in the system, including the protesters themselves. Conformity to standards of newsworthiness in political style, and knowledge of the prejudices and desires of the individuals who determine media coverage in political skills, represent crucial determinants of leadership effectiveness.

The organizational behavior of newspapers can partly be understood by examining the maintenance and enhancement needs which direct them toward projects of civic betterment and impressions of accomplishment.[41] But insight may also be gained by analyzing the role requirements of reporters, editors, and others who determine newspaper policy. Reporters, for example, are frequently motivated by the desire to contribute to civic affairs by their "objective" reporting of significant events; by the premium they place on accuracy; and by the credit which they receive for sensationalism and "scoops."

These requirements may be difficult to accommodate at the same time. Reporters demand newsworthiness of their subjects in the short run, but also require reliability and verifiability in the longer run. Factual accuracy may dampen newsworthiness. Sensationalism, attractive to some newspaper editors, may be inconsistent with reliable, verifiable narration of events. Newspapers at first may be attracted to sensationalism, and later demand verifiability in the interests of community harmony (and adherence to professional journalistic standards).

Most big city newspapers have reporters whose assignments permit them to cover aspects of city politics with some regularity. These reporters, whose

---

Martin, Frank J. Munger, *et al.*, *Decisions in Syracuse: A Metropolitan Action Study* (Garden City, N.Y., 1965) (originally published: 1961), pp. 326-327.

[40] See, e.g., Thompson, *op. cit.*, p. 134, and *passim*; Martin Oppenheimer, "The Southern Student Movement: Year I," *Journal of Negro Education*, 33 (Fall, 1964), p. 397; Cothran, *op. cit.*, p. 72; Pauli Murray, "Protest Against the Legal Status of the Negro," *The Annals*, 357 (January, 1965), p. 63; Allan P. Sindler, "Protest Against the Political Status of the Negroes," *The Annals*, 357 (January, 1965), p. 50.

[41] See Banfield, *op. cit.*, p. 275.

"beats" may consist of "civil rights" or "poverty," sometimes develop close relationships with their news subjects. These relationships may develop symbiotic overtones because of the mutuality of interest between the reporter and the news subject. Reporters require fresh information on protest developments, while protest leaders have a vital interest in obtaining as much press coverage as possible.

Inflated reports of protest success may be understood in part by examining this relationship between reporter and protest leader. Both have role-oriented interests in projecting images of protest strength and threat. In circumstances of great excitement, when competition from other news media representatives is high, a reporter may find that he is less governed by the role requirement of verification and reliability than he is by his editor's demand for "scoops" and news with high audience appeal.[42]

On the other hand, the demands of the media may conflict with the needs of protest group maintenance. Consider the leader whose constituents are attracted solely by pragmatic statements not exceeding what they consider political "good taste." He is constrained from making militant demands which would isolate him from constituents. This constraint may cost him appeal in the press.[43] However, the leader whose organizing appeal requires militant rhetoric may obtain eager press coverage only to find that his inflammatory statements lead to alienation of potential allies and exclusion from the explicit bargaining process.[44]

News media do not report events in the same way. Television may select for broadcast only thirty seconds of a half-hour news conference. This coverage will probably focus on immediate events, without background or explanatory material. Newspapers may give more complete accounts of the same event. The most complete account may appear in the weekly edition of a neighborhood or ethnic newspaper. Differential coverage by news media, and

---

[42] For a case study of the interaction between protest leaders and newspaper reporters, see Michael Lipsky, "Rent Strikes in New York City: Protest Politics and the Power of the Poor," (unpublished Ph.D. dissertation, Princeton University, 1967), pp. 139-49. Bernard Cohen has analyzed the impact of the press on foreign policy from the perspective of reporters' role requirements: see his *The Press and Foreign Policy* (Princeton, N. J., 1963), esp. chs. 2-3.

[43] An example of protest conducted by middle-class women engaged in pragmatic protest over salvaging park space is provided in John B. Keeley, *Moses on the Green*, Inter-University Case Program, No. 45 (University, Ala., 1959).

[44] This was the complaint of Floyd McKissick, National Director of the Congress of Racial Equality, when he charged that ". . . there are only two kinds of statements a black man can make and expect that the white press will report. . . . First . . . is an attack on another black man. . . . The second is a statement that sounds radical, violent, extreme—the verbal equivalent of a riot. . . . [T]he Negro is being rewarded by the public media only if he turns on another Negro and uses his tongue as a switchblade, or only if he sounds outlandish, extremist or psychotic." Statement at the Convention of the American Society of Newspaper Editors, April 20, 1967, Washington, D.C., as reported in *The New York Times,* April 21, 1967, p. 22. See also the remarks of journalist Ted Poston, *ibid.,* April 26, 1965, p. 26.

differential news media habits in the general population,[45] are significant factors in permitting protest leaders to juggle conflicting demands of groups in the protest process.

Similar tensions exist in the leader's relationships with protest targets. Ideological postures may gain press coverage and constituency approval, but may alienate target groups with whom it would be desirable to bargain explicitly. Exclusion from the councils of decision-making may have important consequences, since the results of target group deliberations may satisfy activated reference publics without responding to protest goals. If activated reference publics are required to increase the bargaining position of the protest group, protest efforts thereafter will have diminshed chances of success.

IV. Protest leadership and "third parties"

I have argued that the essence of political protest consists of activating third parties to participate in controversy in ways favorable to protest goals. In previous sections I have attempted to analyze some of the tensions which result from protest leaders' attempts to activate reference publics of protest targets at the same time that they must retain the interest and support of protest organization participants. This phenomenon is in evidence when Negro leaders, recognized as such by public officials, find their support eroded in the Negro community because they have engaged in explicit bargaining situations with politicians. Negro leaders are thus faced with the dilemma that when they behave like other ethnic group representatives they are faced with loss of support from those whose intense activism has been aroused in the Negro community, yet whose support is vital if they are to remain credible as leaders to public officials.

The tensions resulting from conflicting maintenance needs of protest organizations and activated third parties present difficulties for protest leaders. One way in which these tensions can be minimized is by dividing leadership responsibilities. If more than one group is engaged in protest activity, protest leaders can, in effect, divide up public roles so as to reduce as much as possible the gap between the implicit demands of different groups for appropriate rhetoric, and what in fact is said. Thus divided leadership may perform the latent function of minimizing tensions among elements in the protest process by permitting different groups to listen selectively to protest spokesmen.[46]

Another way in which strain among different groups can be minimized is through successful public relations. Minimization of strain may depend upon

---

[45] Matthews and Prothro found, for example, that in their south-wide Negro population sample, 38 percent read Negro-oriented magazines and 17 percent read newspapers written for Negroes. These media treat news of interest to Negroes more completely and sympathetically than do the general media. See pp. 248 ff.

[46] See footnote 31 above.

ambiguity of action or statement, deception, or upon effective inter-group communication. Failure to clarify meaning, or falsification, may increase protest effectiveness. Effective intragroup communication may increase the likelihood that protest constituents will "understand" that ambiguous or false public statements have "special meaning" and need not be taken seriously. The Machiavellian circle is complete when we observe that although lying may be prudent, the appearance of integrity and forthrightness is desirable for public relations, since these values are widely shared.

It has been observed that "[t]he militant displays an unwillingness to perform those administrative tasks which are necessary to operate an organization. Probably the skills of the agitator and the skills of the administrator . . . are not incompatible, but few men can do both well."[47] These skills may or may not be incompatible as personality traits, but they indeed represent conflicting role demands on protest leadership. When a protest leader exhausts time and energy conducting frequent press conferences, arranging for politicians and celebrities to appear at rallies, delivering speeches to sympathetic local groups, college symposia and other forums, constantly picketing for publicity and generally making "contacts," he is unable to pursue the direction of office routine, clerical tasks, research and analysis, and other chores.

The difficulties of delegating routine tasks are probably directly related to the skill levels and previous administrative experiences of group members. In addition, to the extent that involvement in protest organizations is a function of rewards received or expected by individuals because of the excitement or entertainment value of participation, then the difficulties of delegating routine, relatively uninteresting chores to group members will be increased. Yet attention to such details affects the perception of protest groups by organizations whose support or assistance may be desired in the future. These considerations add to the protest leader's problem of risking alienation of protest participants because of potentially unpopular cooperation with the "power structure."

In the protest paradigm developed here, "third parties" refers both to the reference publics of target groups and, more narrowly, to the interest groups whose regular interaction with protest targets tends to develop into patterns of influence.[48] We have already discussed some of the problems associated with activating the reference publics of target groups. In discussing the constraints placed upon protest, attention may be focused upon the likelihood that groups seeking to create political resources through protest will be included in the explicit bargaining process with other pressure groups. For protest groups, these constraints are those which occur because of class and political style, status, and organizational resources.

The established civic groups most likely to be concerned with the problems raised by relatively powerless groups are those devoted to service in the public

---

[47]Wilson, *Negro Politics*, p. 225.

[48]See Wallace Sayre and Herbert Kaufman, *Governing New York City* (New York, 1960), pp. 257 ff. Also see Banfield, *op. cit.*, p. 267.

welfare and those "liberally" oriented groups whose potential constituents are either drawn from the same class as the protest groups (such as some trade unions), or whose potential constituents are attracted to policies which appear to serve the interest of the lower class or minority groups (such as some reform political clubs).[49] These civic groups have frequently cultivated clientele relationships with city agencies over long periods. Their efforts have been reciprocated by agency officials anxious to develop constituencies to support and defend agency administrative and budgetary policies. In addition, clientele groups are expected to endorse and legitimize agency aggrandizement. These relationships have been developed by agency officials and civic groups for mutual benefit, and cannot be destroyed, abridged or avoided without cost.

Protest groups may well be able to raise the saliency of issues on the civic agenda through utilization of communications media and successful appeals or threats to wider publics, but admission to policy-making councils is frequently barred because of the angry, militant rhetorical style adopted by protest leaders. People in power do not like to sit down with rogues. Protest leaders are likely to have phrased demands in ways unacceptable to lawyers and other civic activists whose cautious attitude toward public policy may reflect not only their good intentions but their concern for property rights, due process, pragmatic legislating or judicial precedent.

Relatively powerless groups lack participation of individuals with high status whose endorsement of specific proposals lend them increased legitimacy. Good causes may always attract the support of high status individuals. But such individuals' willingness to devote time to the promotion of specific proposals is less likely than the one-shot endorsements which these people distribute more readily.

Similarly, protest organizations often lack the resources on which entry into the policy-making process depends. These resources include maintenance of a staff with expertise and experience in the policy area. This expertise may be in the areas of the law, planning and architecture, proposal writing, accounting, educational policy, federal grantsmanship or publicity. Combining experience with expertise is one way to create status in issue areas. The dispensing of information by interest groups has been widely noted as a major source of influence. Over time the experts develop status in their areas of competence somewhat independent of the influence which adheres to them as information-providers. Groups which cannot or do not engage lawyers to assist in proposing legislation, and do not engage in collecting reliable data, cannot participate in policy deliberations or consult in these matters. Protest oriented groups, whose primary talents are in dramatizing issues, cannot credibly attempt to present data considered "objective" or suggestions considered "responsible" by public officials. Few can be convincing as both advocate and arbiter at the same time.

[49] See Wilson, *The Amateur Democrats*, previously cited. These groups are most likely to be characterized by broad scope of political interest and frequent intervention in politics. See Sayre and Kaufman, *op. cit.*, p. 79.

V. Protest leadership and target groups

The probability of protest success may be approached by examining the maintenance needs of organizations likely to be designated as target groups.[50] For the sake of clarity, and because protest activity increasingly is directed toward government, I shall refer in the following paragraphs exclusively to government agencies at the municipal level. The assumption is retained, however, that the following generalizations are applicable to the other potential target groups.

Some of the constraints placed on protest leadership in influencing target groups have already been mentioned in preceding sections. The lack of status and resources that inhibit protest groups from participating in policy-making conferences, for example, also helps prevent explicit bargaining between protest leaders and city officials. The strain between rhetoric which appeals to the protest participants and public statements to which communications media and "third parties" respond favorably also exists with reference to target groups.

Yet there is a distinguishing feature of the maintenance needs and strategies of city agencies which specifically constrains protest organizations. This is the agency director's need to protect "the jurisdiction and income of his organization [by] . . . [m]anipulation of the external environment."[51] In so doing he may satisfy his reference groups without responding to protest group demands. At least six tactics are available to protest targets who are motivated to respond in some way to protest activity but seek primarily to satisfy their reference publics. These tactics may be employed whether or not target groups are "sincere" in responding to protest demands.

1. Target groups may dispense symbolic satisfactions. Appearances of activity and commitment to problems substitute for, or supplement, resource allocation and policy innovations which would constitute tangible responses to protest activity. If symbolic responses supplement tangible pay-offs, they are frequently coincidental, rather than intimately linked, to projection of response by protest targets. Typical in city politics of the symbolic response is the ribbon cutting, street corner ceremony or the walking tour press conference. These occasions are utilized not only to build agency

[50] Another approach, persuasively presented by Wilson, concentrates on protest success as a function of the relative unity and vulnerability of targets. See "The Strategy of Protest," pp. 293 ff. This insight helps explain, for example, why protest against housing segregation commonly takes the form of action directed against government (a unified target) rather than against individual homeowners (who present a dispersed target). One problem with this approach is that it tends to obscure the possibility that targets, as collections of individuals, may be divided in evaluation of and sympathy for protest demands. Indeed, city agency administrators under some circumstances act as partisans in protest conflicts. As such, they frequently appear ambivalent toward protest goals: sympathetic to the ends while concerned that the means employed in protest reflect negatively on their agencies.

[51] Sayre and Kaufman, *op. cit.*, p. 253.

constituencies,[52] but to satisfy agency reference publics that attention is being directed to problems of civic concern. In this sense publicist tactics may be seen as defensive maneuvers. Symbolic aspects of the actions of public officials can also be recognized in the commissioning of expensive studies and the rhetorical flourishes with which "massive attacks," "comprehensive programs," and "coordinated planning" are frequently promoted.

City agencies establish distinct apparatus and procedures for dealing with crises which may be provoked by protest groups. Housing-related departments in New York City may be cited for illustration. It is usually the case in these agencies that the Commissioner or a chief deputy, a press secretary and one or two other officials devote whatever time is necessary to collect information, determine policy and respond quickly to reports of "crises." This is functional for tenants, who, if they can generate enough concern, may be able to obtain shortcuts through lengthy agency procedures. It is also functional for officials who want to project images of action rather than merely receiving complaints. Concentrating attention on the maintenance needs of city politicians during protest crises suggests that pronouncements of public officials serve purposes independent of their dedication to alleviation of slum conditions.[53]

Independent of dispensation of tangible benefits to protest groups, public officials continue to respond primarily to their own reference publics. Murray Edelman has suggested that:

> Tangible resources and benefits are frequently not distributed to unorganized political group interests as promised in regulatory statutes and the propaganda attending their enactment.[54]

His analysis may be supplemented by suggesting that symbolic dispensations may not only serve to reassure unorganized political group interests, but may also contribute to reducing the anxiety level of organized interests and wider publics which are only tangentially involved in the issues.

2. Target groups may dispense token material satisfactions. When city agencies respond, with much publicity, to cases brought to their attention representing examples of the needs dramatized by protest organizations, they may appear to respond to protest demands while in fact only responding on a case basis, instead of a general basis. For the protesters served by agencies in this fashion it is of considerable advantage that agencies can be influenced by protest action. Yet it should not be ignored that in handling the "crisis" cases, public officials give the appearance of response to their reference publics, while mitigating demands for an expensive, complex *general* assault on problems represented by the cases to which responses are given. Token

---

[52] See *ibid.*, pp. 253 ff.

[53] See Lipsky, *op. cit.*, chs. 5-6. The appearance of responsiveness may be given by city officials *in anticipation* of protest activity. This seems to have been the strategy of Mayor Richard Daley in his reaction to the announcement of Martin Luther King's plans to focus civil rights efforts on Chicago. See *The New York Times*, February 1, 1966, p. 11.

[54] See Edelman, *op. cit.*, p. 23.

responses, whether or not accompanied by more general responses, are particularly attractive to reporters and television news directors, who are able to dramatize individual cases convincingly, but who may be unable to "capture" the essence of general deprivation or of general efforts to alleviate conditions of deprivation.

3. Target groups may organize and innovate internally in order to blunt the impetus of protest efforts. This tactic is closely related to No. 2 (above). If target groups can act constructively in the worst cases, they will then be able to pre-empt protest efforts by responding to the cases which best dramatize protest demands. Alternatively, they may designate all efforts which jeopardize agency reputations as "worst" cases, and devote extensive resources to these cases. In some ways extraordinary city efforts are precisely consistent with protest goals. At the same time extraordinary efforts in the most heavily dramatized cases or the most extreme cases effectively wear down the "cutting-edges" of protest efforts.

Many New York City agencies develop informal "crisis" arrangements not only to project publicity, as previously indicated, but to mobilize energies toward solving "crisis" cases. They may also develop policy innovations which allow them to respond more quickly to "crisis" situations. These innovations may be important to some city residents, for whom the problems of dealing with city bureaucracies can prove insurmountable. It might be said, indeed, that the goals of protest are to influence city agencies to handle every case with the same resources that characterize their dispatch of "crisis" cases.[55]

But such policies would demand major revenue inputs. This kind of qualitative policy change is difficult to achieve. Meanwhile, internal reallocation of resources only means that routine services must be neglected so that the "crisis" programs can be enhanced. If all cases are expedited, as in a typical "crisis" response, then none can be. Thus for purposes of general solutions, "crisis" resolving can be self-defeating unless accompanied by significantly greater resource allocation. It is not self-defeating, however, to the extent that the organizational goals of city agencies are to serve a clientele while minimizing negative publicity concerning agency vigilance and responsiveness.

4. Target groups may appear to be constrained in their ability to grant protest goals.[56] This may be directed toward making the protesters appear to be unreasonable in their demands, or to be well-meaning individuals who "just don't understand how complex running a city really is." Target groups may extend sympathy but claim that they lack resources, a mandate from constituents, and/or authority to respond to protest demands. Target groups may also evade protest demands by arguing that "If-I-give-it-to-you-I-have-to-give-it-to-everyone."

The tactic of appearing constrained is particularly effective with established civic groups because there is an undeniable element of truth to it. Everyone

[55] See Lipsky, *op. cit.*, pp. 156, 249 ff.

[56] On the strategy of appearing constrained, see Schelling, *op. cit.*, pp. 22 ff.

knows that cities are financially undernourished. Established civic groups expend great energies lobbying for higher levels of funding for their pet city agencies. Thus they recognize the validity of this constraint when posed by city officials. But it is not inconsistent to point out that funds for specific, relatively inexpensive programs, or for the expansion of existing programs, can often be found if pressure is increased. While constraints on city government flexibility may be extensive, they are not absolute. Protest targets nonetheless attempt to diminish the impact of protest demands by claiming relative impotence.

5. Target groups may use their extensive resources to discredit protest leaders and organizations. Utilizing their excellent access to the press, public officials may state or imply that leaders are unreliable, ineffective as leaders ("they don't really have the people behind them"), guilty of criminal behavior, potentially guilty of such behavior, or are some shade of "left-wing." Any of these allegations may serve to diminish the appeal of protest groups to potentially sympathetic third parties. City officials, in their frequent social and informal business interaction with leaders of established civic groups, may also communicate derogatory information concerning protest groups. Discrediting of protest groups may be undertaken by some city officials while others appear (perhaps authentically) to remain sympathetic to protest demands. These tactics may be engaged in by public officials whether or not there is any validity to the allegations.

6. Target groups may postpone action. The effect of postponement, if accompanied by symbolic assurances, is to remove immediate pressure and delay specific commitments to a future date. This familiar tactic is particularly effective in dealing with protest groups because of their inherent instability. Protest groups are usually comprised of individuals whose intense political activity cannot be sustained except in rare circumstances. Further, to the extent that protest depends upon activating reference publics through strategies which have some "shock" value, it becomes increasingly difficult to activate these groups. Additionally, protest activity is inherently unstable because of the strains placed upon protest leaders who must attempt to manage four constituencies (as described herein).

The most frequent method of postponing action is to commit a subject to "study." For the many reasons elaborated in these paragraphs, it is not likely that ad hoc protest groups will be around to review the recommendations which emerge from study. The greater the expertise and the greater the status of the group making the study, the less will protest groups be able to influence whatever policy emerges. Protest groups lack the skills and resource personnel to challenge expert recommendations effectively.

Sometimes surveys and special research are undertaken in part to evade immediate pressures. Sometimes not. Research efforts are particularly necessary to secure the support of established civic groups, which place high priority on orderly procedure and policy emerging from independent analysis. Yet it must be recognized that postponing policy commitments has a distinct impact on the nature of the pressures focused on policy-makers.

IV. Conclusion

In this analysis I have agreed with James Q. Wilson that protest is correctly conceived as a strategy utilized by relatively powerless groups in order to increase their bargaining ability. As such, I have argued, it is successful to the extent that the reference publics of protest targets can be activated to enter the conflict in ways favorable to protest goals. I have suggested a model of the protest process which may assist in ordering data and indicating the salience for research of a number of aspects of protest. These include the critical role of communications media, the differential impact of material and symbolic rewards on "feedback" in protest activity, and the reciprocal relationships of actors in the protest process.

An estimation of the limits to protest efficacy, I have argued further, can be gained by recognizing the problems encountered by protest leaders who somehow must balance the conflicting maintenance needs of four groups in the protest process. This approach transcends a focus devoted primarily to characterization of group goals and targets, by suggesting that even in an environment which is relatively favorable to specific protest goals, the tensions which must be embraced by protest leadership may ultimately overwhelm protest activity.

At the outset of this essay, it was held that conceptualizing the American political system as "slack" or "fluid," in the manner of Robert Dahl, appears inadequate because of (1) a vagueness centering on the likelihood that any group can make itself heard; (2) a possible confusion as to which groups tend to receive satisfaction from the rewards dispensed by public officials; and (3) a lumping together as equally relevant rewards which are tangible and those which are symbolic. To the extent that protest is engaged in by relatively powerless groups which must create resources with which to bargain, the analysis here suggests a number of reservations concerning the pluralist conceptualization of the "fluidity" of the American political system.

Relatively powerless groups cannot use protest with a high probability of success. They lack organizational resources, by definition. But even to create bargaining resources through activating third parties, some resources are necessary to sustain organization. More importantly, relatively powerless protest groups are constrained by the unresolvable conflicts which are forced upon protest leaders who must appeal simultaneously to four constituencies which place upon them antithetical demands.

When public officials recognize the legitimacy of protest activity, they may not direct public policy toward protest groups at all. Rather, public officials are likely to aim responses at the reference publics from which they originally take their cues. Edelman has suggested that regulatory policy in practice often consists of reassuring mass publics while at the same time dispensing specific, tangible values to narrow interest groups. It is suggested here that symbolic reassurances are dispensed as much to wide, potentially concerned publics which are not directly affected by regulatory policy, as they are to wide publics comprised of the downtrodden and the deprived, in whose name policy is often written.

Complementing Edelman, it is proposed here that in the process of protest symbolic reassurances are dispensed in large measure because these are the public policy outcomes and actions desired by the constituencies to which public officials are most responsive. Satisfying these wider publics, city officials can avoid pressures toward other policies placed upon them by protest organizations.

Not only should there be some doubt as to which groups receive the symbolic recognitions which Dahl describes, but in failing to distinguish between the kinds of rewards dispensed to groups in the political system, Dahl avoids a fundamental question. It is literally fundamental because the kinds of rewards which can be obtained from politics, one might hypothesize, will have an impact upon the realistic appraisal of the efficacy of political activity. If among the groups least capable of organizing for political activity there is a history of organizing for protest, and if that activity, once engaged in, is rewarded primarily by the dispensation of symbolic gestures without perceptible changes in material conditions, then rational behavior might lead to expressions of apathy and lack of interest in politics or a rejection of conventional political channels as a meaningful arena of activity. In this sense this discussion of protest politics is consistent with Kenneth Clark's observations that the image of power, unaccompanied by material and observable rewards, leads to impressions of helplessness and reinforces political apathy in the ghetto.[57]

Recent commentary by political scientists and others regarding riots in American cities seems to focus in part on the extent to which relatively deprived groups may seek redress of legitimate grievances. Future research should continue assessment of the relationship between riots and the conditions under which access to the political system has been limited. In such research assessment of the ways in which access to public officials is obtained by relatively powerless groups through the protest process might be one important research focus.

The instability of protest activity outlined in this article also should inform contemporary political strategies. If the arguments presented here are persuasive, civil rights leaders who insist that protest activity is a shallow foundation on which to seek long-term, concrete gains may be judged essentially correct. But the arguments concerning the fickleness of the white liberal, or the ease of changing discriminatory laws relative to changing discriminatory institutions, only in part explain the instability of protest movements. An explanation which derives its strength from analysis of the political process suggests concentration on the problems of managing protest constituencies. Accordingly, Alinsky is probably on the soundest ground when he prescribes protest for the purpose of building organization. Ultimately, relatively powerless groups in most instances cannot depend upon activating other actors in the political process. Long-run success will depend upon the acquisition of stable political resources which do not rely for their use on third parties.

---

[57]Clark, *op. cit.*, pp. 154 ff.

Two Faces of Power

Peter Bachrach
Morton S. Baratz

"Who governs at the local level" has been of central concern to students of local politics for some time. Both political scientists and sociologists have long attempted to discover who has the most direct (or indirect) influence on municipal policy decisions. For example, they have argued about whether it is:

1. Those individuals who hold elected or appointed governmental positions and therefore have the authority to make decisions binding on community residents; or
2. Those who are conceived by others in the community to be influential; or
3. Those who actually participate in making public-policy decisions in various issue areas; or
4. Those who are the most active participants in community groups; or
5. Those individuals who others turn to for political information and advice—the so-called opinion leaders in a community.

In this selection, Peter Bachrach and Morton S. Baratz attempt to place in critical perspective the disagreement between sociologists and political scientists as to the locus of community power. While sociologists, using the reputational approach, have found a highly cohesive power elite composed primarily of economic notables, political scientists employing a decision or policy-making approach continue to find pluralistic, specialized leadership structures.

It should be noted before we proceed further, that in their studies, political scientists have essentially redefined the traditional notion of pluralism. Historically, pluralism included as a necessary condition active citizen participation in local and national affairs and a reasonable equity in the bargaining power of interested individuals and groups. Redefined, pluralism simply refers to viable competition among elites and selected political groups. Despite the fact that political resources are dispersed unequally in most communities and that only a small number of individuals exert direct influence over public-policy decisions, some political scientists still insist on referring to this *situation as pluralism. According to this line of reasoning, citizens still have a great deal of* indirect influence *over their political leaders through elections and the anticipated reaction of leaders to their constituents' attitudes and preferences. While it is possible to demonstrate empirically that participation in the policy-making process is limited to a minority of individuals, it is almost impossible to document indirect citizen influence.*

Bachrach and Baratz argue that although the sociologist and the political scientist have been highly critical of each other's research, *both utilize an approach and make assumptions which predetermine their findings and conclusions. This is an important point to keep in mind, since much research in the social sciences suffers from this same problem, including some of the selections in this volume. Furthermore, Bachrach and Baratz insist that there are two faces of power, neither of which the sociologist sees and only one of which political scientists take into account in their research.*

Pluralists (political scientists) object to the assumptions made by elitists (sociologists) that in every human organization there is a stable, ordered system of power, and object to a perspective which wrongly equates reputed with actual power. Elitists counter with the argument that pluralists provide no objective criteria for selecting "important" issues for study arising in the political arena. Furthermore, according to Bachrach and Baratz, pluralists take no account of the fact that power may be and often is exercised by confining the scope of decision making to relatively safe issues. Thus pluralists have begun by studying the issues rather than the values and biases that might be built into the political system and which, for the student of power, give real meaning to the issues which finally do enter the political arena.

Is a fresh approach to the study of community power needed, one that recognizes both faces of power? Bachrach and Baratz argue that there is such a need. In fact, they outline how one might proceed to study community power, using their revised approach. Would such a study increase our understanding of the nature of power and influence at the local level? How feasible, from a research standpoint, is the Bachrach and Baratz approach?

Is the policy-making process ever closed to certain individuals and groups? Is it important to know about the existing bias in a political system and how, due to the mobilization of such bias, certain groups may be excluded from the policy-making process? Are power and influence ever used to limit the scope of actual policy-making to "safe" issues? What are the implications of these questions, particularly given our ostensible commitment to the realization of democratic politics at the local level?

The concept of power remains elusive despite the recent and prolific outpourings of case studies on community power. Its elusiveness is

Reprinted from *The American Political Science Review*, vol. 56, no. 4 (December 1962), pp. 947-952, by permission of the publisher and authors. This paper is an outgrowth of a seminar in Problems of Power in Contemporary Society, conducted jointly by the authors for graduate students and undergraduate majors in political science and economics.

dramatically demonstrated by the regularity of disagreement as to the locus of community power between the sociologists and the political scientists. Sociologically oriented researchers have consistently found that power is highly centralized, while scholars trained in political science have just as regularly concluded that in "their" communities power is widely diffused.[1] Presumably, this explains why the latter group styles itself "pluralist," it counterpart "elitist."

There seems no room for doubt that the sharply divergent findings of the two groups are the product, not of sheer coincidence, but of fundamental differences in both their underlying assumptions and research methodology. The political scientists have contended that these differences in findings can be explained by the faulty approach and presuppositions of the sociologists. We contend in this paper that the pluralists themselves have not grasped the whole truth of the matter; that while their criticisms of the elitists are sound, they, like the elitists, utilize an approach and assumptions which predetermine their conclusions. Our argument is cast within the frame of our central thesis: that there are two faces of power, neither of which the sociologists see and only one of which the political scientists see.

I

Against the elitist approach to power several citicisms may be, and have been levelled.[2] One has to do with its basic premise that in every human institution there is an ordered system of power, a "power structure" which is an integral part and the mirror image of the organization's stratification. This postulate the pluralists emphatically—and, to our mind, correctly—reject, on the ground that

> nothing categorical can be assumed about power in any community. . . . If anything, there seems to be an unspoken notion among pluralist researchers that at bottom *nobody* dominates in a town, so that their first question is not likely to be, "Who runs this community?," but rather, "Does anyone at all run this community?" The first query is somewhat like, "Have you stopped beating your wife?," in that virtually any response short of total unwillingness to answer will supply the researchers with a "power elite" along the lines presupposed by the stratification theory.[3]

[1] Compare, for example, the sociological studies of Floyd Hunter, *Community Power Structure* (Chapel Hill, 1953); Roland Pellegrini and Charles H. Coates, "Absentee-Owned Corporations and Community Power Structure," *American Journal of Sociology*, Vol. 61 (March 1956), pp. 413-19; and Robert O. Schulze, "Economic Dominants and Community Power Structure," *American Sociological Review*, Vol. 23 (February 1958), pp. 3-9; with political science studies of Wallace S. Sayre and Herbert Kaufman, *Governing New York City* (New York, 1960); Robert A. Dahl, *Who Governs?* (New Haven, 1961); and Norton E. Long and George Belknap, "A Research Program on Leadership and Decision-Making in Metropolitan Areas" (New York, Governmental Affairs Institute, 1956). See also Nelson W. Polsby, "How to Study Community Power: The Pluralist Alternative," *Journal of Politics*, Vol. 22 (August, 1960), pp. 474-84.

[2] See especially N.W. Polsby, *op. cit.*, p. 475f.

[3] *Ibid.*, p. 476.

Equally objectionable to the pluralists—and to us—is the sociologists' hypothesis that the power structure tends to be stable over time.

> Pluralists hold that power may be tied to issues, and issues can be fleeting or persistent, provoking coalitions among interested groups and citizens, ranging in their duration from momentary to semi-permanent. . . . To presume that the set of coalitions which exists in the community at any given time is a timelessly stable aspect of social structure is to introduce systematic inaccuracies into one's description of social reality.[4]

A third citicism of the elitist model is that it wrongly equates reputed with actual power:

> If a man's major life work is banking, the pluralist presumes he will spend his time at the bank, and not in manipulating community decisions. This presumption holds until the banker's activities and participations indicate otherwise. . . . If we presume that the banker is "really" engaged in running the community, there is practically no way of disconfirming this notion, even if it is totally erroneous. On the other hand, it is easy to spot the banker who really *does* run community affairs when we presume he does not, because his activities will make this apparent.[5]

This is not an exhaustive bill of particulars; there are flaws other than these in the sociological model and methodology[6]—including some which the pluralists themselves have not noticed. But to go into this would not materially serve our current purposes. Suffice it simply to observe that whatever the merits of their own approach to power, the pluralists have effectively exposed the main weaknesses of the elitist model.

As the foregoing quotations make clear, the pluralists concentrate their attention, not upon the sources of power, but its exercise. Power to them means "participation in decision-making"[7] and can be analyzed only after "careful examination of a series of concrete decisions."[8] As a result, the pluralist researcher is uninterested in the reputedly powerful. His concerns instead are to (a) select for study a number of "key" as opposed to "routine" political decisions, (b) identify the people who took an active part in the decision-making process, (c) obtain a full account of their actual behavior while the policy conflict was being resolved, and (d) determine and analyze the specific outcome of the conflict.

[4] *Ibid.*, pp. 478-79.

[5] *Ibid.*, pp. 480-81.

[6] See especially Robert A. Dahl, "A Critique of the Ruling-Elite Model," *The American Political Science Review*, Vol. 52 (June 1958), pp. 463-69; and Lawrence J. R. Herson, "In the Footsteps of Community Power," *The American Political Science Review*, Vol. 55 (December 1961), pp. 817-31.

[7] This definition originated with Harold D. Lasswell and Abraham Kaplan, *Power and Society* (New Haven, 1950), p. 75.

[8] Robert A. Dahl, "A Critique of the Ruling-Elite Model," *loc. cit.*, p. 466.

The advantages of this approach, relative to the elitist alternative, need no further exposition. The same may not be said, however, about its defects—two of which seem to us to be of fundamental importance. One is that the model takes no account of the fact that power may be, and often is, exercised by confining the scope of decision-making to relatively "safe" issues. The other is that the model provides no *objective* criteria for distinguishing between "important" and "unimportant" issues arising in the political arena.

II

There is no gainsaying that an analysis grounded entirely upon what is specific and visible to the outside observer is more "scientific" than one based upon pure speculation. To put it another way,

> If we can get our social life stated in terms of activity, and of nothing else, we have not indeed succeeded in measuring it, but we have at least reached a foundation upon which a coherent system of measurements can be built up. . . . We shall cease to be blocked by the intervention of unmeasurable elements, which claim to be themselves the real causes of all that is happening, and which by their spook-like arbitrariness make impossible any progress toward dependable knowledge.[9]

The question is, however, how can one be certain in any given situation that the "unmeasurable elements" are inconsequential, are not of decisive importance? Cast in slightly different terms, can a sound concept of power be predicated on the assumption that power is totally embodied and fully reflected in "concrete decisions" or in activity bearing directly upon their making?

We think not. Of course power is exercised when A participates in the making of decisions that affect B. But power is also exercised when A devotes his energies to creating or reinforcing social and political values and institutional practices that limit the scope of the political process to public consideration of only those issues which are comparatively innocuous to A. To the extent that A succeeds in doing this, B is prevented, for all practical purposes, from bringing to the fore any issues that might in their resolution be seriously detrimental to A's set of preferences.[10]

[9] Arthur Bentley, *The Process of Government* (Chicago, 1908), p. 202, quoted in Polsby, *op. cit.*, p. 481n.

[10] As is perhaps self-evident, there are similarities in both faces of power. In each, A participates in decisions and thereby adversely affects B. But there is an important difference between the two: in the one case, A openly participates; in the other, he participates only in the sense that he works to sustain those values and rules of procedure that help him keep certain issues out of the public domain. True enough, participation of the second kind may at times be overt; that is the case, for instance, in cloture fights in the Congress. But the point is that it need not be. In fact, when the maneuver is most successfully executed, it neither involves nor can be identified with decisions arrived at on specific issues.

Situations of this kind are common. Consider, for example, the case—surely not unfamiliar to this audience—of the discontented faculty member in an academic institution headed by a tradition bound executive. Aggrieved about a long-standing policy around which a strong vested interest has developed, the professor resolves in the privacy of his office to launch an attack upon the policy at the next faculty meeting. But, when the moment of truth is at hand, he sits frozen in silence. Why? Among the many possible reasons, one or more of these could have been of crucial importance: (a) the professor was fearful that his intended action would be interpreted as an expression of his disloyalty to the institution; or (b) he decided that, given the beliefs and attitudes of his colleagues on the faculty, he would almost certainly constitute on this issue a minority of one; or (c) he concluded that, given the nature of the law-making process in the institution, his proposed remedies would be pigeonholed permanently. But whatever the case, the central point to be made is the same: to the extent that a person or group—consciously or unconsciously—creates or reinforces barriers to the public airing of policy conflicts, that person or group has power. Or, as Professor Schattschneider has so admirably put it:

> All forms of political organization have a bias in favor of the exploitation of some kinds of conflict and the suppression of others because *organization is the mobilization of bias.* Some issues are organized into politics while others are organized out.[11]

Is such bias not relevant to the study of power? Should not the student be continuously alert to its possible existence in the human institution that he studies, and be ever prepared to examine the forces which brought it into being and sustain it? Can he safely ignore the possibility, for instance, that an individual or group in a community participates more vigorously in supporting the *nondecision-making* process than in participating in actual decisions within the process? Stated differently, can the researcher overlook the chance that some person or association could limit decision-making to relatively non-controversial matters, by influencing community values and political procedures and rituals, notwithstanding that there are in the community serious but latent power conflicts?[12] To do so is, in our judgment, to overlook the less apparent, but nonetheless extremely important, face of power.

[11] E. E. Schattschneider, *The Semi-Sovereign People* (New York, 1960), p. 71.

[12] Dahl *partially* concedes this point when he observes ("A Critique of the Ruling-Elite Model," pp. 468-69) that "one could argue that even in a society like ours a ruling elite might be so influential over ideas, attitudes, and opinions that a kind of false consensus will exist—not the phony consensus of a terroristic totalitarian dictatorship but the manipulated and superficially self-imposed adherence to the norms and goals of the elite by broad sections of a community. . . . This objection points to the need to be circumspect in interpreting the evidence." But that he largely misses our point is clear from the succeeding sentence: "Yet here, too, it seems to me that the hypothesis cannot be satisfactorily confirmed without something equivalent to the test I have proposed," and that is "by an examination of a series of concrete cases where key decisions are made. . . ."

III

In his critique of the "ruling-elite model," Professor Dahl argues that "the hypothesis of the existence of a ruling elite can be strictly tested only if . . . [t] here is a fair sample of cases involving key political decisions in which the preferences of the hypothetical ruling elite run counter to those of any other likely group that might be suggested."[13] With this assertion we have two complaints. One we have already discussed, viz., in erroneously assuming that power is solely reflected in concrete decisions, Dahl thereby excludes the possibility that in the community in question there is a group capable of preventing contests from arising on issues of importance to it. Beyond that, however, by ignoring the less apparent face of power Dahl and those who accept his pluralist approach are unable adequately to differentiate between a "key" and a "routine" political decision.

Nelson Polsby, for example, proposes that "by pre-selecting as issues for study those which are generally agreed to be significant, pluralist researchers can test stratification theory."[14] He is silent, however, on how the researcher is to determine *what* issues are "generally agreed to be significant," and on how the researcher is to appraise the reliability of the agreement. In fact, Polsby is guilty here of the same fault he himself has found with elitist methodology: by presupposing that in any community there are significant issues in the political arena, he takes for granted the very question which is in doubt. He accepts as issues what are reputed to be issues. As a result, his findings are fore-ordained. For even if there is no "truly" significant issue in the community under study, there is every likelihood that Polsby (or any like-minded researcher) will find one or some and, after careful study, reach the appropriate pluralistic conclusions.[15]

Dahl's definition of "key political issues" in his essay on the ruling-elite model is open to the same criticism. He states that it is "a necessary although possibly not a sufficient condition that the [key] issue should involve actual diagreement in preferences among two or more groups."[16] In our view, this is an inadequate characterization of a "key political issue," simply because groups can have diagreements in preferences on unimportant as well as on important issues. Elite preferences which border on the indifferent are certainly not significant in determining whether a monolithic or polylithic distribution or power prevails in a given community. Using Dahl's definition of "key political issues," the researcher would have little difficulty in finding such in practically any community; and it would not be surprising then if he ultimately concluded that power in the community was widely diffused.

The distinction between important and unimportant issues, we believe, cannot be made intelligently in the absence of an analysis of the

[13] *Op. cit.*, p. 466.

[14] *Op. cit.*, p. 478.

[15] As he points out, the expectations of the pluralist researchers "have seldom been disappointed." *Ibid.*, p. 477.

[16] *Op. cit.*, p. 467.

"mobilization of bias" in the community; of the dominant values and the political myths, rituals, and institutions which tend to favor the vested interests of one or more groups, relative to others. Armed with this knowledge, one could conclude that any challenge to the predominant values or to the established "rules of the game" would constitute an "important" issue; all else, unimportant. To be sure, judgments of this kind cannot be entirely objective. But to avoid making them in a study of power is both to neglect a highly significant aspect of power and thereby to undermine the only sound basis for discriminating between "key" and "routine" decisions. In effect, we contend, the pluralists have made each of these mistakes; that is to say, they have done just that for which Kaufman and Jones so severely taxed Floyd Hunter: they have begun "their structure at the mezzanine without showing us a lobby or foundation,"[17] i.e., they have begun by studying the issues rather than the values and biases that are built into the political system and that, for the student of power, give real meaning to those issues which do enter the political arena.

IV

There is no better fulcrum for our critique of the pluralist model than Dahl's recent study of power in New Haven.[18]

At the outset it may be observed that Dahl does not attempt in this work to define his concept, "key political decision." In asking whether the "Notables" of New Haven are "influential overtly or covertly in the making of government decisions," he simply states that he will examine "three different 'issue-areas' in which important public decisions are made: nominations by the two political parties, urban redevelopment, and public education." These choices are justified on the grounds that "nominations determine which persons will hold public office. The New Haven redevelopment program measured by its cost—present and potential—is the largest in the country. Public education, aside from its intrinsic importance, is the costliest item in the city's budget." Therefore, Dahl concludes, "It is reasonable to expect . . . that the relative influence over public officials wielded by the . . . Notables would be revealed by an examination of their participation in these three areas of activity."[19]

The difficulty with this latter statement is that it is evident from Dahl's own account that the Notables are in fact uninterested in two of the three "key" decisions he has chosen. In regard to the public school issue, for example, Dahl points out that many of the Notables live in the suburbs and that those who do live in New Haven choose in the main to send their children to private schools. "As a consequence," he writes, "their interest in

[17] Herbert Kaufman and Victor Jones, "The Mystery of Power," *Public Administration Review*, Vol. 14 (Summer 1954), p. 207.

[18] Robert A. Dahl, *Who Governs?* (New Haven, 1961).

[19] *Ibid.*, p. 64.

the public schools is ordinarily rather slight."[20] Nominations by the two political parties as an important "issue-area," is somewhat analogous to the public schools, in that the apparent lack of interest among the Notables in this issue is partially accounted for by their suburban residence—because of which they are disqualified from holding public office in New Haven. Indeed, Dahl himself concedes that with respect to both these issues the Notables are largely indifferent: "Business leaders might ignore the public schools or the political parties without any sharp awareness that their indifference would hurt their pocketbooks . . ." He goes on, however, to say that

> the prospect of profound changes [as a result of the urban-redevelopment program] in ownership, physical layout, and usage of property in the downtown area and the effects of these changes on the commercial and industrial prosperity of New Haven were all related in an obvious way to the daily concerns of businessmen.[21]

Thus, if one believes—as Professor Dahl did when he wrote his critique of the ruling-elite model—that an issue, to be considered as important, "should involve actual disagreement in preferences among two or more groups,"[22] then clearly he has now for all practical purposes written off public education and party nominations as key "issue-areas." But this point aside, it appears somewhat dubious at best that "the relative influence over public officials wielded by the Social Notables" can be revealed by an examination of their nonparticipation in areas in which they were not interested.

Furthermore, we would not rule out the possibility that even on those issues to which they appear indifferent, the Notables may have a significant degree of *indirect* influence. We would suggest, for example, that although they send their children to private schools, the Notables do recognize that public school expenditures have a direct bearing upon their own tax liabilities. This being so, and given their strong representation on the New Haven Board of Finance,[23] the expectation must be that it is in their direct interest to play an active role in fiscal policy-making, in the establishment of the educational budget in particular. But as to this, Dahl is silent: he inquires not at all into either the decisions made by the Board of Finance with respect to education nor into their impact upon the public schools.[24] Let it be understood clearly that in making these points we are not attempting to refute Dahl's contention

[20] *Ibid.*, p. 70.

[21] *Ibid.*, p. 71.

[22] *Op. cit.*, p. 467.

[23] *Who Governs?*, p. 82. Dahl points out that "the main policy thrust of the Economic Notables is to oppose tax increases; this leads them to oppose expenditures for anything more than minimal traditional city services. In this effort their two most effective weapons ordinarily are the mayor and the Board of Finance. The policies of the Notables are most easily achieved under a strong mayor if his policies coincide with theirs or under a weak mayor if they have the support of the Board of Finance. . . . New Haven mayors have continued to find it expedient to create confidence in their financial policies among businessmen by appointing them to the Board." (pp. 81-2.)

[24] Dahl does discuss in general terms (pp. 79-84) changes in the level of tax rates and assessments in past years, but not actual decisions of the Board of Finance or their effects on the public school system.

that the Notables lack power in New Haven. What we *are* saying, however, is that this conclusion is not adequately supported by his analysis of the "issue-areas" of public education and party nominations.

The same may not be said of redevelopment. This issue is by any reasonable standard important for purposes of determining whether New Haven is ruled by "the hidden hand of an economic elite."[25] For the Economic Notables have taken an active interest in the program and, beyond that, the socio-economic implications of it are not necessarily in harmony with the basic interests and values of businesses and businessmen.

In an effort to assure that the redevelopment program would be acceptable to what he dubbed "the biggest muscles" in New Haven, Mayor Lee created the Citizens Action Commission (CAC) and appointed to it primarily representatives of the economic elite. It was given the function of overseeing the work of the mayor and other officials involved in redevelopment, and, as well, the responsibility for organizing and encouraging citizens' participation in the program through an extensive committee system.

In order to weigh the relative influence of the mayor, other key officials, and the members of the CAC, Dahl reconstructs "all the *important* decisions on redevelopment and renewal between 1950-58 . . . [to] determine which individuals most often initiated the proposals that were finally adopted or most often successfully vetoed the proposals of the others."[26] The results of this test indicate that the mayor and his development administrator were by far the most influential, and that the "muscles" on the Commission, excepting in a few trivial instances, "never directly initiated, opposed, vetoed, or altered any proposal brought before them. . . ."[27]

This finding is, in our view, unreliable, not so much because Dahl was compelled to make a subjective selection of what constituted *important* decisions within what he felt to be an *important* "issue-area," as because the finding was based upon an excessively narrow test of influence. To measure relative influence solely in terms of the ability to initiate and veto proposals is to ignore the possible exercise of influence or power in limiting the scope of initiation. How, that is to say, can a judgment be made as to the relative influence of Mayor Lee and the CAC without knowing (through prior study of the political and social views of all concerned) the proposals that Lee did *not* make because he anticipated that they would provoke strenuous opposition and, perhaps, sanctions on the part of the CAC?[28]

---

[25] *Ibid.*, p. 124.

[26] *Ibid.* "A rough test of a person's overt or covert influence," Dahl states in the first section of the book, "is the frequency with which he successfully initiates an important policy over the opposition of others, or vetoes policies initiated by others, or initiates a policy where no opposition appears." (*Ibid.*, p. 66.)

[27] *Ibid.*, p. 131.

[28] Dahl is, of course, aware of the "law of anticipated reactions." In the case of the mayor's relationship with the CAC, Dahl notes that Lee was "particularly skillful in estimating what the CAC could be expected to support or reject." (p. 137.) However, Dahl was not interested in analyzing or appraising to what extent the CAC limited Lee's freedom of action. Because of his restricted concept of power, Dahl did not consider that the CAC might in this respect have exercised power. That the CAC did not initiate

In sum, since he does not recognize *both* faces of power, Dahl is in no position to evaluate the relative influence or power of the initiator and decision-maker, on the one hand, and of those persons, on the other, who may have been indirectly instrumental in preventing potentially dangerous issues from being raised.[29] As a result, he unduly emphasizes the importance of initiating, deciding, and vetoing, and in the process casts the pluralist conclusions of his study into serious doubt.

V

We have contended in this paper that a fresh approach to the study of power is called for, an approach based upon a recognition of the two faces of power. Under this approach the researcher would begin—not, as does the sociologist who asks, "Who rules?" nor as does the pluralist who asks, "Does anyone have power?"—but by investigating the particular "mobilization of bias" in the institution under scrutiny. Then, having analyzed the dominant values, the myths and the established political procedures and rules of the game, he would make a careful inquiry into which persons or groups, if any, gain from the existing bias and which, if any, are handicapped by it. Next, he would investigate the dynamics of *nondecision-making*; that is, he would examine the extent to which and the manner in which the *status quo* oriented persons and groups influence those community values and those political institutions (as, *e.g.*, the unanimity "rule" of New York City's Board of Estimate[30]) which tend to limit the scope of actual decision-making to "safe" issues. Finally, using his knowledge of the restrictive face of power as a foundation for analysis and as a standard for distinguishing between "key" and "routine" political decisions, the researcher would, after the manner of the pluralists, analyze participation in decision-making of concrete issues.

We reject in advance as unimpressive the possible criticism that this approach to the study of power is likely to prove fruitless because it goes beyond an investigation of what is objectively measurable. In reacting against

---

or veto actual proposals by the mayor was to Dahl evidence enough that the CAC was virtually powerless; it might as plausibly be evidence that the CAC was (in itself or in what it represented) so powerful that Lee ventured nothing it would find worth quarreling with.

[29] The fact that the initiator of decisions also refrains—because he anticipates adverse reactions—from initiating other proposals does not obviously lessen the power of the agent who limited his initiative powers. Dahl missed this point: "It is," he writes, "all the more improbable, then, that a secret cabal of Notables dominates the public life of New Haven through means so clandestine that not one of the fifty prominent citizens interviewed in the course of this study—citizens who had participated extensively in various decisions—hinted at the existence of such a cabal..." (p. 185).

In conceiving of elite domination exclusively in the form of a conscious cabal exercising the power of decision-making and vetoing, he overlooks a more subtle form of domination; one in which those who actually dominate are not conscious of it themselves, simply because their position of dominance has never seriously been challenged.

[30] Sayre and Kaufman, *op. cit.,* p. 640. For a perceptive study of the "mobilization of bias" in a rural American community, see Arthur Vidich and Joseph Bensman, *Small Town in Mass Society* (Princeton, 1958).

the subjective aspects of the sociological model of power, the pluralists have, we believe, made the mistake of discarding "unmeasurable elements" as unreal. It is ironical that, by so doing, they have exposed themselves to the same fundamental criticism they have so forcefully levelled against the elitists: their approach to and assumptions about power predetermine their findings and conclusions.

Professionalism and Public Participation in Educational Policy Making: New York City, a Case Study

Marilyn Gittell

We know appallingly little about school policy-making, in most cities an issue of critical importance to many citizens. Marilyn Gittell, in the following article, examines five types of policy decisions made in the general area of education, in an attempt to learn something about the distribution of influence in the New York City school system.

Within any school system, the potential participants in educational policy-making are essentially the same. However, the relative influence of each participant may vary considerably from city to city. Gittell's research indicates how insulated from public controls educational policy-making has become in the last two decades in New York. She describes this situation as an abandonment of public education by key forces of potential influence within the city.

Gittell's findings raise a number of serious questions about continued professionalization in the area of education, for the insulation of school policy-making has been brought about by the increased bureaucratization and "overblown" professionalization of the school system. The professional bureaucracy has manipulated its resource of expertise to discourage opposition and the consideration of alternative policies, she concludes. This depoliticalization process has been primarily due to a lack of visibility of decision making, a shortage of information available to the public on most issues, and a lack of available means for meaningful citizen participation. Hence, a decrease in citizen interest and participation in school-policy formulation has taken place.

The relative isolation in which professionals are able to make important policy decisions raises a number of questions about the viability of democratic practices at the local level. Consensus decision-making, whether it be in education or other policy areas, not only limits the discussion of policy alternatives but also inhibits meaningful citizen participation. Therefore, it acts as a very real impediment to policy change. On the other hand, participation by individuals and groups with interests and goals different from the professional administrator's can guarantee that alternatives will at least be discussed, even if they are not acted upon. But such a dialogue can only occur if the decision-making process remains open to participation.

At present, decision-making in the New York City school system can only be described as closed and dominated by a narrow convergent consensual elite. This contrasts sharply with the stereotype we have about the general openness of politics in New York in other policy areas, which perhaps would also turn out to be more myth than fact if the policy-making process in other functional areas was more closely examined.

Decision-making studies and analyses of local power structure in cities have much to contribute to an understanding of the operation of school systems. More intensive studies of decision-making and the distribution of power in school systems can, in turn, contribute significantly to knowledge of how cities are governed. Almost every study of power in large cities points to functional specialization, dispersion of power to specialists in particular areas, and an increased role of the bureaucracy in decision-making. This study of decision-making in the New York City school system concerns itself with the distribution of power, testing the hypothesis of functional specialization and hopefully expanding on its implications.

New York City as a case study

The New York City school system is nominally a dependent school district (that is, the school district does not have independent taxing power), and the city schools and school policy have often been described as strongly susceptible to local political influence.[1]

Concern in New York City with the failures of the education system was brought to a head by legislation introduced in the 1964 session of the Legislature to establish a fiscally independent school system. The Mayor requested the Temporary Commission on City Finances to explore the feasibility of such a plan and to review the general character of the

Reprinted from the *Public Administration Review,* vol. 27, no. 3 (September 1967), pp. 237-251, by permission of the publisher.

[1] Wallace Sayre and Herbert Kaufman, *Governing New York City* (New York: Russell Sage Foundation, 1960), p. 241.

administrative structure in education, with special attention to the role of the Board of Education. An analysis of decision-making in education in New York City was undertaken to determine the impact of fiscal independence on the existing structure. Since no previous study had fully explored the sources and procedures of policy, there was little to go on as to how the school system functioned under its existing structure.

Five *areas* of decision-making were selected for study, on the basis of diversity in the subject dealt with, the widest possible range of participation by those involved in education, and relevance of the policy selected to the overall education function. Generally, exploration of a continuum of policy was considered superior to a single policy decision. Historical data and institutional analysis were utilized in all relevant areas.

Selected for intensive study were: (1) selection of the Superintendent, (2) increases in teachers' salaries, (3) budgeting, (4) school integration, and (5) curriculum development. Other areas of policy were reviewed in a more cursory way, to broaden the scope of the analysis.[2]

Within any school system the potential participants in school policy-making are essentially the same, although actual participation may vary according to the relative power of each in given circumstances. Legal power is usually divided between a board of education and the superintendent. As regards the bureaucracy, distinction must be made among the central administrative bureaucracy and field administrators, top supervisory staff, and middle management. Organizations representing these groups are common in the larger school districts, and their activities can be significant. Teachers and teacher organizations, parents and parent organizations, are potential participants. Specialized education interest groups (ad hoc and permanent) have been active in many communities, and their role can be vital. In the general community there are other potential participants, local, state, and federal officials, civic groups, the press, business organizations, and individual entrepreneurs seeking the rewards of the school system.[3]

The findings of the study emphasize that, in the last two decades, education in New York City has become amazingly insulated from public controls. One could accurately describe the situation as an abandonment of public

[2] An area omitted which later proved worthy of further exploration was school-site selection and construction. The study reviewed this area only as it related to the integration issue and budgeting.

[3] The author analyzed all newspaper items in two daily newspapers for a five-year period, recording all public statements and reports on education policy. These items were categorized by participant and issue, providing a general picture of the public roles and concerns of all participants. A series of detailed, selective interviews with professional staff and Board members was conducted. Data were cross-checked in interviews with participants outside the school system, including staff members of the Public Education Association, United Federation of Teachers, and other civic groups. Lawyers and educators knowledgeable in school affairs were also consulted. A special survey questionnaire was developed for longer interviews with the field superintendents. The files of civic groups were researched for relevant data on specific issues. A search was made of all professional and popular literature for accounts of decision-making in other school systems for comparative purposes.

education by key forces of potential power within the city. Bureaucratization and professionalization are contributing factors. Weber's theory of the emergence of a specialized bureaucracy, monopolizing power through its control of expertise, describes the role of the education bureaucracy in New York City. The claim that only the professionals can make competent judgments has been accepted. Contributing to and perhaps an outgrowth of this attitude is the change in the Mayor's role to one of noninvolvement. Civic and interest groups (other than the specialized education groups) have responded ambivalently; on the one hand, they accept the notion of the professional competence of the bureaucracy, but on the other, express a hopelessness regarding their ability to change the system. The result is narrow or closed participation in large areas of decision-making. Effective influence in these areas is restricted to an inside core of top supervisory personnel in the headquarters staff of the Board of Education. Policy alternatives are rarely discussed or offered, and the inclination to support the status quo is reinforced.[4]

The kind of participation in school policy formulation may fall into one of three categories: 1. *Closed*; only the professionals in the system participate. 2. *Limited*; the Board of Education and/or the Mayor and other special interests such as the Public Education Association, United Parents Association, and the United Federation of Teachers participate. 3. *Open*; all kinds of groups not generally involved in school policy are participants.

The greater part of school policy-making in New York City falls into categories 1 and 2.

The scope of participation has been widened in some instances because of the interests of participants. The teachers' union, for instance, widened participation on the salary issue to include the Mayor because it recognized that it would gain by his participation. The scope of participation was also widened as a result of conflict. The integration issue was not resolved internally in the system, and participation was thrown into the open. In some respects the issue itself can be said to influence participation. But when decisions are not visible, those interests which might potentially become involved do not.

State participation

State minimum standards for education are not an overriding influence in a large city such as New York, which tends to make even greater demands on itself. What influence the state does have results from the state-aid formula, regents' policy, and the administrative rulings of the State Education Commissioner. Recent studies in other states have emphasized the increasing

---

[4] Theodore Lowi, *At the Pleasure of the Mayor* (New York: The Free Press, 1965), p. 199, as well as the Sayre and Kaufman study (*op. cit.*, p. 716) suggested that the system (referring to the citywide power structure) is more favorable to defenders of the status quo than to innovation.

importance of state bureaucracy, particularly the Commissioner, in local education policy.[5]

The State Commissioner was involved in two major policy decisions affecting New York City in recent years. He was instrumental in the removal of the entire Board of Education in 1961. Subsequently, he recommended a change in procedure for selection of the Board. In 1958, his condemnation of de facto segregation in New York City was a catalyst to the initiation of Board policy on school integration. He continued to influence city policy in this regard by outlining the problems of school segregation in a series of reports.[6] In addition to these more overt actions, the Commissioner's influence is manifest in informal contacts with the Superintendent and the staff.

City groups have been notably ineffectual as a force in Albany. One study attributes this failure to the splintering of city educational interest groups. The New York State Educational Conference Board is the strongest and most influential coalition of interest groups in the determination of state education policy. City interests are meagerly represented on the Conference Board, and the state has been able to ignore city education needs without serious political consequences.[7] The general deficiency in leadership in public education in New York is reflected in part in its failure to influence state policy.

City participation

The most significant trend in education in New York City has been the isolation of school administration from city government. In each city administration since the 1940's, complaints of undue city interference have resulted in the delegation of increased responsibility to the Board of Education.

The National Education Assocation condemned Mayor LaGuardia for direct interference with the school system, particularly in personnel policy; the institution of a strict merit system and internal controls over promotions and transfers prevented future Mayors from engaging in similar practices. In 1951, the Strayer-Yavner Report concluded that education policy was controlled by the Board of Estimate, the Mayor, and the Budget Director of the city

[5] Nicholas Masters, Robert H. Salisbury, and Thomas H. Eliot, *State Politics and the Public Schools* (New York: Knopf, 1964), review the role of state educational officers in local school policy in Michigan, Illinois, and Missouri. James Conant's concern with the monopoly of the professional educators is particularly relevant. The professionals run the local school systems, control government policy in state administrative posts, and direct the teachers colleges.

[6] The State Education Commissioner's Advisory Committee on Human Rights and Community Tensions, *Desegregating the Public Schools of New York City* (May 12, 1964), 47 pp.

[7] Stephen K. Bailey, Richard T. Frost, and Paul E. March, *Schoolmen and Politics* (Syracuse: Syracuse University Press, 1961), and Michael A. Usdan, *The Political Power of Education in New York State* (Institute of Administrative Research, Teachers College, Columbia University, 1963).

because of the line-item budget;[8] subsequently the lump-sum budget was adopted, giving the professionals complete control over allocation of funds.[9] Complaints about a political Board were satisfied by the institution of the civic selection panel.[10]

But it is the increased bureaucratization and overblown professionalization of the school system that has had the greatest impact on school policy-making. The professional bureaucracy has manipulated its resource of expertise to discourage opposition and alternative policies. The acceptance of technical expertise as the most relevant, if not the only, basis for sound judgment furthered the depoliticalization of education policy.

The depoliticalization process has been a two-way street. Contributing significantly to it was the last Mayor's (Robert Wagner's) stated desire to delegate complete responsibility for the city's schools to the Board of Education.

Detailed review of newspaper items over the last five years substantiates the Mayor's intention to remove himself from educational policy-making.[11] His public statements were always general, in support of more and better schools. On school integration, he repeatedly stated his desire to leave the matter to the Board of Education and the professional staff. "I subscribe without reservation to the goals of quality integrated education in our schools and of equal opportunity for every child. But the plan, the means, the how, where and what—the timetable, the specific approaches and programs—that is for the educators and for the Board to determine."[12] During the most heated periods of controversy, he met with protest groups but repeatedly refused to intervene.

Requests to the Mayor in 1964 for $45.3 million in additional funds for a More Effective Schools program drew the Mayor to the fringe of the integration issue. The proposal called for obtaining additional funds and services for ten More Effective Schools in ghetto areas. Ultimately, his decision favoring a small appropriation was reached after consultation with school officials and staff members of educational interest groups.

An aide to the Mayor verified that the Mayor had unquestionably shifted responsibility for education policy to the Board of Education. "The Mayor did not want to get involved with school problems," the aide stated, "particularly school integration problems." The Mayor became directly involved only in instances where the Board and some other city agency came into the type of conflict that had to be reviewed and resolved before the Board of Estimate.

The Mayor and the Board of Estimate are major instruments of financial policy, determining overall budgetary appropriation. Their review of the

---

[8] George D. Strayer and Louis Yavner, *Administrative Management of the School System of New York City*, Volume I (October 1951).

[9] *Local Law No. 19* passed by the City Council on April 6, 1962.

[10] *Education Law*, Section 2553, subdivision 1, 2, amended L. 1961.

[11] Scanning of three years of school news stories in two prominent New York City papers reveals that the Mayor's public statements were almost always in response to public pressures.

[12] *New York Times* (March 1, 1965).

education budget, however, has been concerned with the total amount to be allotted. The Mayor's continued involvement in fiscal matters was due more to the fact that the Board wanted to shift responsibility to him than to his own desire to participate. Although the Board of Education is charged with the legal responsibility for determining salaries and has discretion to increase salaries within the total allotted funds, it has not been adverse to relinquishing responsibility to the Mayor for negotiating salaries.[13]

The Mayor, through his negotiators, has twice made direct settlements with the union, in 1961 and 1965.[14] Financial commitments were then met by an additional city appropriation and transfers of funds within the education budget. After the 1965 contract settlement, the Superintendent expressed dismay at the settlement, which far exceeded his planned budgetary allotment for salary increases.

The union, for its part, sees an obvious advantage in shifting salary decisions to city hall. Albert Shanker, president of the union, stated that the union is in a more viable position in negotiating with the Mayor than with the Board. In Chicago, which is a fiscally independent district, the union similarly negotiated its new contract directly with the Mayor.

The Mayor's policy of noninvolvement was reinforced by two major changes in procedure instituted during his administration, the lump-sum appropriation of school funds and the panel selection of Board members.

Under a local law first passed in 1962 and re-enacted each year since then, and by way of a memorandum of understanding with the Mayor, the Board of Education has the power to determine its own allocation of funds. Budget preparation, the allocation and transfer of funds, and post-audit control are internal operations, controlled largely by the top supervisory staff. The Board is the only city agency with such budgetary independence from the municipal government.

Prior to 1961, Board appointments were made directly by the Mayor. Under the new procedure, the nine members of the Board are appointed by the Mayor from a screened list of candidates submitted by a selection panel composed of the heads of 11 educational, civic, and professional organizations. The change, made to deter "political" appointments, followed six years of hearings, numerous scandals, and finally the removal of the Board by the State Legislature.

The Mayor is still forced to take part in school policy in two general areas. The first is on issues in which conflict between major participants cannot be compromised without his involvement. Such issues often concern site selection and provoke sharp differences between the Planning Commission and the Board. Involvement also occurs where key participants decide they have more to gain by the Mayor's participation.

[13] A member of the Board disagreed with this interpretation, suggesting that the Mayor had taken the initiative. The same person, however, confirmed the author's view that the Mayor did not interfere with the Board in education policy. Officers of the United Federation of Teachers confirmed the author's interpretation.

[14] In 1961, the press gave credit to the Superintendent for his successful negotiation on salaries but neglected to explain why the Mayor was involved in the final settlement.

One of the obvious questions which arises in connection with the Mayor's role is whether the precedents established under the Wagner administration over a 12-year period have become so integral a part of the structure that they cannot be changed. Mayor Wagner's role conforms to Banfield's portrait of the Mayor of Chicago as mediator of conflicts, rather than as an initiator of policy.[15] A reform Mayor who cannot rely on party backing is less likely to accept this role and, in fact, must use his power to initiate policy to gather necessary political support. Mayoral noninvolvement has also been based on public deference to professionalism. Mayor Lindsay in his short tenure in office has already faced the charge of "political interference" in an ,attempt to initiate policy in the creation of a civilian police review board and in requiring or attempting to require budgeting accountability in education. Other efforts have been similarly criticized by members of the bureaucracy. The emotional commitment to professionalism, although not inviolate, tends to challenge any suggestion of change or alternate course of action as undue "political interference." The effort of the new Mayor to reassert his policy role represents a direct threat to those who have held almost complete power in decision-making in these areas.

The control of policy by the bureaucracy has been considerably enhanced by the self-removal of other potential participants, particularly civic groups. Any Mayor who decides to become more directly involved in education policy will face serious criticism, not only from the education establishment but from other groups as well. Any movement toward an increased policy role for the Mayor will also involve structural changes. Possibly, a revitalized interest by the Mayor can reactivate civic reformers and public interest sufficiently to expand participation as a basis for reviewing the instruments of policy.

The Board of Education

The nine members of the Board of Education are the official policy-making body for the school system and are responsible for long-range educational planning. Traditionally, the Mayor's appointments had reflected careful consideration of balance of interests, as well as political favor. Catholics, Protestants, and Jews were equally represented, and there was either a Negro or Puerto Rican, or both. Geographic distribution demanded by the by-laws assured borough representation. The religous and racial balances, interestingly enough, are continued in the current selection process:[16]

---

[15] Edward Banfield, *Political Influence* (Glencoe: The Free Press, 1963).

[16] Expectations based on the religious formula were pointed up by an item appearing in the *World Telegram and Sun* of May 29, 1963, reporting criticism expressed by the Catholic Teachers Association of Mayor Wagner's failure to appoint a Catholic to replace a retiring member, Brendan Byrne. Months later, when a Jewish member of the Board retired, a Catholic was appointed to replace him, thereby reestablishing the 3-3-3 balance.

Composition of the Board of Education

Religion	Old Board		New Board	
	1947	*1957*	*1961*	*1965*
Catholic	2	3	3	3
Protestant	3	3	3	3
Jew	3	3	3	3

There was little question prior to 1961 that the Mayor would exercise some measure of control over the Board, and the Board members, in turn, could use their political influence with the Mayor. Strong Board Presidents who were politically oriented served as the channel for communication with the Mayor.[17]

The screening-panel procedure strengthened the role of the civic groups and reduced the discretion of the Mayor. Members of the Board nominated by civic groups are less likely to be intimates of the Mayor and less likely to consult with him on school problems. People outside the formal school structure, interviewed during the study and asked about the new appointment procedure, expressed dissatisfaction with the lack of political "know-how" of Board members. They pointed out that Board members lack personal influence and no longer can play the political role expected of them by school groups. Of the nine members, there are three lawyers, one accountant, one businessman, one labor union official, a civic activist, and two educators.

The Board's role has been largely one of balancing conflicting pressures and interests. It too has become a mediator rather than an initiator of policy. As the spokesman for official policy, the Board nominally participates in all major decisions. It spends a great deal of its time, however, on sensitive issues where the balance of power in the Board has failed to produce consensus. These are not necessarily major areas of policy. For example, site-selection controversies have recently occupied a large amount of Board time.

In the areas selected for study, the Board's role varied from superficial participation in the budget process, to formulation and promulgation of policy, to failure to achieve implementation in school integration. Selecting a Superintendent was the area in which the board has exercised most direct power. Historically, the selection of the Superintendent was a Board function, greatly influenced by its President and subject to the support of high-ranking administrators and education groups. In earlier years, the Mayor had on occasion controlled the appointment. The selection is influenced by the bureaucratic pressure for appointment of an "insider." Three of the last

[17]In the period from 1945 to 1961, the three Board Presidents later moved on to political office. Maxmillan Moss was elected Surrogate in Brooklyn, Arthur Levitt was elected State Controller, and Charles Silver became a personal advisor to the Mayor. This would indicate not only their closeness to the Mayor but their active participation in the Democratic party.

five Superintendents were chosen from the supervisory bureaucracy; the fourth was a former Deputy Mayor and local college president.[18]

The education interest groups, particularly the Public Education Association, have always been concerned with the choice of the Superintendent. Lowi points out that the interest groups in New York City have generally concentrated their attention on appointments, which is confirmed by their involvement in the selection of the Superintendent and Board members.[19] In the past, the Public Education Association has supported, without too much success, the appointment of "outsiders" with high academic credentials. It has always requested a screening panel of educators to assist the Board in the selection process, but in the final analysis the Board President controlled the choice. The Public Education Association has become more influential in the last two appointments than it had been previously. In 1961, the Board accepted the recommendations of the professional panel, selecting a highly regarded "outsider." His failure and dismissal resulted in a return to selection of the highest-ranking person from within the system.

In budgeting, the Board has tended to rely on the budget presented by the Superintendent and his staff. Individual Board members have periodically questioned expenditures, but have also made reference to their lack of information in dealing with intricate budget detail. Generally, the Board views its role as one of assuring city financial support for the total budget, satisfying staff requests and public pressures.

In school integration policy the Board has exhibited a lack of effective follow-through. In 1957 it set a general policy favoring school integration, utilizing rotation of teachers, rezoning, and site selection as the means for achieving their goals. But the Board has failed to effect implementation by the staff. Board members, who were questioned, noted the practical problems obstructing the implementation of their policy. They also pointed to staff inaction as a cause for delay. A member of the Board stated that, were she not on the Board, she would probably be out on the picket line, but dealing with the tough problem of ironing out procedures had taken the edge off her dedication to implementation. A detailed case study of school integration in New York City cites the lack of leadership and determination of the Board and its equivocation after the integration policy was established as a key factor in the failure of that policy.[20]

---

[18] The three Superintendents chosen from the bureaucracy were John Wade, William Jansen, and Bernard Donovan; the fourth mentioned is John Theobald. Of the five, Calvin Gross was the only "outsider" appointed Superintendent. At the time of the Gross appointment, the High School Administrative Assistants Association, the Association of Assistant Superintendents, and the Junior High School Principals Association reminded the Board that "home-grown talent should not be overlooked." *New York Times* (April 25, 1962; July 2, 1962).

[19] Lowi, *op. cit.*, p. 199.

[20] David Rogers, Unpublished manuscript on school desegregation (Center for Urban Education). Sheldon *et al.*, "Administrative Implications of Integration Plans for Schools," in Albert J. Reiss, Jr. (ed.), *Schools in a Changing Society* (New York: The Free Press, 1965).

On the two major salary increases in recent years, the Board has participated in early negotiation but has been satisfied to shift responsibility to the Mayor for final decision-making.

The trend in the Board's participation suggests a diminished role in policy formulation under the new Board. The Board has never fulfilled its obligation for long-range planning, and the new Board has not been any more successful in that area. The lack of a strong Board staff has greatly limited the level and character of its participation. Without staff, the Board cannot realistically challenge or review the programs of the administrative bureaucracy.

It might be more accurate to say that individual members of the Board, as it was formerly constituted, were more involved in policy-making as a result of their own political stature and their association with the Mayor. As the school system has grown larger and more complex and policies demand more specialized knowledge, the Board has had to withdraw from an effective policy role. The bureaucracy and special interest groups have gained power by means of their expertise, while the Board, lacking expertise, has lost power.

Local school boards

In 1961, the Board of Education was empowered to appoint local school board members for 25 district boards.[21] District selection panels submit two or three names for each vacancy to the district superintendents, who pass the list on to the Board for appointment. The activation of local school boards was, in part, a recognition of the inadequacy of the citywide Board and a system too over-centralized to respond to local needs. The local boards, however, were given no real authority in the determination of school policy. Generally, they have acted as community buffers, holding hearings and discussing narrow local issues; they have not had the authority to resolve local problems. Local boards view themselves as preservers of narrow local interests, particularly with regard to integration policy. Officially, the boards rarely act as a body; members are more prone to voice personal views on issues. Local boards do not have the information or facility, much less the authority, to follow through on matters.

The Board of Education has been reluctant to delegate powers to local boards for fear that they would encroach upon its own authority. District superintendents are also hesitant to enhance the position of the local boards because they might interfere with local school administration. The compromise was to assign the local boards the power to hold hearings, which is harmless enough.

Under a 1965 reorganization plan, the 25 boards were increased to 31 to conform with the expanded 31 local districts. The new plan was to include greater emphasis on decentralized policy-making, utilizing the district superintendent and the local boards more effectively. There is no indication, however, that the plan provides for basic prerequisites for redistributing

[21] *Education Law*, Section 2564, amended by L. 1961.

power in the system. Budgeting and personnel policy continue to be centralized, and there is no provision for flexibility in initiating new programs. The
Superintendent indicated, in an interview, that the budgetary limitations, in
themselves, would prevent any effective decentralization of the city school
system, and policy formulation will remain a headquarters responsibility so
long as these conditions are unchanged.[22]

The Superintendent and the bureaucracy

One of the most confusing aspects of school administration in New York
City is the growth in the power of the administrative staff at the same time
that the Superintendent has remained a relatively weak chief executive. In
part, the strength of the bureaucracy has undermined the role of the Superintendent. Several other factors have contributed significantly to this result.
The short tenure in office of the last four Superintendents has undoubtedly
taken its toll. In the last two decades, four Superintendents have held the
office, none with enough time to enhance that office's powers.[23] Open
conflict with the Board was evidenced in two of these administrations, one
resulting in dismissal. The last two Board Presidents have proudly claimed
that they devoted at least 45 hours a week to their jobs, indicating their
day-to-day involvement in school affairs that properly could be left to the
Superintendent and their general lack of reliance on the Superintendent for
policy recommendations. The abandonment of education by civic groups has
been another loss to the Superintendent, who might otherwise use this outside support for developing his own role.

The Superintendent lacks the most essential power of a strong executive,
the power of appointment and removal. The supervisory staff is developed
completely through inbreeding and promotion from the ranks. Tenured
supervisors expect to move to top policy-making jobs, allowing for little
flexibility in appointments. No Superintendent can rely on his own team of
trusted advisors. Appointments from outside the system are almost nonexistent. Loyalties developed within this environment are strong and are based on
how one has received appointment. Top-level Deputy, Associate, and Assistant Superintendents have moved up in divisions of the system, and their
loyalties are based on these associations.

A review of the backgrounds of the 25 top supervisory staff members
showed that they followed a pattern of having served as principals or assistant
principals, were brought into the Board on special assignment, and/or had
served on special committees (usually as a result of contacts already established at headquarters). Assignment to headquarters staff by a school division

[22]The Superintendent recently admitted the need for delegating budget and personnel
power to local district superintendents. *New York Times* (February 20, 1966).

[23]Allan Talbott, "Needed: A New Breed of School Superintendents," *Harpers
Magazine* (February 1966), pp. 81-87.

reinforces the loyalties of staff members to that division and the supervisory staff in that division. In all school reorganization proposals, these loyalties have repeatedly fostered preservation of the status quo.

The Superintendent must cope with these potentially competing interests of his own supervisory bureaucracy.[24] He cannot freely develop his own advisory staff and is encumbered by the appointments and promotions made by his predecessors. Any Superintendent from outside the system, not himself subject to these loyalties, would find his task all the more difficult. In a recent magazine article the author noted, "I am told Calvin Gross could have made a real dent on the New York City schools if only he had a handful of trusted special assistants."[25]

Directives and policy statements issued by the Superintendent on key policies have been attacked by his own supervisory staff, both by their professional organizations and, officially, through organized committees on which they sit.[26] In March of 1964, the Council of Supervisory Associations (the overall organization for all of the individual supervisory organizations, such as the High School Principals' Association, Superintendents' Association, Junior High School Principals' Association, *et al.*) issued one of its many reports condemning policies of the Superintendent and noting his failure to consult with his professional staff before making decisions. The Council recently openly opposed the Princeton plan, school bussing, the dropping of I.Q. examinations, and school pairing, after they were adopted as official policy by the Board and the Superintendent. Invariably, policies which require fundamental institutional change are challenged by the supervisory staff.

The inability of Superintendents to use basic administrative powers is notable. They have thoroughly neglected the budget as a management tool to shape personnel or organization policy. Several days spent in the budget office at headquarters indicated that the budget office staff did not act in an advisory or policy-making capacity. Budget estimates are based essentially on pre-established ratios of books and teachers to pupils, with slight adjustment according to the category of the school. Budget approvals come from division heads and are reviewed in hearings controlled by these same people. The last Superintendent met only once all year with *his* budget director.[27]

In all of the areas studied, the Superintendent played a secondary role as an initiator of policy. He had no direct influence on curriculum, with the exception of support by one administration for complete revision of the elementary school curriculum in the 1950's. Curriculum policy has been left largely to the Curriculum Research Bureau and the Deputy Superintendent.

[24] Personal contact with Board members by the staff is not uncommon. Two years ago the situation was so bad that the Superintendent issued a statement forbidding memos from the supervisory staff directly to Board members. *World Telegram and Sun* (November 15, 1963), p. 47.

[25] Talbott, *loc. cit.*

[26] Both the High School Principals Association and the Junior High School Principals Association have expressed opposition to the 5-3-4 and 4-4-4 organization plans. Several associations opposed the elimination of the I.Q. examination, school pairing proposals, and the comprehensive high school plan.

[27] The new Superintendent appears to be more concerned with administrative matters.

The Superintendent has been most concerned with budget matters and even in that capacity has shown no strong inclination to control the preparation of the budget or to utilize it as a means of controlling his staff. On integration policy, the last two Superintendents have virtually delegated their responsibility to the staff with the result that implementation has not been forthcoming. Although Board policy on integration was established in 1957, no Superintendent has considered his role one of leadership in forcing implementation. The Superintendent, like the Mayor and the Board, became a mediator of disputes, rather than an initiator of school policy.

The administrative staff

The education bureaucracy in New York City consists of two distinguishable groups, the headquarters staff and the operational field staff. The latter includes some 3,000 principals and assistant principals, 31 district superintendents, and 1,300 department chairmen.

The supervisors at headquarters

A precise figure on the size of the headquarters staff is difficult to obtain; it is estimated to be somewhere around 3,000. Close to 800 people at headquarters do not appear on that budget. Although serving as full-time headquarters personnel, they are paid out of local school budgets. A core supervisory group which holds much of the decision-making power includes some 30 headquarters staff members—including the executive Deputy Superintendent, the Deputy Superintendent in charge of instruction and curriculum, the Board of Examiners, 20 of the 30 Assistant Superintendents, and a few of the active directors of special bureaus. With the exception of two Assistant Superintendents who had earlier experience in school systems outside of New York City, this group was bred in the system, many as principals, almost all with long experience at headquarters.

In each of the decision-making areas analyzed for the study, the supervisory staff at headquarters was a primary participant.

In curriculum planning and development, the headquarters staff, lodged in the Bureau of Curriculum Research, exercises almost complete control over curriculum. The Bureau is indirectly influenced by general changes in approach to certain disciplines, i.e., the new math, but for the most part it follows a regular routine of three- to five-year review of curriculum bulletins, revisions, and presentation of new guidelines. The actual implementation of curriculum is dependent upon the action of principals and classroom teachers, and this varies considerably from school to school. Although the Bureau has curriculum assistants attached to its staff on a part-time basis (40 per cent of their time is spent in the district superintendent's office), there is no planned program for assuring implementation. In fact, the director of the Bureau expressed his reservations about their role in implementation.

In budgeting, the distribution and allocation of funds is determined on a division, bureau, and department basis with the staff person in charge the major determinant of his own needs. School appropriations are largely allocated on the basis of pre-established ratios, providing a prescribed number of teachers, specialized personnel, textbooks, and so forth, according to the number of students and the category of school. The district superintendent exercises no discretion in budgeting or in the distribution of personnel. Headquarters personnel monopolize decisions in this area. Old programs are automatically continued, and the adoption of new ones is dependent upon the approval of the Superintendent in charge of a division or bureau. The Superintendent relies on the judgment of the supervisory bureaucracy for evaluation of programs and needs. There is no internal audit except for a rather cursory and technical review by the small budget office staff. There is no procedure for evaluation of performance or elimination of ineffective programs in conjunction with budget. Members of the Board of Education have noted their inability to evaluate the complex budget document and make recommendations, and city review of the budget in the past has been extremely limited.

In another major area of policy, school integration, the supervisory staff has been a major participant as a vetoing group. School integration policy was the only area of school policy explored in the study in which there was wide community participation. This was an outcome of the diverse interests and goals of the participants as well as the delicacy of the problem. The supervisory staff, in its inaction and public disapproval of stated Board policy, contributed inadvertently to that broadening of participation. The Board itself demonstrated its own lack of resolve in promulgating general policy favoring rotation of teachers, school pairing, rezoning, and school reorganization, yet waiting upon the bureaucracy for implementation for eight years. The supervisory staff, for its part, has not only ignored Board policy but has publicly disagreed through statements of policy by their own supervisory organizations. Several of these organizations have opposed each of the proposed plans at one time or another. The More Effective Schools program was the only plan which they supported fully. It was the only plan which would not have interfered with the existing structure because it entailed only the expansion of funds and personnel for selected schools.

In the other two areas studied, salary increases and selection of the Superintendent, one would assume the supervisory staff would have no direct influence. Actually, they are inclined to support fully higher salaries for teachers, since their own salaries hinge on an index based on increases proportionate to those received by the teaching staff. The ability of the supervisory staff to gain statutory legislation establishing the index is a significant indication of its strength. As a group, however, they are not direct participants in salary negotiations.

In the selection of the Superintendent, members of the supervisory staff are indirectly and directly influential. First, they represent the most immediate and likely source of supply, since most Superintendents are selected from their ranks. They are consulted individually by Board members and interest groups for suggestions whenever a Superintendent is appointed.

Their own preference for an "inside" appointment has been a major contributing factor in Board decisions. The Board, of necessity, is concerned with the ability of the staff to relate to the Superintendent. The recent unhappy experience with the selection of an "outsider" will more than likely encourage even greater reliance on the supervisory staff in the selection of the Superintendent.

Board members have indicated their concern with the enormous power of the supervisory staff and the inbred system of selection, but they despair in their inability to change the system.

In other areas studied, tangential to the five decision-making areas, it was evident that the professional headquarters staff, particularly the core of the 30-odd supervisors, were major policy makers. Overcentralization has long plagued the school system, and several studies have stressed the need for thorough administrative reorganization, yet Board support and efforts by the last two Superintendents along these lines have been thwarted by the vested interests of the staff in maintaining the status quo. In school construction and planning, the Assistant Superintendent in charge has successfully ignored Planning Commission recommendations, as well as integration policy, and is relatively free of other controls. He has become the expeditor of school construction. In the assignment of administrative and teaching staffs to schools, the central headquarters staff has recently increased its prerogatives. Much of the power which has been lodged in the central staff has prevented the expansion of the role of the district superintendents, who although nominally supervisory are an anachronism in the system.

District superintendents

Because so much evidence pinpointed power in the professional staff, the author considered it worthwhile to explore more fully the particular role of the supervisors in the field. The district superintendents (31 of them) represent the only means by which the present structure can achieve administrative decentralization and the system's only source of professional liaison with local school needs. A detailed questioning of nine district superintendents suggested that they were not participants in the formulation of school policy. Their ineffectiveness could be attributed to their general lack of budgetary and personnel powers and the inferior caliber of appointments. District superintendents have no discretion in the distribution of funds and the most limited kind of discretion in the assignment of personnel. Their own staffs are small and largely clerical.

The district superintendent acts as a buffer for parent dissatisfaction not resolved by the school principal. Most of the local superintendents interviewed complained that they were not involved significantly in budgeting, curriculum implementation, assignment of personnel, and general formulation of school policy. Very few had meaningful relations with the headquarters staff. Their contact with the schools in the area was limited to periodic school visits and meetings with principals, but rarely with teachers. Even if they could pinpoint special local needs, they felt that there was not much that they could do about dealing with them. The study of the role of the district superintendents verified their dependence on headquarters staff, not only for long-range policy, but in day-to-day decision-making. The variety of directives and forms to be completed for headquarters was a source of severe complaint by the district superintendents. Although a part of the professional bureaucracy, they are probably the least influential as a group. Their lack of participation in policy decisions gives support to the central conclusion of the study, that the central supervisory staff has cornered the power market.

Teacher participation

Because of the power it wields in collective bargaining, the United Federation of Teachers sets major policy. The membership of the union in New York City is over 30,000. It is the official bargaining agent for the city's 50,000 teachers. The union contract determines wide areas of personnel practices, expenditures, and teaching-time allotments. Because salaries and teachers' benefits represent close to half the total education budget, the union is directly involved in matters of finance. The potential power of the union to participate in other policy areas has not been fully realized because of its own choice in concentrating its attention on salary scales and related benefits. Few teachers participate in the most obvious area in which their expertise would be extremely helpful, that is in the development of curriculum. With the exception of a few high school specialists, the Bureau of Curriculum Research has not involved teachers in its programs. There was no evidence to suggest that teachers were consulted on integration policy or the problems of ghetto schools. The union repeatedly voiced its objection to any plan calling for the rotation of teachers, and that has remained a voluntary program. Its only constructive plan was the More Effective Schools proposal. Teachers are not at all involved in budgeting or selection of the Superintendent, either through the union or as individuals.[28]

In 1962, after the first strike in the history of the school system, the United Federation of Teachers negotiated the largest single wage increase ever granted the city's teachers. The United Federation of Teachers gained strength from local union and public support of labor. Its membership expanded considerably as a result of its strike action in 1962, giving it unquestioned priority as collective bargaining agent for the city's teachers. In its negotiations, the union appealed to the Mayor, the Central Labor Council, and the educational interest groups for support. The union has seemingly bypassed the Board and the Superintendent to use its strength where it is most effective—at city hall.

The union can be viewed as representing another large "professional" group in policy-making in education. Its membership comprises the largest group of professionals in the system. In the few limited areas (outside of salary scale and fringe benefits) on which it has taken a public position, the U.F.T. has

[28] In a study of United Federation of Teachers executive board members' perceptions of who makes school policy, most of those questioned attributed little power to the union except in salary matters. In most areas, they cited the Board and the Superintendents as wielders of power. Alan Rosenthal, "Pedagogues and Power," *Urban Affairs Quarterly* (September, 1966).

largely been motivated by a desire to maintain the status quo. It has supported policies which create rigidities in the system and can hardly be considered a proponent of change. Board policy on rotation of teachers was met with an appeal by the union to the Mayor to prevent implementation. The union has publicly and privately fought transfers of experienced teachers to difficult schools. It also questioned the advisability of 4-4-4 school reorganization because the plan threatened the status of the junior high school teacher.[29] In interviews conducted with union leaders, it was clear that they themselves saw a conflict in objective education and professional goals and the narrow interest of the membership. In some instances they expressed concern that their own positions of power in the union might be threatened if they violated those narrower interests.

Local civic and interest groups

As has already been demonstrated, education decision-making is closely circumscribed in the functional specialization characteristic of New York City politics. The professional bureaucracy is answerable only to an organized clientele which reflects the same kind of specialization. Two interest groups in New York City share the responsibility for overseeing education policy, the United Parents Assocation and the Public Education Association. Board membership in both organizations overlaps, and their professional staffs work closely together. The United Parents Association is a central citywide organization made up of delegates elected by school parent associations (who have elected membership in the coordinating agency), while the Public Education Association is a composite group, made up of other interest groups in the city. Board members of the Public Education Association represent the major civic groups in New York City.

The United Parents Association, the membership of which has been drawn largely from middle-class parents, primarily concerned with local school problems and facilities, has directed much of its attention to these ends.[30] In more recent years, site-selection controversies and school integration problems have occupied much of their time. The Association speaks for parents and maintains a direct concern with the immediate effects of policy on local school situations. It has, at times, taken general policy positions on "key issues" and, when possible, makes use of direct influence with Board members. A current member of the Board was an officer of the United Parents Association prior to her appointment and still maintains active communication with the organization. The Association's executive director was recently appointed staff advisor to the Board. The Association has supported the appointment of supervisory staff in the Board of Education and appears to have viable contacts within the bureaucracy. Although it is unlikely that the

[29] Junior high school teachers represent the hard core of union members.

[30] The United Parents Association is a recent recipient of an N.Y.C. Anti-Poverty Operations Board grant to encourage parent participation in schools in underprivileged communities.

Association could stimulate broad citywide parent-group support for certain policies, the threat of its large membership has been used effectively to influence Board decisions.

The Public Education Association is a composite group representing professional education interests in the city, outside of the school system itself. Its activities have centered on the more long-range educational aspects of school policy. Its strategy has been to study special problems in the system and make public recommendations based on these reports. One of the Public Education Association's reports contributed significantly to rethinking and reshaping school policy on vocational schools.[31] In general, the views of United Parents Association and Public Education Association on any issue are never far apart.

In the decisions analyzed for this study, both organizations were participants in selected areas of policy in a most limited way. Their role as overseers of educational policy is generally supportive rather than critical. Their inclination is to work within the structure, never suggesting radical change, and focusing on particular problems. Both groups exercised little influence in the area of curriculum. On occasion, one, or both, have made general statements regarding the need for inclusion of material in the curriculum, or emphasis in a given field, but neither has indicated special concern with curriculum matters. Both have supported increased school expenditures and larger city and state appropriations. The Public Education Association has tended to support greater independence for the school system in all areas, while the United Parents Association seems to prefer continued reliance on city support. Their concern with the school board is only in terms of appropriations for particular programs to which they are committed. They also lobby for state and city support for overall increases in the school budget.

The Citizens Committee for Children, which formerly played a larger role in education affairs, has concentrated its efforts on budget review. Each year the Committee holds hearings in its own offices with the supervisory bureaucracy to review the budget for the next year. Representatives of the United Parents Association and the Public Education Association are usually in attendance. Few changes in the budget result; the exercise serves to solicit interest group support for programs and findings.

The screening-panel device for selection of the Superintendent has given the United Parents Association and the Public Education Association a more direct role in the selection of Board members. Both groups are represented on the panel and exercise a notable influence in the selection process.

The Public Education Association has sought a direct role in the selection of the last four Superintendents. A change in its influence was discernible when the new Board was instituted in 1961. Prior to that time they had not been successful in their pressure to bring in an "outsider," and their recommendations had been virtually ignored. They were, however, a direct influence in the last two appointments.

---

[31] *Reorganizing Secondary Education in New York City*, Education Guidance and Work Committee of the Public Education Association (October, 1963).

Public participation

Public participation in policy-making can come through two obvious channels, voting and/or organized interest groups. In New York City there are no public votes on school issues. The assumption that voting in itself automatically assures meaningful public participation has long been questioned by political scientists. Within the context of a specialized area of decision-making, such as education, the degree of pluralism must be measured in terms of the role and degree of influence of the various public interest groups and elected officials.

As has already been demonstrated, elected officials in New York City play a declining role in education policy-making. Two newspapers in the city report regularly on education matters. Criticism in both has been mild and infrequent. Ethnic and religious groups have been satisfied with adequate representation on the Board. Catholic groups intermittently become concerned with textbooks and curriculum but rely on the Catholic Teachers Association and personal contact with the Board to make their minor demands.

Public participation in school policy formulation is circumscribed by the lack of visible decision-making, the shortage of information available to the public on most issues, and a deficiency in the means for participation. Parent associations are active in individual schools, dealing with highly localized and personalized problems. The highly centralized organization of the school system is a deterrent to communication between parents' groups and policy makers. Parents and teachers, the agents closest to the child, are virtually removed from policy decisions.

The school integration issue is the only area in which public response has been vociferous and active. The integration issue has attracted the widest participation of any policy decision explored.

Local groups of every shade of opinion have organized to oppose or defend individual plans. Among the most vociferous have been the Parents and Taxpayers Association (PAT) and their opposition, Parents and Neighbors United for Integrated-Quality Education (EQUAL). Civil rights groups originally entered the school policy field with the single concern of achieving an integrated system; now they are in the forefront of the demands for decentralization. Local civic groups, chambers of commerce, councilmen, and candidates for public office have voiced strong opinions on proposals. Many of these groups and individuals have never before been involved in school affairs, and their current concern has been limited to the integration issue and its ramifications. Public involvement in the integration issue indicated that more widespread participation results when there is no consensus among those with power and decisions become more visible.

Perhaps the most significant development in school decision-making in the last five years has surrounded the integration issue. Aside from its social and human implications, it has had an important political impact. For the past two decades, superintendents, boards, and school bureaucracies have been free-wheeling, with little outside pressure. They have successfully closed off school policy formulation from elected local government officials and civic groups. The integration issue has broken open the monopoly of power vested in the small core of school officials. It has raised serious questions regarding the role of professionals, their goals and interests in school policy.

Consensus decision-making, confined to the professionals, limits policy alternatives as well as public participation. A balance between professionalism and public participation is the desired end. Conflict between competing forces and differences in interests and goals guarantee the visibility of policy-making and encourage public participation. These are the characteristics of a system which are most likely to produce change and encourage adaptability.

Lowi points out that changes in New York City have come from three sources: (1) a single unpredictable individual, (2) sources outside the city (the state or federal governments), and (3) the reform system or minority party. The last is the most frequent source of innovation.[32] This conclusion would suggest that changes in education will depend on the new Mayor's leadership and perhaps his ability to enlist greater public support and interest in education policy.

Conclusion

In any policy-making structure the role of participants and potential participants is relevant. The resources of particular groups or individuals, and the way they are used, are an essential factor in evaluating power. The usual assumption, that wealth is a primary resource, is denied in educational decision-making in New York City. The key resource appears to be professional expertise. The education bureaucracy has become virtually self-contained, sealed by special training and knowledge. They have expanded their role and limited conflict by manipulation of issues to assert that they are wholly dependent upon expert judgment, which they alone have.

In a rather concise—and, one might say, almost modest—characterization of the educational world in New York City, Sayre and Kaufman noted: "On balance, the school official enjoys an unusual capacity for self-government."[33] In fact, with the exception of the integration issue, there are only three or four areas in which any appreciable outside influence is brought to bear on matters of education policy. Such influence is most direct in regard to the religious and racial balance on the Board of Education and in the distribution of appointments to the supervisory staff. To these items should be added the Mayor's role in the determination of teachers' salaries. Some outside influence can also be seen in the negotiations for individual school locations, the bargaining for school construction contracts, and the granting of minor favors by local district superintendents (in their limited sphere of operation). Basically, however, there are no forces acting to broaden education policy and balance it with other city policy.

As a political subsystem, the New York City school system can only be described as "narrow, convergent, and dominated by a consensual elite." This

---

[32] *Op. cit.,* p. 200.
[33] Sayre and Kaufman, *op. cit.,* p. 285.

description is in sharp contrast to the usual view of New York City politics as "open"—or to the somewhat typical suggestion in this instance by Sayre and Kaufman that "no part of the city's large and varied population is alienated from participation in the system."[34]

For the political scientist, such a disparity poses a basic problem in creating meaningful operational categories by which power can be analyzed. The results of this study indicate the real need to examine how power is exercised in individual areas of activity. Such examinations should explore differences in the distribution of power, the kinds and levels of participation, the degree of integration by citywide elements, and the role of nonprofessional and nonsupportive interest groups. Working from this type of analysis, the methodological concern with pluralist and power elite concepts may be shifted to the development of more quantitative measurements of the determinants of open and closed political systems. Such an approach will also provide greater insights into the sources and possibilities for change in a political system.

[34] *Ibid.,* p. 720.

The Failure of Community Leadership:
Urban Renewal in Toledo

Jean L. Stinchcombe

The importance of leadership to the possibility of policy change in a local community is once again emphasized. A municipality's political leaders not only set the agenda of policy concerns in a community, but also have a great deal of influence on the actual policies pursued by local governmental units. In this selection, from Reform and Reaction: City Politics in Toledo, *Jean Stinchcombe examines the consequences of an amorphous political system and apathetic leadership on urban-renewal programs in Toledo, Ohio.*

Previous research has indicated how difficult it is to bring about school desegregation, fluoridation, and a host of other policy changes without the active involvement and support of key political leaders (decision makers and influentials) in a local community. Additional studies have also indicated that successful urban-renewal programs are associated with leadership capable of negotiating support and facilitating coordinated action. Political leaders must be able to mobilize sufficient resources to overcome opposition to policy change.

Stinchcombe points out that <u>all of the conditions found to be related to successful urban-renewal programs—political leadership, clarity and continuity of direction, administrative competence, and group support</u>—have been lacking in Toledo. Progress in Toledo's urban-renewal projects has been hindered by disagreements over objectives, uncertainty in policy and administrative decisions, resistance from property owners, question and objections from federal officials, demolition difficulties, and an undercurrent of political acrimony. In addition, urban renewal has not engendered a great deal of enthusiasm among political leaders, nor "touched the imagination" of politicians; business leaders have withdrawn their support; black leaders or organizations have shown no particular concern, because few blacks have been displaced by the various projects; and voters have defeated councilmen unpleasantly identified with urban renewal. In effect, no coalition of interests has emerged and given its support to urban renewal in the city.

Why has this been the case? Stinchcombe concludes that the various mayors and renewal administrators have not had the political strength or skill to attract the support of organized interests or the electorate. The governing coalition has proved ineffective because of its inability or unwillingness to overcome Toledo's extreme decentralization of authority. Toledo's reformed institutions, which were intended to assure a positive municipal response to city problems, have proved ineffective in the case of urban renewal. The council manager form of government, with its division of authority between a city council of equals and an administrator, has produced a governmental system which is political without having a locus of power.

In their attempt to remove politics from city government, Toledo's municipal reformers have destroyed political leadership, at least for the present. Has the operation of reformed institutions impeded political change in other local communities? If so, why has this been the case?

Introduction

Toledo's urban renewal program reveals the consequences of an amorphous political system and apathetic private leadership. Federal urban renewal legislation requires a sustained response from the local community which is difficult to maintain without local leadership and interest. Although the 1949, 1954, and 1965 housing laws offer the prospect of substantial federal aid, the planning, initiation, and execution of urban renewal are the responsibility of individual cities.[1] To qualify for federal aid, each community must

From *Reform and Reaction: City Politics in Toledo* by Jean L. Stinchcombe, pp. 129-150. © 1968 by Wadsworth Publishing Company, Inc., Belmont, California. Reprinted by permission of the author and publisher.

[1] For a discussion of the 1949 and 1954 acts and changing federal concepts of urban renewal, see Coleman Woodbury, "Human Relations and Urban Renewal," in Oliver P. Williams and Charles Press, eds., *Democracy in Urban America* (Chicago: Rand McNally & Co., 1961), pp. 489-502.

receive and retain Housing and Home Finance Agency approval of a "workable program" for urban renewal.[2] In executing an urban renewal project, the city must prepare initial plans and surveys, win the approval of the Urban Renewal Administration for loans with which to produce additional surveys and plans, provide the local share (one third) of the project cost, satisfy Urban Renewal Administration requirements on land acquisition, clearance, relocation, and land disposition, achieve the cooperation of the Public Housing Administration and/or attract private developers, and assist mortgage arrangements for redevelopers.

Urban renewal is a complex effort at planned change. The local community must establish its own, often controversial, renewal goals. Questions such as industrial or residential redevelopment, public housing or middle- and upper-income private housing are politically potent. Urban renewal, whatever its objective, is disruptive and damaging to some interests. Community leaders must assess these effects and the possible responses of groups within the city; they must attract the necessary group support to aid in the execution of urban renewal and contribute to redevelopment. In addition, urban renewal requires a measure of continuity and professional competence in city leadership. Local officials must fend for themselves in a diffuse, intricate administrative environment including several federal agencies and many technical restrictions and choices.

Successful urban renewal programs

Studies indicate that successful urban renewal is associated with leadership capable of negotiating support and facilitating coordinated action.[3] Extensive urban renewal programs are most often found in cities with stable, centralized political systems. Robert A. Dahl has emphasized the importance of Mayor Richard Lee's leadership in New Haven's remarkable urban renewal program.[4] In his first term in office Lee made urban redevelopment the central policy of his administration. The mayor's dominant role in this field served to increase his political influence in other areas, such as public education and party affairs. Decision-making by diverse and uncoordinated organizations (or "rival sovereignties," to use Dahl's term) gave way to a durable executive-centered coalition. From 1953 on, Mayor Lee and his urban redevelopment program held the paramount position in local politics. Dahl has described Lee's performance: "He took on more and more of the task of negotiating with the 'Feds'; he knew how to cut through the interminable delays characteristic of bureaucratic agencies, and he exploited statutes and rules to gain concessions for New Haven that cut down the actual contribution the city was required to

---

[2] The "workable program" is to consist of codes and ordinances for building and housing standards; a comprehensive community plan; neighborhood analyses of blight; administrative organizations capable of enforcing codes and executing renewal; financing; relocation plans; citizen participation.

[3] The use of the word "successful" in discussing urban renewal refers to the *extent* of renewal programs rather than their social or aesthetic effects.

[4] See Robert A. Dahl, *Who Governs?* (New Haven, Conn.: Yale University Press, 1961), pp. 115-141.

make. . . . The city was able to move far partly because its agents moved fast."[5] Under the continuing impetus of Lee's leadership, New Haven developed one of the largest urban renewal programs in the country.

Edward C. Banfield has discussed the way in which the Cook County Democratic Party overcame the fragmentation of governmental institutions in Chicago.[6] There, the rival sovereignties were subdued by the "structure of control" achieved by Mayor Daley and his party organization. Formal decentralization in urban renewal and other fields is counteracted by informal centralization. Mayor Daley, like Mayor Lee, committed his administration to urban renewal.[7] Instead of fostering dispersed authority, as his predecessor had done, Mayor Daley used his political and organizational resources to achieve increased coordination in urban renewal. In Chicago, as in New Haven, urban renewal is attached to the fortunes of an adroit politician who has dominated the local scene for approximately a decade (Lee was first elected in 1953, Daley in 1956).

Other examples also confirm the importance of executive power and continuity of leadership. In St. Louis, Mayor Raymond R. Tucker presided over a 12-year period in which massive slum clearance, urban renewal, and other innovations were undertaken. Although he did not have the party organization of either Daley or Lee, Mayor Tucker used the powers of his office (strong mayor) and a reform alliance of business leaders, upper- and middle-income residents, the press, and (some) Negro and union leaders to dominate the policy process.[8] Pittsburgh's renowned urban renewal program benefited from the continuity and cohesion supplied by David Lawrence's Democratic organization.[9] In Newark the development of a successful program was dependent on the support of a mayor occupying a newly strengthened office.[10]

In all of these cases, the political system is centralized. Power is concentrated, either formally, as in Newark, or informally, as in Chicago. In power and prestige the political executives of New Haven, Chicago, Newark, Pittsburgh, and St. Louis stand above other elective officials. The political leaders of these cities are committed to urban renewal and are able to act on that commitment. They have assumed initiative and responsibility in guiding community decisions.

---

[5] Dahl, p. 130.

[6] Edward C. Banfield, *Political Influence* (New York: The Free Press, 1961). See also Martin Meyerson and Edward C. Banfield, *Politics, Planning, and the Public Interest* (New York: The Free Press, 1955).

[7] Peter H. Rossi and Robert A. Dentler, *The Politics of Urban Renewal* (New York: The Free Press, 1961), p. 250.

[8] On the St. Louis political scene, see Robert H. Salisbury, "St. Louis Politics: Relationships Among Interests, Parties, and Governmental Structure," *Western Political Quarterly*, XIII (June 1960), 498-507, and Ernest Calloway, "A Reform Period Closes," *Focus Midwest*, III, Nos. 10 and 11 (1965), 14-15.

[9] Edward C. Banfield and James Q. Wilson, *City Politics* (Cambridge, Mass.: Harvard University and M.I.T. Press, 1963), p. 274.

[10] See Harold Kaplan, *Urban Renewal Politics* (New York: Columbia University Press, 1963). Newark adopted a strong mayor charter in 1954.

The presence of a stable, clear locus of political power has often enhanced the contribution of professional urban renewal administrators. With the assurance of political direction and support, urban renewal professionals can develop the skills and procedures to fulfill the highly technical requirements of the program. Thus Mayor Lee of New Haven provided the political conditions for an effective Development Administrator. Dahl writes:

> No one but the mayor could have given redevelopment the priority it received. In another administration, the Development Administrator could have been frustrated and helpless. In Lee's, the Development Administrator's furious drive and energy found infinite outlets in redevelopment.[11]

Similarly, the administrative staff of the Newark Housing Authority has been a major source of policy and initiative in Newark's urban renewal program. But in Harold Kaplan's judgment, the system rests to a large extent on the mayor's ability to obtain city hall approval of NHA's plans and his willingness to give NHA a free hand in policy formation. Kaplan writes: "The strong mayor charter adopted in 1954 helped stabilize the renewal system by concentrating power at City Hall . . . and relieved NHA of the necessity of dealing directly with the Council."[12]

In addition to its administrative benefits, centralized political leadership of urban renewal has interested and involved community groups in the program. In cities with successful urban renewal programs, mayors have induced the leaders of diverse community organizations to give their endorsement and assistance. Through persuasion, publicity, advisory committees, and political bargaining, Mayors Lee and Daley built community support for renewal. In some cities, business leaders have made significant contributions. For example, powerful leaders in Pittsburgh politics and business have cooperated in a vast urban renewal program, and the business leaders of Newark and St. Louis have been drawn into urban renewal by skilled political leadership.

Urban renewal is, in sum, a political problem. The task of establishing objectives and consolidating support for a difficult community program is essentially political. In cities where leadership is ineffectual, either because of the inadequate formal powers of the mayor or his indifference, urban renewal is unlikely to flourish. In contrast, a strong political leader with an active commitment to urban renewal can supply a crucial stimulus to the program. He can encourage both administrative competence and group support.

---

[11] Dahl, *Who Governs?*, p. 127.

[12] Kaplan, *Urban Renewal Politics*, p. 181. In other cities, stability has been obtained under the council-manager plan. Managers and urban renewal administrators with long tenure and established authority have contributed to the success of urban renewal in Hartford, Connecticut, and Kansas City, Missouri. For a discussion of urban renewal in Hartford, see Carleton F. Sharpe, "Teamwork in Urban Renewal," *Public Management*, XLIV (September 1962), 198-202.

The renewal program in Toledo

In Toledo, all of the conditions related to successful programs—political leadership, clarity and continuity of direction, administrative competence, and group support—have been lacking. The Toledo urban renewal program has been small and halting. By June 1965, approximately $16 million in federal funds had been allotted to urban renewal in Toledo, including projects in the planning stages, underway, and completed.[13] Table 1 indicates the meager extent of the Toledo program in comparison with the programs in 20 leading urban renewal cities.[14]

Table 1. *The twenty leading urban renewal cities and Toledo, 1965*

(1) City	(2) Total federal funds disbursed (in millions of dollars)	(3) Total federal funds reserved (in millions of dollars)	(4) Funds disbursed per capita* (in dollars and cents)
1. New York	122.3	281.1	15.72
2. Chicago	79.8	149.3	22.47
3. Philadelphia	53.2	198.5	26.55
4. Baltimore	37.9	70.8	40.36
5. Boston	37.0	149.5	53.11
6. New Haven	36.5	77.4	239.89
7. Pittsburgh	32.3	99.3	53.49
8. Washington	27.6	82.7	36.12
9. Detroit	26.5	88.5	15.87
10. St. Louis	22.9	57.0	30.58
11. Norfolk	21.7	38.7	71.32
12. Newark	20.0	97.0	49.27
13. Cincinnati	19.5	73.6	38.89
14. Minneapolis	16.0	35.3	33.04
15. Providence	15.2	46.7	73.29
16. Cleveland	15.0	58.9	16.65
17. San Francisco	12.4	93.7	16.80
18. Atlanta	11.7	41.0	24.01
19. Dayton	9.1	25.8	34.58
20. Columbus	8.8	20.7	18.58
21. Toledo	4.0	15.9	12.66

*This is computed by dividing column 2 by the city's 1960 population.
Source: U.S. Housing and Home Finance Agency, Urban Renewal Administration, Urban Renewal Project Directory (Washington, D.C.: March 31, 1965).

[13] Urban Renewal Administration financial estimates and evaluations of progress in Toledo are presented in *The Blade*, July 3, 1965, Section 2, p. 9.

[14] The cities in Table 1 are ranked according to total disbursements of federal funds. Because of this, some cities with smaller totals, but large per capita expenditures do not appear in the table. In Hartford, Connecticut, for example, federal funds disbursed for urban renewal amount to $46.27 per capita. The totals for federal funds reserved indicate the future dimensions of urban renewal programs.

In the years since the passage of the 1949 Housing Act, Toledo has undertaken six urban renewal projects of which one has been completed.[15] The completed project, Gunckel, involved a relatively small clearance area (38 acres) with redevelopment by the Toledo Metropolitan Housing Authority and the expansion of a grade school playground. Other projects now in progress include: Ironville, a 67-acre port-oriented industrial redevelopment project started in 1960; Vistula Meadows, an extensive (99 acres) downtown renewal project started in 1959; Riverview, a small (13 acres) downtown renewal project initiated in 1963; and Roosevelt, a conservation project designated and surveyed in 1962. The oldest project and the one which best reveals Toledo's difficulties in urban renewal is Chase Park, a 127-acre residential redevelopment project three and one-half miles north of the downtown business district.

The Chase Park project

Chase Park was conceived in 1951, when the area was designated a study project of substandard housing. At that time Toledo renewal hopes were focused on plans for a large industrial redevelopment area, the Canton project. In August 1955, an official in the Chicago office of the Urban Renewal Administration advised the director of the Toledo Housing Improvement and Urban Renewal Commission that the Chase Park area would also be an appropriate site for urban renewal. City officials then turned their attention to the Chase Park project, which they visualized as an effort to rehabilitate deteriorating property adjacent to a rat-infested dump. Plans were submitted to federal Housing and Home Finance Agency officials, who questioned the emphasis on rehabilitation instead of clearance and redevelopment.[16] Nevertheless, after a year's delay the Chase Park project received federal approval, a capital grant for two thirds of the cost, and an advance planning loan from the Urban Renewal Administration.[17]

At the local level, controversies were stirring. After an uncertain period in which it had three directors in one year, the Housing Improvement and Urban Renewal Commission began to reconsider the Chase Park project. Proponents of clearance and redevelopment were now in a majority on the commission and on city council. In December 1957, the director of the Housing Improvement and Urban Renewal Commission concluded that it would be necessary to revise the Chase Park plan to meet both the longstanding HHFA preference for redevelopment and the changed appraisal of HIURC members

---

[15] This total does not include two abortive efforts; the Canton Project was dropped in favor of the Chase Park effort, discussed below; the Spring conservation project was dropped for lack of federal approval. The Gunckel project was completed on July 31, 1964.

[16] *The Blade*, December 30, 1956, Section 5, p. 1.

[17] *The Blade*, June 6, 1957, p. 20.

and city councilmen.[18] Instead of being a rehabilitation project with spot clearance, Chase Park was to be a clearance project with spot rehabilitation. In March 1958, the amended application was approved by the HHFA.

In 1958 the city also altered its administrative arrangements. The Housing Improvement and Urban Renewal Commission was replaced by the Urban Renewal Agency, a city department. The role of the former HIUR commissioners was to be fulfilled by a newly established Urban Renewal Advisory Commission, appointed by the mayor with the approval of the city council.

Meanwhile, the Chase Park project was being challenged on new grounds. In the fall of 1958, some councilmen and renewal officials began to consider the industrial potential of the Chase Park area. The chairman of the City Plan Commission and a Democratic city councilman emerged as the leading advocates for a change of plans.[19] They emphasized the proximity of Chase Park to the Maumee River and port development as well as existing industry on the periphery of the project. Those favoring residential redevelopment pointed to nearby parks and residential areas and the greater resale value of residential property. After several months of discussion, city council voted eight to one to approve the Chase Park plans as predominantly residential.[20]

Yet the issue was not settled. While the proponents of industrial redevelopment continued to object to residential plans, citizens living in the vicinity of Chase Park mobilized to resist any change in renewal objectives. In September 1959, two Democratic councilmen staged a desperate effort for industrial development by moving to table the residential project. Their seven colleagues on city council remained unconvinced by arguments that Chase Park is "the most logical place for port-oriented industry," as they voted to proceed with residential redevelopment.[21]

Despite continuing dissension over renewal objectives, Toledo was ready to move into the implementation stage of the Chase Park project in 1960.[22] A fragile Democratic majority had replaced the 8–1 City Manager League council of the previous two years; the Democratic mayor, elected with the support of a maverick Republican and a City Manager League Democrat, had an active interest in urban renewal. During 1960 the city began acquiring property, although it encountered resistance and a law suit from one of the largest property owners in the area.[23] Aside from this difficulty, the project seemed to be advancing at last and the Toledo urban renewal director had reason to believe that "things are going better than we ever dreamed possible."[24] By 1961 a large part of the property had been acquired and the relocation of more than 300 families was proceeding smoothly.

[18] *The Blade*, December 29, 1957, p. 36.

[19] *The Blade*, March 29, 1959, Section 1, p. 2.

[20] This vote took place in December 1958.

[21] *The Blade*, September 9, 1959, p. 1.

[22] For a discussion of continuing dissension over redevelopment objectives see *The Blade*, December 31, 1961, p. 22.

[23] For a review of these difficulties, see *The Blade*, September 12, 1962, p. 3.

[24] *The Blade*, February 3, 1961, p. 17.

Demolition commenced in 1961, a decade after the project had first been discussed. But it soon became evident that hopes for the rapid conclusion of the Chase Park project were premature. In April 1961, after several months of work, demolition was halted by a report that the contractor was selling salvaged siding, windows, and shrubs without authorization. After a conference between the urban renewal director and the contractor, demolition activities resumed.[25] Within weeks, however, new allegations were made. Two city officials, the municipal demolition supervisor and the administrative assistant to the city manager, were found to have been making a little money on the side. The Toledo demolition supervisor had accepted a kick-back of $100.00 in the illicit sale of a garage. In addition, the administrative assistant to the city manager and the demolition supervisor had formed a partnership to buy Chase Park homes and move them elsewhere for sale. Upon disclosure of these activities, the demolition supervisor quickly resigned and the city manager, after some hesitation, called for the resignation of his administrative assistant.[26]

Additional questions led to a second suspension of the contract with Surety Salvage and Lumber Company. The urban renewal director was disturbed by the moving and sale of garages and houses by the demolition contractor; the dismantling of property by unauthorized persons and the sale of salvageable materials on the site also seemed questionable under the contract. But in spite of these and other problems, such as the demolition of 27 houses which the city intended to exempt and resell, Toledo legal and renewal officials recognized that a "loosely drawn" and "ambiguous" contract was at least partly responsible.[27] Thus the city and the contractor again negotiated their differences and demolition resumed.

The city manager attempted to reassure critics by "placing the Chase Park renewal, especially demolition, under the direct supervision of his administration."[28] A registered engineer was to supervise demolition activities and report directly to the city manager. *The Blade* was unimpressed with these moves:

> From the outset, the city ordinance on urban renewal vested in the manager top responsibility for administering the program. And if a registered engineer is required—as Mr. Alspach [the city manager] now finds—why is this necessity discovered so late in the program? . . .
> Although the city administration . . . failed to exercise effective supervision and delayed remedies, this is no occasion for Council to indulge in sanctimonious pronouncements.
> Some councilmen have personally intervened in the selection of urban renewal employees and Council as a whole has seemed more concerned with its own system of overseeing urban renewal projects than with demanding top quality professionals to do the job.[29]

[25] *The Blade*, April 20, 1961, p. 25.
[26] *The Blade*, June 24, 1961, p. 13, and June 26, 1961, p. 1.
[27] *The Blade*, December 31, 1961, p. 22.
[28] *The Blade*, July 3, 1961, p. 1.
[29] *The Blade*, July 5, 1961, p. 20.

The Blade's suspicion that "all was not going well with the project" soon received additional confirmation. In the fall of 1961, demolition activities were suspended as city officials investigated numerous contract violations disclosed by *Blade* reporters. An initial survey of the clearance area revealed 78 instances in which the contractor had failed to remove the foundations of razed buildings to the 36-inch required depth and to comply with specifications for filling excavations and grading surfaces. After inspecting the complete foundations of several supposedly demolished buildings, the city manager commented: "We're in the position of having the wool pulled over our eyes."[30]

Nevertheless, a majority of administrative and elective officials did not think that the project would benefit from a change of contractors. Surety Salvage and Lumber was directed to correct contract violations in 154 of 158 demolished structures at its own expense and to resume demolition under the scrutiny of city supervisors. The city law director assured critics that demolition in Chase Park was actually ahead of schedule; the vice-mayor emphasized city council's responsibility in urban renewal and its determination to correct past mistakes.

A maverick Republican councilman led the opposition to these explanations, contending that Chase Park had long been afflicted with "buck passing, excuses, unnecessary delays, and a high degree of incompetence." Democratic and Republican councilmen supporting the administration countered that the opposition was merely trying to make the city manager, the law director, and the urban renewal director "scapegoats" instead of concentrating on the task of reassuring the public.[31]

As the turmoil over demolition appeared to subside, another issue revived. Although the city had endorsed residential redevelopment in Chase Park three years earlier, in December 1961 the law department recommended that the City Plan Commission approve a major change in previous plans. On the eve of a condemnation suit, the city succumbed to the pleas of the Ayling-Reichert factory and recommended that small industry be allowed to remain in the project area. A *Blade* editorial criticized the sudden shift in which the city asked that a 40-year-old factory be permitted to remain in the center of an area designated for private residential redevelopment.[32]

Others insisted that the factory would preserve jobs and promote industrial development. *The Blade* recalled that it had questioned the original decision to designate the area for residential rather than industrial development. Yet, it concluded, "once the project is undertaken it makes no sense to permit a factory to remain where it has been a nonconforming use since the beginning of zoning."[33] The City Plan Commission refused to accept the recommendation, and *The Blade* offered a critical appraisal of urban renewal in Toledo:

[30] *The Blade*, October 3, 1961, p. 1.
[31] *The Blade*, November 11, 1961, p. 1.
[32] *The Blade*, December 17, 1961, Section 2, p. 4.
[33] *Ibid.*

Toledo has been playing at urban renewal like a dilettante for nearly twelve years. From one administration to another, the city has changed plans and programs so often that it has lost a whole decade of progress during which other communities forged ahead with Federal assistance.[34]

The aura of scandal and incompetence during the Democratic administration of 1960—1961 had contributed to the election of eight Republicans to the city council which assumed office in January 1962. All incumbent Democrats, including the mayor, had been defeated in an election which only one Democrat survived. The new Republican administration listed urban renewal as its top priority. Days after assuming office it was faced with a new problem in demolition operations.[35] A new Republican councilman, Andy Douglas, charged Surety with again violating the contract and defrauding its employees by substandard wages. The councilman cited intimidation and wage cuts suffered by demolition employees. These infractions, added to previous difficulties, led to a cancellation of the $70,000 contract with only half of the job complete. Councilman Douglas, chairman of city council's urban renewal committee, was unsuccessful, however, in his effort to initiate an investigation of urban renewal operations.

The Republican administration hoped to hasten Chase Park progress by the appointment of a new city manager and a revised and improved demolition contract. During the winter months, city officials worked on the task of rewriting the demolition contract, submitting it for federal approval, and seeking bids for a new contractor. Surety Salvage and Lumber Company responded to its dismissal with a law suit asking the Common Pleas Court to prohibit Toledo from hiring another demolition contractor.[36] In March a Common Pleas judge rejected Surety's contention that Toledo had illegally breached the contract.[37] Bids for the demolition of the remaining 161 buildings indicated that the change in contractors would cost the city an additional $23,000. But the revised contract itself was said to be a great improvement, since renewal officials understood it to prohibit the moving and sale of houses and garages.[38]

During the spring of 1962, demolition remained at a standstill and old controversies continued. In April 1962, city council's urban renewal committee revived a recommendation to include public housing for senior citizens in the Chase Park renewal area. Officials for the real estate and building industries (and others) protested the damaging effect of public housing on the prospects for private redevelopment.[39] City council ignored these arguments and approved the recommendation of its urban renewal committee, although

[34] *Ibid.* (Reprinted with permission of Toledo Blade Company. © Toledo Blade Co.)
[35] *The Blade*, January 2, 1962, p. 11.
[36] *The Blade*, January 19, 1962, p. 8.
[37] *The Blade*, March 20, 1962, p. 17.
[38] *The Blade*, March 28, 1962, p. 37.
[39] *The Blade*, April 10, 1962, p. 37.

it had defeated a similar proposal the previous year. At the end of April, city council's urban renewal committee revived another old issue by recommending that the Ayling-Reichert factory be allowed to remain in the Chase Park area under certain conditions. City council rejected this recommendation in a vote calling for the removal of the factory.[40]

In May, after more than four months of delay, demolition resumed with a new contractor, the Cleveland Wrecking Company. Only weeks later a proposal to purchase and ship houses to Michigan for sale to an unnamed buyer brought the work to a standstill again. The city and the contractor were at odds on the terms of the demolition contract, but the question was resolved by the disappearance of the buyer.[41] After this episode *The Blade* commented:

> The Chase Park project may look simple on paper, but it's hard to recall a single undertaking by the city in recent years that got bogged down in such a mass of confusions, frustrations, blunders, and boo-boos as has struck activities in Chase Park.
> . . . If the administration and city council have any thoughts of taking the voters to the top of the mountain and holding up Chase Park as an example of what urban renewal can mean, they had best forget them for the present.[42]

The resignation of the urban renewal director in June left the Republican administration with a critical vacancy. In August 1962, the appointment of Thurmond Hawkins was announced. Although Mr. Hawkins had had no previous experience in urban renewal or city planning, he was said to have been selected for his other professional qualifications. The city manager noted the new director's administrative experience in business and the army. After ending a five-year army career as a major and public relations field representative in Paris, Mr. Hawkins had served in executive and sales capacities in the real estate and insurance business. Moreover, he was secretary of the Republican Central Committee, seventh ward chairman, and a precinct committeeman.[43] *The Blade* castigated the appointment of a real estate and home salesman with no experience in government and administration who "concedes that his background in selling, public relations, and office management encompasses no comparable experience in handling the major contracts or large projects involved in urban renewal."[44]

Demolition, rehabilitation, and relocation continued during 1963. Six of the eight Republican incumbents survived the fall election in which they defended the urban renewal progress achieved by a "competent" and "responsible" administration. Applications for federal approval, loans, and grants on new projects moved more quickly than events in Chase Park,

[40] *The Blade*, April 30, 1962, p. 13, and May 2, 1962, p. 37.

[41] *The Blade*, June 25, 1962, p. 13.

[42] *The Blade*, June 27, 1962, p. 20.

[43] For an account of Hawkins' political positions and activity, see *The Blade*, May 24, 1964, Section C, p. 1.

[44] *The Blade*, July 10, 1964, p. 14.

however. After the completion of clearance and site improvements, Chase Park land was opened for bids in the summer of 1964, with disappointing results. There were only three initial bids on one section of land and no bids at all on about half the acreage advertised for disposition.[45]

In July 1964, federal authorities approved the sale of land to two local redevelopers, Clifford C. Loss, Inc., and Scholz-Chase, Inc. The Loss Company purchased 19 lots on which it began to construct $13,000-$14,000 ranch homes, two of which were opened for display in September 1964. Scholz-Chase purchased 14 acres on which to build a 240-unit apartment complex. Construction, first scheduled to begin in September 1964, had not yet started in September 1966.[46] Other redevelopment in the Chase Park area is by public agencies. The Toledo Metropolitan Housing Authority has constructed a 50-unit housing project for elderly persons, and the Toledo public school system has completed a new elementary school. The final record will indicate that the Chase Park project was at least 15 or 16 years in the making.

Other renewal projects in Toledo

Progress on Toledo's other urban renewal projects has been hindered by many of the problems seen in Chase Park: disagreement over objectives; uncertainty in policy and administrative decisions; resistance from property owners; questions and objections from federal officials; demolition difficulties; and an undercurrent of political acrimony. In addition, a 1914 charter provision (Section 79), which prohibited city expenditures of more than $500,000 on public improvement without voter approval, impeded local financing of urban renewal projects.[47] From 1960 to 1964 the major effort on Ironville (industrial redevelopment) and Vistula Meadows (downtown renewal) was devoted to circumventing Section 79 by subdividing and rearranging the projects.[48] The city was freed from the tortuous process of evading the $500,000 spending limit when the voters repealed Section 79 in May 1964.

In 1966 several large projects entered or approached the execution stage. In Ironville, started in 1960, structures were razed, and the area was finally advertised for redevelopers in 1967. Buildings were also demolished in a one-block area of Vistula Meadows, which will be the site of an experimental public housing project for the aged and handicapped. The city is awaiting federal permission to proceed with land acquisition, relocation, and clearance in the large area remaining. Federal officials expect that Vistula Meadows, in

---

[45] *Ibid.*

[46] For a comment on repeated delays in starting construction, see *The Blade*, September 14, 1966, p. 14. Donald J. Scholz offers his explanation in *The Blade*, September 21, 1966, p. 16.

[47] *The Blade*, June 9, 1963, Section 2, p. 1.

[48] *The Blade*, August 9, 1963, p. 3.

the planning stages since 1959, will be completed in 1972.[49] In October 1965, a demolition contract was signed for Riverview, a three-block downtown renewal project conceived in 1963. Property in the Riverview area was offered and sold to prospective developers in 1966.[50]

The appeal of renewal projects in Toledo

To the politicians

Toledo's urban renewal program has touched the imagination of only one group, the politicians. Yet most politicians have been more intrigued with its possibilities for discrediting the opposition than with its potential for advancing their own ambitions. No Toledo politician has had the power to direct urban renewal in the manner of Mayor Lee of New Haven or Mayor Daley of Chicago. Only two mayors, Michael Damas (D., 1960–1961) and John Potter (R., 1962–1967), have attempted to identify themselves with urban renewal. Mayor Damas, who served during the inglorious demolition activities in Chase Park, did so with disastrous results. His association with the inept administration of urban renewal contributed to the abrupt end of his political career in the only primary defeat ever suffered by a mayor.[51]

John Potter also attached his political fortunes to urban renewal, but with more favorable results. In 1963 Mayor Potter unveiled the Riverview project as his personal contribution to urban renewal in Toledo. In introducing the project, which he described as being inspired by a depressing midnight walk through downtown Toledo, the mayor gave assurances that he had a commitment from a redeveloper who was willing to spend millions to rebuild and revive the area. Later he announced a gift from the Charities Foundation for the purchase of an old post office in the Riverview area. After the 1963 municipal election, Mayor Potter succeeded in removing the dissident Councilman Douglas from the chairmanship of the urban renewal committee and assuming that position himself. The mayor conferred with urban renewal officials in Chicago and Washington, addressed business and citizens' groups, and cajoled local administrators in an effort to facilitate urban renewal. He managed to raise the program from the nadir of ineptitude. Yet he had limited success in accelerating the major projects or interesting community organizations in urban renewal.

The extreme decentralization of the political system, rather than the errors of incumbent mayors, is in large part responsible for the shortcomings of urban renewal in Toledo. The mayor, even when he has had a strong commitment to urban renewal, has not had the authority to dominate the crucial decisions. Power has been dispersed among nine councilmen and several

---

[49] *The Blade*, September 28, 1965, p. 1.

[50] *The Blade*, January 25, 1966, Section 2, p. 1. John Galbreath and Company of Columbus immediately announced its interest in redeveloping the entire area.

[51] Mayor Damas's distinction was noted in *The Blade*, October 24, 1965, p. 1.

administrators. The division of authority between city council and the city manager and between the city manager and the urban renewal director has been unclear. The resulting confusion has engendered a politics of petty reprisal and quarrelsomeness rather than permitting the emergence of a political leader who could confidently stake his career on a record of achievement in urban renewal. Instead of being a field for political achievement, as in New Haven, urban renewal has been an ideal target for attack during the past fifteen years.

To business

The peculiar futility and political backbiting characteristic of urban renewal in Toledo have appealed to few community organizations. The tortuous, uncertain process of making decisions in the absence of executive direction and administrative competence has not created the kind of business support for urban renewal seen in many communities. In New Haven (and other cities with successful programs), political and administrative officials have worked together in a cohesive, centralized effort to achieve coordinated decisions and group support. Thus Mayor Lee employed the Citizens Action Commission with its membership of leading bankers, industrialists, and businessmen to assure acceptability for urban redevelopment.[52] The Newark Economic Development Committee and the Newark Commission on Neighborhood Conservation and Rehabilitation were used to build business support in that city.[53]

In Toledo the Urban Renewal Advisory Commission and the councils for the individual projects have been ineffectual. The potential effect of these groups is negated by the absence of strong political leadership to utilize them. Although many business leaders belong to councils or committees, most of them frankly admit their disinterest in urban renewal. Thus a vice-president in one company said:

> The business leaders, the top people, haven't been very interested in urban renewal. Business people could have done more, much more. The whole program has been entirely too slow. Toledo needs a strong individual to start ramming it through. We need more aggressiveness and a top level executive for the urban renewal agency.

Many executives believe that "more action and less talk" would be the best method to attract the interest of business leaders who have become "bored by years of planning without results." Others argue that business leaders would give more support if "their opinions and assistance had been solicited more frequently and in a more concrete manner."

But the withdrawal of business leaders is also a matter of their own choice. Urban renewal, as one corporation president expressed it, "is an area, which, while it may be desirable, is not a matter of any great concern to business leaders." No specific project or plan has held their interest; no leader has

[52] Dahl, *Who Governs?*, p. 133.
[53] Kaplan, *Urban Renewal Politics*, pp. 70-75.

successfully challenged their detachment. The difficulties of the urban renewal program have confirmed their justification for "not touching it" instead of suggesting the need for increased private interest as well as improved public leadership.

The absence of business support has contributed to Toledo's unimpressive showing in urban renewal. The director of urban development in Pittsburgh has cited the money, time, talent, and interest which business and industry have given to the city's renewal program. No such contribution has taken place in Toledo. A *Blade* editorial commented:

> Here in Toledo urban renewal is plodding along. One reason is that the program simply has not had the active participation and vigorous leadership of the uppermost echelons of our industrial and business community. It has had their vocal support, to be sure; but when it came down to the nuts and bolts of putting a program in shape, of encouraging the city to bring in an experienced professional director, of moving toward substantial investments of private funds in redevelopment projects, of contributing materially in other ways, Toledo's over-all effort suffers immeasurably in comparison to that of Pittsburgh.[54]

To labor

Organized labor's interest in urban renewal has been equally dispirited. In New Haven redevelopment attracted what one labor leader described as universal support from union members and officials.[55] In Toledo labor leaders express differing degrees of dissatisfaction. An official in the Teamsters described Toledo's renewal program:

> It's a business-oriented operation, with little attention to the human aspects. The objective is to clear the property and then turn it over to the real estate speculators. Labor isn't consulted much. They haven't really tried to bring organized labor into the program.

A leader in the Electrical Workers asked: "What urban renewal program? Our system of city government isn't organized for getting things like that done." In the opinion of a UAW official: "John Potter has tried to make urban renewal move and to bring labor in, but he's been sabotaged by Thurmond Hawkins [the urban renewal director]." Officials in the Building Trades Council have found dramatic benefits from redevelopment slow in coming.

Leaders in the various unions are mildly interested in urban renewal and mildly concerned about its slow progress. But few of them think that urban renewal warrants significant attention and support from organized labor.

To Negroes

Because of the slow pace and limited scope of the program in Toledo, it has not displaced significant numbers of Negro residents, as it has in some

[54] *The Blade*, October 20, 1964, p. 16.
[55] Dahl, *Who Governs?*, p. 136.

cities. Thus, urban renewal has not been of particular concern to Negro leaders and organizations. Most prominent Negro leaders in civil rights organizations, religious associations, social agencies, and public positions regard the urban renewal program with satisfaction or indifference: They either praise the program in general terms or confess that they have not followed it closely. Few are interested in the impact of urban renewal on local civil rights problems. Several of the younger leaders, however, are critical and concerned:

> The urban renewal program here is not completely satisfactory from the Negro's standpoint or from anyone else's. Mr. Hawkins does not recognize the Negro as a person. He has not recognized Negro leadership. Even in urban conservation programs in largely Negro areas, there is no consultation. Relocation has not dispersed people enough. Deterioration is increasing rapidly. Housing is a major problem and urban renewal has done nothing to alleviate it. In general, the whole urban renewal program is moving too slowly.

To voters

The voters have had few occasions to record their judgment of urban renewal. Until 1965 Toledo voters did not have the opportunity to express a verdict on a variety of programs through mayoralty elections. But they have defeated councilmen unpleasantly identified with urban renewal. From the response of a wide variety of community organizations, including labor unions, Negro organizations, the Chamber of Commerce, fraternal associations, and nationality clubs, there is reason to believe that popular demand for urban renewal is relatively small. In 1962 only 47.5 per cent of those voting, instead of the required 55 per cent, approved a payroll income tax increase to finance the local cost of slum clearance and urban renewal.

Summary

In Toledo the various mayors and renewal administrators have not had the political strength and skill to attract the support of the organized interests and the electorate. Between the passage of the 1949 Housing Act and 1965, city council has selected six mayors, of whom only two served consecutive terms. Toledo mayors have been ephemeral and powerless in comparison with the executives of cities whose renewal programs have been successful: Mayor Lee of New Haven (1953–); Mayor Daley of Chicago (1956–); Mayor Carlin of Newark (1953–1962); and Mayor Tucker of St. Louis (1953–1965).

The mayors of New Haven, Chicago, and St. Louis succeeded in integrating fragmented decision-making processes in urban renewal and in other fields because they started with considerably more authority than their counterparts in Toledo. They were elective executives and possessed formal powers lacking in Toledo. Chicago has been described as a city with "extreme decentralization of authority";[56] yet the mayor of Chicago, in contrast to the

[56] Banfield and Wilson, *City Politics*, p. 104.

mayor of Toledo, has several essential formal powers, including a veto, which can be overriden only by a two-thirds vote of the aldermen, and an item veto over appropriation acts.[57] In transforming the political system of New Haven from a pattern of "rival sovereignties" to an "executive-centered coalition," Mayor Lee also was aided by formal powers—as well as by his political skill, which Dahl so admires. Dahl mentions "the patronage and wide assortment of other favors and punishments available to the chief executive of the city" and "the resources at the Mayor's disposal [which] are much too great for any dissident faction in his party to overcome."[58] Such could never be said of the mayor of Toledo.

Furthermore, the mayors of Chicago and New Haven could rely on strong party organizations in creating an informal centralization of power. The atrophied party system of Toledo did not provide this alternative. Nor could the mayor of Toledo draw on an active good government alliance, as Mayor Tucker did for many years. Business and labor organizations, active participants in some cities, have provided an uncertain source of community support in Toledo.

On the administrative side, Toledo's urban renewal program has suffered from incompetence and instability. Between the passage of the 1949 Housing Act and 1965, Toledo had five city managers and five urban renewal directors. The managers, lacking decisive directives from the mayor and council, have been unwilling or unable to provide effective supervision of urban renewal. City council and the city manager have deferred to each other for both policy and administrative decisions, with unsatisfactory results. Urban renewal directors, like city managers, have been selected for their political rather than their professional qualifications. In the mid-1960s, a former Republican councilman as manager and a Republican ward chairman and ex-real estate man as urban renewal director reveal the discrepancy between reform ideals and actual practice. These officials have displayed neither the competence nor the "furious drive and energy" of, for example, New Haven administrators.

By his own account, Thurmond Hawkins, the Toledo renewal director, "started from scratch on urban renewal in 1962."[59] Because of the inexperience of its director and staff, the urban renewal agency relied heavily on a New Jersey consulting firm, Candeub and Fleissig, in the preparation of renewal plans and applications. Candeub and Fleissig, hired for their professional skills, submitted report after report to the Urban Renewal Administration only to have them returned for revision.[60]

Toledo's political system is poorly suited to the demands of the urban renewal program, as the 15-year history of the Chase Park project suggests. Reform institutions, which were intended to assure an effective municipal

[57]Meyerson and Banfield, *Politics, Planning, and the Public Interest*, p. 66.

[58]Dahl, *Who Governs?*, p. 111.

[59]Hawkins resigned in May 1966, to become urban renewal director in Rochester, Minnesota. He was replaced by Walter Edelson, a young city planner.

[60]*The Blade*, May 24, 1964, Section C, p. 1.

response to city problems, have yielded the opposite in urban renewal.[61] The council-manager form of government, with its division of authority between a city council of equals and an administrator, has produced a governmental system which is political, without having a focus of power. Contrary to reform expectations, the absence of a preeminent political leader has not facilitated the appointment of a professional administrator; nor has it assured the autonomy and authority of the city manager. Municipal reformers attempted to remove politics from city government and destroyed political leadership instead. The result was most unfortunate for urban renewal.

[61] None of the council-manager cities over 250,000 in population is among the top ten urban renewal cities. The council-manager cities in this population category include four cities of over 500,000: Dallas, Cincinnati, San Antonio, and San Diego. Cities in the 250,000 to 500,000 category include Kansas City, Phoenix, Oakland, Fort Worth, Long Beach, Oklahoma City, Rochester, Norfolk, Miami, Dayton, Wichita, and Toledo. Of the council-manager cities, Norfolk has the most impressive record in urban renewal (see Table 1).

Issue Conflict, Factionalism, and Consensus in Suburban City Councils

Bryan T. Downes

This selection serves to introduce some critical aspects of the decision-making process at the local level. In this article, I examine one specific hypothesis drawn from James S. Coleman's earlier discussion of community conflict. The data are drawn from interviews with local mayors and city councilmen and from the systematic observation of city council meetings in a group of thirty-seven suburban municipalities in the St. Louis Metropolitan Area. These are small communities which have been undergoing quite varied rates of population growth since 1950.

In this research, we were concerned with whether rapid increases in population in a community give rise to exclusive values, divergent interests, and strains which may be reflected in higher levels of issue conflict, factionalism, and hence less consensus in suburban city councils. Most researchers assume population changes do result in increased community conflict. Our task has been to examine whether such conflict "spills over" into the city council.

Although the data lent some tentative support to this hypothesis, I found it necessary to qualify its original form in several important respects. For example, it was apparent that the relationship between population changes and council issue conflict and consensus is a great deal more complicated and certainly less linear than many social scientists have implied in their writings. The real world is never quite as simple as some social scientists would have us believe. Although the types of issues giving rise to suburban council conflict were similar to those found by other researchers, the overall level of issue conflict was generally higher in councils in these suburbs, particularly in very high and medium growth-rate communities. The extent to which issue disagreements carried over in the form of overt council conflict, and the extent to which such conflict was based on enduring council factions, also was at some variance with our initial expectation. Overt council conflict and factionalism were largely restricted to councils with exceptionally high growth rates (over 500 percent from 1950 to 1960).

What is the impact of council conflict and factionalism on the ability of local legislative bodies to process demands made upon them for policy change? Although I did not investigate this question directly, it appears that most suburban councils develop various means for handling conflict arising among council members over issues before them. Most suburban councils strive to reach a consensus before voting on most issues. It is unclear whether intense conflict actually impedes decision-making, but it definitely slows down the legislative process considerably.

Attention is also drawn to the importance of nondecision-making *in communities with low levels of issue conflict. This refers to the process whereby some individuals and groups are able to limit decision-making to relatively noncontroversial matters. In low-conflict suburbs, it appears that decision-making is confined to relatively "safe" issues. This may simply be the result of a great deal of agreement among the participants or it may be that certain groups in these communities are being excluded from the decision process. In effect, the system may be closed to certain individuals and groups. Furthermore, because controversial issues were being kept out of the decisional arena in low-conflict suburbs, city councils were simply not discussing or attempting to act upon many important community problems.*

Introduction

City councils, like most small decision making groups, face a number of basic problems which they must solve or at least cope with if they are to

"Issue Conflict, Factionalism, and Consensus in Suburban City Councils" is expanded by the author from an article which first appeared in *Urban Affairs Quarterly*, vol. 4, no. 4 (June 1969), by arrangement with the Publisher, Sage Publications, Inc. This article is drawn from several chapters of a doctoral dissertation prepared for the Department of Political Science, Washington University (St. Louis), submitted in August, 1966. The author gratefully acknowledges the financial support of the National Science Foundation through Grant No. GS-803 for improving doctoral dissertation research in the Social Sciences. I am also indebted for support to the Political Science Department of Michigan State University.

accomplish their tasks. One particularly critical problem has to do with the manner in which such groups resolve conflict arising between councilmen over issues before the council and promote some degree of consensus among councilmen as they go about making policy decisions.[1]

Relatively little is known about (1) the extent and nature of issue conflict and consensus in suburban city councils, (2) the factors giving rise to conflict and consensus in such political groups, or (3) how conflict provoking issues are handled by city councils. However, social scientists who have recently begun to systematically examine the decision process at different system levels have drawn attention to a number of possible factors which may influence the extent of conflict and consensus in legislative bodies and consequently the behavior of individual legislators. For example, a great deal of research has focused on how factors beyond the institutional boundaries of the legislature, such as external relationships with electoral constituents, parties, interest groups, executive agencies, and those socioeconomic and predispositional attributes that legislators import from the "outside" may influence legislative processes and decisions.[2] On the other hand, social scientists have also emphasized the importance of factors internal to the decision making body, such as group structure, norms of the decision making group, authority relations, influence patterns, and the nature of the issue involved.[3]

Most research at the local level has focused upon how one or more of the above mentioned variables influence the legislative process in city councils.[4] For example, J. Leiper Freeman in his study of voting alignments in one city of nearly 50,000 persons, found that on decisions involving the public works budget the behavior of "Bay City's" councilmen appeared to be influenced by the nature of the issue involved, the internal structure of the council, council norms, and external relationships which councilmen had with constituents, their party, interest groups, the press, and the executive.[5]

[1] On the problem of integration in small political groups see: Richard F. Fenno, "The House Appropriations Committee as a Political System," *The American Political Science Review*, vol. 56, no. 2 (June, 1962), pp. 310-324; and Charles O. Jones, "The Role of the Congressional Subcommittee," *Midwest Journal of Political Science*, vol. 6, no. 4 (November, 1962), pp. 327-344.

[2] For a discussion of these factors see: Heinz Eulau and Katherine Hinckley, "Legislative Institutions and Processes," in James A. Robinson (ed.), *Political Science Annual, An International Review, Volume I—1966* (Indianapolis: Bobbs-Merrill, 1966), pp. 85-93, 114-150.

[3] For a discussion of an "inside model" as opposed to an "outside model" see: *Ibid.*, pp. 93-114. See also the discussion in: James D. Barber, *Power in Committees: An Experiment in the Governmental Process* (Chicago: Rand McNally, 1966).

[4] For example see: J. Leiper Freeman, "A Case Study of the Legislative Process in Municipal Government," in John C. Wahlke and Heinz Eulau (eds.), *Legislative Behavior, A Reader in Theory and Research* (New York: Free Press, 1959), pp. 228-237; and Peter A. Lupsha, "Leadership, Expertise, and Decision-Making in Small Legislative Bodies." Paper prepared for delivery at the 1967 Annual Meeting of the American Political Science Association, Chicago, September, 1967. See also: Robert L. Crain, Elihu Katz, and Donald B. Rosenthal, *The Politics of Community Conflict: The Fluoridation Decision* (Indianapolis: Bobbs-Merrill, 1969); Robert L. Crain, *The Politics of School Desegregation* (Chicago: Aldine, 1968); and James Q. Wilson (ed.), *City Politics and Public Policy* (New York: John Wiley, 1968).

[5] Freeman, *op. cit.*, pp. 235-236.

In another study, which was more specifically concerned with the factors influencing controversy and voting splits on city councils in Los Angeles County, Huckshorn and Young found that age, length of service on the council, occupation, and party affiliation of councilmen were all relevant determinants of council splits.[6] They reported older councilmen were more likely to belong to minority factions, women were more apt to appear on split councils than on unanimous ones, "senior" councilmen tended to be overwhelmed by their "junior" colleagues, there was an almost complete absence of professionals on split councils, and councils dominated by Republicans were least likely to be split.

Although these studies are suggestive, the research reported in this article does not draw very heavily upon either of these two studies. Instead, we turned to the research and writing of James S. Coleman and William Gamson.[7] In separate studies, each of these social scientists draws attention to a variable outside the institutional boundaries of a city's council which appears to be an extremely important condition underlying controversy in certain types of local communities. In *Community Conflict*, Coleman argues that, "whenever a difference in values and interests is created by the influx of new residents, it becomes a potential basis for conflicting response and sets the stage for precipitating incidents."[8] As an example, he cites the case of suburban municipalities lying outside large central cities which in the last ten years have suddenly "mushroomed" with migrants from the city and elsewhere. In such communities, according to Coleman's theory, the stage is set for conflict. Gamson also argues that heavy in-migration may generate "strain" in a community, that is, discontent or dissatisfaction among community inhabitants which may result in rancorous conflict.[9]

In this article, we intend to test a single hypothesis derived from the Coleman-Gamson theory of community conflict in a group of thirty-seven suburban municipalities located in St. Louis County. This is one of the five counties which along with the City of St. Louis make up the St. Louis Metropolitan Statistical Area. These communities ranged in size from a low of 3,089 to a high of 51,249 persons in 1960.[10] We hypothesize that rapid increases in population may give rise to exclusive values, divergent interests, and strains in a community which may be reflected in higher levels of issue

[6]R. J. Huckshorn and C. E. Young, "The Study of Voting Splits on City Councils in Los Angeles County," *The Western Political Quarterly*, vol. 13, no. 2 (June, 1960), pp. 479-497.

[7]James S. Coleman, *Community Conflict* (New York: Free Press, 1957); and William A. Gamson, "Rancorous Conflict in Community Politics," *American Sociological Review*, vol. 31, no. 1 (February, 1966), pp. 71-80.

[8]Coleman, *op. cit.*, p. 7.

[9]Gamson, *op. cit.*, p. 73.

[10]We do not consider this to be a representative sample of suburban communities but rather a universe of municipalities of a certain size in a specific geographic area. For a summary discussion of some of the major characteristics of these communities see: Bryan T. Downes, "Suburban Differentiation and Municipal Policy Choices: A Comparative Analysis of Suburban Political Systems," in Terry N. Clark (ed.), *Community Structure and Decision-Making: Comparative Analyses* (San Francisco: Chandler Press, 1968), pp. 243-267.

conflict and factionalism and hence less consensus in city councils in such municipalities. We are concerned, therefore, with how changes in one aspect of a municipality's context, a factor beyond the institutional boundaries of the city council, affect issue conflict and consensus in small decision making groups.

The municipal context

Our indicator of change in the municipal context is the population growth rate from 1950 to 1960. In measuring our independent variable, we relied upon information gathered by the Bureau of the Census for 1960.[11] The communities studied exhibited a great deal of variation in their rates of population growth. These changes ranged from losses of 15 percent in population to increases of over 3,000 percent during the ten year period. Of the thirty-seven municipalities, six were classified as having *low growth rates*, exhibiting losses in population to increases of 15 percent. In addition, fourteen were classified as having *medium growth rates*, increasing from 16 to 100 percent; eight as having *high growth rates*, increasing from 101 to 500 percent; and five as having *very high rates*, increasing by more than 500 percent. Four of the municipalities were incorporated after 1950, and no figures were available on changes in their populations. Consequently they have been dropped from the analysis which follows.

Originally we also developed a community heterogeneity index, which was a measure of the proportion of foreign born and non-whites in the total population of a municipality.[12] We felt that this index might measure the extent of cleavage or lack of consensus in a municipality based on its ethnic and racial diversity. However, we found very little difference between very high and very low communities when they were ranked on this index. This was primarily due to very low percentages of both foreign born and non-white persons in the total populations of the municipalities studied. For example, the average non-white population in these communities was approximately 1.5 percent. Although there was a somewhat higher percentage of foreign born persons in some of the communities studied, the overall average for all municipalities was quite low, approximately 2.4 percent. Thus the task before us becomes one of explaining differences in issue conflict, factionalism, and consensus in communities which are generally homogeneous with respect to racial and foreign born characteristics but which vary considerably in rate of population increase from 1950 to 1960.

In addition, these communities vary widely in size, density, assessed valuation, social rank, percent young adults, form of government, and percent land which is vacant. However, higher growth rate communities do tend to be

[11] United States Department of Commerce, Bureau of the Census, *County and City Data Book* (Washington, D.C.: U.S. Government Printing Office, 1962).

[12] For a discussion of this index see: Christen T. Jonassen and Sherwood H. Peres, *Interrelationships of Dimensions of Community Systems* (Columbus: Ohio State University Press, 1960), p. 31.

somewhat smaller, less densely populated municipalities with higher percentages of young adults. On the other hand, lower growth rate suburbs tend to be larger, more densely populated communities with fewer young adults. We found little relationship between a municipality's rate of population increase and its social rank or per capita assessed valuation.

Issue conflict, factionalism, and consensus

Issue conflict can be conceptualized in a number of different ways.[13] In a general sense it involves a struggle over values and claims to scarce resources in which the aim of the antagonists is to neutralize or in some cases eliminate their rivals.[14] Such conflict is most generally manifest in local communities when demands are made upon elected political leaders for substantial expansion or contraction in the net scope or way of functioning of local government.[15] For example, demands for the adoption of fluoridation, zoning changes, capital improvements, expansion of park and recreational facilities, and increases in salaries of city personnel may all generate a great deal of conflict not only among community residents but also among city councilmen.

However, not all communities are beset by conflict of this sort. Huckshorn and Young found that real splits on controversial issues appeared in only twenty of the fifty-one cities they studied.[16] In these twenty cities, eight split on some aspect of zoning, with the most typical situation being a disagreement among councilmen over the rezoning, for industrial purposes, of a residential area or an underdeveloped area adjacent to a residential tract. Councils in an additional six cities were split over personnel and administrative questions. In most instances these disagreements were the result of opposition to the city manager form of government, opposition to the establishment of a chief administrator's office, lack of confidence in a particular member of the city's administration by one or more members of the council, or disagreement over the adoption of new personnel or administrative techniques. The remaining six councils were split over such issues as capital improvements, annexation, intergovernmental problems, and recreational facilities.

In the research reported in this article, we are primarily concerned with examining issue conflict as it occurs among city councilmen, that is, disagreements among councilmen which arise over issues before the council.

[13] Definitions of concepts such as "conflict", including the one which we adopted, should be thought of as being neither true nor false; but rather as apt or inept, clear or vague, fruitful or useless.

[14] This is very similar to the definition set forth in: Lewis Coser, *The Functions of Social Conflict* (New York: Free Press, 1956), p. 8.

[15] See the discussion of this notion in: Robert E. Agger, Daniel Goldrich, and Bert E. Swanson, *The Rulers and the Ruled: Political Power and Impotence in American Communities* (New York: John Wiley, 1964), pp. 6-10.

[16] Huckshorn and Young, *op. cit.*, pp. 484-486.

Such disagreements grow out of controversy over decisions which a council is called upon to make and are usually settled by the vote of a majority defeating a minority of councilmen. However, we are also concerned with the extent to which such issue disagreements are based on the existence of enduring council splits or factions. Decisions over such issues are also controversial but differ from the aforementioned type of disagreements in that conflict and ultimately voting patterns are the result of enduring factional splits on the council.[17]

In addition, William Gamson has argued that, "the same issue—for example, fluoridation—may run its course in undramatic fashion in one town, but prove to be a trigger for an explosive confrontation in another town with seemingly similar characteristics."[18] One of the factors which may be quite important in either circumventing or controlling such explosive confrontations between councilmen, has to do with the way in which issue conflict is handled by the council. We assume that if a council is able to cope with issue disagreements among its members and promote some degree of consensus, then it will probably have a greater capacity to process demands made upon it. This assumption is based on an extensive examination of the findings of small group research.[19]

However, far from being only a negative factor which impedes a council's task effectiveness or leads to breakdowns in a group's functioning, issue conflict may fulfill a number of more positive functions.[20] For example, in some councils a great deal of issue conflict may be quite functional for the group in that it contributes to the maintenance of the council and prevents withdrawal of councilmen from the group. A full airing of the issues may simply be an integral part of the decision making process in some communities. In this study, then, we will be concerned with both the functions and dysfunctions of issue conflict, that is, those consequences of issue disagreements which affect the task performance of city councils.[21]

In approaching the study of issue conflict, factionalism, and consensus in suburban city councils, several different types of data were collected.[22] First, information was gathered through lengthy personal interviews with some 210

[17]For a discussion of this distinction between (1) non-controversial, unanimous decisions; (2) controversial, organized majority decisions; and (3) controversial, factional alliance decisions see: Freeman, *op. cit.*, pp. 230-232.

[18]Gamson, *op. cit.*, p. 71.

[19]For example see: W.J.H. Sprott, *Human Groups* (Baltimore: Penguin Books, 1958); Michael S. Olmstead, *The Small Group* (New York: Random House, 1959); Sidney Verba, *Small Groups and Political Behavior* (Princeton: Princeton University Press, 1961); Barry E. Collins and Harold Guetzkow, *A Social Psychology of Group Processes for Decision-Making* (New York: John Wiley, 1964); John W. Thibaut and Harold H. Kelley, *The Social Psychology of Groups* (New York: John Wiley, 1961); and Bernard Berelson and Gary A. Steiner, *Human Behavior: An Inventory of Scientific Findings* (New York: Harcourt, Brace, and World, 1964), pp. 325-361.

[20]See the entire discussion in: Coser, *op. cit.*

[21]*Ibid.*, p. 8.

[22]The data reported in this article represent only a small proportion of the total information collected during the fall and winter of 1965-66 from census materials, questionnaries, interviews with city councilmen and mayors, and the systematic observation of city councils in the thirty-seven suburban communities.

councilmen and mayors.[23] In attempting to learn about the extent of issue conflict and factionalism, councilmen were asked about (1) the types of issues giving rise to disagreements, (2) the existence of council factions, (3) reasons for factional cohesion, and (4) reasons why there was a lack of enduring factional divisions in their councils. Indicators of consensus in city councils included councilmen's perceptions of the way in which the council handles issues before it, unanimity of group decision making, and how the council works out disagreements which arise over various issues. In examining this data city councilmen are the basic empirical unit of analysis. However, because we are primarily interested in characterizing the extent of issue conflict and consensus in suburban city councils, councils become the theoretical unit of analysis.[24]

Second, data has also been gathered through the systematic observation of council meetings. This information will be used as a supplement to the interview data.[25] During a five month period from October 1965 to March 1, 1966, at least two meetings of each of the thirty-seven councils were systematically observed by the principal investigator or one of two individuals employed and trained to assist in this phase of the project.[26] We used an observation protocol originally developed by Professor Harold Guetzkow and his associates for their 1950 study of small face-to-face decision making groups in government and industry.[27] This protocol was subsequently revised for purposes of this analysis.[28]

The observer kept a running account of the substantive content of the meeting, the time spent on all agenda items, and the manner in which the council handled and disposed of the various issues before it.[29] At the

[23] In the thirty-seven municipalities finally included in the study there were 279 possible respondents—mayors, city councilmen, aldermen, and trustees. Of these 279 individuals, seventy-six percent (210) agreed to be interviewed. The interviews with these individuals lasted approximately one and one-half hours.

[24] This distinction is briefly discussed in: Heinz Eulau, *The Behavioral Persuasion in Politics* (New York: Random House, 1963), pp. 13-19.

[25] For a discussion of the utility in using multiple data collection techniques to gather data on and measure similar phenomena see: Eugene J. Webb, Donald T. Campbell, Richard D. Schwartz, and Lee Sechrest, *Unobtrusive Measures: Non-reactive Research in the Social Sciences* (Chicago: Rand McNally, 1966).

[26] I am aware that the observer is required to undertake a degree of inferential interpretation which may seriously jeopardize the reliability of these ratings. However, an attempt was made to thoroughly familiarize the observers with the protocol and the definitions of the various dimensions which they were called upon to use. In addition, extensive pretesting and discussion of the protocol enabled each observer to develop an appropriate frame of reference and an awareness of the relevant behavioral cues for each rating.

[27] *Instruments and Manuals, Field Observation of Business and Government Conferences, 1949* (Ann Arbor: University Microfilms Publication No. 1904, 1949).

[28] For a more detailed discussion of this and other instruments used in this study (and their reproduction) see: Bryan T. Downes, "Suburban Differentiation and Municipal Policy Choices: A Comparative Analysis of Suburban Political Systems" (Unpublished doctoral dissertation, Washington University, 1966), pp. 348-388.

[29] Discussion at council meetings is usually guided by a formal agenda which is made up prior to the meeting by the city clerk, mayor, or city manager. The subject matter headings on the average city council agenda include: reading of the minutes and opening remarks; comments and petitions from citizens; reports of officers, standing and special

conclusion of the meeting the observer rated the council on over fifty variables. These variables were incorporated into a series of ten point scales on such aspects of the group's process as conflict and consensus, group structure and problem solving process, and member satisfactions with various aspects of the council meeting.[30] Of particular interest to this analysis are the observer's perception and interpretation of (1) the extent of overt council conflict, (2) council cohesion, and (3) the thoroughness and efficiency of the council problem solving process.[31]

Council issue conflict and factionalism

On the basis of their study of four Michigan middle-sized cities, Oliver P. Williams and Charles Adrian concluded that local city councils, with perhaps the exception of legislative bodies in large cities, are faint modified copies of those at the state and national levels.[32] By the single fact that they are manned by amateurs, conducting city business in their spare time, it is difficult for councilmen to supply active leadership. Instead of providing leadership for proposals, councilmen more often simply oppose proposals put forward by the mayor, city manager, or other councilmen. Therefore, the council's authority rested in its perogative of saying "no" when its concurrence was indispensible.[33]

In addition, in the four city manager cities Williams and Adrian studied, there were few issues coming before the councils which were regarded by councilmen as involving nonroutine or controversial decisions.[34] The data in Table 1 cause us to tentatively question the generalizability of this finding. For instance, fifty-nine percent of the councilmen in the thirty-three cities we studied reported there had been recent issues before their councils which had given rise to disagreements.[35]

---

committees; unfinished business; new business; reading of correspondence and announcements; and adjournment.

[30] For purposes of analysis the rating scales were later collapsed into five point scales.

[31] We have discussed only a small proportion of the total observation data which were collected. In addition, I have only used information from the first observations which were done by the principal investigator.

[32] Oliver P. Williams and Charles Adrian, *Four Cities: A Study in Comparative Policy Making* (Philadelphia: University of Pennsylvania Press, 1963), pp. 291-295.

[33] Duane Lockard, *The Politics of State and Local Government* (New York: Macmillan, 1963), p. 324.

[34] Williams and Adrian, *op. cit.,* p. 293.

[35] In presenting the data in this article, I have chosen to rely on a discussion of the data as it is arrayed in contingency tables, that is, to stay very "close" to the data. Although both contingency and gamma coefficients were computed in an attempt to measure the degree of association between rate of population increase and the various dependent variables, neither of these measures proved very satisfactory. Both measures were affected, although somewhat differently, by the arrangement of the data. The contingency coefficient tended to consistently *overstate* and the gamma coefficient *understate* the degree of association between two variables. For the methodological purists in our midst the contingency coefficients for each of the tables are as follows: Table 1 (C = .48), Table 2 (C = .66), Table 3 (C = .57), Table 4 (C = .59), Table 5

It is apparent, however, that the hypothesis derived from the Coleman-Gamson theory about the conditions underlying community controversy is tentatively supported by the data in Table 1, although with several interesting qualifications. Municipalities undergoing rapid population expansion do have city councils characterized by more issue conflict than councils in more stable communities. This is particularly true of councils in very high (more than 500 percent) and medium (16-100 percent) growth rate communities. In the former, over ninety percent of the councilmen indicated there had been recent issues before the council which had given rise to disagreements between councilmen, and in the latter, sixty-five percent indicated there had been such disagreements. Contrary to our initial expectation, in municipalities with high growth rates (101-500 percent) only thirty-five percent of the councilmen reported recent issue disagreements.

Table 1.   *Population increase, 1950-60, and councilman's perception of issue disagreements*

Have there been any issues recently giving rise to disagreements?	Low		Medium		High		Very high		Total	
	N (6)*	%	N (14)*	%	N (8)*	%	N (5)*	%	N (33)*	%
No	16	55	28	35	29	63	4	10	77	40
Yes	13	45	52	65	16	35	34	90	115	59
Don't know	0	0	0	0	1	2	0	0	1	1
Total	29	100	80	100	46	100	38	100	193	100

These figures represent the number of municipalities falling into each category. They are set forth in most tables in this article.

The observation data on the extent of overt conflict at public council meetings, allow us to further qualify the Coleman-Gamson derived hypothesis. Overt conflict refers to the extent to which a council's interaction is characterized by important differences of opinion—issue disagreements—among council members, substantive or personal in origin.[36] For example, although in medium growth rate communities councilmen reported higher levels of disagreement over recent issues which they had considered, such disagreements definitely do not appear to carry over to council meetings. On the other hand, in very high growth rate suburbs issue disagreements do carry over and become an integral part of the council proceedings. In these communities four of the five councils were rated as having much overt conflict among council members during their meetings. Overall, sixty-seven percent of the councils were rated as having little or no overt conflict during meetings.

(C = .58), Table 6 (C = .53), Table 7 (C = .60). All statistics were computed before tables were collapsed. For a discussion of the problems involved in using the contingency coefficient see: Sidney Siegal, *Nonparametric Statistics for the Behavioral Sciences* (New York: McGraw-Hill, 1965), pp. 196-202.

[36] Leonard Berkowitz and Harold Guetzkow, "Manual for Overall Observers," in *Instruments and Manuals, op. cit.,* p. 27. This definition is very similar to the one developed for issue conflict.

What types of issues give rise to disagreements among councilmen? The two most conflict provoking issues in the suburbs studied revolve around questions of zoning and planning or city personnel and salaries, with the former being twice as likely to provoke disagreements as the latter (Table 2). This generally corresponds to the findings reported by Huckshorn and Young cited earlier in the article.[37] In very high and medium growth rate communities zoning and planning questions were most likely to give rise to issue conflict. Forty-seven percent of the councilmen in the former and thirty-four percent in the latter indicated these issues gave rise to conflict in their councils. In high growth rate communities zoning and planning questions were conflict provoking but less so than in either very high or medium growth rate communities. On the other hand, when disagreements did occur in low growth rate communities, either fiscal or personnel issues were most likely to give rise to such disagreements among council members.[38]

In order to ascertain whether issue disagreements were the result of enduring splits or factions on the council, we asked councilmen whether there was more or less the same line-up when disagreements occurred in their councils. A faction, in this case, is simply a subgroup of councilmen who have common interests, usually in opposition to the principles or aims of other councilmen and/or the council's leadership.

Table 2. *Population increase, 1950–60, and councilman's perception of types of issues giving rise to issue disagreements*

Types of issues giving rise to disagreements	Low		Medium		High		Very high		Total	
	N (6)	%	N (14)	%	N (8)	%	N (5)	%	N (33)	%
Miscellaneous: sidewalks and streets; increasing services; storm sewers; and stop signs	0	0	9	11	3	7	4	10	16	8
Budget, tax rate	5	18	4	5	1	2	3	8	13	7
Personnel, salaries	5	18	9	11	2	4	9	24	25	13
Zoning, planning	0	0	27	34	8	17	18	47	53	27
Not relevant	18	64	30	38	32	70	4	10	86	44
Total	28	100	80	99*	46	100	38	99*	193	99*

*Rounding error.

[37]Huckshorn and Young, *op. cit.*, pp. 484-486.

[38]The issue of city personnel refers primarily to problems such as raising the salaries of existing city employees or the hiring of additional personnel by the municipality.

Table 3.   Population increase, 1950—60, and councilman's
perception of factional splits

If so, what is the line-up?	Low		Medium		High		Very high		Total	
	N (6)	%	N (14)	%	N (8)	%	N (5)	%	N (33)	%
Names one, two, or three factions	11	38	27	34	9	20	31	82	77	40
No factions	17	58	52	65	36	78	7	18	113	58
Don't know	1	4	1	1	1	2	0	0	3	2
Total	29	100	80	100	46	100	38	100	193	100

As Table 3 indicates most councilmen, a majority of fifty-eight percent, reported that no factions or splits existed in their councils. However, in very high growth rate suburbs eighty-two percent of the councilmen reported factions existed and that their councils tended to split in a particular manner on most all issues. Thus in very high growth rate communities issue disagreements appear to be largely a function of enduring factions and these cleavages affect the extent of conflict on most issues. On the other hand, in medium growth rate communities issue disagreements did not appear to be the result of enduring council splits.

In most councils which were split, councilmen reported the existence of two recurring factions. Very few councils were split by only a single faction or by more than two factions. When these same councilmen were asked about why factions were cohesive, fifty percent indicated that faction members tended to think along the same lines—there was ideological congruence among them—and twenty-two percent that faction members were friends. In those legislative bodies which were not divided by factions, councilmen indicated that either disagreements existed but they varied from issue to issue or that there was generally more cooperation than controversy among councilmen. Generally, in low and high growth rate communities councilmen indicated the latter reason for lack of council divisions, while in medium growth rate communities councilmen reported that although disagreements existed they varied from issue to issue and were not based on factional alliances.

When councils were rated on the extent to which the group members appeared bound together because of feelings of we-ness or belonging to the group—their cohesiveness—we found that in high and low growth rate communities councils were consistently more cohesive (Table 4).[39] On the other hand, in very high and medium growth rate municipalities, legislative bodies were rated as less cohesive. This was particularly true of councils in very high growth rate communities.

In summary, it was our initial intent to test a single hypothesis derived from the Coleman-Gamson theory about the relationship between population

[39] Berkowitz and Guetzkow, op. cit., p. 28.

Table 4. *Population increase, 1950–60, and observation of council cohesion*

Council cohesion	Low		Medium		High		Very high		Total	
	N	%	N	%	N	%	N	%	N	%
Very cohesive	4	66	7	50	5	62	2	40	18	54
Somewhat cohesive	1	17	6	43	3	38	2	40	12	36
Not very cohesive	1	17	1	7	0	0	1	20	3	10
Total	6	100	14	100	8	100	5	100	33	100

increases and council conflict. In examining how variation in population growth was related to councilmen perceptions of issue conflict and council factions we found the following relationships to exist.[40] First, we did find a very strong positive relationship between rate of population increase and issue conflict and enduring council factions, but with several important qualifications. Generally, very high and medium growth rate suburbs, particularly the former, had more issues coming before their councils which gave rise to disagreements. However, it was only in very high growth rate communities that such issue conflict was likely to be a function of the existence of enduring council factions. Thus it would appear that only in the most rapidly growing communities, those whose populations increased by more than 500 percent from 1950 to 1960, are exclusive values, divergent interests, and strains that result from such an influx of new residents reflected in the council decision process in not only exceptionally high levels of disagreement over issues but also controversy based on enduring factional alliances. Although medium growth rate communities also had a great deal of issue conflict among city councilmen, such disagreements were seldom based on enduring splits among council members. In these municipalities conflict did not appear to be dysfunctional, that is, overt conflict did not carry over to council meetings nor was issue conflict based on factional alliances. In these councils issue disagreements did occur and appeared to be a necessary part of the decision making process. Perhaps if councilmen were not allowed to express dissent, they might feel compelled to withdraw from the group. Issue conflict in these councils may have served a group maintaining function.

Finally, we found that zoning and planning as well as city personnel and salaries were the issues most likely to give rise to council disagreements in these communities. In very high growth rate suburbs councilmen are continually called upon to make decisions on how vacant land will be used, that is, on zoning and planning matters. This is primarily due to the existence of open spaces and lower population densities. Medium growth rate

[40]In interpreting these relationships we have drawn upon further analysis of the data which the principal investigator and/or his students have undertaken.

communities, despite their higher densities and lack of vacant land were also more likely than either high or low growth rate suburbs to have disagreements over zoning and planning questions. In the case of these municipalities, such disputes most often took the form of requests to rezone residential property for industrial or commercial purposes or to allow the construction of multiple dwellings. One of these communities was also extensively involved in urban renewal. In low growth rate communities, on the other hand, zoning and planning questions were not important conflict provoking issues primarily because few of these communities had any land to develop, nor were they committed to redevelopment through rezoning and/or renewal of land. However, resources are scarce in these communities; therefore, budget and tax issues or the addition of city personnel and salaries of city officials were important issues which when they were raised could provoke council disagreements.

The handling of issues and council unanimity

How do councils handle issues before them? Does the process of handling issues vary according to the type of issue being discussed? How do councils go about working out issue disagreements? How often does unanimity occur in city councils and on what kinds of issues do councilmen vote unanimously? These are the questions we will examine in this section. They are also questions about which political scientists know very little.

Do communities undergoing rapid increases in population handle issues differently than more stable communities in which political patterns may be less amorphous? As Table 5 indicates, in communities undergoing more rapid population increases, councils tend to handle issues primarily by discussing them before the public (at their meetings), or more openly than councils in lower growth rate suburbs. They rely less on the use of committees and discussion in private and more on discussion before the public. This more open handling of issues, particularly in very high growth rate communities wherein councils are divided by factions, provides a ready made forum for venting issue disagreements. The greater reliance on committees and private discussion, particularly in medium growth rate suburbs, provides a better means for handling issue disagreements which arise between councilmen. In these councils issue disagreements are not allowed to spill over into the public meetings but are handled behind closed doors. However, most councilmen (74 percent) reported that the process of handling an issue varied according to the type of question being discussed. This was true of councilmen in all communities regardless of their rate of population increase.

When councilmen were asked about how their councils tended to work out disagreements over conflict provoking issues, we found a rather clear-cut pattern (Table 6). In very high growth rate suburbs, councilmen were much more likely to report they simply voted on issues giving rise to disagreements at their public meetings. In other communities, councilmen indicated they

Table 5. *Population increase, 1950–60, and how the council handles issues brought before it by individuals or groups*

How does the council handle issues brought before it?	Low		Medium		High		Very high		Total	
	N (6)	%	N (14)	%	N (8)	%	N (5)	%	N (33)	%
Discuss in public, in private, and refer to committee	12	41	36	45	17	37	16	42	81	42
Discuss in public and in private	2	7	13	16	6	13	2	5	23	12
Discuss in private only	7	24	4	5	2	4	0	0	13	7
Discuss before public	7	24	25	31	21	46	20	53	73	38
Other	1	4	2	3	0	0	0	0	3	1
Total	29	100	80	100	46	100	38	100	193	100

most often attempted to work out their differences in private before taking a final vote on the conflict provoking issue. This was the primary procedure followed by councils in low growth rate communities although it was also emphasized by councilmen in medium and high growth rate suburbs.

Table 6. *Population increase, 1950–60, and how the council works out issue disagreements*

How does the council work out issue disagreements?	Low		Medium		High		Very high		Total	
	N (6)	%	N (14)	%	N	%	N (5)	%	N (33)	%
We try to talk out our differences at the public meeting and then vote	3	10	13	16	9	20	7	18	32	16
We try to talk out our differences in private and then vote	19	66	36	45	20	43	13	34	88	46
We simply vote	6	20	29	36	17	37	17	45	69	36
Other	1	4	2	3	0	0	1	3	4	2
Total	29	100	80	100	46	100	38	100	193	100

In higher growth rate suburbs councilmen indicated that unanimity in making policy decisions occurred somewhat less often than it did in communities whose populations were growing less rapidly. In very high growth rate suburbs unanimity occurs least often according to reports of councilmen. On the other hand, in low growth rate communities sixty-nine percent of the councilmen reported that their councils made unanimous decisions very often. This is probably due to large measure to the fact that in lower growth rate communities there was less issue conflict and/or factionalism and issues were discussed in private or referred to committees before action was taken on them, whereas in communities whose populations were expanding most rapidly, both council issue conflict and factionalism were very high and issues were also handled more openly. When asked what type of issues their councils voted on unanimously, in higher growth rate suburbs councilmen generally indicated that unanimity occurred most often on noncontroversial or routine issues. This was particularly true of councilmen in very high growth rate suburbs. In contrast, in lower growth rate communities, councilmen tended to vote unanimously on most all issues.

Finally, when councils were observed, they were rated on the extent to which there was an incisive attack on problems and efficient work on solutions—the thoroughness and efficiency of their problem solving process (Table 7). Not surprisingly, in higher growth rate communities, particularly those with very high growth rates, the thoroughness and efficiency of the problem solving process was rated as quite low, as not very thorough and efficient. On the other hand, in lower growth rate municipalities, the thoroughness and efficiency of the problem solving process tended to be rated higher.

Table 7.   *Population increase, 1950—60, and observation of the thoroughness and efficiency of the problem solving process*

Thoroughness and efficiency of the council problem solving process	Low		Medium		High		Very high		Total	
	N	%	N	%	N	%	N	%	N	%
Always— incisive attack on problems and efficient work on solutions	3	50	4	29	3	37	2	40	12	36
Sometimes	3	50	10	71	3	37	1	20	14	43
Seldom	0	0	0	0	2	25	2	40	7	21
Total	6	100	14	100	8	99*	5	100	33	100

*Rounding error.

Conclusion – *article in contrained by small # of communities examined;*

Most previous research on decision making in small political groups has focused on internal aspects of such groups and examined how group structure, norms, etc., affect the behavior of group members. There are few studies which analyze the impact of external factors on group processes and behavior.

In this study we have undertaken a preliminary analysis of how changes in one aspect of a municipality's context, rate of population growth, affects issue conflict, factionalism, and consensus in small decision making groups, in this case, city councils in thirty-seven suburban communities. Our working hypothesis was derived from the Coleman-Gamson theory of community conflict. We hypothesized that rapid increases in population may give rise to exclusive values, divergent interests, and strains in a community which may be reflected in higher levels of issue conflict and factionalism and hence less consensus in city councils in such municipalities. Although our data lent some tentative support to this hypothesis we found it necessary to *qualify the hypothesis* in several important respects.

Table 8 summarizes our findings. It is apparent, at least in the suburban communities we studied, that the relationship between population changes and issue conflict and consensus in city councils is a great deal more complicated and certainly less linear than many social scientists have implied in their writings. Although the types of issues giving rise to conflict are similar to those found by other researchers, the overall level of issue conflict is generally higher in councils in these suburbs, particularly in very high and medium growth rate communities.[41] The extent to which issue disagreements carried over in the form of overt council conflict and the extent to which such conflict was based on enduring council factions, also was at some variance with our initial expectations. Overt council conflict and factionalism were largely restricted to councils with exceptionally high growth rates (over 500 percent). Although we cannot at this point say conclusively why some councils have more conflict and factions, or are less cohesive, we can suggest several possible reasons for the patterns which we found. A great deal of further research is suggested, however.

It is obvious from these data that very high growth rate communities have very distinctive councils, not only in the extent of issue disagreements and overt conflict, factionalism, and their general lack of consensus, but also in the more open manner in which issues are handled and the lack of unanimity in decisions made. In these communities divergent values and interests created by new inhabitants, who vary considerably in socioeconomic status and background, are reflected in the council decision process. In such municipalities *potential* sources of cleavage in the community are reflected in *actual* factional splits on the council, factions made up of councilmen who think basically alike.

[41] Huckshorn and Young, *op. cit.*

Table 8. Summary of issue conflict, factionalism, and consensus in suburban city councils

Issue conflict, factionalism, and council consensus	Population increase, 1950–60			
	Low	Medium	High	Very high
Council issue conflict	Medium	High	Low	Very high
Types of issues giving rise to issue conflict	Personnel and salaries; budgets and taxes	Zoning and planning	Zoning and planning	Zoning and planning
Observation of overt council conflict	Little or none	Little or none	Little or none	Much overt conflict
Existence of enduring council factions	Low +	Low +	Low	Very high
Observation of council cohesion	High	Medium	High	Low
Handling of issues	Least open	Less open	Open	Most open
Unanimity of decision making	Very high	High to medium	High to medium	Medium to low
Observation of the thoroughness and efficiency of the problem solving process	Thorough	Less thorough	Less thorough	Least thorough

Although medium growth rate communities also have higher levels of issue disagreements in their councils, these disagreements vary from issue to issue and are not based on factional alliances. Hence cohesion is higher in these councils as is unanimity of decision making. Most issue disagreements in these councils are handled in private and not aired before public meetings. Thus issue disagreements are less likely to spill over into the public arena. With few exceptions, these communities are the natural habitat of the middle class. Their councils, as a result, are made up of fewer professionals and are more likely to have councilmen with dissimilar partisan attachments.[42] Both of these factors, according to Huckshorn and Young, may provide a basis for issue disagreements. However, in these communities such disagreements do not appear to seriously impede the task effectiveness of the city councils.

High growth rate communities present a serious problem. According to the Coleman-Gamson theory, councils in these municipalities should have a great deal of issue conflict as well as exhibit factional splits. But they obviously do not. One possible explanation for this anomaly is that high growth rate communities are either very high or very low in social rank. Although both types of communities have undergone large population changes in recent years, new residents who move into these communities tend to be of the same

[42] For a discussion of the characteristics of councilmen in communities of different social rank see: Bryan T. Downes, "Municipal Social Rank and the Characteristics of Local Political Leaders," *Midwest Journal of Political Science*, vol. 12, no. 4 (November, 1968), pp. 514-537.

socioeconomic status as older residents and have values, interests, and attitudes which are very similar to older community residents. In these suburbs, then, both old and new residents are generally in agreement on what they want their city to be like and what city government should be doing. They are committed to maintaining the existing social character of their communities and keeping governmental services at a minimum, although the reasons for these positions differ considerably in the two types of municipalities. Thus there is more similarity than diversity of values and interests among residents in high growth rate suburbs.

This is quite different than the situation in both very high and medium growth rate suburbs. In these municipalities, old and new residents vary considerably in backgrounds and socioeconomic status, which gives rise to greater diversity in values, interests, and attitudes among community residents. One might conclude that in very high growth rate suburbs there appears to be disagreement over both community goals and appropriate means for achieving such goals, while in high and low growth rate municipalities there is general agreement on both goals and means. In medium growth rate communities there is agreement on community goals but generally a great deal of disagreement over appropriate means for achieving such goals.

One of the more interesting facets of the data presented in this article is the extent to which observation data (1) provide additional support for findings based on the responses of councilmen to a series of interview questions, and/or (2) allow us to further qualify and interpret such information. For example, the observation of overt council conflict enabled us to examine the extent to which issue disagreements and/or factional splits carried over and disrupted council meetings. In the case of very high growth rate communities we found that conflict was definitely an integral part of the council's decision making process. Such councils were not only likely to have very high levels of overt group conflict but also members in opposition roles and to be less cohesive. On the other hand, in medium growth rate communities, issue conflict did not carry over to council meetings. Consequently, these councils were rated as being more cohesive and as having a more thorough and efficient problem solving process than councils in very high growth rate communities. It is obvious that one might get a very false impression of the extent, nature, and varying forms that issue conflict and consensus can take by simply relying on observation data alone. Interview and observations together, however, do facilitate our understanding of the decision making process in councils characterized by varying levels of conflict and consensus.

Because of the negative connotations attached to terms like issue conflict, overt conflict, and/or factionalism, one should be very careful in interpreting the data presented in this article.[43] For example, most communities which did not exhibit a great deal of issue conflict were rather dull, stagnant, and unchanging. On the other hand, many suburbs exhibiting a great deal of issue conflict were among the most vital, stimulating, and rapidly changing

---

[43]This point is made in: Gamson, *op. cit.*, p. 81.

communities studied.[44] Although the manner in which these latter communities were handling issues coming before them might not appear to be the most "thorough and efficient," they were at least attempting to come to grips with important community wide problems. On the other hand, although there was greater cohesion and consensus among councilmen in high and low growth rate suburbs, councilmen in these communities, particularly those of lower social rank, were simply not discussing or attempting to act upon important community problems. In these communities, decision making is confined to relatively "safe" issues on which there is a great deal of agreement. Many important and more controversial issues are simply kept out of the decisional arena. Hence the *non-decision making process*, that is, the process whereby some individuals and groups are able to limit decision making to relatively non-controversial matters, may be exceedingly important in these suburban municipalities.[45] The absence of conflict, therefore, is no necessary indication of a "better" or an "ideal" suburban community.

[44] These judgments are based upon analysis of a great deal of information about each of the suburban municipalities studied.

[45] For a discussion of the importance of non-decision making see: Peter Bachrach and Morton S. Baratz, "Two Faces of Power," *The American Political Science Review,* vol. 58, no. 4 (December, 1962), pp. 947-952. See also: Peter Bachrach and Morton S. Baratz, *Power and Poverty: Theory and Practice* (New York: Oxford University Press, 1970).

School Desegregation and School Decision-Making

Robert L. Crain
David Street

This study, conducted in eight large Northern cities, raises a number of important questions about decision-making in education. First, because there has been little research on the school desegregation issue, many misconceptions have arisen. Most common is the belief that intense conflict over this issue is unavoidable because civil rights leaders want major concessions which white voters are too prejudiced to give. This study indicates that intense conflict over school desegregation is avoidable in some circumstances.

The groups pressing for school desegregation are more interested in symbolic than real changes in school policy. Most simply desire the prevention of discrimination in allocating students to schools and the acceptance by the school system that integration is desirable in principle. As a result, in many cities there is relatively little opposition to school desegregation. Therefore, the school system has some freedom to establish a policy that will prevent conflict.

Although the initial response of the school superintendent to demands for school desegregation is usually quite hostile and defensive, demonstrations or threats of demonstrations by civil rights groups soon result in the active consideration of the issue by the school board. When controversy threatens, the school board takes over decision-making responsibility. The initial response of the board to demands for school desegregation is critical, for it sets the tone for the remainder of the encounter, according to Crain and Street. If the board agrees to acquiesce to civil rights demands, conflict can be avoided. The attitudes held by board members about school desegregation and the extent to which board members agree on an appropriate course of action, therefore, have an important effect on the resolution of this conflict.

Though these findings appear to be somewhat different from those reported by Gittell in her article above, on closer examination we see they are not. In New York, the school board acted as a mediator rather than as an initiator of educational policy. Its role was largely restricted to balancing conflicting interests and pressures. This is precisely the role which school boards played in the eight cities Crain and Street studied. In fact, the difficulties encountered in the eight cities in implementing school desegregation were directly related to one of the basic inadequacies in the organizational capacities of large city schools—that is, their inability to change. This is, of course, one of Gittell's basic points.

In the future, there is a great possibility of intense conflict in many central-city school systems. Civil rights and neighborhood groups in the ghetto have already become less interested in token school integration. Instead, these groups are demanding they be allowed to participate in educational decision-making. They also want the quality of education in neighborhood schools drastically upgraded. Given the general unresponsiveness of educational institutions to such demands, the stage seems set for intense and bitter conflict. However, as Crain and Street point out, positive action by educational leaders could avert such a confrontation. What is the likelihood that school boards and administrators will respond positively to the new demands of ghetto residents? What impact will demonstrations, sit-ins, boycotts, and threats of violence have on the initial response of educational leaders? What other factors will influence their response?

In many ways the school desegregation issue is an ideal context in which to examine the general question of how school systems make policy decisions. First, it is an issue of some importance, so that the decision-making process uncovered can be assumed to be a nontrivial one. Second, it is a relatively new issue, so that the system can make decisions without much reference to traditional decision-making rules; this means that the social scientist need not be greatly concerned with the impact of prior historical accidents. Finally, the issue has arisen in nearly every large city with only minor differences among cities in the way in which it has been raised and with such idiosyncratic factors as the taxing power of the system being of minor importance. This means that the setting is almost ideal for comparative analysis.

This paper principally discusses some of the conclusions of a comparative study of integration in eight Northern large city school systems carried out by the National Opinion Research Center in 1965.[1] Data were gathered by teams of graduate students who spent ten man-days in each city interviewing school administrators, school board members, civil rights leaders, political leaders, members of the civic elite, and other informants. The cities were selected by a modified random sampling design from the cities having a population between 250,000 and 1,000,000 of which at least 10 percent was Negro. The findings are supplemented by observations made in the course of research on the social organization of the large city school system carried out principally in the Chicago schools.[2]

The issue

Very little research has been devoted to the school desegregation issue as a problem in policy-making. Consequently, almost everyone, including most social scientists, have been dependent upon the popular media for information about the issue. This has produced a widespread acceptance of some important misconceptions. Perhaps the most common is the view that intense conflict over school desegregation is unavoidable because civil rights leaders want major concessions which the white voters are too prejudiced to give. This statement contains, we believe, three errors: First, our findings indicate that in some circumstances intense conflict is avoidable. In the eight cities studied, three (Newark, Baltimore, and St. Louis) have at least temporarily resolved their conflict with the civil rights movement. In three other cities

"School Desegregation and School Decision-Making" by Robert L. Crain and David Street is reprinted from *Educating an Urban Population* (1967), pages 136-154, edited by Marilyn Gittell, by permission of the Publishers, Sage Publications, Inc.

[1] This research is reported in Robert L. Crain, Morton Inger, Gerald A. McWorter, and James J. Vanecko, *School Desegregation in the North: Eight Comparative Case Studies of Community Structure and Policy Making*, Chicago: National Opinion Research Center, Report #110A. The research was sponsored by the U.S. Office of Education.

[2] This research was supported by the Russell Sage Foundation. Major findings will be reported in David Street, *The Public Schools and Metropolitan Change*, forthcoming publication.

(Pittsburgh, San Francisco, and Buffalo), the controversy has cooled down and shows promise of being resolved. In the two remaining cities the controversy is still raging. Second, our data indicate that most civil rights leaders will be satisfied (or at least call off their attacks) if they receive even minimal concessions. Third, survey data have indicated relatively little opposition to school desegregation in national samples of white voters.[3]

In short, the school system has some freedom to establish a policy which will prevent conflict. This is not the same as saying that the school system has the power to develop a policy which will actually alter the basic nature of the schools' treatment of Negro students; indeed, we doubt that any big city school system can do this. Thus, it will be necessary to divide our discussion into two sections: first, viewing school desegregation as an issue of symbolic politics, and then looking at the actual outputs of the school system—the extent of school integration and the extent to which educational opportunities can in fact be equalized.

Symbolic politics: the demands of the civil rights movement

Traditional civil rights groups have pressed for school integration in all eight cities studied in the NORC research. To these groups the integration issue means two things: (1) the prevention of discrimination in allocating students to schools; and (2) the acceptance on the part of the school system of the principle that integration is desirable. Beyond these rather minimal goals, the civil rights leaders would prefer, of course, a maximum amount of actual integration, but most of them view true integration as a nearly unattainable goal.[4] If the school system can be persuaded to make racial integration one if its major goals, the civil rights groups will have achieved an important victory, for this commitment exerts normative pressure on the total community to accept the principle of racial equality and to define the efforts to segregate Negroes as illegitimate. Thus, for the traditional civil rights movements, the written policies and pronouncements of the school system are important regardless of their impact. (Of course, if the system took no efforts to implement the policy, the civil rights leaders would raise the cry of hypocrisy.) The civil rights groups would probably endorse the definition of integration given by the Pittsburgh Urban League: "We regard a community as integrated when opportunities for the achievement of respect and the distribution of material welfare are not limited by race."

One is tempted to draw parallels between the school desegregation issue and labor-management negotiations. The major difference is that the corporation is required by law to negotiate with a labor union, while the school board is

[3] For a general review of these and other survey data, see Paul B. Sheatsley, "White Attitudes Toward the Negro," *Daedalus*, 95 (Winter, 1966), 217-238; and Harriet B. Erskine, "The Polls: Race Relations," *Public Opinion Quarterly*, 26 (1962), 137-148.

[4] It is for this reason that we have chosen to use "desegregation" rather than "integration" in the title of this paper.

not. The school board is in the position of the corporation of four decades ago, when management had to decide whether it was wise or morally proper to negotiate with labor unions. The Northern school board is not required to recognize the civil rights movement as legitimate, and indeed many whites who appear otherwise unprejudiced do not consider it so. But another problem is that even when the school system decides that negotiation is proper, the question remains of whom to recognize as the true spokesmen for the civil rights movement. For these two reasons, actual back-room negotiations with the civil rights movement are not common. In our eight cities, only two school systems have been able to maintain this sort of communication with the civil rights groups. This means that we will have to analyze the school systems' policy-making as taking place with only limited private face-to-face communications between the "negotiators."

The first stage of the desegregation decision: the school superintendent as decision-maker

We shall see that the policy decision on desegregation is made by the school board, not the superintendent. However, in each case the board attempted to avoid making a decision for as long as possible. The typical school board seems to operate in a highly pragmatic, fire-fighting fashion. It has limited time, resources, and information with which to make policies, and the result is that it seems not to have a clear policy perspective but primarily makes *ad hoc* decisions as issues become "hot."[5] In the case of desegregation, none of the eight school boards took action when the issue was first raised, and this placed the burden of decision-making on the superintendent. Of ten superintendents who served in the eight cities during the racial controversy, seven can be said to have acted autonomously without board direction to reject demands made by the civil rights movement, while three urged the board to take a liberal position. This comes as no surprise. It is now fashionable to accuse superintendents as a group of being narrowminded and arrogant in their dealings with civil rights leaders. As our data indicate, superintendents do not uniformly reject civil rights demands, but enough do to require us to discuss this point.

The statements of school superintendents frequently stress three themes. The first is that the appropriate stance should be "color blindness"—the refusal to pay any attention to race. This sometimes leads to statements that racial census of school children is illegal or at least immoral. Coupled with this concern with color blindness is the stress placed on a narrow definition of the function of the school as "educational" rather than "social." The third theme which recurs (although with somewhat less frequency) is an extreme defensiveness and an intolerance for "lay" criticism. Lay persons are

---

[5] Support for this hypothesis is provided by L. L. Cunningham, "Decision-making Behavior of School Boards," *American School Board Journal* (February, 1962).

dismissed as unqualified to make recommendations, and their criticisms are frequently answered with flat disagreement or with vague, overly detailed, and off-the-point replies.

Of course, these reactions are common to all organizations which must meet criticism, but the educators go further than most public officials in reacting defensively to political demands. Educational administrators are insistent on defining themselves as professionals and have an entrenched ideology that grants lay control but stresses the importance of the teaching certificate and "educational experience" as the boundary between the expert and the layman. In part, the response to the demands for integration is only another instance of the professionals' tendency—developed through generations of conflict over political interference, progressive education, charges of communism in the schools, and other issues—to perceive any criticism as an "attack upon education."

Further, civil rights demands also strike deeply at one of the most firmly held tenets of the ideology of the large city superintendent: universalism. In the development of the large city schools, insistence on equality of programs for all populations in the city marked a dramatic accomplishment as it gave the schools protection from the pleas for special treatment from various political and ethnic groups. Without this universalism, Northern schools would be more segregated than they are; even after World War I, biracial high schools still discriminated against their Negro students in extracurricular activity participation.[6] Yet, demands by the civil rights movement give the lie to the assumption of universalism, thereby provoking a defensiveness around a highly salient theme and, often, the administrators' counterattack that civil rights demands are themselves a case of special pleading. The defensive response may also be increased by the superintendent's knowledge that even if he were wholly committed to making integration a prime value of the schools, many of his personnel are too traditionalistic, too prejudiced, or too recalcitrant to make the needed adjustments without great resistance.

Thus, we can understand the superintendents' initial defensive response. But in most cases, the school board has little difficulty taking control of the decision from the superintendent. Why is this? The answer seems to lie in what areas the superintendents can make believable claims to expertise. On many issues—for example, curriculum construction, textbook selection, or design of facilities—the superintendents' judgments generally go unchallenged, not only because they usually fall into areas of indifference but also because the superintendents' accumulation of detailed information, his technical background, and his appeals to standard or good practice argue well for honoring his professional claims. On such issues, the superintendent in effect runs the schools. Any criticism in these areas may cause the superintendent to accuse the board of interference with his administrative role.

But it is only in the extreme case of Benjamin C. Willis in Chicago that a superintendent has been willing to take the stand that he must have

---

[6] J. H. Tipton points out that in the late 1940s Negro students were not allowed to use the swimming pool in one high school in Gary, Indiana. See his *Community in Crisis*, New York: Columbia Teachers College, 1953.

autonomy or he will resign over a racial issue.[7] This is understandable, for there is not truly marketable expertise on racial integration anywhere, and there is certainly little claim possible in this area from within the education profession. Therefore, the superintendent, after his initial negative response, often finds his upstaging by the board to be the least awkward exit.

In addition, the origins and backgrounds of the large city superintendents generally do not provide them with a sensitivity to urban social change and problems and to the current revolution of rising racial expectations in the large cities which would lead these men to play a leadership role in the absence of professional claims. Evidence bearing on this point comes from the biographies of the eleven big city superintendents contained in *Who's Who*. Of the ten whose birth date was given, the mean age was fifty-seven. Nine of the eleven began as teachers, and only one finished graduate school before beginning his career. Six of the ten American-born superintendents were from very small cities or farms, and none of the eleven attended a first-rank undergraduate college. Seven of the eleven began their teaching in small towns, and much of the administrative experience of all but four had been outside the large cities.

While many of these men had been administrators in smaller, suburban, and often vanguard or experimental school systems, their experiences in the large cities have not stimulated their desire to be experimental. The financial problems of the large city systems, the sheer administrative problems of size, scale, and change, and the often inert middle-level personnel and principals (who frequently are political appointees left over from an earlier era) tend to move these superintendents toward an emphasis upon a traditionalistic philosophy of education that stresses the three R's, the standard neighborhood school, and "sound programs." When racial and other social changes place new demands on the schools, these superintendents generally are unable to articulate a leadership ideology dealing with integration and broadened welfare goals.

The second stage of the controversy: the school board takes over

In the typical city studied, the civil rights movement first approaches the board cautiously over a period of a year or two, making statements and testifying at hearings. In general, the school system does not respond to this; the issue is still below the level of saliency. The integrationists then step up their campaign, and their demands are rejected by the school superintendent at this point. When the movement replies to this with demonstrations or threats of demonstrations, the school board begins to take the issue seriously and responds in a variety of ways. At this point, the second stage of the

[7]Willis' temporary resignation was apparently triggered by a taxpayer's suit charging that he had arbitrarily changed a voluntary transfer plan designed by the board to further integration. The incident is described in Joseph Pois, *The School Board Crisis*, Chicago: Aldine Press, 1964, pp. 109-114.

controversy has begun. The board has taken over racial policy-making. In six of the eight cities it is possible to find a point at which the superintendent's recommendations were ignored or a point when he was instructed to alter his policy. In the other two cases, the system changed superintendents without changing its policy, so that we must assume that the board supplied policy continuity to the system.

The first response made by the school system during this second phase we call the "key response," because it sets the tone for the remainder of the conflict. This key response by the board seems to be made with almost complete autonomy. One might expect the community political and civic elites to exert great influence, but we have only one clear case where this was done successfully. In two cases, the school board seemed to ignore the recommendations of the mayor; in another case, the community's most prominent industrialist was flatly rebuffed. It is not possible to describe all the actions taken by various actors in this short paper, but in general it seems clear that there is less direct influence exerted on the board than one would expect and that attempts to influence the board usually are not very successful.

The most complex question is: To what extent can the civil rights movement control the outcomes of the school desegregation decision by their use of power? The evidence seems to indicate that they have surprisingly little influence. The civil rights movement can force the school system to deal with the issue, of course; few if any of these systems would have done anything about civil rights if they had not been pressured by the movement. Generally, the movement is successful in part—that is, the system will usually desegregate schools to some limited extent, and all of the eight cities have adopted a policy statement advocating integration. But concessions may be minimal and may come so late and be given so grudgingly as to be nearly meaningless.

Apparently, there is little that the civil rights leadership in a typical city can do to prevent this. Once the key response of the board is taken, the process is "locked in." If the key response is conciliatory, continued low-keyed civil rights activity will extract additional concessions; if the key response is negative, the civil rights movement will retaliate with demonstrations, but this usually leads to an escalation of the conflict and the school board's subsequently becoming more reluctant to negotiate or make additional concessions. The only way in which the movement can control the outcome is by introducing a new authority—for example, the state government may step in to order desegregation, and this is sometimes very effective.

Altogether, the findings mean that the school board usually is nearly autonomous in its policy-making on racial issues. It generally is not effectively influenced by political or civic leadership, by its superintendent, or even by the behavior of the civil rights movement, despite the fact that the decision on race is probably the issue of greatest immediate importance to the largest number of actors.

In order to demonstrate this conclusion, the research staff of the eight-city study ranked the cities on four variables: the level of civil rights activity prior to the key response, the level of civil rights activity after the key response, the degree to which the key response indicated a willingness to acquiesce to the civil rights demands, and the final level of acquiescence of the board to the demands made. Acquiescence is based on the number of demands met and the general public tone taken by the schools with respect to the civil rights movement. Put another way, the research staff attempted to rank the cities according to the degree to which a typical civil rights leader would feel satisfied with the response of the school system. The eight cities varied greatly in their acquiescence. In Pittsburgh, for example, the school board reacted very early to civil rights demands with a transfer plan which integrated two previously all-white schools. When demands for integration reappeared later, the school board committed itself, in a long and candid statement, to integration; adopted some short-range integration programs; and began planning for large scale educational parks as the long run answer to the integration question. In Baltimore, a demand for the elimination of overcrowding in Negro schools led to a summer of negotiation between the civil rights leaders and the school board, resulting in a decision to transport 4,000 Negro students and eliminate all double-shift schooling in the system, effective only six months after the issue was first raised. These two school systems are scored at the top of the acquiescence scale. At the opposite extreme, two school boards have refused to meet any of the demands for integration made, despite repeated demonstrations and pressure from other governmental officials. These two systems are located at the bottom of the scale.

Figure 1 diagrams the rank-order correlations between the initial level of civil rights activity, the acquiescence of the key response, the level of civil rights activity following the key response, and the total level of acquiescence of the school system. The correlations indicate that the key response is not dependent upon the level of civil rights activity directed at the board, and also that the key response predicts quite accurately the final amount of acquiescence of the school system. If the rank correlations are accurate, they indicate that the civil rights movement principally responds to the behavior of the school system rather than being a cause of the character of the school system's behavior.

This is only indirect evidence that the boards can be quite autonomous in their decision. We also have some direct evidence of this. In Figure 2, the eight boards have been ranked by a combination of two closely correlated variables: the percentage of the board members having high socioeconomic status (men from large businesses, corporation lawyers, or professionals) as against the percentage who are professional politicians or related in other ways to the political parties in their city. (High-status men are, or course, generally independent of the parties.) This single variable predicts quite well the final level of acquiescence of the school system. Since the variable is clearly independent of the actual decision situation, this seems to be strong evidence.

The autonomy of the nonpolitical board is not so surprising. However, the five boards which are partly or wholly made up of political appointments are

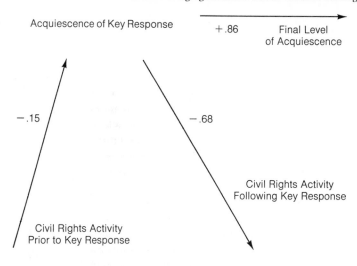

Figure 1. *Rank-order correlations between civil rights activity and acquiescence of school boards to civil rights demands.*

also largely autonomous. Two of these boards are elected boards in cities where political power is quite decentralized. In a third city, the mayor's recommendations seem to have been largely ignored. In another, the mayor's appointments have disagreed strongly with each other and have involved the city in a lengthy controversy. In the fifth city, the mayor seems to have maintained control over the school system, and here the board has been persuaded twice to change its position on a racial issue.

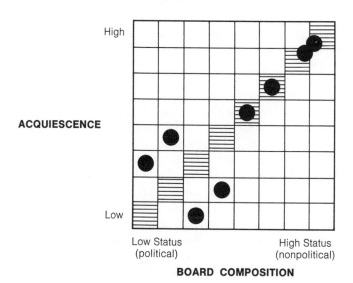

Figure 2. *Status and political activity of school board members and acquiescence to civil rights demands. (Note: The two boards in the upper right are tied on both rankings.)*

It is usually assumed that political leaders wish to maximize their power and, therefore, detachment from school politics may seem surprising; but the mayor who tries to run the schools would be taking a great risk for a very small reward.

Before considering the implications of these findings, we also should consider why it is that the civic board is more acquiescent than the political board. The answer is a simple but empirical one: On our measures, the civic board members are more liberal on racial issues and the political board members are more conservative. This is not a trivial statement, because it is certainly not necessary that there be a high correlation between the personal attitude of government officials and their public actions. In fact, a similar study of Southern school boards indicates that there is at best a weak correlation between racial attitudes and behavior regarding school deseg-regation.[8] The presence of this high correlation in the North indicates the extent to which the school desegregation issue is unstructured. In the absence of clear legal guidelines for action, of efficient communication between the contesting parties, and of a coherent educational ideology to draw upon, the school board members are "on their own" in deciding what to do. Board members are very conscious of this; more than one has publicly appealed for a decision by a local or Federal court to clarify the situation. Buffalo, New York, furnishes a striking example of what this kind of clarification by an authority can do. The state commissioner of education, James E. Allen, demanded that the board desegregate the schools, and immediately the board became a cohesive decision-making body even though it had been torn by internal conflict for well over a year prior to his intervention.

The lack of structure and clarity in the civil rights arena is, we think, also reflected in the fact that heterogeneous school boards and boards with a history of internal conflict have the greatest difficulty in meeting civil rights demands. Only two of the eight boards have contested elections for membership (five are appointed while another is *de facto* appointed by a slating committee); these two boards were the least acquiescent, probably because of their heterogeneity and the pressures on the boards to make their disagreements public. The board with internal conflict cannot acquiesce to the demands made on it for two reasons: First, it cannot agree on what is being asked of it, and what strategies are available to it; second, it cannot prevent public controversy which polarizes the community and further limits the alternatives available to it.

The great debate over community power structure hinges about the amount of autonomy which governmental officials have and the extent to which the civic elite are able to influence policy. The findings of this research suggest that it is possible for government officials to have great autonomy and at the same time for the civic elite to have great influence. In the case of the schools, the nature of the local civic elite is a principal factor in determining

---

[8] See Robert L. Crain, Morton Inger and Gerald A. McWorter, "School Desegregation in New Orleans: A Comparative Study in the Failure of Social Control," Chicago: National Opinion Research Center, Report #110B.

the composition of the school board, and thus the elite indirectly controls policy, even though it makes little or no effort to influence any single decision (and probably could not do so if it tried). The three most acquiescent cities all have high-status schools boards, and the civic elite in all three cases plays an important role in locating school board members. These three cities have elites which are highly active across a wide range of local policy issues. In the other five cities, the elites are weaker, and the result is that school board members are selected either from the ranks of the political parties, or from the leadership of voluntary organizations, or in order to represent various ethnic groups.

Even the degree of heterogeneity and internal conflict in the school board has its roots in the structure of the political parties and the nature of the elite. The conflict-ridden boards which resist desegregation appear in cities with weak political parties, for example. Thus, the school board is autonomous in its decision-making procedure, yet the degree of acquiescence of the school system is determined by the overall political structure of the city.

Symbolic politics and real outputs

To this point we have not discussed the real outputs of the school system's racial policy—the actual changes in quality of education or the actual increase in the number of students in integrated schools. It is not difficult for a school system to adopt a racial policy which will partially satisfy civil rights leaders without actually making a large impact on the operation of the schools. (These symbolic victories may have a considerable impact on the attitudes and behavior of individual Negro students, but this is outside the range of the two studies). Conversely, it is also possible for the school system to have in operation policies which increase school integration without satisfying the civil rights groups. In two cities, Negro students were routinely bussed into white schools, but the school adamantly refused to state that such integration was desirable, and the board in each case was subject to a great deal of attack.

The actual amount of integration is, of course, small. Among the eight cities, the greatest acquiescence, as judged by the research staff, was in Pittsburgh, Baltimore, and St. Louis. In Pittsburgh, the school system has succeeded in remaining on cordial terms with the civil rights leaders and has committed itself wholeheartedly to integration; but to date, Pittsburgh has done little to increase integration. St. Louis and Baltimore have adopted bussing programs which have successfully relieved overcrowded Negro schools, but less than 5 percent of the Negro students are directly involved. In the eight cities, the proportion of Negro elementary school children attending schools which are at least 90 percent Negro varies from a low of 30 percent in San Francisco to a high of 86 percent in St. Louis; the median for the eight cities is 68 percent. If the largest cities—Chicago, Detroit, Cleveland, Philadelphia, Washington, and New York City—had been included in the study, the picture would look even bleaker.

The school board may commit itself to a policy of integration but find its efforts to implement this policy restricted by a number of factors outside of its control. The superintendent may undermine the design and implementation of the policy through his role in developing technical details of the plan. Voluntary plans for pupil-transfer may have a minimal effect because of a lack of interest among Negro parents, or may even further segregation by allowing whites to transfer out of integrated schools. (This is another example of universalism; transfer plans explicitly based on the race of the pupils involved are quite *avant-garde*.) Or track systems or practices of homogeneous grouping, discriminatory or not, may segregate pupils rigidly within the "integrated" school. And in cities where racial tensions are especially high, such as in Chicago and Cleveland, Negro students attending white schools have been assaulted, and it is often a community prophecy (and in part a self-fulfilling one) that integrated schools will become all Negro.[9]

More important, the school system cannot control its own personnel. The heart of successful integration is the classroom teacher, and many big city teachers do not feel comfortable teaching Negro students or handling an integrated class. Further, it is a big city tradition that the integrated school is a "changing" school, where teachers transfer out, morale drops, and high-level programs are phased out as no longer appropriate to the clientele.

The difficulties encountered by the school systems in implementing effective integration go beyond the particular personality problems of the individual actors. They are tied to basic inadequacies in the organizational capacities of the large city school systems for adapting to social change. Briefly, these inadequacies include the following:

1. A bureaucratic rigidity flowing from the statutory and quasi-legal restrictions placed on the school systems by states and accrediting associations. These restrictions limit the scheduling of the school year, prescribe certain courses and curricula, bureaucratize teacher recruitment, etc. This rigidity is related to the great emphasis upon universalism, a stress which in large part is a heritage of many cycles of reform. The result is administration by numbers: an attempt at innovation becomes merely an elaborate formula for assigning X numbers of specialists to Y numbers of schools. Another example is the procedure of allowing teachers to pick whatever schools they want on the basis of seniority, a practice which usually undermines the "difficult" school. And a crucial result is the highly standardized curriculum, which exists despite obvious differences in the needs of different schools.

2. The fact that teachers are basically solo practitioners. Unlike most professions, teaching offers relatively little opportunity for collegial contact which could provide the opportunity not only for respite but for communication of new practices and the development of

[9] Each of these problems is potentially subject to remediation as shown, for example, in St. Louis's ability to bus approximately 2,600 Negro students into white schools in 1965-1966. The bussing program seems to have an informal "quota"; none of the integrated schools is over 40 percent Negro. After the initial shock, there has been virtually no opposition in this border city, and bussing of Negro students is now taken for granted.

new attitudes. In-service training tends to be restricted to short-term workshops which are likely to have a minimal impact on teacher attitudes relevant to racial change. Yet, intensive resocialization procedures are apparently essential because of the conventional perspectives with which persons enter teaching.[10] Further, rewards for the teachers are largely ascriptive, based on seniority and on graduate work which in most schools of education is not oriented to the problems of urban education. As solo practitioners, the teachers frequently are reluctant to have anyone enter their classrooms, including subprofessionals or volunteers who could play a significant role. Principals and middle-level administrators face similar problems of poor lateral and vertical communication except on purely administrative matters.

3. Given these patterns, the large city school systems have very primitive mechanisms of control, which limit them severely in producing change. These systems are overcentralized in the sense that standardized curricula and administration by formula do not provide enough fiscal and administrative autonomy to permit "decentralized" administrators to vary their programs to local needs with any real facility. Yet they are undercentralized in the sense that it is very difficult for decisions made at the top of the organization to alter the traditional operating procedures. This is particularly the case in cities where principals or other personnel have become highly entrenched in their positions; the man who has been principal of the same school for twenty years is not responsive to supervision. Commitment to the status quo is often heightened by inbreeding and by the associations of principals and other personnel which act as mutual protective associations.[11]

4. Also limiting the school system in producing innovations in racial practices and programs for the deprived is their general weakness in research and development. The large systems have numerous special projects for dealing with Negro pupils, and many have generated a sense of success and excitement. But evaluation research is usually poor, and attempts to expand the program to other schools are so haphazardly administered that few survive to become incorporated into standard operating procedure.

Cumulatively, these characteristics of the large city school system imply that more adequate integration of the large city schools will require not only higher levels of leadership in broadening and pursuing educational goals, but also substantial transformations in the organizational format.

---

[10]The tendency for even city-bred teacher trainees to have quite negative orientations toward the challenges of "problem schools" in the inner city is described in Bryan Roberts, "The Effects of College Experience and Social Background on Professional Orientations of Prospective Teachers," unpublished dissertation, University of Chicago, 1964. Findings of an experiment conducted by Bruno Bettelheim in cooperation with the Russell Sage project indicate that teachers' difficulties in dealing with Negro children who present behavior problems flow not principally from racial prejudice but from social class views in which the teacher assumes that the children are unlikely to learn. The Bettelheim work also seems to demonstrate that really intensive in-service training can produce a reduction in these stereotypic views.

[11]For a discussion of the power of this sort of clique, see W. S. Sayre and H. Kaufman, *Governing New York City*, New York: W. W. Norton & Company, Inc., 1965, 279-280.

Conclusion

It has often been said that in a large and complex organization the leadership does not have control over the operation of the system. These data indicate that there is considerable truth in this. Control over the classroom teacher is limited by the fact that she cannot be supervised directly and by the nature of her contract and the character of her professional organization. Control over individual principals is limited because supervision must be from a distance and by a strict universalism in administration. The board cannot supervise a school superintendent unless he supplies information to them, presents the full range of policy alternatives, and permits the board to believe that it knows something about how to run a school system. Similarly, the men who select the school-board members must defer to them as "experts" once the selection has been made.

On the other hand, we do see a clear line of influence which runs from the top of the system to the bottom. When members of the mayor's staff or members of the civil elite choose school-board members (and in most cities they do choose them), they have in mind an operational image when they say they want a "good man" for the job. It is hardly a surprise that they get the kind of man they want most of the time. These men then control the schools "image" on racial matters and to a limited extent this style can filter down to the classroom. The board selects the superintendent, and some boards have definite criteria in mind; if he does not meet them, he may then be subject to what one board member called a "learning experience." And the superintendent, through his choice of subordinate administrators and his use of policy directives and public relations, can project a "style" into the school system. Granted there is no close isomorphism between this "style" and the actual day-to-day operations of the schools, but at least there is some order in the system.

Additional suggested readings:
the policy-making process

Robert E. Agger, Daniel Goldrich, and Bert E. Swanson, *The Rulers and The Ruled: Political Power and Impotence in American Communities* (New York: John Wiley, 1964).

Peter Bachrach, and Morton S. Baratz, *Power and Poverty: Theory and Practice* (New York: Oxford University Press, 1970).

Harry A. Bailey, Jr. (ed.), *Negro Politics in America* (Columbus: Charles E. Merrill Books, 1967).

Edward C. Banfield, *Political Influence: A New Theory of Urban Politics* (New York: The Free Press, 1961).

Edward C. Banfield, and James Q. Wilson, *City Politics* (New York: Random House, 1963).

Alvin Boskoff and Harmon **Zeigler**, *Voting Patterns in a Local Election* (Philadelphia: J. B. Lippincott Co., 1964).

Stokely Carmichael and Charles V. Hamilton, *Black Power: The Politics of Liberation in America* (New York: Random House, 1967).

Terry N. Clark (ed.), *Community Structure and Decision Making: Comparative Analyses* (San Francisco: Chandler Press, 1968).

Robert L. Crain, *The Politics of School Desegregation: Comparative Case Studies of Community Structure and Policy-Making* (Chicago: Aldine, 1968).

Robert L. Crain, Elihu Katz, and Donald B. Rosenthal, *The Politics of Community Conflict: The Fluoridation Decision* (Indianapolis: Bobbs-Merrill Co., 1969).

Robert A. Dahl, *Who Governs?: Democracy and Power in an American City* (New Haven: Yale University Press, 1961).

Morris Davis and Marvin G. Weinbaum, *Metropolitan Decision Processes: An Analysis of Case Studies* (Chicago: Rand McNally, 1969).

Bryan T. Downes, "Municipal Social Rank and the Characteristics of Local Political Leaders," *Midwest Journal of Political Science*, vol. 12, no. 4 (November 1968), pp. 514-538.

——, "Black Protest and Urban Racial Violence: Confrontation Politics," in James A. Riedel (ed.), *State and Local Politics* (Waltham, Mass.: Blaisdell, 1970).

E. S. Evans, "Ghetto Revolts and City Politics," in Louis H. Masotti and Don R. Bowen (eds.), *Riots and Rebellion: Civil Violence in the Urban Community* (Beverly Hills: Sage Publications, 1968), pp. 389-407.

William A. Gamson, "Reputation and Resources in Community Politics," *The American Journal of Sociology*, vol. 72, no. 2 (September 1966), pp. 121-131.

Charles E. Gilbert, *Governing the Suburbs* (Bloomington: Indiana University Press, 1967).

Marilyn Gittell, "Community Control of Education," *Proceedings of the Academy of Political Science*, vol. 29, no. 1 (July 1968), pp. 60-71.

——, *Participants and Participation: A Study of School Policy in New York City* (New York: Praeger, 1968).

—— and Alan G. Hevesi (eds.), *The Politics of Urban Education* (New York: Praeger, 1969).

Norval D. Glenn and Charles M. Bonjean, *Blacks in the United States* (San Francisco: Chandler Press, 1969).

Jeffrey K. Hadden, Louis H. Masotti, and Victor Thiessen, "The Making of the Negro Mayors 1967," *Trans*-action, vol. 5, no. 3 (January/February 1968), pp. 21-30.

Willis D. Hawley and Frederick M. Wirt (eds.), *The Search for Community Power* (Englewood Cliffs, N.J.: Prentice-Hall, 1968).

Roscoe Hill and Malcom Feeley (eds.), *Affirmative School Integration: Efforts to Overcome De Facto Segregation in Urban Schools* (Beverly Hills: Sage Publications, 1967).

R. J. Huckshorn and C. E. Young, "The Study of Voting Splits on City Councils in Los Angeles County," *The Western Political Quarterly*, vol. 13, no. 2 (June 1960), pp. 479-497.

Floyd Hunter, *Community Power Structure: A Study of Decision Makers* (Chapel Hill: University of North Carolina Press, 1953).

M. Kent Jennings, "Parental Grievances and School Politics," *Public Opinion Quarterly,* vol. 32, no. 3 (Fall 1968), pp. 363-378.

M. Kent Jennings and Harmon Zeigler, "Class, Party, and Race in Four Types of Elections: The Case of Atlanta," *The Journal of Politics,* vol. 28, no. 2 (May 1966), pp. 391-407.

Gladys M. Kammerer and John M. DeGrove, "Urban Leadership During Change," *The Annals of the American Academy of Political and Social Science,* vol. 353 (May 1964), pp. 95-106.

William R. Keech, *The Impact of Negro Voting: The Role of the Vote in the Quest for Equality* (Chicago: Rand McNally, 1968).

Milton Kotler, *Neighborhood Government: The Local Foundations of Political Life* (Indianapolis: Bobbs-Merrill Co., 1969).

Everett Carll Ladd, Jr., *Negro Political Leadership in the South* (Ithaca: Cornell University Press, 1966).

——, *Ideology in America: Change and Response in a City, a Suburb, and a Small Town* (Ithaca: Cornell University Press, 1969).

Michael Lipsky, *Protest in City Politics* (Chicago: Rand McNally, 1970).

Donald R. Matthews and James W. Prothro, *Negroes and the New Southern Politics* (New York: Harcourt, Brace & World, 1966).

Martin Oppenheimer, *The Urban Guerrilla* (Chicago: Quadrangle Books, 1969).

Robert Presthus, *Men At The Top: A Study in Community Power* (New York: Oxford University Press, 1964).

Francine F. Rabinovitz, *City Politics and Planning* (New York: Atherton Press, 1969).

Robert H. Salisbury, "Urban Politics: The New Convergence of Power," *The Journal of Politics,* vol. 26, no. 4 (November 1964), pp. 775-797.

Jerome Skolnik, *The Politics of Protest* (New York: Ballantine Books, 1969).

Jean L. Stinchcombe, *Reform and Reaction: City Politics in Toledo* (Belmont, Calif.: Wadsworth, 1968).

Chuck Stone, *Black Political Power in America* (Indianapolis: Bobbs-Merrill Co., 1968).

Supplemental Studies for the National Advisory Commission on Civil Disorders (Washington, D.C.: U.S. Government Printing Office, July 1968). This is one of the most comprehensive studies to date of racial attitudes in American cities and suburbs.

Roland L. Warren (ed.), *Politics and the Ghettos* (New York: Atherton Press, 1969).

Arthur I. Waskow, *From Race Riot to Sit-In: 1919 and the 1960's* (Garden City, N. Y.: Doubleday & Co., 1967).

James Q. Wilson, *Negro Politics: The Search for Leadership* (New York: The Free Press, 1960).

Basil G. Zimmer and Amos H. Hawley, "Opinions on School District Reorganization in Metropolitan Areas: A Comparative Analysis of the Views of Citizens and Officials in Central City and Suburban Areas," *Southwestern Social Science Quarterly,* vol. 21, no. 3 (September 1968), pp. 483-495.

——, *Metropolitan Area Schools: Resistance to District Reorganization* (Beverly Hills: Sage Publications, 1968).

Part four   Local differences and public policy in central cities and suburbs

In the introductory essay I distinguished three types of policy outcomes: *public policy*, or the actions of government; *policy outputs*, which represent the service levels affected by these actions, and *policy impacts*, which involve the effect policy has on people's lives, the alleviation of particular problems, and/or citizen demands for policy change. The articles in this section generally restrict their attention to public policy. They examine how differences in the context in the formal rules, procedures, and political structures, and/or in the policy-making process result in variation not only in the policy problems confronting central cities and their suburbs but also in the public policies which they actually pursue. On the whole, they are concerned with *explanation*, that is, with why policy problems arise and/or why local governments do or do not undertake specific public policies.

One of the very real problems in the social sciences, and particularly in political science, is the lack of clear, concise, meaningfully defined concepts. Lewis J. Froman has argued that if policy analysis is to be taken out of the problem-oriented, case-study, and often normative framework in which it is most often found, and raised to the level of scientific inquiry, then we must have an adequate conceptualization not only of the various factors which influence public policy but of public policy itself. Without this, and as Hennessey will show in the conclusion, explanation is seriously hampered.

The public-policy problems facing central cities and their suburbs are many and varied. Many central cities and some older suburbs are attempting to redevelop a deteriorating physical plant. On the other hand, suburbs and some younger central cities are frequently caught up in the process of developing vacant land and meeting demands for more governmental services. James Q. Wilson, in the opening selection, discusses some of the relevant aspects of the urban problem. This problem, according to Wilson, as well as a human component, has psychological and technical components. He argues quite persuasively that there has been little real understanding of the relative importance of each component and consequently little successful attack on the paramount human problems of city dwellers. Instead, we have been far too concerned with reclaiming land and real estate.

I have adhered to a functional analysis of public policy in this section. No attempt has been made to be exhaustive, however. Rather than review each of the articles, I will simply discuss the relationships examined in each one. First, Campbell and Meranto investigate the important effect contextual changes can have on educational policy. They are particularly concerned with the impact population changes have had on the growing disparity between needs and resources in many central-city school districts. In addition, much of the material on racial violence and social disorganization points to the important influence contextual conditions, such as overcrowding, poor housing, lack of jobs, low incomes, and so on, can have on problems involving race, welfare, poverty, crime, and violence.

Second is the extent to which formal rules, procedures, and governmental structures have an independent effect on public policy. For example, Lineberry and Fowler empirically document the different fiscal policies pursued by cities with reformed and unreformed governmental structures. Unreformed cities simply tax and spend more. Greenstone and Peterson investigate the impact reformed and unreformed institutions have on the distribution of goods and services and/or political power. These are the two somewhat contradictory goals of the war on poverty Cities with unreformed institutions are much more effective at getting and distributing material benefits, while communities with reformed structures are more adept at distributing power.

Third is the important influence citizen political attitudes and behavior can have on certain policy decisions. Scott, for example, documents how citizen and leader opposition to radical proposals for metropolitan governmental reorganization has led to their defeat at the polls, where citizen approval is required for the success of any policy change.

Finally, we turn to the relationship between political leadership and public policy. We have already called attention to the importance of vigorous political leadership if policy change is to take place. Clark returns to this question in his examination of how the centralization/decentralization of influence in 51 local communities affected public policy in four issue areas.

When these important determinants of public policy are combined with those discussed in previous selections, the problem of explaining why particular central cities and suburbs pursue divergent public policies becomes quite complex. It is important, therefore, to design with great care any study which attempts to explain public policy. A useful strategy is to begin by investigating the impact of the most proximate determinants of public-policy decisions, that is, the various dimensions of the policy-making process. Particularly important to examine are the attitudes and behavior of political leaders and the role they play in mobilizing sufficient resources to overcome opposition to policy change. Why have researchers not adopted this strategy more often?

In conclusion, these selections also point out some of the very real constraints on governmental action. Particularly important is the inability of local units of government to respond positively to current citizen and leader demands for new services and programs without receiving substantial technical and monetary assistance from higher levels of government.

The Urban Problem and the War on the Cities

James Q. Wilson

Although you may not agree with James Q. Wilson's attempt to distinguish various aspects of the urban problem or the policy alternatives he sets forth to deal with the problems facing many of our nation's central cities and some older suburbs, they do provide an excellent basis for class discussion.

Wilson argues that federal policy toward the cities has always been plagued by lack of agreement on goals and clear understanding of priorities. What have we been trying to accomplish in the cities? Does federal policy seek to raise standards of living, maximize housing choices, revitalize the commercial centers of our central cities, end suburban sprawl, eliminate discrimination, reduce traffic congestion, improve the quality of urban design, check crime and delinquency, strengthen the effectiveness of local planning, and/or increase citizen participation in local government?

The initial impetus to this selection was the Demonstration Cities legislation proposed in 1966 by President Lyndon Johnson. In commenting on the proposed legislation, known after enactment as the Model Cities Program, Wilson points out how it appears to be an effort to create a new slum policy that will, at least in a few cities, put social and human goals ahead of physical ones. It also involves putting various interests—the poor, intellectuals, and some bureaucrats—now struggling for power against the old urban-renewal coalition of downtown businessmen, mayors, and most bureaucrats, into a new coalition for urban renewal.

With these introductory remarks, Wilson turns to his central concern--what indeed is the urban problem? According to Wilson, there are at least three components to this problem, all of which are of course related. First, the psychological component *refers to problems resulting from the "revolution of rising expectations" among certain segments of our urban population. Such a problem cannot be solved in the short run, at least not without a drastic rethinking of priorities and a massive reallocation of resources. Second, there is a* technical component *to the urban problem, created because people are living together in highly interdependent, dense settlements in an industrial society. These two components can also be considered political problems, since their solution requires cooperative action by independent governmental units.*

Third, and most important according to Wilson, is the human component, *the problems of the poor who reside in our central cities. Wilson argues that we have only recently realized there is a human component to the urban problem. Hence most federal programs have been misdirected. They have been primarily concerned with reclaiming land and real estate, and not with the real problems of the poor in our society.*

Wilson sets forth an alternative policy, one which would not necessarily scrap existing federal programs but only require their redirection. Such a policy would begin by recognizing that different types of urban problems exist, some of which, like poverty, are as much rural as urban problems, and others, like the gap between expectations and achievements, are problems which government cannot do anything about, at least in the short run.

Wilson concludes by discussing the basic components of his alternative policy. Has Wilson left anything out? Would the urban poor object to Wilson's alternative policies? Why would they object? Does Wilson's agenda for action simply represent more of the same old paternalism which ghetto groups are objecting to? Should we also be concerned with creating conditions that will facilitate meaningful involvement of the poor in decision-making? Might a more equitable distribution of decision-making power, enabling local community groups to begin working on internal ghetto problems and thereby giving the poor a personal stake in their community, be one of the most effective means of mitigating further ghetto violence?

Introduction

What indeed, is the "urban problem"? The language of crisis with which this subject is normally discussed—"sick cities," "the urban crisis," "spreading blight"—is singularly unilluminating. I doubt that most residents of most American cities would recognize in such terms a fair description of the conditions in their communities. Since such words are usually uttered or printed in Washington, D.C., or New York City, perhaps the most we can infer is that life is tough in these two places—though the staggering expense the authors of such words are willing to incur in order to live in the very center of these cities suggests that the "crisis" is at least bearable.

Reprinted from James Q. Wilson, "The War on Cities," *The Public Interest*, no. 3 (Spring 1966), pp. 31-44, by permission of the publisher and author. © 1966 by National Affairs, Inc.

Viewed in historical perspective, and taking American cities as a whole, the conditions of urban life have, by most measures, been getting steadily better, not worse. Nationally, the proportion of families under the poverty line—for purposes of argument, let us take that as a family income of $3,000 a year in constant dollars—declined from 31 percent to 19 percent between 1950 and 1963, and the decline was the greatest in the cities (in the rural areas of our country, by contrast, about *half* the families still live at or near the poverty line). Since the Second World War, there has been a more or less steady decline in the proportion of housing units that are substandard; this improvement has been greatest in the cities, least in the rural areas. (In 1960, less than 3 percent of the dwelling units in cities of 50,000 population and over were dilapidated by Census Bureau standards.) The "flight to the suburbs" has made most people better off—the middle-income family finds the peace and privacy of a suburban home, the lower-income family takes over the larger, sounder structures vacated in the central city. The proportion of young people who drop out of school before getting a high school diploma has been declining steadily, both absolutely and relatively, for about the last twenty years. Certain forms of violent crime—murder and forcible rape—have declined in rate for the last several decades, though other forms of crime (assault, theft) may have increased (no one knows for certain, because crime statistics are neither completely reliable nor standardized for the changing age composition of the population).

American cities have fully participated in the prosperity of the country — indeed, they have participated more than the rural areas; and this no doubt accounts for the fact that, whatever problems the cities have, people are moving to the cities in very large numbers. But it would be a mistake to try to be unreservedly optimistic about these aggregate trends. Certain classes of people within cities continue to confront problems, and these problems vary with the size and kind of the city in question. Three of these problems are especially noteworthy.

High expectations

First, there is what might be called the "psychological urban problem"—i.e., our expectations are increasing faster than our achievements. As more affluent suburbs spring up, with neat lawns and good schools, the apparent gap between the quality of life in the central city and at the periphery increases. The suburbanites, adjusting rapidly to residential comfort, become more discontented with the conditions that surround the places where they work in the central city, even though these conditions are also (on the average) improving. Those city dwellers who cannot, for reasons of income or race, move to the suburbs, grow increasingly envious of those who can; the prizes of worldly success are held up before their eyes but out of their reach.

Because whites are gaining, in income and housing, faster than Negroes (though they are gaining also), the gap between the two groups is widening. (The full-employment economy of World War II narrowed the gap because of the need to fill manpower shortages; the under-employment prosperity of the 'fifties widened the gap; a continued Vietnamese war and the re-emergence of labor shortages may once again reduce the gap.) Moreover, within the Negro community itself, greater progress is being made in schooling than in income. The fact of Negro life is that a high school diploma is worth less to a Negro than to a white person, and the disparity is most obvious precisely where educational progress has been the greatest—in the cities.

In addition, the central city has remained the place where important members of the commercial and intellectual elite live. This is the group which, more than any other, sets the tone and provides the rhetoric of public discussion on "urban problems." By habit and tradition, it prizes the cultural amenities of the large central city and it tends to resent the spread of lower-class people into areas where these cultural and commercial institutions are established—even though that spread has been caused by the very increases in freedom and prosperity which the elite itself values. In the resulting distress, we see the conflict between the two major functions of the central city—on the one hand, the maintenance of a highly urbane style of life and of a concentrated and diverse market for the exchange of wealth and ideas; on the other hand, the provision of a place in which the lower classes, especially the immigrant lower classes, are housed, employed educated, and by slow degrees assimilated to the standards of civility of American society. It is no longer possible to keep these two functions geographically separate within the central city, because it is no longer possible to confine the lower classes to high-density ghettoes—they have moved out into low-density ghettoes, thereby consuming much more land area than before, including land around or near the city's universities, hospitals, museums, and theaters.

The psychological urban problem cannot be solved, it can only be coped with. Indeed, it has been caused precisely because so many other problems *have* been coped with, if not solved. Efforts to lessen the gap between expectations and achievements will, in the short run, only make the discontent produced by that gap more acute. That is one of the inevitable tensions in a society committed to self-improvement.

Technical problems, political solutions

The second kind of urban problem might be called the "technical" problem. By this I mean both that the problems are created because people are living in highly interdependent, dense settlements in an industrial society and that the solutions to these problems are technically feasible. If the problems are not solved, it is not for lack of knowledge. It might be more meaningful, indeed, to call them "political" problems, inasmuch as the obstacles to their solution are largely political.

These problems result partly from the fact that we are constantly getting in each other's way or otherwise committing various nuisances. We pollute the air with soft coal soot and with hydrocarbons from automobile exhausts; we pollute rivers and lakes with industrial and residential sewage; we congest city streets with cars, and sidewalks with pedestrians. The problems are also in part the result of consuming natural resources—e.g., open space and park land—and of making future generations bear the cost of this consumption. (Or to say the same thing in other words: we spend less on urban—and suburban—beauty than would be spent if everyone who will at some time enjoy that beauty were here now to vote on the matter.) Finally, the "technical" problem is also the result of an imbalance between the costs and benefits of various essential local services—education, police protection, welfare, and the like. Everyone would agree that supplying such services is a common responsibility which one should not be able to escape simply by moving away from the place where such facilities are maintained. Yet this is exactly what many of us do when we leave the central city for the suburbs. If the central city is to continue to perform its traditional functions of housing, employing, educating, policing, and supporting the poor and the disadvantaged (and the only alternative is to spread the poor and the disadvantaged throughout the suburbs), then it must be able to tap the taxable wealth of all of us.

What all these problems—nuisances, scarce collective resources, fiscal imbalance—have in common is that they result from a situation in which the costs and benefits of urban life are imperfectly related. People who get the benefits of consuming attractive land, driving cars on city streets, or cheaply disposing of waste products and junked cars, do not pay their fair share of the costs of vital central city services. Similarly, people who inhale the foul air, gaze at the ruined landscape or the junked cars, or put up with the traffic congestion, have no way of being reimbursed for having these annoyances inflicted on them.

There is no reason in principle why these problems cannot be solved or significantly alleviated. We know, or can discover, techniques for stopping pollution; the crucial task is devising an appropriate combination of legal sanctions, tax policies, and incentives that will make these techniques effective. Open space and other unique natural resources can be conserved by public purchase, by easements, and by tax policies. Those persons who are determined to produce ugliness in parts of the city where ugliness is out of place (and this is not everywhere; every city, like every home, ought to have some place—the equivalent of Fibber McGee's closet—where we can store necessary ugliness) can be restrained by fines, taxes, and laws from carrying on those activities, or can be induced by subsidies to hide the ugliness by appropriate devices. There is nothing very difficult about hiding or getting rid of junked automobiles—provided that the people who are pleased by the absence of junk are willing to share the necessary cost of achieving the result. Even the design of private buildings can be improved by rewarding builders who leave open spaces around their buildings and who hire good architects and artists. The fiscal imbalance between public needs and public resources in the central city can be corrected by using a combination of transfer payments and user charges to insure that the suburbanite who uses the central city pays his fair share of the cost of that use and that everyone, regardless of whether he uses the facilities, pays his fair share of the cost of supplying essential common services such as education, police protection, and the like.

Traffic congestion is a somewhat more complicated matter, for it is not obvious in what precise sense it constitutes a problem. Congestion arises because many people want to use limited space; in a sense, as Martin Meyerson and Edward Banfield point out (*Boston: The Job Ahead*), congestion is a means by which we ration access to a scarce resource (i.e., a desirable central city location) just as the price system is a way we ration the enjoyment of most other commodities (e.g., Cadillacs). The only way congestion could be eliminated entirely is to reduce the attractiveness of a given location to the point that no one will want to go to any one place any more than he will want to go to any other. Clearly this is both impossible and undesirable—central locations are central precisely because there are certain things people want to do in the company of large numbers of other people, or because large numbers of customers or workers are necessary to carry on various activities.

But congestion can be reduced if we provide other ways of rationing access besides traffic jams. One way—politically risky, but nonetheless likely to grow in favor—is to assess a charge on automobiles driven into central city locations, the amount of such a charge either to be based on the full cost of accommodating the car (parking space, police and fire protection, road use), in which case it is simply a user charge, or to reflect some penalty cost selected to deter the use of cars rather than merely to finance their accommodation.

The other strategy to deal with congestion is, of course, to subsidize mass transit facilities. The enthusiasm with which this proposal has been embraced by most public spokesmen suggests that their advocacy is based as much on an emotional dislike for automobiles (especially those parts made of chromium) as it is on a sober assessment of the comparative costs and benefits of various transportation programs. There are no doubt communities where the development of this kind of mass transit makes sense, either because of the population densities involved, or the investment already sunk in train tracks and equipment, or both. It is also perfectly clear, as John Meyer, John Kain, and Martin Wohl point out in their comprehensive study, *The Urban Transportation Problem*, that the vast majority of American cities could not possibly support a rail-based system without staggering subsidies. In fact, most communities would be better served by a mixed transportation plan that relied on a combination of user charges on automobiles entering the central city, high-speed bus service in reserved lanes on existing roadways, and various mechanical devices to regulate the flow of cars on and off expressways. The prosperity that produced the massive shift away from the train and bus and to the private car cannot be reversed by public policy; its effects, however, can be regulated.

The Negroes in the city

The third sense in which there is an urban problem is the most important. It results from the fact that the large central cities are where the immigrant lower classes congregate.

Today, with Negroes constituting the most important part of the urban lower class, the challenge to the central city is greater than ever before, because the Negroes create a unique set of problems. Unlike most previous migrants, they are marked by color. Furthermore, the Negro came originally from a slave culture in which he had no opportunity to acquire a complete range of political, economic, and social skills, and in which his family was subjected to systematic disruption and abuse. Unlike other immigrants—even other colored immigrants, such as the Chinese and Japanese—the Negro began his migration to the central city lacking the relevant skills and experience, and with a weakened family structure. Urbanization, of course, places further strains on community and family ties. The result is a central-city population with little money, few skills, a weakened capacity to cope with large bureaucratic institutions, and high rates of social disorder—crime, broken homes, alcoholism, narcotics addiction, illegitimacy, delinquency, and unemployment.

The argument over the details of the Moynihan Report on the Negro family has to some extent obscured its most important implication, which I cannot believe anyone will reject: if all Negroes were turned white tomorrow, they would still have serious problems. Whether these problems are more the result of a weak family structure, or of the impact of urbanization, or of the past history of discrimination, or of a depressed economic position, is very hard to say. But I suspect that whatever the cause, there are few aspects of this problem which will not be cured—or will not cure themselves—in time.

In time. In how much time? And what does one do in the meantime? I incline to the view that in the long run the acculturational problem of the Negro—i.e., the problem of being unable, as an individual or a family, and as compared with previous migrants to the cities, to cope with the fact of poverty—will be reduced by improvements in income and education; habits will change as class changes, though more slowly. Perhaps I say this because it is easier to think of changing class position than cultural values, though altering the former is hard enough. Perhaps I say it because of the great and obvious differences between middle-class and lower-class Negroes, differences much greater than those between middle-class and lower-class whites. And perhaps I am wrong.

But whatever the strategic factor is, we cannot as yet say we have discovered it. The best that can be said in our favor is that we are perhaps the only free society which has ever tried to change a large racial minority by massively upgrading its condition. The debate about what the goal of "equality" means—whether a random distribution of Negroes throughout the city and the social structure, or a distinctive Negro enclave with guaranteed rights of entry and departure, or some combination of the two—is less interesting to me than the fact that, wherever we want to go, we don't know how to get there. And for the present, the urban Negro is, in a fundamental sense, *the* "Urban Problem."

If there were no Negroes in our large cities, or if the only difference between Negroes and whites were the accident of skin color, the rate of serious crime in our cities would immediately be cut by about a third. The welfare rolls would be cut by a like amount. The population of our state prisons would be cut by more than one-fourth. No one can be sure how many fewer narcotics addicts or alcoholics there would be, but no one could argue the reduction would be negligible. The number of "dilapidated" homes would be further reduced by about 30 percent.

What we don't know

If solutions to the technical problems facing our cities are impeded because our motivation does not yet equal our knowledge, then solutions to our fundamental problems are impeded because our understanding does not yet match our motivation. A dramatic crisis—an epidemic of deaths resulting from smog, for example—will quickly produce the motivation necessary to move swiftly on many of the technical problems. But we have already had our crisis with respect to the fundamental problems—Watts, for example—and the result has only been a frantic and futile search for "answers." There is no ready-made knowledge stored up in our universities or foundations on how to prevent a Watts, or even on what causes a Watts. The malaise of lower-class life in the central cities has been a matter of scholarly concern for several decades, but there is not much scholarly wisdom to show for it, except a general—and probably sound—belief that higher incomes, more education, and less discrimination are desirable things. For thirty years, various experiments have been conducted in an effort to reduce juvenile delinquency; although we have occasionally been successful in eliminating gang warfare (primarily by disarming and policing the gangs), no one has been able to reduce the apparent rates of the most common form of delinquency, theft. We know that the rates of certain "private" crimes—murder, for example—cannot be changed no matter what tactics the police may use. We suspect that certain "street" crimes (auto theft, or purse snatching) can be reduced by "saturation" police patrol, but no one knows whether what occurs is actually a reduction or simply a displacement of the crime to other parts of the city—or, if a reduction, whether it can be made permanent. No one is yet precisely certain what effect segregated schools have on Negro children, or how much of the slower rates of learning of these children is the result of family background (which is very hard to change) or of the school experience (which is somewhat easier to change). We do not even know how much narcotics addiction there is, much less what to do about it on any large scale. Above all, we do not know how much urban pathology is in some sense inevitable and how much space, therefore, our central cities must expect to reserve for the derelicts, the alienated, and the unaspiring poor.

One would suppose that we know most about one prerequisite for progress among the lower classes—employment opportunities. Yet, although the debate between the proponents of achieving full employment by stimulating aggregate demand and those who insist that we need structural change (job retraining, family allowances, vocational education, public works) has been raging for a decade or more, neither side has convinced the other. More importantly, *neither* strategy has been seriously tried. Until the war in Vietnam required a greater use of our industrial capacity, the federal government did not attempt as vigorously as it might, through tax and fiscal policies, to create a full employment economy—in part from fear of inflation, in part from a concern over the international balance of payments. Nor have the structuralists tried a program of public works, guaranteed incomes, worker resettlement, and vocational education on a scale sufficient to test the feasibility of eliminating the so-called "pockets of poverty." The war on poverty contains some of the elements of a "structuralist" strategy—for example, the Job Corps as a way of developing skills and motivation, and Project Head Start as a long-term attack on rates of learning—but it will be some time before we know how successful they are and to what extent such methods can be generalized.

Alternative policies

Federal policies have moved only by halting steps in a direction that acknowledges that the "urban problem" is not primarily, or even significantly, a housing problem. The rent supplement program is a recognition of the need to deal directly with the cause of slum housing—i.e., the fact that there are people who cannot afford non-slum housing. The call for legislation to bar discrimination in the housing market is a recognition of the need to reduce the inflated prices of Negro housing by giving Negroes access to the entire housing market. (Although the principle is sound, not much is likely to happen as a result of such a statute; open occupancy laws already on the books in many states and cities have not broken up the Negro enclaves, partly because housing outside such enclaves sometimes costs more than housing inside them.) But for the present, these and other modifications are largely frosting on a tasteless cake. The major thrust of federal policy is now, and always has been, a commitment to maintain and enhance the physical shells of existing American cities—adding, where appropriate, a few new towns to handle the overflow. The desire to make all American cities "livable" not only exaggerates the extent to which cities are now "unlivable," but it thoughtlessly lumps together all cities—whether or not they continue to serve any functions, whether or not there are any rational grounds for conserving them at public expense, and even whether or not the local leadership conceives of urban conservation as driving the poor across the city line into somebody else's city.

It was long argued that urban interests deserved a cabinet department, just as agricultural interests had one. It is a disturbing analogy. For thirty years the Department of Agriculture has, in effect, been committed to the preservation of farms regardless of how inefficient or economically unsound they became. Now there are signs that pressure from mayors and downtown business interests may move the Department of Housing and Urban Development even farther toward a policy of guaranteeing the perpetual existence of the central business district of every American city, no matter how inefficient or economically unsound they may become.

There is nothing sacrosanct about the present patterns or functions of urban life; cities, like people, pass through life cycles during which their values and functions change. But the implicit commitment of our new Department to physical structures, rather than to concrete human needs, makes it almost impossible for it to distinguish between cities which need help and cities which do not; any city "needs" help if it says it does. The result is that while the rhetoric of the "urban crisis" is aimed at the great national and regional centers of commerce, culture, education, and government—Washington, New York, Philadelphia, Boston, Los Angeles—the reality of federal programs can be found in Barre, Vermont, and Wink, Texas. *Over half of all cities with urban renewal projects have populations of less than 25,000* (in this respect, HUD is more democratic than the Department of Agriculture; whereas the latter was of more help to the big than to the small farmer, the former is subsidizing the smaller as well as the larger cities).

There is an alternative policy which could direct federal activities. It would require, not the scrapping of existing federal programs, but only their redirection. Such a policy would begin with a recognition of the different kinds of "urban problems"—some of which, like poverty, are as much rural as urban problems, and others of which, like the gap between expectations and achievements, are not problems that government can do anything about. Such a policy would, I suggest, contain the following elements:

First, the federal government would assume responsibility for placing a floor under the capacity of Americans to acquire a minimally satisfactory level of personal and family amenities—housing, food, clothing, medical care. Where possible, guaranteeing such resources to every family would be done by combining aggregate fiscal policies which produce full employment with direct income transfers—in the form, say, of a negative income tax, family allowances, or rent subsidies—such that each family has maximum free choice as to the type and location of its housing. Some conservatives will of course object that this is a "dole," productive of moral debilitation. I submit that, unless we are willing to tolerate privation, we of necessity must have some sort of dole; the real question is whether it will be one which minimizes choice and maximizes bureaucratic intervention in private lives (as is the case with public housing projects and many welfare programs) or one with the opposite characteristics. As far as moral debilitation is concerned, I have found no compelling psychological or theological evidence that the souls of the poor are in greater danger from government subsidies than are the souls of businessmen, intellectuals, and farmers, all of whom have been enjoying government largesse for some time.

I am under no illusion that the problems of the central-city poor, white and Negro, will vanish because we adopt an income maintenance strategy. All I am suggesting is that whatever else must be done to cope with poverty, there will be little progress unless the one indisputable component of poverty—low incomes—is dealt with by methods more effective and less debasing than those which require husbands to first desert their wives and children before these latter can apply for welfare.

Second, public power and public funds would be used to provide those common benefits (or, as the economists say, collective goods) which are enjoyed, and thus must be paid for, by everybody. Fresh air, pure water, open spaces, park land, and police protection are the most common examples of indivisible benefits, to achieve which public powers must be exercised. Ironically, it is in this area (where even in the days of Adam Smith it was agreed that public intervention was required) that federal action has been the slowest in developing. The reason, of course, is understandable enough; most collective goods require control over those aspects of community life—the education of the young, the policing of the city, and the use of land—which Americans have long insisted be kept in local hands. So long as most of us lived and worked in the same place—i.e., the central city—purely local control of these matters may have made sense. What services we used as we travelled to and from work we also paid for through taxes. Upper-middle-class citizens with a strong interest in (and a healthy capacity to pay for) common benefits, such as parks and the like, lived in—and often governed—the central city. With the exodus to the suburbs, and our self-segregation into radically different kinds of communities on the periphery, differences in preferences and income which used to co-exist within a single taxing authority now are separated by political boundaries. If the incidence of costs and benefits of various collective goods is to be equalized throughout the metropolitan area, some higher taxing authority must assume responsibility for transfer payments. There are only two such authorities—the state and the federal government.

Third, where possible, central cities facing a fiscal crisis ought to receive block grants from state or federal governments in order to help defray the cost of servicing the poor, providing decent education and police protection, etc. At the present time, cities must commit themselves to a whole range of federally conceived programs in order to get money they urgently need, even though many of these programs may be either irrelevant or harmful to the interests of parts of the city's population. Cities with an eroding tax base seize upon urban renewal as the only way to get federal support for that tax base, even though it is a clumsy and inefficient way—it requires destroying homes or businesses, allowing land to lie vacant for long periods of time, and pushing people who consume high levels of local services into neighboring cities where they cause the whole dreary cycle to be repeated. The already-enacted federal aid to education program is a step in the right direction, though the amounts will surely have to be increased. Even if one were to accept the dubious proposition that the cities could be rebuilt to retain or lure back the middle classes—a proposition that lies at the bottom of much of the urban renewal strategy—any but the most blind partisans ought to concede that what drives the middle classes out of the city in the first place may have much less to do with the physical condition of the buildings than with the quality of the public schools and the level of public safety. Subsidizing these institutions, rather than the rents the middle classes have to pay, strikes me as both fairer (since it will help the poor as well as the better off) and more likely to produce results.

Fourth, the federal government ought to encourage, through special incentives, cities to experiment with various user charges as a way of making certain that non-residents pay their fair share of the services they use in the cities where they work or shop, and that residents have a more precise and personal way than voting for or against the mayor to indicate how much of a particular local service they really desire for themselves. At the present time, large groups of people get something for nothing—non-residents who park on the city's streets, for example, or residents who, owning no taxable property, enthusiastically vote for more and more free public facilities. The whole burden is thrown on the property-tax payer, and he cannot sustain it.

Fifth, urban renewal and other land clearance programs can be used as a tool to aid in providing common benefits (by assembling land and financing good design for public buildings, schools, and the like) and as a way of eliminating hazardous or unsalvageable structures. If renewal is to do more than this, then to insure against the excesses of the past it ought to be hedged about with the most explicit restrictions. If decent low-cost housing is to be torn down for high-cost housing, then it should be done only when either a clear collective benefit (e.g., a new park) will result or when *surplus* low-cost housing can be removed. The latter would require a prior showing that the vacancy rate among low-cost housing units in that city or area is high enough to make possible the absorption of displaced families without serious economic loss, and that a close study of the social structure of the affected neighborhood reveals it to be primarily a place with high transiency rates where strong family life and neighborhood ties have not developed. And if a subsidy is conferred on the developer and his new upper-income tenants, then provision ought to be made to recapture that subsidy over time—perhaps by making the federal contribution a long-term loan rather than a grant (this was actually proposed when the original legislation was first debated in Congress) or by allowing the city to adopt special tax measures to recover the subsidy for itself.

Conclusion

It is possible to conceive of a rational policy for dealing with so-called "urban" problems, once one begins to realize that the word "urban" is less relevant than the word "human." And perhaps this is implied in the Demonstration Cities Program proposed by the President, though the details are still sufficiently vague to make its real significance unclear. Leaving aside the obvious contradictions in the "guidelines" for determining whether a city is qualified to participate (for example, the incompatibility between maximum "coordination" achieved by a "single authority with adequate powers" and "widespread citizen participation" in the demonstration area or the conflict between maximum employment of indigenous workers and the development of labor-saving technologies), one may take the optimistic view that the Demonstration Cities Program is simply a fancy way of describing a new federal effort to impose federal standards on the local use of renewal money, so that renewal projects are more likely to serve legitimate national objectives rather than what ever purposes, good or bad, local leaders cook up. The demand for more local "co-ordination" and "planning" may be a tactic for creating an organized local constituency for HUD. A good case can be made for such intentions, but it is doubtful that a Congress sensitive to local interests and pressures is going to let HUD or anyone else get away with it entirely. And this, or course, should provide a good political reason for shifting federal efforts more in the direction of universalistic programs (maintaining the incomes of all poor, and subsidizing services—like education—that provide general benefits) and away from particularistic programs (tear down some buildings and subsidize others). So long as programs are designed to achieve particular effects in particular places, they will frequently be used by local groups to the disadvantage of the poor and powerless, or to produce effects that the federal taxpayer ought not have to pay for. And so long as HUD has no consistent federal policy, Congress will be able to insist that policies be set at the local level.

There is a bureaucratic as well as political reason for favoring universalistic programs—large bureaucracies are not very good at performing complex tasks requiring the exercise of a great deal of co-ordination over disparate activities, the accomplishments of which cannot be easily measured or evaluated. Direct income transfers, block grants to local governments, and increased reliance on individual choice are ways of reducing the impossible burdens on government agencies, most of which are (necessarily) staffed by men of average attainments. Making full allowance for the good intentions behind the Demonstration Cities Program, its central problem—apart from (though related to) the obscurity as to its goals and the mystery as to its means—is that it is an effort to improve on old programs, not by changing them or by substituting a wholly new strategy, but by creating a new apparatus to show how, by "co-ordination" (i.e., more administration), the job can be done better. But the failures of the past sixteen years have been precisely the failures of administration—of seeking inappropriate or incompatible goals, or of being unable to attain given goals, or of failing to take into account the consequences of working toward these goals. Overcoming the weaknesses of administration by providing more administration is likely to succeed only if extraordinary men do the administering. There are such men, but not many; simply hoping that enough of them wind up in HUD strikes me as, to say the least, imprudent.

For almost two decades we have been "attacking" the problems of the city—almost literally—by mounting successive assaults against various real and imagined difficulties. Each assault force has had its own leadership and ideology and the weaknesses of each have been the signal for a new assault, under different leadership and with a new ideology. First came public housing, then urban redevelopment, then urban renewal, and now the demonstration program. The old assaults of course never vanished, they just moved over a bit (not without complaints) to let the newcomers in. The common objective is to capture and hold central-city real estate; the differences in tactics concern the number of fronts on which the fighting is to proceed. In general, each successive assault has had broader objectives—the current President's message calls for a change in the "total environment." The motto is, "more is better." Perhaps it will all work out, if humane weapons are used and we evacuate the wounded. But I suspect that in the confusion the real enemies—poverty, ignorance, despair—may slip away, to live and strike again in another place.

The Metropolitan Education Dilemma: Matching Resources to Needs

Alan K. Campbell
Philip Meranto

This article examines how selected contextual changes in the metropolis influence both the quantity and quality of educational services large central cities are able to provide. Alan Campbell and Philip Meranto begin by delineating those contextual changes which have important consequences for the performance of the education function. They examine the characteristics of the people who reside in metropolitan America, and examine in particular the sorting-out process which gives rise to significant differences in the socioeconomic characteristics of central-city and suburban populations.

What have been the effects of this redistribution process? Recent contextual changes in most metropolitan areas have definitely had an impact on the provision of educational services. For example, a chief problem confronting central-city school systems involves their need for sufficient resources to educate the large numbers of so-called disadvantaged students in their school districts. To what extent are central cities capable of raising the necessary resources to adequately perform their educational functions? If the central cities cannot extract such resources from local assets, where are these resources to come from?

Obviously, the fiscal crisis currently confronting many large city school systems would not be as critical if cities had at their disposal an ample supply of fiscal resources. However, the declining tax base of many central cities and demands for a wider range and higher quality of public services give rise to a very real disparity between needs and resources. This disparity is nowhere more apparent than in the area of education.

What public-policy alternatives exist, and to what extent are they politically feasible? The most obvious solution would be to redistribute the population so as to reduce the concentration of disadvantaged pupils in central cities. Is this physically and politically feasible? Another solution would be to create educational parks or campuses which would contain a larger, more hetero- geneous school population. Is this monetarily and politically feasible?

No matter what the possibility of pupil redistribution, however, the central need is, and will remain, additional fiscal resources. Such resources must be procured from either the states or the federal government. The fundamental question, therefore, really revolves around the ability of federal and state governments to raise additional revenue, and their willingness to redistribute these resources according to need. *If this is not done, no major improvement in the situation confronting central-city school systems can be expected. What is the likelihood that the federal partners will undertake such action? States frequently collect and distribute funds to local school districts, but how willing have they been to redistribute such resources on the basis of need?*

Introduction

The metropolitanization of American society has gained widespread attention in recent years from a notable variety of scholars, popular writers, and public officials. Some scholars have preoccupied themselves with tracing the historical roots of metropolitanism, while others have attempted to demonstrate empirical relationships between metropolitanism and the social, economic, and political dimensions of society. Popular writers have inter- preted some of these findings for the general public, and they have usually stressed the so-called "decay" of large American cities and the multitude of problems plaguing these urban centers. While journalists and scholars have been describing and analyzing the metropolitan phenomenon, public officials have been struggling with its policy implications. For these officials, the fact of metropolitanism, however dimly perceived, complicates many of the problems with which they must deal and influences many of the decisions they make.

The extent of this concern with one of the major forces of change in postwar America has been beneficial but, on occasion, misleading. On the one hand, it has stimulated popular interest and knowledge of the changing character of American culture. Further, it has prompted a wide assortment of research efforts about the causes and consequences of metropolitanism. On the other hand, there has been a tendency to see nearly all of the changes and problems which characterize contemporary America as consequences of the metropolitan process. Too often the interrelationships between substantive

"The Metropolitan Education Dilemma: Matching Resources to Needs" by Alan K. Campbell and Philip Meranto is reprinted from *Educating an Urban Population* (1967), pages 15-36, edited by Marilyn Gittell, by permission of the Publisher, Sage Publications, Inc.

problems and metropolitanism have been blurred rather than clarified by this kind of perception. Similarly, there has been a tendency to assume that the problems involved in the provision of any public service (education, welfare, health, transportation, and so forth) are all related to or result from metropolitanism. This is not the case. With every function there are problems that would exist even if the country had not become metropolitan. Further, the fact of metropolitanism is not a problem in itself, but the dynamics which underpin it and the patterns which accompany it may be perceived by individuals and groups within the society as creating problems, and in many instances the problems thus perceived can be solved only by public action.

The tendency to equate both social change and functional concerns with metropolitanism is evident in the field of education. Much of the literature which purports to discuss the implications of metropolitanism or urbanism for education is, instead, simply a catalog of the substantive issues which characterize the education function. The metropolitan component of the problems is often assumed to be self-evident, and no effort is made to demonstrate the relationship between metropolitanism and the substantive issues.

It is the primary purpose of this article to delineate those aspects of metropolitanism which produce important consequences for the performance of the education function in large urban centers. Such an analysis necessitates, first, an investigation of basic population trends and an examination of the distributional results of these trends on income, educational attainment, race, and the nature of school population. Second, the relationships between these population attributes and the provision of educational services are analyzed, as are the relationships between education needs and the quantity and quality of resources available in the various parts of the metropolis. And finally, the public policy alternatives are examined in terms of their ability to meet the demonstrated needs.

Characteristics of metropolitan America

The most often cited statistic about metropolitanism is the growing proportion of the American population which lives in metropolitan areas.[1] By 1964 this proportion had reached 65 percent, and projections indicate that it will approach 70 percent by 1970. A simultaneous phenomenon, perhaps of even greater significance for the education function, is the redistribution of people between the central city and its suburbs. There has been a gradual but

---

[1] The Census Bureau definition of the metropolitan area and of its component parts is followed throughout this article. That definition is as follows: "Except in New England, a standard metropolitan statistical area (an SMSA) is a county or group of contiguous counties which contain at least one city of 50,000 inhabitants or more or 'twin cities' with a combined population of at least 50,000. In addition to the county, or counties, containing such a city or cities, contiguous counties are included in an SMSA if, according to certain criteria, they are essentially metropolitan in character and are socially and economically integrated with the central city." In New England, towns are used instead of counties.

consistent decrease in the proportion of total metropolitan population which lives within central cities. In 1900 over 60 percent of the metropolitan population lived within central cities; by 1965 this share had declined to under 50 percent.

This decline in the proportion of the metropolitan population living in central cities represents for many cities, particularly those in the largest metropolitan areas, an absolute decline in the central city population. Table 1 illustrates this fact by presenting the percent of population change for both central city and outside central city between 1950 and 1960 for selected large cities. The few instances of an increase in central city population were caused, in most cases, by annexation rather than by population growth within the original boundaries of the central city. Clearly, the population within the largest metropolitan areas is decentralizing.

Table 1. Population change in 15 largest SMSAs central city and outside central city: 1950-1960

SMSA	Central city		Outside central city	
	1960	Percent change since 1950	1960	Percent change since 1950
New York	7,781,984	−1.4	2,912,649	75.0
Chicago	3,550,404	−1.9	2,670,509	71.5
Los Angeles*	2,823,183	27.1	3,919,513	82.6
Philadelphia	2,002,512	−3.3	2,340,385	46.3
Detroit	1,670,144	−9.7	2,092,216	79.3
Baltimore	939,024	−1.1	787,999	72.4
Houston	938,219	57.4	304,939	44.8
Cleveland	876,050	−4.2	920,545	67.2
Washington	763,956	−4.8	661,911	87.0
St. Louis	750,026	−12.5	1,310,077	51.9
Milwaukee	741,324	16.3	452,966	41.7
San Francisco†	1,159,932	−4.5	1,075,495	55.0
Boston	697,197	−13.0	1,892,104	17.6
Dallas	679,684	56.4	403,997	30.7
New Orleans	627,525	10.0	240,955	109.6
United States (all SMSAs)	58,004,334	10.7	54,880,844	48.6

*Includes Long Beach.
†Includes Oakland.
Source: U. S. Bureau of the Census, U. S. Census of Population: 1960. Vol. I, Characteristics of the Population, Part A. *Number of inhabitants, Table 33.*

The significance of these shifts for the education function would be substantial even if the population redistribution between central city and suburbs was random relative to the socioeconomic characteristics of the people involved. But this is not the case. The shifting is not only a matter of numbers of people; it also involves a sorting-out process. In general, it is the poor, less educated, nonwhite Americans who are staying in the central city and the higher income, better educated, whites who are moving out, although this description must be qualified somewhat in terms of the size of the metropolitan area and region of the country in which it is located. The larger the metropolitan area, however, the more accurate is this description.[2]

This sorting-out process has resulted in a median family income for central city residents in 1959 which was 88.5 percent of outside central city income; $5,940 for central cities, compared to $6,707 for the suburbs. Although median family income for both central city and outside central city residents has grown since 1959, the gap is widening, with central city median family income in 1964 at $6,697, while for outside central city areas it was $7,772, a proportionate relationship of 86.2 percent.[3]

These nation-wide averages hide important differences between metropolitan areas which can be explained, in part, by differences in population size. Overall, the larger metropolitan areas have higher family incomes than the smaller ones. In metropolitan areas having populations of over 3 million—the largest size category—the percent of families earning over $10,000 a year is almost double the percent earning less than $3,000 a year. Further, it is only in this category that the central cities have a higher proportion of their population over $10,000 than under $3,000.

The large metropolitan areas have less poverty proportionately than the small ones. This finding, however, is not as significant for the performance of the education function as is the contrast between central cities and their suburbs. It is the large, relatively affluent areas which possess the greatest income disparity between central cities and their suburbs. In the size category of over 3 million, for every 100 families in central cities earning under $3,000, there are 127 earning over $10,000. In the suburbs, the comparable number of families with an income over $10,000 is 312 for every 100 families earning under $3,000. In other words, there are 185 more families with income over $10,000 in the suburbs for every 100 families under $3,000 than is true for the central cities. The magnitude of this difference in income distribution between central city and outside central city declines as the size of the area decreases and, in fact, reverses itself for the two size-categories below 250,000 population.

The differences in income characteristics between central cities and their suburbs is reflected in the educational attainment of the respective populations. Again, the contrast between central city and suburbs is substantial: 40.9 percent of central city pupils have completed four years of high school or more, while outside the central cities the comparable percentage is 50.9. Once more the differences are greatest when one examines the data for individual large metropolitan areas (Table 2).

The explanation for the income and education differences between central city and suburb rests in part on differences in the distribution of nonwhite population within metropolitan areas.[4] Although the nonwhite component of

[2] For a complete discussion of these differences relative to size and region, see Advisory Commission on Intergovernmental Relations, *Metropolitan Social and Economic Disparities: Implications for Intergovernmental Relations in Central Cities and Suburbs,* Washington, D.C.: U.S. Government Printing Office, 1965.

[3] U.S. Bureau of the Census, *Consumer Income,* Series P-60, No. 48, April 25, 1966.

[4] The terms nonwhite and Negro are used interchangeably in this article since Negroes constitute 92 percent of the nonwhite classification as defined by the Census Bureau.

Table 2. Educational attainment of persons 25 years or older in 15 urbanized areas
by residence, by color: 1960 (four years of high school or more, in percent)

Urbanized area*	Central city	Urban fringe*	Central city nonwhites
New York	36.4	48.7	31.2
Chicago	35.3	53.9	27.3
Los Angeles	53.4	53.4	43.6
Philadelphia	30.7	48.0	23.6
Detroit	34.4	47.5	26.5
Baltimore	28.2	42.3	19.7
Houston	45.2	50.1	26.2
Cleveland	30.1	55.5	28.1
Washington	47.8	67.5	33.5
St. Louis	26.3	43.3	20.2
Milwaukee	39.7	54.4	26.0
San Francisco	49.4	57.9	39.1
Boston	44.6	55.8	36.2
Dallas	48.9	56.4	25.2
New Orleans	33.3	44.6	15.0
All urbanized areas	40.9	50.9	28.3

*This table utilizes urbanized area and urban fringe as units due to the availability of data. The Census Bureau defines an urbanized area as "the thickly settled portions of the SMSA." The urban fringe constitutes the urbanized area minus the central city. Source: Computed from U. S. Bureau of the Census, U. S. Census of Population: 1960, General Social and Economic Characteristics, Washington, D. C.: U. S. Government Printing Office, 1961; and U. S. Census of Population and Housing: 1960, Census Tracts, Washington, D. C.: U. S. Government Printing Office, 1961.

the American population has now distributed itself between metropolitan and nonmetropolitan areas in approximately the same proportion as the white population, the distribution within metropolitan areas follows a quite different pattern. It is well known that the proportion of nonwhites in central cities has been increasing, while the proportion in the suburban areas has been declining. This larger proportion of Negro population in central cities helps to account in part for the differences in educational achievement and income between central cities and suburbs. Due to a history of discrimination in all aspects of life, the Negro has a lower income and less education than does his white neighbor. In central cities, for example, the 1964 median family income for Negroes was $4,463, while for whites it was $7,212. In 1964 the percentage of all Negroes twenty-five years old and over having completed four years of high school was 17.1; the comparable percentage for whites was 31.3.

The impact of the growing proportion of nonwhite population in central cities is intensified for the schools by the even higher proportion of public school enrollment which is nonwhite. This difference in population and enrollment proportions is a result of age distribution, family composition, and the greater tendency of white parents to send their children to private and parochial schools. Table 3 shows, for 1960, the proportion of the total population of the largest cities which was nonwhite and the proportion of

Table 3.   Nonwhite population contrasted with nonwhite school enrollment
for 15 largest cities: 1960

City	Percent nonwhite of total population	Percent nonwhite of school population	Difference in proportions of nonwhite school enrollment and nonwhite population
New York	14.0	22.0	8.0
Chicago	22.9	39.8	16.9
Los Angeles	12.2	20.5	8.3
Philadelphia	26.4	46.7	20.3
Detroit	28.9	42.9	14.0
Baltimore	34.7	50.1	15.4
Houston	22.9	30.2	8.7
Cleveland	28.6	46.1	17.5
Washington	53.9	77.5	23.6
St. Louis	28.6	48.8	20.2
Milwaukee	8.4	16.2	7.8
San Francisco	14.3	30.5	16.2
Boston	9.1	16.4	7.3
Dallas	19.0	26.0	7.0
New Orleans	37.2	55.4	18.2

Source: U. S. Bureau of the Census, U. S. Census of Population: 1960, Selected Area Reports, Standard Metropolitan Statistical Areas and General Social and Economic Characteristics, 1960.

public school enrollment which was nonwhite. The ratio of nonwhites to whites is considerably higher in the school population than in the total population, and indications are that this is becoming increasingly the case.

The sorting-out process which produces significant differences in socio-economic characteristics between central city and suburban populations is the chief background factor against which the educational implications of metropolitanism must be examined. To the extent that these differences in characteristics produce different kinds of educational problems, the fact of metropolitanism is important to the provision of educational services.

Population composition and educational problems

The redistribution process described in the preceding section has left the central city school system with a disproportionate segment of pupils who are referred to as "disadvantaged," and this appears to be a trend that is continually increasing. These students are disadvantaged in terms of the income level and educational background of their parents, their family composition, and their general home environment. To the extent that education of the disadvantaged is a more complex phenomenon than the education of middle-income pupils, the central city school systems face a different and more serious set of problems than do suburban education systems.[5]

In the immediate postwar period, the most striking phenomenon in education related to the metropolitanization of the country was the impact on suburban areas of a rapidly increasing population. The suburbs, however, responded well to the challenge and rapidly met the new requirements in building the necessary physical facilities and the provision of a teaching staff. The significance of the suburban expansion for the central city schools, however, was only dimly, if at all, perceived. It is now clear that the suburbanization of the country, by draining the higher income families and much economic activity from the central cities, produced greater problems for education in central cities than it did for the suburbs.

As the proportion of disadvantaged students in the central cities has increased, there has been a simultaneous increase in what are known in the community as "undesirable" schools, schools to which parents would prefer not to send their children. Many of these schools are so characterized because of the large proportion (in many cases, nearly 100 percent) of the students who are Negro. Because of population trends and the residential pattern of most of our cities, it is increasingly difficult to rearrange district lines to achieve what is referred to as "racial balance" among schools. As a result, more and more central city schools are being designated as "undesirable."

The underlying cause for the undesirable label in educational terms, however, is low income, not race. Several studies have now substantiated that the single most important determinant of educational achievement is family income.[6] In the high correlation between income and test scores, income undoubtedly is a proxy, and a fairly accurate one, for a combination of factors—family characteristics, educational attainment of parents, home environment. When white parents resist sending their children to undesirable schools, this is not necessarily a racial issue, although it is often difficult to separate the racial and educational questions which currently surround controversies over central city schools.

The undesirable schools are unattractive not only to parents but also to first-rate teachers. Teachers seek to be assigned to the "better" schools within the city system, and many abandon central city districts entirely for more

[5] For a sampling of the literature which deals with this topic see Frank Riessman, *The Culturally Deprived Child,* New York: Harper and Row Publishers, Incorporated, 1962; Judith R. Kramer and Seymour Leventman, *Children of the Gilded Ghetto,* New Haven: Yale University Press, 1961; A. Harry Passow (Ed.), *Education in Depressed Areas,* New York: Teachers College, Columbia University, 1963; and C.W. Hunnicutt (Ed.), *Urban Education and Cultural Deprivation,* Syracuse, N.Y.: Syracuse University Press, 1964.

[6] Patricia Sexton, *Education and Income: Inequalities in Our Public Schools,* New York: The Viking Press; H. Thomas James, J. Alan Thomas, and Harold J. Dyck, *Wealth, Expenditures and Decision-Making for Education,* Stanford, Calif.: Stanford University Press, 1963; Fels Institute of Local and State Government, University of Pennsylvania, *Special Education and Fiscal Requirements of Urban School Districts in Pennsylvania,* 1964; and Jesse Burkhead, *Cost and Performance in Large City School Systems,* forthcoming publication of Metropolitan Studies Center, Syracuse University, as part of the Carnegie supported study of Large City Education Systems, 1967.

attractive suburban districts. Furthermore, central city systems find it increasingly difficult to attract choice graduates of the universities as new teachers.

The resource needs for central cities relate not only to teachers but to other educational needs as well. Cities have much older school plants than do suburbs, and the site costs for building new schools within central cities are substantially higher than those for the suburbs. In addition, there is greater competition within the cities for resources for such noneducation functions as police protection, street maintenance, and welfare than is true in the suburban areas. These noneducation needs compete for the same resources which the central city schools need to meet their pressing educational problems.

This set of central city education problems exists in a society which is in need of a continuous improvement in its educational output. The very fact of metropolitanization implies extended specialization in a society which is increasingly complex. The need, therefore, is for a better and better educated work force. To some extent, the suburban areas have responded to this need through the gradual improvement and sophistication of its curricula and teaching. Curriculum improvement in central cities, however, is much less discernible and is particularly lacking in the education of the disadvantaged.[7]

The answer to this problem does not rest with providing education with a different purpose for disadvantaged pupils. A suggestion by James Conant that disadvantaged pupils should be concentrated in vocational education hardly seems appropriate.[8] Improvement in the quality of vocational education is needed, but it should not be made especially for the disadvantaged. Among the disadvantaged, there are those who are capable of achieving high educational accomplishment in a great variety of fields and options, and in terms of equity the opportunities should be the same for them as for other pupils. Further, it is apparent that the greatest employment growth of the future will be in the white-collar occupations, not in vocational fields offered by most of today's vocational schools.

One of the central issues confronting large city schools, therefore, becomes the allocation of sufficiently massive resources to the field of education for the disadvantaged to help them overcome their present handicaps. To what extent are large central cities capable of providing the resources needed to meet these problems and where are these resources to come from if the central cities cannot provide them from local assets?

The availability of resources

The educational problems confronting large cities would not be nearly as critical if cities had at their disposal an ample supply of resources to deal with these difficulties. But this is not the case. The metropolitan process has not

[7]William W. Wayson, *Curriculum Development in Large City Schools,* forthcoming publication of Metropolitan Studies Center, Syracuse University, as part of the Carnegie supported study of Large City Education Systems, 1967.

[8]James B. Conant, *Slums and Suburbs,* New York: The New American Library, 1964, pp. 33-49.

only redistributed the population in a way that presents the central cities with a population having special educational difficulties; the process has simultaneously operated to weaken the local resource base which must be used to meet their needs.

It has already been noted that the central city component of the metropolitan area population has lower income levels than the population outside the central city. This pattern is particularly significant because it has become increasingly apparent that income is the single most important variable in explaining the expenditure levels of a community for both educational and noneducational services.[9] To a large extent, it is the income available which influences the ability of a governmental unit to meet the service requirements of its population. Central cities are simply losing ground in this respect, while their functional needs are simultaneously increasing.

Metropolitanism is characterized by the decentralization of economic activities from the core city to the surrounding areas, as well as by decentralization of population. Evidence of this trend can be found by examining the distribution of economic activity within specific metropolitan areas over time. For example, an investigation of the proportion of manufacturing carried on in the central city portion of twelve large metropolitan areas demonstrates that the central city percentage has clearly declined over the past three decades, particularly in the post-World War II period. Whereas the twelve cities accounted, on the average, for 66.1 percent of manufacturing employment in 1929, this proportion decreased to 60.8 percent by 1947 and then declined to less than half (48.9 percent) by 1958.[10]

A similar decentralizing trend for retail activity can be demonstrated by examining the growth of retail store sales in the metropolitan area as a whole, in the central city, and in the central business district of the core city for the period 1948 to 1958. Such a comparison was made for a sample of twenty-two large cities. It was found that with the exception of one (Birmingham, Alabama), the entire metropolitan area had increased its retail sales more than had the central city and far more than the central business district. This evidence illustrates that the historical dominance of the central city and its business district over regional retail activity is on the decline.[11] The patterns for manufacturing employment and retail sales reflect the fact that economic activity, like population, has migrated from the central city outward. This push for dispersal is related to a number of factors, including the need for physical space, the introduction of new industrial processes, the ascendance of the automobile and truck as means of transportation and shipping, the

[9] Alan K. Campbell and Seymour Sacks, *Metropolitan America: Fiscal Patterns and Governmental Systems,* forthcoming publication, Metropolitan Studies Center, Syracuse University, 1966.

[10] See Raymond Vernon, *The Changing Economic Function of the Central City,* New York: Committee for Economic Development, 1960; and U.S. Bureau of the Census, *Census of Manufacturing, 1958.* The cities include: Baltimore, Boston, Chicago, Cincinnati, Cleveland, Detroit, Los Angeles-Long Beach, New York, Philadelphia, Pittsburgh, St. Louis, and San Francisco-Oakland.

[11] See U.S. Bureau of the Census, *Census of Business, 1958* for the twenty-two cities which reported all three figures.

building of vast highway systems, and the spreading of the population throughout the metropolis.[12]

The consequences of this economic migration for the tax base of the central city have been widely discussed. As industries continue to move outward, taxable assessed valuation, the source of local property taxes, has barely held its own in many cities and has actually declined in several large cities. For example, in a recent five-year period, the percent changes in taxable assessed valuation for seven cities were as follows: Baltimore, -10.5 percent; Boston, -1.2 percent; Buffalo, -1.0 percent; Detroit, -2.0 percent; St. Louis, +1.1 percent; Philadelphia, +2.8 percent; and Cleveland -3.4 percent.[13] These changes in taxable valuation do not yield the necessary resources to deal with the problems facing these urban centers.

Table 4.   Five-year changes in per pupil taxable assessed valuation

	Percent of change over a five-year period*	
City	City	State (minus cities listed)
Baltimore	−19.3	10.2
Boston	− 5.3	*Not available*
Buffalo	− 8.6	26.1
Chicago	− 6.0	−0.2
Cleveland	− 9.9	4.2
Detroit	− 5.7	3.4
Houston	− 2.8	18.9
Los Angeles	5.1	5.6
Milwaukee	− 9.6	−1.1
New York City	32.4	26.1
Philadelphia	− 0.6	13.6
Pittsburgh	2.2	13.6
St. Louis	−10.6	3.1
San Francisco	5.9	5.6

*Change is for the most recent five-year period for which data are available.
Source: Research Council of the Great Cities Program for School Improvement, The Challenge of Financing Public Schools in Great Cities, *Chicago, 1964.*

Translated into educational terms, the recent performance of the tax base in large cities has not kept pace with the growth or nature of the school population in these cities. Indeed, an examination of the per pupil taxable valuation over a five-year period shows that ten large cities out of fourteen experienced a decrease in this source of revenue. Since local property taxes are the most important source of local educational revenues, large city schools can barely meet ordinary education needs let alone resolve the problems resulting from the shifting population distribution. (See Table 4.)

[12] Edgar M. Hoover and Raymond Vernon, *Anatomy of a Metropolis,* Garden City, N.Y.: Doubleday and Company, Inc., 1962.

[13] The Research Council of the Great Cities Program for School Improvement, *The Challenge of Financing Public Schools in Great Cities,* Chicago, 1964.

There is an additional factor which weighs against the capacity of central cities to meet their pressing educational needs. The postwar intensification of urbanization and metropolitanization has resulted in a demand for a wider range and higher quality of public services than at any other time in the nation's history. These demands are particularly great in the largest cities, where the necessity for providing a wide variety of welfare, public safety, sanitation, traffic control, and street maintenance services has been most pressing. The fact that central cities have responded to these demands is reflected in the data included in Table 5. An investigation of the fiscal patterns in thirty-six Standard Metropolitan Statistical Areas revealed that for the year 1957, the central cities in these areas were spending $25.66 more per capita in total expenditures than the communities in the outlying areas. Unfortunately for education systems, this difference was not due to higher educational expenditures in the central cities. In fact, their education expenditures were $27.82 per capita less than what was spent on education in the corresponding suburban areas. It was in the noneducational category that the central city exceeded the outside central city area in expenditures. In this sample, central cities spent about $53.00 more per capita on noneducation services than their surrounding communities. Further, this difference is largely due to the "all other" classification, which includes the traditional municipal services that cities, unlike suburban communities, must provide. The cost and number of noneducational governmental services tend to increase with the size and density of a district and to consume a larger proportion of the budget in major cities where many services are provided for nonresidents as well as for residents. It is reasonable to suggest that this "municipal overburden" is supported at the expense of the education function.[14]

The figures in Table 5 also show that the central cities were supporting these expenditure levels by taxes that were $23.29 per capita higher than in areas outside the cities. In contrast, the cities received about $5.00 per capita less in total intergovernmental aid and, most importantly, $12.31 less per capita in education aid than did suburban areas, where income was higher. In other words, not only are central cities pressed to support a large array of services by a relatively shrinking tax base, but they tax themselves more heavily to do so and they receive less intergovernmental aid than the more wealthy communities in their metropolitan area. This fiscal pattern borders on the ironic when it is realized that central city education systems must compete for educational resources with suburban school districts which have higher income levels and receive a greater amount of state aid. In fact, the state aid system actually works to intensify rather than to resolve the educational crises facing large city school systems.

The multitude of fiscal difficulties faced by the central cities results in a lower per student expenditure in the cities than in surrounding suburbs.

---

[14] David C. Ranney, *School Government and the Determinants of the Fiscal Support for Large City Education Systems,* unpublished doctoral dissertation, Syracuse University, 1966.

Table 5.   *Fiscal characteristics: central city and outside central city areas,*
36 sample SMSAs: 1957

Per capita	Central city	Outside central city	Differences central city −outside central city
Total general expenditure	$185.49	$159.83	25.66*
Education expenditure	58.02	85.84	−27.82†
Current	49.16	61.72	−12.56†
Capital	8.86	24.12	−15.26†
Noneducation expenditure	127.48	73.95	53.53†
Total highways	16.55	14.41	2.14
Health and hospitals (current)	14.84	7.09	7.55†
Public welfare	10.22	8.34	1.88†
All other	85.70	43.80	41.90†
Taxes	109.07	85.78	23.29†
Property tax	92.06	78.58	13.48
Nonproperty tax	17.01	7.20	9.81†
Proxy variables			
Nonaided education expenditure (education taxes)	42.24	56.43	−14.19†
Nonaided noneducation expenditure (noneducation taxes)	108.33	60.39	47.94†
Total aid	34.65	39.72	− 5.07
Education aid	16.12	28.43	−12.31†
Noneducation aid	18.60	11.83	6.77*
Exhibit:			
Per capita income	1,998.86	2,280.50	−281.64*

*Significant at .05 level of confidence.
†Significant at .01 level of confidence.
Note: Totals do not add because of unallocated aid. All figures in per capita terms unless otherwise indicated.
Source: Alan K. Campbell and Seymour Sacks, op. cit.

Specifically, an examination of the thirty-seven largest metropolitan areas in the country indicated that the central city school districts in 1962 were spending an average of $144.96 less per pupil than their suburban counterparts.[15] This considerable difference in expenditures per student between central city and suburb would be serious even if the educational problems were the same for the two type areas; but, as has already been demonstrated, such is not the case.

It is not known what amount of additional resources per student would be necessary to provide an adequate education for the culturally disadvantaged. On the basis of studies yet to be published, it is clear that the present small amounts of additional resources being used in some cities for what is generally referred to as "compensatory education" are accomplishing very little.[16] The additional resources currently being allocated to these programs are simply not sufficient.

[15] For a breakdown by individual city, see the Sacks-Ranney article in this issue.
[16] Jesse Burkhead, op. cit.

In this respect it is interesting to note the amount per student which is being expended in the urban Job Corps Centers which have been established by the Federal Anti-Poverty Program to provide a meaningful education for disadvantaged pupils. Present costs for establishing and organizing the centers amount to $10,500 per student per year.[17] It is estimated that once the camps are in full operation and their costs level off, the expenditures per student will be reduced to $7,350 per year. Even if the subsistence cost (which in the regular public school system is absorbed by parents) is subtracted from this $7,350 figure, there remains a vast gap between the resulting figure and what is currently being spent in central city public schools. Assuming that the subsistence costs are $3,000 per year, this leaves a per pupil education expenditure of approximately $4,350. This figure presents a vivid contrast to education expenditures in many cities. New York City, for example, with the highest large central city expenditures per pupil in the country, expended $603.95 per pupil in 1961-1962, while Chicago spent $409.78 per student.

Obviously the quantity of resources being put into Job Corps education exceeds what is available or likely to become available for general central city education. Nevertheless, it does point the direction which must be followed if the disadvantaged schools in our central cities are to come near accomplishing their educational purposes. Such educational services as extensive counseling of individual students, small, specialized classes, and effective job training, all of which are furnished by the Job Corps, are not provided cheaply. The Job Corps Center at Camp Kilmer, New Jersey, has a student enrollment of approximately 2,000 and a teaching and administrative staff of about 450, a student-professional ratio of about 4.5 students to 1 professional. The present ratio in larger city school systems is between 25-30 students to 1 professional.

It may be argued that comparing general public schools to the Job Corps schools is not realistic, since the Job Corps concentrates on those whom the regular schools failed. The point, however, is that the regular school systems failed these students, in part because they did not have the resources to provide the kind and quality of education needed. The obvious need is for more resources and an allocation system which recognizes the areas and students with special needs.

This analysis of the resources available for central city education demonstrates the disparity between needs and resources. There is little indication that present trends will substantially alter these circumstances; in fact, there is good reason to believe that the situation is becoming more serious. If these trends are to be modified, imaginative public policy decisions must be identified and pursued. What public policy alternatives exist and to what extent are they politically feasible?

Public policy implications

A variety of means exists for attacking the lack of fit between educational needs and resources. Some of these are politically more feasible than others.

[17]"The Job Corps," *The New Yorker*, May 21, 1966, p. 112f.

Perhaps the most obvious solution would be to redistribute the population so as to reduce the concentration of disadvantaged pupils in cities. The demand for racial integration within public education points in this direction. There are, however, both physical and political obstacles to this course of action which, at the moment, appear to be insurmountable. First, the disadvantaged are concentrated in wide geographic areas within many cities. To redistribute these pupils throughout the city and throughout the metropolitan area, which would be necessary to achieve integration in the future, would require a transportation network so extensive and costly that it is both physically and politically impractical.

Obviously, there are neighborhood school districts where the redrawing of attendance areas within cities and perhaps the redrawing of district lines between cities and suburbs would substantially alter the present student balance in the schools. Where this is the case, however, political resistance is likely to be stiff. The recently discovered attachment of many people to the neighborhood school has produced powerful political support for present district lines and attendance areas. To assume that such changes could be accomplished on a metropolitan-wide basis is unrealistic.

There is, in fact, an inverse relationship between the intensity of political opposition to accomplishing some redistribution of pupils and the size of the area and proportion of the population involved. In cities where the proportion of disadvantaged students, particularly the proportion of Negro students, is relatively low (thereby making the redrawing of attendance area lines a meaningful alternative), the political resistance seems capable of preventing any substantial changes. Boston is a good example of this situation: On the other hand, where the political strength of the disadvantaged is great enough to initiate some change, the high proportion of students and large areas involved present a practical limitation on how much can be accomplished in this manner.

An alternative to the decentralization of disadvantaged students is the much-discussed creation of education parks or campuses which would contain many more pupils than the present single-building schools. By drawing on a larger enrollment area, school campuses would be able to concentrate services and would contain a more heterogeneous population, thereby, presumably, providing a higher quality of education for all students.

The concentration of disadvantaged students also would be lessened by the return of middle-income families to cities from the suburbs. It had been anticipated by some students of urban affairs that urban renewal would contribute to such a return. This reversal of the outward flow of people would have been beneficial in two ways: The mix of students in the schools would be improved and the tax base for supporting education would be strengthened. However, the contribution of urban renewal to revitalizing the central city has not been great. Much of the current disappointment over urban renewal has resulted from the lack of recognition of the importance of low-quality education as one of the primary factors motivating the move out of the city. It seems apparent that physical redevelopment, unless it is accompanied and closely interrelated with a variety of social improvements, particularly improvements in public education, will not attract the suburban-ite back to the city.

Whatever the possibility of pupil redistribution, the central need is and will remain additional resources for the education of the disadvantaged. Whether educated where they are presently located or elsewhere, the disadvantaged have special education needs. To meet these needs, which is the only way of guaranteeing equality of educational opportunity, additional resources are required.

The present allocation pattern of state aid does little to accomplish this. In fact, the aid pattern runs exactly counter to the need pattern. It is possible that as reapportionment is accomplished and as the nature of the problem becomes more evident, state aid formulas will be revised to correspond more closely with needs. It is important to note, however, that reapportionment will result in a much greater gain in representation for the suburbs than it will for central cities.[18] It may be that the suburban representatives will recognize their stake in an improved central city education system; but if they do not, the present pattern of higher aid to the suburbs may well be accentuated rather than reversed by reapportionment.

Perhaps the single most significant policy response to the set of problems described here has been the response of the Federal government as reflected in the Elementary and Secondary Education Act of 1965.[19] This program, combined with the antipoverty program, has given recognition for the first time to the problem of allocating more resources to education for the disadvantaged. However, although the concept underpinning the legislation is sound, the amount of aid provided for large cities is relatively small in relation to the need. In the case of New York City, for instance, the new Federal aid amounts to only 6.2 percent of total 1962 education expenditures. For Chicago, the figure is 2.9 percent, for Los Angeles 2.6 percent, with the highest figure among the fifteen largest cities being for New Orleans, where the new aid will amount to 17.5 percent of 1962 school expenditures. This program is clearly moving in the right direction; the task is to fortify it with enough money so that it can have a substantial impact.

Whatever means are used to provide the resources for the provision of adequate education services, they will have to come, in large part, from the middle- and higher-income suburbanites. If, therefore, the suburbanites resist

---

[18] Robert S. Friedman, "The Reapportionment Myth," *National Civic Review*, April, 1960, pp. 184-188.

[19] Title I of this law, which accounts for about $1.06 billion of the approximately $1.3 billion authorized, provides for grants to be made to local school districts on the basis of 50 percent of the average per pupil expenditures made in their state for the school year 1963-1964 multiplied by the number of five- to seventeen-year-old children in the local school district from families with an annual income below $2,000, or with a higher income resulting from aid to dependent children relief payments. Local districts receive their proportion of the funds under this formula only after plans they have submitted indicating how they will meet the special educational needs of disadvantaged students are approved by their state education department. The politics surrounding the enactment of this legislation are analyzed in Philip Meranto, *The Politics of Federal Aid to Education in 1965: A Study in Political Innovation*, unpublished doctoral dissertation, Syracuse University, 1966.

a redistribution of population or a redrawing of school district lines to create a more equitable balance in the present pupil ability distribution, the alternative—if the problem is to be met—is greater Federal and state taxes paid by persons of middle and high income.

The fundamental issue, therefore, really revolves around the ability and willingness of Federal and state governments to raise revenue and redistribute the resources according to need. If this is not done, no major improvement in the situation confronting central city school systems can be expected.

There remains, of course, the issue of the ability of school systems to make good use of additional resources. This question, which is discussed elsewhere in this issue, relates to the kinds of changes needed in both curriculum and teaching techniques if the educational disadvantages of many young people are to be overcome.

However that question is answered, the fact remains that quality education for all will not be accomplished until the resources are found to do the job.

Reformism and Public Policies in American Cities

Robert L. Lineberry
Edmund P. Fowler

In this selection, Robert Lineberry and Edmund Fowler examine whether governments that are products of the reform movement behave differently from those with unreformed institutions, even if the socioeconomic composition of their populations is similar. They are primarily concerned with the consequence of variation in the formal rules and procedures adopted by local units of government—form of government, type of constituency, and partisanship of elections—upon taxation and expenditure policies. How do you think the adoption of particular rules and procedures might affect public-policy decisions?

Although Lineberry and Fowler find very little difference in the socio-economic contextual characteristics of cities operating under either reformed or unreformed rules and procedures, they do find that, with the exception of partisan mayor council and ward cities which appear less willing to commit

What does
this mean?

their resources to public purposes than their reformed counterparts,
unreformed cities spend more and tax more than reformed cities.

They argue that when a city adopts reformed structures, it is governed more
on the basis of a rationalistic theory of administration and less in terms of
conflict among various interests. Lineberry and Fowler conclude, therefore,
that reformed cities are less responsive than unreformed cities to socio-
economic cleavages in their populations. When reformism is viewed as a
continuous variable, the political structures of the reform syndrome have an
additive effect—the greater the reformism, the lower the responsiveness. This
conclusion, which is very questionable, given the data Lineberry and Fowler
present, should be viewed as a hypothesis in need of further testing. In order
to adequately test such a hypothesis, what sort of data would you have to
collect?

Lineberry and Fowler further argue that the goal of the reformers has been
essentially realized. When a city adopts nonpartisan elections, at-large
constituencies, and manager government, it becomes less responsive to the
enduring conflicts of political life. According to their argument, reforms serve
to decrease the salience of "private regarding" demands and instead increase
the relative influence of "public regarding" agencies like the local press.
Political reforms have a significant impact on decreasing decision-making
conflict because electoral institutions of reformed governments serve to
insulate public-policy making from demands arising out of cleavages and
conflicts in the population.

Whether you agree or disagree with Lineberry's and Fowler's interpretation
of their data, the selection does raise a number of important questions about
the political implications of adopting particular formal rules and procedures.
Have Lineberry and Fowler presented sufficient evidence to indicate why
these factors bring about the taxing and expenditure patterns they found?
What is it about a city's form of government and its formal electoral
procedures which bring about particular policy choices?

In evaluating the findings of this selection, one should also consider the
conclusions drawn by Glen W. Fisher after he had examined revenue and
expenditure patterns in five large cities. Perhaps the most important factor
influencing variation in expenditures in these cities had to do with differences
in the responsibilities assigned to each one by their respective state
legislatures, and the extent to which they share responsibility with other
governmental units for the performance of such functions as sewage disposal,
hospitals, parks, and housing. An additional factor causing fluctuation in
expenditure levels had to do with differences in capital outlays undertaken
each year. Finally, the size of funds provided by the particular state (and in
some cases the federal government), along with the flexibility of the state
government in allowing their local municipalities to levy nonproperty taxes,
also gave rise to significant variation in expenditures. Formal rules and
procedures may be one very relevant determinant of revenue and expenditure
policies, but not necessarily of those discussed by Lineberry and Fowler.
Those that they particularly focus on may also be important, but unless

sufficient explanatory evidence is presented, we must look upon their findings with a great deal of skepticism.

A decade ago, political scientists were deploring the "lost world of municipal government" and calling for systematic studies of municipal life which emphasized the political, rather than the administrative, side of urban political life.[1] In recent years, this demand has been generously answered and urban politics is becoming one of the most richly plowed fields of political research. In terms originally introduced by David Easton,[2] political scientists have long been concerned with inputs, but more recently they have focused their attention on other system variables, particularly the political culture[3] and policy outputs of municipal governments.[4]

The present paper will treat two policy outputs, taxation and expenditure levels of cities, as dependent variables. We will relate these policy choices to socio-economic characteristics of cities and to structural characteristics of their governments. Our central research concern is to examine the impact of political structures, reformed and unreformed, on policy-making in American cities.

I. Political culture, reformism, and political institutions

The leaders of the Progressive movement in the United States left an enduring mark on the American political system, particularly at the state and

Reprinted from *The American Political Science Review*, vol. 61, no. 3 (September 1967), pp. 701-716, by permission of the publisher and authors. The authors are indebted to Professors Robert T. Daland, James W. Prothro, William R. Keech and James Q. Wilson for comments on an earlier draft of this paper. For assistance in statistical and methodological questions, the advice of Professor Hubert Blalock and Mr. Peter B. Harkins has been invaluable. The authors, of course, assume responsibility for all interpretation and misinterpretation.

[1] Lawrence J.R. Herson, "The Lost World of Municipal Government," *The American Political Science Review*, 51 (June, 1957), 330-345; Robert T. Daland, "Political Science and the Study of Urbanism," *ibid.*, 491-509.

[2] David Easton, "An Approach to the Analysis of Political Systems," *World Politics*, 9 (April, 1957), 383-400.

[3] Edward C. Banfield and James Q. Wilson, *City Politics* (Cambridge: Harvard University Press and the MIT Press, 1963); see also James Q. Wilson and Edward C. Banfield, "Public-Regardingness as a Value Premise in Voting Behavior," *The American Political Science Review*, 58 (December, 1964), 876-887.

[4] See, for example, Thomas R. Dye, "City-Suburban Social Distance and Public Policy," *Social Forces*, 4 (1965), 100-106; Raymond Wolfinger and John Osgood Field, "Political Ethos and the Structure of City Government," *The American Political Science Review*, 60 (June, 1966), 306-326; Edgar L. Sherbenou, "Class, Participation, and the Council-Manager Plan," *Public Administration Review*, 21 (Summer, 1961), 131-135; Lewis A. Froman, Jr., "An Analysis of Public Policies in Cities," *Journal of Politics*, 29 (February, 1967), 94-108.

municipal level. In the states, the primary election, the referendum, initiative and recall survive today. The residues of this *Age of Reform*,[5] as Richard Hofstadter called it, persist in municipal politics principally in the form of manager government and at-large and nonpartisan elections. The reformers were, to borrow Banfield and Wilson's phrase, the original embodiment of the "middle class ethos" in American politics. They were, by and large, White Anglo-Saxon Protestants reacting to the politics of the party machine, which operated by exchanging favors for votes.[6]

It is important that we understand the ideology of these reformers if we hope to be able to analyze the institutions which they created and their impact on political decisions. The reformers' goal was to "rationalize" and "democratize" city government by the substitution of "community oriented" leadership. To the reformers, the most pernicious characteristic of the machine was that it capitalized on socio-economic cleavages in the population, playing on class antagonisms and on racial and religious differences. Ernest S. Bradford, an early advocate of commission government with at-large elections, defended his plans for at-large representation on grounds that

> ... under the ward system of governmental representation, the ward receives the attention, not in proportion to its needs but to the ability of its representatives to 'trade' and arrange 'deals' with fellow members. ... Nearly every city under the aldermanic system offers flagrant examples of this vicious method of 'part representation.' The commission form changes this to representation of the city as a whole.[7]

The principal tools which the reformers picked to maximize this "representation of the city as a whole" were the commission, and later the manager, form of government, the nonpartisan election and the election at-large. City manager government, it was argued, produced a no-nonsense, efficient and business-like regime, where decisions could be implemented by professional administrators rather than by victors in the battle over spoils. Nonpartisan elections meant to the reformer that state and national parties, whose issues were irrelevant to local politics anyway, would keep their divisive influences out of municipal decision-making. Nonpartisan elections, especially when combined with elections at-large, would also serve to reduce the impact of socio-economic cleavages and minority voting blocs in local politics. Once established, these institutions would serve as bastions against particularistic interests.

Banfield and Wilson have argued that the "middle class ethos" of the reformers has become a prevalent attitude in much of political life. The middle class stands for "public regarding" virtues rather than for "private

[5] (New York: Alfred A. Knopf, 1955).

[6] John Porter East, *Council Manager Government: The Political Thought of Its Founder, Richard S. Childs* (Chapel Hill: University of North Carolina Press, 1965), p. 18.

[7] Ernest S. Bradford, *Commission Government in American Cities* (New York: Macmillan, 1911), p. 165.

regarding" values of the ethnic politics of machines and bosses. The middle class searches for the good of the "community as a whole" rather than for the benefit of particularistic interests.[8] Agger, Goldrich and Swanson, in their study of two western and two southern communities have documented the rise of a group they call the "community conservationists," who "see the values of community life maximized when political leadership is exercised by men representing the public at large, rather than 'special interests.' "[9] Robert Wood has taken up a similar theme in his penetrating analysis of American suburbia. The "no-party politics of suburbia" is characterized by "an outright reaction against partisan activity, a refusal to recognize that there may be persistent cleavages in the electorate and an ethical disapproval of permanent group collaboration as an appropriate means of settling disputes."[10] This ideological opposition to partisanship is a product of a tightly-knit and homogeneous community, for "nonpartisanship reflects a highly integrated community life with a powerful capacity to induce conformity."[11]

Considerable debate has ensued over both the existence and the consequences of these two political ethics in urban communities. Some evidence has supported the view that reformed governments[12] are indeed found in cities with higher incomes, higher levels of education, greater proportions of Protestants and more white-collar job-holders. Schnore and Alford, for example, found that "the popular image of the manager city was verified; it does tend to be the natural habitat of the upper middle class." In addition, manager cities were "inhabited by a younger, more mobile population that is growing rapidly."[13]

More recently, Wolfinger and Field correlated socio-economic variables— particularly ethnicity and region—to political structures. They concluded that "the ethos theory is irrelevant to the South . . . inapplicable to the West . . . fares badly in the Northeast . . ." and that support for the theory in the Midwest was "small and uneven."[14] Region proved to be a more important predictor of both government forms and of policy outputs like urban renewal expenditures than did the socio-economic composition of the population.

---

[8]Banfield and Wilson, *op. cit.*, p. 41.

[9]Robert Agger, Daniel Goldrich, and Bert E. Swanson, *The Rulers and the Ruled* (New York: John Wiley and Sons, 1964), p. 21.

[10]Robert C. Wood, *Suburbia: Its People and Their Politics* (Boston: Houghton Mifflin Co., 1959), p. 155.

[11]*Ibid.*, p. 154.

[12]We refer to cities characterized by commission or manager government, nonpartisan elections, and at-large constituencies as "reformed." Our use of the term is historical and no value position on reformism's merits is intended. To refer to reformed cities as "public regarding" or "middle class" is, it seems, to assume what needs to be proved.

[13]Leo Schnore and Robert Alford, "Forms of Government and Socio-Economic Characteristics of Suburbs," *Administrative Science Quarterly*, 8 (June, 1963), 1-17. See also the literature cited in Froman, *op. cit.*

[14]Wolfinger and Field, *op. cit.*, pp. 325-326.

In our view, it is premature to carve a headstone for the ethos theory. It is our thesis that governments which are products of the reform movement behave differently from those which have unreformed institutions, even if the socio-economic composition of their population may be similar. Our central purpose is to determine the impact of both socio-economic variables and political institutions (structural variables) on outputs of city governments. By doing this, we hope to shed some additional illumination on the ethos theory.

II. Research design

Variables

The independent variables used in this analysis, listed in Table 1, consist of relatively "hard" data, mostly drawn from the U.S. census.[15] These variables were selected because they represent a variety of possible social cleavages which divide urban populations—rich vs. poor, Negro vs. white, ethnic vs. native, newcomers vs. old-timers, etc. We assume that such social and economic characteristics are important determinants of individual and group variations in political preferences. Data on each of these independent variables were gathered for each of the two hundred cities in the sample.[16]

Table 1. Independent variables

1. Population, 1960
2. Per cent population increase or decrease, 1950-60
3. Per cent non-white
4. Per cent of native population with foreign born or mixed parentage
5. Median income
6. Per cent of population with incomes below $3000
7. Per cent of population with incomes above $10,000
8. Median school years completed by adult population
9. Per cent high school graduates among adult population
10. Per cent of population in white collar occupations
11. Per cent of elementary school children in private schools
12. Per cent of population in owner-occupied dwelling units

Our principal theoretical concern is with the consequences of variations in the structural characteristics of form of government, type of constituency

[15] The source for the first nine variables is *The County and City Data Book* (Washington: United States Bureau of the Census, 1962). For the last three variables, the source is Orin F. Nolting and David S. Arnold (eds), *The Municipal Yearbook 1965* (Chicago: International City Managers' Association, 1965), pp. 98 ff.

[16] We used a random sample of 200 of the 309 American cities with populations of 50,000 or more in 1960. All information on the forms of government and forms of election are drawn from *The Municipal Yearbook, 1965, op. cit.*

and partisanship of elections. The variable of government form is unambiguous. Except for a few small New England towns, all American cities have council-manager, mayor-council or commission government. There is, however, somewhat more ambiguity in the classification of election type. By definition, a "nonpartisan election is one in which no candidate is identified on the ballot by party affiliation."[17] The legal definition of nonpartisanship conceals the wide variation between Chicago's and Boston's nominal nonpartisanship and the more genuine variety in Minneapolis, Winnetka and Los Angeles.[18] We will quickly see, though, that formal nonpartisanship is not merely an empty legal nicety, but that there are very real differences in the political behavior of partisan and nonpartisan cities, even though we are defining them in legal terms only.[19]

Our classification of constituency types into only two groups also conceals some variation in the general pattern. While most cities use either the at-large or the ward pattern of constituencies exclusively, a handful use a combination of the two electoral methods. For our purposes, we classified these with district cities.

The dependent variables in this study are two measures of public policy outputs. A growing body of research on local politics has utilized policy measures as dependent variables.[20] The present research is intended to further this study of political outputs by relating socio-economic variables to expenditure and taxation patterns in cities with varying political structures.

The dependent variables are computed by a simple formula. The measure for taxation was computed by dividing the total personal income of the city into the total tax of the city, giving us a tax/income ratio. Similarly, dividing expenditures by the city's aggregate personal income gave us an expenditure/income ratio as the measure for our second dependent variable. These measures, while admittedly imperfect,[21] permit us to ask how much of a city's income it is willing to commit for public taxation and expenditures.

[17]Banfield and Wilson, *op. cit.,* p. 151.

[18]For Minneapolis, see Robert Morlan, "City Politics: Free Style," *National Municipal Review,* 49 (November, 1949), pp. 485-490; Winnetka, Banfield and Wilson, *op. cit.,* p. 140; Los Angeles, Charles G. Mayo, "The 1961 Mayoralty Election in Los Angeles: The Political Party in a Nonpartisan Election," *Western Political Quarterly,* 17 (1964), 325-339.

[19]At least one other variable may produce a given institutional form in a city—the legal requirements of a state government, which vary from state to state and may even vary for different kinds of cities within the same state. We have not taken account of this variable because systematic information on comparative state requirements in this area was unavailable to us. However, Wolfinger and Field consulted several experts and eliminated cities which are not given free choice over their institutions. Nevertheless, a comparison of our figures with theirs revealed no important differences.

[20]See footnote 4, *supra.*

[21]We recognize that these are only rough indicators of city finance policies. Definitions of taxation vary from city to city and what may be financed from taxes in one city may be financed from fees in another. Expenditures present a more complex problem because the types and amounts of state transfer payments vary from state to state according to state laws, the division of governmental labor in a state, the incomes and sizes of cities, not to mention political factors at the state level. We think it important,

Hypothesis

Much of the research on city politics has treated reformed institutions as dependent variables. Although we shall briefly examine the social and economic differences between reformed and unreformed cities, our principal concern will be to explore the *consequences* for public policy of political institutions. From our earlier discussion of the political culture of cities we hypothesized that:

    1. The relationship between socio-economic cleavages and policy outputs is stronger in unreformed than in reformed cities.

This hypothesis focuses on the intention of the reformers to minimize the role of particularistic interests in policy making.

III. Reformed and unreformed cities: a comparison

The economic and social contrasts between reformed and unreformed cities have been the subject of much research,[22] and for our purposes we may be brief in our treatment. We divided the independent variables into three groups, one measuring population size and growth, a second containing social class indicators and a third including three measures of social homogeneity. The means and standard deviations for each variable by institutional category are found in Table 2.

It should initially be noted that population size and growth rate fairly clearly separate the reformed from the unreformed cities. As Alford and Scoble have amply documented,[23] the larger the city, the greater the likelihood of its being unreformed; the faster its growth rate, the more likely a city is to possess manager government, nonpartisan and at-large elections. These differences are largely accounted for by the fact that very large cities are most likely to (1) have unreformed institutions and (2) be stable or declining in population. Since neither of these variables emerged as

---

however, that our independent variables explain a large proportion of the variation in municipal outputs as we measured them. No doubt one could explain an even larger proportion of the variation in measures which specify different functional responsibilities of cities. At least these measures constitute a starting point, and we hope others will improve on them.

The source of our output measures was *The County and City Data Book, op. cit.*

[22] See, for example, Robert Alford and Harry Scoble, "Political and Socio-Economic Characteristics of American Cities," *The Municipal Yearbook 1965, op. cit.*, pp. 82-97; Sherbenou, *op. cit.*; John H. Kessel, "Governmental Structure and Political Environment," *The American Political Science Review*, 56 (September, 1962), 615-620.

[23] Alford and Scoble, *op. cit.* The particularly large differences found between the populations of reformed and unreformed cities reflect the fact that New York City and several other urban giants are included in the sample.

particularly important predictors of our output variables, we relegated them to secondary importance in the rest of the analysis.

The data in Table 2 indicate that reformed cities (at least those over 50,000) do not appear to be "the natural habitat of the upper middle class." While reformed cities have slightly more educated populations and slightly high proportions of white collar workers and home ownership, unreformed

Table 2.   Comparison of the means (and standard deviations) of socio-economic characteristics of reformed and unreformed cities

Independent variable	Government type					
	Mayor-council		Manager		Commission	
Population						
Population (10^3)	282.5	(858.6)	115.7	(108.0)	128.6	(115.2)
% change, 1950-60	36.4%	(118.8)	64.1%	(130.4)	18.5%	(36.7)
Class						
Median income	$6199.	(1005.0)	$6131.	(999.6)	$5425.	(804.4)
% under $3000	15.3%	(7.0)	17.3%	(6.9)	21.5%	(7.9)
% over $10,000	16.9%	(7.2)	17.5%	(6.7)	12.5%	(3.7)
% high school graduates	40.7%	(10.8)	48.1%	(8.9)	41.6%)	(10.4)
Median education (yrs.)	10.7	(1.1)	11.4	(.89)	11.0	(2.1)
% owner-occupied dwelling units	54.9%	(15.1)	57.3%	(13.6)	54.6%	(13.7)
% white collar	44.1%	(9.0)	48.1%	(7.1)	44.2%	(7.6)
Homogeneity						
% nonwhite	10.6%	(11.5)	11.6%	(10.8)	16.5%	(14.9)
% native with foreign born or mixed parentage	19.7%	(9.9)	12.4%	(8.3)	11.7%	(10.7)
% private school attendance	23.5%	(11.9)	15.3%	(11.8)	16.6%	(11.8)
	N = 85		N = 90		N = 25	

Independent variable	Election type			
	Partisan		Nonpartisan	
Population				
Population (10^3)	270.8	(1022.1)	155.8	(198.7)
% population increase 1950-1960	17.1	(40.1)	58.3%	(136.1)
Class				
Median income	$5996	(904.5)	$6074	(1045.5)
% under $3000	16.8%	(7.1)	17.2%	(7.2)
% over $10,000	16.1%	(6.1)	16.7%	(7.0)
% high school graduates	40.5%	(9.2)	45.3%	(10.6)
Median education (yrs.)	10.6	(1.1)	11.2	(1.2)
% owner-occupied dwelling units	51.5%	(14.4)	57.7%	(13.8)
% white collar	43.5%	(7.5)	46.7%	(8.3)
Homogeneity				
% nonwhite	13.0%	(11.9)	11.5%	(11.8)
% native with foreign born or mixed parentage	17.5%	(10.7)	14.7%	(9.6)
% private school attendance	24.1%	(13.6)	16.9%	(11.3)
	N = 57		N = 143	

Table 2—(Continued)

Independent variable	Constituency type			
	District		At-large	
Population				
Population (10^3)	246.9	(909.8)	153.6	(191.2)
% population increase 1950-1960	23.1%	(36.4)	59.1%	(143.7)
Class				
Median income	$6297	(965.2)	$5942	(1031.9)
% under $3000	14.7%	(6.5)	18.2%	(7.6)
% over $10,000	17.7%	(7.1)	16.0%	(6.6)
% high school graduates	43.6%	(10.9)	44.4%	(10.4)
Median education (yrs.)	10.9	(1.1)	11.2	(1.2)
% owner-occupied dwelling units	55.1%	(14.4)	56.9%	(14.5)
% white collar	45.2%	(9.4)	46.3%	(7.5)
Homogeneity				
% nonwhite	9.8%	(10.6)	13.0%	(12.3)
% native with foreign born or mixed parentage	18.9%	(9.4)	13.4%	(9.7)
% private school attendance	23.2%	(12.5)	16.6%	(11.7)
	N = 73		N = 127	

cities have generally high incomes. In any case, whatever their direction, the differences are not large. What is striking is not the differences between the cities but the similarities of their class composition.

Homogeneity is easily one of the most ambiguous terms in the ambiguous language of the social sciences. We have followed Alford and Scoble who used three measures of homogeneity: for ethnicity, the per cent of population native born of foreign born or mixed parentage; for race, the per cent nonwhite; and for religious homogeneity, the per cent of elementary school children in private schools. The last measure, while indirect, was the only one available, since data on religious affiliation are not collected by the Census Bureau.

With the exception of race, reformed cities appear somewhat more homogeneous than unreformed cities. While the differences in homogeneity are more clear-cut than class differences, this hardly indicates that reformed cities are the havens of a socially homogeneous population. Although the average nonpartisan city has 16.9 per cent of its children in private schools, this mean conceals a wide range—from 2 to 47 per cent.

Our findings about the insignificance of class differences between reformed and unreformed cities are at some variance with Alford and Scoble's conclusions. There is, however, some support for the argument that reformed cities are more homogeneous. While we used cities with populations of over 50,000, their sample included all cities over 25,000; and varying samples may produce varying conclusions. The only other study to analyze cities over 50,000 was Wolfinger and Field's and our conclusions are generally consistent with theirs. We differ with them, however, on two important questions.

First, Wolfinger and Field argued that what differences there are between unreformed and reformed cities disappear when controls for region are introduced: "The salient conclusion to be drawn from these data is that one can do a much better job of predicting a city's political form by knowing what part of the country it is in than by knowing anything about the composition of its population."[24] Since regions have had different historical experiences, controls for region are essentially controls for history, and more specifically, historical variation in settlement patterns. The problem with this reasoning, however, is that to "control" for "region" is to control not only for history, but for demography as well: to know what region a city is in *is* to know something about the composition of its population. Geographical subdivisions are relevant subjects of political inquiry only because they are differentiated on the basis of attitudinal or socio-economic variables. The South is not a distinctive political region because two surveyors named Mason and Dixon drew a famous line, but because the "composition of its population" differs from the rest of the country.

It is therefore difficult to unravel the meaning of "controlling" for "region" since regions are differentiated on precisely the kinds of demographic variables which we (and Wolfinger and Field) related to reformism. Cities in the Midwest, for example, have a much higher proportion of home ownership (64%) than cities in the Northeast (44%), while northeastern cities have more foreign stock in their population (27%) than the Midwest (16%). Hence, to relate ethnicity to political reformism and then to "control" for "region" is in part to relate ethnicity to reformism and then to control for ethnicity. Consequently, we have grave reservations that the substitution of the gross and unrefined variable of "region" for more refined demographic data adds much to our knowledge of American cities. "Controlling" for "region" is much more than controlling for historical experiences, because region as a variable is an undifferentiated *potpourri* of socio-economic, attitudinal, historical and cultural variations.[25]

We also differ with Wolfinger and Field in their assertion that their analysis constitutes a test of the ethos theory. As we understand it, Banfield and Wilson's theory posits that particular attitudes are held by persons with varying sociological characteristics (ethnic groups and middle class persons, in particular) and that these attitudes include preferences for one or another kind of political institution. But relating the proportion of middle class persons in a city's population to its form of government says nothing one way or another about middle class preferences. An important part of understanding, of course, is describing and it is certainly useful to know how reformed cities differ from unreformed cities.

[24] *Op. cit.*, p. 320.

[25] In statistical parlance, the problem with "region" as an independent variable might be described as treating a complicated background variable as the first variable in a specific developmental sequence. But, as Blalock argues, ". . . *one should avoid complex indicators that are related in unknown ways to a given underlying variable.* Geographical region and certain background variables appear to have such undesirable properties": Hubert M. Blalock, *Causal Inferences in Nonexperimental Research* (Chapel Hill: University of North Carolina Press, 1964), p. 164 (italics in original).

In our view, however, such tests as Wolfinger and Field used cannot logically be called explanations, in any causal sense. The most obvious reason is that they violate some important assumptions about time—order: independent variables are measured with contemporary census data, while the dependent variables are results of decisions made ten to fifty years ago. Moreover, this problem is multiplied by the difficulty of inferring configurations of political power from demographic data. Presumably, their assumption is that there is a simple linear relationship between sheer numbers (or proportions) of, say, middle class persons and their political power: the larger the size of a group in the city's population, the easier it can enforce its choice of political forms. At least one prominent urban sociologist, however, has found empirical support for precisely the opposite proposition. Hawley concluded that the smaller the proportion of middle class persons in a city, the greater their power over urban renewal policies.[26] Similarly, it may also be dubious to assume that the size of an ethnic population is an accurate indicator of influence of ethnic groups. Although we recognize the importance of describing the socio-economic correlates of political forms, the logical problems involved suggest the need for a good deal of caution in interpreting these differences as explanations.[27]

In any case, the question of why the city adopts particular structures is of less interest to us than their consequences for public policy. It is to this analysis that we now turn.

IV. Policy outputs and the responsiveness of cities

We are now in a position to take three additional steps. First, we can compare the differences in policy outputs between reformed and unreformed cities. Second, we can assess the cumulative impact of socio-economic variables on these policy choices. Finally, we can specify what variables are related in what ways to these output variables. In essence, we can now treat political institutions, not as dependent variables, but as factors which influence the *level* of expenditures and taxation and the *relationship* between cleavage variables and these outputs.

Differences between reformed and unreformed cities' outputs

Contrary to Sherbenou's conclusions about Chicago suburbs,[28] our data indicate that reformed cities both spend and tax less than unreformed cities, with the exception of expenditures in partisan and nonpartisan cities. It

---

[26] Amos Hawley, "Community Power and Urban Renewal Success," *American Journal of Sociology,* 68 (January, 1963), 422-431.

[27] See also the exchange between Banfield and Wilson and Wolfinger and Field in "Communications," *The American Political Science Review,* 60 (December, 1966), 998-1000.

[28] Sherbenou, *op. cit.,* pp. 133-134.

appears that partisan, mayor-council and ward cities are less willing to commit their resources to public purposes than their reformed counterparts. What is of more importance than the difference in outputs, however, is the relative responsiveness of the two kinds of cities to social cleavages in their population (Table 3).

Table 3. Mean values of tax/income and expenditure/income ratios, by structural characteristics

Structural variables	Taxes/ income	Expenditures/ income
Election type		
Partisan	.032	.050
Nonpartisan	.030	.053
Government type		
Mayor-council	.037	.058
Manager	.024	.045
Commission	.031	.057
Constituency type		
Ward	.036	.057
At-large	.027	.049

The responsiveness of cities

We have argued that one principal goal of the reform movement was to reduce the impact of partisan, socio-economic cleavages on governmental decision making, to immunize city governments from "artificial" social cleavages—race, religion, ethnicity, and so on. As Banfield and Wilson put their argument, the reformers "assumed that there existed an interest ('the public interest') that pertained to the city 'as a whole' and that should always prevail over competing, partial (and usually private) interests."[29] The structural reforms of manager government, at-large, and nonpartisan elections would so insulate the business of governing from social cleavages that "private regarding" interests would count for little in making up the mind of the body politic. But amid the calls of the reformers for structural reforms to muffle the impact of socio-economic cleavages, a few hardy souls predicted precisely the opposite consequence of reform: instead of eliminating cleavages from political decision-making, the reforms, particularly the elimination of parties, would enhance the conflict. Nathan Matthews, Jr., a turn-of-the-century mayor of Boston, issued just such a warning:

> As a city is a political institution, the people in the end will divide into parties, and it would seem extremely doubtful whether the present system, however illogical its foundation be, does not in fact produce better results, at least in large cities, than if the voters divided into groups, separated by property, social or religious grounds.[30]

[29] *Op. cit.*, p. 139.
[30] Quoted in Banfield and Wilson, *op. cit.*, p. 154.

Matthews recognized implicitly what political scientists would now call the "interest aggregation" function of political parties.[31] Parties in a democracy manage conflict, structure it, and encapsulate social cleavages under the rubric of two or more broad social cleavages, the parties themselves. "Parties tend to crystallize opinion, they give skeletal articulation to a shapeless and jelly-like mass . . . they cause similar opinions to coagulate . . ."[32] The parties "reduce effectively the number of political opinions to manageable numbers, bring order and focus to the political struggle, simplify issues and frame alternatives, and compromise conflicting interests."[33] Since parties are the agencies of interest aggregation, so the argument goes, their elimination makes for greater, not lesser, impact of social cleavages on political decisions.

Political scientists have recently confirmed Matthews' fears, at least with regard to electoral behavior in partisan and nonpartisan elections. Evidence points to the increased impact of socio-economic cleavages on voting when a nonpartisan ballot is used than when the election is formally partisan. Gerald Pomper studied nonpartisan municipal elections and compared them with partisan elections for the New Jersey State Assembly in Newark. He concluded that the "goal of nonpartisanship is fulfilled, as party identification does not determine the outcome. In place of party, ethnic affiliation is emphasized and the result is 'to enhance the effect of basic social cleavages.' "[34] If (1) this is typical of other American cities and if (2) electoral cleavages can be translated effectively into demands on the government in the absence of aggregative parties, then we might assume that the reformed institutions would reflect cleavages more, rather than less, closely than unreformed ones.

Essentially, then, there are two contrasting views about the consequences of municipal reform. One, the reformers' ideal, holds that institutional reforms will mitigate the impact of social cleavages on public policy. The other argues that the elimination of political parties and the introduction of other reforms will make social cleavages more, rather than less, important in political decision-making.

The measurement of responsiveness

We have hypothesized that socio-economic cleavages will have less impact on the policy choices of reformed than unreformed governments. Thus, one

[31] For a discussion of the concept of interest aggregation, see Gabriel Almond, "Introduction: A Functional Approach to Comparative Politics," in Gabriel Almond and James S. Coleman (eds.), *The Politics of Developing Areas* (Princeton: Princeton University Press, 1960), pp. 38-45.

[32] Maurice Duverger, *Political Parties* (New York: Science Editions, 1963), p. 378.

[33] Frank J. Sorauf, *Political Parties in the American System* (Boston: Little, Brown and Co., 1964), pp. 165-166.

[34] Gerald Pomper, "Ethnic and Group Voting in Nonpartisan Municipal Elections," *Public Opinion Quarterly,* 30 (Spring, 1966), p. 90; see also, J. Leiper Freeman, "Local Party Systems: Theoretical Considerations and a Case Analysis," *American Journal of Sociology,* 64 (1958), 282-289.

could do a better job of predicting a city's taxation and expenditure policy using socio-economic variables in partisan, mayor and ward cities than in nonpartisan, manager and at-large cities. Operationally, we will test this hypothesis by using multiple correlation coefficients. Squaring these coefficients, called "multiple R's," will give us a summary measure of the total amount of variation in our dependent variables explained by our twelve independent variables.[35] The results of the correlation analysis are summarized in Diagrams 1 and 2.

On the whole, the results of the correlation analysis strikingly support the hypothesis, with the exception of commission cities. Thus, we can say, for example, that our twelve socio-economic variables explain 71 per cent of the variations in taxation policy in partisan cities, and 49 per cent of the variation in nonpartisan cities. In commission cities, however, socio-economic variables predict substantially more variation in both taxes and expenditures than in the unreformed mayor-council cities.[36] The anomaly of commission governments is interesting, for they present, as we will see, marked exceptions to virtually every pattern of relationships we found. The substantial explanatory power of these socio-economic variables is not altered, but confirmed, by examining the variables independently. The rest of the correlations show a consistent pattern: reformed cities are less responsive to cleavages in their population than unreformed cities.

If one of the premises of the "political ethos" argument is that reformed institutions give less weight to the "private regarding" and "artificial" cleavages in the population, that premise receives striking support from our analysis. Our data suggest that when a city adopts reformed structures, it comes to be governed less on the basis of conflict and more on the basis of the rationalistic theory of administration. The making of public policy takes less count of the enduring differences between White and Negro, business and labor, Pole and WASP. The logic of the bureaucratic ethic demands an impersonal, apolitical settlement of issues, rather than the settlement of conflict in the arena of political battle.

V. *To spend or not to spend*

If efforts to expand or contract the scope of government stand at the core of municipal political life,[37] they are nowhere better reflected than in the

---

[35] It is possible that the difference between any two correlations may be a function of very different standard deviations of the independent variables. A quick look at Table 2, however, suggests that this is not likely to affect the relationships we find.

[36] Wolfinger and Field, *op. cit.*, p. 312, ". . .omit the commission cities from consideration since this form does not figure in the ethos theory." Historically, however, commission government was the earliest of the structures advocated by the Progressives and is quite clearly a product of the reform era. While history tells us that commission cities can not legitimately be excluded from the fold of reformism, they appear to be its black sheep, characterized by low incomes, low population growth and large proportions of nonwhites. In fact, they present a marked contrast to both mayor-council and manager cities.

[37] Agger *et al.*, *op. cit.*, pp. 4-14.

Diagram 1. *Proportion of variation explained (R^2) in taxation policy with twelve socio-economic variables, by institutional characteristics**

Independent variables	Structural variables	Dependent variable
	Reformed institution	
	Government: commission 62%	
	Government: council-manager 42%	
	Election: nonpartisan 49%	
	Constituency: at-large 49%	
Twelve socio-economic variables		Tax/income ratio
	Unreformed institution	
	Government: mayor-council 52%	
	Election: partisan 71%	
	Constituency: ward/mixed 59%	

*In the total sample, the twelve independent variables explained 52% of the variation in taxes.

Diagram 2. *Proportion of variation explained (R^2) in expenditure policy with twelve socio-economic variables, by institutional characteristics**

Independent variables	Structural variables	Dependent variable
	Reformed institution	
	Government: commission 59%	
	Government: council-manager 30%	
	Constituency: at-large 36%	
	Elections: nonpartisan 41%	
Twelve socio-economic variables		Expenditure/income ratio
	Unreformed institution	
	Government: mayor-council 42%	
	Constituency: ward/mixed 49%	
	Elections: partisan 59%	

*In the total sample, the twelve independent variables explained 36% of the variation in expenditures.

taxation and expenditure patterns of cities. A generation ago, Charles Beard wrote, "In the purposes for which appropriations are made the policies of the city government are given concrete form—the culture of the city is reflected. Indeed, the history of urban civilization could be written in terms of appropriations, for they show what the citizens think is worth doing and worth paying for."[38] Pressures to expand and contract government regulations and services are almost always reflected one way or another in the municipal budget. Labor, ethnic groups, the poor and the liberal community may press for additional services and these must be paid for; the business community may demand municipal efforts to obtain new industry by paring city costs to create a "favorable business climate"; or businessmen may themselves demand municipal services for new or old business. In any case,

[38] Charles A. Beard, *American Government and Politics* (New York: Macmillan, 1924, 4th edition), p. 727.

few political conflicts arise which do not involve some conflict over the budget structure.

Class variables and public policies

Part of the political rhetoric associated with the demand for a decrease in the scope of the national government is the argument that the initiative for policy-making should rest more with the state and local governments. Opposition to high federal spending levels, as V.O. Key has demonstrated, is found more often among persons with middle class occupations than among blue-collar workers.[39] It is not inconceivable that the middle class argument about state and local responsibility might be more than political rhetoric, and that at the local level, middle class voters are willing to undertake major programs of municipal services, requiring large outlays of public capital. Wilson and Banfield have argued that the "public regarding" upper-middle class voters in metropolitan areas are often found voting for public policies at variance with their "self-interest narrowly conceived," and that "the higher the income of a ward or town, the more taste it has for public expenditures of various kinds."[40] Similarly a longitudinal study of voting patterns in metropolitan Cleveland found that an index of social rank was positively correlated with favorable votes on welfare referenda.[41] If these data reflect middle class willingness to spend on a local level, they might indicate that the "states' rights" argument was more than ideological camouflage: middle class voters stand foursquare behind public expenditures at the local level even when they oppose those expenditures from the national government. Therefore, we hypothesized that:

2a. The more middle class the city, measured by income, education and occupation, the higher the municipal taxes and expenditures.

In line with our general concern of testing the impact of political structures on municipal policies, we also hypothesized that:

2b. Unreformed cities reflect this relationship more strongly than reformed cities.

With respect to hypothesis 2a, the data in Table 4 on three middle class indicators are unambiguous and indicate a strong rejection of the hypothesis. However we measure social class, whether by income, education or

[39] V. O. Key, *Public Opinion and American Democracy* (New York: Alfred A. Knopf, 1961), p. 124.
[40] Wilson and Banfield, *op. cit.*, p. 876. Footnote 5 in the same article conveniently summarized research supporting this proposition.
[41] Eugene S. Uyeki, "Patterns of Voting in a Metropolitan Area: 1938-1962," *Urban Affairs Quarterly*, 1 (June, 1966), 65-77.

Table 4. *Correlations between middle class characteristics and outputs in reformed and unreformed cities*

Correlations of	Government type			Election type		Constituency type	
	Mayor-council	Manager	Com-mission	Partisan	Non-partisan	Ward	At-large
Taxes with:							
Median income	−.13	−.24	−.19	.03	−.19	−.17	−.22
White collar	−.23	−.12	−.62	−.21	−.33	−.30	−.32
Median education	−.36	−.22	−.08	−.45	−.24	−.48	−.18
Expenditures with:							
Median income	−.19	−.32	−.43	−.04	−.32	−.23	−.34
White collar	−.24	−.23	−.58	−.18	−.39	−.32	−.35
Median education	−.32	−.36	−.26	−.36	−.38	−.44	−.32

occupation, class measures are negatively related to public taxes and expenditures.

It is possible, however, that income does not have a linear, but rather a curvilinear relationship with municipal outputs. Banfield and Wilson argue that "In the city, it is useful to think in terms of three income groups—low, middle, and high. Surprising as it may seem to Marxists, the conflict is generally between an alliance of low-income and high-income groups on one side and the middle-income groups on the other."[42] If the relationship between income and expenditure is curvilinear, then we should expect to find that proportions of both low and high income groups were positively correlated with outputs. Our data, however, lend no support to this notion of a "pro-expenditure" alliance. Rather, the proportion of the population with incomes below $3000 is positively correlated with expenditures in all city types (although the relationships are small) and the proportion of the population in the above $10,000 bracket is negatively correlated with expenditures. Summing the two measures and correlating the combined measure with outputs produced no correlation greater than 0.15 and the relationships were as likely to be negative as positive. Tests for nonlinearity also suggested that no such coalition exists in the cities in our analysis.

To be sure, aggregate data analysis using whole cities as units of analysis is no substitute for systematic survey data on middle class attitudes, but it is apparent that cities with larger middle class population have lower, not higher expenditures. As we emphasized earlier, the "ethos theory" deals with attitudes and the behavior of individuals, while our data deal with cities and their behavior. The coalition suggested by Banfield and Wilson, however, is not discernible at this level of aggregation in these cities.

Hypothesis 2b is not consistently borne out by the data. In fact, the relationships between middle class variables and outputs are, if anything, stronger in the reformed cities than in their unreformed counterparts. One would not want to make too much of the data, but a large body of literature

[42] Banfield and Wilson, *op. cit.,* p. 35.

on city politics, which we discuss below, suggests that reformed institutions maximize the power of the middle class.

We originally assumed that the proportion of owner-occupied dwelling units constituted another measure of middle class composition, but it soon became apparent that it was only weakly related to income, occupation and education measures. Nevertheless, it emerged as the strongest single predictor of both expenditure and taxation policy in our cities. We hypothesized that:

> 3a. Owner-occupancy and outputs are negatively correlated, and
> 3b. Unreformed cities reflect this relationship more strongly than reformed cities.

Hypothesis 3a is consistently borne out in the data presented in Table 5. These relationships were only slightly attenuated when we controlled for income, education and occupation. No doubt self-interest (perhaps "private regardingness") on the part of the home owner, whose property is intimately related to the tax structure of most local governments, may account for part of this relationship. Moreover, home ownership is correlated (almost by definition) with lower urban population density. High density, bringing together all manner of men into the classic urban mosaic, may be itself correlated with factors which produce demands for higher expenditures— slums, increased needs for fire and police protection, and so on.

Table 5.   *Correlations between owner occupancy and government outputs in reformed and unreformed cities*

Correlations of owner occupancy with:	Government type		Election type		Constituency type	
	Mayor-council	Manager	Com-mission	Partisan	Non-partisan	Ward	At-large
Taxes	−.57	−.31	−.73	−.64	−.45	−.56	−.48
Expenditures	−.51	−.23	−.62	−.62	−.40	−.50	−.40

In confirmation of hypothesis 3a, the unmistakable pattern is for unreformed cities to reflect these negative relationships more strongly than the manager, nonpartisan and at-large cities, although commission cities show their usual remarkably high correlations.

Homogeneity variables and public policies

Dawson and Robinson, in their analysis of state welfare expenditures, found strong positive relationships between the ethnicity of a state's population and the level of its welfare expenditures.[43] If this is symptomatic

---

[43] Richard E. Dawson and James A. Robinson, "The Politics of Welfare," in Herbert Jacob and Kenneth Vines (eds.), *Politics in the American States* (Boston: Little, Brown and Co., 1965), pp. 398-401.

of a generalized association of ethnic and religious minorities with higher expenditures, we might find support for the hypothesis that:

> 4a. The larger the proportion of religious and ethnic minorities in the population, the higher the city's taxes and expenditures.

And, if our general hypothesis about the impact of political institutions is correct, then:

> 4b. Unreformed cities reflect this relationship more strongly than reformed cities.

The correlations between ethnicity, religious heterogeneity and outputs (see Table 6) are, with one exception, positive, as predicted by hypothesis 4a. These associations may reflect the substantial participation by ethnic groups in municipal politics long after the tide of immigration has been reduced to a trickle.[44] The relatively intense politicization of ethnic groups at the local level,[45] the appeals to nationality groups through "ticket balancing" and other means, and the resultant higher turnout of ethnic groups than other lower status groups,[46] may produce an influence on city government far out of proportion to their number.

Table 6. Correlations between ethnicity and religious heterogeneity and outputs in reformed and unreformed cities

	Government type			Election type		Constituency type	
Correlations of	Mayor-council	Manager	Com-mission	Partisan	Non-partisan	Ward	At-large
Taxes with:							
Ethnicity	.49	.26	.57	.61	.43	.56	.40
Private school attendance	.38	.15	.37	.33	.37	.41	.25
Expenditures with:							
Ethnicity	.36	.02	.21	.48	.21	.44	.13
Private school attendance	.34	−.01	.07	.25	.24	.40	.05

We found when we related all twelve of our independent variables to outputs in various city types that the associations were much weaker in cities we have labeled reformed. The correlations for ethnicity and religious homogeneity show a generally similar pattern, with commission cities exhibiting their usual erratic behavior. The data, then, show fairly clear support for hypothesis 4b.

[44] Raymond Wolfinger, "The Development and Persistence of Ethnic Voting," *The American Political Science Review,* 59 (December, 1965), 896-908.

[45] Robert E. Lane, *Political Life* (Glencoe, Ill.: The Free Press, 1959), pp. 236-243.

[46] *Ibid.*

The third variable of our homogeneity indicators—per cent of population non-white—had almost no relationship to variation in outputs, regardless of city type. We found the same weak correlations for the poverty income variable, which was, of course, strongly related to the racial variable. An easy explanation suggests that this is a consequence of the political impotence of Negroes and the poor, but one should be cautious in inferring a lack of power from the lack of a statistical association.

We have dealt in this section with factors which are positively and negatively related to spending patterns in American cities. While social class variables are associated negatively with outputs, two measures of homogeneity, private school attendance and ethnicity are related to higher taxes and spending. Examining the strengths of these correlations in cities with differing forms, we found some support for our general hypothesis about the political consequences of institutions, especially for the homogeneity variables and the home ownership variable. Interestingly, however, this was not the case with class variables.

VI. Reformism as a continuous variable

The central thrust of our argument has been that reformed governments differ from their unreformed counterparts in their responsiveness to socio-economic cleavages in the population. Logically, if the presence of one feature of the "good government" syndrome had the impact of reducing responsiveness, the introduction of additional reformed institutions should have an additive effect and further reduce the impact of cleavages on decision-making. We therefore decided to treat "reformism" as a continuous variable for analytic purposes and hypothesized that:

> 5. The higher the level of reformism in a city, the lower its responsiveness to socio-economic cleavages in the population.

We utilized a simple four-point index to test this hypothesis, ranging from the "least reformed" to the "most reformed." The sample cities were categorized as follows:

1. Cities with none of the reformed institutions (i.e., the government is mayor-council, elections are partisan and constituencies are wards).
2. Cities with any one of the reformed institutions.
3. Cities with two of the reformed institutions.
4. Cities with three reformed institutions (i.e., the government is either manager or commission, elections are nonpartisan and constituencies are at-large).

We can not overemphasize the crudity of this index as an operationalization of the complex and abstract concept of "reformism." Nonetheless, we think some of the relationships we found are strongly suggestive that reformism may in reality be a continuous variable.

To test this hypothesis, we took four variables which had moderate-to-strong correlations with our dependent variables and computed simple correlations in each reform category. If our hypothesis is correct, the strength of the correlations in Table 7 should decrease regularly with an increase in reform scores. While there are some clear exceptions to the predicted pattern of relationships, there is some fairly consistent support for the hypothesis. Even when the decreases in the strengths of the correlations are irregular, there is a clear difference between cities which we have labeled "most reformed" and "least reformed."

Again, we would not want to attach too much importance to the results of this rough-and-ready index. But, the patterns support our previous argument about the impact of reformism: the more reformed the city, the less responsive it is to socio-economic cleavages in its political decision-making.

Table 7. *Correlations between selected independent variables and output variables by four categories of reformism*

	Reform scores			
Correlations of	*1 (least reformed)*	*2*	*3*	*4 (most reformed)*
Taxes with:				
Ethnicity	.62	.41	.50	.34
Private school attendance	.40	.32	.28	.25
Owner-occupancy	−.70	−.39	−.54	−.44
Median education	−.55	−.27	−.32	−.13
Expenditures with:				
Ethnicity	.51	.27	.41	.05
Private school attendance	.46	.23	.16	.08
Owner-occupancy	−.67	−.30	−.54	−.38
Median education	−.49	−.19	−.38	−.37

discuss this?

VII. A causal model and an interpretation

A causal model

The implicit, or at times explicit, causal model in much of the research on municipal reformism has been a simple one: socio-economic cleavages cause the adoption of particular political forms. A more sophisticated model would include political institutions as one of the factors which produce a given output structure in city politics. We hypothesize that a causal model would include four classes of variables: socio-economic cleavages, political variables (including party registration, structure of party systems, patterns of aggregation, strength of interest groups, voter turnout, etc.), political institutions (form of government, type of elections and types of constituencies), and political outputs. Diagram 3 depicts one possible causal model.

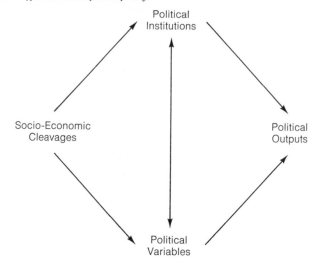

Diagram 3. A hypothesized causal model

This study has of necessity been limited to exploring the linkages between socio-economic cleavages, political institutions and political outputs. We found that political institutions "filter" the process of converting inputs into outputs. Some structures, particularly partisan elections, ward constituencies, mayor-council governments and commission governments, operate to maximize the impact of cleavage indicators on public policies. We conclude by discussing some of the reasons why different structures have varying impacts on the conversion process.

An interpretation

Three principal conclusions may be derived from this analysis.

1. Cities with reformed and unreformed institutions are not markedly different in terms of demographic variables. Indeed, some variables, like income, ran counter to the popular hypothesis that reformed cities are havens of the middle class. Our data lent some support to the notion that reformed cities are more homogeneous in their ethnic and religious populations. Still, it is apparent that reformed cities are by no means free from the impact of these cleavages.

2. The more important difference between the two kinds of cities is in their behavior, rather than their demography. Using multiple correlation coefficients, we were able to predict municipal outputs more exactly in unreformed than in reformed cities. The translation of social conflicts into public policy and the responsiveness of political systems to class, racial, and religious cleavages differs markedly with the kind of political structure. Thus, political institutions seem to play an important role in the political process—a role substantially independent of a city's demography.

3. Our analysis has also demonstrated that reformism may be viewed as a continuous variable and that the political structures of the

reform syndrome have an additive effect: the greater the reformism, the lower the responsiveness.

Through these political institutions, the goal of the reformers has been substantially fulfilled, for nonpartisan elections, at-large constituencies and manager governments are associated with a lessened responsiveness of cities to the enduring conflicts of political life. Or, as Stone, Price and Stone argued in their study of changes produced by the adoption of manager governments, the council after the reform "tended to think more of the community as a whole and less of factional interests in making their decisions."[47]

The responsiveness of a political institution to political conflicts should not be confused with the "responsibility" of a political system as the latter term is used in the great debate over the relative "responsibility" of party systems.[48] In fact, the responsiveness of political forms to social cleavages may stand in sharp contrast to "responsible government" on the British model. Presumably, in American cities, partisan elections, ward constituencies, and mayor-council governments maximize minority rather than majority representation, assuring greater access to decision-makers than the reformed, bureaucratized and "de-politicized" administrations.

Partisan electoral systems, when combined with ward representation, increase the access of two kinds of minority groups: those which are residentially segregated, and which may as a consequence of the electoral system demand and obtain preferential consideration from their councilmen; and groups which constitute identifiable voting blocs to which parties and politicians may be beholden in the next election. The introduction of at-large, nonpartisan elections has at least five consequences for these groups. First, they remove an important cue-giving agency—the party—from the electoral scene, leaving the voter to make decisions less on the policy commitments (however vague) of the party, and more on irrelevancies such as ethnic identification and name familiarity.[49] Second, by removing the party from the ballot, the reforms eliminate the principal agency of interest aggregation from the political system. Hence, interests are articulated less clearly and are aggregated either by some other agency or not at all. Moreover, nonpartisanship has the effect of reducing the turnout in local elections by working class groups,[50] leaving officeholders freer from retaliation by these groups at the polls. Fourth, nonpartisanship may also serve to decrease the salience of "private regarding" demands by increasing the relative political power of

---

[47]Harold Stone, Don K. Price and Kathryn Stone, *City Manager Government in the United States* (Chicago: Public Administration Service, 1940), p. 238.

[48]The standard argument for party responsibility is found in the works of E.E. Schattschneider, esp. *Party Government* (New York: Farrar and Rinehart, 1942) and in the report of the Committee on Political Parties of the American Political Science Association, *Toward a More Responsible Two-Party System* (New York: Rinehart, 1950).

[49]See Pomper, *op. cit.*; and Freeman, *op. cit.*

[50]Robert Salisbury and Gordon Black, "Class and Party in Partisan and Nonpartisan Elections: The Case of Des Moines," *The American Political Science Review*, 57 (September, 1963), 584-592.

"public regarding" agencies like the local press.[51] And when nonpartisanship is combined with election at-large, the impact of residentially segregated groups or groups which obtain their strength from voting as blocs in municipal elections is further reduced.[52] For these reasons, it is clear that political reforms may have a significant impact in minimizing the role which social conflicts play in decision-making. By muting the demands of private-regarding groups, the electoral institutions of reformed governments make public policy less responsive to the demands arising out of social conflicts in the population.

The structure of the government may serve further to modify the strength of minority groups over public policy. It is significant in this respect to note that commission governments, where social cleavages have the greatest impact on policy choices, are the most decentralized of the three governmental types and that manager governments are relatively the most centralized.[53] From the point of view of the reformer, commission government is a failure and their number has declined markedly in recent years.[54] This greater decentralization of commission and of mayor-council governments permits a multiplicity of access points for groups wishing to influence decision-makers.[55] It may also increase the possibilities for collaboration between groups and a bureaucratic agency, a relationship which has characterized administrative patterns in the federal government. As a result of this decentralization, group strength in local governments may be maximized.

It is important in any analysis of reformism to distinguish between the factors which produce the *adoption* of reformed institutions and the *impact* of the new political forms once they have been established. We can offer from our data no conclusions about the origins of reformed structures, for it is obviously impossible to impute causation, using contemporary census data, to events which occurred decades ago. Once a city has institutionalized the reformers' ideals, however, a diffused attitude structure may be less helpful in explaining the city's public policy than the characteristics of the institutions themselves. With the introduction of these reforms, a new political pattern may emerge in which disputes are settled outside the political system, or in which they may be settled by the crowd at the civic club at the periphery of the system.[56] If they do enter the political process, an impersonal, "non-political" bureaucracy may take less account of the conflicting interests and pay more attention to the "correct" decision from the point of view of the municipal planner.

[51] One newspaperman said of nonpartisan politics that "You can't tell the players without a scorecard, and we sell the scorecards": Banfield and Wilson, *op. cit.*, p. 157.

[52] Oliver P. Williams and Charles Adrian, *Four Cities* (Philadelphia: University of Pennsylvania Press, 1963), pp. 56-57.

[53] Alford and Scoble, *op. cit.*, p. 84.

[54] In our view, the failure of the commission government to achieve the intended reforms is more plausible as an explanation of its demise than its administrative unwieldiness—the conventional explanation.

[55] Williams and Adrian, *op. cit.*, pp. 30-31.

[56] Carol E. Thometz discusses the role of the "Civic Committee" in decision-making in Dallas: See *The Decision-Makers* (Dallas: Southern Methodist University Press, 1963).

These conclusions are generally consistent with the ethos theory developed by Banfield and Wilson. If one of the components of the middle class reformers' ideal was "to seek the good of the community as a whole" and to minimize the impact of social cleavages on political decision-making, then their institutional reforms have served, by and large, to advance that goal.

Reformers, Machines, and the War on Poverty

J. David Greenstone
Paul E. Peterson

In this article we again return to the question of the differential effects of particular forms of government on the distribution of power, on political style, on the overall policy-making process, and on policy outcomes in central cities and suburbs. Whereas political scientists of an earlier generation believed political reforms designed to weaken urban political machines would benefit the poor, some contemporary scholars have taken an opposite view. Nevertheless, these two perspectives share certain common insights. In explaining why the initial implementation of local poverty programs funded under the Economic Opportunity Act of 1964 (OEO) varied in New York, Chicago, Los Angeles, and Philadelphia, Greenstone and Peterson propose to use these insights.

They argue that in its first two years (1964-1966), the war on poverty pursued two not entirely compatible goals: (1) to end poverty by distributing various material perquisites (benefits), and (2) to end the virtual exclusion of low-income groups from political life by distributing political power. Has the poverty program been able to realize these two goals? It has not, according to Greenstone and Peterson, largely because of differences in the style of politics in reform and machine cities. In the former, reformers have dispersed power, whereas in the latter the machine has centralized political power among a few of its own leaders. Although many reformers did centralize formal authority in the hands of the mayor or city manager, this has not necessarily offset the overall dispersion of power to a wide range of individuals, groups, and agencies. However, this very dispersion of power has had important latent consequences unforeseen by the reformers. The more pluralistic reform regimes have found it difficult to secure agreement among all the centers of power. The dispersal of power has made the rapid acquisition and distribution of resources more difficult. On the other hand, the centralization of political power by the machine has enabled city officials to move quickly and decisively in obtaining and distributing material resources. Consistent with their historical backgrounds, then, reform cities have generally been more successful at distributing power, while machine cities have been more adept at distributing material resources.

Greenstone and Peterson contend that three considerations—the upper-class bias of both reform and machine politics, the different approaches of political machines and reformers to distributing power and perquisites, and the scholarly disagreement on the proper role of the mass population—are all relevant for explaining intercity variation in the administration of community-action programs. They also point out that in a manner typical of federal programs in the decentralized American political system, OEO policies tend to reinforce rather than bring about changes in the prevailing political pattern in each city studied.

In the short run, Greenstone and Peterson believe, maximizing citizen participation in political decision-making—that maximum feasible participation of the poor required by OEO programs—tends to impede the alleviation of poverty. However, they point out that ultimately the solution to poverty may depend on increasing the political power of precisely those disorganized and politically unsophisticated low-income neighborhood groups who are just beginning to participate meaningfully in the poverty program. In fact, it may be more useful for the poor to organize so they can demand greater economic assistance in the future. Once neighborhood and minority groups develop viable political organizations, they will be able to compete more effectively in the larger polity for scarce political resources. This is precisely what black power advocates are attempting to do. How has federal policy encouraged political organization among the urban poor?

Machines and reformers in city politics

S.M. Lipset has observed that:

> . . . the political intellectual, the man of ideas, is nowhere very interested in defending inconsistencies, and every *status quo* is full of inconsistencies. Only by attacking the limitations of his political and social order can he feel he is playing a fruitful creative role.[1]

Reprinted from *City Politics and Public Policy*, edited by James Q. Wilson, by permission of the Publisher, John Wiley & Sons, Inc., and the authors. © 1968. The authors wish to express their appreciation to the Russell Sage Foundation for making possible this research. Mr. Peterson would like to express similar appreciation to the Woodrow Wilson Foundation.

[1] S.M. Lipset, *Political Man* (Garden City, New York: Doubleday, 1963), p. 345.

Accordingly, scholarly analyses of city politics have varied inversely with the changes in the political life of American cities. From the late nineteenth century to World War II, political scientists viewed with alarm the concentration of power achieved by organized political parties.

While relying on the votes of the poor, the machine cooperated in their exploitation by more privileged groups. As Ostrogorski said, machines only insured "the power of plutocracy . . . in the political sphere."[2] Machines often provided large personal profits to individual racketeers, speculators, and businessmen. Basing their power on control of lower-class voters, the most successful members of the machine emulated their robber baron contemporaries in accumulating personal fortunes. The motto of George Washington Plunkitt of Tammany Hall, a master at procuring "honest graft," was "I seen my opportunities and I took 'em."[3] Merton, himself a sympathetic interpreter of the machine, observed that one of the machines' "latent functions" was to provide a locus of political power with which the business community could negotiate.[4] At the height of their power, moreover, machines were not noted for instituting massive new government services that redistributed wealth collectively in the urban lower classes.

Throughout the twentieth century, however, the machines' power has declined, partly in response to rising education and income levels, the greater political influence of the news media, and increasing bureaucratization of welfare programs. Of equal importance, the reform movement, adopting the views of Ostrogorski and others, weakened or destroyed party machines by transforming the politics of many American cities. Reform innovations, such as nonpartisan elections and a civil service merit system, often eliminated patronage and reduced graft, two bulwarks of machine power.

As the power of the machine declined, new scholars, in keeping with Lipset's observation, began to depict favorably the political machine as the articulator of the wants of the immigrant, working-class population. They have cited the views of machine politicans such as Plunkitt himself:

> If a family is burned out I don't ask whether they are Republicans or Democrats, and I don't refer them to the Charity Organization Society which would investigate their case in a month or two and decide they were worthy of help about the time they are dead from starvation. I just get quarters for them, buy clothes for them if their clothes were burned up, and fix them up till they get things runnin' again. . . . The

---

[2] M. Ostrogorski, *Democracy and the Organization of Political Parties,* II (Garden City, New York: Doubleday, 1964), p. 299. Ostrogorski was far from alone in his bitter attack on the "machine." Other critics include James Bryce, *The American Commonwealth II* (New York: Macmillan, 1895), and Roy V. Peel, *The Political Clubs of New York City* (New York: G.P. Putnam's Son, 1935). Of great influence in this generally critical attitude toward the party organization was Robert Michels' *Political Parties* (New York: Collier Books, 1962), which documented the oligarchical tendencies within the Social Democratic parties in Europe.

[3] William L. Riordan, *Plunkitt of Tammany Hall* (New York: E.P. Dutton, 1963), p. 3.

[4] Robert Merton, *Social Theory and Social Structure* (Glencoe, Illinois: Free Press, 1957), pp. 75-76.

consequence is that the poor look up to George W. Plunkitt as a father, come to him in trouble and don't forget him on election day.[5]

Simultaneously these contemporary scholars saw reform innovations favoring more privileged groups in the community, and they began to view this movement with increasing suspicion.[6] Hofstadter's influential analysis of *The Age of Reform* spelled out the middle-class, Protestant basis of the Progressive movement as a reaction to the value system of lower-class, Catholic immigrants. Hofstadter argued that:

> On one side [the reformers] feared the power of the plutocracy, on the other the poverty and restlessness of the masses. But if political leadership could be firmly restored to the responsible middle classes who were neither ultra-reactionary nor, in T.R.'s phrase, "wild radicals," both of these problems could be met.[7]

Political scientists have added that the reformers' structural changes contributed to middle-class domination of city politics. In nonpartisan elections the lower-class voters, lacking a middle-class sense of civic duty, stayed at home, for there was no organization to stir them to political action.[8] Business-oriented civic associations and daily newspapers became the bulwark for many office-seekers.[9] City-wide elections favored politicians with independent sources of income.[10] The new city manager, with an invariably middle-class background found himself most at home with leaders in the business community.[11] Finally, these new scholars have suggested, the declining strength of party organizations encouraged an interest group politics, often favorable to large corporations and businessmen's associations.

In our view this critique of reform movement overlooks several of its important attributes. Certainly the reformers initially attacked both the machine's accumulation of power and its defense of privilege. Social workers such as Jane Addams and muckrakers such as Lincoln Steffens called for public policies which would improve the position of the entire lower class.[12] Earning the enmity of businessmen, they advocated better schools, garbage collection, and other services in poor areas, as well as the abolition of

---

[5] Riordan, pp. 27-28.

[6] For example, see Eugene C. Lee, *The Politics of Nonpartisanship* (Berkeley: University of California Press, 1960).

[7] Richard Hofstadter, *The Age of Reform* (New York: Alfred A. Knopf, 1959), p. 238.

[8] Lee, pp. 139-140. Also, Oliver P. Williams and Charles R. Adrian, "The Insulation of Local Politics under the Nonpartisan Ballot," *American Political Science Review,* LIII (December, 1959), pp. 1059-1061.

[9] Edward C. Banfield and James Q. Wilson, *City Politics* (Cambridge: Harvard University Press, 1963), Chap. 21.

[10] Lee, pp. 76-84.

[11] See John Bartlow Martin, "The Town That Tried Good Government," in Edward C. Banfield, ed., *Urban Government* (New York: The Free Press of Glencoe, 1961), pp. 276-284. Reprinted from *Saturday Evening Post,* October 1, 1955.

[12] The best source for the views of the muckrackers is in Lincoln Steffens, *The Autobiography of Lincoln Steffens* (New York: Harcourt, Brace & World, 1931).

sweatshops and child labor. The comparatively progressive policies of Theodore Roosevelt and Woodrow Wilson were in many ways the product of the reform movement.

Nevertheless, the reformers' paternalistic attitude toward the lower classes, their reluctance at times to engage in ethnic politics, and their indifference to the immediate material needs of individual immigrants prevented them from developing a reliable lower-class constituency. Following World War I, the social conscience of the reform movement was conspicuously absent; as the entire political system became more conservative, reform focused more on corruption than on general social ills. Reformers were more successful in altering political structures than in redistributing wealth to the poor.

We conclude that each scholarly tradition was more accurate in its critique than in its defense, since both the machine and the reform movement had conservative consequences. For businessmen "on the make," machine politics provided franchises and special privileges. For their better established successors good government seemed both efficient and morally praise-worthy.[13] The machine *controlled* the lower-class vote, while somewhat later the reformers' structures *reduced* it. By drastically reducing party competi-tion each protected vital business interests from significant political inter-ference. Their consequences were similar to those of the one-party system of 1896, which, as Burnham shows, dramatically reduced and disoriented the electorate in national and state party politics from 1900 to the New Deal.[14]

Indeed, once the question of favoritism for particular classes is set aside, the two scholarly traditions actually agreed on certain differences between machine and reform politics in the allocation of political values. Machines directly tied their governmental outputs to the maintenance of their organization. The machine was willing and able to distribute governmental resources to individuals, but the criterion of distribution was not whether the individual was deserving or fell within the category prescribed by the relevant law but whether the individual contributed to the political success of the organization. For rich and poor alike, partisan political criteria were the universal standards for distributing values. At the same time, the patronage system meant that party campaign workers staffed the city's administrative bureaucracy. Both policy and personnel practices, then, served to obliterate the distinction between input and output structures. The early scholarly tradition condemned these practices of the machine as an abuse of governmental power for partisan aggrandizement. Modern revisionists have noticed the importance of these practices in serving the individual wants of an immigrant, working-class population.

The reformers, on the other hand, have studiously tried to separate the input and output structures. By eliminating patronage, exposing graft and corruption, and rigorously adhering to the letter of the law, reformers have

[13] Banfield and Wilson, p. 265. For an illuminating discussion of the transformation of American reform, see Michael Rogin, *The Intellectuals and McCarthy: The Radical Spectre* (Cambridge, Mass.: MIT Press, 1967), Chap. 7, especially pp. 202-207.

[14] Walter Dean Burnham, "The Changing Shape of the American Political Universe," *American Political Science Review*, LIX (March, 1965), pp. 7-28.

consciously conformed to explicit legal criteria in distributing government outputs.[15] These steps, Ostrogorski believed, would mean the reinvigoration of democratic processes. More recent scholars, however, have emphasized the advantages such changes confer on the middle and upper classes in urban politics.

These differences in style had important consequences for urban political systems as such. Whereas the machine centralized political power in its own hands, the reformers overtly attempted to disperse this power to "better government" civic associations, the civil service, the press, and (through the initiative, referendum, and recall) to individual voters. Many reformers did centralize formal *authority* in the hands of the mayor or city manager, but these steps by no means fully offset the overall dispersion of power.[16] In sum, the machine concentrated power among a few of its own leaders, while the reform movement dispersed power to a wide range of individuals, groups, and agencies.

But this very dispersion of power produced latent consequences unforeseen by reformers. The centralization of political power by the machine enabled city officials to move quickly and decisively in obtaining and distributing material resources. The machine's distribution system may not have followed Weberian bureaucratic norms, but its cohesive, centralized structure of power enabled it to move efficiently in overcoming political barriers to the establishment of governmental programs. Once a program was established, a reform administration could employ a bureaucracy committed to principles of scientific and efficient management. But these more pluralistic reform regimes found it exceedingly difficult to secure agreement among all the centers of power who could veto their suggestions. The dispersal of power, in other words, made the rapid distribution of resources more difficult.

Both the upper-class bias common to reformers and machines and the scholarly consensus on the different political processes characteristic of machine and reform politics suggest that the real dispute between the two scholarly perspectives reflects an underlying clash of political values. Defenders of reform voiced a nineteenth century Jeffersonian optimism: widespread political participation meant good citizenship, vigorous republican government, and sound public policies.[17] The vote buying, vote stealing, and sheer organizational strength of the machine led Ostrogorski to argue that:

> Where the Machine is supreme, republican institutions are in truth but an idle form, a plaything wherewith to beguile children. . . . It is no longer "a government of the people, by the people, and for the people."[18]

[15] An excellent discussion of the goals of these municipal reformers can be found in Banfield and Wilson, pp. 138-186.

[16] Banfield and Wilson, pp. 101-111.

[17] An excellent statement of the views of nineteenth-century theorists on democracy as distinguished from the pluralist viewpoint is given in Jack L. Walker, "A Critique of the Elitist Theory of Democracy," *American Political Science Review*, LX (June, 1966), pp. 285-296.

[18] Ostrogorski, p. 300.

Reflecting the pessimistic theories of mass society characteristics of the twentieth century, critics of reform believed the public interest is better served by limiting direct mass participation in policy making. This theory argues that such direct participation as that currently generated by interracial tension too often leads to confrontations that not only make compromise of diverse interests difficult but also prevent political leaders from disregarding "public opinion at crucial moments when public opinion or intensely moved parts of it, is out of line with long-term national interests."[19] By contrast, machine control of the electorate through ethnically balanced tickets and material payoffs to individual voters reduces the accessibility of city officials to mass pressures and any temptation to demagoguery.[20]

We contend that these three considerations—the upper-class bias of both reform and machine politics, the different approaches of machines and reform to distributing power and perquisites, and the scholarly disagreement on the proper political role of the mass population—are all relevant for analyzing the intercity variation in the administration of community action programs.

Community action programs: distributing material perquisites or political power?

The war on poverty is one of the clearest examples of a post-New Deal welfare state program designed to redistribute material perquisites to lower-class citizens. Community Action Programs were expected by law to give "promise of progress toward eliminating poverty . . . through developing employment opportunities, improving human performance, motivation, and productivity, or bettering the conditions under which people live, learn, and work."[21] But the legislation conceived of poverty as a political as well as an economic condition. In a celebrated phrase it required that Community Action Programs be "developed, conducted and administered with the maximum feasible participation of residents of the areas and members of the groups served."[22] While some personnel in the federal Office of Economic Opportunity (OEO) were concerned only with finding more jobs and better services for the poor, other officials, together with certain civil rights organizations, saw this "maximum feasible participation" phrase as an opportunity to increase the political power of the Negroes and other disadvantaged citizens. According to the OEO's Community Action Workbook, for example, a "promising method" of implementing "maximum feasible participation" was

[19] Banfield and Wilson, p. 345.

[20] Edward C. Banfield, *Political Influence* (New York: The Free Press of Glencoe, 1961), pp. 260-262.

[21] U.S. Congress, *An Act to Mobilize the Human and Financial Resources of the Nation to Combat Poverty in the United States,* Public Law 88-452, 88th Cong., 2nd Sess., 1964, p. 9.

[22] *Ibid.*

"to assist the poor in developing autonomous and self-managed organizations which are competent to exert political influence on behalf of their own self-interest."[23]

According to the view that poverty was a political as well as an economic condition, low-income groups lacked financial resources, social prestige, and easy access to decision makers. Such groups continue to be known for low voter turnout where parties are weak and for the ease with which their vote can be "controlled" by strong party organizations. Most important of all, the poor have had few autonomous organizations which articulate their collective demands and maximize their electoral influence—requisites for becoming more than a "potential group" in urban politics.[24] "Maximum feasible participation" was thus interpreted as the organized and active pursuit of political power.

In practice, the OEO was constrained by the decentralized American political system to administer the "war on poverty" through local community action agencies, keeping for itself only the power to choose among the proposals submitted for its approval. Consequently, its attempt to disperse political power to the poor was confined to the formalistic requirement that representatives of the poor—chosen "whenever feasible" in accord with "traditional democratic approaches and techniques"—comprise approximately one-third of the policy-making body for local Community Action Agencies.[25] Although its actual effectiveness is far from clear, presumably this requirement would stimulate the growth of indigenous organizations, increasing the political power of the poor. In any case all the major political actors—the OEO, the big city mayors, reform and civil rights leaders, interested Republicans, congressmen, and articulate members of neighborhood groups—regarded the question of representation as potentially significant.

The duality of viewpoints within the OEO was reflected in the pattern of cleavage in all four cities. In 1964 and 1965 the four incumbent mayors regarded poverty as an economic condition and resisted those in OEO who sought to disperse political power. Initially, the mayors each formed a committee to centralize decision-making among key members of their administrations.[26] When OEO sought to disperse political power by including representatives of the poor on the policy-making body, Wagner of New York articulated the common mayoral reaction in testimony before a congressional committee:

> When I testified a year ago, I urged that the local governing bodies, through their chief executives or otherwise, should have the ultimate

[23] Office of Economic Opportunity, *Community Action Workbook* (Washington, D.C., 1965), III. A. 7.

[24] This term is drawn from David Truman, *The Government Process* (New York: Alfred A. Knopf, 1965), pp. 511-516.

[25] Office of Economic Opportunity, *Community Action Program Guide* (Washington, D.C., 1965), I, p. 18.

[26] Characteristically, the extreme decentralization in Los Angeles required the participation of other governmental units even at the beginning.

authority, as they have the ultimate responsibility, for . . . the conduct and operation of the anti-poverty program.[27]

Similarly, the executive committee of the U.S. Conference of Mayors resolved:

> *Whereas,* no responsible mayor can accept the implications in the Office for Economic Opportunity Workbook that the goals of this program can only be achieved by creating tensions between the poor and existing agencies and by fostering class struggle; . . . NOW THERE-FORE BE IT RESOLVED that the Administration be urged to assure that any policy . . . assure the continuing control of local expenditures relative to this program by the fiscally responsible local officials.

The mayors had sound political reasons for viewing poverty as an economic condition. An antiquated tax structure had created severe financial burdens for city administrations. Demands of the poor and minority groups for costly changes in education, for expansion of hospitals and public health services, expensive vest pocket parks, and improved welfare services obviously strained local budgets.[28] Mayors, therefore, welcomed federal aid designed to alleviate the economic plight of slum residents who might resort to direct action and even violence. To be sure, the Community Action Program was far from a complete answer to these problems; the resources available were both too few and too restricted.[29] As practical politicians, however, the mayors regarded any program alleviating economic poverty as better than none; besides, the accompanying publicity would give at least the appearance of action.

By contrast, attacking poverty as a political condition appeared exceedingly risky. Dispersing power to the poor would only increase their demands for more governmental services, which were already in short supply. Even worse, these demands of new autonomous organizations would inevitably antagonize other urban interests and weaken the mayor's own position. Complaints about police brutality and calls for a civilian review board had aroused the ire of police departments. Public housing authorities had often objected to the formation of militant tenant groups demanding more responsiveness to the wishes of residents. Principals and teachers generally opposed public pressure against traditional educational practices, especially when generated by poorly educated slum dwellers. Real estate interests bitterly attacked picketing, demonstrations, and rent strikes aimed at better maintenance of tenement housing. Private welfare agencies have disliked the development of autonomous organizations that compete for clients, funds, and staff. Few mayors

[27]U.S. Congress House Committee on Education and Labor, *Hearings, Examination of the War on Poverty Program,* 89th Cong., 1st Sess., 1965, p. 483.

[28]For an interesting discussion of needs, plans, and possibilities in New York City, see Thomas P.F. Hoving, "Think Big About Small Parks," *New York Times Magazine* (April, 1966), pp. 12-13, 68-72. Changes in welfare policies—and their costs—are discussed by Richard A. Cloward and Frances Fox Piven, "The Weight of the Poor: A Strategy to End Poverty," *The Nation,* CCII (May, 1966), pp. 510-517.

[29]The legislation forbade use of poverty funds for primary or secondary education and limited OEO's educational activities largely to Head Start programs.

desired to antagonize any of these entrenched interests; independent militant groups spawned by the war on poverty might well arouse most of them.

Understandably, then, the mayors in all four cities simultaneously conceived of poverty as a purely economic condition and sought to centralize power during the initial development of the poverty program. In each case, however, the chief executive encountered opposition from those who conceived of poverty as a political condition as well. These included neighborhood organizations, certain settlement houses, the more militant civil rights groups, liberal Republicans, and, in Philadelphia, some industrial unions. When OEO revealed that it would withhold funds until the poor were represented on policy-making bodies, these groups held meetings and rallies calling for dispersal of power to the poor. Significantly, their demands were also articulated by two supporters of the reform tradition, who, as our previous analysis would suggest, favored a further dispersal of political power. Newspapers, almost everywhere a stalwart of reform, were particularly important, since one of the few weapons neighborhood groups have is the unfavorable publicity that they can create for the mayor. News stories focusing on the role of the poor and official reluctance to involve them were published in each of the four cities. The *Philadelphia Bulletin* devoted an average of eight column inches per day to the controversy in the four months before the final decision on the structure of the program. In each of the cities except Los Angeles, at least one major paper backed the critical view of the mayor expressed in news stories with editorial support of varying enthusiasm for participation by the poor.

Favorable coverage of the demands of neighborhood groups reflected the traditional commitment of newspapers to the reform cause.[30] More specifically, in New York City, Republican Congressman John Lindsay had announced as a reform candidate for mayor. Many newspapers were preparing to support him against Democrat Paul Screvane, the man Wagner had chosen both to supervise the poverty program and to succeed him as mayor. In Philadelphia both the major newspapers were in bitter opposition to the former Democratic ward politician who had become mayor. In Chicago the Republican-oriented newspapers were willing to attack the mayor, although his formidable political strength made them hesitant and selective in their criticism.

Still more vigorous support for representation of the poor was provided by the liberal political clubs who had become the major organizational arm of the reform movement. Not only were the clubs ideologically committed to dispersion of power, but in all four cities they were to some degree antagonistic to the incumbent mayor. In both Los Angeles and New York relatively pro-reform candidates had emerged in the forthcoming mayoral election. The Independent Voters of Illinois and their one alderman on the council vigorously supported participation by the poor in Chicago's program.

---

[30] Another motive may have been the penchant of newspapers for controversial issues which boost circulation. But since any number of problems can be made controversial and interesting to newspaper readers, this goal is not a sufficient explanation for newspaper focus on this particular issue.

Philadelphia's more influential Americans for Democratic Action, which disliked Mayor Tate's ward politician image, lent the neighborhood groups office space, staff, materials, and the prestige of a middle-class, intellectual organization. Of the four Los Angeles area congressmen who opposed Mayor Yorty's efforts to assure official control of the program in early 1965, three were identified with reform clubs in California. (The fourth represented the one Negro district in the state.)

The reformers had their greatest impact in New York City. Democratic Congressman William Fitts Ryan, a leading Manhattan reformer who had recently announced his candidacy for mayor, attacked his rival Paul Screvane for "visions of a new patronage pool." In the spring of 1965 Ryan called for representation of the poor on the policy-making body and for administration of the programs by "democratically" selected local boards. That summer, the Republican candidate, Congressman John Lindsay, adopted the campaign style of a reformer, charging that "City Hall is now setting up a structural monstrosity" and favored instead "prompt steps to increase representation of the poor on the Council."[31]

The dual commitment within the OEO to both economic and political solutions to poverty thus became a matter of open political controversy in the four cities. The mayors held to the conception of poverty as an economic condition and sought to consolidate their power over this program. By contrast, reform groups saw poverty as in part a political condition and supported the dispersal of power to representatives of the poor. Resolution of this conflict varied according to the relative strength of the combatants. This in turn led to intercity variations in the outputs of the community action program.

Intercity variation: the attack on political poverty

In light of the contrasting machine-reform traditions in the four cities, we hypothesized a considerable variation in the local poverty programs funded by OEO. The federal agency would presumably be most successful in distributing power to the poor in reform cities, given the existing dispersion of power. On the other hand, machine cities would probably be more successful at distributing material resources. In order to test this hypothesis, we first assessed the city's *dispersion of political power,* which reflected the existing strength and past success of the reform movement. As an index of power dispersion, we used the strength of the dominant party organization, which in all cases was that of the Democratic party. The four cities were ranked as follows: Chicago (with the strongest organization), Philadelphia, New York, and Los Angeles.

---

[31] A third Congressman from New York City who contributed to the debate on the poverty program was Adam Clayton Powell. While he cannot be considered part of the reform movement, his political style (which relies on issues rather than on patronage for support) resembles that of the reform clubs. See James Q. Wilson, "Two Negro Politicians: An Interpretation," *Midwest Journal of Political Science,* IV (November, 1960), pp. 349-369.

Both qualitative and quantitative data support this rank ordering. In Chicago the mayor was also the leader of the dominant Democratic organization, whose loyal congressional delegation was noted for unrivaled cohesion. Reformers were chronically ineffective, while the Republicans had been an insignificant force in city politics since the 1930's. The Philadelphia Democratic organization also had a relatively united congressional delegation, and in the 1963 mayoral election the organization had elected James H.J. Tate, a ward committeeman, as mayor. On the other hand, the organization lacked Chicago's extensive state and local patronage and after his election Mayor Tate and the party chairman fell into a dispute, reflecting in part the greater influence (compared to Chicago) of reform Democrats in city-wide elections. In 1965, a Republican-reform candidate was elected to the city's district attorney with the support of the Americans for Democratic Action; and in 1966 an independent gubernatorial candidate came within a few thousand votes of carrying Philadelphia in the Democratic primary.

The New York Democratic party organization had so much less cohesion than either Chicago or Philadelphia that the opposition attacked the "bosses" rather than the "boss." Not only had reformers periodically been elected mayor since 1902, but the organization was defeated in the mayoral race both in 1961 by a reform-supported coalition within the party and in 1965 by Republican-reform opposition. Moreover, the New York Democratic congressional delegation had little unity. The Los Angeles party organization was even more feeble. The city was governed by a nonpartisan mayor who had limited formal powers and operated under a rigid merit system. Nor were state and county governments sources of significant patronage. Legally handicapped in local politics and denied all effective patronage, the formal party organization could not be meaningfully compared even to their New York counterparts. By 1964, the informal Democratic organizations, which had developed over the previous twelve years, were quarreling with each other and were themselves internally divided.

Since these factors have also affected electoral behavior, analyses of election data confirm these considerations. V.O. Key once noted that:

> . . . among the sure districts for each party, there were many in which the organization was so strong that no aspirant dared challenge its man in the primary while in many others the organization was so weak that a primary fight could occur.[32]

Drawing on Key's insight, we examined in each city both the number of candidates per available Democratic nomination to the lower house of the state legislature and the proportion of the vote obtained by the losing candidates. We thus obtained an index of the strength of the organization by considering perhaps the very core of its political power—its ability to monopolize effectively the path to public office.[33] The calculations were based on

[32]V.O. Key, Jr., *American State Politics* (New York: Alfred A. Knopf, 1963), p. 181. Wilson, too, has noted, "The absence of real primary contests is probably as good an indication as any of the power—both actual and imputed—of the machine." James Q. Wilson, *Negro Politics* (New York: Free Press of Glencoe, 1960), p. 45.

[33]The number of candidates aspiring for political office is, to be sure, related to the probability of the party's winning the general election. Where the party has little chance,

the 1958-1964 elections—that is, the four preceding the period when major decisions affecting the poverty program were made.

Even this crude measure of organizational strength sharply differentiates the four cities, as shown in Table 1. Chicago's powerful organization so discouraged insurgent candidates that over three-fourths of the races were uncontested. The party's power to prevent contests declined somewhat in Philadelphia, fell even more in New York, and reached a low point in Los Angeles, where scarcely more than one-half the elections were uncontested. The impact of the regular organization's strength on the voters is further demonstrated in those elections which were contested. In only 8 percent of all cases did opposition candidates in Chicago receive 20 per cent or more of the vote. This figure increased to 23 per cent in Philadelphia, to 33 per cent in New York and in Los Angeles to 43 per cent. Additional details in Table 1 emphasize these intercity differences still more, but it is clear that this quantitative index conforms to the qualitative data on the strength of the dominant party in the four cities.

We hypothesized that the rank order of cities on this index of power dispersion would be directly associated with the intercity variation in the distribution of power to the poor through community action. In order to

Table 1. Percentage of vote cast for losing candidates in Democratic primaries for lower house of state legislature (1958—1964)

Percentage cast for losing candidates	Possible contests (percent)			
	Chicago	Philadelphia	New York	Los Angeles
No opposition	77.5	67.1	61.2	51.7
1—19	14.5	9.9	6.1	5.2
20—39	8.0	20.4	16.5	20.7
40—59*	0.0	2.6	16.2	12.1
60—	0.0	0.0	0.0	10.3
Total	100.0	100.0	100.0	100.0
Number of possible contests	(138)	(152)	(260)	(58)

*In contests involving three or more candidates, the losers together can receive more than 50 percent of the vote.

there may be only one candidate, however weak the organization. But here we are comparing the dominant party organization in each city. Since the Democratic party does well in all four cities in general elections, there are few "safe" Republican seats; thus, this factor should not pose a problem for our intercity comparison.

Special calculations were required in the multimember districts in Philadelphia and Chicago. Here the number of candidates running was calculated in terms of the available Democratic nominations. If three candidates ran in a two-member district, only one race was said to be contested. If four or more ran, both seats were considered contested. In calculating the percentage vote for losing candidates in these two-member districts, the procedures were as follows. Where three candidates ran, the opposition's percentage was calculated by taking the vote of the losing candidate as a percentage of the combined vote of this losing candidate and the weakest winning candidate. Where four or more candidates ran, the percentage for one race was calculated by dividing the vote of the strongest losing candidate by his vote *plus* the vote of the weakest winning candidate. The opposition's percentage in the contest for the second seat was the following ratio: the total vote of all losing candidates, except the strongest, over this numerator plus the vote of the strongest winning candidate. In this way, contests in multimember districts were compared to those in single-member districts.

measure this power distribution through community action we constructed an index based on the following three indicators: *first,* the percentage of neighborhood and minority group representatives on the city-wide community action agencies; *second,* the relative influence of the city administration over the selection of these representatives; and *third,* the degree to which the representatives could be held accountable by an organized constituency.

Chicago officials rejected uncontrolled participation of representatives as unwarranted. By March, 1966, only 8 per cent (six of seventy-eight) of the members of the decision-making committee even formally represented the poor. Moreover, these representatives were chosen directly by the staff of the Chicago poverty program, providing only *controlled* representation. Even though OEO in the summer of 1966 insisted on twice this number of low-income representatives, no substantial change in the process of selection was implemented. The controlled selection process prevented the representatives from developing any autonomous relations with their constituency.

Direct elections were held in Philadelphia to select the representatives of the poor to twelve neighborhood committees. Each committee chose one representative to the city-wide committee, giving the poor 40 per cent representation on a thirty member body. The process of selection in Philadelphia was virtually *free of control* by either the city administration or the party organization. But it failed to encourage the *organization* of the poverty program's clients. Turnout in the first poverty election amounted to only 3 per cent of the eligible voters and the vote itself revealed a "friends-and-neighbors" pattern.[34] Without an organized constituency for whom the representatives could speak and to whom they could be held accountable, they lacked both the power and the continuing mandate to influence decisively either the poverty program or city politics in general. Developments in Los Angeles resembled the Philadelphia pattern. The poor were given 35 per cent representation on the policy-making body (seven out of twenty members). The representatives were chosen in an *uncontrolled* election but less than 1 per cent of the eligible electorate participated. The winners, once again, had only limited and *unorganized* contact with their constituents.

In New York under the Wagner administration, client representatives were entitled to thirty-two out of one hundred seats on the policy-making body and another ten seats were awarded to such neighborhood nonprofit organizations as Haryou-Act and Mobilization for Youth. But before the poor filled all these seats, which would have given them 42 per cent representation, the Lindsay administration in the summer of 1966 created a new structure which gave 50 per cent representation to neighborhood organizations. Community conventions attended by delegates of neighborhood organizations were used to select the representatives of the poor; since the process was

---

[34] The term is taken from V.O. Key, Jr., *Southern Politics* (New York: Alfred A. Knopf, 1949). Analysis of election data on Philadelphia's poverty election discloses the same tendency to vote for one's neighbor when organization is lacking that Key found in many southern states.

relatively free of official control, it encouraged *uncontrolled, yet organized* representation. While this process in some cases enabled established agencies and churches to influence the selection of representatives, more often it brought out leaders interested in developing new organizations with a protest orientation and militancy unrivalled in other cities. The leaders were at once free of official control yet capable to speak for a fairly well organized body of constituents.

Thus, Table 2 shows the New York program most fully realized the uncontrolled, but organized, representation of the poor. The greatest control over the representation occurred in Chicago, while Philadelphia and Los Angeles fell in between these two extremes.[35]

Table 2. *Percentage and type of representation of low-income groups on community action agencies' policy-making committees*

City	Percentage representation	Type of representation
Chicago	8	City controlled
Los Angeles	35	Uncontrolled, but disorganized
Philadelphia	40	Uncontrolled, but disorganized
New York	50	Uncontrolled and organized

When we cross-tabulated the index of party strength against the propensity of community action to distribute power, the curvilinear relationship presented in Figure 1 emerged. Since we hypothesized a direct or linear relationship, this finding forced us to reconsider the intervening political processes in the four cities. As we shall show, this curvilinear relationship was produced by the unexpectedly complex effect of power dispersion on *the mayor's resources, the mayor's interests,* and *the flow of demand inputs.*

The stronger the party organization, the greater the resources of the mayor in bargaining with other political actors. The relations between the mayor and OEO provide a particularly graphic example. Chicago's Mayor Daley, through his unified congressional delegation, could force OEO to withdraw suggestions that the poor be given meaningful representation. But in cities where power was more dispersed, the mayor had fewer resources in his negotiations with Washington. In New York and Los Angeles, where reform had been most successful, several congressmen publicly opposed the mayor's attempt to centralize power over the program. Thus, the mayor's political *resources* were a critical intervening variable. The relationship between power dispersion and the political *interests* of the mayor was more complicated. Where power was centralized, as in Chicago, the mayor's primary goal was to maintain the party organization which kept him in power. His machine, which had been the sole significant political force in low-income areas, did not welcome the growth of

[35] Work now in progress on more precise indicators of the increase in the political power of the poor due to the community action program tentatively suggests that in fact there was more participation in Los Angeles than in Philadelphia. The less refined indicators of formal participation presented here were unable to distinguish between the two cities.

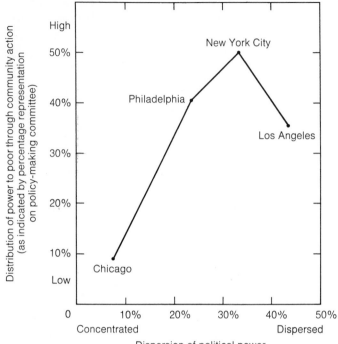

Figure 1.   Dispersion of political power and distribution of power to poor through community action

independent neighborhood organizations. Once such groups received federal poverty funds, they would have an interest in acquiring the political power to assure additional funding later. Thus politicized, they might begin to campaign for their friends and against their enemies, eventually entering their own candidates and threatening traditional party bastions. Saul Alinsky, a militant organizer of the poor, has argued that "City Hall obviously won't finance a group dedicated to fierce political independence and to the servicing of its own self-interests as it defines them."[36] Such considerations, while most prominent in Chicago, also affected the interests of Mayor Tate in Philadelphia and, to a lesser extent, Wagner in New York.

But with the election in New York of Republican-reform Mayor John Lindsay, the political interests of the city administration there were significantly altered. In fact, new community organizations in low-income neighborhoods are probably least threatening to reform mayors such as Lindsay, *who are elected over the opposition of a political machine that has not been completely destroyed.* Such mayors have depended largely on the newspapers, the prestigious civic associations, and middle-class reform clubs for support against the hostile party organizations. But they have lacked a

[36] Steven M. Loveday, *Wall Street Journal,* February 18, 1966.

stable organization to mobilize voters in low-income areas where a weakened but potentially troublesome party organization has existed and, as in St. Louis, may regain power. By supporting funds for community groups in low-income areas and listening to the demands they make for better services, reform mayors may well have been able to expand their own voting constituencies. At least they created new problems for hostile party organizations.

All of this seemed to apply with particular force if the reform mayor supporting participation of the poor was also a Republican, as was John Lindsay. The Democratic Negro or Spanish-speaking residents living in the lowest-income areas often demanded desegregated housing and education as well as more opportunities for employment as skilled workers. Such policies often threatened Democratic Italian, Polish, and Irish groups more than Republicans in silk-stocking neighborhoods.[37]

At least until 1966, the machine's distribution of material benefits to particular individuals enabled the Democratic leaders to ignore some of the Negroes' demands for improved public service, thus helping maintain the loyalty of white ethnic groups. But if new community organizations were to make more universalistic demands for better public services, it would not be as easy to maintain the Negroes' Democratic solidarity. Indeed, an alliance between Republicans and reformers, occurring in 1965 in both New York and Philadelphia, led to significant Negro defection in local elections from the Democrats. In comparison with many of the white supporters of the Democratic regular party organizations, reform groups have an ideological commitment to the goals of integration and dispersal of political power to the poor. A further political link between the well-to-do and the poorest voting groups may lie in their "public-regarding" values toward major civic expenditures, as distinguished from the more "private-regarding" values held by Catholic ethnic groups.[38] Indeed, this coalition would parallel the tacit partnership between big business and Negro groups in many southern cities. In New York City the extensive but far from total dispersion of political power induced the mayor to encourage a program aimed at the political conditions of poverty.

In Los Angeles, unlike New York, power is so dispersed that the mayor has little to gain by a further distribution of power to low-income groups. The city's nonpartisan elections and utter organizational fluidity have so destroyed party structures as to eliminate them as political threats. No political considerations, in other words, offset the manifold ways in which autonomous community groups could create new administrative problems for the mayor of a large city.[39]

[37] Because of this tension between low income whites and Negroes, Samuel Lubell argued in 1964 that "for some years to come the likely pattern of political conflict promises to be stormier at the local and state levels than at the presidential level." Samuel Lubell, *White and Black: Test of a Nation* (New York: Harper & Row, 1964), p. 160.

[38] James Q. Wilson and Edward C. Banfield, "Public-Regardingness as a Value Premise in Voting Behavior," *American Political Science Review*, LVIII (December, 1964), pp. 876-887.

[39] *Supra*, pp. 275-276.

A curvilinear relationship also obtained between the dispersion of political power and the articulation of opposition demands. Centralized power in Chicago prevented opposition demands from flowing easily through the system. Newspapers and even politicians of opposite political persuasion did not give neighborhood groups their support, lest they antagonize the mayor needlessly. Even existing protest groups which thrive on public controversy had to concentrate their attention on one or two issues—education and housing—lest they overcommitted their limited resources. As Bachrach and Baratz have argued, this "other face of power" prevented controversial issues from arising.[40] In Philadelphia, and still more in New York, less concentrated political power enabled private welfare agencies, Republicans, reformers, and leading newspapers to support neighborhood groups seeking power for themselves. Encouraged by such support, the neighborhood groups formed city-wide *ad hoc* committees which gave organization and focus to the scattered demands of neighborhood groups. As the level of controversy rose, the mayors were forced to concede substantial representation to the poor, particularly in New York City.

In Los Angeles, on the other hand, the extreme dispersal of political power actually handicapped the demands of neighborhood groups for more power. The reform clubs had no local bosses to attack, which weakened their interest in stimulating competing community organizations. Their candidate for mayor, James Roosevelt, gave significantly less support to representation of the poor than Ryan and Lindsay had in New York City. Similarly, with no machine left to reform, Los Angeles newspapers had little incentive to encourage participation. Consequently, they supported the incumbent mayor and opposed the neighborhood groups in the controversy. As a result, disorganization of the city's political and social structures left the opposition with few channels through which their demands could flow. More successful than their eastern counterparts, Los Angeles reformers so individualized power that, like Humpty Dumpty, it could not readily be put back together again—even to achieve reform purposes.

To summarize, in Chicago the confluence of three factors—the mayor's resources, his interests, and the flow of demands—all acted to reduce the distribution of power in the community action program. The mayor had both the interests and the resources to minimize representation for minority groups. Meanwhile, the opposition found it difficult to enlist political support for its demands. In New York City, power was distributed in the community action programs under Lindsay because the mayor's interests coincided with this policy. Even under Wagner the mayor's resources were so limited that demands for representation of the poor, which flowed easily through the political system, could not be ignored. Intermediate levels of power dispersion in the community action structures appeared in both Philadelphia and Los Angeles but for very different reasons. Although both mayors opposed extensive representation of the poor by autonomous organized groups, Mayor

---

[40]Peter Bachrach and Morton S. Baratz, "Two Faces of Power," *American Political Science Review*, LVI (December, 1962), pp. 947-952.

Tate in Philadelphia had far more resources than Mayor Yorty of Los Angeles with which to resist these demands. On the other hand, the availability of important allies provided protest groups in Philadelphia with channels for making their demands felt. In Los Angeles, these channels were unavailable. It is this *varying* combination of mayoral resources and interests together with the flow of political demands which produced the curvilinear relationship between existing power dispersion and the further distribution of power in the community action program.

Intercity variation: the attack on economic poverty

Our second hypothesis was that machine cities would obtain and expend community action dollars more quickly than reform cities. To test this hypothesis we again used party strength as our index of the dispersion of political power, cross-tabulating it this time against the community action dollars per poor family granted to the city by the OEO during the first two years of the program.[41] The relationship is presented in Figure 2. The per capita grant to each city at least provides a good measure of the speed with which each city initiated a relatively sizeable attack on poverty as an economic condition through OEO's program.[42]

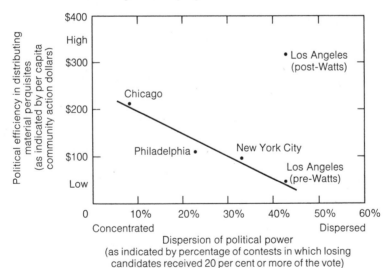

Figure 2. Dispersion of political power and political efficiency in distributing material perquisites

[41] The amount of community action dollars granted to each city for the fiscal years 1964-1965 and 1965-1966 was obtained directly from the OEO. The number of poor families in each city is the number of families with incomes of less than $3000 per year given in the 1960 census.

[42] These figures by themselves do not directly support the contention that a particular city distributed more material services to the poor than any others. The city that

Significantly enough, this quantitative measure correlates with the more qualitative and impressionistic data on the four local programs, particularly the speed and efficiency with which the community action activities were inaugurated. Thus Chicago, which received the highest amount per poor family—$211—was able to put its neighborhood centers, the main focus of its program, into operation as early as March, 1965. Philadelphia, which secured only $112 in federal funds per low-income family, did not select an executive director until April, 1965, and the program did not begin until the following summer. Even then most money was channeled through other agencies, such as the schools and the recreation department, because the poverty agency was not able to establish its own program quickly. New York acted still more slowly since it received only $101 per poor family and used this amount only haphazardly and after long delays. Its first Progress Center was not opened until March, 1966—one year later than the Chicago center. At the end of the 1965-1966 fiscal year, $12 million remained undistributed. The most spectacular delays occurred in Los Angeles which, at the end of the first fiscal year, did even more poorly, having been granted less than half as much per poor family as any of the other three cities—only $25 per poor family (calculated at the two-year rate of $50 in Figure 2). During this period the community action program barely got under way in the face of the many-sided and complicated conflict that pervaded the first year of the program.

But this linear relationship between centralized political power and the distribution of material perquisites was dramatically altered by the social explosion in Los Angeles at the beginning of the second fiscal year of the program. During the second year the city became the most favored of the four, receiving $158 per poor family (calculated on the graph at the two year rate of $316). The Watts riots, the most violent of all Negro outbursts, so disturbed OEO officials that comparatively vast sums of money were allocated to the city. But in light of the poverty program's expressed goal of reducing urban violence, through the elimination of economic poverty, the disruption of the usual operation of structural variables, such as the dispersion of political power, was scarcely surprising.

But with this exception, the linear relationship did obtain between the centralization of political power in the city and the capacity of the authorities to secure and distribute material perquisites through the community action program. The intervening variables seem fairly clear. All mayors felt it was in their *interest* to obtain as much money as possible and to spend it as quickly as possible. In this way favorable publicity would replace carping criticism. The key variable thus became the resources of the mayor to attain this goal, which as we have seen, depended directly on the

---

received the most money per low income family may have spent a much higher percentage for the benefit of relatively advantaged rather than poor citizens. But since there was no persuasive evidence for this contention, it was more reasonable to assume that approximately the same per cent of poverty funds actually benefited the poor in all four cities. If this is so, then we may conclude that those cities that obtained more money from Washington did do more to ameliorate the *economic* needs of the poor.

dispersion of political power within the city. With centralized political power, the mayor could bargain effectively with OEO officials. In particular, Mayor Daley's cohesive congressional delegation placed him in an enviable position in comparison to his New York or Los Angeles counterpart. But of equal and perhaps greater importance, the mayor needed power to still internal dissent so that he could quickly establish this new program. One potential source of dissent was the demand for the representation of the poor on the board; where this controversy flourished, it delayed the implementation of the program. But other factors contributed to program delay as well. In Philadelphia, Mayor Tate delayed selecting his executive director because he was unable or unwilling to choose between competing Negro factions. In New York City, the opening of neighborhood centers and sites for Head Start, the educational program for preschool children, was delayed by other city bureaucracies too entrenched to be forced to cooperate by a politically weak mayor. The Los Angeles conflict combined tensions among competing governmental jurisdictions with the struggle between neighborhood organizations and the mayor.

In summary, the strength of party organization affected both the amount of federal funding and the speed and efficiency with which local agencies were established to disburse the funds. Since machines were historically dependent on the efficient payment of material benefits to their various supporters, it is not surprising to find that greater organizational strength increases the mayor's ability to obtain and distribute poverty funds. By contrast, the far greater concern of reform movements for "democracy" and "honesty" in political processes and structures, as opposed to the distribution of material outputs, explains the less effective distribution of funds by poverty agencies in cities with strong reform traditions.

Democracy in urban America: power,
perquisites, and "class bias"
reconsidered

This investigation of the community action program sustains the points of agreement between the early critics of machine politics and its more recent scholarly defenders. The tendency of machine cities to use material perquisites to concentrate power (condemned by the early and heralded by the later scholarly tradition) directed the program toward solving the economic dimension of poverty. For the most part, the stronger the machine, the greater the tendency toward distributing material perquisites rather than power. The reform tradition's propensity to disperse power even at the cost of rapid implementation of governmental programs (endorsed by the early scholars but criticized by recent social scientists) led reform cities to concentrate their attack on the political conditions associated with poverty. For the most part, the stronger the reform movement, the easier it was for neighborhood groups to gain political influence but the harder for the city to inaugurate programs intended to alleviate the economic plight of the poor. It is worth emphasizing, however, that in Los Angeles—before the Watts riots—neither the political nor the economic conditions of poverty were significantly alleviated by the program. The complete triumph of reform seems .to have reduced the political system's capacity to achieve even reformist goals.

If our empirical investigation validates the consensus of the two scholarly traditions on the different political processes of reform and machine politics, it remains to assess the class bias of these two structures with regard to the community action program. In fact, community action within the war on poverty provides a case where both reform and machine administrations were explicitly directing benefits to the poor. Their common pattern of upper-class bias, in other words, was measurably reduced. This relatively greater concern for the lower classes than in the past reflects the New Deal revolution in the American party system which made the dominant national party, the Democrats, responsive to the disadvantaged urban masses. Specifically, the Johnson administration provided that federal funds be explicitly directed *by law* to a low-income clientele. Moreover, the 90 per cent federal share of the cost spared substantial expense for local taxpayers, minimizing much potential community opposition. This trend has been reinforced by the growing numbers and sophistication of urban Negro and Spanish-speaking voters. Far more than earlier urban immigrants, these groups have begun to demand political solutions for their economic and social problems. But because of the present differences in the class biases of machine and reform politics, this change has not occurred to the same extent or in the same way in all four of our cities.

As an autonomous political organization determined to maintain its centralized power, pre-New Deal machines were reluctant to become too dependent on any one social stratum—even the politically powerful business class. They balanced upper-class money against lower-class votes. By contrast, the reformers, simply by dividing ånd distributing power among various social groups, produced a political process which more nearly reflected the general upper-class dominance of the social system. Unlike the lower classes in machine cities, those experiencing reform rule received less in the way of both psychic rewards (such as ethnic balance on electoral slates) and particularistic material benefits. But in this post-New Deal period, the machine's same concern to maintain its independence leads it to oppose an independent position of political power for minority and low-income groups despite the rise of the welfare state. As a result, low-income groups in reform cities may eventually use their greater power to secure more far-reaching collective material rewards, such as substantial increases in city services. Just as reform politics was *relatively* more favorable to upper classes in the past, it may now—at least potentially—be *relatively* more favorable than machine politics to low-income groups.

Admittedly, the significant participation of the poor requires an extreme effort on the part of poverty officials and neighborhood leaders. Even in New York City, participation of community groups was only beginning in 1966.

Yet the city's program at times neared the point of complete administrative breakdown. At least in the short run, maximizing the value of participation appeared to come only at considerable cost in alleviating economic poverty. On the other hand, the long-run solutions to economic poverty may depend on increased political power of precisely these presently disorganized and politically unsophisticated low-income neighborhood groups. Rather than limited economic assistance over the short run, it may be more beneficial for the lower classes to stimulate neighborhood and minority groups to demand future economic assistance on a far more massive scale.

Finally, the varied experience of the community action program in the four cities shows that the conflict of basic political values between the two scholarly traditions over mass participation in political action parallels a continuing conflict within the American political system. As we have seen, this conflict produced a critical ambiguity in OEO's own goals. In Kornhauser's terms, the pessimistic adherents of contemporary pluralism within OEO sought to reduce the vulnerability of existing political and social elites to mass discontent and pressure by attacking the economic basis of poverty.[43] The more optimistic adherents of Jeffersonian participatory democracy sought to incorporate these same masses as effective actors in the political community by providing for the "maximum feasible participation" of the program's clientele.

We have tried to show that this ambivalence within OEO was substantially magnified by the differences imposed by the reform and machine traditions in the different cities. In a manner typical of federal programs in the decentralized American political system, OEO policies conformed to and thus reinforced the prevailing political pattern in each local community. Where the dominant party machine still had centralized political power, OEO concentrated on its goal of restraining and pacifying the lower class by improving its economic condition. In cities where an historically successful reform tradition had dispersed power, federal administrators partially realized their Jeffersonian goal of increasing citizen participation in political life.

The continuing impact of these historical differences on contemporary efforts to end urban poverty suggests how deeply rooted has been the fear of the democratic masses in a large and necessarily impersonal republic. This presumably modern issue was not only raised by de Tocqueville in the age of Jackson, but it was also debated (although less explicitly) by the Hamiltonians and Jeffersonians of the preceding generation. Moreover, as our analysis points out, the issue of mass participation in political life was also a covert but perhaps the critical issue between machines and reformers in American urban politics even before it emerged as the mass society theory of many modern political philosophers in Europe and the United States. We have argued here that this theoretical question has reemerged as a significant political issue in contemporary American politics.

[43]William Kornhauser, *The Politics of Mass Society* (New York: The Free Press of Glencoe, 1959).

Community Structure, Decision-Making, and Public Policy in Fifty-One American Communities

Terry N. Clark

Political leaders play a critical role in contemporary societies. The need for "enlightened" political leadership is nowhere more apparent than in our nation's troubled cities, particularly given the complexity of the problems they face. It is important that we continue to examine, as previous selections have already done, the role played by urban political leaders in attempts to successfully cope with city problems.

Social scientists have expended a great deal of time studying "who governs" or the structure of power and influence at the local level. A more important question, however, particularly for political scientists is: Who governs, where, when, and with what effects, in central cities and suburbs? This question focuses attention on those characteristics of a community which predispose it toward one or another pattern of influence. It also meets one particularly well-taken criticism of earlier studies of community power—that they failed to portray the impact of varying patterns of influence on public-policy decisions. The structure of municipal influence, then, is best understood by examining its causes as well as its consequences.

In this article, Terry N. Clark examines the centralization of influence in a number of local communities. This is an important selection because it reports some initial findings on one of the first large-scale comparative attempts to quantitatively examine the impact of community leadership on public-policy decisions. Clark specifically tests a number of propositions in which community contextual and political characteristics of the structure are related to the centralization/decentralization of influence. Then he examines the impact of these factors on budget and urban-renewal expenditures in 51 American communities.

Drawn from 22 different states, these communities ranged in size from 50,000 to 750,000 persons. Information on the policy-making process in these municipalities was gathered through interviews with a standard panel of community informants. An "ersatz decisional method" was used to identify actors initiating, supporting, opposing, and negotiating in four different issue areas—urban renewal, the election of the mayor, air pollution, and the antipoverty program. The degree to which actors overlapped from one issue area to the next was combined with the total number of actors *across issue areas to provide a measure of the centralization of influence—or what Clark refers to as the centralization of decision-making. By my use of the term* decision-making, *what would you conclude that Clark has really studied and attempted to measure?*

Not surprisingly, and as Clark had predicted, larger, more economically diversified cities with governmental structures favoring citizen participation (unreformed) had more decentralized patterns of decision-making. *Political influence, then, is more centralized in reformed than in unreformed cities. From your reading of previous selections, would you have expected such a finding? Why?* A decentralized decision structure in turn led to a higher level of budget expenditures and larger urban-renewal programs. *Does this conclusion differ from that presented by Lineberry and Fowler? If so, why?*

Clark concludes that these findings generally support his theory about how community contextual and political structural characteristics are related to decision-making patterns, but contradict his hypotheses regarding public policy. However, for fragile decisions—*that is, decisions on issues like fluoridation and school desegregation, which are difficult to successfully implement after they have come under general attack by outspoken local groups—the more centralized the decision-making structure, the more likely municipalities were to undertake such policies. Why does the decentralization of influence lead to the defeat of certain public-policy issues?*

During much of the 1950's and early 1960's, studies of community decision-making were largely concerned with conceptualizing and measuring the leadership and influence patterns within local communities. The central question of the research tended to be a variation of Who Governs? (Dahl, 1961) Almost all empirical investigations took the form of case studies of individual communities. However, by the end of the 1950's, some researchers had begun to undertake comparative studies of two or more communities. There were several reasons for this new trend: discontent with the limited generalizations possible from case studies; a persuasion that the methodological difficulties of measuring "power structures" could be at least partially resolved by comparative research; and—not a negligible factor—increased research funds. Initially, the questions posed by these comparative studies were essentially the same as those in the earlier case studies. Nevertheless, systematic differences began to emerge between the decision-making patterns of various communities, and a broader range of questions gradually came to be perceived as essential for understanding community decision-making processes. To comprehend adequately Who Governs, it is necessary to

This is a revised and expanded version of an article with the same title published in the *American Sociological Review*, vol. 33, no. 4, (August 1968), pp. 576-593, reprinted by permission of the publisher and author.

ascertain not only Who Governs, but also Where, When, and With What Effects? (Clark, 1967a) This series of questions focuses attention on those structural characteristics of a community which predispose it toward one or another pattern of decision-making. It also meets one particularly well-taken criticism of the earlier studies: their failure to portray the impact of one or another pattern of decision-making on concrete community outputs. The influence structure of a community is best understood by examination of its *causes* as well as its *consequences*.

With the guiding questions reformulated in this fashion, researchers began to elaborate a series of comparative propositions to specify answers for these general questions under varying conditions.[1] Although until very recently it has been easier to elaborate propositions than to test them, a number of procedures for "testing" propositions have been devised.

A first, admittedly crude, procedure is to compare two or three case studies of individual communities which have been conducted by different persons, focusing on the concomitant variations in community structures, decision-making patterns, and outputs (Rossi, 1968). But although superior to generalizing from a single case, this procedure has definite limitations. Besides the problem of whether varying research methods can yield comparable results, the simple lack of information on theoretically important variables constitutes a formidable obstacle.

A second, improved variation of this procedure is the comparison of results from two, three, or four communities which have been investigated by the same researcher, or team of researchers, using directly comparable methods and collecting identical data (Presthus, 1964; Agger et al., 1964; Adrian and Williams, 1963). While this procedure has been more successful than the first, significant advances have been made by using both procedures, as well as by combining them. But while contrasting results from a small number of communities may provide excellent stimulation for generating propositions as well as illustrative support for them, such a limited number of cases make it virtually impossible to sort out the complex interplay of variables.

A third type of procedure is the quantitative comparison of relatively large numbers of case studies (Walton, 1966; Walton, 1968; Gilbert, 1968; Clark et al., 1968). Here, as when examining smaller numbers of studies, problems of comparability loom large, while, to compound the difficulty, missing information inevitably lowers the "n" of any given correlation. But despite its drawbacks, this procedure permits more systematic comparisons than do the first two.

A fourth procedure, and the most satisfactory one for testing comparative propositions, is the quantitative study of large numbers of communities, collecting identical data in each case using directly comparable research methods. While the value of this procedure has been recognized for some time, only quite recently has it been possible to mobilize the necessary human and financial resources for an undertaking utilizing this approach.

---

[1] Cf. Clark (1967a) and the works cited there.

The 51-community study

This article is a first report on a study in which 51 American communities were investigated using the field staff of the National Opinion Research Center at the University of Chicago. To date this is by far the largest study of its kind. The background history of the study has already been reported elsewhere (Clark, 1968:Chap. 22; Rossi and Crain, forthcoming), and will be passed over here except to note that it was a joint undertaking of the International Studies of Values in Politics and the NORC Permanent Community Sample.

The 51 communities were sampled on the basis of region and population size. Table 1 presents some of the basic characteristics of the 51 cities. Representing 22 different states, their population size ranged from 50,000 to 750,000; the mean was 250,786. Cities in this range were selected in order to eliminate the somewhat unique metropolises and the smaller communities for which basic census-type statistics were not readily available. Median income ranged from $4,323 to $9,132, and median school years completed from 8.8 to 13.3. Percent foreign born ranged from 1 to 19. The extent to which cities included a sizable poor, uneducated, and often nonwhite population sector also varied a good deal: the percent with incomes under $3,000 ranged from 4 to 33; those having completed fewer than five years of formal education

Table 1.   *Selected characteristics of 51 communities*

Characteristics	Mean	N	Minimum value	Maximum value
Total population*	250,786	51	50,498	750,026
Median income*	6,186.04	51	4,232.00	9,132.00
Median school years completed*	11.05	51	8.80	13.30
Percent foreign born*	7.82	51	1.00	19.00
Percent non-white*	11.82	51	0.00	41.00
Percent income under $3,000*	15.86	51	4.00	33.00
Percent unemployed*	5.04	51	2.00	8.00
Percent Jewish†	2.44	49	0.04	17.69
Percent Catholic†	18.57	51	1.02	56.91
Percent Protestant†	23.67	51	7.60	65.30
League of Women Voters membership‡	268.33	49	0.	995.
General budget expenditures, 1957§	33,633.039	51	1,537.00	217,110.00
Urban renewal expenditures, 1962 ‖	39,148.636	51	0.	167,627.00

*Source: County City Data Book (*Washington, D.C.: U.S. Government Printing Office,* 1966). *Data are for central cities and independent cities in 1960.*

†Source: Churches and Church Membership in the United States (*New York: National Council of the Churches of Christ in the USA, 1956). Figures are for members of religious institutions; in some cases they are only estimates.*

‡*Supplied by Washington headquarters of the League of Women Voters. Data are for cities, as of January 1, 1967. Thanks are due to Mrs. Paul Cleveland for making these data available.*

§ Source: U.S. Census—Compendium of Municipal Finances (*Washington, D.C.: U.S. Government Printing Office, 1960*).

‖Source: Urban Renewal Project Characteristics (*Washington, D.C.: Department of Housing and Urban Development, 1965*).

varied from 1 to 14 percent; nonwhites were less than one percent in one city, but represented 41 percent of the population in another.

These are the rankings of the communities on a few of the approximately 300 variables obtained for each community. Principal sources for these data were the U. S. Census and such derivative publications as the *County City Data Book* and the *Compendium of Municipal Finances*, as well as various urban renewal and public health reports, and *The Municipal Yearbook*. Certain data, however, were obtained from less conventional sources. For example, we were interested in the possible importance of the religious affiliation of the population and procured religious data from a relatively little known source: the reports of the National Council of the Churches of Christ. These data are less precise than one might desire: in some cases they are only estimates; generally they were compiled in 1952; and they are not reported by city but by county. Because the religious figures were obviously crude, we initially had strong doubts about using them at all; we decided to include them provisionally, however, because they varied so much from one place to another. Percent Roman Catholic, for example, ranged from 1 to 56. As will be shown below, the number of Catholics residing in an area seems to lead to some very interesting consequences. Then because of the extensive discussions from Tocqueville to the present about the role of voluntary organizations in community life, we sought membership figures on as many organizations as possible that might conceivably influence community decision-making patterns. In certain communities—such as Dallas and Pitts-burgh—there is a single organization which reputedly brings together many leading citizens of the community and which plays a leading role in public affairs. In a case study of such a community, information on this kind of organization is of course vital. But since such organizations are not found everywhere, and since their composition and functions vary considerably from one community to the next, information on such organizations is extremely difficult to interpret meaningfully for a systematic comparative study. Ideal are membership figures for an organization which is found in virtually all communities, and which undertakes generally comparable activities everywhere. The Parent-Teachers Association was one candidate, but as vigorously local organizations, PTA's are organized around individual school districts. There is no national PTA organization in a position to supply membership figures. We considered several other voluntary organizations, but either they were not comparable across communities or membership figures for our sample were impossible to obtain. The League of Women Voters, however, was ideal from several standpoints. It is perhaps the most important single civic voluntary organization in American communities. It frequently becomes involved in significant local issues. While not identical, the activities of the League from one community to the next are carefully circumscribed by the National organization: the local chapter in at least one of our communities had been disbanded after involvement in activities beyond those sanctioned by the national leadership. The national headquarters also maintains careful membership figures on the local organizations, and generously made them available to us for analysis. In our 51 communities membership ranged from zero to 995.

Data collection procedures

In addition to these data from central sources, we conducted a series of interviews to collect additional information on matters such as political organization and decision-making.

In earlier studies (cf. Crain et al., 1966) and on the basis of preliminary fieldwork in several communities, we found about a dozen persons from different community sectors particularly well informed about community affairs. These were not necessarily the most active *participants*, but were generally knowledgeable *informants*. Attempting to collect as much information as possible, but to maximize reliability and validity while minimizing costs, we decided to interview eleven strategically placed informants in each community:[2] the mayor, the chairmen of the Democratic and Republican parties, the president of the largest bank, the editor of the newspaper with the largest circulation, the president of the chamber of commerce, the president of the bar association, the head of the largest labor union, the health commissioner, the urban renewal director, and the director of the last major hospital fund drive.

Interview schedules for the various informants concentrated on their particular institutional realms, but most interviews also contained a core set of items dealing with general community issues.

The professional field staff of NORC conducted the interviews in January 1967, generally with one interviewer in each community. In an effort to maximize reliability, interviewers were provided with a general report about the study as well as detailed interview instructions, including a list of substitutes for unavailable interviewees.

Issue areas and decision-making

To maintain inter-community comparability, in each community these same informants were interviewed about the same four issues: urban renewal, the election of the mayor, air pollution, and the anti-poverty program. These four particular issues were selected because they tend to involve different types of community actor in differing relationships with one another.[3] A mayoral election, for example, tends to mobilize the various community sectors along traditional lines of political cleavage as detailed by studies of voting behavior: income, education, religion, and so forth.

[2] Various measures of reliability and validity for the study are presently being prepared; they will be reported in subsequent papers.

[3] Cf. the theoretical discussions in Clark (1968: Chap. 3) and Lowi (1964).

Urban renewal, on the other hand, is an issue that varies considerably. It may divide a community along traditional political lines, but, due to the importance of outside funds, it may also become a general distributive issue whereby virtually all members of the community benefit from funds supplied largely by the Federal government.

The anti-poverty issue is similar to urban renewal in reliance on outside funds, thus necessitating no reallocation of community resources. But unlike urban renewal, which may be turned toward diverse subsectors of the community, depending on the content of the program, the anti-poverty program is largely oriented toward assisting the poorer sectors of the community (although there may be substantial indirect benefits to other sectors).

Air pollution, on the other hand, requires direct and often expensive sacrifices by the industrial sector of the community for the benefit of the community as a whole.

Two issues—mayoral election and air pollution—are largely local and tend to involve the redistribution of local resources, although the directions and amounts of reallocation are subject to varying definitions. The two other issues—urban renewal and poverty—principally involve distribution within the community of resources supplied from outside. The latter two issues also imply close relationships with higher-level governmental officials outside the community.

All four issue areas need the support of local government to implement basic decisions. And, of course, insofar as any decision-making structure exists within a community, it will channel and redirect the activities within these various areas.[4]

But it is just this decision-making structure which is illuminated by comparison of the patterns of influence in the four different issue areas. We attempted to measure the community decision-making structure by using what we termed "the ersatz decisional method."

We examined the number of major actors involved in each issue area, and the degree to which decision-makers overlapped from one issue area to the next: for each issue area, we posed a series of questions inquiring essentially:

1. Who initiated action on the issue?
2. Who supported this action?
3. Who opposed this action?[5]
4. What was the nature of the bargaining process; who negotiated with whom?
5. What was the outcome? Whose views tended to prevail?

The cross-classification of the five decisional stages with the four issue areas generated a twenty-cell matrix for each community. From this was constructed our index of centralization. Most theoretical discussions of centralization of authority, pluralism (here understood as decentralization), and

---

[4] We understand by *decision-making structure* the patterned distribution of *influence* exercised in a community, in contrast to the patterned distribution of *resources,* which is better referred to as a *power structure.* (Cf. Clark, 1968: Chap. 3)

[5] If there were more than two "sides" to an issue, the third (or fourth) side was treated as a second (or third) distinct "opponent."

related concepts (cf. Dahl, 1961; Presthus, 1964; Clark, 1967b) have isolated two basic dimensions, both of which are included in our index. The first is *participation:* the larger the number of actors involved in community decision-making, the greater the decentralization. Second is *overlap:* the less similar the cluster of actors in one issue area to those in adjoining issue areas, the greater the decentralization. To combine these conceptual dimensions in a single index, we counted the number of actors named by our informants, but we counted each actor only once even if he was named in more than one issue area. When we obtained the number of actors by summing as described above, we divided by the number of issue areas present in the community because in a few communities a particular issue area did not exist. There were 5 communities in which the issue of air pollution was absent, 2 for urban renewal, and 1 for the poverty program.

A few examples may clarify this procedure. Consider first a situation which most writers would label highly centralized or monolithic: a community where the mayor initiated action on a decision, was supported by the downtown businessmen, and opposed by the labor unions and the newspaper. The mayor was the major "entrepreneur" in bargaining between the various groups. And the mayor-businessmen coalition prevailed. Under such circumstances, the total number of actors in the issue would be four: mayor, businessmen, labor unions, and newspaper. If these same four actors, again playing the same roles, were the only ones involved in the other three issues, there would still only be a total of four actors in all issue areas, which, dividing by the number of issue areas, yields a final score of one for the community. This centralized community would thus rank near the bottom of our scale of decentralization. On the other hand, if we consider a situation generally regarded as more decentralized, where, for example, five different actors were involved in each issue area, the total number of actors would be twenty, and, dividing by the number of issue areas, the community score comes to five. Applying this same procedure, we computed a decentralization score for each of the 51 communities. The minimum score was 3.25, the maximum 9.38, and the mean 6.79.

A few comments are perhaps in order on some of the points of ambiguity we confronted in operationalizing centralization of decision-making, and the solutions we finally decided upon. One is the problem of identifying distinct actors. For example, in one community three labor leaders might be named as actors, while in another only "the labor unions" would be specified. We reasoned that different individuals of closely similar status should not be counted the same as three individuals from three different sectors of the community. Therefore we devised a code of some 73 community statuses, and we considered that a separate actor would be counted for each status named. But two persons occupying the same status were counted only once. A single individual could thus be counted as two actors if he were named in two different issue areas as occupant of two distinct statuses (e.g., county judge and chairman of a neighborhood organization). Some might disagree with this interpretation, but we reasoned that it was more logical to weight by the involvement of community institutions than by individual persons.

Another ambiguity concerns conflicting or missing information from different informants. Our solution was to count each new status mentioned by any informant as a new actor, but if a status were mentioned several times by different informants, it was still counted only once. There were, however, slight but systematic differences in the number of actors which our different informants would name. For this reason, we constructed weights for the different informants based on the mean number of different actors they named which were not mentioned by any other informant. The weights were constructed for the informants in the 36 communities in which there were no missing informants, and are presented in Table 2. Then in the 15 communities where one or more informants were unavailable for an interview, the centralization index score for that community was increased by the amount of the weight for the missing informant(s).

Another point relates to what might be termed the dynamics of the decision-making process: Within a given issue area, how should one conceive the relationships between the various stages of a decision? Is initiating action more important than supporting it, or does a heavy involvement of actors at the opposition stage imply greater conflict and a more decentralized decision-making process? If the answer to these last two questions were a clear affirmative, it would imply, methodologically, a disproportionate weighting of the actors involved at the initiation and opposition stages. But given the absence in this area of any theory sufficiently rigorous to permit the researcher to assign specific weights, we followed the conservative alternative of assigning equal value to every actor in the issue area regardless of the stage at which he became involved.[6]

Community structure, decision-making, and outputs

An earlier article (Clark, 1967a) formulated a series of 34 propositions relating community structural characteristics (demographic, economic,

Table 2. *Mean number of community actors named by each informant in addition to those named by all other informants, and number of communities in which the informant was not able to be interviewed*

Informant	Mean no. of actors	No. of communities unavailable
Chamber of Commerce President	*2.08*	*0*
Labor Council president	*2.14*	*3*
Newspaper editor	*1.81*	*1*
Bar Association president	*2.69*	*6*
Democratic Party chairman	*1.50*	*2*
Republican Party chairman	*1.53*	*1*
Mayor	*1.53*	*6*

[6] Ruth Moser, a University of Chicago graduate student, has experimented with alternative weighting schemes in a Master's Essay completed as part of the Comparative Study of Community Decision-Making (Moser, 1967).

legal-political, cultural, etc.) to centralized and decentralized patterns of decision-making. Subsequently (Clark, 1968: Chap. 5), refining certain of these propositions, we added several others relating decision-making patterns to outputs, and subsumed a number of the discrete propositions under a more general formulation:

> The greater the horizontal and vertical differentiation in a social system, the greater the differentiation between potential elites, the more decentralized the decision-making structure, which without the establishment of integrative mechanisms leads to less coordination between sectors and a lower level of outputs.

The empirical analysis reported in the present paper was primarily oriented toward testing the earlier propositions and the general formulation. We therefore focused on variables for which some theoretical proposition had already been elaborated, although we were prepared to include other variables that might account for significant variance in any of the dependent variables. A large zero-order correlation matrix was inspected, and variables isolated about which we had specific hypotheses or which correlated highly with the measure of centralization of decision-making. Due to the high intercorrelation of many variables, we performed a series of factor analyses to isolate clusters of variables and then from each cluster selected one or two with high factor loadings. Performance of regression analyses reduced the number of independent variables still further. We finally ended with eight, which together generated multiple correlation coefficients of 0.475 to 0.840 with centralization of decision-making and the two policy output variables. The variables and output measures used are the following:[7]

> *Population size* refers simply to the total number of community inhabitants.
>
> *Community poverty* was reflected in percent of population with incomes under $3,000, percent with fewer than five years of education, percent unemployed, and percent non-white. Since all four measures were highly intercorrelated, to simplify the analysis we used simply percent with income under $3,000 as an indicator for this cluster.
>
> *Industrial activity* was represented by the percent of manufacturing establishments in the community with more than 20 employees.
>
> *Economic diversification* comprised a dichotomous classification of communities ranked by Nelson (1955) as diversified or financial, and all other communities.[8]
>
> *Highly educated population* was simply the median number of years of schooling completed by the community residents.
>
> *Catholic population* was the number of members of the Roman Catholic Church in the county, standardized by the county population.
>
> *Civic voluntary organization activity* was based on membership in the League of Woman Voters. Community membership figures were standardized by community population size.

[7] The source for information about each variable is indicated under Table 1, except for the governmental characteristics, taken from *The Municipal Yearbook 1966* (Chicago: International City Managers Association, 1966).

[8] A dummy variable format was used when correlating qualitative with quantitative variables (cf. Draper and Smith, 1966).

The *Index of governmental reformism* was constructed from the three governmental characteristics traditionally associated in the United States with "reform" government: the professional city manager, non-partisan elections, at-large electoral constituencies (Banfield and Wilson, 1963; Adrian and Press, 1968:Chap. 8). The score for a community was the number of these characteristics present.[9]

Decentralized decision-making structure has already been discussed.

General budget expenditures were the total budget expenditures of the local community government on all items, standardized by population size.

Urban renewal expenditures were the total expenditures from Federal and local sources on urban renewal projects in the community (1965), standardized by the size of the population.

Table 3 presents the zero-order correlation matrix (of product moment correlations) for these eleven variables.

To test our propositions and evaluate the relative importance of each variable in the model, we computed the relationships among all variables utilizing a graphic variation of multiple regression analysis, path analysis.[10] We refer the reader to the works cited for a more general consideration of the method, and note here only that path analysis is a procedure for representing a causal model of the relationships among a number of different variables. Arrows pointing in the direction of assumed causation connect the variables to one another. Straight arrows represent lines of causation, while double-headed bowed arrows indicate simple intercorrelations not implying dependency relationships. The numerical figure above each arrow leading away from a variable represents the separate contribution made by that variable in each of the directions indicated. Path coefficients may vary from +1 to -1, a negative sign indicating a negative contribution. In addition to these arrows connecting interrelated variables, there is an arrow for a residual error term for each variable dependent on others in the model. Residual error terms may vary from 1 to 0; the larger the error term the smaller the amount of variance in the dependent variable explained by the model.[11]

Although over a long enough period none of the variables is without some influence on the others, at any given point in time we may, without undue

---

[9] This same procedure was used by Lineberry and Fowler (1967) except that they included commission government as a reform characteristic. In a personal communication Lineberry agreed that our weighting scheme is probably more appropriate.

[10] Path analysis, although developed in the 1920's by the geneticist Sewall Wright, has remained a seldom utilized statistical technique. The work of Simon (1957) and Blalock (especially 1961) stimulated interest in causal models, while Duncan's recent article (1966) brought path analysis as used in genetics to the attention of contemporary sociologists. Raymond Boudon's outstanding study (1967) is to date the most thorough treatment of path analysis and its relationships to more traditional statistical procedures. With the increasing concern in the social sciences for specifically causal models, and the ease of data processing made possible by high speed computers, path analysis may well become widely used in the near future.

[11] The path coefficients in Tables 4 through 8 constitute a complete path analysis diagram with all traditional elements included. The difficulties of reading such a complex diagram led us to break it down into five separate parts, each of which corresponds to a single dependent variable.

Table 3.   Zero order correlation matrix of eleven
variables of the model

Variables	X_1	X_2	X_3	X_4	X_5	X_6	V	W	Y	Z_1	Z_2
X_1 Population size											
X_2 Community poverty	.276										
X_3 Industrial activity	-.104	-.141									
X_4 Economic diversification	.516	.334	-.154								
X_5 Highly educated population	-.238	-.339	-.339	.027							
X_6 Catholic population	.037	-.441	.204	-.236	-.322						
V Civic voluntary organization	-.427	-.269	.049	-.335	.490	.083					
W Reformist government	-.199	.077	-.332	.143	.625	-.425	.276				
Y Decentralized DMS	.384	-.031	-.008	.347	-.332	.254	-.275	-.548			
Z_1 General budget expenditures	.310	-.100	-.062	-.045	-.057	.610	.042	-.015	.237		
Z_2 Urban renewal expenditures	.213	.060	-.050	.086	-.040	.252	-.005	-.053	.260	.435	

difficulty, order most of the variables in a causal sequence.[12] Six variables relate to the demographic composition and economic base of the community and, for the present analysis, may be conceived as generally constant: population size, community poverty, industrial activity, economic diversification, educational level of the population, and percent population Catholic. We shall examine in turn the impact of each of these independent varibles on five dependent variables: the level of civic voluntary organization activity, the form of government, patterns of community decision-making, general budget expenditures, and urban renewal expenditures.

Civic voluntary organization activity (Table 4)

As one would expect from the literature on voluntary organizations (cf. Hausknecht, 1962), the educational level of the population strongly

---

Each of the five tables also contains the corresponding regression equation, including the intercept, the unstandardized regression coefficients for each variable, and (in parentheses) the standard error of each regression coefficient. Linear least squares regression was used in every case; although we were prepared to utilize transformed variables, none were sufficiently skewed to justify transformation.

The five path analysis diagrams associated with Tables 4-8 could not be included here for reasons of space; they may be obtained by writing to the author.

[12] There are one or two cases that follow in which the causal sequence is not as clearcut as indicated by the path analysis diagrams. While fully recognizing this point, we

influences the level of civic voluntary organization activity. The next most influential variable was not so predictable: the size of the Catholic population. While the percent of the community residents who were Roman Catholics shows no zero-order correlation with voluntary organization activity, when the other variables are controlled in the model the influence becomes quite sizable. The impact of the extent of poverty in the community changed even more radically from the zero-order relation—from a -0.269 correlation to a +0.311 path coefficient. We might interpret this finding as suggesting that potential members of the League of Women Voters generally do not reside in areas with extensive poverty, but when there is poverty in their communities, they tend to become active in civic affairs.

Reform government (Table 5)

Our findings about the socioeconomic correlates of reform government characteristics are generally similar to those reported by earlier students of the subject (Kessel, 1962; Alford and Scoble, 1965; Wolfinger and Field, 1966; Lineberry and Fowler, 1967). The most influential variable by far is the educational level of the population: more highly educated populations tend to have reform governments. As Wolfinger and Field point out, this is most characteristic of Western communities: our index correlated 0.645 with a dummy variable for communities in the Western states. We should call attention, however, to the relationships between reformism and two variables not utilized by earlier authors. The correlation (zero order) with reformism of percent Catholic is—0.425, and that of civic activity is 0.276. Both of these relationships would seem to offer support for the traditional "public regardingness" thesis. However, when the other variables (but not region) in the model are introduced, the relationships between these two variables and reformism virtually disappear. This should presumably be interpreted as implying that when Catholics move into communities (in the West or elsewhere) with highly educated populations, they assimilate a political culture of reformism. Correspondingly, potential League members in such communities may become less active, since they are reasonably content that the victory for reform has already been won. Still, the present data force these interpretations to remain highly tentative.

The decision-making structure (Table 6)

As we remarked above, the present study was oriented principally toward investigating the causes and consequences of community decision-making patterns. Accordingly, a larger number of specific propositions had been

---

felt that it was valuable to attempt causal statements wherever possible instead of speaking merely in terms of associations. Our interpretations may then be more directly validated or revised by future studies.

Table 4.   Correlations and path coefficients for the dependent variable:
civic voluntary organization activity (V)

Independent variable	Zero order correlation	Path coefficient
Highly educated population: X_5	.490	.744
Catholic population: X_6	.083	.369
Community poverty: X_2	−.269	.311
Economic diversification: X_4	−.335	−.232
Industrial activity: X_3	.049	.213
Population size: X_1	−.427	−.208
Residual	. . . .	.716

R = .699   Variance explained = 43%

$$V^* = -1031.8581 - 0.000122\, X_1 + 5.8659\, X_2 + 3.5166\, X_3 - 58.3283\, X_4 + 85.2983\, X_5$$
$$(0.000079)\quad (2.9738)\quad (2.0055)\quad (33.8527)\quad (17.6693)$$
$$+\ 3.0859\, X_6$$
$$(1.2286)$$

*Regression coefficients unstandardized; standard errors in parentheses.

Table 5.   Correlations and path coefficients for the dependent variable:
index of reform government (W)

Independent variable	Zero order correlation	Path coefficient
Highly educated population: X_5	.625	.617
Community poverty: X_2	.077	.265
Population size: X_1	−.199	−.182
Economic diversification: X_4	.143	.110
Industrial activity: X_3	−.332	−.075
Catholic population: X_6	−.425	−.062
Civic voluntary organization activity: V	.276	.012
Residual	. . . .	.698

R = .716   Variance explained = 40%

$$W^* = -5.744202 - .000001\, X_1 + .0469\, X_2 - .0116\, X_3 + .2592\, X_4 + .6645\, X_5 + .0001\, V$$
$$(.000001)\quad (.0122)\quad (.0192)\quad (.3243)\quad (.2026)\quad (.0014)$$

*Regression coefficients unstandardized; standard errors in parentheses.

formulated in this area than for the others. Because the more general theoretical considerations relating to each proposition have been treated in detail elsewhere (especially in Clark, 1968), we here limit the presentation to the propositions themselves and a discussion of the extent to which they were or were not supported by the empirical findings.

An idea that has been advanced on several occasions[13] is that *the larger the number of inhabitants in the community, the more decentralized the decision-making structure.* But the proposition has not been substantiated on several occasions when it has been subjected to empirical test—to the great dismay, generally, of those forced to present the results (cf. Clark, 1968:96 ff.). It is therefore heartening to be able to report that the earlier theory seems to have been stronger than its empirical tests: we found a firm

[13] For documentation, see Clark (1967a: proposition 1).

Table 6.   *Correlations and path coefficients for the dependent variable:*
decentralized decision-making structure (Y)

Independent variable	Zero order correlation	Path coefficient
Index of reform government: W	-.548	-.586
Economic diversification: X_4	.347	.477
Industrial activity: X_3	-.008	-.213
Community poverty: X_2	-.031	-.220
Highly educated population: X_5	-.332	-.061
Civic voluntary organization activity: V	-.275	.105
Population size: X_1	.384	.066
Catholic population: X_6	.254	.000
Residual	. . . .	.676

R = .738   Variance explained = 47%

$$Y^* = 11.5429 + .0000 X_1 - .0462 X_2 - .0393 X_3 + 1.3340 X_4$$
$$(.000001) \quad (.0273) \quad (.0219) \quad (.3751)$$
$$-.2062 X_5 + .0012 V - .6959 W$$
$$(.2254) \quad (.0015) \quad (.1748)$$

Regression coefficients unstandardized; standard errors in parentheses.

zero-order correlation between community population size and decentralization of decision-making.

But for most of us who had theorized about population size, size *per se* is not generally thought of as the crucial variable, but various phenomena associated with it, among which the foremost is perhaps structural differentiation. With increasing size, differentiation tends to advance in the whole range of community institutions: economic, political, cultural, etc. Differentiation in the economic sphere has led to the following proposition (Clark, 1968:102): *The more diverse the economic structures within a community, the more decentralized the decision-making structure.* Here too, however, empirical support has often been lacking. But once again our findings provide strong support for the theorized relationship: the more economically diversified communities definitely have more decentralized decision-making structures.

Although differentiation of governmental institutions is less clear than differentiation in the economic sector, the characteristics of reform government may be interpreted as tending toward a less differentiated pattern than the "unreformed" alternatives of our index. Reform government is less differentiated when the set of political institutions are considered as a distinct subsystem of the total community. But if we consider the general functions performed by the political subsystem for the rest of the community system, we must recognize the political subsystem generally, and reform government institutions more specifically, as an important mechanism of integration. These considerations[14] suggest that reform governmental characteristics should lead to more centralized patterns of decision-making, as indeed they do. Reform government has the strongest relationship with centralization of any variable in the model.

[14] See Clark (1968: 107 ff.) for further discussion.

Reform government, in turn, is strongly correlated with a highly educated community population. But, the zero correlation of education with decentralization is negative. This would seem, at first, to contradict our proposition that *the higher the educational level of community residents, the more pluralistic the decision-making structure* (Clark, 1968:119). When the other variables in the model are introduced, however, the negative association disappears. But the proposition is still not supported.

Another variable closely related to a highly educated population is the level of civic voluntary activeness. We had postulated that *the greater the density of voluntary organizations in the community, the more decentralized the decision-making structure* (Clark, 1968:115). The negative zero-order correlation between civic activeness and decentralization implies rejection of the proposition; but in the causal model, the relationship—although quite weak—was positive. Highly educated populations thus tend to lead to both reform governments and higher levels of civic activity. But while the first tends toward centralization of decision-making, the second tends, perhaps, toward decentralization. Correspondingly, the general proposition about higher education leading to decentralization is not supported by the present evidence; still, the intermediate links in the causal chain need to be specified more precisely before the proposition can be verified or rejected.

A final proposition which we were able to test suggested that *the higher the degree of industrialization in a community, the more decentralized the decision-making structure* (Clark, 1968:107). The path coefficient in our model, while not very strong, suggests the opposite relationship. Even if strongly negative, however, the substantive meaning of such a finding would not be self-evident. By international standards, the United States is obviously a highly industrialized country. But such effects of industrialization as those implied by the proposition do not necessarily make themselves felt in the areas immediately surrounding large industrial installations. The more indirect consequences of industrialization—wealth, leisure time, education, more harmonious social relations—are apparently more important in effecting a decentralized pattern of decision-making than industrial activity *per se*. And when these indirect benefits are separated ecologically from industrial establishments, the relationship stated in the proposition will no longer strictly hold. One solution would be to reformulate the proposition to apply to larger ecological units—Standard Metropolitan Statistical Areas or regions. But here, the differences within the United States are so small when compared to those between the U.S. and communities in other countries that it seems preferable provisionally to retain the proposition as it stands, but to seek comparable data from communities in less industrialized countries in order to test it. Several projects are presently underway which should make this feasible in the near future (see Clark, 1968: Chap. 22).

Policy outputs (Tables 7-9)

Until quite recently, neither theoretical nor empirical work on community decision-making has been concerned with systematically relating decision-making patterns to policy outputs.[15] Consequently, the number of propositions in this area was smaller than those predicting patterns of decision-making from community structural characteristics.

One basic proposition, however, for which some support exists,[16] is that *the more centralized the decision-making structure, the higher the level of outputs.* But our findings with regard to both general budget and urban renewal expenditures were precisely the opposite of those predicted by this proposition. The fact that certain studies have supported the proposition suggest that it is not necessarily wrong, but more likely incomplete; it may apply only to certain types of decisions.

The types of decisions that have been the subject of earlier studies that have supported the proposition have been fluoridation, school desegregation, and urban renewal. One characteristic of these types of decisions which apparently differentiates them from our two policy outputs is their *fragility.* Fluoridation studies have continually stressed the difficulty of successfully implementing fluoridation programs after they have come under general attack from outspoken local community groups. The same is true of school desegregation. And, if we are to judge from the earlier case studies of urban renewal programs, and the quantitative data for the 1950's presented by Hawley, this would seem to have been the case for urban renewal as well—at least until recently. Since an important component of fragility is the newness of any particular program to a community, fragility, *ceteris paribus,* should decrease over time. For with time, community residents become increasingly accustomed to the presence of a particular activity, the personnel associated with the program establish continuing relationships with other community sectors, initial projects have a chance to be completed, and later projects improved through experience from the earlier ones—the program activities become legitimated. School desegregation and urban renewal both seem to have become less fragile issues than they were a decade ago.

In a decentralized community, a small but discontented group is much more likely to be able to find a sympathetic ear of at least one of the leaders, or potential leaders, of the community than it would be in a more centralized community where the leadership is strong enough to be able to ignore mild opposition. In the case of a sufficiently fragile issue, active opposition by even a small discontented group may delay or even halt action on the issue. A weak government, or at least one which must govern with participation and active consent of many supporting groups, is more likely to have difficulty in carrying out fragile decisions than a stronger one. Or, slightly restated, *for fragile decisions, the more centralized the decision-making structure, the higher the level of outputs.*

But if the effects of decentralization may be to lower the level of outputs in fragile decisions, by no means is this necessarily the case in less fragile decisions. Although compromise on a fragile issue may result in a complete

---

[15] See, however, the articles in Section VII of Clark (1968).
[16] See Hawley (1968), Gamson (1968), Rosenthal and Crain (1968), Crain et al. (1966), and Clark (1968:92 ff.).

stalemate, compromise on a less fragile issue is likely simply to lead to its modification. For such less fragile issues as budget construction or (established) urban renewal programs, as increasing numbers of outside pressures develop, each pleading for an increase in a particular section of the budget, or special treatment in the urban renewal program, compromise is likely to be in the direction of further expansion of these programs. And in more decentralized communities, where more pressure can be brought to bear by a larger number of groups, the expansion of outputs should be greater. These last considerations suggest, then, that *for less fragile decisions, the more centralized the decision-making structure, the lower the level of outputs.*

Insofar as budget construction and more established urban renewal programs may be classified as less fragile decisions, their size should increase with decentralization of the decision-making structure. And this we found in fact to be the case.

Decentralization of decision-making, however, is not the only factor behind budget and urban renewal expenditures in American communities. By far the most influential variable was one which has been virtually ignored by every major study of factors affecting community budget expenditures of which we are aware: the percent of the community residents who are members of the Roman Catholic Church. The zero-order correlation of percent Catholic and budget expenditures was high—0.610—but instead of declining in importance when the other variables in the model were introduced, as one might have expected, a phenomenally strong path coefficient of 0.922 was generated. This was the strongest single path coefficient in our entire analysis. The path coefficient from percent Catholic to urban renewal expenditures was not quite so impressive, but it was still easily the strongest single path in Table 7. As we suggested above, the figures that we used for religious affiliation seem to have remained unknown to most social scientists (although they are not

Table 7. *Correlations and path coefficients for the dependent variable:*
urban renewal expenditures (Z_1)

Independent variable	Zero order correlation	Path coefficient
Catholic population: X_6	.454	.620
Community poverty: X_2	.136	.527
Population size: X_1	.392	.340
Decentralized decision-making structure: Y	.350	.291
Highly educated population: X_5	−.297	.282
Economic diversification: X_4	.050	−.235
Industrial activity: X_3	.119	.181
Index of reform government: W	−.308	.052
Civic voluntary organization activity: V	−.051	.025
Residual	. . . .	.708

R = .705   Variance explained = 40%

$$Z_1{}^* = -581.9180 + .001\,X_1 + 6.7657\,X_2 + 2.0347\,X_3 - 40.1232\,X_4$$
$$(.00006)\quad (2.2836)\quad (1.5096)\quad (28.0434)$$
$$+ 22.0305\,X_5 + 3.5293\,X_6 + .0169\,V + 3.8038\,W + 17.7491\,Y$$
$$(17.2175)\quad (.9209)\quad (.1061)\quad (13.4547)\quad (10.0208)$$

Regression coefficients unstandardized; standard errors in parentheses.

Table 8. *Correlations and path coefficients for the dependent variable: general budget expenditures* (Z_2)

Independent variable	Zero order correlation	Path coefficient
Catholic population: X_6	.610	.922
Index of reform government: W	-.015	.521
Community poverty: X_2	-.100	.422
Economic diversification: X_4	-.045	-.408
Decentralized decision-making structure: Y	.237	.394
Highly educated population: X_5	-.057	.382
Population size: X_1	.310	.369
Civic voluntary organization activity: V	.042	-.126
Industrial activity: X_3	-.062	.097
Residual	. . . .	.544

R = .840   *Variance explained = 66%*

$$Z_2{}^* = -459.3432 + .0001\,X_1 + 3.8870\,X_2 + .7850\,X_3 - 50.0548\,X_4$$
$$(.0000) \quad (1.2558) \quad (.8301) \quad (15.4211)$$
$$+\ 21.4175\,X_5 + 3.7679\,X_6 - .0618\,V + 27.1004\,W + 17.2776\,Y$$
$$(9.4679) \quad (.5064) \quad (.0584) \quad (7.3988) \quad (5.5105)$$

*Regression coefficients unstandardized; standard errors in parentheses.

new). That they are somewhat old, and necessarily somewhat inexact, should simply lower their correlations with other variables. But that such strong relationships persist even with a crude measure seems remarkable testimony to the importance of a hitherto neglected variable.

How are we to explain these findings? Our first reaction was that there may have been errors in the data, but all figures were checked twice and found to be correct. Our second concern was multicollinearity. We thus examined the zero-order correlations between percent Catholic and other variables in order to search out possible strong associations between Catholicism and some other unanalyzed factor. Zero-order correlations show that communities with large numbers of Catholic residents are often in the Northeast, less often in the South, reasonably high in population density, slightly more industrialized, and have populations that are somewhat less educated, and less frequently Protestant, but have a relatively *small* percent of the population with incomes under $3,000. From these findings one might infer that the Catholic communities tend toward the private-regarding ideal-type of Banfield and Wilson, but, although percent Catholic correlated -0.425 with reform governmental institutions, strongly Catholic communities only tend slightly toward having a Democratic mayor (0.378).

Searching for factors that might be more significant than Catholicism in explaining high community expenditures, we introduced into our standard regression model, one or two at a time, region, population, density, various measures of industrial activity, percent Protestants and Jews in the population, and the party of the mayor. But none of these factors—to our surprise—seriously decreased the impact of percent Catholic membership—the path coefficient from percent Catholic to budget expenditures never dropped below 0.730.

Percent Catholic was also quite consistently influential when, instead of the general budget figure, expenditures on separate budget items were analyzed: for a total of 23 separate items, it was the most influential single variable for nine items, and the second or third most influential for five others. Its influence was virtually zero for six items (highways, highway capital outlays, sewerage, parks and recreation, libraries, and general public buildings), and negative for just two (sewerage capital outlays and total utility expenditures). Thus the impact of Catholics on budget expenditures derives not from just a few items, but is found quite consistently on about two-thirds of all budget items.

We then tried to specify what kinds of Catholics were most likely to spend public funds. Much of the literature on ethnic politics suggests that, among Catholics, it is the Irish who have been most consistently involved in politics. But there is little support in the literature for the proposition that Irish Catholics spend more than other national groups (Gosnell, 1968; Glazer and Moynihan, 1963; Levine, 1966).

To specify the relative importance of the various national groups, we computed sixteen measures based on the number of foreign born persons and persons with at least one parent born in Ireland, Germany, Poland, Mexico, Italy, Western Europe (UK, Ireland, Norway, Sweden, Denmark, Switzerland, France), Central Europe (Germany, Poland, Czechoslovakia, Austria, Hungary, Yugoslavia), and Southern Europe (Greece, Italy, Yugoslavia). These eight figures for each community were then standardized by dividing by 1) the total number foreign born and persons with foreign or mixed parents, and 2) the total community population. As the figures we used were from the 1960 census, we were concerned that certain groups, especially Irish and Germans, would be underrepresented because these figures would reflect immigration only after the last part of the nineteenth century. But although the Irish were probably more underrepresented in these figures than most other national groups, they still emerged as the most important national group. When the sixteen standardized figures were introduced one at a time into our path analysis model for general budget expenditures, only the two Irish figures were significant. With Irish as a percentage of the total community population included in our model, the path coefficient for percent Catholic dropped to 0.362; the path coefficient for Irish was 0.501. (See Table 9.) No other national group or combination of national groups significantly decreased the percent Catholic relationship. The distinctiveness of Irish Catholics, at least with regard to this issue, suggests that the currently widespread practice in discussions of city politics of lumping together persons under such categories as "ethnics," "immigrants," or even "private regarding" groups may be highly misleading.

It has been abundantly documented in public opinion studies that Catholics prefer the Democratic over the Republican party (Campbell et al., 1964: Chap. II; Converse, 1966), that they are favorably disposed toward increased governmental activities (Lenski, 1961:152), and that they support more extensive welfare state activities (Lenski, 1961:154). However, the importance of Catholicism in influencing actual policy outcomes to our

Table 9. Budget expenditures model with Irish as a percent of the total community population included: dependent variable, general budget expenditures (Z_2)

Independent variable	Zero order correlation	Path coefficient
Index of reform government: W	-.004	.542
Percent Irish: X_7	.679	.501
Population size: X_1	.330	.365
Percent Catholic: X_6	.573	.362
Economic diversification: X_4	-.007	-.255
Community poverty: X_2	.007	.243
Decentralized decision-making structure: Y	.216	.208
Civic voluntary organization activity: V	-.045	-.047
Highly educated population: X_5	-.166	-.039
Industrial activity: X_3	-.013	.030

R = .848   Variance explained = 72%

$$Z_2{}^* = 3.5899 + .0000\ X_1 + .0162\ X_2 + .0018\ X_3 - .2257\ X_4 - .0159\ X_5$$
$$\quad (.0000) \quad (.0091) \quad (.0059) \quad (.1075) \quad (.0658)$$
$$+ .0107\ X_6 + .1779\ X_7 - .0260\ V + .2036\ W + .0658\ Y$$
$$\quad (.0058) \quad (.0618) \quad (.0667) \quad (.0531) \quad (.0409)$$

Regression coefficients unstandardized; standard errors in parentheses.

knowledge has not been previously demonstrated in such striking fashion. It is to be hoped that future studies will more often include religious variables in their analysis.

But let us compare our findings somewhat more systematically with those reported by earlier research on community budget expenditures.[17] Probably the most frequently analyzed variables, not surprisingly, are those associated with wealth. When data from individuals are aggregated, most often in national studies, personal income has generally been strongly associated with budget expenditures (Brazer, 1959; Sachs and Hellmuth, 1961; Campbell and Sachs, 1967). Studies of a state or a region have been able to make use of locally compiled figures for per capita assessed value of property of individual communities, and have found strong relationships with budget expenditures (Bollens, 1961; Sachs and Hellmuth, 1961; Scott and Feder, 1957; Fisher and Fairbanks, 1968). These findings concur with our 0.382 path coefficient from education to budget expenditures; the coefficient was 0.337 from education to urban renewal expenditures. (The path coefficient for median income, when it was used in the model instead of median education, was lower than that of education.)

Most of the rest of our findings, however, are interesting in the ways in which they differ from earlier research. Studies of suburbs around New York and Philadelphia, for example, showed that measures of the industrial activity of the community were extremely important in explaining governmental expenditure levels (Wood, 1964:40ff.; Williams et al., 1965:91ff.). Our

---

[17]There are practically no studies which systematically examine the determinants of urban renewal expenditures. Duggar (1961) is a partial exception, but he included no community structural characteristics in his analysis.

findings suggest that the tendency of a community to spend more than others nearby by taxing its industries is more a suburban than a general phenomenon. Various measures of industrial activity—the proportion of manufacturing establishments with more than 20 employees, per capita value added by manufacturing, percent of industrial establishments with 20 or more employees—were introduced one at a time into our model, but were all of small importance.

Hawley observed several years ago that the proportion of the SMA population residing in the central city was more important in predicting budget expenditures than the city population (Hawley, 1951), and Brazer (1959) reported the same relationship for large American cities. This proportion was not important for our sample, however, presumably because of the inclusion of more independent and smaller communities than in the studies by Hawley and Brazer.

The other variables included in our model which exercised some influence on budget expenditures were economic diversification (negatively), the size of the poverty sector (positively), and the total population size (positively). Voluntary organization activity, however, showed no impact on budget or urban renewal expenditures.

Conclusion

Without following Comte too closely, we may suggest that the study of community decision-making has developed in a series of three stages. After a power-elitist stage inspired by Hunter and Mills, and a pluralist stage influenced by Dahl, a comparative stage now seems to be in the offing. This third stage does not just pose new questions but new types of question: no longer content with Who Governs?, the query is extended to Who Governs, Where, When, and With What Effects? A body of propositions specifying answers to these questions under varying conditions is growing, inspired by theoretical advances in several substantive areas as well as by empirical studies of decision-making, employing a broad variety of methods. For example, small numbers of separate case studies conducted by separate persons are compared qualitatively, or larger numbers quantitatively, or a single person may investigate three or four communities using comparable research procedures. But while any source of inspiration for a theory may be in some sense legitimate, it is imperative that somewhat more rigorous procedures be utilized to "test" propositions, if they are to be verified, reformulated, or rejected. And to sort out interrelationships among many variables, a reasonably large number of communities must be studied.

This paper reports on the most extensive systematic investigation of community decision-making undertaken to date: 51 communities of varying sizes and dimensions throughout the United States were studied using directly comparable research methods. Ranging in population size from 50,000 to 750,000, the communities also varied a good deal in income, education, religion, civic voluntary association activity, form of government, budget expenditures, and urban renewal expenditures. A professional interviewer from NORC collected information about the decision-making structure of each community by interviewing about a dozen persons whom earlier research had identified as particularly knowledgeable informants about community affairs. In each community occupants of homologous positions were questioned about decision-making in four contrasting issue areas: urban renewal, mayoral elections, air pollution control, and antipoverty programs. An "ersatz decisional method" was used to collect information about the initiators, supporters, opponents, and other actors involved in decision-making in each issue area. An index of centralization of decision-making was computed, based on the amount of overlap of actors from one issue area to the next and on the total number of actors involved in all issue areas.

Using these data, it was possible to test a series of previously formulated propositions relating community structural characteristics to decision-making patterns and to community outputs. The procedure used to specify interrelationships among the variables in the statistical model was a graphic variation of multiple regression analysis: path analysis.

These findings, on the whole, supported our general formulation:

> The greater the horizontal and vertical differentiation in a social system, the greater the differentiation between potential elites, the more decentralized the decision-making structure, which without the establishment of integrative mechanisms leads to less coordination between sectors and a lower level of outputs.

Horizontal differentiation of basic community structures was best reflected in the economic sphere in *economic diversification* and to some extent in the political sphere in the *index of reform government*. Differentiation was also generally associated with *population size*.

Differentiation between potential elites, although not measured very precisely, was to some extent indicated by active *civic voluntary associations*, these in turn reflecting the degree of development of a potential elite group outside of and in addition to leaders of political parties, higher civil servants, and leaders of other community institutions who may rather easily become involved in community decision-making.

Decentralized decision-making was positively associated with *economic diversification, population size,* and (very slightly) active *civic voluntary associations,* and negatively associated with the *index of reform government.* All of these relationships are consistent with our reasoning that the greater the structural support for a plurality of potential elites, the more decentralized the decision-making structure.

Our best indicator of the strength of *community integrative mechanisms* was the *index of reform government*, which tended to lead to higher outputs.

Where specification and revision of the general formulation seemed most necessary was in the relationship of the antecedent variables to the *level of outputs*. In contrast to our hypothesis, *decentralization of decision-making* was positively associated with both *budget expenditures and urban renewal expenditures*. We suggested one alternative interpretation of this finding, but further study of community outputs is certainly imperative before we can formulate more precise propositions relating community characteristics to various types of community outputs. It is necessary here, as for the other causal mechanisms suggested, to specify the actual content and structure of the processes involved—using various procedures. At this point we may turn to the highly detailed case study, which can once more perform an indispensable function. Content analysis and attitude questionnaires can also be profitably employed to relate political cultural variables to the largely structural variables utilized in our model. In this regard, analysis of social and cultural characteristics of community leaders should be especially profitable. Then, too, replication of these findings is no doubt in order—in smaller and larger American communities, and in societies outside the United States marked by differing structural and cultural patterns of local community decision-making. Only in this way will it be possible to generate and verify a more general theory of decision-making.

References

Charles R. Adrian and Charles Press, *Governing Urban America* (New York: McGraw-Hill, 1968).

Charles Adrian and Oliver P. Williams, *Four Cities* (Philadelphia: University of Pennsylvania Press, 1963).

Robert E. Agger, et al., *The Rulers and the Ruled* (New York: Wiley, 1964).

Robert Alford and Harry Scoble, "Political and socio-economic characteristics of American Cities," *The Municipal Yearbook 1965* (Chicago: International City Managers Association, 1965), pp. 82-97.

Hubert Blalock, *Causal Inferences in Non-Experimental Research* (Chapel Hill: University of North Carolina Press, 1961).

John C. Bollens (ed.), *Exploring the Metropolitan Community* (Berkeley and Los Angeles: University of California Press, 1961).

Raymond Boudon, *L'analyse mathematique des faits sociaux* (Paris: Plon, 1967).

Harvey Elliot Brazer, *City Expenditures in the United States* (New York: National Bureau of Economic Research, 1959).

Alan Campbell and Seymour Sacks, *Metropolitan America* (New York: The Free Press, 1967).

Angus Campbell, et al., *The American Voter* (New York: Wiley, 1964).

Terry N. Clark, "Power and community structure: who governs, where, and when?" *The Sociological Quarterly*, 8 (Summer 1967), pp. 291-316.

——, "The concept of power: some overemphasized and underrecognized dimensions," *Southwestern Social Science Quarterly* (December 1967), pp. 271-286.

Terry N. Clark (ed.), *Community Structure and Decision-Making: Comparative Analyses* (San Francisco: Chandler, 1968).

Terry N. Clark, et al., "Discipline, method, community structure and decision-making: the role and limitations of the sociology of knowledge," *American Sociologist* 3 (August, 1968), pp. 214-217.

Robert L. Crain, et al., *School Desegregation in the North* (Chicago: National Opinion Research Center, 1966).

Phillip E. Converse, "Religion and politics: the 1960 election," pp. 96-124 in Angus Campbell, et al., *Elections and the Political Order* (New York: Wiley, 1966).

Robert A. Dahl, *Who Governs?* (New Haven: Yale University Press, 1961).

N. R. Draper and H. Smith, *Applied Regression Analysis* (New York: Wiley, 1966).

George Duggar, "The relationship of local government structures to urban renewal," *Law and Contemporary Problems*, 26 (Winter 1961), pp. 49-69.

Otis Dudley Duncan, "Path analysis: sociological examples," *American Journal of Sociology*, 72 (July 1966), pp. 1-16.

Glenn W. Fisher and Robert P. Fairbanks, *Illinois Municipal Finance* (Urbana: University of Illinois Press, 1968).

William A. Gamson, "Rancorous conflict in community politics," pp. 197-214 in Terry N. Clark (ed.), *Community Structure and Decision-Making: Comparative Analyses* (San Francisco: Chandler, 1968).

Claire W. Gilbert, "Community power and decision-making: a quantitative examination of previous research," pp. 139-158 in Terry N. Clark (ed.), *Community Structure and Decision-Making: Comparative Analyses* (San Francisco: Chandler, 1968).

Murray Hausknecht, *The Joiners* (New York: Bedminster, 1962).

Amos H. Hawley, "Metropolitan population and municipal government expenditures in central cities," *Journal of Social Issues*, 7, pp. 100-108 (1951).

——, "Community power and urban renewal success," pp. 393-406 in Terry N. Clark (ed.), *Community Structure and Decision-Making: Comparative Analyses* (San Francisco: Chandler, 1968).

John H. Kessel, "Government structure and political environment," *American Political Science Review*, 56 (September 1962), pp. 615-620.

Gerhard Lenski, *The Religious Factor* (Garden City, N.Y.: Doubleday-Anchor, 1961).

Robert L. Lineberry and Edmund P. Fowler, "Reformism and public policies in American cities," *American Political Science Review*, 61 (September 1967, pp. 701-716.

Theodore I. Lowi, "American business, public policy, case studies, and political theory," *World Politics*, 16 (July 1964), pp. 677-715.

Ruth Moser, "Correlates of decision-making in eighteen New England communities," Unpublished Master's Essay, Department of Sociology, University of Chicago (1968).

Howard J. Nelson, "A service classification of American cities," *Economic Geography*, 31 (July 1955), pp. 189-210.

Robert Presthus, *Men at the Top* (New York: Oxford University Press, 1964).

Donald B. Rosenthal and Robert L. Crain, "Structure and values in local political systems: the case of fluoridation decisions," pp. 215-242 in Terry N. Clark (ed.), *Community Structure and Decision-Making: Comparative Analyses* (San Francisco: Chandler, 1968).

Peter H. Rossi, "Power and community structure," pp. 129-138 in Terry N. Clark (ed.), *Community Structure and Decision-Making: Comparative Analyses* (San Francisco: Chandler, 1968).

Seymour Sachs and William F. Hellmuth, Jr., *Financing Government in a Metropolitan Area* (New York: Free Press, 1961).

Stanley Scott and Edward L. Feder, *Factors Associated with Variations in Municipal Expenditure Levels* (Berkeley: Bureau of Public Administration, University of California, 1957).

Herbert A. Simon, *Models of Man* (New York: Wiley, 1957).

John Walton, "Substance and artifact: the current status of research on community power structure," *American Journal of Sociology*, 71 (January 1966), pp.684-699.

——, "Differential patterns of community power structure: an explanation based on interdependence," pp. 441-462 in Terry N. Clark (ed.), *Community Structure and Decision-Making: Comparative Analyses* (San Francisco: Chandler, 1968).

Robert C. Wood, *1400 Governments* (New York: Doubleday-Anchor, 1964).

Oliver P. Williams, et al., *Suburban Differences and Metropolitan Policies* (Philadelphia: University of Pennsylvania Press, 1965).

Raymond E. Wolfinger and John Osgood Field, "Political ethos and the structure of city government," pp. 159-196 in Terry N. Clark (ed.), *Community Structure and Decision-Making: Comparative Analyses* (San Francisco: Chandler, 1968).

Policy-Making for the Police: Dilemmas of Police Administration

James Q. Wilson

A great deal has been written recently about the role police have played in precipitating incidents of collective racial violence. These outbursts have produced tremendous havoc and destruction in many American cities since 1963. Robert M. Fogelson has argued that most of the 1960s' "riots" were triggered by commonplace, reasonable, and even trivial police actions. He feels that police actions have evoked such an extraordinary response from blacks because of their tremendous resentment and antagonism toward police in the ghetto.

One of the primary reasons why blacks so keenly resent the police, according to Fogelson, is due to either real or alleged police brutality. This involves the excessive use of force against civilians. Another, no less important reason, though much less well known, involves police harassment *or denial of ordinary respect to blacks because of their color and assumed criminality. A third, somewhat ironic reason, particularly in view of the first two grievances, is that Negroes believe that* ghettos are not adequately protected. *Many blacks feel that police maintain much less rigorous standards of law enforcement in black ghettos and also treat complaints and appeals with much less urgency in Negro areas than in white neighborhoods. Finally, resentment is further intensified because most blacks believe they are* powerless to protest and remedy the grievances *they have about police practices.*

It is quite clear that unless such grievances are redressed, blacks are prepared and willing to respond to unjust police action with continued confrontation and violence, no matter what the cost. As Fogelson observes:

> *So long as they are arrested without due cause, they will challenge ordinary arrests; so long as they are subjected to verbal abuse and excessive force, they will shout back racial obscenities and launch out-and-out assaults; and so long as they are denied redress, they will protest and, if need be, protest violently.*

What is surprising, according to Fogelson, given the extreme vulnerability of the police in urban America and the wide range of violent means available to disaffected minorities, is that blacks have thus far acted with such restraint toward the police. However, since late 1968, such restraint has given way to systematic attempts by some black extremists to kill police operating in the ghetto. Snipings and "shoot outs" are occurring with greater frequency in many central cities.

Why have the police been unable to change their tactics, strategies, goals, and behavior? In this very provocative yet pessimistic piece, James Q. Wilson argues that policy-making for the police is complicated by the fact that police departments are organized for at least two objectives, one of which produces conflict and the other of which cannot be attained. The first objective, which Wilson labels order-maintenance, involves the handling of disputes or behavior which threatens to produce disputes. Such disputes take place among persons who disagree over what ought to be right or proper conduct or over the assignment of blame for what is agreed to be wrong or improper conduct. The second objective is law enforcement or the application of legal sanctions, usually by the arrest of persons who injure or deprive innocent victims. The dilemmas facing police administration, according to Wilson, arise out of their inability to obtain agreement on what constitutes satisfactory performance of the first objective, and their difficulty in finding a strategy which would permit the realization of the second.

Wilson argues that substantial and lasting improvement in police-community relations are not likely unless there is a change in the class composition of our central cities, that is, until the position of lower-class residents is substantially upgraded. Only then will the street crime rate and the incidence of public disorder in central cities decline substantially. In effect, the solution to the problem of "law and order" does not lie solely with the police. This and other conclusions reached by Wilson raise a number of important questions about the performance of the police function in our cities. His conclusions, which should be considered further, also emphasize the need to rethink many of the proposals currently being considered by urban policy-makers for changing police training and practices.

Policy making for the police is complicated by the fact that, at least in large cities, the police department is an organization with at least two objectives, one of which produces conflict and the other of which cannot be attained.[1] The dilemmas facing police administrators arise out of their inability to obtain agreement on what constitutes satisfactory performance of the first objective, and their difficulty in finding a strategy which would permit the realization of the (agreed-upon) second objective. (There are, of course, additional objectives which a police department serves—providing certain nonpolice services and handling large-scale disorders, for example. The former is treated in some detail in the article by Herman Goldstein in this symposium.)

Objectives

The first objective I call *order maintenance*—the handling of disputes, or behavior which threatens to produce disputes, among persons who disagree over what ought to be right or seemly conduct or over the assignment of blame for what is agreed to be wrong or unseemly conduct. A family quarrel, a noisy drunk, a tavern brawl, a street disturbance by teenagers, the congregation on the sidewalk of idle young men (especially in eccentric clothes or displaying an unconventional demeanor)—all these are cases in which citizens disagree as whether or how the police should intervene. If the police do intervene, one party or another is likely to feel harassed, outraged, or neglected. Though a law may have been broken, as with an assault inflicted by a husband on his wife, the police do not perceive their responsibilities as involving simply the comparing of a particular behavior to a clear legal standard and making an arrest if the standard has been violated. For one thing, the legal rule is, in many order-maintenance cases, ambiguous. A "breach of the peace" implies a prior definition of "peace," and this is a matter on which persons commonly disagree. For another thing, even when

Reprinted from the *Public Administration Review*, vol. 28, no. 5, (September/October 1968), pp. 407-417, by permission of the publisher.

[1] This article is in part adapted from material that will appear in my book-length study of the police, *Varieties of Police Behavior* (Cambridge: Harvard University Press, 1968).

the legal standard is clear enough—as with an assault—the "victim" is often not innocent (indeed, he may have called for the police because he was losing a fight he started) and thus the question of *blame* may be to the participants more important than the question of "guilt" and they will expect the officer to take this into account. Finally, most order-maintenance situations do not result in an arrest—the parties involved wish the officer to "do something" that will "settle things," but they often do not wish to see that settlement entail an arrest. And in any case the infraction is likely to be a misdemeanor and thus, in many states, the officer cannot make a valid arrest unless the illegality was committed in his presence or unless the victim is willing to sign a complaint. As a result, the officer cannot expect a judge to dispose of the case; the former must devise a substantive solution for a disorderly event which the latter will never hear of.

The second objective is *law enforcement*—the application of legal sanctions, usually by means of an arrest, to persons who injure or deprive innocent victims. A burglary, purse snatch, mugging, robbery, or auto theft are usually crimes committed by strangers on persons who did not provoke the attack. Though there is, in these matters, a problem of finding the guilty party, once guilt is established there is no question of blame. For almost all such law-enforcement situations, the officer is expected to either make an arrest or act so as to prevent the violation from occurring in the first place. His task is the seemingly ministerial and technical act of either apprehending or deterring the criminal. The difficulty is that the officer lacks the means—the information, primarily—to apprehend or deter more than a very small fraction of all criminals. Leaving aside murder, rape, and aggravated assault—in which a high proportion of suspects are known or even related to their victims—few major crimes such as burglary and robbery that are of primary concern to the citizen are "cleared by arrest." In 1965 only 38 per cent of all *known* robberies and 25 per cent of all *known* burglaries were cleared by arrest, and even that figure is artifically high. The household victimization study done by the National Opinion Research Center for the President's Commission on Law Enforcement and Administration of Justice[2] showed that in 1965 there were over three times as many burglaries and 50 per cent more robberies than were reported to and recorded by the police; thus, the adjusted clearance rates are only about 8 per cent for burglary and 24 per cent for robbery. But even those figures may be too high, for, as Skolnick points out, there are often strong organizational pressures leading detectives to induce arrested burglars and robbers to "cop out" to as many offenses as possible in order to boost the clearance rate.[3]

There is, of course, no way to measure the number of crimes prevented by police activity, but the number is not likely to be large. Crimes of passion that occur in private places (many, if not most, murders, rapes, and serious

---

[2]Philip H. Ennis, *Criminal Victimization in the United States*, a report to the President's Commission on Law Enforcement and Administration of Justice (Washington, D.C.: U.S. Government Printing Office, 1967), p. 13.

[3]See Jerome H. Skolnick, *Justice Without Trial* (New York: Wiley, 1966), pp. 167-181.

assaults are in this category) probably happen at a rate independent of the nature or intensity of police activity. Crimes of stealth, such as burglary and many forms of larceny, may in unknown ways be affected by police activity, but the effect is probably not great—no city, whatever its police strategy, has been able to show any dramatic reversal in the rising rates of reported thefts. There is some evidence that certain kinds of street crimes—muggings, purse snatches, holdups of taxi and bus drivers, and the like—can be reduced by very intensive police patrol, the use of officers disguised as cabbies or lady shoppers, the formation of citizen auxiliaries, and the like. But even with these crimes, which surely are the ones most disturbing to the average person, two problems exist. First, no one is confident that what appears to be a reduction is not in fact a displacement of crime (to other places or to other forms of crime), or that if a reduction genuinely occurs it will persist over time.[4] And second, the kinds of police activities apparently best adapted to suppressing street crime—intensive patrols, close surveillance of "suspicious" persons, frequent street stops of pedestrians and motorists, and so on—are precisely those most likely to place the police in conflict with important segments of the community—primarily with persons who because of their age, race, or social class are regarded (and, as far as the evidence goes, correctly regarded) as most likely to commit criminal acts. In short, in the one aspect of law enforcement where there may be opportunities for substantial deterrence, the police are obliged to act in a way which, like their actions in order-maintenance situations, is most likely to bring them into conflict with the citizen.

The dilemmas of police administration arise out of the difficulty confronting a chief who seeks policies which can guide his men in performing the order-maintenance function and a technique which will prove efficacious in serving the law-enforcement function. The conflict over how the police should behave in order-maintenance cases results from differing expectations as to the appropriate level of public or private order and differing judgments over what constitutes a just resolution of a given dispute. In a homogeneous community, where widely shared norms define both the meaning of order and the standards of justice (who is equal to whom and in what sense), the police role is comparatively simple. But where the community, usually because of differences of class or race, has no common normative framework, the police have no reliable guides to action and efforts to devise such guides will either be half-hearted or sources of important public controversy. The conflict that arises over the performance of the law-enforcement function, on

---

[4] A "get-tough" policy by the police in Miami was reported to have led to a drop in street crimes, at least in one area of the city (*New York Times*, February 19, 1968). When off-duty police officers began to work as taxi drivers in New York City, there was a drop in the number of robberies and assaults against cabbies (*New York Times*, February 20, 1968). After the stories appeared, however, it was reported that these street crimes had begun to show an increase, though they had not yet risen to the level they attained before the counter-measures were adopted. We know very little about how great a reduction in crime is the result of criminal perceptions of police intent and how much the result of the direct consequences of police actions, nor have we tried (except in a very few cases) to measure the persistence of such improvement as does occur.

the other hand, arises out of the lack of any technique by which crime can be reduced significantly and without incurring high costs in terms of other values—privacy, freedom, and so forth. The dispute about the law-enforcement function is, unlike the dispute over order maintenance, not over ends but over means.

Criticisms

Organizations to which society gives tasks that cannot be performed to the satisfaction of society suffer not only certain frustrations but some fundamental administrative problems as well. The criticisms directed at the police are well known and often sound, but conditions giving rise to these criticisms are frequently not well understood by the critic. For example, police departments are frequently charged with hiring unqualified personnel, suppressing or manipulating crime reports, condoning the use of improper or illegal procedures, using patrol techniques that create tensions and irritation among the citizens, and either over-reacting (using too much force too quickly) or under-reacting (ignoring dangerous situations until it is too late) in the face of incipient disorder. All of these criticisms are true to some extent, though the extent of the deficiencies is often exaggerated. But let us concede for the moment that they are all true. Why are they true?

Explanations vary, but commonly they are some variation on the "bad men" theme. Unqualified, unintelligent, rude, brutal, intolerant, or insensitive men, so this theory goes, find their way (or are selectively recruited into) police work where they express their prejudices and crudeness under color of the law. Though a few of the commanding officers of the department may try to improve matters, on the whole they are ineffective. At best they invent paper palliatives—empty departmental directives, superficial community relations programs, one-sided internal disciplinary units—which do little more than offer a chance for issuing favorable, but misleading, publicity statements about the "new look." And at worst, the theory continues, such administrators exacerbate tensions by encouraging, in the name of efficiency or anti-crime strategies, various techniques, such as aggressive preventive patrol, that lead to the harassment of innocent citizens. The solution for these problems is, clearly, to hire "better men"—college graduates, Negroes, men who can pass tests that weed out "authoritarian" personalities, and the like. And those on the force should attend universities, go through sensitivity training, and apply for grants to develop "meaningful" community relations programs.[5]

Some critics go even further. Not only do the police fail to do the right thing, they systematically do the wrong thing. Not only do the police fail to prevent crime, *the police actually cause crime.* Not only do the police fail to

---

[5] Various proposals for changing police practices are reported in the President's Commission on Law Enforcement and Administration of Justice *Task Force Report: The Police* (Washington, D.C.: U.S. Government Printing Office, 1967), p. xi, and the National Advisory Commission on Civil Disorders *Report* (Washington, D.C.: U.S. Government Printing Office, 1968), chapter XI.

handle riots properly, *the police cause riots.* Presumably things might improve if we had no police at all, but since even the strongest critics usually recognize the need for the police under some circumstances, they are willing to permit the police to function provided that they are under "community control"—controlled, that is, by the neighborhoods (especially Negro neighborhoods) where they operate. If police departments are at best a necessary evil, filled with inept or intolerant men exploiting the fact that they are necessary, then the solution to the problem of abuse is to put the police under the strictest and closest control of those whose activities they are supposed to regulate.

The view taken in this paper is quite different from at least the more extreme of these arguments. If all big-city police departments were filled tomorrow with Negro college graduates and placed under the control of the neighborhoods they are supposed to control, most of the problems that exist today would continue to exist and some in fact might get worse. The crime rate would not go down; indeed, owing to police timidity about making arrests among people who have a voice in their management, it might go up marginally. Police involvement in conflict and disorder would have no happier outcomes, because most disorder—family or neighbor quarrels—does not involve the community nor would the community necessarily have any better idea how to resolve it than do the police now. Perceived police abuse and harassment might decline in the neighborhood, but since each neighborhood would have its own police, the amount of abuse and harassment perceived by a person from one neighborhood entering a different neighborhood (say a Negro entering a white area, or vice versa) might increase. The conflict between neighborhood residents who want more police protection (small businessmen, home-owners, older people) and those who want less (teenagers, transients, young men hanging on street corners) would remain and the police would tend, in the eyes of one group, to serve the standards of the other.

There would, of course, be some improvements. The police might have better information about the neighborhood if they were controlled by it and thus, in the event of large-scale disorders, be able to distinguish more accurately between solid citizens and trouble makers. They might also be more alert to the customs of the area and thus prepared to tolerate behavior (street-corner gatherings, loud noises) which the neighborhood tolerates, even though in other places such behavior might be regarded as breaches of the peace. And college-educated men might display more civility in routine encounters, handling incidents more impersonally and people more politely.

But it is difficult to say that such gains would be more than marginal. Some police departments (such as those on the West Coast) already have large numbers of men with some college training, but these departments (Oakland and Los Angeles, for example) are frequently criticized by Negroes for being "too tough," "too impersonal," "gung ho," and the like. (There may be no causal relation between police education and Negro criticism, but it is possible that while college men are more civil, they also have a stronger sense of duty.) It is not clear that departments with large numbers of Negroes patrolling Negro areas have experienced less community tension than departments with few Negroes, or that in any given encounter a Negro officer behaves much differently from a white one. This is not an argument against hiring Negro police officers; on the contrary, there are in my view compelling reasons for having as many as possible patrolling Negro areas. But their value would, in my opinion, be primarily symbolic (no less important for that!) and their presence would not make substantially easier the policy-making or administrative problems of the police. Nor are the consequences of different patrol and community relations policies clear. Some departments (San Francisco, Chicago) have made a major community relations effort, but they seem to fare no better than those (such as Philadelphia or Albany) with a "get tough" policy. Departments which use aggressive preventive patrol and have strict traffic enforcement policies (such as Los Angeles) produce criticism and experience disorders, but so do departments (such as Boston) which are less aggressive or strict. Though there are these differences in police practices,[6] it is not clear how they affect the management of order, the enforcement of laws, or the maintenance of good community relations.

Nature of police function

The difficulty in managing the police arises, in my view, less from the quality of men recruited or the level at which authority is exercised and more from the nature of the police function. Mental hospitals provide a useful comparison to the police in this regard. Like the police, they are regarded as essential; like the police, they are routinely and repeatedly condemned for failures and inadequacies. The indictment of such institutions found, for example, in Ivan Belknap's book, has become commonplace.[7] The appalling conditions to be found in hospital wards, the apparent callousness and brutality of the staff, the denial of rights and privileges, the shortage of qualified psychiatric and medical staff, and (equally important) the inability of such professional staff as exists to control the practices of the hospital—all these circumstances have been described, and the accounts are no doubt in large measure correct. Repeated efforts at reform have been made. Budgets have been increased, hospitals have been reorganized, better-qualified personnel have been sought, staff services have been increased, and volumes of research have been published. And yet each decade sees essentially the same lamentable conditions exposed and the same indignation unleashed. With the failure of successive reform efforts, the prescriptions have become more radical. At first the need was thought to be for "better men" and "more money." Then the attack shifted to the professional staff itself—doctors and

---

[6] Differences in patrol styles or strategies are described and to some degree explained in Wilson, *op. cit.*, chapters IV-VII.

[7] Ivan Belknap, *Human Problems of a State Mental Hospital* (New York: McGraw-Hill, 1956). It is striking to note the similarities between Belknap's description of mental hospital attendants and my description of patrolmen in large cities—see especially Belknap, pp. 115, 116, 138, 152, 154, and 170.

others were charged with "causing" mental illness, or at least retarding its elimination. The hospital was administration-centered; it should become patient-centered.[8]

In an incisive review of the literature on mental hospitals, Perrow concludes that the reason for the failure of reform has not been bad men or low budgets or improper organization or incompetent management (though all of those things may exist); the central problem is that we do not know how to cure mental illness. The problem is not one of ideology, but of technology. The hospitals are given a task they cannot perform, yet they must try to perform it, for the alternative (doing nothing) seems even worse.[9] The most important recent improvement in mental hospital care was the result of an advance in medical technology—the development of tranquilizer drugs. Changes in organization, leadership, and in the men recruited to hospital tasks have rarely produced significant or lasting results from the patient's point of view. To be sure, some hospitals manage to treat the inmates humanely—these are often small, heavily staffed hospitals with patients who can afford the high costs of such facilities. Bestial practices can be eliminated, but it costs a lot of money and requires large concentrations of scarce talent. But even in these circumstances, the improvement in the mental health of the patient does not seem to be much greater than whatever improvement occurs in less intensive (and less expensive) programs.[10]

The parallel with the police is striking. Abusive practices or indifference to citizen needs can be eliminated, but it typically requires a community that (like the intensive-treatment hospital) is small, expensive, and cooperative. In short, it requires a middle-or upper-middle class suburb. Some advocates of community control over the police argue that it is the close supervision of the police by the suburban community that accounts for the good relations between police and citizens to be found there; if one duplicates those political conditions in the central city—if one, in short, "suburbanizes" the central-city neighborhoods—comparable improvements in police-citizen relations will occur. My research suggests that it is not the degree or kind of control that produces this effect in the suburbs, it is the class composition of the community. In a homogeneous, middle-class suburb there is relatively little public disorder; consequently the police rarely need intervene in situations of high conflict. When the chief law enforcement problem involves crimes of stealth (burglary and larceny) rather than street crimes (assaults, robberies, muggings), the police need not practice aggressive preventive patrol or otherwise keep persons on the streets under close surveillance; accordingly,

[8]See the excellent analysis in Charles Perrow's, "Hospitals: Technology, Structure, and Goals," in James G. March's (ed.) *Handbook of Organizations* (Chicago: Rand McNally, 1965), pp. 916-946, and the accounts of certain "elite" hospitals practicing "milieu therapy" in W. Caudill's *The Psychiatric Hospital as a Small Society* (Cambridge: Harvard University Press, 1958), R. N. Rapoport, et al., *Community as Doctor* (London: Tavistock, 1960), and A. H. Stanton and M. S. Schwartz's *The Mental Hospital* (New York: Basic Books, 1954).

[9]See Perrow, *op. cit.*, pp. 925, 926, 930, 934.

[10]Rapoport, et al., *op. cit.*, p. 208.

it is rare for a suburban resident walking the streets at night to feel he is being "harassed." Finally, a socially homogeneous middle-class area provides the police with relative unambiguous cues as to who should be regarded as a "suspicious person" and thus who should be made the object of police attention. Teenagers hanging around a suburban ice-cream parlor late at night or a Negro in the back alley of an all-white residential community would be viewed suspiciously by the police and citizenry alike. Though this suspicion may be, in the particular case, unjust to the teenagers or the Negro, acting on the basis of it does not bring the police into conflict with the community. (But though an affluent suburb may provide the conditions that reduce the likelihood of police-citizen conflict or of police abuses of their authority, it does not provide the conditions that make the management of such disorder as exists or the prevention of such crimes as occur any easier. In short, high-status communities permit the police to solve their ideological but not their technological problems.)

The policy implications of this argument are clear, though gloomy. Substantial and lasting improvements in police-community relations are not likely until and unless there is a substantial and lasting change in the class composition of the central city population—i.e., until the street-crime rate and the incidence of public disorder in the central cities becomes closer to that in the middle-class suburbs. Only then will it be possible to reduce substantially the police-community tension generated by practices like aggressive preventive patrol and the use of gross indicators such as race and apparent class as clues to criminal potential.

Racial complication

Race complicates the issue, of course, and renders it more explosive. A black person is more likely to be regarded as lower-class or otherwise suspicious than a white person, and thus a law-abiding and peaceful Negro is more likely to be treated as if he were potentially lawless and disorderly than an equivalent white person. Innocent Negroes so treated will naturally feel a deep sense of injustice. It is sometimes argued that this would not happen if police officers were not prejudiced. No doubt many officers are prejudiced (indeed, one study indicates that the vast majority are) and this prejudice may make matters worse.[11] But the crucial point is that large numbers of

---

[11]Donald J. Black and Albert J. Reiss, Jr., "Patterns in Police and Citizen Transactions," in *Studies of Crime and Law Enforcement in Major Metropolitan Areas*, a report to the President's Commission on Law Enforcement and Administration of Justice (Washington, D.C.: U.S. Government Printing Office, 1967), Vol. II, Section I, pp. 132-139. Observers working under the direction of Black and Reiss in Boston, Chicago, and Washington, D.C., reported that 72 per cent of all white officers and 28 per cent of all Negro officers volunteered "highly prejudiced" or "prejudiced" comments about Negroes. There was, however, no clear relationship between attitude and behavior: "A recurring theme in the observer's reports was the great disparity between the verbalized attitudes of officers in the privacy of the patrol car, and the public conduct of officers in encounters with Negroes and members of other minority groups" (p. 138). After observing police behavior, Black and Reiss conclude that

innocent Negroes would still be treated in (to them) unjust ways even if all policemen were entirely free of race prejudice so long as a disproportionate number of Negroes are lower class. Violent crime and disorder are predominantly (though not exclusively) lower-class phenomena;[12] Negroes are disproportionally (though far from exclusively) lower class; a black skin, therefore, will continue to be a statistically defensible (though individually unjust) cue that triggers an officer's suspicion. Among the consequences of this generalization will be continued police suspicion of blacks and continued Negro antagonism toward the police.

The point is perhaps more easily understood if we examine other cues to which police respond and other forms of prejudice which they may have. Young people commit a disproportionate share of many kinds of crime, especially crimes against property. Being young is therefore a statistically useful cue to an officer who is scanning a population in search of persons more likely than others to commit, or to have committed, a crime. In addition, it is quite possible that the police have "youth prejudice"—that is, they may impute to young people even more criminality than in fact they possess, just as officers having race prejudice impute to Negroes more criminality than in fact they display. But if all officers were cured of "youth prejudice," young people would still be singled out for special attention and suspicion. The difference, of course, is that young people outgrow their youth, while Negroes cannot outgrow their blackness.

The best evidence that race prejudice is not the crucial factor can be found in the behavior of Negro police officers. There has been no systematic study of such men, but my observations suggest that black policemen are as suspicious and tough in black neighborhoods as white officers. Indeed, in the long run Negroes have an advantage over youth. It may be possible to improve the class position of Negroes so that the crime rates found among them will be no higher (and perhaps even lower) than the rates found among whites. Then there will be no reason, other than prejudice, why an officer would treat a Negro differently from a white. By contrast, there is probably no way even in principle to reduce greatly the crimogenic properties of youth and therefore no way even in principle to make the police less suspicious of young people.

If the fundamental problem is one of class (admittedly greatly complicated by the problem of race), what can a police administrator do in the short run while he waits for society somehow to solve the class problem? If the point of view presented here is correct, not a great deal. But since even marginal gains

"Policemen generally do not disproportionately behave aggressively or negatively toward Negroes," though they do "disproportionately behave amiably or postively toward white citizens" (p. 56).

[12] A good summary of the evidence on the disproportionately lower-class origin of assaultive crime is Marvin E. Wolfgang's *Crimes of Violence,* a report to the President's Commission on Law Enforcement and Administration of Justice (1967), pp. 166-169. Additional evidence based on direct observation can be found in Walter B. Miller's "Violent Crimes in City Gangs," *Annals,* Vol. 364 (March 1966), pp. 96-112, and "Theft Behavior in City Gangs," in Malcolm W. Klein's *Juvenile Gangs in Context* (Englewood Cliffs, N.J.: Prentice-Hall, 1967), p. 34.

are desirable when conditions are (or are widely thought to be) deplorable, it is worth considering palliatives however slight may be their benefits.

First, the police should recognize clearly that order maintenance is their central function—central both in the demands it makes on time and resources and in the opportunities it affords for making a difference in the lives of the citizens. Hunting criminals both occupies less time (at least for the patrolmen) and provides fewer chances for decisive action. How well disputes are settled may depend crucially on how competent, knowledgeable, and sensitive the police are; how fast the crime rate mounts is much less dependent on the level and nature of police activity. (As will be argued below, other than by reducing the size of the lower class the best way society can affect the crime rate may be through the court and correctional systems rather than through the police.)

Order-Maintenance Function

A police department that places order maintenance uppermost in its priorities will judge patrolmen less by their arrest records and more by their ability to keep the peace on their beat. This will require, in turn, that sergeants and other supervisory personnel concern themselves more with how the patrolmen function in family fights, teenage disturbances, street corner brawls, and civil disorders, and less with how well they take reports at the scene of burglary or how many traffic tickets they issue during a tour of duty. Order maintenance also requires that the police have available a wider range of options for handling disorder than is afforded by the choice between making an arrest and doing nothing. Detoxification centers should be available as an alternative to jail for drunks. Family-service units should be formed which can immediately assist patrolmen handling domestic quarrels. Community-service officers should be available to provide information, answer complaints, and deal with neighborhood tensions and rumors.

Patrolmen who are given the order-maintenance function will obviously require a great deal of information about their beats—more than can be obtained by riding around in a patrol car or rotating frequently among several beats. Obtaining this knowledge will be made easier by the decentralization of the patrol function so that local commanders deal with local conditions subject to general policy guidelines from the police administrator. This decentralization need not always take the form of proliferating precinct station houses—these facilities, as traditionally used for mustering the watch, jailing prisoners, and keeping records, are expensive. Many of them, indeed, were built in a period when patrolmen, like firemen, slept in when they had night duty. Smaller, less elaborate, and more numerous "store-front" police offices scattered throughout central-city neighborhoods might prove more effective and less expensive. Officers assigned to a particular neighborhood ought to remain in that area for long periods of time, rather than experience frequent rotation among neighborhoods. An even more radical experiment might be to assess the value of having patrolmen actually live in certain key areas. For example, some officers might be encouraged, on a volunteer basis, to live in public housing projects. To make such an assignment more attractive and to increase the pay of the officer, he could be given the apartment rent-free or at a substantial discount.

Such decentralization of function requires the strengthening of the command system if it is not to produce inconsistent behavior, political intervention, and corruption. Supervisory officers, especially watch commanders, ought to have more authority to assign, direct, and evaluate their officers. Mechanical, fixed assignments and evaluation solely by written examinations decrease the possibility of inducing patrolmen to take seriously their order-maintenance function and lead them instead to emphasize following the safe routine, memorizing the penal code and departmental rule book, and "pushing paper"—filing reports, writing tickets, and so forth.

At the same time, if patrolmen are expected to devote themselves primarily to the most conflict-laden, unpleasant parts of their task, there must be rewards available that are commensurate with the burdens. At present, the major rewards open to the patrolman—promotion, higher pay, specialized duty—all take him out of the patrol force and place him in supervisory posts, criminal investigation, or headquarters staff units. If the patrol function is the most important and difficult job in the department, the best men ought to be rewarded for doing it well in ways that leave them *in* the patrol force and on the street. It should be possible to obtain substantial pay increases while remaining a patrolman, just as it is now possible to win higher salaries in the Federal Bureau of Investigation while remaining a special agent.

Getting good men to serve, not only in the police department, but in those police roles that are the most demanding, may produce only a marginal gain, but we are largely ignorant of how to achieve even that. Almost no systematic research has been done to define and measure those qualities characteristic of officers best able to keep the peace. Entrance examination in many states and cities may not measure any relevant quality other than (perhaps) general literacy, familiarity with a police handbook, or some knowledge of current events. Indeed, there is hardly any evidence that they measure even these traits very accurately. How—or indeed, whether—such tests can be more useful is a matter on which we know very little, and perhaps a modest amount of research would be in order (though I would not be surprised if such research turned out to be inconclusive).

Policy statements

If able men are found and assigned to neighborhood patrol forces under conditions that will facilitate their understanding of neighborhood conditions and personalities and if they are rewarded for successful performance of the peace-keeping function, what in concrete terms will these men actually do? How, in short, does one keep the peace? Some have argued that police departments ought to develop and issue policy statements that will give some guidance to officers who must necessarily exercise wide discretion with respect to matters where legal codes contain few applicable rules.[13] To the extent this is possible, of course it should be done, and it is not being done at all in many departments. But it would be a mistake to assume that policies can be found that will provide meaningful guides to action in most situations of real or potential disorder. The most feasible rules perhaps are those which tell the patrolman what *not* to do—don't use racial epithets, don't hit a man except in self-defense, don't grasp a man's arm or shoulder unless it is necessary to complete an arrest or prevent violence, and so forth. But relatively few rules can be devised that tell a patrolman what he *should* do with quarrelling lovers, angry neighbors, or disputatious drunks. This is not because the police have had little experience with such matters (on the contrary!) or even because they do know in a given case what to do (they may), but because so much depends on the particular circumstances of time, place, event, and personality. No psychiatrist would attempt to produce, much less use, a "how-to-do-it" manual for these cases, and he has the advantage of dealing with people at his leisure, over long periods of time, and in moments of relative calm. The best that can be done is to list "factors to be taken into account," but in the concrete case everything depends on *how* they are taken into account.

In the broadest terms, the patrolman in performing his order-maintenance function is neither a bureaucrat nor a professional, and thus neither increased bureaucratization nor increased professionalism will be of much value. He is not a bureaucrat in that he does not and cannot apply general rules to specific cases—there are no general rules, and thus his discretion is wide. (In performing his law-enforcement function, by contrast, he can act more nearly like a bureaucrat—the legal rules defining a crime are relatively unambiguous and the officer's discretion, especially if it is a serious crime, is narrow.) On the other hand, the patrolman is not a professional—there is no organized group of practitioners (as there is with doctors or physicists) who can impart to him by education certain information and equip him by apprenticeship with certain arts and skills that will make him competent to serve a "client" when the latter cannot be the sole judge of the quality of the service he receives. Nor do such external reference groups (professional societies) exist to certify that the patrolman is competent or to make him subject to a code of ethics and a sense of duty.

The patrolman is neither a bureaucrat nor a professional, but a member of a *craft*. As with most crafts, there is no generalized, written body of special knowledge; learning is by apprenticeship, but the apprenticeship takes place on the job rather than in an academy; the primary reference group from which the apprentice wins (or fails to win) respect are his colleagues on the job, not fellow members of his discipline wherever they may be; and the members, conscious of having a special skill or task, think of themselves as set apart from society and in need of restrictions on entry. But unlike other

---

[13] See President's Commission on Law Enforcement and Administration of Justice, *Task Force Report: The Police* (Washington, D. C.: U. S. Government Printing Office, 1967), pp. 21-27.

members of a craft—carpenters, for example, or journalists—the police work in an environment that is usually apprehensive and often hostile, and they produce no product (like a finished house or a well-written newspaper) the value of which is evident and easily judged.

An attempt to change a craft into a bureaucracy will be perceived by the members as a failure of confidence and a withdrawal of support and thus strongly resisted; efforts to change them into a profession will be seen as irrelevant and thus in great part ignored. Such gains as can be made in the way the police handle citizens are not likely to come primarily from either proliferating rules (i.e., bureaucratizing the police) or sending officers to colleges, special training programs, or human relations institutes (i.e., "professionalizing" the police). Instead, the most significant changes will be in organization and leadership in order to increase the officer's familiarity with and sensitivity to the neighborhood he patrols and rewarding him for doing what is judged (necessarily after the fact) to be the right thing rather than simply the "efficient" thing.

Law-enforcement function

These recommendations leave out of account the law-enforcement function of the police. This has been deliberate, partly because the crook-catching, crime-stopping function is so often exaggerated. But obviously there is a law-enforcement function, and it is in any given case hard to separate from the order-maintenance function. Law enforcement ideally should be organized differently from order maintenance, however. It is, for example, more suitably managed through centralized command structures, the issuance of explicit rules, and the specialization of tasks (burglary details, homicide details, traffic enforcement divisions, and so forth). Perhaps a police department should make the two functions even more separate than they are now. For example, there is some impressionistic evidence that such tactics worsen police-community relations.[14] Perhaps the roving patrol force should be composed of men different from those in the neighborhood patrol force, so that the tensions created by the former could be directed away from the role performed by the latter. Or perhaps intensive street patrol in a particular area could be done under the guidance of and on the basis of tactical intelligence furnished by neighborhood patrol officers who are best able to distinguish between innocent and suspicious behavior and between decent citizens and "bad actors."

But in crime prevention not too much should be expected of the police. I doubt that any deployment, any strategy, or any organizational principles will permit the police to make more than a slight or temporary reduction in the rate of most common crimes. As the police themselves are fond of saying, "we don't cause crime," and, as I would like to see them add, "we can't stop crime." They can and should make arrests and they can and should

[14] *Report* of the National Advisory Commission on Civil Disorders (1968), chapter 11.

investigate suspicious circumstances. But I know of no police administrator who is optimistic that they can make more than marginal gains, however they behave. It would be well, therefore, not to "over-sell" proposed improvements in police manpower, organization, training, equipment, or tactics. Already too many citizens share the rather dangerous view that if only we "unleashed" the police we could "stop crime"—dangerous because if we act on that assumption we are likely to produce only frustrated expectations and deeper passions.

Indeed, it might be well if we shifted the focus of our legitimate concern to the behavior of those institutions that dispose of criminals once arrested—the courts and the correctional and probation systems. For all offenses other than the most trivial, the vast majority of the persons processed by these institutions are repeaters. According to one estimate, 87.5 per cent of all persons arrested for nontraffic offenses have been arrested before.[15] The average person arrested will be arrested 7.6 times in his lifetime.[16] The problem of recidivism is obviously of the greatest importance—if we fail to induce a person after his first arrest to avoid crime, there is a strong chance we will have to arrest him six or seven more times; how many more times we *should* arrest him for crimes we do not learn of is anyone's guess. In the simplest cost-effective terms, a dollar invested in the right correctional program is likely to have a higher marginal product than a dollar invested in the right police program.

But what is the "right program"? Do we have a correctional technology capable of significantly reducing the recidivism rate? I am not sure we do, or that we ever will, but I suspect that we have not tried very hard to find out. There have been some promising experiments with community-based, heavily staffed programs in California, Utah, and New Jersey, but there appears to be little organized effort to repeat these experiments elsewhere, or if they are repeated to evaluate them rigorously, or if they are evaluated to institutionalize what we learn from them.[17] In our preoccupation with the crime problem, we have come to identify it either as wholly a "social" problem (which can only be solved in three or four generations by programs which might—no one quite seems to be sure how—eliminate the lower classes) or as a "police" problem which can be solved only by taking the "handcuffs" off the police and "cracking down." I am certainly not opposed to ameliorating social problems or to increasing public support for the police, but I would like to see at least an equivalent amount of attention given to improving the way existing institutions now manage the offenders who have already shown by their actions that antipoverty programs are yet to have a therapeutic

[15] Ronald Christensen, "Projected Percentage of U.S. Population With Criminal Arrest and Conviction Records," in President's Commission on Law Enforcement and Administration of Justice, *Task Force Report: Science and Technology* (Washington, D.C.: U.S. Government Printing Office, 1967), Appendix J, p. 220.

[16] *Ibid.*, p. 227.

[17] President's Commission on Law Enforcement and Administration of Justice, *Task Force Report: Corrections* (Washington, D.C.: U.S. Government Printing Office, 1967), chapter 4, especially pp. 38-39, 41-42.

effect, and by their appearance in court that they have not managed to escape the police.

Metropolitan Governmental Reorganization Proposals

Thomas M. Scott

A great deal has been written about the need for metropolitan governmental reorganization in the last fifty years. Reformers and good-government groups have deplored the fragmentation of political authority existing in most metropolitan areas and the resulting "irrational" manner in which resources are allocated. This selection points up some of the very real obstacles to achieving radical political structural changes in the metropolis.

Citizens have continued to reject radical attempts at structural reorganization, primarily because they do not view the existing fragmented system as one beset by crisis, as do reformers and their allies. In fact, Scott Greer has argued that those interested in reforming metropolitan government, if they are to be successful, must (1) somehow mobilize a winning party to fight on partisan grounds for metropolitan government, or (2) so educate the voters at large that the questions will precede the answers and the problems the solutions, or (3) avoid direct democracy, where citizens vote in referendum. The first two are unlikely, whether due to partisan differences between central cities and their suburbs or due to a political culture which does not support metropolitan governmental reorganization. On the other hand, the third is most likely—"deviously, covertly, we may achieve metropolitan government," argues Greer. According to Thomas R. Dye, when cooperation does take place between local communities, it usually occurs only between governmental units whose populations are similar in socioeconomic status.

In this selection, Thomas Scott reviews various proposals for metropolitan reorganization. He distinguishes these proposals in terms of their "radicalness." For Scott, a radical reorganization proposal is one that involves (or is perceived as involving) substantial changes in existing political arrangements for large numbers of people. According to this criterion, county reorganization, metropolitan federation, annexation, and consolidation are all considered radical. Such proposals pose a threat, either real or imaginary, to the political-governmental world which citizens, governmental employees and officials, and political leaders have learned to live with and like. Change threatens their very existence.

Support for such proposals most often comes from civic groups, central-city newspapers, and ideologically oriented good-government groups whose campaigns are waged primarily through the mass media rather than by face-to-face appeals to individual voters. Vigorous opposition easily leads to the defeat of radical metropolitan reorganization in most instances. In fact, the thesis advanced by Scott is that radical reorganization has been possible in Miami, Nashville, Atlanta, and Newport News only because of special or unusual circumstances which caused political leaders and citizens to respond "abnormally" to the reform proposal. In other words, they must be treated as deviant cases and explained separately from what Scott characterizes as the normal response pattern—intense opposition by leaders and citizens directly affected by such plans.

Scott points out that normal metropolitan areas handle their problems incrementally, in a piecemeal fashion, and prefer to pursue policies at the least radical end of the metropolitan reorganization continuum, where voter approval is not required (single-purpose special districts, contracts for services, intermunicipal cooperation, shifting functions to other units, etc.). Use of these "solutions," along with increased federal involvement, means that problems never reach a point where they give rise to demands by large numbers of citizens and their leaders for radical change in the status quo. Nevertheless, Scott argues that metropolitan areas in which more radical reorganization has taken place may function as "showcases" or "experiments." As awareness and understanding of these reorganizations develop, radical proposals, assuming they do not fail in the experimental areas, may begin to look less and less threatening to citizens and their political leaders.

Is radical metropolitan structural reorganization really the answer to the many and varied problems confronting central cities and their suburbs? Is fragmentation of political authority in the metropolis the real problem? Are there other means for overcoming the fragmentation of political authority in the metropolis which might be less threatening to citizens and political leaders?

Introduction

As metropolitan areas continue to expand and develop, attention is turned increasingly to governmental reorganization as a way of solving public problems. Most of the standard texts in American state and local government describe the various alternatives: annexation, consolidation, transferring of functions, special districts, "federated metro" proposals, etc.[1] In addition, a growing body of literature discusses the successes and failures of these alternatives in specific metropolitan areas.[2] The casual reader of these works, however, is likely to be struck by the seemingly haphazard manner in which alternatives have been proposed, accepted, rejected, and compromised in various metropolitan areas. What is needed at this point, and what this essay attempts to do, is to offer a tentative explanation of the process of governmental reorganization as it is occurring in the contemporary metropolis.

Once developed, metropolitan governmental reorganization may take many sizes and shapes, but it must come into being either by decision of the official governmental units involved (state legislatures, county boards, city councils, etc.) and/or by voter referendum. Experience to date suggests that relatively minor reorganization is likely to be consummated by the official governmental units while major changes require voter ratification. Experience also suggests that voter approval is hard to come by; indeed, when given the opportunity, voters have often turned down metropolitan governmental reorganization proposals, especially those involving radical change.

The May 1962 report of the President's Advisory Commission on Intergovernmental Relations, *Factors Affecting Voter Reactions to Governmental Reorganization in Metropolitan Areas*, describes efforts to reorganize government in eighteen metropolitan areas between 1950 and 1961 (see Table 1 for summary). Eight or nine proposals, depending on how one keeps score, were accepted by the voters during this period. The rest were defeated. Closer examination of the Commission report reveals important differences between the proposals accepted and those rejected. In all ten cases where voters turned down reorganization plans, significant, indeed radical, changes had been proposed. Five plans involved city-county consolidation which meant total political elimination of the core city and suburban communities.[3] In three of these cases (Albuquerque, Durham, and Knoxville) the proposal was overwhelmingly defeated in the central city and in the surrounding

---

[1] For example, see: Charles Adrian, *State and Local Governments* (New York: McGraw-Hill, 1960), chap. 12; Duane Lockard, *The Politics of State and Local Government* (New York: Macmillan, 1963), chap. 16; Russel Maddox and Robert Fuquay, *State and Local Government* (Princeton: Van Nostrand, 1962), chap. 22.

[2] John C. Bollens (ed.), *Exploring the Metropolitan Community* (Berkeley: U. of California Press, 1961); David A. Booth, *Metropolitics: The Nashville Consolidation* (East Lansing: Institute for Community Development and Services, Michigan State U., 1963); Winston Crouch and Beatrice Dinerman, *Southern California Metropolis* (Berkeley: U. of California Press, 1963); John C. Grumm, *Metropolitan Area Government: The Toronto Experience* (Lawrence: Governmental Research Center, U. of Kansas, 1959); Scott Greer and Norton Long, *Metropolitics: A study of Political Culture* (New York: Wiley, 1963); Roscoe Martin and Frank J. Munger, *Decisions in Syracuse* (Bloomington: Indiana U. Press, 1961), parts 2 and 4; Henry Schmandt, Paul Steinbicker, and George Wendel, *Metropolitan Reform in St. Louis* (New York: Holt, Rinehart and Winston, 1961); Edward Sofen, *The Miami Metropolitan Experiment* (Bloomington: Indiana U. Press, 1963).

[3] The five were Albuquerque—Bernalillo County, New Mexico, 1959; Durham—Durham County, North Carolina, 1961; Knoxville—Knox County, Tennessee, 1959; Macon—Bibb County, Georgia, 1960; and Richmond—Henrico County, Virginia, 1961.

Table 1.   *Summary of metropolitan reorganization proposals and their
acceptance or rejection*

Radicalness of proposal	Metropolitan area	Voters' reaction	
		yes	no
Minor changes	Erie County—Buffalo	x	
	Denver Capital District	x	
	Oneida County—Utica	x	
	Onondaga County—Syracuse	x	
County reorganization	Lucas County—Toledo		x
Metro-federated	Cleveland		x
	Miami—Dade County	x	
	Nashville—1958		x
	Nashville—1962	x	
	St. Louis		x
Annex and federation	Atlanta	x	
Annexation	Louisville		x
Consolidation	Albuquerque—Bernalillo Co.		x
	Durham—Durham Co.		x
	Knoxville—Knox Co.		x
	Macon—Bibb Co.		x
	Newport News—Warwick	x	
	Richmond—Henrico Co.		x

county areas. In Bibbs County, Georgia (Macon), and Henrico County, Virginia (Richmond), the core cities passed the consolidation proposal, but it was defeated in the suburbs.

Three of the ten unsuccessful attempts (Cleveland, Nashville—1958, and St. Louis) involved variations of the federated-metro scheme which transferred some functions to a metropolitan-wide governmental unit and retained the remainder in the local municipalities. In Cleveland and St. Louis the plan was resoundingly defeated in the central cities and suburbs. In Nashville—1958, the proposal passed in the central city but was lost in the suburbs.

The last two of the unsuccessful reorganization attempts were unique. A basic feature of the Louisville "Improvement Plan" included the annexation of some 68,000 suburban residents to the central city. This proposal, while carrying in Louisville proper, was defeated overwhelmingly in 29 of the 31 suburbs. The Lucas County (Toledo), Ohio, attempt involved a "significant change in the structure of county government." It was voted down by a better-than-two-to-one margin in the central city and in the surrounding county areas.

On the other hand, many of the proposals receiving favorable voter reaction required *relatively* less radical governmental change. Three involved a reorganization of county government, but included strong safeguards for municipal autonomy; ". . . the charter stated that local governmental functions, facilities, and powers were not to be transferred, altered, or impaired."[4]

The 1961 Denver Metropolitan Capital Improvements District involved a metropolitan sales tax to facilitate the financing of capital improvements. It was defeated in the suburbs but carried well enough in Denver to give it the over-all simple majority required by state law. However, the Colorado Supreme Court later declared the enabling legislation under which the plan was passed to be in violation of the Colorado Constitution. The successful Seattle multipurpose district plan of 1958 is a modified and compromised version of an earlier unacceptable proposal, and its powers and functions are in reality quite modest.

Only four of the metropolitan reorganization attempts receiving voter approval appear to involve more or less radical change. In 1950, Atlanta with the approval of both city and county voters succeeded in annexing 87,000 suburban residents as part of the Fulton County Improvement Plan. The consolidation of the two first-class cities, Newport News and Warwick, Virginia, in 1957 appears to be another radical change, especially when the name of the newly created unit was to be Newport News. The Miami-Dade County federation and the 1962 metropolitan plan for Nashville-Davidson County are the other two radical reorganizations that have achieved voter approval.

This brief and sketchy review suggests the idea of a continuum based on the degree of "radicalness" of the various metropolitan governmental reorganization proposals. (See Figure 1.)

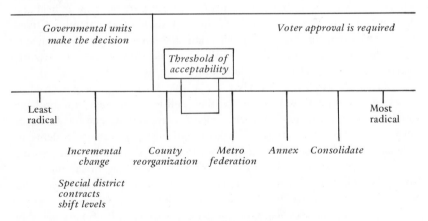

Figure 1. Continuum of radicalness of metropolitan
governmental change

---

[4] The three were Erie County (Buffalo), New York; Oneida County (Utica), New York, and Onondaga County (Syracuse), New York. See Advisory Commission on Intergovernmental Relations, *Factors Affecting Voter Reactions to Governmental Reorganization in Metropolitan Areas* (May, 1962), pp. 45, 59, and 61.

On the "least radical" end of the continuum are those proposals involving relatively minor changes, such as intermunicipal cooperative agreements, interunit contracts-for-services, transfers of functions to county and state levels, single-function special districts, etc. As Figure 1 indicates, these reorganizations, while not necessarily uncontroversial, are normally ratified by governmental decision-makers (city councils, county boards, state legislatures).

The more comprehensive proposals are located toward the more radical end of the continuum where state and/or local law requires voter approval. While county reorganization plans such as those in Syracuse, Buffalo, and Utica, are not especially radical and are likely to be ratified at the polls, metropolitan federations, large-scale annexations, and most consolidations represent more drastic change and, with the few exceptions noted, have been turned down by the voters. Experience to date suggests that voters are willing to accept moderate but not radical change. One might say that there is a "threshold of voter acceptability" located somewhere along the continuum of radicalness indicating the point beyond which, generally speaking, citizens are not likely to approve metropolitan governmental change.

Metropolitan reorganization: some examples

Several questions are raised immediately by this formulation. What does it mean to say that some proposals are considered to be more "radical" than others, i.e., what is it about these plans that makes them more radical and thus, presumably, less acceptable? Is the "threshold of acceptability" fixed at a certain point, or does it vary over time and from one metropolitan area to another? How can this analysis explain the "deviant" cases; e.g., Atlanta, Newport News—Warwick, Miami, and Nashville—1962?

A radical reorganization proposal is one that involves (or is perceived as involving) substantial change in existing political arrangements for large numbers of people. It may affect elected, appointed, and civil service governmental positions. It may alter the citizenship status of residents of various municipalities. It may realign governmental services and the existing tax structure. In short, it threatens (or is perceived as threatening) the political-governmental world that citizens, governmental employees and officials, and political leaders have learned to live with and like. They know how the system operates, what to expect from it, and how to function within it. Change threatens their very existence. Thus, suburbs threatened with loss of identity and decision-autonomy, suburban business threatened with loss of patronage, suburban and county officials and employees threatened with loss of jobs and status, central city political leaders threatened with dilution of electoral support, etc., have usually resisted any and all kinds of metropolitan reorganization attempts.

Conversely, support for such proposals has generally come from civic groups, core city newspapers, and ideologically oriented, "good-government" organizations. The campaigns have been waged primarily in the mass media and not in the direct face-to-face, door-to-door style characteristic of hard-fought political struggles. The antagonists of reorganization see the proposals as directly threatening specific elements in their political-governmental lives and are willing to supply the effort needed to insure defeat, while the supporters of such plans, seeing them vaguely as providing a "better day ahead" do little more than reinforce each other through intellectual public debate and the editorial pages of the city newspapers.[5]

In fact, the similarities in the patterns of support and opposition to reorganization proposals in most metropolitan areas lead one to conclude that intensive opposition by actors directly affected is the *normal* way for the political system to respond to such plans. Furthermore, there is every reason to anticipate that this vigorous opposition will *normally* succeed in defeating the lukewarm ideological fervor and activity of the reorganization proponents. Incidentally, it should be noted that this struggle usually bypasses a large portion of the electorate who exclude themselves both from the pre-vote dialogue and from the decision at the polls.[6]

If the "normal" response to radical metropolitan reform proposals is vigorous reaction by those directly affected, ineffectual intellectual-oriented activity by ideologues, and disinterest by most, why have some of these proposals been accepted; notably, Miami, Nashville—1962, Atlanta—1950, and Newport News? And, does this mean that radical change will not occur in other metropolitan areas?

The thesis advanced in this essay is that radical reorganization was possible in these four areas because special or unusual circumstances in each caused them to respond "abnormally" to the reform proposal. In other words, they must be treated as deviant cases and explained separately from what has been identified as the "normal" response pattern. Unfortunately, the literature of political science does not adequately discuss the Atlanta and Newport cases. However, available evidence does support the notion that both situations were unique. By 1950, the city of Atlanta had spread into two counties, Fulton and DeKalb, and much of the suburban population growth was in unincorporated areas surrounding the central city. While the counties were unable to tax the populated areas more heavily, they did provide them with city-level services. A survey conducted at the time indicated that only one area in Fulton County outside of Atlanta paid as much in taxes as it received in services from the county. This meant, of course, that Atlanta taxpayers were paying the lion's share of the cost of city-level services for suburban dwellers, and explains why the suburbanites resisted both incorporation and annexation by Atlanta. Among other things this situation had led to an extraordinary number of formal cooperative agreements between the city and the county in areas such as welfare,

[5] See especially, Bollens, *op. cit.*, Booth, *op. cit.*, Greer, *op. cit.*, Martin and Munger, *op. cit.*, and Sofen, *op. cit.*

[6] Advisory Commission Report, *op. cit.*, p. 71, shows that the average turnout for the 18 referenda was less than 25 per cent of the voting-age population and none exceeded 41 per cent.

water, sewers, courts, libraries, fire, police, schools, bond programs, and hospitals as well as development of a general plan of improvement by the Local Government Commission of Atlanta and Fulton County.

The Commission's plan was a carefully worked out compromise and it avoided the main sources of anticipated resistance by: (1) excluding DeKalb County even though it was an integral part of the developing metropolitan area (because it did not want to be involved in the governmental integration proposals); (2) providing for the annexation of *unincorporated* areas to Atlanta and not disturbing existing municipalities; (3) judiciously dividing and arranging governmental functions and services and carefully providing for the job and salary protection and seniority and pension rights of existing municipal and county employees. The Commission Plan required an advisory election which carried in Atlanta by 90 per cent and in the unincorporated areas of Fulton County by 57 per cent.

The unusual features of the Atlanta case include the substantial development of unincorporated suburban areas and the compromised nature of the integration proposal which undercut the potential opposition of the recalcitrant county, existing suburban municipalities, and city and county employees.[7]

The Newport News—Warwick, Virginia, case is also unique. In 1950, the peninsula area of Virginia contained five units of local government; the cities of Hampton and Newport News, the counties of Elizabeth City and Warwick, and the town of Phoebus. A referendum to consolidate all five units failed at that time although it carried in Newport News and Warwick County. Subsequently, Newport News continued to annex unincorporated territory and the threat of such annexation led to the consolidation of Elizabeth City County, Hampton, and Phoebus into a new city of Hampton and the incorporation of Warwick County to Warwick City.

In 1956 a citizen's group proposal to consolidate the three remaining units of government failed to receive the required support in each of the units when Hampton defeated the proposal 7,048 to 6,192. The referendum had not received the wholehearted support of the three city councils and in addition there was some opposition to the proposed name of the new complex. (The vote on the integration proposal included a vote on the name as well.)[8]

Following the 1956 defeat with its demonstrated lack of support for integration in Hampton, the cities of Newport News and Warwick voted to consolidate. The referendum, which carried very strongly in Newport News and by 54 per cent in Warwick did *not* include a proposed name for the newly consolidated unit. In a subsequent election the name, "Newport News," was accepted despite some opposition from the citizens of Warwick.[9]

[7] See Lynwood M. Holland, "Atlanta Pioneers in Merger," *National Municipal Review*, 41 (1952), 182.

[8] Weldon Cooper and Chester Bain, "Three-City Merger Sought in Virginia," *National Municipal Review*, 45 (1956), 443.

[9] See News and Notes, *National Municipal Review*, 46 (1957), 409 and 526.

Again, while the analysis of the consolidation struggle is far from complete it is clear that the peculiarities of the geographical situation, the history of slow but steady governmental integration, and the willingness to compromise by excluding the reluctant unit were important conditions that contributed to the ultimate merging of Newport News and Warwick.

By contrast, the other two successful radical reorganizations, Miami and Nashville, have been thoroughly studied. Edward Sofen describes the unique social-political-economic characteristics of Dade County, Florida, at the time the "Metro" federated plan was approved. Tourism was the backbone of the economy, population turnover and mobility were high, community traditions were relatively low, and the number of established municipalities was quite small. Consequently, Sofen notes that

> Miami was able to create a metropolitan government with the very type of support that failed in other parts of the nation because of . . . [these ecological conditions] . . . —particularly the absence of powerfully established political parties, labor organizations, and ethnic groups—and because Miamians have long been accustomed to depend on such non-party sources as the newspapers for political leadership.[10]

Even under these unique circumstances, however, the "Metro" proposal received a slim majority of the 26 per cent of eligible voters participating in the election. One might conclude that any organized opposition such as would be found in a "normal" metropolitan area (labor, parties, municipal officials, etc.) could easily have caused the defeat of the plan. In other words, the success of the reorganization referendum in Dade County is the result of the county's being a unique metropolitan area responding in an abnormal way to the proposal.

The Nashville case is equally unique and interesting. David Booth first describes a normal metropolitan area responding normally in 1958 to a federated metropolitan reorganization proposal. The plan was supported by the city newspapers, the Nashville Chamber of Commerce, the League of Women Voters, the Citizen's Committee for Metropolitan Government, and other similar groups. Furthermore, "no attempt was made to organize a 'grass-roots' organization in support of the proposal. . . ."[11]

> The opposition to the consolidation plan was much more clandestine, remaining largely silent and hidden until about a week before the vote, when it unleashed a bitter whirl-wind attack. The plan was attacked on many grounds and was even alleged to be inspired by the communist plot to take over the world. Spot announcements on the radio were used to urge defeat of the proposal. Leaflets were given out on the streets and on buses and also through the county school teachers to their pupils. Apparently, most of the opposition came from some members of the Quarterly County Court [the county legislative body], from county school teachers' organizations and from private suburban

---

[10] Sofen, *op. cit.*, p. 86.

[11] Booth, *op. cit.*, p. 20.

fire and police companies which would have been largely driven out of business with the adoption of the plan. The proposal was also opposed by many suburban merchants and businessmen, who apparently feared renewed competition from the central business district, in the event of consolidation. . . .

As has often been the case elsewhere, the defeat of Metro in the Nashville area was caused by an adverse vote outside the central city.

The defeat was not surprising and, in many ways, was typical of the failures of other consolidation plans. . . .[12]

By 1962, however, the situation had changed radically. The city and county had raised taxes to meet immediate demands. The city had adopted a vehicle tax on all automobiles using city streets in an attempt to force suburban commuters to help finance city services. Needless to say, the county residents were not pleased. Soon after the 1958 metro referendum, the city annexed seven square miles of contiguous industrial and commercial property and in 1960 Nashville annexed 82,000 suburban residents without their approval. The annexations were very unpopular because they deprived the county of valuable human and commercial resources while forcing the original city taxpayers to pay for the upgrading of services required by the newly annexed territories. The annexees were extremely resentful since they did not want to be citizens of Nashville and they regarded the annexations as a "sell-out" by the Nashville mayor and his political organization.

Resentment over taxation and fear of annexation created renewed interest in the federated proposal as a modified way to protect suburban communities. The plan was reintroduced and a vigorous campaign for its adoption mounted. Booth compares the 1958 and 1962 campaigns:

> In 1958, the situation lacked urgency. The question was nebulous and hinged on the desirability of adopting an abstract solution to real and anticipated problems. In 1962, the issues were critical and clear-cut, though they varied for different groups. For the voter in the old core city, the question was whether or not to keep Ben West as mayor. A vote for the Charter was a vote against the mayor.
>
> For the voter in the newly annexed areas, the issue was whether to become a first-class citizen in a new metropolitan government, or to retain the second-class, under-represented status inherent in annexation. Another issue was whether to retain a mayor who had broken his pledge (to give the people a vote on annexation) or whether to drive him from office, in order to choose new political leaders.
>
> For the voter in the rest of the county, there were also two issues: whether he wanted to be liable to annexation at any time, yet receive no guarantee of better services, or whether he wanted to adopt Metro, which guaranteed services within one year. . . . The second issue was a choice between taxation without representation . . . (the vehicle tax) and a new plan, wherein each voter would participate in the election . . . of the new council. . . .[13]

[12] *Ibid.*, pp. 20-21.
[13] *Ibid.*, pp. 86-87.

The final vote was quite different from the outcome in 1958. Voting was heavy; the plan was defeated in the old core city, but won well enough in the newly annexed areas and in the county to assure adoption.

These four case studies support the basic argument of this thesis, namely that voter approval of more radical metropolitan reorganization will occur only in unusual or "abnormal" circumstances. In Atlanta, the final integration proposal represented a carefully conceived compromise that protected as many as possible of the existing social and political interests. In Newport News–Warwick, reorganization came only after a long history of consolidation proposals, defeats, counter proposals, and compromises. In Miami an amorphous social-economic-political structure did not provide the usual basis for organized opposition and the plan was approved by a largely disinterested electorate. In Nashville–1962 strong reaction to a series of political events caused a dramatic change of attitude on the part of city and county voters. The issues changed from the vague ideological speculations of the "good government" groups in 1958 to the hard, tough, self-interest motivations of 1962, and in heavy voting the proposal won handily.

By contrast, the studies of the "normal" metropolitan responses to radical proposals (Cleveland, Nashville–1958, and St. Louis) give no indication of unique or special conditions that might have affected and altered the anticipated outcomes. Bollens and Schmandt in summarizing these reform campaigns suggest that "for the most part, the same classes of protagonists, the same evolutionary steps (from study commission, through official charter-drafting board to public vote), the same demographic and political factors, and the same type of public response were present in each instance."

They specify these common patterns: (1) metropolitan reform has been the product of good government groups and has not resulted from grass-roots dissatisfaction or leadership by public officials; (2) the general public is indifferent; (3) mass-based interest groups are rarely committed as either supporters or opponents; (4) major reorganization proposals are unlikely to succeed without organized political support; (5) voters who support metropolitan reform are usually drawn from higher socio-economic categories; and (6) campaigns conducted by good government groups and civic notables seldom establish effective communication with a mass audience.[14]

How then do "normal" metropolitan areas respond to their problems, if, as the evidence suggests, they are not capable of radical reorganization? As most observers have noted, they deal with their problems incrementally, preferring, for the most part, those reponses at the "least radical" end of the continuum where voter approval is not required; e.g., single-purpose special districts, contracts for service, shifting functions to other units, etc. These solutions, along with increased federal involvement, mean that problems never develop to the point where they activate and mobilize large-scale public demands. Thus, in the "normal" metropolitan area support for radical change is not

[14]John Bollens and Henry Schmandt, *The Metropolis: Its People, Politics, and Economic Life* (New York: Harper and Row, 1965), pp. 521 ff.

sufficient to overcome the active opposition of the various combinations of self-protecting interests and change is therefore relatively undramatic.

However, these facts of metropolitan political life are not necessarily permanently fixed. Indeed, there is evidence of an additional element in the process we have been describing, an element involving intergovernmental "learning." While Toronto, Miami, and Nashville—1962 have been described and explained as deviant cases, they also serve as functioning "showcases" or "experiments" of radical reorganization.[15] Newspapers, educators, associations of public officials and employees, civic groups, etc. become aware of, study, and disseminate information on these experiments. For example, in the Minneapolis-St. Paul area there is active interest in the Toronto and Dade County plans and various civic groups are supporting travel to these areas so that civic leaders may investigate their virtues on a first-hand basis. Even the experience of defeating such a proposal serves to educate the voting public. Greer cites evidence from St. Louis that suggests a "general friendliness to the notion of future efforts at metropolitan integration," following the 1959 defeat.[16]

As awareness and understanding develop, the radical reorganization proposals may begin to look less and less radical (assuming they do not fail in the experimental communities). Adjustments and compromises designed to fit the peculiar needs of a given metropolitan area may be made, and this may lead to a reduction of fears and perceived threats. If reorganization proposals become less threatening, anticipated opposition may be reduced, shifting the threshold of voter acceptability toward the more radical end of the continuum. When and if this learning and adjustment process occurs, "normal" metropolitan areas may be more likely to adopt major reorganization plans.

To summarize the analysis: normal metropolitan areas with central city-suburban conflicts, competing political parties, interest groups, governmental employees, etc., will tend to respond to governmental reorganization proposals in one of three ways: (1) relatively minor—incremental change will be accomplished without voter participation (depending on state and local law); (2) relatively minor changes requiring referenda will be approved; (3) relatively radical proposals will be defeated by the vigorous opposition of actors directly affected over the ineffective campaigns of ideologically committed "good-government" groups. With few exceptions recent metropolitan reorganization proposals have followed this pattern.

Radical reorganization plans tend to be approved only in areas with unusual social-economic-political characteristics, such as Atlanta, Newport News, Miami, and Nashville—1962. These cases are unique and must be explained as deviations from the normal patterns. However, they are also "living proof" of the viability and, perhaps, desirability of radical change and thus they function as innovators in the common political culture. As more and more individuals and groups learn of the innovation, the norms of this culture may change,

[15] Toronto (and Winnipeg) has not been discussed, but it is here classified as a deviant case because the provincial government developed the federated plan and voter response was not involved in its implementation.

[16] Greer, *op. cit.*, p. 163.

resistance may be diminished and voter acceptance may increase. As this learning and diffusing process continues, metropolitan areas with more normal characteristics may find it politically possible to accept relatively radical reorganization proposals.

Practically speaking, this analysis suggests that in the near future radical metropolitan change will continue to win voter approval only under unique circumstances. In the meantime, "normal" metropolitan areas (as most are) will forestall crises by dealing with their problems in a piecemeal manner. Eventually, as awareness grows and new ideas become more widely diffused, what we now regard as innovative will become simply another of the many alternative solutions to modern urban problems and additional metropolitan areas will be more likely to reorganize their governmental structures.

Additional suggested readings: local differences and public policy

Michael Aiken and Robert R. Alford, "Community Structure and Innovation: The Case of Public Housing," *The American Political Science Review*, vol. 64, no. 3 (September 1970), pp. 843-864.

, "Comparative Urban Research and Community Decision-Making," *The New Atlantis*, vol. 1, no. 2 (Winter 1970), pp. 85-110.

Alan A. Altshuler, *The City Planning Process: A Political Analysis* (Ithaca: Cornell University Press, 1965).

David J. Bordua (ed.), *The Police: Six Sociological Essays* (New York: John Wiley, 1967).

Alan K. Campbell and Seymour Sacks, *Metropolitan America: Fiscal Patterns and Governmental Systems* (New York: The Free Press, 1967).

Jim Chard and Jon York (eds.), *Urban America: Crisis and Opportunity* (Belmont, Calif.: Dickenson, 1969).

Kenneth Clark and Jeannette Hopkins, *A Relevant War Against Poverty: A Study of Community Action Programs and Observable Social Change* (New York: Harper & Row, Publishers, 1968).

James W. Clarke, "Environment, Process and Policy: A Reconsideration," *The American Political Science Review*, vol. 63, no. 4 (December 1969), pp. 1172-1182.

"The Conscience of the City," *Daedalus*, vol. 97, no. 4 (Fall 1968).

Michael N. Danielson, *Federal-Metropolitan Politics and the Commuter Crisis* (New York: Columbia University Press, 1965).

Thomas R. Dye, "Urban Political Integration: Conditions Associated with Annexation in American Cities," *Midwest Journal of Political Science*, vol. 8, no. 4 (November 1964), pp. 430-446.

——, "City-Suburban Social Distance and Public Policy," *Social Forces*, vol. 44, no. 1 (September 1965), pp. 100-106.

——, "Governmental Structure, Urban Environment, and Educational Policy," *Midwest Journal of Political Science*, vol. 11, no. 3 (August 1967), pp. 353-380.

Thomas R. Dye and Brett W. Hawkins (eds.), *Politics in the Metropolis: A Reader in Conflict and Cooperation* (Columbus: Charles E. Merrill Books, 1967).

Heinz Eulau and Robert Eyestone, "Policy Maps of City Councils and Policy Outcomes: A Developmental Analysis," *The American Political Science Review*, vol. 62, no. 1 (March 1968), pp. 124-143.

Glenn W. Fisher, "Revenue and Expenditure Patterns in Five Large Cities," *Quarterly Review of Economics and Business*, vol. 3, no. 3 (Autumn 1963), pp. 61-72.

Lyle C. Fitch and Associates, *Urban Transportation and Public Policy* (San Francisco: Chandler Press, 1964).

Robert M. Fogelson, "From Resentment to Confrontation: The Police, The Negroes, and the Outbreak of the Nineteen Sixties Riots," *Political Science Quarterly*, vol. 83, no. 2 (June 1968), pp. 217-247.

Lewis A. Froman, Jr., "An Analysis of Policies in Cities, " *The Journal of Politics*, vol. 29, no. 1 (February 1967), pp. 94-108.

Daniel R. Grant, "The Metropolitan Governmental Approach: Should, Can, and Will It Prevail?," *Urban Affairs Quarterly*, vol. 3, no. 3 (March 1968), pp. 103-110.

Scott Greer, "The Rational Model, The Sociological Model, and Metropolitan Reform," *Public Opinion Quarterly*, vol. 27, no. 2 (Summer 1963), pp. 242-249.

——, *Metropolitics: A Study of Political Culture* (New York: John Wiley, 1963).

Charles V. Hamilton, "The Politics of Race Relations," in Charles U. Daly (ed.), *Urban Violence* (Chicago: The University of Chicago Center for Policy Study, 1969).

Harold Kaplan, *Urban Renewal Politics: Slum Clearance in Newark* (New York: Columbia University Press, 1963).

——, *Urban Political Systems: A Functional Analysis of Metro Toronto* (New York: Columbia University Press, 1967).

H. R. Mahood and Edward L. Angus (eds.), *Urban Politics and Problems: A Reader* (New York: Charles Scribner's, 1969).

Peter Marris and Martin Rein, *Dilemmas of Social Reform: Poverty and Community Action in the United States* (New York: Atherton Press, 1967).

Louis H. Masotti and Don R. Bowen, *Riots and Rebellion: Civil Violence in the Urban Community* (Beverly Hills: Sage Publications, 1968).

Daniel P. Moynihan, *Maximum Feasible Misunderstanding: Community Action in the War on Poverty* (New York: The Free Press, 1969).

Wilfred Owen, *The Metropolitan Transportation Problem* (New York: Doubleday & Co., 1966).

Lee Rainwater and William L. Yancey, *The Moynihan Report and the Politics of Controversy* (Cambridge: M.I.T. Press, 1967).

Austin Ranney (ed.), *Political Science and Public Policy* (Chicago: Markham, 1968).

Report of the National Advisory Commission on Civil Disorders (New York: Bantam Books, 1968).

Robert H. Salisbury, "The Dynamics of Charter Politics in St. Louis," *Midwest Journal of Political Science*, vol. 5, no. 3 (August 1961), pp. 260-275.

Arnold Schuchter, *White Power/Black Freedom: Planning the Future of Urban America* (Boston: Beacon Press, 1968).

Bruce L. R. Smith, "The Politics of Protest: How Effective is Violence?," *Proceedings of the Academy of Political Science*, vol. 29, no. 1 (July 1968), pp. 111-128.

Sterling Tucker, *Beyond the Burning: Life and Death of the Ghetto* (New York: Association Press, 1968).

Urban America Inc. and The Urban Coalition, *One Year Later: An Assessment of the Nation's Response to the Crisis Described by the National Advisory Commission on Civil Disorders* (New York: Praeger, 1969).

Oliver P. Williams, Harold Herman, Charles S. Liebman, and Thomas R. Dye, *Suburban Differences and Metropolitan Policies: A Philadelphia Story* (Philadelphia: University of Pennsylvania Press, 1965).

Robert C. Weaver, *The Urban Complex* (Garden City: Doubleday & Co., 1966).

James Q. Wilson, *Varieties of Police Behavior: The Management of Law and Order in Eight Communities* (Cambridge: Harvard University Press, 1968).

————(ed.), *Urban Renewal: The Record and the Controversy* (Cambridge: M.I.T. Press, 1966).

————(ed.), *City Politics and Public Policy* (New York: John Wiley, 1968).

———— (ed.), *The Metropolitan Enigma: Inquiries into the Nature and Dimensions of America's "Urban Crisis"* (Cambridge: M.I.T. Press, 1968).

Robert C. Wood, *1400 Governments: The Political Economy of the New York Metropolitan Region* (Garden City: Doubleday & Co., 1961).

Conclusion   Studying local politics and public policy

How can the questions raised and the hypotheses suggested in the preceding discussion be investigated? How can you learn more about local politics, particularly the nature of the policy-making process and the various phenomena which influence municipal policy outcomes? What follows is a brief and very straightforward discussion of how one might proceed. Obviously, the particular strategy adopted in any given class will depend on its size and composition plus the structure of the course. By dividing responsibilities, a class working together can go a long way toward investigating many of the dimensions of the policy-making model discussed in the introductory essay; however, students working alone will need to restrict their attention to more manageable projects. In addition, a graduate course in local, urban, or metropolitan politics would probably undertake more systematic and intensive research than an undergraduate survey course.

First, begin by reading Roland L. Warren's *Studying Your Community*, which has recently been rewritten and published in paperback.[1] Although done from a sociological perspective, it does discuss local political life and how it can be studied. In addition, politics is placed within the larger context of the total community. This volume also contains a great deal of information about local municipalities, as well as citing sources you can turn to for additional data.

Second, for those interested in a more rigorous formulation of how social science research should be conducted, I suggest you examine *Foundations of Behavioral Research* and *Research Methods in Social Relations*.[2] Some highly

---

[1] Roland L. Warren, *Studying Your Community* (New York: Free Press, 1965).

[2] Fred N. Kerlinger, *Foundations of Behavioral Research* (New York: Holt, Rinehart, and Winston, 1965); and Claire Selltiz, et al., *Research Methods in Social Relations* (New York: Holt, Rinehart, and Winston, 1959).

G E S U   P A R I S H   Milwaukee, Wisconsin

PASTORS: Jesuit Fathers Robert Purcell, George Bischof-
   berger, Walter Boehme, Ervin Czarnecki, John Halloran,
   David Haschka, Kenneth Herian, Norbert Loehr, Pat Walsh.
PARISH OFFICE: 1210 West Michigan St., Milwaukee, Wis.
   Office Phone: 224 - 7101. Residence 224 - 7700.
SUNDAY MASSES
   Upper Church: 9:00 a.m., 10:30, 12:00 noon, 4:30 p.m.
                 and 5:45 p.m.
   Lower Church: 6:00 a.m., 7:30, 11:00 a.m.
WEEKDAY MASSES
   Lower Church: 6:15 a.m., 7:00, 7:45, 8:30, 11:15,
                 12:00 noon, 4:30 p.m. and 5:30 p.m.
   Saturday: 4:30 and 5:45 p.m. are the anticipated
             Sunday Masses in the upper church.
CONFESSIONS
   Weekdays: 11:30 to 12:30 and 4:30 to 5:30 p.m.
   Saturdays, Thursday before First Friday, & Vigils
   of Holy Days: 11:30 to 12:30 and 3:30 to 5:30 p.m.
                 and 7:30 to 8:30 p.m.

Dear Friends,

     One of the specially good things about the
Easter liturgy is that the "flavor lasts."
Each day of the week following Easter there are
reminders loud and clear that Jesus DID rise
from the dead. This life given him in his
Resurrection is the life he shares with us, so
in very truth and right now we are a risen
people. We should remember this, specially on
those "down days." Even on those days, through
our union with Jesus, we are somehow and joyfully
"up."

     It is with this spirit of optimism in Jesus
risen that we pray for vocations to the priest-
hood and the religious life. Numbers surely
have declined in the past few years, but the
power of Jesus and his Holy spirit has not. Pray
that truly Spirit-filled people will heed God's
call to serve his Church.

                    Fr. Purcell, S.J.

APRIL 24, 1977
Roman Rite: Third Sunday of Easter
Eastern Rites: Third Sunday after Holy Pasch
(Myrrh-Bearing Women)

Are We Paying Too Much Attention to Abortion?

Father Hugh J. O'Connell, C.SS.R.

The question is sometimes asked, even by Catholics: "Why so much attention to abortion? There are many other important social issues, such as honesty in government, freedom of speech and press, antidiscrimination, the elimination of poverty, crime, unemployment, etc. Why do the bishops and so many Catholic groups seem to focus attention on this one problem?"

THE FUNDAMENTAL RIGHT

The answer is that *the right to life is the most fundamental and basic of all human rights.* Without it, no other human right has any meaning. If you're not alive, you cannot enjoy freedom of speech or conscience, freedom of housing, freedom of education, or anything else of value.

The proabortion view, as contained in the Supreme Court decision of 1973, is a breakthrough of the pagan outlook which denies that human life is sacred and under the sole dominion of God. It asserts the competence of the State to decide who will live and who will die.

Such a position opens the door to a number of other attacks on the right to life, such as euthanasia, the killing of deformed or retarded children, and the elimination of those who are "useless" or aged. We have seen such opinions put into practice in Nazi Germany. Even in our own country, bills advocating euthanasia have been introduced into state legislatures.

DOES THE UNBORN CHILD POSSESS HUMAN LIFE?

From the viewpoint of science, there cannot be the slightest question that the unborn child, even in its earliest stages, possesses human life. Certainly, by every

(Continued on back page.)

appropriate but seldom-used methods for studying individual, group, and community behavior are discussed in *Unobtrusive Measures: Nonreactive Research in the Social Sciences.*[3]

Third, a rereading of previous selections will provide a point of departure for selecting questions for further investigation plus guidelines for an appropriate methodology. In this regard, one can also consult the suggested readings at the end of each major section. For example, if you were interested in studying nondecision-making, first reread the selection by Bachrach and Baratz in Part Three, plus other selections which address themselves to the question of who governs at the local level. Then read their more detailed, recently published study of nondecision-making, *Power and Poverty: Theory and Practice,* which is based on research conducted in Baltimore.[4]

Once you have decided what to study and have reached some conclusion about how the research will be conducted, you are ready to collect some background information. Begin by checking the *local library* to see if any materials have been written about the particular community or communities you intend to study. Frequently you will find at least one journalistic account which traces its historical development. Of course more background information is generally available on larger municipalities, particularly central cities. However, you will find very little, if any, information on local politics. Topics such as citizen political attitudes and participation, group political activities and coalition formation, local political leadership, and council decision-making are seldom discussed in these publications.

Next, read the *local newspapers.* Most local newspaper publishers will also give you access to their back issues. From newspaper accounts one can frequently learn a great deal about a municipality, particularly its major policy problems, controversial policy issues, important groups and their political activities, community influentials, and so on.

In addition, most city governments publish various *documents and reports.* Free copies are usually available, or they can be read at city hall. Particularly important is the city's annual report. This document will give you a fairly detailed breakdown of sources of municipal revenue, as well as how such revenue is spent in any given year. You can also get some idea of the size and scope of a particular municipal government's operations, including personnel, services provided, and so on. However, in smaller communities, particularly suburbs, this source of information is less complete and hence less useful.

Meanwhile, you can also *attend city council and/or local school board meetings.* These meetings, which can give you a real "feel" for local politics, are open to the public and are held weekly in central cities and bi-monthly in most suburban municipalities. At these meetings you can get some idea of the kinds of policy issues currently being considered and consequently those which are not under consideration; the formal role(s) played by the various decision makers; the kinds of issues, if any, which give rise to controversy; the

---

[3] Eugene J. Webb, et al., *Unobtrusive Measures: Nonreactive Research in the Social Sciences* (Chicago: Rand McNally, 1966).

[4] Peter Bachrach and Morton S. Baratz, *Power and Poverty: Theory and Practice* (New York: Oxford University Press, 1970).

degree of consensus among councilmen and citizens over the proper role of local government; individuals and groups who appear before the council and make demands; the openness and style of the council decision process; and so on.

Obviously, there is more to local politics and the policy-making process than can be observed in city councils and/or school board meetings. To get at more informal aspects or dimensions of the policy-making process, such as group activities, political communications, power and influence relationships, you will have to *formally interview or informally discuss* these questions with various political leaders and key informants (see Terry N. Clark's discussion in Part Four on how to identify these latter individuals). For example, in smaller communities the local newspaper editor is always a good, although not always unbiased, source of information. In larger municipalities you can talk with individual reporters who cover local political affairs. Heads of established groups like the Chamber of Commerce, League of Women Voters, the N.A.A.C.P., the Urban League, labor unions, neighborhood associations, and so on are another useful source of information about how public-policy decisions get made in particular municipalities. The mayor, city councilmen, the city administrator, department heads, plus citizens who are members of city commissions and/or study groups, are usually willing to talk with students, although not always frankly.

Before interviewing these individuals and taking their time, however, you should have clearly in mind the various topics you would like to discuss. If it is impossible to get access to these people—and this is a particularly critical problem with large numbers of students—invite some of these individuals to speak to the class. Provide ample time for questions and class discussion, otherwise these presentations may not prove very satisfactory. If there is a controversy "brewing" in the community, the classroom provides an ideal forum in which the various interested parties can be brought together for a panel discussion of the particular issue.

Although this is far from an exhaustive discussion of some of the possibilities for increasing your understanding of local politics, it may prove suggestive to those who wish to venture into the "real world" to conduct research. We now turn to our two concluding selections. In these, both Timothy Hennessey and James Clarke address themselves to important questions which also relate, in a more rigorous way, to the conduct of political research at the local level.

Theory and Concept Formation in Comparative Urban Research

Timothy M. Hennessey

For the first part of our conclusion, we turn to a critical essay by Timothy M. Hennessey. He is primarily concerned with the problem of conceptualization, particularly with the negative impact which the concept "political ethos" has had on theoretical progress in urban politics. This is an important selection because it raises a number of basic theoretical questions about comparative urban research and also draws your attention to various conceptual inadequacies in several selections in Part Four. One should not conclude from this discussion, however, that "political ethos" is the only ambiguously defined concept in the literature. Many, if not most, of the concepts discussed in the introductory essay and in the selections are still in the preliminary stages of conceptual refinement. In fact, a great deal of time and thought will have to be devoted to both clarifying and developing valid measures for these concepts before they will contribute much either to empirical theory or to overcoming the noncumulative nature of most current research in urban politics.

First, Hennessey argues, and I think rightly so, that for research to be theoretically meaningful it must be guided by concepts which have been clearly and precisely defined. In order to support this position, he examines the negative consequences which the "ethos theory" of political behavior has had for theory construction and hence explanation in urban politics. After reading his critique, one should realize that it is far better for social scientists to be wrong than ambiguous and hence misunderstood in their research, particularly if we are to have meaningful theoretical progress in the social sciences.

Second, one of the very real problems with the concept of "political ethos" is the imprecise manner in which it has been measured. This problem follows quite logically from the ambiguous use of the concept by various researchers. For example, even though the concept refers to specific attitudinal predispositions of individuals in particular social groups in our society, such attitudes have seldom been measured directly. Instead, they are most often inferred from the aggregate characteristics of such groups. As Hennessey points out, such a procedure is extremely risky as well as methodologically invalid. Query: Do most individuals in a particular social, economic, or political group share the same attitudes on all or even a few political questions? It is very important, then, when conducting research to develop both valid and reliable measures (indicators) for the concepts being used in the particular study. However, this can only be accomplished if the concepts themselves are clearly and precisely defined.

Finally, throughout his discussion Hennessey notes how individual values can influence empirical research—from the initial selection of a problem for study to the final interpretation of the evidence collected. He also points out how by focusing undue attention on formal rules, procedures, and governmental structures, the reformist tradition has served to direct attention away from systematic empirical investigation of the policy-making process, including nondecision-making and political change at the local level. Yet despite such attention, we still know very little about how and why formal rules and procedures or governmental structures influence the policy-making process and policy outcomes.

It is heartening to see that in the last several years students of local government and politics are finally beginning to direct their attention away from the reformer's static concerns to the systematic comparative analysis of political processes and, to some extent, political change. The adequacy of our explanations and hence our understandings of local politics can only be enhanced as a result of this refocusing of attention.

The works of Key, Deutsch, and Lipset, Trow and Coleman, to cite only a few, reveal the importance of comparative political analysis in the process of theory construction.[1] In this sense, theory is viewed as an attempt to invent explanations and consists of a set of logically interrelated concepts and hypotheses that represents a systematic view of a problem by specifying the relationships among variables. But the theoretical utility of the comparative method is only as good as the concepts which inform the comparisons. Hence, researchers ought to be particularly sensitive to the adequacy of the concepts they use in their research. This paper addresses itself to this general problem by demonstrating the harmful consequences for theoretical progress in comparative urban politics represented by Edward Banfield and James Q. Wilson's Ethos Theory. In particular, their "theory" exhibits a degree of conceptual confusion directly proportional to its influence on the study of

Reprinted from the *Midwest Journal of Political Science*, vol. 14, no. 4 (November 1970), by permission of the Wayne State University Press and author. The author would like to thank the following people for their helpful comments on an earlier draft: Robert Alford, David Bell, Bryan Downes, Ada Finifter, Alan Grimes, William Hannah, Brett Hawkins, Susan Lawther, Robert Lineberry, Vincent Ostrum, Liz Powell, Charles Press, Leslie Roos, and Donald Searing. The author would also like to thank James Q. Wilson for his courteous, constructive disagreement.

[1] V.O. Key, *Southern Politics* (Vintage, 1949); Karl Deutsch, *Nationalism and Social Communication* (Cambridge: MIT Press, 1953); and, Seymour Lipset, Martin Trow and James Coleman, *Union Democracy* (Glencoe: Free Press, 1956). For a fascinating and controversial discussion of the role of comparative method in theory construction see Barney Glaser and Anselm Strauss. *The Discovery of Grounded Theory: Strategies for Qualitative Research* (Chicago: Aldine, 1967).

urban politics and this relationship, in turn, has seriously inhibited cumulative research. After a brief explication of concept formation, we shall turn to a discussion of the Ethos formulation and its consequences for empirical inquiry.

I. *Concept formation*

There is no science that deals with the objects of its concern "in toto." Of necessity it selects certain dimensions of the problem and attempts to establish relationships among them. The initial stage in this attempt at making observed relationships meaningful is the process of concept formation. In this sense, concepts are a traditional part of the theoretical machinery of the investigator which help him sharpen his focus and which provide convenient analytic categories under which a wide range of activity and seemingly diverse phenomena can be subsumed.

There appears to be some agreement that the process of concept formation begins with the problem of "recognition": the tentative and frequently intuitive identification of important qualities or aspects of the situation being studied. Out of this attempt to understand the problematic phenomena, a notion or concept develops, albeit an extremely vague one, to account for the particular behavior or behaviors in question.[2] At this point, the concepts should be analytic and sufficiently generalized to designate the characteristics of the concrete entities but not the entities themselves. They should also be "sensitizing"; that is, they should yield a "meaningful" picture of the phenomena.[3] Ultimately, however, concepts must be judged by their usefulness as theoretical tools. First and foremost they should reveal the fundamental character of the phenomena. But the greater the distance between one's concepts and the world of observation to which they are designed to refer, the greater is their capacity for being misunderstood. Hence, the vague imagery which characterized the early stages of concept formation must be clarified and brought more nearly in line with empirical measures.[4]

The preceding observations are particularly relevant to Banfield and Wilsons' Ethos formulation since the latter represents an instance where such vague imagery has not been brought sufficiently into line with empirical measures. Their unclear explication has led to a number of problems. First, the ethos concept *came to be defined quite differently by different*

---

[2] For an insightful discussion of the process of concept formation see Paul Lazarsfeld, "Evidence and Inference in Social Research" in Daniel Lerner (ed.), *Evidence and Inference* (Glencoe, Illinois: The Free Press, 1958), pp. 107-138.

[3] The "sensitizing" aspects of concepts are discussed in Herbert Blumer, "What Is Wrong with Social Theory?" *American Sociological Review*, 19 (February, 1954), 39 and Barney Glaser and Anselm L. Strauss, *op. cit.*, pp. 190-199.

[4] We are referring here to reducing any ambiguity and vagueness in the concepts and are not suggesting that their "openness of meaning" be reduced. For this distinction see Abraham Kaplan, *The Conduct of Inquiry: Methodology for Behavioral Science* (San Francisco: Chandler, 1964), pp. 62-71.

investigators;[5] the scope of the concept's applicability came to be a function of implicit choices made by the individual scholar to study one thing rather than another.[6] This selection delineated the range of the concept's applicability. The unclear nature of the formulation also permitted the *values of the individual investigators to enter into research at the verification stage.* It is at this vaguely articulated stage that values most easily influence research leading the researchers to accept or reject hypotheses on the basis of insufficient and/or inadequate evidence.[7] In sum, *both of these difficulties have inhibited the cumulative character of research in urban politics.*

II. The Ethos Theory: a case of faulty concept formation

The very influential Ethos Theory[8] proceeds from the rather misleading and simplistic assumption that urban cleavages coalesce around two opposite conceptions of the public interest.[9] One conception derives from the middle

[5] See Donald Searing, "Values in Empirical Research: A Behavioralist Response," *Midwest Journal of Political Science,* (Forthcoming, Feb. 1970) p. 14. Timothy Hennessey discusses this problem by noting the different research applications of the concepts "public policy" and "political development" in his: "Considerations of Theory and Concept Formation in Comparative Political Analysis," paper delivered at the annual meeting of the Midwest Political Science Association, Ann Arbor, Michigan, April 24-26, 1969.

[6] Several scholars have critically observed how the values of different researchers have influenced the study of "community power" in urban politics. See in particular: Peter Bachrach and Morton Baratz, "Two Faces of Power," *The American Political Science Review,* 56, 4 (December, 1962), pp. 947-952 and John Walton. "Discipline, Method and Community Power: A Note on the Sociology of Knowledge," *American Sociological Review,* 31, 5 (October, 1966), pp. 684-690.

[7] This discussion relies heavily on distinctions in Searing, *op. cit.,* pp.10-12.

[8] The Ethos Theory is articulated in Edward C. Banfield and James Q. Wilson, *City Politics* (Cambridge: Harvard University and MIT Press, 1963) and James Q. Wilson and Edward C. Banfield, "Public Regardingness as a Value Premise in Voting Behavior," *American Political Science Review,* 58, 4, (December, 1964), pp. 876-887. For some indication of the influence of Banfield and Wilson's ethos formulation, see the central position it occupies in the following research: Terry N. Clark, "Community Structure, Decision-Making, Budget Expenditures and Urban Renewal in 51 American Communities," *American Sociological Review,* 33, 4 (August, 1968), pp. 584-589; Terry N. Clark (ed.), *Community Structure and Decision Making: Comparative Analyses* (San Francisco: Chandler, 1968), pp. 108, 146, 159-195, 215-216, 233, 269; Robert L. Crain, Elihu Katz and Donald B. Rosenthal, *The Politics of Community Conflict: The Fluoridation Decision* (New York: Bobbs-Merrill, 1969), pp. 74, 159-160, 165, 179-180, 196-197; Raymond Wolfinger and John Osgood Field, "Political Ethos and the Structure of City Government," *American Political Science Review,* 60, 2 (June, 1966), pp. 306-326; Robert Lineberry and Edmund Fowler, "Reformism and Public Policies in American Cities," *American Political Science Review,* 61, 3 (September, 1967), pp. 701-716; James Q. Wilson (ed.), *City Politics and Public Policy* (New York: John Wiley and Sons, 1968), pp. 13, 186-188, 218; and Robert Alford and Eugene Lee, "Voting Turnout in American Cities," *American Political Science Review,* 62, 3 (September, 1968), pp. 810-813. This list is not meant to be exhaustive, simply illustrative.

[9] The Ethos Theory is not a "theory" in any formal sense since it is not logically interconnected. It might best be viewed as a concept. Moreover, the ethos formulation is

class ethos which favors "good government"; that is, government which is efficient, impartial, devoid of favoritism and characterized by a strong executive and model legal codes. The logic of the middle class ideal does not refer simply to value premises underlying the citizen's attachment to the political system "but also 'implies' a preference for certain institutional arrangements such as nonpartisan and at-large elections, the council-manager form, master planning and metropolitan area organization."[10] The other conception derives from the "immigrant ethos"; that is, the propensity to identify with the ward or neighborhood rather than the city as a whole. This latter orientation involves a propensity to look to politicians for "help" and "favors": it is less concerned with efficiency and impartiality and more with the local politicians' readiness to confer material rewards.

A. Logical structure of the Ethos Theory

Although there are a number of confusing and contradictory aspects of the Ethos formulation, one fundamental problem stands out. Since Banfield and Wilson indicate that public and private regarding orientations represent different concepts of the public interest, their argument is *contingent* upon some theory of the public interest. As we shall see, without such a conception, issues tend to be selected *ad hoc* and their public regarding or private regarding characteristics left up to the intuition of the reader. Yet, beyond citing Banfield's earlier efforts, no such theory is offered.[11] While admitting that construction of such a theory is a monumental task, it seems clear that it is incumbent upon the originators of the ethos notion to offer a theory of the public interest which refers to objective indicators of its various dimensions in terms of which issues can be selected to test the "Ethos."[12]

---

basically of the political culture genre. For examples of this type of explanation in urban politics see: Robert Agger, Daniel Goldrich and Bert C. Swanson, *The Rulers and the Ruled*, (New York: John Wiley and Sons, 1964), pp. 544, 554, 563-568; Robert Presthus, *Men at the Top* (New York: Oxford University Press, 1964), pp. 320-367; Oliver P. Williams and Charles R. Adrian, *Four Cities* (Philadelphia: University of Pennsylvania Press, 1963), p. 293; Robert C. Wood, *1400 Governments* (Cambridge: Harvard University Press, 1964), pp. 72, 160, 167, 188, 216. For the use of the political culture idea in cross-cultural research see also Edward C. Banfield, *The Moral Basis of a Backward Society* (New York: The Free Press, 1958), pp. 10, 103, 123, 139, 156, 166; Gabriel Almond and Sidney Verba, *The Civic Culture* (Princeton: Princeton University Press, 1963); Lucian Pye, *Politics, Personality and Nation-Building* (New Haven: Yale University Press, 1963); Harry Eckstein, *Division and Cohesion in Democracy: A Study of Norway*, (Princeton: Princeton University Press, 1966); Lucian Pye and Sidney Verba (eds.), *Political Culture and Political Development* (Princeton: Princeton University Press, 1965).

[10] Banfield and Wilson, *op. cit.*, p. 330.

[11] Banfield's efforts at constructing a theory of the public interest are presented in Martin Myerson and Edward Banfield, *Politics, Planning and the Public Interest* (New York: The Free Press, 1955), pp. 285-329.

[12] For some of the severe problems in theories of the public interest see Glendon Schubert, *The Public Interest: A Critique of the Theory of a Political Concept* (New

Now the ethos formulation seems to be an example of the most common type of environmental explanation in social theory; that is, it involves group culture as an environmental variable and some notion of membership as a mapping (socialization) variable.[13] Ethnic group membership or (social class membership) acts as a mapping variable which has the value of 0 or 1. Its causal force can be conceived as exposure to, or embedding in, some group culture or "Ethos." Hence, some extra-individual process determines the position of these ethnics; that is, it operates only on those who are exposed or socialized into it or who are located in a social setting that supports such an ethic.

Once the argument is reduced to these simple components, several difficulties can be isolated. It is unclear, for example, whether the difference in the two ethics is due to ethnicity, social class or some unspecified combination of the two. Moreover, it is not clear if a combination of ethnicity *and* working class status is the origin of the private regarding ethos. If it is a combination of the two, why should upward mobility produce a change in ethos? Banfield and Wilson might argue that since private-regardingness is a consequence of ethnic consciousness, it disappears when middle class status is achieved. But several studies indicate that upward mobility does little to change ethnic consciousness.[14]

If we take social status to be the major factor in determining the two ethics, there are other difficulties. We have already observed that group awareness is necessary to provide the subcultural milieu in which the socialization or mapping process takes place. While it is possible to grasp the role of ethnicity in this regard, how does the notion of "middle class" or "Anglo-Saxon" provide such group awareness? Even if we accept "middle class" as a meaningful notion in the development of an ethos, Banfield and Wilson never unequivocally specify whether the public regarding ethos is characteristic of the middle class, the upper-middle class or the upper class. Some of these difficulties would seem to be surmounted if we assume that "middle class" means upper-middle class. In certain passages, they indicate that the important dividing line is between professional and business people on the one hand and lower status people on the other. Yet, the largest part of their

---

York: The Free Press, 1960). For a critique of Banfield's theory in particular see Schubert, *Ibid.,* pp. 206-211. For a general discussion of the public interest notion by several scholars see the articles in Carl J. Friedrich (ed.), *The Public Interest* (New York: Atherton Press, 1962). Schubert summarizes the views of many scholars on the utility of such a concept when he notes that: "If the public interest concept makes no operational sense, notwithstanding the efforts of a generation of capable scholars, then political scientists might better use their time nurturing concepts that offer greater promise of being useful tools in the scientific study of politics." *Ibid.*

[13]"Mapping Variable" is used here in the sense employed by Stinchcombe; that is, since group attachment varies from one person to another, in a sense it "maps" this environmental on the individual's cognitive system.See Arthur Stinchcombe, *Constructing Social Theories* (New York: Harcourt, Brace & World, 1968), p. 204.

[14]On the persistence of ethnic identification see: Raymond Wolfinger, "The Development and Persistence of Ethnic Voting," *American Political Science Review,* 59 (December, 1965) pp. 896-908. Michael Parenti, "Ethnic Politics and the Persistence of Ethnic Identification," *American Political Science Review,* 61, 3 (September, 1967), pp. 717-726.

argument contradicts this. This is especially apparent in their discussion of the likelihood that the middle class will, in the long run, assimilate the lower classes which suggests that they include everyone with a white collar occupation in the middle-class in terms of the two ethics.[15]

Finally, the "theory" does not specify the environments in which the "mapping" or socialization process takes place; that is, what is it about immigrant subcultures which makes them more "private-regarding"? Were these cultural values imprinted in the "old country" or through interaction in subcultures in this country, or what?

B. Testing the theory

Wilson and Banfield indicate that the central proposition suggested by their theory is the following: "Some classes of voters (provisionally defined as "subcultures" constituted on ethnic and income lines) are more predisposed to rest their choices on some conception of the public interest or the welfare of the community. . . . the voting behavior of some classes of voters tends to be more public regarding and less private (self-family) regarding than that of others." Moreover, "to test this hypothesis, it is necessary to examine voting behavior in situations where one can say that a certain vote could not have been private-regarding. . . . If the voter nevertheless casts such a vote and if there is evidence that the vote was not in some sense accidental, then it *must* be presumed that his action was based on some conception of the public interest."[16] In support of these propositions Banfield and Wilson consider several sets of referenda. There are a number of problems with their tests, all of which reflect ambiguities in the basic formulation.

First, the logic of their argument is directed at the level of individual voter choice, yet Banfield and Wilson draw inferences concerning the existence of public or private regardingness on the basis of aggregate voting statistics. By using such a procedure they are guilty of the ecological fallacy; that is, the fallacy of making inferences about individual behavior on the basis of correlations between higher level aggregates such as voting statistics, median family income, percent owner occupied, etc.[17]

Banfield and Wilson suggest that "public-regardingness" is manifested in support for expansion of many government services that may not benefit the individual, but which will increase his taxes. In these instances, if the individual nevertheless votes for such increased services, he cannot be said to be acting in a "private regarding" manner and, hence, must be voting in the "public interest." In support for this "theory," they offer two referenda, one on a County Hospital and the other on a Welfare Building because the taxes

[15] See Wolfinger and Field, *op. cit.*, p. 308, for a similar observation.

[16] Wilson and Banfield, *op. cit.*, p. 876. The emphasis on "must" is my own.

[17] For a discussion of the ecological fallacy see: W.S. Robinson, "Ecological Correlations and Behavior of Individuals," *American Sociological Review* (June, 1950), pp. 351-357. It is only fair to note that Banfield and Wilson are aware that survey data would be a more appropriate data base than voting statistics. Nevertheless, the particular study in question does contain an ecological fallacy.

necessary for their construction were to be assessed against different publics: the Hospital from property taxes and the Welfare Building from sales tax. In other words, the homeowner would bear the burden of financing the Hospital whereas both the homeowners and renters would be taxed for the Welfare Building. They suggest that if the homeowners support the hospital, they are public regarding since their behavior in this instance cannot be construed as private-regarding as it costs them something. The data below (see Table 1)[18] are interpreted as support for their theory since a large percentage of the high income group supported the measure at a cost to themselves whereas an even higher percentage of the low income renters supported a measure which cost them nothing but from which they would benefit. The latter group presumably voted in accordance with their self-interest narrowly conceived.

But in their search for situations in which the behavior of one class of voters, (namely the upper and middle class homeowners) could not be construed as "private regarding," they have so structured the "test" that the other class of voters (the middle and low income renters) is precluded from the possibility of behaving in a "public regarding" manner. Put another way, given the test how could the middle and low income renters have behaved in a public regarding manner? Would voting against the county hospital bill have been an indicator of public regardingness? It is hard to imagine how the "public interest" would have been served by such a vote. In short, since the two groups are not subjected to the same stimuli and cost parameters, it is

Table 1. *Voting behavior of four major economic groups compared in Cook County*

	Percent "yes" vote	
	County	State welfare
	Hospital (1957)	Building (1958)
	(%)	(%)
High income homeowners		
Winnetka	64	76
Wilmette	55	70
Lincolnwood	47	64
Middle income homeowners		
Lansing	30	54
Bellwood	21	55
Brookfield	22	51
Middle income renters		
Chicago Ward 44	65	71
Chicago Ward 48	61	72
Chicago Ward 49	64	74
Low income renters		
Chicago Ward 2	88	73
Chicago Ward 3	87	76
Chicago Ward 27	87	78

[18] Wilson and Banfield, *op. cit.,* p. 886.

impossible to know how the lower SES renters would have behaved had their cost parameters been the same as the homeowners.

In other words, inferences of the sort drawn by Banfield and Wilson should be drawn only in cases where all groups were subjected to the *same* not different stimuli. Hence if both groups had been taxed for the hospital as well as the welfare building and a large percentage of the middle and lower class renters had voted against such a proposal then Banfield and Wilson might have some ground for their claims. But on the basis of their tests, all they can validly conclude about the Hospital Referendum is that the different behavior elicited (percentage of yes votes) was a function of different stimuli (taxation – no taxation). Indeed, on the issue where all the groups are subjected to the same stimuli (the Welfare Building) very little difference can be noted except that the middle income homeowner is the least public regarding. Judging from both referenda, the middle income homeowners have little taste for expenditures of any kind! If the high income homeowners are compared with the middle income renters very little difference appears on either of the referenda. Which of these are we to credit with the public regarding virtues? Given these considerations one can only conclude that the tests are so poorly designed as to be of doubtful value in establishing the validity of their thesis.

Following their notion of social status as an indicator of the public regarding ethic, the authors cite in support of their theory positive correlations between "yes" votes on a number of referenda and median family income. But, at the same time, they display, but for some reason do not discuss, scattergrams showing *negative* correlations between percent owner occupied and "yes" votes on a sewer referendum in Chicago and a referendum on increased hospital facilities in Cleveland.[19]

Finally, they use social status variables to examine the relationship between "yes" votes on a proposition to approve a $300 bonus for veterans of the Korean War and median family income.[20] The predicted positive correlation does not occur: the relationship yielded a strong negative correlation (-.71). This seems to be a particularly clear-cut instance where the Ethos Theory does not correctly predict voting behavior. Furthermore, it might be construed as a blatant instance of private regardingness among the upper classes. That is, given the inequities of the draft, in which fewer upper class sons are drafted owing to deferments of one sort or another, members of the upper-class would benefit less from such a bonus and, therefore, voted against it. But Banfield and Wilson have a different explanation. To account for this finding, they introduce a variation on their concept of "public-regardingness" by interpreting the finding as follows: "upper income Anglo-Saxons, and to a lesser degree, Jews, tend to *vote on public regarding grounds against* some proposals, notably those like veterans, bonuses and city employees/pension benefits and pay increases that they regard as serving "special interests" rather than "the community as a whole."[21] But again, since Banfield and

[19] *Ibid.*, p. 878-879.
[20] *Ibid.*, p. 881.
[21] *Ibid.*, p. 886.

Wilson provide no theory of the Public Interest it is impossible to know what sorts of issues are in the "Public Interest." If veterans bonuses are "Special Interests," was the G. I. Bill a "Special Interest"? And what about welfare programs, are these "special interests" since they mainly serve the poor? Hence, while it is relatively easy to see that sewers and hospitals benefit the community as a whole there is a wide range of issues the status of which is not clear in terms of the Ethos Theory.

In short, the data on social class lend little support to the Ethos Theory: there is as much evidence against as for the proposition. With respect to the influence of ethnicity, the evidence is also mixed. In several instances, homeownership is a better predictor than ethnicity. Moreover, whatever rigor was present in the tests involving social status is not present in the tests for ethnicity. The data simply indicate that some ethnics have a greater propensity to support certain expenditures than do others. Now while this is an interesting finding, it hardly warrants the significance the authors attach to it. Most importantly, the Ethos Theory does not help us explain *why* one ethnic group should be more supportive than another. For example, in a particularly surprising oversight, the authors fail to show how their theory explains why Negroes should be more enthusiastic for public expenditures than other ethnics and why this could be the case even among Negro homeowners. Wilson and Banfield make no attempt to tie this rather interesting finding into their discussion except to suggest that the Negro vote may be in some sense irrational. As they put it: "In passing it is worth noting that Negroes are two or three times more favorable toward urban renewal— despite the fact that they are commonly the chief victims of land clearance programs."[22]

The preceding critique should make readily apparent the serious problems which can arise when poorly formulated assumptions are treated as axioms and derived theorems. Not only was their failure to delineate the precise dimensions of the Ethos Theory reflected in their unsatisfactory verification enterprise but such confusion permitted subsequent researchers to attribute quite different meanings to the formulation, depending on their particular research goals. In the sections which follow we shall show how research undertaken in the name of the Ethos Theory has had a non-cumulative quality as well as noting the theoretically harmful consequences of this development.

III.   Some conceptual loose ends: the making of a straw man

The research of Wolfinger and Field[23] purports to be a test of Banfield and Wilson's Ethos Theory. More accurately, these scholars create a "straw man" and commence to demolish it. Moreover, in the process of constructing the

---

[22] *Ibid.*, p. 884.
[23] Raymond Wolfinger and John Osgood Field, "Political Ethos and the Structure of City Government," *American Political Science Review*, 60 (June, 1966), pp. 306-326.

test, they expand the Ethos Theory to include preferences for formal structural arrangements as well as attitudinal predispositions.[24] And although there is evidence that Banfield and Wilson did not intend to suggest that the two ethics be translated into institutional form, they leave sufficient loose ends in their formulation to permit such an interpretation.[25] There are several places, for example, where they make references to the "logic" of the theory calling for different institutional arrangements.[26] Such imprecise language permits Wolfinger and Field to represent the theory as containing an institution focus.

In order to test the theory, Wolfinger and Field proceed to treat formal governmental structure and selected policies as their dependent variables and ethnicity, as measured by the percent of the cities' population that is foreign born, as their major independent variable.[27] These associations are then examined for each major region of the U.S.[28] Their tests include the hypothesized relationships shown below.[29]

The dependent variables

	Private-regarding	Public-regarding
Form of government	Mayor	Manager
Type of ballot	Partisan	Nonpartisan
Method of electing councilmen	Wards	At-large
Size of council districts	Small	Large
Civil service coverage	Less	More
City planning expenditures	Low	High
Urban renewal	Low	High

On the basis of the tests, they are prepared to draw the following inferences:

> If the hypothesized relationship between ethnicity and a given political form is not found, three conclusions can be considered: a) a preference for that form is not part of the ethos; b) the ethos is not related to ethnicity; c) the two ethics are not translated into political reality.[30]

[24] They argue that the private regarding ethic calls for mayors, partisan ballots and ward elected councilman, etc., whereas the public regarding ethic calls for city managers, at-large elections, nonpartisan ballot, etc.

[25] See Wilson and Banfield, "Communications," *American Political Science Review*, 61 (December, 1966), pp. 998-999.

[26] See Banfield and Wilson, *op. cit.*, p. 330.

[27] The other independent variables are measures of social class, median family income, and education level. They examine these relationships in 272 cities all of which are over 50,000 in population. Cities with Commission forms of government are excluded from the sample as the authors feel the Ethos Theory does not include such structures. Wolfinger and Field, *op. cit.*, p. 312.

[28] They examine the degree of association between percent foreign born for each dependent variable while controlling for the other independent variables.

[29] Wolfinger and Field, *op. cit.*, p. 310.

[30] *Ibid.*, p. 312.

When the relationship between ethnicity and form of government is examined *within* regions this eliminates most of the original positive relationship. The relationship between ethnicity and form of government is considered to be a regional phenomena. Region, moreover, proved to be a better predictor of public policies such as urban renewal and level of civil service than did ethnicity. They conclude, therefore, that there is no nationally relevant level of ethnicity with which one form of government is likely to predominate.[31]

Now the "straw man" referred to above, is constructed from several elements. Aside from the inclusion of formal structures, one of the most serious misinterpretations of the Ethos Theory is the use of percent foreign born as the sole objective indicator of ethnicity. Since the largest part of the Ethos Theory is an attempt to demonstrate variation in preferences *between* different ethnic groups, by using percent foreign born, Wolfinger and Field are concealing the very source of the variation in question. Such a measure places in one category such diverse groups as Jews, Irishmen, Germans, Italians, French Canadians, etc. The same may be said of the group they label "American" which includes poor Negroes, New England Yankees, hillbillies, etc.

Another problem concerns the following inference by Wolfinger and Field: "contrary to specific propositions in the Ethos Theory, some of the political forms and policies are not manifestations of either ethos." But these inferences are based on faulty logic and violate some rather obvious caveats about time-series ordering: the independent variables are measured with 1960 census data, while the dependent variables are based on the results of choices made ten to fifty years ago.[32] Data of this kind can never answer the question of why a city adopted one set of formal governmental structures rather than another. Given the inappropriateness of these measures, it is not difficult to see how Wolfinger and Field manage to "disprove" the Ethos Theory.

IV. The Ethos Theory transformed: the role of formal structures

We have seen how Wolfinger and Field expanded the scope of the Ethos Theory to include formal structures. Many other scholars have also been

---

[31] It is not clear precisely what is involved in the concept "Region." Regions have had different historical traditions, in one sense, controlling for region is controlling for history. But as Lineberry and Fowler note, "The problem with this reasoning is that to 'control' for region is to control not only for history, but for demography as well: to know what region a city is in *is* to know something about the composition of its population. Geographic subdivisions are relevant subjects of political inquiry only because they are differentiated on the basis of attitudinal or socioeconomic variables." Lineberry and Fowler, *op. cit.*, p. 707. For an informative discussion of "Region," see Bruce Russett, *International Regions and International System* (New York: Rand McNally, 1967), pp.1-20.

[32] For similar observations, see Lineberry and Fowler, *op. cit.*, p. 707 and Wilson and Banfield, "Communications . . . .," *op. cit.*, p. 999. Moreover, it is not convincing to

interested in the role of such structures, and their concerns can be summarized around three fundamental questions, all of which claim to be informed by the Ethos Theory. The questions are as follows:

1. What is it about the social characteristics of cities which predisposes the citizens to prefer one formal governmental structure over another?
2. What can the formal structure of a city's government tell us about the "public" and "private regarding" attitudes of its citizens which might prove useful in explaining public policy?
3. What role do these formal governmental structures play in explaining the relationship between a city's social characteristics and public policy?

Wolfinger and Field's research is an example of an attempt to answer the first question.[33] Their inquiry, however, was by no means the first effort in this direction. In this connection, it is important to note the work of Sherbenou, Kessel, Schnore and Alford, and Alford and Scoble.[34]

The work of several of these scholars suffers from the same time series difficulty we noted in Wolfinger and Field. Moreover, the theoretical worth of most of these studies is severely limited by being explicitly or implicitly based on static models: that is, a number of different variables are offered to account for formal structural characteristics. While some may find it useful to know how the characteristics of "reformed" cities differ from "unreformed cities," to know the labels of phenomena and to know their distribution is not to explain them.

The work of Crain, Katz and Rosenthal[35] represents an attempt to answer the second question. In order to explain why some communities decide in favor of fluoridation and others do not, they conducted a comparative study of a number of American municipalities. They found that:

---

argue, as Wolfinger and Field do, that the % of ethnics has not significantly changed in the last fifty years since the people involved are simply not the *same* people as fifty years ago.

[33] To be as accurate as possible, Wolfinger and Field do devote a small portion of their paper to the relationship between ethnicity and selected public policies, e.g., level of civil service coverage, city planning expenditures per capita, and urban capital grants per capita. But the major thrust of their article is addressed to the relationship between social environment and formal structures.

[34] See Edgar L. Sherbenou, "Class, Participation, and the Council-Manager Plan," *Public Administration Review*, 21 (Summer, 1961), pp. 131-135; Leo F. Schnore and Robert Alford, "Forms of Government and Socio-Economic Characteristics of Suburbs," *Administrative Science Quarterly*, VIII (1963), pp. 1-17; John H. Kessel, "Governmental Structure and Political Environment: A Statistical Note about American Cities," *American Political Science Review*, 56, 3 (September, 1962), pp. 615-620; Robert Alford and Harry M. Scoble, "Political and Socio-Economic Characteristics of Cities," *The Municipal Year Book, 1965* (Chicago: The International City Managers' Association, 1965), pp. 82-97. Sherbenou found high property values in Chicago to be related to the manager form, while the less expensive homes had the mayor form. Kessel found the mayor form to occur most frequently in cities with large percentages of ethnics. Schnore and Alford report a similar finding for a large number of suburbs, but the relationship is of a much lower level of magnitude. The two latter studies found manager forms in predominately white collar settings.

[35] Crain, *et. al., op. cit.*

In all regions, administrative adoptions of flouridation are most frequent in manager cities, followed by partisan mayor-council cities. Referenda are more characteristic of the manager and non-commission forms. In general, partisan mayor-council cities and commission cities are less likely to act altogether, and there is some suggestion that the commission form is most hesitant of all.[36]

In an attempt to explain the relationship between form of government and fluoridation, they suggest that a general community ethos of "progressivism" (reformism) may constitute an adequate explanation.[37] They then make inferences about the "political culture" of the community using the form of government as the major indicator, e.g., reformed structures indicate a progressive community.

But there are several problems with this approach. In particular, since decisions to adopt one form of government rather than another were made many years prior to the fluoridation decision, it is patently invalid to make inferences about current attitudinal predispositions using such formal structures as indicators. A hypothetical example of the problem would be to infer that since Southern California has an abundance of city managers, citizens who reside in such cities have public-regarding or progressive attitudes. But, since these structures were chosen years ago, and since the population of much of California is very fluid, there is simply no basis for assuming that attitudes which prevailed at the time of the form's adoption still prevail, or even that a large percentage of the same people still reside in the community. Moreover, there is ample evidence to show that political behavior in parts of Southern California which have reform institutions is far from "progressive."[38]

A large part of the trouble underlying the fluoridation study and other such studies is the treatment of formal institutional structures as equivalent to social structure variables. It is difficult to grasp how *formal* structures can have the same conceptual status or scientific utility as such dynamic social structure variables as social class and education. But such an approach has advantages for the researcher because, by treating formal governmental structures as part of the social structure, essentially historical choices appear to be constantly up to date, although this is clearly not the case.

---

[36] Crain, *Ibid.*, p. 165.

[37] When the authors examined this possibility they found the over-all picture to be more complex than the simple "Progressivism" argument. When they examined the relationship between form of government and votes on various issues or community decisions on "Progressive" measures, they found evidence that the city-manager form was more "Progressive" than the others. The city-manager government was more likely to have embarked on: urban renewal, a planning program, a capital budget for major expenditures, and fluoridation adoptions. However, "Progressivism" seemed to have little value in explaining the pattern among the other three forms of government, or in explaining the bond-issue votes in city-manager cities. Among the mayor-council cities, for example, they found the nonpartisan ones more likely to be involved in planning and urban renewal, but less likely to adopt fluoridation (Crain, *Ibid.*, p. 169).

[38] On the prevalence of conservatism in Southern California see Raymond E. Wolfinger and Fred I. Greenstein, "The Repeal of Fair Housing in California: An Analysis of Referendum Voting," *American Political Science Review*, 62, 3 September, 1968), pp. 753-769.

V. Environment, governmental structure, and policy outputs

In an imaginative and methodologically sophisticated effort to answer the third question, Lineberry and Fowler incorporate the Ethos Notion into a process model. Their objective is to determine: "the impact of both socio-economic variables and political institutions (structural variables) on outputs of city governments. By doing this, we hope to shed some additional illumination on the Ethos Theory."[39]

In order to establish these influences they use twelve socio-economic variables as indicators of environmental inputs and then compute multiple correlation coefficients for "reformed" and "unreformed" cities using taxes and expenditures as the dependent variables. They find the coefficients to be lower for the "reformed" cities and attribute this to the influence of reformism. These findings are a function of several key concepts and propositions all of which come directly from the reformist ideology. Indeed, the authors suggest that this is only appropriate:

> It is important that we understand the ideology of these reformers if we hope to be able to analyze the institutions which they created and their impact on policy decision.[40]

In one sense, this is a puzzling statement. It seems to be analogous to asserting that a necessary condition for analyzing the American Congress or the Supreme Court is to understand the intentions of "the founding fathers." Clearly, such knowledge is not a necessary precondition for empirical research on formal institutions. There is another sense, however, in which their remarks can be interpreted. The ideology of the reformers may suggest concepts and variables which can be incorporated into working hypotheses. This would seem to be their intention. Drawing heavily on the Ethos Theory, they base their process model on the following propositions:

1. The less social *homogeneity* in the city, the more *cleavage.*
2. The more *cleavage,* the more *conflict.*
3. The more *conflict,* the more *private-regarding demands* on governmental structures.
   A. Since reformed structures are designed to reduce the influence of partisan, socio-economic cleavages and substitute administrative efficiency in the service of the "public interest," it follows that:
4. The higher the level of *Reformism,* the less *responsive* the governmental structures to these conflicts and private-regarding demands.[41]

Of all the concepts in these propositions, however, only two are directly measured: "homogeneity" and "responsiveness," the rest are imputed or

---

[39] This article is reprinted in Part Four.

[40] *Ibid.,* p. 701.

[41] *Ibid.,* p. 713. These propositions were extracted from Lineberry and Fowler.

inferred from reformist ideology *via* the Ethos Theory. There are no objective indicators whatever for such dynamic political features of the model as "cleavage," "conflict," and "private-regarding demands." Moreover, many of the central concepts bring into the model pejorative connotations intended by the reformers. We shall return to this important point when we discuss some of the normative implications of the model.

Let us turn to one of the concepts for which indicators are provided: namely, "responsiveness." This is measured by computing multiple R's for the twelve socio-economic variables. But since Lineberry and Fowler use only this gross measure and never discuss the contribution of each of the variables, they are forced to take the position that "reformed" cities are less responsive to *all* group demands. But this seems to fly in the face of common sense, which suggests that different institutional arrangements might favor different interests.[42] Lineberry and Fowler try to get around this difficulty by drawing on the Ethos Theory which suggests that only *some* elements, which they term minorities, actually make selfish demands while others who are "public regarding" care for the good of the community as a whole!

A closely related problem concerns the concept of "cleavage." Lineberry and Fowler work with twelve indices which "represent a variety of possible social cleavages which divide urban populations."[43] Now although this list most probably does contain indicators of cleavage, the authors never tell us which ones are the indicators. In no case do they provide evidence that these items are indices of social conflict to say nothing of politically relevant demands.

A. Reformism as a type concept

Lineberry and Fowler make clear that formal political structures are not treated as independent variables but as *factors* which influence the level of expenditures and taxation and the relationship between these "cleavage" variables and outputs.[44] In short, *these structures are crucial in the process* by which environmental inputs are transformed into outputs.[45] And since these structures refer to operative variables, the reformed-unreformed classification seems to have the status of a type concept: that is, these two categories are a way of indicating that in each instance some large number of variables go together so that specific values of one are associated with specific

---

[42] See Wolfinger and Field, "Communications," *op. cit.,* p. 228. One might choose to weaken the case by conceding that in some instances a summary measure (in this case the multiple R), could legitimately refer to a *net balance of forces* rather than that all of the forces are in the same direction.

[43] Lineberry and Fowler, *op. cit.,* p. 703.

[44] *Ibid.,* p. 707.

[45] It is clear that they do *not* wish to treat these forms as *parameters;* that is, as determinants that are known or expected to influence dependent variables but which, in the investigation at hand, are made or assumed not to vary. See Neil Smelser, *Essays in Sociological Explanation* (Englewood Cliffs, New Jersey: Prentice-Hall, Inc., 1968), p. 16.

values of the other.[46] In short, type-concepts of this sort are convenient ways of writing a function of two or more variables in such a way that interaction effects may be simply stated.

Lineberry and Fowler never indicate, however, what variables make up each category. Had they initially determined what combination of variables they wished to represent by the notions of "reformed" and "unreformed," the propositions they suggest would have a great deal more theoretical worth than propositions such as: "the more reformism, the less responsiveness." Hypotheses could then be formulated which refer not only to such a crude category as "reformism" but to some combination of variables to which the designation refers. Such an approach would suggest why, for example, the commission form of government should or should not go in the reform category *prior* to the analysis rather than after, as was the case with the research in question.

The first test of such a type concept is that the variables which make it up are, in fact, connected.[47] Clearly, it is impossible to perform such a test with "reformism" since information on such variables is not provided by any research reviewed here.[48] The important point is that because the reformers were not primarily interested in political science as science, they never specified the variables to which these type-concepts were designed to refer. Banfield and Wilson and subsequent researchers have never filled this lacuna. Hence, when political scientists use these types as concepts, their research

[46] For a discussion of type-concepts, see Stinchcomb, *op. cit.*, p. 48, and Paul F. Lazarsfeld and Allan H. Barton, "Qualitative Measurement in the Social Sciences: Classification, Typologies, and Indices" in Daniel Lerner and Harold D. Lasswell (eds.), *The Policy Sciences* (Stanford: Stanford University Press, 1951), pp. 155-193. For an interesting recent attempt at typological formulation in political science, see Arend Lijphart, "Typologies of Democratic Systems," *Comparative Political Studies*, No. 1 (April, 1968), pp. 3-45. For a critical review of typologies in sociology, see John C. McKinney, *Constructive Typology and Social Theory* (New York: Appleton-Century-Crofts, 1966).

[47] Recent studies evaluating Max Weber's type-concept of bureaucracy have discovered that some of the variables used to construct this type-concept were, in fact, associated, while others were not. The concept then had to be broken down into two different type-concepts, "rational" and "bureaucratic" or "professional" and "bureaucratic administration." See Stanley Udy and Arthur Stinchcombe in Peter Blau and Richard Scott, *Formal Organizations* (San Francisco: Chandler, 1962), pp. 207-208.

[48] This statement is not meant to imply that there have been no attempts to determine the empirical dimensions of these types. Several studies have shown that the idealized picture of council government does not and cannot account for extensive variation in practice among manager cities and the considerable deviation of these cities from the model. Gladys Kammerer and her associates have shown that the popular election of the mayor is a crucial factor in the actual functioning of the manager plan and its deviation from ideal practice. See Gladys Kammerer, *et. al., City Managers in Politics: Analysis of Manager Tenure and Termination* (University of Florida: Monographs, No. 13, 1962). For other preliminary attempts to get at this problem see Charles Adrian, "Leadership and Decision-Making in Three Manager Cities," *Public Administration Review*, Vol. 18 (Summer, 1958), and Wallace Sayre, "The General Manager for Large Cities," *Public Administration Review*, Vol. 14 (Autumn, 1954). Kammerer has also suggested that the approach of organizational decision-making may be helpful in associating crucial variables associated with different governmental forms. See Gladys Kammerer, "Role-Diversity of City Managers," *Administrative Science Quarterly*, Vol. 8 (March, 1964).

yields propositions and hypotheses which are ultimately of little theoretical utility because such designations refer to *complex arrangements of unspecified variables which somehow or other influence behavior.* To put it another way, the argument is analogous to asserting that differences in the formal governmental structures of Great Britian, France and the United States lead somehow to different types of public policy. In fact, disagreement over the merits of the parliamentary versus the presidential system has been a traditional concern of students of comparative politics. But again, although these formal structures probably do make a difference it is *necessary to specify what it is about these structures* which brings about variation in public policy.

B. The Ethos Theory as a model
of politics

Lineberry and Fowler claim confirmation for what is essentially an elitist model; that is, one which deemphasizes the role of the masses while stressing the wisdom and skill of political leaders.[49] For example, they infer "cleavages" from low homogeneity measures when all this need imply is diversity. They then assume that cleavages lead to "private-regarding demands" rather than simply interest articulation. Their concepts consistently denote disunity, bitterness, conflict and narrowly conceived self-interest. In short, they paint a bleak picture of governments confronted with *threatening social environments.* The Ethos Theory suggests an answer, however: reform structures will insulate the governments from such "artificial" cleavages. Lineberry and Fowler reach the same conclusion on the basis of their research:

> If one of the premises of the "political ethos" argument is that reformed institutions give less weight to the "private regarding" and "artificial" cleavages in the population, that premise receives striking support from our analysis. Our data suggest that when a city adopts reformed structures, it comes to be governed less on the basis of conflict and more on the basis of the rationalistic theory of administration. The making of public policy takes less count of the

[49]For a discussion of elitist models see Jack L. Walker, "A Critique of the Elitist Theory of Democracy," *American Political Science Review,* 60 (June, 1966), pp. 285-294. Positions formulated by Banfield and Wilson in literature not examined in detail here also could fall in the elitist category. Indeed, they appear to be in emphatic opposition to broad politicization of issues because this exacerbates conflict and lessens the available space for managing decisions. Their notion of pluralism is that of a controlled pluralism of elites. In short, they maintain that popular participation is inefficient because it clogs the machinery through which issues can be resolved: In particular, see Wilson's argument in *The Amateur Democrat: Club Politics in Three Cities* (Chicago: University of Chicago Press, 1962), pp. 340-370, and James Q. Wilson, *Negro Politics* (New York: Free Press, 1960). Some have argued that the distinction between those who prefer traditional machine politics to reform politics is overstated since they are both essentially elite formulations. See David Greenstone and Paul Peterson, "Reformers, Machines and the War on Poverty," in James Q. Wilson (ed.), *City Politics and Public Policy* (New York: Wiley, 1968), pp. 267-292.

enduring differences between White and Negro, business and labor, Pole and WASP. The logic of the bureaucratic ethic demands an impersonal apolitical settlement of issues, rather than the settlement of conflict in the arena of political battle.[50]

and again:

With the introduction of these reforms, a new political pattern may emerge in which disputes are settled outside the political system, or in which they may be settled by the crowd at the civic club at the periphery of the system. If they do enter the political process, an impersonal, "nonpolitical" bureaucracy may take less account of the conflicting interests and pay more attention to the "correct" decision from the point of view of the municipal planner.

These conclusions are generally consistent with the Ethos Theory developed by Banfield and Wilson. If one of the components of the middle class reformer's ideal was "to seek the good of the community as a whole" and to minimize the impact of social cleavages on political decision-making, then their institutional reforms have served, by and large, to advance that goal.[51]

The authors offer no measures of "conflict," "private-regardingness" nor the "public interest," and their inferences are based solely on the differences between two multiple correlation coefficients and the implicit model of democracy suggested by the Ethos Theory. But if one employs *an alternative model of democracy*, a more populist model for example; different inferences follow from the same measures and data. If low homogeneity is viewed simply as an indicator of diversity, and diversity, in turn, as an indicator of a variety of interests, then "conflict" and "cleavage" need not cloud the picture. Further, if we make the assumption that "responsible" government makes public policy in accordance with some notion of what the public feels it needs rather than what "insulated" decision-makers see as "correct" decisions, then a proposition might be formulated which states: the less "responsive" the structure to diverse social interests, *the less "responsible" it is to the needs of the citizen.* In short, it is not so much that Lineberry and Fowler do not meet the conditions of their own model as it is that they fail to test the conditions of possible competing models.

VI. Community structure, decision-making, and policy outputs

Terry Clark applied the ethos notion in a different manner than Lineberry and Fowler by incorporating it into a model of the relationship between community structure, decision making, budget expenditures and urban renewal in 51 American communities.[52] He obtained one indicator of

[50] Lineberry and Fowler, *op. cit.*, p. 710.

[51] *Ibid.*, p. 716.

[52] This article is reprinted, with minor revisions, in Part Four.

"ethos" through an index of governmental reformism which was included with demographic, economic and cultural factors in the "Community Structure" concept. Decision making was investigated through questionnaires administered to a standard panel of community informants. An "Ersatz Decisional System" was used to identify actors initiating, supporting, opposing, and negotiating in four different issue areas. The degree to which actors overlapped from one issue area to the next and the total number of actors across all issue areas were combined in a measure of centralization of decision-making.[53]

By adopting a pluralist posture Clark also proceeds from a different model of politics than Lineberry and Fowler. In particular, he equates decentralization in decision-making with pluralism. When he examines the relationship between the index of governmental reformism and the degree of centralization he finds the strongest positive relationship in the model.[54] If we were to conceptualize reform structures as indicators of public regardingness, as several students of urban politics have done, then on the basis of Clark's findings, we might formulate the following proposition: *The more reformed the structure, the less pluralistic its decision making.*[55]

Moreover, if one uses propensity to support expenditures as an indicator of public regardingness, it is interesting to note that Clark found "decentralization" to be strongly (positively) correlated with budget expenditures and urban renewal expenditures, while the index of governmental reformism was negatively correlated with these same expenditures. In short, Clark's research suggests that reform structures are not only characterized by a lack of pluralism in decision-making but are quite restrictive in relation to public expenditures.

Clark also includes per-cent Catholic as an indicator of the ethnicity component of the ethos formulation. He does this despite the fact that Banfield and Wilson were referring to attitudinal propensities among particular ethnic groups many of whom were not Catholic, e.g., Negroes, Jews, etc. Nevertheless, Clark proceeds with the measure and finds:

> The correlation (zero-order) with reformism of per-cent Catholic is -0.425 and that of civic activity is 0.276. Both of these relationships would seem to offer support for the traditional "public-regardingness" thesis. However, when the other variables are introduced, the relationships between these two variables and reformism disappear.[56]

Clark's findings do not support his interpretation of the ethos formulation. But instead of noting this, he feels compelled to search for ways of interpreting these results as supportive of the ethos notion. He observes that

[53] *Ibid.*, p. 580.

[54] David Greenstone and Paul Peterson suggest a different picture of reform structures. They see decision-making in these forms as dispersed among a wide range of individuals and groups. See their: "Reformers, Machines, and the War on Poverty" in James Q. Wilson (ed.), *City Politics and Public Policy, op. cit.*, p. 271.

[55] It should be noted that this is not Clark's argument but my own: I am extrapolating from his findings.

[56] Clark, *op. cit.*, p. 585.

This should presumably be interpreted as implying that when Catholics move into communities (in the West or elsewhere) with highly educated populations, they assimilate a political culture or reformism. Correspondingly, potential League members in such communities may become less active, since they are reasonably content that the victory for reform has already been won.[57]

Per-cent Catholic also emerges as the single most important variable in explaining budget expenditures. The path coefficient from per-cent Catholic to budget expenditures never dropped below .73. This finding does not derive from a few items but was found consistently on about two-thirds of all budget expenditures.[58] Although Clark finds this relationship very puzzling he chooses to leave it up to the reader to interpret. Given Clark's interpretation of "Ethos," his results are consistently unsupportive of the Banfield and Wilson formulation. But, again, since Banfield and Wilson never intended per-cent Catholic to be used as a valid indicator of Ethos, we can only judge that Clark's use of the measure is another blatant example where the ethos concept is utilized according to the personal preferences of the investigator.

VII. Attitudinal dimensions of the Ethos Theory: evidence from survey data

It has been six years since Banfield and Wilson first introduced the ethos notion. In that time, private and public regardingness has not been directly measured with survey data. Recently, however, Hawkins and Prather have used survey data to devise a scale to measure private regarding attitudes.[59] Their findings give strong support to the idea that private-regardingness is an empirically discernable attitudinal dimension independent of related concepts.

These scholars also investigated social group differences in private regardingness. They categorized their respondents by ethnicity (number of grandparents born abroad) and social class and then located them on the scale. They found that *ethnicity was negatively related to private regardingness.*[60] This pattern is, of course, at variance with Banfield and Wilson's generalizations about the linkage between ethnicity and public regardingness. But the Hawkins and Prather findings do correspond with the Lineberry-

---

[57] *Ibid.,* p. 585.

[58] *Ibid.,* pp. 587-588.

[59] The subjects in their study were 162 students in an introductory political science class at a state university. Hawkins and Prather point out that the sample is conceptualized as an "explanatory" survey designed to examine relationships among variables relevant to the Ethos Theory, not a descriptive survey designed to describe precisely one or more characteristics of some defined population. See Brett W. Hawkins and James E. Prather, "Measuring Private Regardingness," paper delivered at the 1969 annual meeting of the Southern Political Science Association, Hotel Deauville, Miami Beach, Florida, November 5-8, 1969.

[60] *Ibid.,* pp. 14-15.

Fowler study which showed ethnicity to be positively correlated with expenditures.

Moreover, Hawkins and Prather found a *positive correlation between social class and private regardingness.*[61] This finding also corresponds with Lineberry and Fowler[62] who found a negative relationship between class and expenditures, and is at variance with Banfield and Wilson's Cleveland and Chicago findings. Indeed, the ecological correlations reported by the latter suggest that high income groups are public regarding (i.e., pro-expenditure).[63]

In sum, while the research of Hawkins and Prather supports the existence of "private regardingness" their attitudinal data and the aggregate data of others, do much to place in question the ethos explanation of such attitudinal predispositions. That is, ethnicity and social class do not relate to expenditures in the predicted direction. Yet Banfield and Wilson might argue, as they did with Wolfinger and Field, that ethnicity is not a measure of the attitudinal predispositions of any *particular* ethnic group. Indeed, they might recommend that more survey data be gathered on Negroes, Jews, Poles, Czechs, etc. With such a hypothetical rejoinder research employing the ethos notion could conceivably continue indefinitely.

VIII. Summary

Recent research on the Ethos Theory has moved away from Banfield and Wilson's original concern with the role of attitudinal predispositions as predictors of voting behavior in mass publics. Instead, current efforts have assumed a more *formalist-elitist* thrust. The research tends to be formalistic because it concentrates on the public policy correlates of formal institutional arrangements. Such a focus *begs the whole question of political process* by failing to specify what features of these structures contribute to one type of policy rather than another. Moreover, scholars such as Lineberry and Fowler use the ethos formulation to support an essentially elitist model. They suggest that the most progressive governments are precisely those that are the least responsive to changes in and demands from mass publics. Sources of change apparently originate in the minds of an insulated elite. Yet they offer no theory of elite decision-making in terms of which to understand how such decisions are arrived at. Terry Clark has made some tentative steps in this direction. But his scheme of simply counting the circulation and overlap of

---

[61] *Ibid.,* pp. 15-16.

[62] Lineberry and Fowler, *op. cit.,* p. 711.

[63] Many comparative studies show a positive relationship between class and city expenditures. See, for example Harvey Brazer, *City Expenditures in the United States* (New York: National Bureau of Economic Research, Inc., 1959); Alan K. Campbell and Seymour Sacks, *Metropolitan America: Fiscal Patterns and Governmental Systems* (New York: Free Press, 1957); and Thomas R. Dye, "Governmental Structure, Urban Environment, and Educational Policy," *Midwest Journal of Political Science, 11* (August, 1967), pp. 353-380.

elites around selected policies does not get at the dynamics of decision-making in terms of the needs of the political system as a whole.

This last distinction is important. In most cases, governmental and political changes benefit some people and disadvantage others and no one can really blame the citizens for defending their interests. But an analysis of politics which views cleavage and conflict as somehow abnormal, as Lineberry and Fowler do, is dangerously restrictive because it may serve to discourage investigation into the impact of alternative programs and patterns of organization on the relative position of all the participants in the political process. The middle class ethos, which presumably informs the behavior of these elites may be based on a level of affluence and security which permits the middle class to limit interclass conflict, to avoid solutions leading to significant change and to substitute stalemate and harmless debate.

IX. Conclusion

This inquiry was based on the assumption that theoretically grounded comparative research is in large part a function of conceptual sophistication. And since proofs are so long and life is so short, it is essential that research be informed by concepts which seem strategic to theory construction. The most general conclusion that emerges from this study is that poorly formulated conceptual schemes such as the Ethos Theory, are particularly ill-suited to occupy such a strategic position.

The presumption that scientific discovery and theory are cumulative has been a cherished canon of the behavioral belief system. And cumulative research presupposes some intersubjectivity in formulating and applying concepts. Yet when concepts are fuzzy, their definition and measurement becomes a function of the personal preferences of the individual researcher. This, in turn, permits different formulations of what are sometimes understood to be the same questions. Such procedures can obviously inhibit scientific growth, as Stinchcombe observes in the following passage:

> For a social theorist, ignorance is more excusable than vagueness. Other investigators can easily show I am wrong if I am sufficiently precise. They will have much more difficulty showing by investigation what, precisely, I mean if I am vague. I hope not to be forced to weasel out with, but I didn't mean that! Social theorists should prefer to be wrong rather than misunderstood. Being misunderstood shows sloppy theoretical work. A theory to be useful must be specific enough to be disproved.[64]

Such vagueness is all too apparent in the Ethos formulation and this has harmed the cumulative potential of research in comparative urban politics. Indeed, we have noted how frequently *definition, application* and *verification*

[64] Stinchcombe, *op. cit.*, p. 6.

procedures tended to be largely a matter of the particular investigator's individual needs. As a result, all of the following have, at one time or another, been considered valid indicators of Banfield and Wilson's Ethos Theory: per-cent ethnic, per-cent Catholic, social class, formal structural arrangements, expenditure patterns, and "private-regardingness" attitude scales. In actuality, however, they represent quite different problems being investigated under the "Ethos" rubric.

Almost thirteen years have passed since Norton Long accused political scientists of losing sight of important issues in local government and politics.[65] Herson's review of textbooks on municipal politics provided a bill of particulars and specifications buttressing the indictment.[66] In that time, the study of urban politics has advanced far beyond the anecdotal quality of the early literature. Yet the research reviewed here suggests that much more needs to be done in order to create meaningful concepts to facilitate theoretical based comparative research.

[65]Norton Long, "Aristotle and the Study of Local Government," *Social Forces,* Vol. 24, No. 3 (Autumn, 1957), pp. 287-310.

[66]Lawrence J.R. Herson, "The Lost World of Municipal Government," *American Political Science Review,* 51, (June, 1957). See also Robert T. Daland, "Political Science and the Study of Urbanism," *American Political Science Review,* (June, 1957), pp. 491-509.

Environment, Process, and Policy:
A Reconsideration

James W. Clarke

In this final selection, James W. Clarke raises a number of important questions regarding an appropriate strategy for future empirical political research at the local level. First, Clarke draws our attention to the rather divergent findings of case and aggregate studies which have attempted to explain variation in municipal policy outcomes. You have only to review selections in previous sections to document such differences. On the one hand, the case study approach draws attention to the importance of various political variables, particularly dimensions of the policy-making process, as determinants of public policy. On the other hand, studies employing the aggregate approach emphasize the importance of contextual variables and/or formal rules, procedures, and governmental structures. In particular, the social and economic characteristics of the units studied and their form of government are found to be consistently associated with municipal policy.

Clarke reviews several reasons for these apparently contradictory findings. First, because each approach tends to ignore certain factors, it probably exaggerates the importance of those variables which it does consider. Second, in many cases, particularly in the aggregate studies, indicators are too crude or insensitive to reflect the specific dimension being considered. Third, most comparative studies have been unable to control for differences in local policy which result from state and federal restrictions on policies rather than from local prerogatives. Finally, it may simply be that environmental factors are important determinants of some policies, such as revenue and expenditures, which are largely dependent on the economic potential or resource base of a community. Query: Do these same environmental variables have as much influence on policies, such as open housing, fluoridation, school desegregation, planning, urban renewal, public housing, referenda decisions, and so on, which more closely reflect the basic values of municipal residents and their political leaders?

Next, and in an attempt to reconcile the diverse findings of past research, Clarke examines some of the correlates of change in governmental form in forty-three third-class cities in Pennsylvania. His general hypothesis stipulates that variations in the social, economic, and political characteristics of local communities are associated with the decision to alter or retain existing forms of government. His findings basically support the linkage model hypothesized by Lineberry and Fowler in their selection in Part Four. In this instance, political phenomena appear to function as intervening variables linking various environmental factors to referenda outcomes.

Clarke's findings suggest that political-process variables are important explanatory factors in comparative urban research. In addition, while his analysis demonstrates that environmental variables are not unimportant, it does emphasize how their relative importance must be assessed against that of relevant and meaningful political variables. Dimensions of the policy-making process—such as citizen political attitudes and behavior; group activities and the formation of coalitions; political leadership; power and influence relationships; and so on—which are often recognized but rarely included in large-scale comparative urban research, must be incorporated into future study designs. Are there other relevant political variables which should also be included? Why should they be incorporated into future research?

Clarke concludes by suggesting the following research strategy. In the future, researchers should attempt to merge the two approaches. "In short, an effort must be made to include those variables which have been shown in the case study literature to have theoretical and political relevance into aggregate comparative studies." If this is an appropriate strategy for future research, why has it not been adopted sooner? What factors might impede successful utilization of such a revised approach? What kinds of costs are involved? What benefits might be forthcoming both in the short and long run?

It seems that if our understanding of local government and politics is to be increased and the adequacy of our explanations enhanced, then a merging of the case study and aggregate approaches is definitely needed. Similarly, and as I argued in the introductory essay:

> *... decision makers operating within different institutional and community settings should be compared as they make decisions on various types of public-policy questions. Such a revised approach requires a merging of earlier perspectives. It also requires a sampling of local municipalities, decision makers, and public-policy issues. To continue undertaking diverse studies at the local level will be theoretically meaningless unless they are concerned with explaining a common dependent variable, such as public policy and/or other policy outcomes.*

The research agenda seems clear, I suggest we turn our attention to it.

In recent years a growing body of research has used multivariate statistical techniques to examine the relationship between aggregate environmental characteristics and the public policies of state and local governments. This research has been concerned primarily with isolating or demonstrating the social, economic, and political correlates of either public policies (e.g., expenditures, revenues and referenda issues) or governmental structures (viz., form of government, size of election districts and type of ballot).[1]

One advantage of the aggregate approach, beyond the relative accessibility of data, is that it permits a systematic, comparative study of states or cities. On the local level this comparative approach provides a convenient supplement to the earlier case study approach which was concerned with the political processes and issues of particular cities.

A number of hypotheses have been suggested by studies employing either the case study or aggregate approaches. In those observations dealing with government structure, attention is usually directed to the council-manager plan as an example of progressive government. That is, city governments which are reform-oriented are likely to be found in more affluent, better educated, homogeneous, middle-class cities. The notion is that the middle class prefers a more efficient, professional city administration. Conversely, the mayor-council plan is usually associated with older, machine-type politics

Reprinted from *The American Political Science Review*, vol. 63, no. 4 (December 1969), pp. 1172-1182, by permission of the publisher and author. This research is a by-product of a larger study supported by a U.S. Public Health Service Research Grant (IFS AP33, 924-01). Special thanks are due my graduate assistant, David H. Vomacka, for his help in processing these data.

[1] A good discussion of this literature can be found in Herbert Jacob and Michael Lipsky, "Outputs, Structure, and Power: An Assessment of Changes in the Study of State and Local Politics," *Journal of Politics,* 30 (May, 1968), 510-538.

which allegedly reflects the preferences of the less affluent, less-educated, working class and ethnic minorities who are most concerned about political representation.[2]

The question of how to categorize commission government has presented a problem. Despite the fact that it was one of the earliest manifestations of the reform movement, its popularity has declined steadily, and it is rapidly fading into obscurity throughout most of the country.[3] Curiously enough, in spite of its decline in the last four decades and its rather marked politicization in those cities in which it does remain, scholars continue to consider both commission and council-manager governments analytically as reform governments. Indications of the weaknesses in such a combination are apparent in some of the anomalous relationships revealed and recognized in a recent study by Lineberry and Fowler.[4]

I. General statement of problem

Two ideas emerge from the case and aggregate studies of public policies in cities. The results of the case studies suggest that political variables are important determinants of public policy. More specifically, political decision-making and interaction processes appear to be the key variables which must be studied in order to understand policy outcomes.[5] Conversely, the results of aggregate comparative studies on the state and local levels indicate that policy outcomes are more closely associated with the social and economic characteristics of the units of analysis. These studies suggest that environmental rather than political variables appear to be much more important as policy determinants.[6]

[2] Perhaps the best known statement of this view is found in Edward C. Banfield and James Q. Wilson, *City Politics* (Cambridge: Harvard University Press and Massachusetts Institute of Technology Press, 1963); and their article, "Public-Regardingness as a Value Premise in Voting Behavior," *The American Political Science Review*, 58 (December, 1964), 876-887.

[3] Charles R. Adrian, *Governing Urban America* (2nd ed., New York: McGraw-Hill Book Company, Inc., 1961), pp. 214, 217-218.

[4] For example, they found that commission governments did not fulfill the objectives of institutional reform, i.e., this form of government seems to reflect rather than reduce the impact of social cleavages. Robert L. Lineberry and Edmund P. Fowler, "Reformism and Public Policies in American Cities," *The American Political Science Review*, 61 (September, 1967), 701-716.

[5] See, for example, Robert J. Mowitz and Deil S. Wright, *Profile of a Metropolis* (Detroit: Wayne State University Press, 1962); and Robert Dahl, *Who Governs? Democracy and Power in an American City* (New Haven: Yale University Press, 1961).

[6] See, for example, Richard E. Dawson and James A. Robinson, "Interparty Competition, Economic Variables and Welfare Politics in the American States," *Journal of Politics*, 25 (May, 1963), 265-298; Richard I. Hofferbert, "The Relation Between Public Policy and Some Structural and Environmental Variables in the American States," *The American Political Science Review*, 60 (March, 1966), 73-82; and Thomas R. Dye, "Governmental Structure, Urban Environment, and Educational Policy," *Midwest Journal of Political Science*, 11 (August, 1967), 353-380. For an exception to this general finding, see Ira Sharkansky, "Economic and Political Correlates of State

There are several possible explanations for these somewhat contradictory conclusions. First, it may be that some variables are ignored in either approach, thus exaggerating the importance of those variables which are considered. For example, most case studies ignore or at least do not treat systematically the social and economic variables employed in the aggregate approach. The opposite emphasis is present in the aggregate studies, i.e., decision-making or process variables tend to be ignored. Second, and this applies mainly to the aggregate studies, it may be that the indicators which are used to measure process variables are simply too crude or insensitive to reflect the dimensions being considered. Attempts to quantify what are essentially behavioral variables frequently encounter this problem. Third, comparative studies of cities have been unable to control adequately for differences in local policies which may reflect state and Federal restrictions rather than local prerogatives. Thus state laws limiting the discretion of city governments can only confound attempts to explain the policies of these governments if this factor is not considered. Closely related to this problem is the fact that controls for time are rarely employed. Particularly in studies of reformism, cities are often classified as reformist or not regardless of when or how the particular charter was adopted. It is unlikely that events such as these, many of which occurred around the turn of the century, can be considered the same as events occurring at mid-century.[7] Finally, it may be that environmental factors are important determinants of policies, such as revenue and expenditure policies, which are substantially dependent on the economic potential of communities. But are these same environmental variables equally important in influencing policies which reflect more closely the manifest political values of a community (e.g., elections for public office and certain referenda decisions)?

Lineberry and Fowler, in their study of reformism in American cities, suggest that:

> The implicit, or at times explicit, causal model in much of the research on municipal reformism has been a simple one: socio-economic cleavages cause the adoption of particular political forms. A more sophisticated model would include political institutions as one of the factors which produce a given output structure in city politics. We hypothesize that a causal model would include four classes of variables: socio-economic cleavages, political variables (including party registration, structure of party systems, patterns of aggregation, strength of interest groups, voter turnout, etc.), political institutions (form of government, type of elections and types of constituencies), and political output.[8]

This study represents an effort to examine, with one modification, such a model of reformism. That modification is that the single policy output, or

Government Expenditures: General Tendencies and Deviant Cases," *Midwest Journal of Political Science*, 11 (May, 1967), 173-192. See also the discussion of this question in Jacob and Lipsky, *op. cit.*, pp. 511-517.

[7]On this point, see, Jacob and Lipsky, *op. cit.*, p. 518.

[8]Lineberry and Fowler, *op. cit.*, p. 714.

dependent variable, in this study involves change or innovation in a political institution form of government.

II. Setting

Forty-three third-class cities in Pennsylvania have been selected for study. In 1957, the Optional Third-Class City Charter Law was signed providing all third-class cities with the option to adopt new municipal charters—either a mayor-council or council-manager plan.[9] If the local electorate chose to keep its existing commission form of government, which until 1957 had been required by state law, it could do so.[10] Under these conditions, the state laws of Pennsylvania provide a common legal framework for these cities. That is, in 1957, all forty-three cities were governed by commission governments, and all were provided with the same opportunity to adopt new charters under the law. This, perhaps more than anything else, directs attention to the characteristics of individual communities in seeking some explanation for their action or inaction on the charter question.[11]

The time period considered is the years from 1957, when the Optional Charter Law was adopted, through 1966. During this period, nine cities voted to adopt new charters. Six cities adopted the mayor-council plan. Three adopted the council-manager plan. Twelve other cities attempted unsuccessfully to adopt new charters.[12] There was no new charter activity in the remaining twenty-two cities.

Broadly defined, the dependent variable to be examined is municipal reform or change. As indicated earlier, the usual and inappropriate distinction between reform and non-reform government is not used. Thus, both the new options, council-manager or mayor council, are considered innovative or representative of political change, while the commission plan only represents the status quo.

The setting of this study approaches a quasi-experimental situation. All forty-three cities function within the constraints imposed by Pennsylvania law. Each city was provided with the same option, at the same time, to consider new charters. Furthermore, the controlled time period during which the cities were examined minimizes the effects of demographic or other environmental fluctuations. Control of these factors permits a more accurate assessment of the environmental and political influences on local public policy.

[9] Hereafter referred to as the Optional Charter Law.

[10] Under the law, a city could place a proposal to elect a charter study commission before the voters either by ordinance or petition. If a commission were elected by popular vote, it could, after a study period, recommend either a mayor-council or council-manager charter, or it could recommend retention of the existing commission plan. A recommendation for a new charter was then placed before the people in a referendum.

[11] Other structural variables usually considered in studies such as this were not relevant. Pennsylvania law requires partisan, at-large elections in all third-class cities.

[12] One of these cities, at the time of this writing had not had the opportunity to vote. It was coded as an "active" rather than a new charter city.

III. Research design

The purpose of this study is to examine those variables which are related to the consideration and adoption of new political forms. In a broader perspective, the analysis deals with the correlates of political change on the local level. The general hypothesis is that variations in the social, economic and political characteristics of communities are associated with the decision to alter or retain existing forms of government. The forty-three cities selected for the study are treated as a statistical population of third-class cities in Pennsylvania.[13]

The study attempts to answer two questions: (1) What are the correlates of charter-reform activity in the forty-three cities? (2) Among those cities which were active, what variables are associated with the outcomes of this activity? Twelve independent variables were selected for analysis because of their prominence in the local and state policy literature (see Table 1).[14] Aside from the familiar variables (1-8), variables 9-11 require some further clarification below:

Metropolitan classification

The cities are classified as central, independent, or suburban cities. A central city is the largest city of 50,000 or more, located within a Standard Metropolitan Statistical Area (SMSA). Suburbs are cities above 10,000 located within SMSA's. Independent cities are cities above 10,000 located outside SMSA's.[15] This classification is treated as a dichotomous variable comparing central and independent cities to suburbs.

Table 1. Independent variables

---

1. *Population, 1960 (10^3).*
2. *Median gross rentals, 1960.*
3. *Real estate values, 1960 (per capita).*
4. *Median income, 1960 (10^2).*
5. *Median school years completed by the adult population, 1960.*
6. *Percentage white collar, 1960.*
7. *Percentage nonwhite, 1960.*
8. *Percentage of the native population of foreign or mixed parentage, 1960.*
9. *Metropolitan classification (1960).*
10. *Employment-residence ratios (1960).*
11. *Percentage absentee-owned industry (1965).*
12. *Local interparty competition (1955-1966).*

---

[13] The 1960 census populations of these cities range from 10,667 to 138,440. Five cities were excluded from the study because they have dropped below the legal population minimum of 10,000 required for third-class cities.

[14] Variables 1 through 10 were taken from *The Municipal Yearbook 1963* (Chicago: The International City Manager's Association, 1963) and *The County and City Data Book 1962* (Washington: U.S. Department of Commerce, Bureau of Census, 1962). All data are taken from the 1960 census.

[15] *The Municipal Yearbook 1963*, p. 97.

Employment-residence ratios

This is the ratio of total employment to resident employment. It measures the extent to which a city is dependent upon a nonresident labor force.[16]

Percentage absentee-owned industry

The degree of absentee-owned industry is measured by the percentage of the total local work force employed by absentee-owned firms. The location of the firm's home office was used to determine whether the firm is absentee or locally owned, i.e., if the home office is located outside the city, it is considered to be an absentee-owned firm.[17]

Local interparty competition

This variable is defined as the relative percentage of city elective offices held over the twelve year time period by the minority party. This was determined by consulting *The Pennsylvania Manual* for the years included in the study and recording for each two year period the number of offices held by both parties.[18] These numbers were then totaled for the twelve year period and the percentage of local offices held by the minority party was calculated for each city. The index ranges from 0 (least competitive) to 50 percent (most competitive) where control was equally divided between the parties.

The dependent variable—charter reform activity—is treated as a dichotomous variable, i.e., reform activity is dichotomized on the basis of its presence or absence in each city. The minimal condition required for a city to be classified as "active" was that it had, either by petition or ordinance, placed the question of whether or not to elect a charter study commission before the local electorate.[19]

Two methods were used to explore the second question. First, results were classified in terms of success, i.e., either adoption or rejection of the charter proposals, and operationalized as a dichotomous variable.[20] Second, the percentage of the popular vote approving the proposal was used as the

---

[16]*Ibid.*, p. 92.

[17]The employment information and home office location were taken from the *Pennsylvania Industrial Directory 1965* (Harrisburg, Pennsylvania: Department of Internal Affairs, 1965).

[18]"Lists of Public Officials" (Harrisburg, Pennsylvania: Department of Property and Supplies), Vols. 92-97.

[19]Twenty-one of the forty-three cities were defined as active.

[20]Rejection was defined to include, in addition to electoral defeat, the failure of a charter study commission either to submit a recommendation or to recommend retention of the commission plan. One of these conditions was met in twenty-five cases involving twenty cities. Five cities experienced two campaigns. In the analysis, the second effort in these five cities was treated as a separate event.

dependent variable in the twenty-two cases where the public did have an opportunity to vote on the issue.[21]

Four political process variables—type of proposal, city hall response, fear of the higher costs of reform government and voter turnout—were included in the analysis. These variables are commonly considered in the case study literature on municipal reform and metropolitan reorganization,[22] but they are not often included systematically in comparative studies. They are treated in this analysis as dichotomous variables.[23]

As stated above, the twenty-two charter referenda occurred over the years from 1957 to 1966. Because of this extended time period, newspaper accounts seemed to offer the most reliable and comprehensive information concerning the campaigns. Local newspapers, in each of the cities in which the referenda occurred, were examined for the time period beginning with the ordinance or petition leading to the election of a charter study commission through to the date the referendum was held.[24]

The four process variables were defined as follows:

1. *Type of proposal.* This was defined and coded simply as either a mayor-council (1) or council-manager (0) plan.

2. *City hall response.* This variable was dichotomized as opposition (0) or lack of opposition (1) to the proposal. Opposition was defined subjectively as any number of councilmen or city employees who, actively and overtly, opposed the charter reform proposal to a degree, sufficient in itself, to keep the issue consistently before the public. In those cities where city hall was divided on the issue, the dominant response, in terms of publicity, was coded.

3. *Cost issue.* This variable was defined as either the presence (0) or absence (1) of a fear of higher costs under a reform government, as reflected in newspaper accounts and political advertisements.

4. *Voter turnout.* This variable was included in the analysis in a more conventional manner.[25] Voter turnout was defined as the percentage of the total registered voters in each community who voted on the local charter referendum.

---

[21] The twenty-two referenda occurred in nineteen cities. Again, the second referendum in three of the cities was treated as a separate event with conditional changes treated as new information.

[22] For example, see David A. Booth, *Metropolitics: The Nashville Consolidation* (East Lansing, Michigan: Michigan State University, Institute for Community Development, 1963), pp. 37-56; and Brett Hawkins, "Public Opinion and Metropolitan Reorganization in Nashville," *Journal of Politics*, 28 (May, 1966), 408-418.

[23] The risks involved in dichotomizing such complex variables are recognized and accepted in view of the new information which may be revealed about the interrelationship of these variables and the standard environmental indicators in determining policy outcomes.

[24] The duration of reform activity usually ranged from a year to eighteen months. Additional information on some campaigns was found in published and unpublished documents made available by the Bureau of Research and Information of the Pennsylvania Department of Community Affairs, Harrisburg, Pennsylvania.

[25] For an analysis of the correlates of voter turnout, see Robert R. Alford and Eugene C. Lee, "Voting Turnout in American Cities," *The American Political Science Review*, 62 (September, 1968), 796-813.

Simple, partial and multiple correlations are used to describe the relationships. In addition, cumulative coefficients of determination are reported to indicate the relative variation explained by each independent variable.

IV. Reform and socio-economic
indicators: some propositions

There is a substantial body of literature which discusses the environmental correlates of municipal reform.[26] No attempt will be made here to discuss that literature. Rather, only the major conclusions will be summarized in the form of propositions.[27]

1. *Population size.* Larger cities are more likely to consider and adopt new charters than smaller cities (Alford and Scoble; Kessel).
2. *Social Class.* Cities with larger middle-class populations—as measured by occupation, education and income—are more likely to consider and adopt new charters (Banfield and Wilson; Schnore; Alford and Scoble; Kessel).
3. *Social heterogeneity.* Cities with larger non-white and ethnic populations are less likely to consider and adopt new charters (Banfield and Wilson; Kessel; Schnore and Alford; and Alford and Scoble).
4. *Economic potential.* Cities with greater economic potential—as measured by per capita market value of real estate, median gross

---

[26] Examples of such studies are: Edgar L. Sherbenou, "Class, Participation, and the Council-Manager Plan," *Public Administration Review,* 21 (Summer, 1961), 131-135; John H. Kessel, "Government Structure and Environment: A Statistical Note about American Cities," *The American Political Science Review,* 56 (September, 1962), 615-620; Oliver P. Williams and Charles R. Adrian, *Four Cities: A Study in Comparative Policy Making* (Philadelphia: University of Pennsylvania Press, 1963), pp. 287-288; Leo F. Schnore, *The Urban Scene: Human Ecology and Demography* (New York: The Free Press, 1965) pp. 184-199; Robert R. Alford and Harry M. Scoble, "Political and Socioeconomic Characteristics of American Cities," *The Municipal Yearbook 1965* (Chicago: The International City Manager's Association), pp. 82-97; Charles S. Liebman, "Functional Differentiation and Political Characteristics of Suburbs," *American Journal of Sociology,* 66 (March 1961), 485-490; Raymond E. Wolfinger and John Osgood Field, "Political Ethos and the Structure of City Government," *The American Political Science Review,* 60 (June, 1966), 306-326; Thomas R. Dye, "Urban Political Integration: Conditions Associated with Annexation in American Cities," *Midwest Journal of Political Science,* 8 (November, 1964), 430-446; Thomas R. Dye, Charles S. Liebman, Oliver P. Williams and Harold Herman, "Differentiation and Cooperation in a Metropolitan Area," *Midwest Journal of Political Science,* 7 (May, 1963), 145-155; and Amos H. Hawley, "Community Power and Urban Renewal Success," *American Journal of Sociology,* 68 (January, 1963) 422-431; and Leo F. Schnore and Robert R. Alford, "Forms of Government and Socio-Economic Characteristics of Suburbs," *Administrative Science Quarterly,* 8 (June, 1963), 1-17.

[27] The propositions listed are logically derived from the studies indicated in footnote 26, *supra.* These propositions are not empirically derived because most of this literature deals specifically with government structure rather than political change. Thus, the results of the examination of these propositions do not bear directly on the findings from which they were derived.

rentals and larger employment residence ratios—are more likely to consider and adopt new charters (Williams and Adrian; Sherbenou).

5. *Absentee-owned industries.* Cities with greater proportions of the work force employed in absentee-owned firms are less likely to consider and adopt new charters[28] (Williams and Adrian, Kessel).

6. *Metropolitan classification.* Central and independent cities are more likely to consider and adopt new charters than suburban cities. This proposition is drawn from Schnore's finding that the commission plan is more common in "older, less modernized" suburbs where many problems are not recognized or acknowledged.[29] Third-class suburban cities in Pennsylvania tend to fit this description. It may be also that the status quo or "caretaker" orientation of some suburbs is a result of the suburban dependence on central city resources and services.[30]

7. *Interparty competition.* Cities with more competitive party structures are more likely to engage in reform activity but less likely to adopt new charters. There is a scarcity of research on local party competition from which to draw hypotheses. Proposition 7 is based on the suspicion that challenges to the controlling party, such as structural changes, are more likely in competitive cities because of the minority party's efforts to exploit any opportunity to weaken the control of the majority party. At the same time, it is doubtful that a weak minority party could mobilize sufficient support to carry a proposal which was opposed by the majority.

V. Reform activity and environmental indicators: some findings

A step-wise correlation program was used to analyze these data.[31] In Table 2, the independent variables are ranked in terms of the relative variance produced in the dependent variable—reform *activity*. It is clear that metropolitan class and population size are the most important environmental correlates of reform activity. The remaining ten variables, in combination, contribute only an additional 22 percent to the explained variance in the dependent variable. It appears that the effects of social class and heterogeneity, economic potential, and absentee ownership are marginal in determining the presence or absence of charter reform activity.

---

[28] See also, Ernst A. Barth, "Community Influence Systems: Structure and Change," *Social Forces,* 40 (October, 1961), "Absentee-Owned Corporations and Community Power Structure," *American Journal of Sociology,* 61 (March, 1956), 413-419; Robert O. Schulze. "The Role of Economic Dominants in Community Power Structure," *American Sociology Review,* 23 (February, 1958), 3-9.

[29] Schnore, *op. cit.,* p. 190.

[30] See for example, Amos Hawley, "Metropolitan Populations and Municipal Expenditures in Central Cities," *Journal of Social Issues,* 7 (1951), 100-108. The reference to "caretaker" government is taken from the Williams and Adrian typology, *loc. cit.*

[31] For a brief explanation, see Note, Table 2. A complete description of the program is available in W.J. Dixon (ed.), *Biomedical Computer Programs* (Los Angeles: Health Sciences Computing Facility, Department of Preventive Medicine and Public Health, School of Medicine, University of California, 1964), pp. 49-59.

Table 2. *Cumulative multiple correlations between selected environmental variables and reform activity in forty-three Pennsylvania cities*

Environmental variables	Activity index		
	Multiple R	Multiple R^2	Increase in R^2
Metropolitan class	.48	.23	.23
Population size	.58	.33	.10
All variables*	.74	.55	.22

Note: *In this program, variables are ranked in terms of their overall explanatory power (i.e., the variance produced in the dependent variable). If a variable is unrelated to the dependent variable, it is excluded from the equation. When a number of independent variables are not truly independent, i.e., when they are highly intercorrelated, the importance of one or more of these variables may be minimized. For example, if variables A, B, and C are highly intercorrelated and their effects on variable D are being analyzed, the computer may rank variable A highly and as a result, deemphasize the importance of variables B and C. This would result because B and C did not contribute a sufficient additional increment to the variance explained by A. For a more detailed explanation, see Hubert M. Blalock,* Social Statistics *(New York: McGraw-Hill, 1960), pp. 346-351.*
Variables which independently account for less than a 7 percent increase in R^2.

Although the total variation explained by the environment is not high (55 percent), metropolitan classification and population size together account for 33 percent of the total variation. This finding provides some support for Propositions 1 and 6, which, when combined, might be termed a stress-dependence hypothesis. That is, larger cities may generate greater demands for services which are not easily handled in the rather decentralized administrative structure inherent in commission governments. The resulting stress may provide at least the inclination to consider structural changes. Further, as indicated above, the dependence of suburban cities on central city resources may result in a reduction in demands placed on suburban governments and a corresponding status quo orientation.[32]

VI. Environment indicators and reform outcomes: some findings

Attention is now directed to this question: once political change is formally considered, as reflected in the activity index, what are the environmental correlates of the results of this consideration (i.e., the variables associated with passage or defeat)? The results reported in Table 3 reveal that the

[32] A further justification for this explanation is that population size is not strongly associated with any other environmental variable, and is only marginally associated with metropolitan classification (r = .33). It is possible that ethnicity (r = -.49) and race (percentage nonwhite, r -= -.33) are exerting an indirect influence through metropolitan classification. These correlations indicate that there is a tendency for the suburban cities to have larger ethnic and non-white populations. But, the correlations between both these variables and the activity index are low, although directionally consistent (r_e = .29) (r_{ew} = .25), and they proved to be rather inconsequential in the step-wise analysis.

relationship between outcomes and metropolitan class is consistent with the earlier findings, but the explanatory importance of population size has diminished. A possible explanation is that this is a consequence of the fact that larger cities tended to be active while smaller cities remained inactive (i.e., larger cities were more likely to attempt to exercise their new charter options than smaller cities). In this measure, where only active cities are considered, the variation in population size is not as great.

The effects of absentee-ownership require some explanation. The relationship is negative.[33] It appears that there is a tendency to reject new charter proposals in cities where a larger proportion of the local economy is controlled by absentee-owned firms.[34] This finding is consistent with Proposition 5. Further, there is evidence of support for Proposition 4. Economic potential, as reflected in rentals and real estate values, appears to be a factor of some importance. New charter proposals tend to have a higher probability of success in cities with greater economic potential.

The most important conclusion which can be drawn at this point is that central and independent cities with greater economic potential and lower levels of absentee-ownership are more likely to adopt new charters. It is interesting to note that neither the social indicators nor interparty competition (Propositions 2, 3 and 7) is associated with reformism as it is measured in two separate indices.

VII. Environmental and political indicators and referenda outcomes: some propositions and findings

Thus far, interparty competition was the only explicitly political variable included in the analysis.[35] Now the four additional political process variables are introduced in the analysis of twenty-two charter referenda: (1) type of proposal, (2) city hall response, (3) fear of excessive costs, and (4) voter turnout.[36] The dependent variable in this case is the percentage of the popular vote approving the new charter proposal.

The textbook literature on urban politics provides an abundant supply of insights into the politics of municipal reform.[37] In brief, it is suggested that

[33] The partial correlation coefficient between absentee-ownership and activity outcomes is -.45.

[34] Recall that rejection here does not necessarily mean electoral defeat, but any of the means of rejection indicated earlier, *supra,* footnote 20.

[35] Incomplete newspaper coverage is the reason other political variables were not included. Newspaper coverage improved greatly after it was established that a referendum would be held.

[36] Recall again that "reform outcomes" (passage/defeat) refer to the twenty-five cases in which decisions were made either by the charter commission, (e.g., recommendation to retain the commission plan) or in a referendum. At this point, *only* referenda decisions (defined as the percentage of the vote for the proposal) are considered.

[37] See, for example, Adrian, *op cit.,* ch. 8; and Edward C. Banfield and James Q. Wilson, *City Politics, op cit.,* ch. 13.

Table 3. *Cumulative multiple correlations between selected environmental variables and reform outcomes in twenty-five attempts**

Environmental variables	Outcomes (passage-defeat)		
	Multiple R	Multiple R^2	Increase in R^2
Rentals	.47	.22	.22
Metropolitan class	.63	.40	.18
Absentee-ownership	.73	.53	.13
Real estate values	.78	.60	.07
All variables†	.86	.74	.14

*See footnote 20.
†Variables which independently account for less than a 7 percent increase in R^2.

council-manager proposals are usually opposed by incumbent city administrations and local politicians. This opposition often has its basis in the understandable reluctance to sacrifice or relinquish political influence (e.g., patronage) to a professional manager. Perhaps the most common criticism of the manager plan is that it costs too much. Opponents of manager proposals often exploit the public's fear of excessive costs during reform campaigns. If this fear becomes a salient issue for the electorate, it is probable that it will be reflected in a higher voter turnout comprised of a disproportionately large number of negative voters.[38]

The following propositions are drawn from this literature:

8. City hall opposition is associated with council-manager proposals.
9. The fear of higher costs of reform government is associated with council-manager proposals and city hall opposition.
10. Higher voter turnouts are associated with council-manager proposals, city hall opposition, and the fear of higher costs.
11. Referendum defeat is associated with council-manager proposals, city hall opposition, fear of excessive costs and larger voter turnouts.

Beyond examining these specific propositions, the overriding question raised here involves the relative importance of political process variables when they are evaluated simultaneously with the environmental set.

Propositions 8, 9 and 10 are examined in Table 4. The substantial association between these variables tends to confirm the hypothesized relationships, if one agrees with a logical sequence of events. That is, when council-manager proposals were offered, in most cases city hall responded negatively. Usually this opposition was mobilized in counter-campaigns to dramatize the alleged excessive costs of council-manager government. Alerted to the alleged financial burden council-manager government would create,

[38] A study of fluoridation referenda indicates that higher voter turnout is associated with the defeat of these referenda. See Maurice Pinard, "Structural Attachments and Political Support in Urban Politics: The Case of Fluoridation Referendums," *American Journal of Sociology*, 68 (March, 1963), 513-526.

*Table 4. Simple correlations among political variables
in twenty-two campaigns*

	City hall response	Type of proposal	Cost issue	Percent voter turnout
City hall response (1 = support, 0 = opposition)	—	.72	.83	−.53
Type of proposal (1 = mayor, 0 = manager)		—	.76	−.56
Cost issue (1 = no, 0 = yes)				−.57

taxpayers expressed their fears by turning out in larger numbers to vote against the proposal. It appears that if local public officials oppose a charter proposal and subsequently provide a nucleus for resistance, opposition in the community at large is more likely to develop.[39]

With reference to Proposition 10, larger voter turnouts are clearly associated with council-manager proposals, city hall opposition and the fear of excessive costs of reform government. Conversely, smaller voter turnouts are associated with mayor-council proposals, city hall support, or at least lack of opposition, and the absence of the cost issue.

Proposition 11 is considered in the final phase of the analysis, when both environmental and political variables are combined to assess their relative importance as correlates of referenda outcomes. The results reported in Table 5 provide evidence of the rather striking relative importance of political process variables. Four of the sixteen variables included in the analysis, three political process variables and population size, account for 75 percent of the variation in the percentage positive vote, i.e., the percentage of votes cast *for* the adoption of new charters.

Several conclusions can be drawn from these results. Of greatest significance, is the relative strength of the political process variables. With the exception of population size (a positive relationship), the explanatory capacity of the environmental set of variables appears to be quite limited. Again, the weakness of association between the dependent variable and indicators of social class, social heterogeneity and interparty competition is noteworthy in view of the importance accorded these variables in the literature. Beyond this, it appears safe to conclude that there is some empirical support for Proposition 11.

With reference to Proposition 11, perhaps some further clarification is due. A larger positive vote on the charter question is associated with mayor-council proposals, absence of the cost issue, and lower voter turnout.[40] The

[39]This is consistent with the findings that the position of the mayor is closely associated with the outcomes of fluoridation referenda. See David B. Rosenthal and Robert L. Crain, "Executive Leadership and Community Innovation: The Fluoridation Experience," *Urban Affairs Quarterly*, 1 (March, 1966), 39-57.

[40]The simple correlation between voter turnout and the percentage positive vote is negative, r = −.53.

Table 5. *Cumulative multiple correlations between selected environmental and political variables and the percentage positive vote in twenty-two referenda*

Environmental and political variables	Percentage positive vote		
	Multiple R	*Multiple R^2*	*Increase in R^2*
Cost issue	.69	.47	.47
Population size	.76	.57	.10
Type of proposal	.82	.68	.11*
Voter turnout	.87	.75	.08
All variables†	.98	.96	.21

*The apparent non-sequential ordering is due to rounding. The difference in R^2 between the second and third variables is .0033.
†Variables which independently account for less than a 7 percent increase in R^2.

reduced importance of city hall response as an independent variable is a function of the statistical fact that this variable is highly correlated with two of the other process variables, viz., type of proposal and the cost issue (see Table 4). In the case of three such variables in a multiple correlation equation, the explanatory overlap is considerable (see Note, Table 2).

VIII. Environmental and political variables: a relative assessment

Thus far, an attempt has been made to determine the correlates of variously defined dependent variables which measure different dimensions of structural change or reformism. The analysis has shown that, in general, the relative importance of environmental variables declined when political process variables were considered simultaneously in the analysis of referenda outcomes. Population size was the single exception.

At the conclusion of their study, Lineberry and Fowler suggest that ". . . political institutions 'filter' the process of converting [socio-economic] inputs into [political] outputs."[41] They hypothesize that political variables perform a similar "filter" or linkage function. If the Lineberry-Fowler model is valid, one would expect to find a convincing relationship between the environmental set and the political process variables. Table 6 shows that there is such a relationship between a subset of the environmental set and the political variables. More specifically, indicators of economic potential (rentals, income, real estate values, and employment-resident ratios) and race (percentage nonwhite) are most closely associated with the political variables. Cities with greater economic potential and larger non-white populations are more likely to receive and vote on mayor-council proposals. Consequently, city officials are less likely to oppose these proposals and the cost issue remains dormant. This combination of events results in lower voter turnouts and greater acceptance potentials for reform proposals.

[41] *Op. cit.*, p. 715.

*Table 6. Simple correlations between environmental and
political variables in twenty-two referenda*

Environment	Type of proposal	City hall response	Cost issue	Voter turnout
Rentals	.27	.42	.41	−.53
Income	.31	.30	.18	−.52
Real estate values	.35	.14	.33	−.43
Employment/residence ratios	.07	.33	.49	−.39
Nonwhite	.48	.43	.29	−.32
Party competition	−.03	−.19	−.20	.20
Metro class	.17	.18	.22	.17
Absentee-ownership	.19	−.11	−.14	−.16
Education	−.13	.06	.11	−.13
Ethnicity	−.17	−.25	−.02	.07
White collar	−.28	.00	−.03	−.07
Population	.29	−.01	.11	−.03

There is some evidence, reported earlier, that reform activity is less likely to occur in more racially diverse cities, viz., suburbs.[42] However, this evidence must now be qualified by adding that when reform activity does occur, the size of the nonwhite minority is positively associated with mayor-council proposals which have a greater probability of acceptance. It may be that economically viable and racially diverse cities find mayor-council government more compatible with a need to provide an arena for the arbitration of potentially conflicting interests.

Population size and metropolitan class, which were shown earlier to have some determinant effect on reform activity and outcomes (see Tables 2, 3 and 5), are not related in any meaningful way to the political variables. A plausible interpretation of this, noted earlier, is that population size and metropolitan class exert an independent influence on reformism.[43] Larger central and independent cities are more likely to consider and adopt reform policies simply as a result of a sheer physical need for administrative innovation. In short, their size, relative proximity to parasitic suburbs, or as is the case with independent cities, their relative geographical isolation may provide sufficient pressures for structural change or administrative innovation regardless of other social, economic, and political variables. The remaining environmental indicators appear to be only tenuously related to the political variables.

IX. Summary and conclusions

An important feature of this study is its quasi-experimental design. Both the time sequence and legal constraints are uniform for each city included in

[42] See footnote 32, *supra.*
[43] *Supra,* p. 1177-78.

the analysis. Thus, any distortion, which is quite probable when these factors are not controlled, has been eliminated.

The findings reported are generally consistent with the linkage model hypothesized by Lineberry and Fowler.[44] The analysis has shown that some of the political variables recognized in the Lineberry and Fowler model—viz., structure of party systems (interparty competition), patterns of aggregation (type of proposal and cost issue), strength of interest groups (city hall response) and voter turnout—were, with the exception of interparty competition, important determinants of referenda outcomes. Beyond this, the relative importance of environmental variables declined when these political variables were considered simultaneously in the analysis. There is some evidence that these political variables function as intervening variables linking a subset of the environmental indicators to referenda outcomes. Finally, some standard social indicators, viz., education, ethnicity, and occupation, were shown to be conspicuously weak in their association with reformism throughout the analysis.

These findings suggest the importance of political process variables in comparative urban research. On the surface, it may seem that this finding is contrary to those of a number of studies which have indicated the limited influence of political variables on policy outputs at both the state and local levels.[45] A possible explanation for these somewhat divergent findings is that previous policy output research has been limited almost exclusively to analyses of revenue and expenditure policies which, quite plausibly, would be associated with variables reflecting the economic potential or the tax base of states and localities. However, the relationships which exist between these socio-economic variables and policies which represent explicitly political values (e.g., candidate preferences or essentially noneconomic issues such as fluoridation and municipal reform) may not be as direct or important as they are in those policies which must be made within the parameters set by the economic potential of the state. It is probable, and certainly worthy of further research, that the explanatory importance of socio-economic and political process variables will vary with the type of policy being considered. When noneconomic policies are considered, a stronger association is revealed between political process variables and, in this case, referenda outcomes. These process variables reflect the attitudinal and behavioral dimensions of city politics to a greater degree than the socio-economic variables.

Another explanation for these differences is that perhaps too much consideration is being given to the relative availability of political data rather than the theoretical relevance of these data to the problem being examined.

[44] *Loc. cit.*

[45] See, for example, Herbert Jacob, "The Consequence of Malapportionment: A Note of Caution," *Social Forces*, 43 (December, 1964), 256-261; Thomas R. Dye, "Malapportionment and Public Policy in the States," *Journal of Politics*, 27 (August, 1965), 586-601, and *Politics, Economics and the Public: Policy Outcomes in the American States* (Chicago: Rand McNally, 1966); Richard I. Hofferbert, "The Relation Between Public Policy and Some Structural and Environmental Variables in the American States," *The American Political Science Review*, 60 (March, 1966), 73-82; and Jacob and Lipsky, *op. cit.*, 511-517.

The result is that political variables are usually defined operationally in structural rather than behavioral or interactional terms. To this extent, the behavioral dimension of politics is being ignored, not assessed, in the policy output studies and the results may be simply a product of the methodology.

What this analysis has demonstrated is not that environmental variables are unimportant, but rather that their importance must be assessed in combination with relevant and meaningful political variables; that is, political process variables which are often recognized but rarely included in comparative urban research. Despite the reservations one may have about the validity of dichotomous variables in defining complex political phenomena, the costs of excluding such variables may far exceed the satisfaction which may be derived from more rigorously defined, more readily accessible but inconsequential indicators. In short, an effort must be made to include those variables, which have been shown in the case study literature to have theoretical and political relevance, into aggregate comparative studies. The theoretical limitations of case study analysis are well-known. More attention should now be directed to the explanatory limitations of simple input-output analysis in which no attempt is made to determine the independent and intervening effects of political process variables.